THE COURAGE

TO HEAL

Other Books by the Authors

Ellen Bass

I NEVER TOLD ANYONE: WRITING BY WOMEN SURVIVORS OF CHILD SEXUAL ABUSE (COEDITOR)

NO MORE MASKS!: AN ANTHOLOGY OF POEMS BY WOMEN (COEDITOR)

Laura Davis

THE COURAGE TO HEAL WORKBOOK: FOR WOMEN AND MEN SURVIVORS OF CHILD SEXUAL ABUSE

THE COURAGE
TO HEAL

A GUIDE FOR WOMEN SURVIVORS
OF CHILD SEXUAL ABUSE

ELLEN BASS and
LAURA DAVIS

PERENNIAL LIBRARY

HARPER & ROW, PUBLISHERS, New York
Cambridge, Philadelphia, San Francisco, Washington
London, Mexico City, São Paulo, Singapore, Sydney

Workshops and Lectures

Ellen Bass and Laura Davis offer training seminars and educational programs about child sexual abuse nationally. Ellen also offers workshops for survivors, groups for partners, and training for counselors. For a schedule of upcoming lectures, workshops, and seminars, or if you are interested in bringing one to your area, please write to us at the address below.

The authors welcome any feedback or responses to *The Courage to Heal* but regret that they are unable to answer individual letters.

Ellen Bass and Laura Davis
P.O. Box 5296
Santa Cruz, CA 95063-5296

Copyright acknowledgments follow the Index.

THE COURAGE TO HEAL. Copyright © 1988 by Ellen Bass and Laura Davis. All rights reserved. Printed in the United States of America. No part of this book may be used or reproduced in any manner whatsoever without written permission except in the case of brief quotations embodied in critical articles and reviews. For information address Harper & Row, Publishers, Inc., 10 E. 53rd Street, New York, N.Y. 10022. Published simultaneously in Canada by Fitzhenry & Whiteside Ltd., Toronto.

Copyeditor: Katherine G. Ness
Designer: Laura Hough
Index by Meryl Schneider for Riofrancos & Co., Indexers

Library of Congress Cataloging-in-Publication Data

Bass, Ellen.
   The courage to heal.

   Bibliography: p
   Includes index.
   1. Child molesting—United States.   2. Women—United States—Psychology.   3. Adult child abuse victims—United States.   I. Davis, Laura.   II. Title.
HQ72.U53B37   1988   616.85′83   87-45598
ISBN 0-06-055105-4   89 90 91 92   RRD   10 9 8 7 6 5 4 3
ISBN 0-06-096234-8 (pbk.)   90 91 92   RRD   12

CONTENTS

Acknowledgments *9*

Preface *13*

Introduction: Healing Is Possible *19*

About the Stories in This Book *25*

Using the Writing Exercises *27*

PART ONE. **TAKING STOCK**

Effects: Recognizing the Damage *33*

Coping: Honoring What You Did to
   Survive *40*

PART TWO. **THE HEALING PROCESS**

An Overview *57*

The Decision to Heal *60*

The Emergency Stage *65*

Remembering *70*

Believing It Happened *86*

Breaking Silence *92*

Understanding That It Wasn't Your
   Fault *104*

The Child Within *111*

5

Trusting Yourself   *116*
Grieving and Mourning   *118*
Anger—The Backbone of Healing   *122*
Disclosures and Confrontations   *133*
Forgiveness?   *149*
Spirituality   *155*
Resolution and Moving On   *161*

PART THREE. **CHANGING
PATTERNS**

The Process of Change   *173*
Self-Esteem and Personal Power   *178*
Feelings   *191*
Your Body   *207*
Intimacy   *223*
Sex   *239*
Children and Parenting   *270*
Families of Origin   *289*

PART FOUR. **FOR SUPPORTERS
OF SURVIVORS**

The Basics   *315*
For Family Members   *318*
For Partners   *321*
For Counselors   *345*

PART FIVE. **COURAGEOUS
WOMEN**

An Introduction   *357*
Judy Gold   *359*
Eva Smith   *367*
Soledad   *373*
Evie Malcolm   *381*
Anna Stevens   *387*
Kyos Featherdancing   *394*
Lorraine Williams   *400*
Randi Taylor   *405*
Alicia Mendoza   *410*
Annette   *417*
Diane Hugs   *422*
Krishnabai   *425*
Michelle and Artemis   *431*
Mary McGrath   *441*
Gizelle   *446*

Healing Resources   *458*
Bibliography   *466*

Index   *487*

Don't run away from it. Don't bury it. Don't try to produce a different reality getting all strung out on something, or eating your way through your feelings. Don't slash your wrists. Just deal with it, because it's going to keep coming back if you continue living anyway. It's painful, but you just have to keep going. It's just part of life, really.

—Soledad, 28-year-old survivor

Give as much commitment to healing as you did to surviving for the last ten or fifteen years.

—Dorianne, 35-year-old survivor

There's more than anger, more than sadness, more than terror. There's hope.

—Edith Horning, 46-year-old survivor

ACKNOWLEDGMENTS

We would like to thank the hundreds of survivors and partners who answered our ads, returned our calls, and shared their stories with us. We are also grateful to the participants in Ellen's workshops who generously allowed us to tell their stories and describe their struggles. Their courage and determination inspired us and deepened our own commitment. This book would not exist without them.

There are many people who've provided invaluable assistance to us in completing this project. Together, we'd like to thank:

Janet Goldstein, our editor at Harper & Row, for her incredible support, brilliance, dedication, and her unwavering belief in this book from the beginning.

Katherine Ness, production editor extraordinaire, whose care, thoughtfulness, and attention went beyond the call of duty; Laura Hough, whose creative attention to design made for a beautiful book; and to our literary agent, Charlotte Raymond, for her ongoing encouragement and support.

Sandra Butler, Lucy Diggs, Jeanne Mayer Freebody, Dorothy Morales, Nona Olivia, Kay Slagle, and Daniel Sonkin for their invaluable criticism of the manuscript as a whole. And Lucy Diggs for extensive line editing, and for cooking a fine Christmas dinner.

Lola Atkins, Janet Bryer, Jesse Burgess, Mariah Burton-Nelson, Pandora Carpenter, Lauren Crux, Carol Anne Dwight, Rashama Khalethia, Edith Kieffer, Ellen Lacroix, Donna Maimes, Wendy Maryott-Wilhelms, Rose Z. Moonwater, Pat Pavlat, Amy Pine, Robin Roberts, Helen Resneck-Sannes, Ariel Ellen Shayn, Roger Slagle, Deborah Stone, and Karen Zelin for their careful reading of portions of the manuscript.

Kristina Peterson, Margaret Hill, Pat Saliba, and Emily Joy Hixson, Laura's housemates, for love and patience all those days when Ellen slept in the living room and the dining room table was piled with papers.

Among the survivors we'd like to thank for their contributions are: Janice Avila, Rachel Bat Or, Shelley Bennet, Eileen Daly, Natalie Devora, Martha Elliott, Jill Fainberg, Ely Fuller, Ann Marie Godwin, Jayne Habe, Barbara Hamilton, Margaret Hawthorn, Rashama Khalethia, Edith Kieffer, Krishnabai, Dorianne Laux, Jennierose Lavender, Suzanne Leib, Cristin Lindstrom, Julie Martchenke, Erin May, Sharrin Michael, Janet Hanks Morehouse, Nina Newington, Kathleen O'Bannon and her daughter Maureen Davidson, Lynn Slade, Kay Slagle, Catherine Stifter, Teresa Strong, Josie Villalpando, and Diana Wood.

Others whose contributions have helped along the way: Jane Ariel, Beth Beurkens, Diana Bryce, Judy Butler, Don Cotton, Gabby Donnell, Linda Eberth, Sandi Gallant, Diane Hugs, Adrianne Chang Kwong, Julie Robbins, Kathleen Rose, Sue Saperstein, Theresa Tollini, Donna Warnock, Mary Williams, and Linda Wilson.

The Fessenden Educational Fund, for help with expenses.

Ellen Bass

I have received such abundant encouragement and support that I can't name everyone, but I would particularly like to thank:

All the workshop participants who taught me what survivors need in order to heal.

Mildred Bass, my mother, for giving me the wholehearted love and commitment every child deserves. And Sarah Wolpert, her mother, for giving that to her. So much of what I have to give to survivors I received from them.

Josephine Clayton, for being a second mother to me, when I needed one very much.

Pat Pavlat, my therapist, for being a model of excellence. And for inspiring me to climb Angel's Landing.

Florence Howe, for teaching me the basics of facilitating groups: respect for each person's feelings and thoughts. And for opening so many doors.

Marty Bridges, for promoting the first I Never Told Anyone workshops; Pam Mitchell, for bringing them to Boston; and Becky Northcutt, for bringing it all back home.

Susan Bass, for vigorously encouraging me to write this book, against all my protestations.

Laura Davis, for pushing me past what I thought were my limits.

Saraswati Bass Nelson, for making me care so much.

And Janet Bryer, for loving my eccentricities instead of my virtues and for teaching me to fool around.

Laura Davis

Writing my first book on an issue of such deep and personal significance has been possible only because of the tremendous love and support I have received. I'd like to thank:

Karen Zelin for being everything a best friend should be, Natalie Devora for many kinds of sustenance, Barbara Cymrot, Dafna Wu, and Ruby for being family, Nona Olivia for humor, encouragement, and wisdom, Aurora Levins Morales for cooking me duck and telling me to write, Roberta Rutkin for teaching me to honor my creativity.

Janet Bryer and Saraswati Bass Nelson

for patience, love, countless wonderful meals, and always making me feel at home.

Abe Davis, my father, for creative inspiration, his quick wit, and most of all his unyielding faith in me.

Linda Eberth for teaching me that healing was possible, even for me.

Dagny Adamson, Marcy Alancraig, Ophelia Balderama, Theresa Carilli, Kimberly Jane Carter, Lynn Chadwick, Diane Costa, Carol Anne Dwight, Brandy Eiger, Toke Hoppenbrouwers, Diane Hugs, Shama Khalethia, Wendy Maryott-Wilhelms, Helen Mayer, Jennifer Meyer, Nina Newington, Kathleen Rose, Paula Ross, Jane Scolieri, Ray Gwyn Smith, Catherine Stifter, Deborah Stone, and Cheryl Wade for friendship, encouragement, and belief in this project.

Irena Klepfisz, Sandy Boucher, and Tillie Olsen for inspiration, wisdom, and encouraging me to write.

Rick Eckel, Alan Burton, and all the reporters at *Youth News* for patience and flexibility.

Dorothy Morales for wisdom and generosity.

Melanie Joshua for helping me stay in my body.

And finally my coauthor, Ellen Bass, for a million things, but mostly for changing her mind and saying yes.

PREFACE

Ellen Bass

I first heard that children were abused in 1974, when a young woman in my creative writing workshop pulled a crumpled half-sheet of paper out of her jeans pocket. Her writing was so vague, so tentative, that I wasn't sure what she was trying to say, but I sensed that it was important. Gently, I encouraged her to write more. Slowly she revealed her story. In pieces, on bits of paper, she shared the pain of her father's assaults, and I listened.*

Shortly afterward, another woman told me her story. And then another. And another. There were no groups for survivors of child sexual abuse then. The word "survivor"

was not yet in our vocabulary. But as they sensed that I could understand their stories, more and more women shared them with me. The psychologist Carl Rogers once said that when he worked through an issue in his life, it was as if telegrams were sent to his clients informing them that they could now bring that subject to therapy. Once I became aware of child sexual abuse, it was as if women knew that I was safe to talk to.

I was stunned by the number of women who had been sexually abused. I was deeply moved by the anguish they had endured. And I was equally impressed by their integrity, their ability to love and create through such devastation. I wanted people to know about this, about their strength and their beauty.

In 1978, three months after my first child was born, five women from my workshops and I began collecting stories for *I*

---

* This woman, Maggie Hoyal, went on to become a fine writer, and her story, "These Are the Things I Remember," is included in *I Never Told Anyone* (see the Bibliography).

Never Told Anyone: Writings by Women Survivors of Child Sexual Abuse. By 1983, when it was published, I had learned a great deal about the healing process. One of the things I learned was that writing itself was healing.

I decided to offer a group for survivors and designed the I Never Told Anyone workshops. I tried to create an environment safe enough for women to face their own pain and anger so they could begin to heal. At the first workshop, I mainly listened. I wanted to learn what survivors needed to talk about, what they needed to hear. Women wrote about their experience of being sexually abused, and read what they had written to the group. The simple opportunity to share with other survivors was profoundly healing.

The women who came to the workshops had no historical reason to trust. As children they had learned that their trust would be taken advantage of. And yet in the groups, they trusted.

This book, like the workshops, is based on the premise that everyone wants to become whole, to fulfill their potential. That we all, like seedlings or tadpoles, intend to become our full selves and will do so if we are not thwarted. People don't need to be forced to grow. All we need is favorable circumstances: respect, love, honesty, and the space to explore.

Since I began the I Never Told Anyone workshops, I have worked with hundreds of survivors across the country. I've facilitated workshops for partners of survivors and offered training seminars for professionals who work with survivors. I have solidified my understanding of what it takes to heal from child sexual abuse. This is the knowledge I want to share with you here.

I am not academically educated as a psychologist. I have acquired counseling skills primarily through practice. Since 1970, when I began working as a counselor and group facilitator, I've had the opportunity to train with a number of excellent therapists. But none of what is presented here is based on psychological theories. The process described, the suggestions, the exercises, the analysis, the conclusions, all come from the experiences of survivors.

I am also the partner of a survivor. In the beginning of our relationship we struggled with issues of trust, intimacy, and sexuality common to many couples and exacerbated by the effects of sexual abuse. Now, several years later, the problems that caused us both such anguish are no longer wrenching. Sexual abuse no longer overshadows our relationship. I want to tell you this because when you are in the thick of the pain, it's hard to believe that it will ever change. Yet it does. And it does not take forever.

As my grandmother used to say, "No one gets cheated from trouble." I was not sexually abused as a child, but I too have had pain to heal from. In the three years since beginning this book, I have made major personal changes. I live in the same house, with the same family, doing the same work. But I am not the same. Inspired by the survivors I worked with, I followed their example. Slowly, repetitively, step-by-step, little by little, my old fears, my desperate places, my limiting ways of coping, have receded. After saying "Healing is possible" to hundreds of survivors, it occurred to me that it was possible for me too.

Sometimes people ask, "Don't you find it depressing always to be thinking about child sexual abuse?" But I don't think so much about the abuse. I think about the healing.

The opportunity to be a part of women's healing feels a little like assisting at a birth. It's awesome to touch the miracle of life so closely. When women trust me with their most vulnerable, tender feelings, I am aware that I hold their spirit, for that moment, in my hands, and I am both honored and thrilled.

I want to see us all become whole—and not stop there. As we become capable of nurturing ourselves and living rich personal lives, we are enabled to act creatively in the world so that life can continue—the eucalyptus trees, the narcissus, the sunfish, the squirrels, seals, hummingbirds, our own children.

—*Ellen Bass*

Laura Davis

I remember calling Ellen one day a few months after I'd first remembered the incest. I counted the rings—two, three, four—she had to be home! She had to be! Five, six, seven—if I didn't talk to her right now, I knew I couldn't last through the afternoon. Eight, nine, ten—well, maybe she was outside folding the laundry and was just slow getting to the phone. Eleven, twelve, thirteen—I cannot stand another moment of this pain. My heart hurts and I can't take any more. Fourteen, fifteen . . .

"Hello, this is Ellen," she said, cheery and calm.

"Ellen, this is Laura. Look, you've got to tell me just one thing. Will I ever get through this? Is there ever an end? I can't take it anymore, and if you'll just tell me I can get to the other side, I'm sure I can last through the week." I was talking fast, my sentences piling up on each other.

"Hello, Laura. I'm glad you called." Her voice was smooth, reassuring. "And yes, you can make it. Healing is possible. You're already well on your way."

"Well on my way? How can you say that? I can't sleep, and when I do, it's all I dream about. I can't think about anything else. Every child I see on the street reminds me of incest. I can't make love, I can't eat, my whole body feels like a giant piece of rubber. I'm crying all the time. My whole life is flashbacks, going to therapy, and talking about incest. Half the time I don't even believe it happened, and the other half I'm sure it was my fault."

"It did happen, Laura. Look at what you're going through. Would anyone willingly choose to go through this torture? Why would you ever want to invent something this bad? You were just a little girl, Laura. He was what—seventy years old? You were a victim. You were innocent. You didn't do anything. It wasn't your fault."

Over and over, Ellen repeated those simple phrases: "It wasn't your fault. I believe you. Healing is possible. You're going to make it. You're going to be okay."

I expressed every doubt I could think of. Then I made up some new ones. I knew other survivors didn't make up this sort of thing, but I was the exception. I'd always been the exception, all my life.

"You can fight it all you want, Laura," she said finally, "but the door's been opened, and you're in the healing process whether you like it or not."

There was a long silence. Then I said, "Isn't there any way out?"

"The only way out is through, honey, I'm sorry."

I was quiet for a long time. "But it hurts, Ellen. It hurts so much."

"I know, Laura. I know. But there's a way through this stuff, and I know you're going to find it."

I wanted to write this book for probably the same reasons you are picking it up now —I felt a tremendous amount of pain in my life, and I wanted it to stop. Six months before I approached Ellen about collaborating, I had my first memories of being sexually abused by my grandfather when I was a child. Since that time, my life had fallen apart. My lover was leaving me. I was becoming increasingly estranged from my family. I was sure I was going crazy. I needed to understand what was happening to me. I needed to talk to other women who had been through it. Out of that need, my desire to write this book was born.

During the first year of our collaboration, it was my task to gather other women's stories. Ellen and I placed ads in papers, wrote to the women who'd come to her workshops, put out the call by word of mouth. I screened hundreds of calls and spent days on the phone listening to the stories of survivors, some of whom had never told anyone about their abuse before they read our ad, saw our poster.

Even though many of the women I interviewed had been actively healing for years, our conversations were never easy. One woman came to my house with a bag of food and ate from it for the whole three hours we talked. Another had to get stoned to tell me her story. A third burned sage and cedar, cleansing the room to make it safe. Sometimes the women cried. Sometimes we both did.

The honesty and courage of these women continually gave me hope. When I found it impossible to make love because of flashbacks, I'd ask a woman I was interviewing how she had healed her sexuality. When I started to wish I could shove the memories back where they came from, a woman would tell me that healing was the greatest miracle in her life.

As the months went by and the number of interviews grew, it became clear that there were tremendous similarities in the stories. The black ex-nun from Boston and the ambassador's daughter from Manila described the stages of their healing process the same way. A pattern started to emerge. What I was going through made sense.

As I moved along in my own healing, my relationship to the book changed. The acuteness of my own needs began to fade. It became increasingly important for me to communicate what I was learning. I began to talk more freely about the book with people I met. Within the first few minutes of any conversation, I'd be asked why I was writing it, and it would all be out on the table: "Because I'm a survivor myself."

Many people quickly changed the conversation or turned away. But an astonishing number responded with stories of their own: "It happened to me too." "My best friend says her swimming coach used to touch her." "My neighbor's kid reported her father just last week."

There are many phases involved in writing a book. For me, they have felt just like the stages of the healing process. With each new juncture I'd freeze, certain that I couldn't possibly jump over the next hurdle. I couldn't confront my family. I couldn't begin to write. Then I'd take that first terrifying step forward, and be set in motion again.

Throughout the first year, I wrote nothing about my own experience as a survivor. Ellen began the first draft while I kept busy transcribing and editing the interviews. Underneath, I knew that this book was as much about my life as it was about theirs, but I successfully avoided the inevitable moment when I, too, would have to speak my truth.

I remember the day very clearly. It started with a sentence I came across in one of Ellen's drafts. I was lying on the floor of her living room, reading through "Disclosures and Confrontations" with a red marker in my hand. Ellen was explaining the fact that family members may be sympathetic when first told about sexual abuse, only to turn on the survivor later on. She had used me as her example:

When Laura told her mother about the incest, her mother's first reaction was to send her one of her favorite nightgowns, so that Laura would be comforted; but after she'd thought about it for a while, she called Laura back and she said . . .

After that, Ellen had left a blank. She'd forgotten the exact content of the call.

When I read what she had written, my breakfast curled up into a tight little ball in my stomach. I started to tremble, and then I started to sweat. Anxiety shot from my stomach straight through my head. The fact that I was writing a book about my experiences in healing from incest could no longer be denied, abstracted, placed in a vague never-never land. There was the sentence, clear as day. "This is about me! This is about my life. That's *my* mother she's talking about."

"You'll have to rewrite that part," Ellen said with studied casualness. "It'll be much better in the first person."

I picked up the manuscript, and I crossed out the "Lauras." It wasn't easy to do it because I was holding my breath and my hand was shaking. Every time the word "Laura" appeared, I substituted the word "I." And whenever I saw the word "her," I put in

"my." Then I finished the sentence. When I was done, it read:

When I called my mother and told her I had remembered the incest, her first reaction was to tell me she loved me and supported me. She had an old favorite nightgown. It was cotton, well loved and broken in. She said she was going to send it to me in the mail, so I'd have something that smelled like her, since she couldn't be with me to comfort me in person.

A week after the nightgown arrived, my mother called me at four in the morning, waking me out of a sound sleep. She was screaming: "I've been up all night, and you're going to be up all night too! My father would never have done anything like that! You're just making this up to destroy me! You've just jumped on the incest bandwagon. You've always been into the 'in' thing. It's all because you're a lesbian. You all hate men. You all hate your families. You just want to kill me! You couldn't have done anything worse if you'd shot me."

The words flew out in a torrent, filling the whole side margin and curving around into all the available space at the top of the page. They wavered before my eyes, a field of red. "I did it," I said to Ellen, my voice high and tight. "Wanna hear it?"

"Sure," she said. "What have you got?"

I read it to her. She pretended not to notice the tremor in my voice. "Sounds better," she said. "Sounds a whole lot better."

For days after I wrote those words, I lived in a state of raw, unparalleled terror. I became convinced that Ellen did not really want to write the book with me. It was clear the whole collaboration was going to fall through. There was a conspiracy against me. Every day my anxiety increased, more and more out of proportion.

It wasn't until my friend Aurora, who is a very wise writer, invited me over for roast duck, fed me, soothed me and listened to me, that I quieted down enough to hear her say, over and over, in a hundred different ways, "Yes, Laura, it seems that you and Ellen will have to talk, *but what about those sentences you wrote?*"

It's been my experience that every time the subject of incest comes up in any kind of personal way, I reexperience the terror I felt as a child being abused. It's the same terror I saw in the faces of the women I interviewed when we finally sat down, small talk and tea finished, and I nudged them, my voice gentle: "What happened to you?" It's the fear I've seen flash across the faces of other women who ask what my work is, and who cannot bear to speak to me once they've heard the answer. It's the terror that's silenced us.

This book has been a way for me to break silence. But it has been more than that. It has been a steady source of inspiration and amazement for the past two and a half years. It has taught me that it is possible to take something that hurt me so deeply and turn it around. I hope it teaches you the same.

—Laura Davis

INTRODUCTION:
HEALING IS POSSIBLE

He pulled his hand out of my pants and spit on his fingers and rubbed them together. He didn't even seem aware of me. The sound of his spitting made me sick. Then he put his hand back down my pants and started to say something in that singing voice he used.

The front screen door slammed and his hand ripped out of my pants like it was burned. Then he turned on me and whispered harshly, "Don't you say anything to your mother ever. If you do, you'll be sorrier than you've ever been in your life."

—Maggie Hoyal, from "These Are the Things I Remember"

I can't scream, I can't speak, I can't breathe. My mouth, my whole face aches from his thrusts. I cannot see him, only huge arms, only dark brown hair around a wet red penis, pushing and pushing. I kick at the chair. I scratch his arms and skin comes off in my nails. He laughs, pressing harder, pushing his penis down my throat. Kiss it, kiss it.

—Experience Gibbs, from "1952, and Other Years"

Then one afternoon when I was just waking up from a nap, he sat next to me on the side of the bed. He put his big heavy fingers in my pants and began rubbing my clitoris. I had no idea what he was trying to do. He asked, yet sort of told me, "It feels good, doesn't it?" All I knew was I couldn't say no. I felt powerless to move. I said Yes.

—Karen Asherah, from "Daddy Kanagy"*

If you have been sexually abused, you are not alone. One out of three girls, and one out of seven boys, are sexually abused by the time they reach the age of eighteen. Sexual abuse happens to children of every class, culture, race, religion, and gender. Children are abused by fathers, stepfathers, uncles, brothers, grandparents, neighbors, family friends, baby-sitters, teachers, strangers, and sometimes by aunts and mothers.† Although women do abuse, the vast majority of abusers are heterosexual men.‡

All sexual abuse is damaging, and the trauma does not end when the abuse stops.

---

* All quotes are from Ellen Bass and Louise Thornton, eds., *I Never Told Anyone: Writings by Women Survivors of Child Sexual Abuse* (New York: Harper & Row, 1983).

† For sources on the scope of child sexual abuse, see *Conspiracy of Silence* by Sandra Butler, *The Best Kept Secret* by Florence Rush, *Sexually Victimized Children* and *Child Sexual Abuse* by David Finkelhor, and *The Secret Trauma* by Diana E. H. Russell. Listed in the "About Sexual Abuse" section of the Bibliography, these books cite a variety of studies you can refer to for more complete statistics.

‡ See footnote on pages 96–97.

If you were abused as a child, you are probably experiencing long-term effects that interfere with your day-to-day functioning.

However, it is possible to heal. It is even possible to thrive. Thriving means more than just an alleviation of symptoms, more than band-aids, more than functioning adequately. Thriving means enjoying a feeling of wholeness, satisfaction in your life and work, genuine love and trust in your relationships, pleasure in your body.

Until now, much of the literature on child sexual abuse has documented the ravages of abuse, talking extensively about "the tragedy of ruined lives," but little about recovery. This book is about recovery—what it takes, what it feels like, how it can transform your life.

People say "time heals all wounds," and it's true to a certain extent. Time will dull some of the pain, but deep healing doesn't happen unless you consciously choose it. Healing from child sexual abuse takes years of commitment and dedication. But if you are willing to work hard, if you are determined to make lasting changes in your life, if you are able to find good resources and skilled support, you can not only heal but thrive. We believe in miracles and hard work.

HOW CAN I KNOW IF I WAS A VICTIM OF CHILD SEXUAL ABUSE?

When you were a young child or teenager, were you:

- Touched in sexual areas?
- Shown sexual movies or forced to listen to sexual talk?
- Made to pose for seductive or sexual photographs?
- Subjected to unnecessary medical treatments?
- Forced to perform oral sex on an adult or sibling?
- Raped or otherwise penetrated?
- Fondled, kissed, or held in a way that made you uncomfortable?
- Forced to take part in ritualized abuse in which you were physically or sexually tortured?
- Made to watch sexual acts or look at sexual parts?
- Bathed in a way that felt intrusive to you?
- Objectified and ridiculed about your body?
- Encouraged or goaded into sex you didn't really want?
- Told all you were good for was sex?
- Involved in child prostitution or pornography?*

---

* Between 500,000 and 1,000,000 children are involved in prostitution and pornography in this country; a high percentage of them are victims of incest. See *Sex Work: Writings by Women in the Industry,* edited by Frédérique Dellacoste and Priscilla Alexander (Pittsburgh: Cleis Press, 1987).

If you are unable to remember any specific instances like the ones mentioned above but still have a feeling that something abusive happened to you, it probably did (see "But I Don't Have Any Memories," page 81).

Women who come to Ellen's workshops are often afraid that their abuse wasn't bad enough for them to be qualified to participate. They will say, "It wasn't incest—it was just a friend of the family," or "I was fourteen and it only happened once," or "He just showed me movies," or "It was with my brother. He was only a year older than me."

Such statements are a measure of the gross minimizing of abuse done in our society.

The fact that someone else has suffered from abuse more severe than your own does not lessen your suffering. Comparisons of pain are simply not useful.

There are many ways of minimizing sexual abuse. A particularly offensive one is to claim that if a man didn't force his penis into some opening of your body, you weren't really violated. This is not true. The severity of abuse should not be defined in terms of male genitals. Violation is determined by your experience as a child—your body, your feelings, your spirit. The precise physical acts are not always the most damaging aspects of abuse. Although forcible rape is physically excruciating to a small child, many kinds of sexual abuse are not physically painful. They do not leave visible scars.

Some abuse is not even physical. Your father may have stood in the bathroom doorway, making suggestive remarks or simply leering when you entered to use the toilet. Your uncle may have walked around naked, calling attention to his penis, talking about his sexual exploits, questioning you about your body. Your tennis coach may have badgered you into telling him exactly what you did with your boyfriend. There are many ways to be violated sexually.

There is also abuse on the psychological level. You had the feeling your stepfather was aware of your physical presence every minute of the day, no matter how quiet and unobtrusive you were. Your neighbor watched your changing body with an intrusive interest. Your father took you out on romantic dates and wrote you love letters.

Nor is frequency of abuse what's at issue. Betrayal takes only a minute. A father can slip his fingers into his daughter's underpants in thirty seconds. After that the world is not the same.

BUT I DON'T REMEMBER

Children often cope with abuse by forgetting it ever happened. As a result, you may have no conscious memory of being abused. You may have forgotten large chunks of your childhood. Yet there are things you do remember. When you are touched in a certain way, you feel nauseated. Certain words or facial expressions scare you. You know you never liked your mother to touch you. You slept with your clothes on in junior high school. You were taken to the doctor repeatedly for vaginal infections.

You may think you don't have memories, but often as you begin to talk about what you do remember, there emerges a constellation of feelings, reactions, and recollections that add up to substantial information. To say "I was abused," you don't need the kind of recall that would stand up in a court of law.

Often the knowledge that you were abused starts with a tiny feeling, an intuition. It's important to trust that inner voice and work from there. Assume your feelings are valid. So far, no one we've talked to thought she might have been abused, and then later discovered that she hadn't been. The progression always goes the other way, from suspicion to confirmation. If you think you were abused and your life shows the symptoms, then you were.

GETTING SUPPORT

No matter how committed you are, it is extremely difficult to heal from child sexual abuse in isolation. Much of the damage experienced is the result of the secrecy and silence that surrounded the abuse. Trying to heal while perpetuating that lonely silence is nearly impossible.

It is essential that you have at least one other person with whom you can share your pain and your healing. That person may be another survivor, a member of a support group, or a counselor. He or she could be a nurturing partner or family member, or a sibling who was also abused. Ideally, you will have a combination of many resources. (For help in finding support, see "Healing Resources," page 458.)

WHERE ARE YOU NOW?

You may be reading this book at any point in the healing process. You may not yet have identified yourself as a survivor. You may be just starting to make the connection between sexual abuse and its effects in your life. On the other hand, you may be years into an active healing process. Or you may simply want an affirmation of how far you've come. This book can provide specific suggestions, support, and validation no matter where you are in the healing process.

WHAT READING THIS BOOK WILL BE LIKE

Reading this book can be a cathartic healing experience. As you begin to realize that your life makes sense, and that you are not the only one who has suffered, you may experience a tremendous feeling of relief. But relief is not the only response you may have.

In the course of writing this book, we shared parts of the manuscript with many survivors. In response, women have gone out and confronted abusers, renewed their commitment to heal, or shared honestly with their partner for the first time. Some have had breakthroughs in their sexuality. Others have stopped blaming themselves.

Women have also reported feeling terrified, furious, and anguished. Others have connected with forgotten pockets of grief and pain. Women reported having nightmares, flashbacks, new memories. One survivor, a recovering alcoholic, began to crave alcohol as she read. Another woman began fighting with her lover. Several went back to therapy. All said their lives were changed.

If you have unfamiliar or uncomfortable feelings as you read this book, don't be alarmed. Strong feelings are part of the healing process. On the other hand, if you breeze through these chapters, you probably aren't feeling safe enough to confront these issues. Or you may be coping with the book the same way you coped with the abuse—by separating your intellect from your feelings. If that's the case, stop, take a break, talk to someone for support, and come back to it later. It's important that you don't "bear" this book the way you bore the abuse: numb and alone. If you come to a part that stops you, you may be having a hard time with the material in that section. Don't force yourself to read it. Try a different chapter.

As you read, it's important to look inside, paying attention to your own thoughts and feelings. The idea of developing such a relationship with yourself may be foreign to you. As women, we've been taught to meet the needs of others, that focusing on ourselves is selfish. But healing requires a willingness to put yourself first.

The other morning, when Ellen listened to the messages on her answering machine, there was one that said, "I called to let you know that I really *am* healing. And this is the sweetest feeling I have ever known—to be whole."

You deserve this feeling.

ABOUT THE STORIES IN THIS BOOK

Over two hundred survivors volunteered to be interviewed for this book. Out of these, we talked to fifty women in depth. We could not tell everyone's story in its entirety, but we have included portions of each woman's experience.

We have also included stories from the participants of the I Never Told Anyone workshops, as well as workshops for partners and for counselors. All these women and men generously gave us permission to include their experiences.

The survivors presented here represent a broad range of women. You will meet women who vary in terms of age, economic background, race, and sexual preference. Some are in committed relationships, others are single; there are mothers and non-mothers; women who were abused under different circumstances and by different perpetrators. You will read about women who are at different stages of the healing process and women whose approaches to healing have varied.

The quotes and stories included throughout this book come from survivors and the partners of survivors. Throughout the text, you will see many unidentified quotes. Each quote stands alone and represents one person's experience. Sometimes two or more survivors speak on a single page.

We chose not to place a name with every quote because it would have been unwieldy. Yet when it was essential to the story or when someone specifically asked to be identified, we did use names. We wanted to respect each person's right to choose whether they wanted to use their real name, a pseudonym, or no name at all. (For more on the use of pseudonyms, see "Names or Pseudonyms: The Right to Choose," page 357.) As authors, we also had personal experiences we wanted to share. At those times we identify ourselves by our first names.

The creative writings are primarily by survivors or supporters of survivors—partners, friends, and counselors. The others are poems we thought would have significance for survivors.

Although we've included the experiences of male partners and supporters, we chose not to address male survivors directly. Many boys are abused, and male survivors need and deserve support in their healing, but we wrote this book for women because women's experiences were what we understood best. Since most of the healing process is universal, we hope men who read this book will find it helpful. There is a growing movement of support for male survivors, and we've included some references in the "Resources for Male Survivors" section of the Bibliography.

USING THE
WRITING EXERCISES

In the I Never Told Anyone workshops Ellen leads for adult survivors of child sexual abuse, ten to twenty women come together in an environment of support, confidentiality, and safety to explore their feelings, mourn their violation, gather their strength, and celebrate their survival.

Participants are asked to write about being sexually abused as children. So often survivors have had their experiences denied, trivialized, or distorted. Writing is an important avenue for healing because it gives you the opportunity to define your own reality. You can say: This did happen to me. It was that bad. It was the fault and responsibility of the adult. I was—and am—innocent.

By going back and writing about what happened, you also reexperience feelings and are able to grieve. You excavate the sites in which you've buried memory and pain, dread and fury. You relive your history.

WHY WRITING?

One handy thing about writing is that it's almost always available. At three in the morning, when you're alone or you don't want to wake your partner, when your friend's out of town, when your counselor's answering machine is on and even the cat is out prowling, your journal is there. It's quiet, cheap, and portable. A journal can help you figure out how you feel, what you think, what you need, what you want to say, how you want to handle a situation, just by writing it through.

ANYONE CAN USE WRITING

Using writing as a healing tool can be helpful whether or not you participate in an organized workshop with other survivors. You don't need to think of yourself as a writer or even like to write. You may have had a limited education. Perhaps you can't spell or think you're a terrible writer.

Some survivors have special blocks associated with writing. If your mother read your private diary, if your father was an English teacher and always criticized your written work, if your best friend passed your intimate letters around the junior high school cafeteria, then you may be wary of putting words on paper. But all of us have a deep need for self-expression. Yours may take forms other than writing, but if you'd like to try writing as one method of healing, even previous blocks need not stand in the way. Many women who have been reluctant to write have done these exercises—and benefited enormously.

TIME AND PLACE

Choose a time and place where you won't be interrupted. Though it may take some arranging, you deserve such a time. Half an hour is a good actual writing time for each exercise. Although you can write for longer if you want, setting a specific time can help you feel comfortable.

Since writing about sexual abuse can bring up strong feelings, don't squeeze in your half-hour of writing time between picking the kids up from school and starting dinner. Make sure you give yourself a little time afterward to absorb the impact of the writing.

BEING HEARD

Writing itself is very helpful, but sharing what you've written is important too. After you write, read your writing to someone who will listen attentively and be responsive. *Make sure you protect yourself by not choosing anyone who will reabuse you in any way.*

If there's no one you can read to right away, read out loud to yourself—at least you will be reading to one attentive listener. Just saying the words out loud can make them more real.

If you read your writing to someone who has no experience in listening to personal writing, tell that person what you need. You may say that you'd like them not to criticize or judge what you say. You may want them to ask questions, to help you talk about it more, or you may want them simply to listen quietly. You may want comforting and you may not. People usually respond in more satisfying ways when you tell them what you want.

THE BASIC METHOD

Try to forget everything you've ever been told about writing. What you're going to do is a kind of free writing, or stream-of-consciousness writing. It's not about making art or polished crafting or trying to make sense to someone else. Rather it's a way to short-circuit some of your censors to get to what you need to say.

Write without stopping. Go at a pace that's comfortable for you, and don't stop. If you get stuck or can't think of anything to say, you can write "This is the stupidest exercise I ever heard of," or "I'm hungry—I wonder if time's up yet." One woman who was writing about her abuse stopped every few lines and wrote "I cannot say any more," and then went on to say more. Allowing herself to refuse to go on, saying no, made it possible for her to go one more step each time.

You needn't use full sentences. You needn't spell or punctuate properly. It can be in English or in another language. Sometimes if another language was spoken when you were a child you will remember in that language. If you were abused before you learned to talk, your writing may come out as baby talk.

THE WRITING EXERCISES

The Effects . . . . page 39
Coping . . . . page 54
What Happened to You . . . . . . page 83
The Child Within . . . . page 115
Grieving . . . . page 121
Disclosures and
    Confrontations . . . . page 148
Reconstructing Family
    History . . . . page 154
Changing Patterns . . . . page 177
Your Family Now . . . . page 306

PART ONE
TAKING STOCK

EFFECTS: RECOGNIZING
THE DAMAGE

People have said to me, "Why are you dragging this up now?" Why? WHY? Because it has controlled every facet of my life. It has damaged me in every possible way. It has destroyed everything in my life that has been of value. It has prevented me from living a comfortable emotional life. It's prevented me from being able to love clearly. It took my children away from me. I haven't been able to succeed in the world. If I had a comfortable childhood, I could be anything today. I know that everything I don't deal with now is one more burden I have to carry for the rest of my life. I don't care if it happened 500 years ago! It's influenced me all that time, and it does matter. It matters very much.

—Jennierose Lavender, 47-year-old survivor

The long-term effects of child sexual abuse can be so pervasive that it's sometimes hard to pinpoint exactly how the abuse affected you. It permeates everything: your sense of self, your intimate relationships, your sexuality, your parenting, your work life, even your sanity. Everywhere you look, you see its effects. As one survivor explained:

It's like those pictures I remember from *Highlights for Children* magazine. The bicycle was hidden in a tree, a banana was growing from someone's ear, and all the people were upside-down. The caption underneath said, "What's wrong with this picture?" But so many things were disturbed and out of place, it was often easier to say, "What's right with this picture?"

Many survivors have been too busy surviving to notice the ways they were hurt by the abuse. But you cannot heal until you acknowledge the areas that need healing.

Because sexual abuse is just one of many factors that influenced your development, it isn't always possible to isolate its effects from the other influences on your life. Is your self-esteem low because you were a Black child raised in a racist society? Because you grew up in a culture that devalues women? Because your mother was an alcoholic? Or because you were molested when you were nine? It's the interplay of hundreds of factors that make you who you are today.

The way the abuse was handled when you were a child has a lot to do with its subsequent impact. If a child's disclosure is met with compassion and effective intervention, the healing begins immediately. But if no one noticed or responded to your pain, or if you were blamed, not believed, or suffered further trauma, the damage was compounded. And the ways you coped with the abuse may have created further problems.

Not all survivors are affected in the same way. You may do well in one area of your life, but not in another. You may be competent at work and in parenting but have trouble with intimacy. Some women have a constant nagging feeling that something is wrong. For others, the damage is so blatant that they feel they've wasted their lives:

As far as I'm concerned, my whole life was stolen from me. I didn't get to be who I could have been. I didn't get the education I should have gotten when I was young. I married too early. I hid behind my husband. I didn't make contact with other people. I haven't had a rich life. It's not ever too late, but I didn't start working on this until I was thirty-eight, and not everything can be retrieved. And that makes me very angry.

The effects of child sexual abuse can be devastating, but they do not have to be permanent. As you read this chapter, you may find yourself nodding your head—"Uh-huh, me too"—recognizing, perhaps for the first time, the ways in which the abuse affects your life. Look at the following lists and ask yourself how you've been affected. Such recognition will probably be painful, but it is, in fact, part of the healing process.

SELF-ESTEEM AND PERSONAL POWER

When you were abused, your boundaries, your right to say no, your sense of control in the world, were violated. You were powerless. The abuse humiliated you, gave you the message that you were of little value. Nothing you did could stop it.

If you told someone about what was happening to you, they probably ignored you, said you made it up, or told you to forget it. They may have blamed you. Your reality was denied or twisted and you felt crazy. Rather than see the abuser or your parents as bad, you came to believe that you did not deserve to be taken care of, that you in fact deserved abuse. You felt isolated and alone.

Many abused kids are told directly that they'll never succeed, that they're stupid, or that they're only good for sex. With messages like these, it's hard to believe in yourself.

WHERE ARE YOU NOW?

- Do you feel that you're bad, dirty, or ashamed?
- Do you feel powerless, like a victim?
- Do you feel different from other people?
- Do you feel there's something wrong with you deep down inside? That if people really knew you, they'd leave?
- Do you ever feel self-destructive or suicidal? Or that you simply want to die?

- Do you hate yourself?
- Do you have a hard time nurturing and taking care of yourself? Are you able to enjoy feeling good?
- Do you find it hard to trust your intuition?
- Do you feel unable to protect yourself in dangerous situations? Have you experienced repeated victimization (rape, assault, battery) as an adult?
- Do you have a sense of your own interests, talents, or goals?
- Do you have trouble feeling motivated? Are you often immobilized?
- Are you afraid to succeed?
- Can you accomplish things you set out to do?
- Do you feel you have to be perfect?
- Do you use work or achievements to compensate for inadequate feelings in other parts of your life?

FEELINGS

As a child you could not afford to feel the full extent of your terror, pain, or rage. The agony would have been devastating. You could not have done arithmetic with other second-graders had you known the depth of your sorrow. And you could not think about killing your father when you relied on him to feed you.

Because your innocent love and trust were betrayed, you learned that you could not rely on your feelings. The feelings you expressed may have been disregarded or mocked. You were ignored, told you had nothing to worry about, molested again.

If the adults around you were out of control with their feelings, you got the message that feelings led to violence or destruction. Anger meant beatings or furniture thrown across the room.

You may have learned to block out physical pain, because it was too devastating or because you did not want to give the abuser the satisfaction of seeing you cry. But since you can't block feelings selectively, you simply stopped feeling.

WHERE ARE YOU NOW?

- Can you recognize your feelings? Tell the difference between them?
- Do you have trouble expressing your feelings?

- Do you value feelings or see them as an indulgence?
- Are you comfortable with anger? Sadness? Happiness? Calm?
- Do you feel confused much of the time?
- Do you experience a wide range of emotions or just a few?

- Are you prone to depression? Nightmares? Panic attacks?
- Have you ever worried about going crazy?
- Are you afraid of your feelings? Do they ever seem out of control?
- Have you ever been violent or abusively angry?

YOUR BODY

Children learn about the world through their bodies. When you were sexually abused, you learned that the world was not a safe place. You experienced pain, betrayal, and conflicting sensations of arousal. Children often learn to leave their bodies to avoid these feelings—or they numb themselves as best they can.

WHERE ARE YOU NOW?

- Do you feel present in your body most of the time? Or are there times when you feel as though you've left your body?
- Do you ever use alcohol, drugs, or food in a way that concerns you?

- Do you have a full range of feelings in your body? Or do you sometimes go numb?
- Are you aware of the messages your body gives you (hunger, fear, tiredness, pain)? Do you respond to them?
- Do you have a hard time loving and accepting your body? Do you feel at home in it?
- Do you have any physical illnesses that you think might be connected to your abuse?
- Do you enjoy using your body in activities such as dance, sports, or hiking?
- Have you ever intentionally hurt yourself or abused your body?

INTIMACY

The building blocks of intimacy—giving and receiving, trusting and being trustworthy—are learned in childhood. If children are given consistent loving attention, they develop skills for establishing and maintaining nurturing relationships. Unfortunately, if you were abused, your natural trust was skewed by adults who misused your innocence. You were told, "Daddy's only touching you because he loves you" or "I'm doing this so you'll be a good wife to your husband someday." You grew up with confusing messages about the relationship between sex and love, trust and betrayal.

WHERE ARE YOU NOW?

- Do you find it difficult to trust anyone? Do you have close friends?
- Can you imagine a healthy relationship?
- Is it difficult for you to give or receive nurturing? To be affectionate?
- Are you afraid of people? Do you feel alienated or lonely?
- Do you tend to get involved with people who are inappropriate or unavailable?
- Have you ever been involved with someone who reminds you of your abuser?
- Do you often feel taken advantage of?
- Do you find that your relationships just don't work out?
- Do you have trouble making a commitment? Do you panic when people get too close?
- Do you find you're able to get close to friends, but can't seem to make things work with a lover?
- Do you find yourself clinging to the people you care about?
- Do you repeatedly test people?
- Do you expect people to leave you?
- Can you say no?

SEXUALITY

When children are sexually abused, their natural sexual capacity is stolen. You were introduced to sex on an adult's timetable, according to an adult's needs. You never had a chance to explore naturally, to experience your own desires from the inside. Sexual arousal became linked to feelings of shame, disgust, pain, and humiliation. Pleasure became tainted as well. And desire (the abuser's desire) was dangerous, an out-of-control force used to hurt you.

Children often leave their bodies during sex with the abuser. You numbed yourself or disappeared. You disconnected from sexual feelings.

When abuse was coupled with affection, your needs for nurturing were linked with sex. You didn't learn to meet these needs in other ways.

WHERE ARE YOU NOW?

- Are you able to stay present when making love? Do you go through sex numb or in a panic?
- Do you try to use sex to meet needs that aren't sexual? Can you accept nurturing and closeness in other ways?
- Do you find yourself avoiding sex or going after sex you really don't want? Can you say no?
- Do you feel your worth is primarily sexual?
- Are you sexual with partners who respect you? Have you ever had partners who sexually abused you?
- Have you been a prostitute? Or used your sexuality in a way that had elements of exploitation?
- Do you experience sexual pleasure? Sexual desire? Do you think pleasure is bad?

- Do you ever think sex is disgusting or that you're disgusting for enjoying it?
- Are you turned on by violent, sadistic, or incestuous fantasies?
- Do you find you need to control everything about sex to feel safe?

- Do you ever experience flashbacks to the abuse?
- Do you have sex because you want to, or only because your partner wants it?
- Have you ever been sexually abusive?

CHILDREN AND PARENTING

If the abuse took place within your own family, or if your family did not protect and support you, you grew up in a dysfunctional family. You did not have the benefit of healthy role models. Until you actively face your abuse and begin to heal from it, you are likely to repeat the same kind of parenting you had as a child.

WHERE ARE YOU NOW?

- Do you feel uncomfortable or frightened around children?

- Have you ever been abusive, or feared you might be?
- Do you find it hard to set clear boundaries with children? To balance their needs with your own?
- Do you have a hard time feeling close to your children? Are you comfortable being affectionate with them?
- Have you had trouble protecting the children in your care?
- Are you overprotective?
- Have you taught your children to protect themselves? Have you talked to them honestly about sex?

FAMILIES OF ORIGIN

Relationships are distorted in incestuous families. The essential trust, sharing, and safety are missing, and in their place there is secrecy, isolation, and fear. If you were abused by a family member, you may have been made the family scapegoat, repeatedly told that you were crazy or bad. You may have felt isolated, cut off from nurturing contact with others.

Since alcoholism and other dysfunctional patterns often accompany sexual abuse, you may have had to cope with these problems as well. Adult responsibilities may have been forced on you.

If the abuse took place outside your family and you weren't adequately heard, you got the message that your pain wasn't important, that you couldn't rely on your family to protect or understand you.

WHERE ARE YOU NOW?

- Are you satisfied with your family relationships? Or are they strained and difficult?
- Is the sexual abuse acknowledged in your family? Do the people in your family support you?

- Do you feel crazy, invalidated, or depressed whenever you see your family? Have you been rejected by your family?
- Have you confronted your abuser or told other family members about your abuse?
- Do you feel safe when you're with your family?
- Do you expect the people in your family to change? To take care of you? To see your point of view? To believe you? Do you keep hoping?
- Does incest still go on in your family?

YOU CAN HEAL FROM THE EFFECTS OF ABUSE

If you feel overwhelmed reading this chapter, remember that you have already lived through the hardest part—the abuse itself. You have survived against formidable odds. The same abuse that undercut you has also provided you with many of the inner resources necessary for healing. One quality every survivor can be confident of having is strength. And with an understanding of what it takes to heal, that strength leads directly to determination. As one woman stated: "No one's gonna fuck with me no more."

WRITING EXERCISES: THE EFFECTS

(See the basic method for writing exercises on page 28.)

Write about the ways you're still affected by the abuse. What are you still carrying in terms of your feelings of self-worth, your work, your relationships, your sexuality? How is your life still pained, still limited?

Write about the strengths you've developed because of the abuse. Think of what it's taken for you to survive. What are the qualities that enabled you to make it? Perseverance? Flexibility? Self-sufficiency? Write about your strengths with pride.

COPING: HONORING WHAT YOU DID TO SURVIVE

My whole life has pretty much been coping.

—35-year-old survivor

Coping is what you did to survive the trauma of being sexually abused. There is a continuum of coping behaviors. You may have run away from home or turned to alcohol or drugs. You may have become a super-achiever, excelling in school and taking care of your brothers and sisters at home. You may have forgotten what happened to you, withdrawn into yourself, or cut off your feelings. With few resources for taking care of yourself, you survived with whatever means were available.

Many survivors criticize themselves for the ways they coped. You may not want to admit some of the things you had to do to survive. But coping is nothing to be ashamed of. You survived, and it's important to honor your resourcefulness.

While some of the ways you've coped have developed into strengths (being successful at your work, becoming self-sufficient, developing a sense of humor, being good in a crisis), others have become self-defeating patterns (stealing, drug or alcohol abuse, compulsive overeating). Often one behavior will have both healthy and destructive aspects. Healing requires that you differentiate between the two. Then you can celebrate your strengths while you start changing the patterns that no longer serve you.

As you read through these different ways of coping, you'll find some that are general, common to almost all survivors. Others are specific and may or may not be familiar to you. Identifying the ways in which you've coped is an essential first step in making satisfying changes in your life.

THE BASICS

MINIMIZING

Minimizing means pretending that whatever happened wasn't really that bad. It means saying "My dad's a little pissed off," when in fact he just smashed an armchair to bits. Kids growing up surrounded by abuse often believe that everyone else grows up the same way. Doesn't every father tuck his daughter into bed like that?

Yeah, I minimized it. "Hey, so your dad puts his prick in your mouth? What's the big deal? Hey!" Up until five years ago, people would say to me, "Were you from an abusive family?" and I'd say, "No!" After all, I didn't die. I was in the hospital with broken bones, but I didn't die. There was blood all over the place but at least I made it.

RATIONALIZING

Rationalizing is the means by which children explain away abuse. "Oh, he couldn't help it. He was drunk." They invent reasons that excuse the abuser. "Four kids was just too much for her. No wonder she didn't take care of me." Rationalizing keeps the focus on the abuser:

There's a part of me that always wants to figure out "Why the hell did he

What My Father Told Me
by Dorianne Laux

Always I have done what was asked, melmac
dishes stacked on rag towels, the slack
of a vacuum cleaner cord wound around my hand,
laundry hung from a line.
There is much to do always, and I do it. The iron
resting in its frame, hot in the shallow pan
of summer as the basins of his hands push
the book I am reading aside.
I do as I am told, his penis like the garden
hose, in this bedroom, in that bathroom, over
the toilet or my bare stomach. I do
the chores, pull weeds out back, finger
stinkbug husks, snail
carcasses, pile dead grass in black bags.
At night his feet are safe on their pads, light
on the wall to wall as he takes the hallway
to my room.
His voice, the hiss of lawn sprinklers, wet
hush of sweat in his hollows, the mucus
still damp in the corner of my eyes as I wake.
Summer ended. Schoolwork didn't suit me.
My fingers unaccustomed to the slimness
of a pen, the delicate touch it takes
to uncoil the mind.
History. A dateline pinned to the wall.
Beneath each president's face, a quotation.
Pictures of buffalo and wheat fields, a wagon train
circled for the night, my hand raised to ask the question
Where did the children sleep?

do it? What could have hurt this poor man so terribly that he would have to resort to these things?" That's a way of dramatizing his story instead of mine. It's a way of trying to forgive him, instead of allowing the real anger and fury I feel.

DENYING

Denying is turning your head the other way and pretending that whatever is happening isn't, or what has happened didn't. It is a basic pattern in alcoholic families. It's almost universal where incest is concerned. "If I just ignore it long enough, it will go away."

Denial can also be a way to avoid telling anyone about the abuse. It's often more comfortable for a child to deny reality than to face the fact that the adults around her won't protect her, and in fact may harm her.

One woman remembered the time a neighborhood boy told her everyone knew that her father had been beating her the night before. They'd all heard her screaming. "I told him, 'Oh, that wasn't me. My father would never beat me.' "

Some survivors acknowledge that they were abused but deny that it had any effect. "I told my therapist I'd already dealt with it," one woman said. "He believed me."

FORGETTING

Forgetting is one of the most common and effective ways children deal with sexual abuse. The human mind has tremendous powers of repression. Many children are able to forget about the abuse, *even as it is happening to them:*

I had a visual image of a closet in my mind. I shoved everything that was happening to me into the back of that closet, and I closed the door.

This capacity to forget explains why so many adult survivors are unaware of the fact that they were abused. (For a more thorough explanation of this phenomenon, see "Remembering," page 70.) Some survivors remember the abuse but forget the way they felt at the time. One woman, repeatedly molested throughout her childhood by her stepfather and her brother, said, "I had totally and completely repressed that it had even been uncomfortable."

SPLITTING

We use the term "splitting" to describe two different feeling states. Although only the first usage fits the clinical definition, we use "splitting" both ways because survivors so often do.*

---

* Clinically, "splitting" refers to the tendency to view people or events as either all good or all bad. It is a way of coping that allows a person to hold opposite, unintegrated views. For example, the child separates the father whom she depends on for love and protection from the father who abuses her. This allows her to preserve an image of the "good" father, but at great cost. She is left identifying herself as "bad" in order to make sense of the abuse.

"Splitting" also describes the feeling the survivor has when she separates her consciousness from her body, or "leaves" her body.

LACK OF INTEGRATION

One of the by-products of forgetting is a feeling of being divided into more than one person. There is the little girl having the good childhood, but underneath there is the child who's prone to nightmares and sees people hiding in the corner of the room.

Many survivors continue this pattern into adulthood. On the inside you feel evil and bad, and know that something is very wrong, but on the outside you present a different front to the world. Laura remembers:

At twenty-one I was lying in my bed, unable to get up, watching the bugs march across my sheets, thinking I would either kill myself or go crazy. A half-hour later, I turned around and wrote my mother another cheery letter about how well I was doing. I was desperate to maintain the facade.

But the facade is often very thin. A fifty-six-year-old psychotherapist explains the way she acted out the split in her life:

Growing up, I did everything super-right. I was an overachiever. I was an A student all through college. I was a Fulbright scholar in London. I was considered a huge success.

I developed a total false personality based on what you were supposed to be, and hid myself. My interpersonal relationships were exchanges of displays, nothing more. I got by because of money and status.

I knew I was sick. I knew there was something hideously wrong with me. Underneath that false personality was a blankness, and underneath the blankness was a tremendous rage. I was sure that if I ever allowed my behavior to manifest any sign of the problems I had inside, everything would crumble entirely and I'd end up in an insane asylum or police lockup.

In cases of extreme abuse, this kind of splitting can result in the development of multiple personalities (see "Multiple Personalities," page 423).

LEAVING YOUR BODY

Children who are abused or battered often numb their bodies so they will not feel what is being done to them. Others actually leave their bodies and watch the abuse as if from a great distance.

It's like I actually rise up out of my body. I could feel myself sitting in a chair, and I could feel myself floating up out of my body. That's exactly what it is, like being suspended in midair. I know that my body is in the chair, but the rest of me is out of my body.

(For more on this kind of splitting, see "From Splitting to Being in Your Body," page 209.)

CONTROL

Control is a thread that runs through the lives of many survivors:

I have a tremendous attachment to things going my way. It feels like I'm going to die if I don't get my way. There

Two Pictures of My Sister
by Dorianne Laux

If an ordinary person is silent
it may be a tactical maneuver.
If a writer is silent, he is lying.
——*Jaroslav Seifert*

The pose is stolen from Monroe, struck
in the sun's floodlight, eyes lowered,
a long-stemmed plastic rose between her
          teeth.
My cast-off bathing suit hangs in folds
over her ribs, straps cinched, pinned
at the back of her neck. Barefoot
on the hot cement, knock-kneed, comical
if it weren't for the graceful
angles of her arms, her flesh soft
against the chipped stucco.

The other picture is in my head.
It is years later.
It is in color.
Blond hair curls away from the planes of her
          face
like wood shavings. She wears a lemon
          yellow
ruffled top, denim cutoffs,
her belly button squeezed to a slit
above the silver snap.

She stands against the hallway wall
while Dad shakes his belt in her face.
A strip of skin has been peeled
from her bare shoulder, there are snake
lines across her thighs, a perfect curl
around her long neck.
She looks through him as if she can see
behind his head. She dares him.
Go on. Hit me again.
He lets the folded strap unravel to the floor
and holding it by its tail bells the buckle
off her cheekbone.
She does not move or cry or even wince
as the welt blooms on her temple
like a flower opening frame by frame
in a Disney film.
It lowers her eyelid with its violet
petals and as he walks away only her eyes
move, like the eyes of a portrait that follow
          you
around a museum room, her face a stubborn
moon that trails the car all night, stays
          locked
in the frame of the back window
no matter how many turns you take,
no matter how far you go.

are a lot of small, everyday interactions that make me feel tremendously out of control.

When survivors grow up in a chaotic environment they often go to great lengths to keep their lives in order:

My shoes have to be put back in the same place at night. My room is always neat. When I come to work in the morning, I have this whole routine of putting the pen in a certain place, my keys in a certain place. Wherever I can maintain control, I do it, because there were so many places as a kid where I didn't have any control.

Such control can be positive. Good organization is an asset if you're a manager, a mother, or a worker. The negative side can be a lack of flexibility, and difficulty in negotiating or compromising.

CHAOS

Survivors sometimes maintain control by creating chaos. If your behavior is out of control, you force the people around you to drop what they're doing to respond to your latest problems. In this way, you get attention (though negative) and in effect become the person calling the shots. Laura's father always told her, "A family is a dictatorship run by its sickest member."

Like children of alcoholics, survivors are often good at both resolving and generating crises:

They say that humans tend to gravitate toward what is comfortable, what they know. If this is true, then it explains why more often than not you find survivors in the midst of chaos. Not only are they familiar with it, they handle it beautifully. I could handle any extraordinary circumstance and in fact felt in my element in those situations. But put me into the everyday world and I was very freaked-out. I have always been hysterical in the midst of normalcy.

Before I found out that I was a survivor, I wondered why my life was filled with traumatic situations. Not only did I not have any middle ground, I was terrified at the thought of it. Whenever my life would calm down, I would start wishing for something major to happen so I could feel at home. While other people were looking for ways to put

themselves on the edge, I could never get off it.

—Jerilyn Munyon

While this capacity to handle crises can make you a good emergency-room worker or ambulance driver, it can also be a way you keep yourself from feeling. If you are addicted to intensity and drama, you might make a dynamic, charismatic performer, but you may also be running from yourself.

SPACING OUT

Survivors have an uncanny capacity to space out and not be present. There are many ways to do this:

I walked into walls and doors and furniture a lot, because I wasn't in my body, but a few bruises were a small price to pay for oblivion.

Whenever something scares her, one survivor finds an object in the room and stares at it—just as she did when she was being molested:

I have total recall of the most intimate details of different rooms I've been in. I can't remember who I was talking to or what we were talking about, but I sure can tell you exactly what the window looked like!

The problem with this kind of distancing is that you cut yourself off, not only from pain but from the richness of life and human feeling. You avoid the pain but miss everything else as well:

I spent a lot of my life spacing out and disappearing. I pride myself on how slick I am. I have been known to sit there and be totally gone and then to come back and have no idea where I am in a conversation. I'll have been talking the whole time. And what's really weird is that most people don't even notice I'm gone!

During an interview, both Laura and this survivor demonstrated their abilities to space out. Laura says:

We were laughing about how good we both were at disappearing and I turned and asked her how much of the time she had been present during the interview. "Oh, about 70 percent," she answered. "What about you?"

"Oh, about 65 percent. I'm having a hard day." We laughed. There we were, two incest survivors doing an interview about healing and neither of us was fully there. We made a pact on the spot to stop at any point either of us started to disappear and to talk about what had triggered it.

BEING SUPER-ALERT

As a child, tuning into every nuance of your environment may have saved you from being abused. You may always be aware of where you are in a room. You may sit where you can watch the entrance, making sure no one can come up behind you. You might also be hyper-aware of the people around you, always anticipating their needs and moods. One woman said she was a confirmed gossip for just this reason. If she kept track of what

everyone was doing around her, no one could ever surprise her again.

Hyper-awareness can be an asset. Survivors have become excellent therapists, sensitive doctors, ground-breaking reporters, perceptive parents, compassionate friends. One survivor works in a crime lab analyzing evidence in sexual assault cases. She says her extra level of awareness makes her great at the job. Other survivors have developed psychic abilities from their sensitivity. Yet this state of constant alertness can be wearing. We all need to relax sometimes.

HUMOR

A tough sense of humor, a bitter wit or sense of cynicism, can get you through hard times. As long as you keep people laughing, you maintain a certain protective distance. And as long as you keep laughing, you don't have to cry:

For years I used humor to deflect the pain and the shame I felt talking about incest. The humor was, of course, the gallows variety. It often pointed out the absurdity of the American Ideal, the family surrounded by a white picket fence—with blood dripping down the painted slats where the daughters had been sacrificially skewered. It was my way of telling the truth about something I wasn't sure anyone would believe if they hadn't lived through it.

Once I asked my therapist about my use of humor. It didn't seem right to laugh about these things. He told me, "Humor is only one way of dealing with tragedy. Other people destroy themselves or others, or they start fires or drink themselves to death. Of all the possible ways there are to deal with deep pain, you have chosen one that is fairly harmless and that affirms life with laughter. Not a bad choice. Not a bad choice at all."

Humor can be an asset. People enjoy you. You may keep yourself from being depressed. You might even become a comedian or a performer. The goal is to use humor effectively, without hiding behind it.

BUSYNESS

Staying busy can be a way to avoid being in the present moment, to avoid feelings. Many survivors live their whole lives according to the lists they write first thing in the morning. As one woman remarked, "I often mourn for a pace of life that I've never had."

ESCAPE

As a child or an adolescent, you may have made attempts to run away. If you were more passive, there was escape through sleep, books, and television. Many adult survivors still read obsessively. One woman said, "I'd buy a junk novel and read it till I fell asleep, usually for a good thirty-six hours at a stretch." Others spend hours in front of the TV.

If you couldn't afford to believe the abuse was really happening, you could make believe something else was going on. Sometimes children create fantasies that explore their desire for power in a powerless situation. One woman dreamed of a little house she could live in all by herself, with locks on all the doors. Another spent her childhood dreaming of revenge:

I'd watch *Perry Mason* to get ideas about how to kill my father. It was really the best of times. Every day I would get a new method. However the person was murdered on *Perry Mason* that day, I would go to bed that night, and that's how I would kill my father. One time on *Perry Mason* this guy killed his wife by knocking an electric fan into the bathtub. I imagined electrocuting him like that. I remember really vividly fantasizing about putting ground glass in the meatloaf. I was the cook. I thought about stabbing him, shooting him. Every night I killed him in another way.

Many survivors continue an intense fantasy life when they grow up:

As an adult these changed to vindication fantasies, fantasies about having power in the world, revenge fantasies. I can work myself into a state of sobbing over something in a fantasy. I love fantasies about dying and everyone regretting all the wrongs they'd ever done to me. They're just an updated version of what I did as a kid. I can be lost in fantasy for hours. It's a lot safer to work things out in my head than to change things in the world.

Yet fantasies can be the source of a rich creative life. One teenager needed to escape so badly, she believed *Star Trek* was real. When the series was taken off the air, she began to hear the voices of the characters in her head and started writing her own episodes. Today she is a successful science fiction writer.

WHEN THE PAIN GETS TOO GREAT

MENTAL ILLNESS

Problems occur when the line between fantasy and reality blurs. For many survivors "going crazy" makes a lot of sense:

I've been mentally disturbed all my life. Mental hospitals were more like a respite for me because they got me away from my family. It was just an extension of the running away. I had no control in my life whatsoever. What my father didn't control, my mother controlled. It wasn't my life. I was in this body, but it was like I was this puppet, and everybody else pulled the strings. *I had to get sick to get away.* I just kept going further and further in my head, so I wouldn't have to deal with reality at all.

SELF-MUTILATION

Self-mutilation is one way survivors control their experience of pain. Instead of the abuser hurting you, you hurt yourself. One woman beat herself severely with a belt. Another carved into her leg with a knife:

I've wanted to hurt myself, to cause myself pain, and the way I usually think of doing that is cutting myself with a knife. It's a feeling that the pain inside is so bad, that if I cut myself, it'll come out. Lots of times I have images of putting my fists through glass, and I just think watching the blood go down the glass would make the pain go away somehow. It's like you're a balloon pushed full and you need to pop open a little. It seems like once you do it, it gets easier to do it again and again. It's like any other addiction.

Lots of times I get the urge when I have a new memory. I start to feel so out of control. If I cut myself, other people will know the pain I'm in. Otherwise they don't notice, especially since I try to cover it up emotionally.

The other thing is that physical pain distracts from the emotional pain. So I could focus on that instead of the emotional pain, which makes me feel so trapped and hopeless.

For information on stopping a pattern of self-mutilation, see "From Self-Mutilation to Self-Care," page 219.

SUICIDE ATTEMPTS

Suicide sometimes seems like the only option left in a life that feels out of control:

I've been suicidal many, many times and have been serious about it, but there is something in me that doesn't want to die. I've slashed a razor blade down a vein, and the blood just spurted out, but I didn't die. I took twenty-eight meprobamate, which is a strong tranquilizer. Half of that should have killed me but I didn't die. I have a very strong will to live.

Attempts at suicide are not always so overt. One woman spent her childhood saying the prayer "If I should die before I wake" with her fingers crossed. (If you're feeling suicidal see "Don't Kill Yourself," page 202.)

ADDICTION AND ISOLATION

Addictions are common ways of coping with the pain of sexual abuse. They are usually self-defeating and self-destructive. You can be addicted to dangerous situations, to crisis, or to sex. You may have turned to drugs, alcohol, or food to keep the memories down, to numb feelings. Addictions must be curbed if you want to heal. (For more on fighting addictions, see "From Addiction to Freedom," page 216.)

Isolation is often coupled with addictions. If no one is close to you, no one can hurt you anymore. Survivors often shut others out, creating a half-life of their own making.

Before I Remembered the Abuse: Sunny's Story

I started drinking with my mother in the afternoons after school. Her cocktail hour started with *Merv Griffin*. She was disabled, so when I came home from school, she'd say, "Make me a drink." And then one day she started to say, "Make us a drink." It wasn't until I was seventeen and went away to college that I started having blackouts and getting more serious about my drinking.

I never was a party-goer. I rarely went to bars. I did my drinking alone at home. I drank until I passed out, or until the bottle was empty. It was always the last time I was going to do it, so why not finish it off?

I did the same thing with eating. I wouldn't eat anything in the morning, because every day started out with me on a diet. I might go till two or three in the afternoon, and then I'd start eating. Instead of eating a meal like a normal person, I'd buy half a gallon of ice cream or a dozen doughnuts, and consume a huge quantity of food in a short period of time. It never tasted good. I just felt bad about myself, and the eating would make me feel worse. I'd feel horrible, that I'd failed. And then I'd say, "Well, I'll start tomorrow."

Before I went to AA and got sober, I felt that I was the only person in the world who felt the things I felt, who did the things I did, who lived the way I lived. I lived like a rat. I dressed normal, and I had a job, and I had nice apartment, but I would go home on Friday, shut the drapes, lock the door, watch old movies and drink and eat.

I wouldn't ever watch anything current —like the news, or a parade, or a baseball game. Only old movies that were fantasies. Or soap operas. The characters were like my family. I especially liked the fact that they aired on holidays, because I could have Christmas and Thanksgiving with *All My Children*.

I would only get dressed to go to the store. There was a liquor store one block from the house and I would drive the one block. Sometimes I wouldn't even make it home. I'd have to stop the car and get into whatever it was that I had bought. Sometimes I wouldn't even get dressed. I would put a coat over my nightgown and drive to the store.

I felt bad about living that way, but I tried not to think about my life. I knew there was something wrong with it, but I couldn't put my finger on it. I knew other people didn't live that way. I'd think that someday I'd do something about it. But not today.

I had no friends. I knew only a small handful of people. I remember thinking if I died, the first person to know it would be the landlady when I didn't pay my rent on the first of the month. There was really nobody in my life. No one I cared about. I was incredibly isolated. And I continued to feel that way until I went to Alcoholics Anonymous.

EATING DIFFICULTIES

Eating difficulties often result from abuse. Young girls who were sexually abused sometimes develop anorexia and bulimia. In a rigidly controlled family system where the abuse is hidden and all appearances are normal, anorexia or bulimia can be a cry for help. For girls who've been pressured into sex they didn't want, growing into a woman's body can be terrifying. Anorexia and bulimia can be an attempt to say no, to assert control over their changing bodies.

Compulsive overeating is another way of coping. Survivors may feel that being large will keep them from having to deal with sexual advances.

I've been overweight since I was nine. I remember exactly the day I started eating. It was the day my step-father fingered me in front of other people. He took off my bathing suit and under the guise of drying me off, got his fingers inside of me. I felt completely exposed and I remember I started eating that day. And I really ballooned.

I frequently eat very consciously to gain weight to cover me, to protect me. When I lose weight, I feel totally ex-posed and naked. I can't stand it. There's a lot of heartache in being so overweight. It affects every part of your life, but I still need the protection.

Another survivor said, "I kept eating so I wouldn't have to talk about what had happened. I just made sure my mouth was always full."

Compulsive eating is not necessarily related to body size. Some large women are not overeaters and some thin women binge compulsively. In our culture fat is a stigma, but we all have naturally different body sizes. Being large is not necessarily an indication of anything emotional or problematic. An excellent resource on the oppression and liberation of large women is *Shadows on a Tightrope* (see the "Your Body" section of the Bibliography).

For more on anorexia, bulimia, and compulsive overeating, see "Eating Difficulties," page 217.

LYING

When children are told never to talk about the abuse, or don't want people to know what's really going on at home, they become adept at lying. Many adult survivors are compulsive liars, the abuse remaining the biggest lie of all.

STEALING

Stealing is a totally absorbing activity. It enables you to forget everything for a brief moment—including the abuse. It is a way to create distraction or excitement, to re-create the feelings you had when you were first abused—guilt, terror, the rush of adrenaline. Stealing is also a way of defying authority, an attempt to take back what was stolen, to even the score. It can also be a cry for help:

> I worked at being a thief for a year and a half. When I first quit drinking, it was a way of coping. I didn't steal because I wanted the stuff—I got a terrific high from it. Unfortunately, it only lasted for about thirty seconds, and so I kept having to repeat the act.
>
> I embezzled from the company I worked for. I worked an insurance fraud that was grand larceny. And I shoplifted. I accumulated so much stuff that I started throwing it away. My car was full of loot. I never got caught.
>
> I stopped stealing five years ago on Christmas Day. I hadn't had one day where I hadn't stolen anything in a long time. All the stores were closed that day, so it seemed like a good day to begin. I finally called someone from AA and told them I had this problem. Just telling seemed to release me.

GAMBLING

Gambling is a way to maintain the hope that life can magically change. It's a way to act out the longing that your luck will shift, that there will be justice: if you win big, you will finally get your due.

Gambling is also a thrill, a way to escape the difficulties and challenges of day-to-day life by entering another world—one that is totally consuming and in which the risks and payoffs are well defined.

WORKAHOLISM

Survivors often feel an overwhelming need to achieve, to make up for the badness they feel is hidden inside. Excelling at work is something that they can control and that's given a lot of support in our high-achieving culture. While working to excess can show a strong motivation to succeed, it can also be a way to avoid an inner life or a connection to the people around you:

> I became 100 percent work. I got into graduate school and just turned off to sharing or closeness with anyone. I was in a really intense MBA program, and I was determined to be perfect. If I wasn't at work with my job, I was working on school, which was supposed to get me further ahead in my job. During that two-year period, I raised my income $19,000 a year. It was all that mattered. It was the only place left where I could prove I was worth anything.

SAFETY AT ANY PRICE

While some survivors have felt compelled to go out and overcome every obstacle, others have chosen security. They are the obedient daughters, honor students, good wives, and selfless mothers. They take few risks, sacrificing opportunities for protection. Opting for security can provide you with grounding and stability, but it may mean giving up your ambitions and dreams.

One of the most common ways for

women to find safety is through their families:

> I married a man who would be stable, who wouldn't leave me, and above all, would not be intrusive. He was the rock. I felt myself to be on such shaky ground. We had a traditional marriage. I didn't really have to do anything. I just clung to my husband. He was a high-status high achiever, and I shone in his glory for a long time. I lived in his protectorate for twenty-two years and that's how I survived.

AVOIDING INTIMACY

If you don't let anyone close to you, no one can hurt you. As one woman said, "You can't be in an abusive relationship if you don't get in relationships." Another added, "I kept myself safe *and* alone."

Survivors go to great lengths to limit intimacy. One woman said, "I can stop being friends with someone and never think twice about it." Another had relationships only with men who lived a great distance from her: "One of them was a plane ride away. The other one didn't have a car. That was really good."

Some survivors avoid intimacy in less overt ways, seeming open and friendly on the surface but hiding real feelings inside. One survivor had a "Ten Official Secrets List" which she freely shared:

> I'll tell people things about myself that seem too personal to share, but I don't really trust them or get close to them. They don't know what I feel inside. I hardly ever share that.

While avoiding intimacy keeps you safe —and sometimes leads to positive traits such as independence and autonomy—it also means missing out on the rewards that healthy relationships can bring.

GIVE ME THAT OLD-TIME RELIGION

Safety can also be found by attaching yourself to a belief system that has clearly defined rules and boundaries:

> I'm addicted to religion and theology. I was married in a Chasidic Jewish wedding. I can "do" any ethnic group that you like. I am addicted to groups. I am a sponge. Put me somewhere where people are nice to me, and I'll learn their whole scene better than they can do it themselves.
>
> I converted to being Jewish when I was twelve. I did Orthodox Chasidic Jew for nine years. Kept a kosher house, kept Shabbos, all of it. Eventually, I got bored with doing Jewish, and I switched over to Swami Satchidananda. I did yoga. I went to India and lived in an ashram.

More traditional religion can provide an anchor as well. The lure of divine forgiveness can be a powerful pull for the survivor who still feels the abuse was her fault.

Marilyn's Story: Being Born Again

I found some security in a born-again Baptist group when I was about fifteen. The evangelist talked about how bad we all were and how our sins could all be forgiven.

Everybody went to Bob Jones University with the pink and blue sidewalks, where the boys walked on the blue and the girls walked on the pink. We all wanted to go to Bob Jones. It was the ultimate. We were always out on the streets, evangelizing, handing out tracts, witnessing to all our friends.

Church was a release. It gave me the structure—if you do this and this, then you will be okay. There are formal do's and don'ts that you get from the pulpit, and then there are informal ones you get from your friends. You know which stores to buy your clothes in and which clothes to buy. You know which kinds of nightgowns to wear. You know which kinds of sexual activities with your husband are all right, which ones are not allowed. You all cook the same things. You raise your children in the same way. The point being that if you do those things, you're going to be all right.

I thoroughly believed that God intervened in the details of everything I did, including grocery shopping. I believed that as long as I was walking in the Light, nothing was going to happen to me that God wouldn't allow. I knew that if I couldn't make a decision, all I had to do was wait and God would tell me. I took no responsibility for my life—it was wrong for me to do so. What I had to do was find God's will in everything I did. I'd go to the store, and the sofa I had been looking at would be on sale, and it was God's will that I buy it.

I used to teach Bible studies for women. The teachings I lived by and taught for so many years were *Fascinating Womanhood* and *The Total Woman*. I just cringe when I think of those women, and I hope they have discarded what I taught them. One of them would be a little rebellious, and I would tell her she'd better knuckle under to her husband. I would quote scripture and verse.

I allowed no doubt. None. I just lapped those things up because they gave me great security. I knew I'd be forgiven for what a bad person I was.

COMPULSIVELY SEEKING OR AVOIDING SEX

If abuse was your sole means of getting physical contact when you were a child, you may continue to look for closeness only in sexual ways. You may become promiscuous or try to meet nonsexual needs through sex.

While some survivors use sex as an escape, or experience it as an addiction, many go to great lengths to avoid sexuality.

I intentionally married a man who was basically asexual. He was the three-time-a-year man, and he was absolutely perfect. When we wanted to get pregnant, I took my temperature. The conception of my children was as close to artificial insemination as you can get.

Others numb their bodies so they no longer respond:

Part of the way I coped with the fact that some of the incest felt good was by saying, "It will never feel good. Sex will never feel good, because it felt good when it shouldn't have." So I don't ever feel. I don't pay attention to sex. I don't care about it and it doesn't make me feel anything. The other person is happy when it's done. And I can't wait until I'm out of the situation so I don't have to do it again.

YOU CAN CHANGE

When you were a child, you did not have many options. Now you have more resources. You can recognize self-destructive patterns. You can pick and choose among your coping behaviors. You can discard the ones that no longer work for you and keep the positive skills you've developed. (See Part Three for specific suggestions for changing patterns of coping.)

Not everyone has the same opportunities. If you coped in a way that gets positive recognition—by being super-nurturing or successful in work—your options may be broader than if you turned to drugs as a way to get by. If you are incarcerated in prison or a mental hospital, you clearly will not have the same control over changing your life. If your health has been ravaged by eating disorders, you will face real limitations. And of course your economic and social status, race, and sexual preference all influence your opportunities.

The starting point for everyone, however, is to look at the ways you coped and to forgive yourself. You have no reason to be ashamed. You did the best you could as a child under impossible circumstances. You have earned the name "survivor." Now you are an adult with the power to change. From a place of acceptance and love you can do so.

WRITING EXERCISE: COPING

(See the basic method for writing exercises on page 28.)

You've read about different ways that people have coped. Some of these you will identify with. There may be others not mentioned that have been recurring themes in your life. This is an opportunity for you to write about your experience of coping—how you remember it, how you're still doing it, how it's affected your life. Write with as much detail as you can, always from the perspective of honoring what you did.

Take half an hour to write.

PART TWO

THE HEALING

PROCESS

AN OVERVIEW

"Don't give up." That's the best thing I could tell somebody who just remembered she was a survivor. That's the most important thing right in the beginning. There are people who have lived through it, and as trite, and as stupid, and as irrelevant as it sounds to you right now, you will not be in so much pain later. Even not so far in the future. If you made it this far, you've got some pretty good stuff in you. So just trust it, no matter what outside messages you get. You're the only person who can tell yourself what you need to do to heal. *Don't give up on yourself.*

Survivors often come to Ellen's workshops expecting to pay their money, invest one weekend, and be healed. One woman said, "I thought once I told someone what had happened to me, that would be the end of it. I wanted to get well, and of course it was going to happen overnight."

We live in a society of instant mashed potatoes, microwave ovens, one-hour dry cleaning. We are taught to expect results immediately. But deep change takes time.

The healing process is a continuum. It begins with an experience of survival, an awareness of the fact that you lived through the abuse and made it to adulthood. It ends with thriving—the experience of a satisfying life no longer programmed by what happened to you as a child. And in between is the subject of this book: the healing process.

Until recently, survivors have had to

make the journey with no map, no guarantees, and few role models. These women have been pioneers. Their courageous acts of healing have taught us much.

We have learned that healing is not a random process. There are recognizable stages that all survivors pass through. The next chapters will provide you with a map of those stages, enabling you to see where you are, what you've done already, and what's yet before you.

We've presented the stages in a particular order, but you will probably not experience them that way. Few survivors finish stage #1 and then move on to stage #2. Healing is not linear. Rather, it is an integral part of life. As one survivor said, "No matter what happens, I can turn it into my healing."

THE STAGES

Although most of these stages are necessary for every survivor, a few of them—the emergency stage, remembering the abuse, confronting your family, and forgiveness—are not applicable for every woman.

The Decision to Heal. Once you recognize the effects of sexual abuse in your life, you need to make an active commitment to heal. Deep healing happens only when you choose it and are willing to change yourself.

The Emergency Stage. Beginning to deal with memories and suppressed feelings can throw your life into utter turmoil. Remember, this is only a stage. It won't last forever.

Remembering. Many survivors suppress all memories of what happened to them as children. Those who do not forget the actual incidents often forget how it felt at the time. Remembering is the process of getting back both memory and feeling.

Believing It Happened. Survivors often doubt their own perceptions. Coming to believe that the abuse really happened, and that it really hurt you, is a vital part of the healing process.

Breaking Silence. Most adult survivors kept the abuse a secret in childhood. Telling another human being about what happened to you is a powerful healing force that can dispel the shame of being a victim.

Understanding That It Wasn't Your Fault. Children usually believe the abuse is their fault. Adult survivors must place the blame where it belongs—directly on the shoulders of the abusers.

Making Contact With the Child Within. Many survivors have lost touch with their own vulnerability. Getting in touch with the child within can help you feel compassion for yourself, more anger at

A common analogy for the healing process is that it's like a spiral. You go through the same stages again and again; but traveling up the spiral, you pass through them at a different level, with a different perspective. You might spend a year or two dealing intensely with your abuse. Then you might take a break and focus more on the present. A year or so later, changes in your life—a new relationship, the birth of a child, graduation from school, or simply an inner urge—may stir up more unresolved memories and feelings, and you may focus in on it again, embarking on a second or a third or a fourth round of discovery. With each new cycle, your capacity to feel, to remember, to make lasting changes, is strengthened.

your abuser, and greater intimacy with others.

Trusting Yourself. The best guide for healing is your own inner voice. Learning to trust your own perceptions, feelings, and intuitions forms a new basis for action in the world.

Grieving and Mourning. As children being abused, and later as adults struggling to survive, most survivors haven't felt their losses. Grieving is a way to honor your pain, let go, and move into the present.

Anger—the Backbone of Healing. Anger is a powerful and liberating force. Whether you need to get in touch with it or have always had plenty to spare, directing your rage squarely at your abuser, and at those who didn't protect you, is pivotal to healing.

Disclosures and Confrontations. Directly confronting your abuser and/or your family is not for every survivor, but it can be a dramatic, cleansing tool.

Forgiveness? Forgiveness of the abuser is *not* an essential part of the healing process, although it tends to be the one most recommended. The only essential forgiveness is for yourself.

Spirituality. Having a sense of a power greater than yourself can be a real asset in the healing process. Spirituality is a uniquely personal experience. You might find it through traditional religion, meditation, nature, or your support group.

Resolution and Moving On. As you move through these stages again and again, you will reach a point of integration. Your feelings and perspectives will stabilize. You will come to terms with your abuser and other family members. While you won't erase your history, you will make deep and lasting changes in your life. Having gained awareness, compassion, and power through healing, you will have the opportunity to work toward a better world.

THE DECISION TO HEAL

If you enter into healing, be prepared to lose everything. Healing is a ravaging force to which nothing seems sacred or inviolate. As my original pain releases itself in healing, it rips to shreds the structures and foundations I built in weakness and ignorance. Ironically and unjustly, only I can pay the price of having lived a lie. I am experiencing the bizarre miracle of reincarnating, more lucidly than at birth, in the same lifetime.

—Ely Fuller

The decision to heal from child sexual abuse is a powerful, life-affirming choice. It is a commitment every survivor deserves to make. Although you may have already experienced some healing in your life—through the nurturing of a foster family, the caring of an intimate partner, or the satisfaction of work you love—*deciding* to heal, making your own growth and recovery a priority, sets in motion a healing force that will bring to your life a richness and depth you never dreamed possible:

For the first time I'm appreciating things like the birds and the flowers, the way the sun feels on my skin—you know, really simple things. I can read a good book. I can sit in the sun. I don't ever remember enjoying these things, even as a little kid. I've woken up. If this hadn't happened, I'd still be asleep. So for the first time, I feel alive. And you know that's something to go for.

****

I am here now. I don't have my thoughts and feelings planed off into the future, or wasting away because of some memories. I am here right now. I am experiencing every bit of my life and I'm not wasting any of it.

****

This has given me the opportunity to look at me. I am emotionally more open. I've learned so much. It's not all bad. You do heal. And you do become stronger. I don't know what it would take to flatten me, but it would have to be something really big. I am, in fact, a survivor.

The commitment to heal rises from a different set of life circumstances for each survivor. A young girl who turns her father in for molesting her may be ordered by the court to go to therapy. A twenty-five-year-old woman may get married and suddenly find that she can't maintain the intimacy she felt with her husband before their wedding. A thirty-year-old may start to feel crazy when her daughter reaches the age she was when her own abuse began. An older woman might decide to heal at the funeral of her abuser.

Other women describe themselves "bursting apart at the seams," or "hitting bottom" before they decide to heal. One woman didn't get help until she was hospitalized for eating difficulties: "I actively avoided getting a therapist for years. I didn't start dealing with it until I couldn't *not* deal with it." Healing isn't always a matter of choice:

It was a compulsion. I think everybody has a compulsion to grow and to be whole. I think everybody has a compulsion to seek relief from pain.

A single human interaction may be the impetus to heal. One survivor decided to heal because a friend told her, "I don't trust you. I never feel you're telling me the truth. I can't trust you with my feelings because I don't know what you're doing with them." The survivor was shocked. First, because it was true, and second, because she thought she'd done a good job of faking it. "I felt she'd crawled inside my head and seen what was really there. She put words to what I'd been feeling all my life. So I went to therapy."

Another woman decided to heal when her younger sister killed herself. "She didn't make it. I had to understand what had happened to her, and give myself the tools to make sure it couldn't happen to me."

One young survivor said she was motivated to heal because of a class assignment:

I was twenty years old. I was in a psych class doing a research project on the aftereffects of incest on survivors. Now, most people just wouldn't choose that kind of subject! But the stuff was pushing up from the inside. I wanted to annihilate my grandfather. I just wanted to castrate him by the time I finished this paper. I thought writing the paper would heal me from it, but my feelings were just erupting all over the place. By the time I presented the paper, I fell apart. I'd been contemplating therapy for a while, and a few days later I found a therapist.

A survivor who'd been a Carmelite nun described her decision to heal as a need to clarify her reasons for living in the convent.

"I loved the convent, but somehow I distrusted my choice to be there. Until I worked out the sexual abuse, I felt I would never know if I was really choosing this life out of health, and out of all the good things that religious life should be chosen from. I wanted to believe that whatever I chose to do, I was doing it for all the right reasons."

IT'S NOT EASY

While it is always worth it, healing is rarely easy. Choosing to work on abuse-related issues will raise questions you never planned to ask and will give answers you didn't expect. Once you commit yourself, your life won't be the same:

My therapist was not the kind of person who would lie to me. He would say, "I can't give you any guarantees. I don't know if you're going to feel better after you talk about this. You could feel a lot worse." And it was hard to make that leap, to decide that it didn't matter which way it went, that the leap itself was the important thing.

I was giving up a person who was really a very viable, powerful, self-reliant human being. There were a lot of positive things about those negative aspects of my personality. And I didn't want to give them up. Maybe it wasn't the best way of coping, but at least I was used to it. I felt incredibly vulnerable having to let go in order to make the room to create a new person. Into what void would I be thrown if I let go of this stuff? I felt like a raw muscle walking around for a long time.

You may wonder if it's worth it to take the risk. But as one survivor simply put it, "Taking that risk was the most promising choice I had."

Often the decision to heal wreaks havoc with marriages and intimate relationships, dealings with parents, other relatives, sometimes even your children. It can be hard to function, to go to work, to study, to think, to smile, to perform. It can even be hard to sleep, to eat, or simply to stop crying:

If I'd known that anything could hurt this much or could be this sad, I never would have decided to heal. And at the same time you can't go back. You can't unremember. I spent so many years not hurting at all. It's like I don't have the coping mechanisms for hurting. I have the coping mechanisms for *not* hurting. And that's been real hard.

Sometimes the early stages of healing are so filled with crisis that women have a hard time accepting the fact that they made a choice at all. When Laura remembered her abuse and made her first call to a therapist, she made the decision to heal. But it didn't feel that way to her:

For a long time, I felt like a victim of the process. This was something I'd chosen? No way! Remembering the incest was something that had happened *to* me. The memories were like one of those plastic raincoats that come in a two-inch package. Once I opened them up, I could never fold them neatly back inside. The whole thing felt out of my control, like being swept up in a hurricane.

There are certain major decisions we make not really knowing what we're getting into. Healing from sexual abuse is one of them:

> Though sometimes I want to crawl into a dark place and hide from reality, and other times I want to give up completely, I go on. I don't know where this "healing" will lead me. I live on other people's hopes. I live on other people's faith that life will get better. I continue to wonder whether it is worth it, but I go on. This, then, is healing.

Deciding to actively heal is terrifying because it means opening up to hope. For many survivors, hope has brought only disappointment.

Although it is terrifying to say yes to yourself, it is also a tremendous relief when you finally stop and face your own demons. There is something about looking terror in the face, and seeing your own reflection, that is strangely relieving. There is comfort in knowing that you don't have to pretend anymore, that you are going to do everything within your power to heal. As one survivor put it, "I know now that every time I accept my past and respect where I am in the present, I am giving myself a future."

EVERYONE DESERVES TO HEAL

Aside from the obstacles we've already mentioned, some women face additional factors that hinder their commitment to naming their abuse or healing from it. Age, race, religious background, and other factors all influence the decision to heal.

They'll Use It Against Us: Rachel Bat Or's Story

Rachel Bat Or is a forty-one-year-old lesbian who lives in Oakland, California. She works with abuse survivors, helping them reclaim their strength. Born to Jewish parents, she was abused by all four members of her family—her mother, father, brother, and grandfather. Through the course of her own healing and her work with other survivors, Rachel has seen a reluctance on the part of many Jewish women to acknowledge that they were abused, and therefore to commit to healing.

Compared to many of our parents' lives of poverty or escape from anti-Semitic countries, whatever happens to us gets played down. As long as we have a roof over our heads, we have clothes and food, then nothing that happens to us can be as bad, because they lived with rats, in incredible poverty, the families often separated in traveling to America. And so no matter how awful we feel inside of us, we feel we can't say that out loud because our parents had it so much worse.

Then the stereotypes of Jewish women are that we're loud and pushy and that the men are gentle and hardworking. And so we're taught to feel sorry for the men and blame the women. So if the men—our fathers or brothers—are abusing us, there isn't that instantaneous hatred, because they're so exalted in the religious teachings and the culture. So it's very hard for us to hold on to that anger.

And then there's the myth that Jewish men are not alcoholics or batterers. So if our family is different, that can't be admitted.

The next thing is, "What will the neighbors say? We're Jewish." Because we have to protect our religion from being criticized, we ignore whatever happens in our family. If there are any problems, it's the whole religion that gets looked on, not just our family. We know that. It's not some myth.

And then there's the last thing that puts us in a real quandary: There's the us/them dichotomy. If we do tell about whatever happens to us, it's usually to the "them," someone who's not Jewish, who's outside the family, who doesn't respect our family, and so we lose the "us" security. It's hard to go to a "them." And maybe we can muster our courage and do that, but then we lose any of the benefits we do get from being an "us."

It's Never Too Late: Barbara Hamilton's Story

Barbara Hamilton is sixty-five years old. She was molested by her father in childhood. She grew up, married, raised six children, and now has grandchildren and great-grandchildren as well. Unknown to Barbara until a few years ago, when she started talking about her own molestation, some of her children and grandchildren were also molested, either by her father or by other perpetrators. She talks about the difficulties older women have in making the commitment to heal.

When you get older, especially as a woman, you deal with rejection on all sides. Society devalues you, and you fall right into that as a victim. Being a survivor ties right into that sense of isolation. It went underground for all those years I was raising my family, but as I got more and more alone, and as the insecurity in my life increased *because* I was an older woman, it all came back up. I had to realize that it hadn't been resolved. All I'd done is acknowledge that it

happened. It hadn't really been touched. And I had fifty years of pushing it away.

Don't wait. Don't wait, because it won't go away. It always comes back, and it gets harder. But older woman deserve to heal too. There must be thousands like me who are living under it just like I was. And though the focus of all the books is toward younger women, I don't think you're ever too old. You may be infirm. It may be too hard that way. You won't have the same experiences as a young person. As an older woman, you probably won't ever be able to confront your abuser. But it's worth it. I feel so much better about myself.

In spite of the horror, in spite of the tragedy, in spite of the weeks of sleepless nights, I'm finally alive. I'm not pretending. I feel real. I'm not playing charades anymore. I wouldn't go back to the way I was for anything. I'm really like a different person. I'm where I am, and I'm making the most of it. I *know* I'm courageous now. I found out I had it in me to face this. It's just not ever too late. Look what Grandma Moses did at ninety-five. There's still hope.

It's like going from black-and-white to color, and you never even knew you were in black-and-white. We all thought black-and-white was great all those years that all we had was black-and-white. Do you remember the first time you saw Technicolor? The first time you wore those 3-D glasses? Eventually you get to where life is Technicolor, and it's worth it.

If you say "Why should I bother? I've coped this far," I'd say to you, "You *haven't* coped. You haven't even lived a fraction of yourself. You may be smothering an artist. You may be smothering all kinds of self-expression that needs to come out for your sake, and for others. Why not give it a chance?"

THE EMERGENCY STAGE

Q: Was your healing process an obsessive one?

A: Are you kidding? In the beginning, I'd go to an incest conference for two days and then sit up all night reading Michelle Morris's book *If I Should Die Before I Wake*.

The emergency stage feels like this: You walk out the door to go to work, and you fall on the steps and break your leg. Your spouse tries to drive you to the hospital, but the engine of your car blows up. You go back to the house to call an ambulance, only to find you've locked yourself out. Just as a police car pulls over to give you some help, the big earthquake hits, and your home, your spouse, your broken leg, and the police car all disappear into a yawning chasm.

Many women go through a period when sexual abuse is literally all they can think about. You may find yourself talking about it obsessively with anyone who will listen. Your life may become full of practical crises which totally overwhelm you. You may find yourself having flashbacks uncontrollably, crying all day long, or unable to go to work. You may dream about your abuser and be afraid to sleep:

I just lost it completely. I wasn't eating. I wasn't sleeping. I did hold down a job at Winchell's Donuts. But I was afraid to stay in the house alone. I would go out in the middle of the night and hide somewhere, behind a Dipsy dumpster or something. I had terrible nightmares about my father. I was having all kinds of fantasies. I'd hear the sound of my father's zipper coming down, the click of the buckle. Then I'd imagined all this blood. Physically, I was a mess. I had crabs. I hadn't bathed in a month. I was afraid of the shower.

Total obsession with sexual abuse is more likely if you've forgotten your abuse. When Laura had her first memories, the shock alone was enough to fixate her on incest for several months: "I hadn't had many real memories of my childhood, it was true, but I had created a picture I could brag about, of those early golden years. It's not that all those good things I remembered hadn't happened. It's just that I had somehow forgotten the fact that I had been sexually abused too.

"Breaking through my own denial, and trying to fit the new reality into the shattered framework of the old, was enough to catapult me into total crisis. I felt my whole foundation had been stolen from me. If this could have happened and I could have forgotten it, then every assumption I had about life and my place in it was thrown up for question."

Remembering, for Laura, was a veritable earthquake. Women often describe the early stages of their healing as a variety of natural disasters: "It was like being lifted up in a twister." "It was like being caught in an avalanche." "It was a volcano erupting."

I felt like I was standing in a room, looking at the floor. I was shattered all over it, and I had to go through and pick up the pieces and put them back together. Look at each one and say, "This is me," put it on, and say, "This is where it goes." Or, "Nope, wrong place." Then I'd have to find the place where it really fit. I was picking up pieces of my life and looking at them, saying, "Do I want to keep this? Is it of any use to me anymore? When will the pain stop?"

The emergency stage is not something you choose, yet it must be ridden through to the other side. It cannot be ignored. As one survivor aptly remarked, "It's like learning a new word. Within days, you start seeing it in everything you read, and you never saw it before in your life."

The Emergency Stage: Catherine's Story

Catherine first faced the fact that she had been sexually abused in a therapy group for alcohol co-dependents. She called a therapist and said, "I need to come to therapy because I'm an incest survivor."

Three months later Catherine quit her job. She had a verbally abusive boss and decided, "I was going to eliminate any stress I could, and so I quit."

At that point, the emergency stage kicked in with full force. "I didn't have any daily responsibilities anymore. I didn't have to be personable for anyone. That's when the despair really had a chance to surface. I started feeling this uncontrollable sadness.

"I dropped everything else in my life. It was like there were large six-foot-high letters in my living room every day when I woke up: *INCEST!* It was just so much in the forefront of my mind that I felt that everyone knew I was an incest victim. I thought I looked like one. I was sure everybody would know the real reason why I was such a creep. I was in constant fear of telling anyone that's what I was in therapy for, because I was so ashamed."

Catherine also disconnected from most of the people in her life. "I had no energy to deal with other people or their problems. My reserves had been drained dry. I withdrew my social time with acquaintance-type people. Then I started to rely more on the people I felt were really true friends. I told them more about my therapy and what I was discovering. The people I used to call up and say, 'Hi. Let's go roller skating,' I didn't bother to call anymore."

Catherine felt completely drained and slept ten or twelve hours a night. "For a long time, all I cared about was going to sleep and being able to wake up the next day."

There were certain emergency things she did to take care of herself during these early stages. "I had to find people who would sit with me no matter what I felt like. I had one friend who'd been beaten when she was a kid. She understood. I could call her up when I felt horrible, and she'd let me come over to just eat and watch TV. It was okay to go over there and feel shitty. She knew what was going on, but we only discussed if it I brought it up.

"I also had to find a safe place to be alone. I went for walks in the woods. I ran a lot. I'd go for twenty- or thirty-mile bike rides. I spent a lot of time outdoors by myself. It felt a lot safer than being at home where someone might need something from me."

Catherine's self-esteem was also hard hit. Like many survivors, she experienced a profound sense of disorientation. "It was the most awkward feeling, to have to try out everything I'd been familiar with. I had to

prove to myself that I could go to the store or drive my car, *and* be an incest victim, all at the same time. I had to spend time in my own house thinking, 'Now I know I'm an incest victim, and yes, I still live here, and yes, my cats still like me.' Outside, it all looked the same, but inside, it was just scrambled. I felt like I was in a vacuum for a whole year, and all that was in front of me were flashbacks and crying."

An essential lifeline for Catherine during the emergency stage was her connection to her therapist. "The only thing that saved me when I felt totally cut off from everything was that I had my therapist's phone number written many places, all over my house. I had it up on the mirror in the bathroom. I had it in my journal. I had it in books that I was reading. I'd stuff it in there on little pieces of paper. I just burned it in my memory, so at any time I could stop and call her. And many times, just making the call and getting her answering machine, and being able to leave a message in my real voice, in my cracking, crying voice, that I needed her to call me, let me know that I could reach out. It reminded me that there was actually something other than my pain and depression. There was actually somebody up on the ledge and I could reach out to her. I knew she would call me eventually, and I could hold out till then."

In Catherine's life, it took many months before the pressure lessened. "After about a year, something shifted for me. I was able to lift my head up a little bit and notice that the season had changed. I started to realize that even though I was an incest survivor, I could go on with my life. I wanted to pick up all the things I had dropped the year before. I was able to say, 'I'll only go to therapy once a week and think about incest twenty hours a week, instead of going twice a week and thinking about incest one hundred hours a week.' I had a choice. I could stop myself from thinking about it at times. It was a tremendous relief."

SURVIVING THE EMERGENCY STAGE

The important thing to remember is that the emergency stage is a natural part of the healing process and will come to an end. The nature of crisis is that it overwhelms you; while you are in it, it is all you can see. But there will be a time when you will not think, eat, and dream sexual abuse twenty-four hours a day. And if you are in the emergency stage, that time will not come a moment too soon.

- **Don't hurt or try to kill yourself.** You deserve to live. If you start feeling suicidal or self-destructive, reach out. (And read "Don't Kill Yourself," page 202.)
- **Know that you're not going crazy.** What you're going through is a recognized part of the healing process. (If you find yourself in a panic, read "Panic," page 201.)
- **Find people you can talk to.** Don't try to bear it alone.
- **Get skilled professional support.** (If you don't know where to look, see "Healing Resources," page 458.)
- **Get support from other survivors.** It's unlikely that anyone other than another survivor can listen as much as you'll need to talk.
- **Allow yourself to obsess.** Don't make things worse by hating yourself for being where you are.

- **Do as many nice things for yourself as possible.** (For suggestions, see "Nurture Yourself: The Teddy Bear's Picnic," page 187.)
- **Drop what isn't essential in your life.** Release the pressure any way you can. This means dropping unsupportive people, quitting activities, lightening your work load, getting extra child care.
- **Create a safe area in your home.** You need at least one place where you feel safe. (For suggestions, see "Create a Safe Spot," page 203.)
- **Watch your intake of drugs and alcohol.** Repeatedly numbing your feelings will only prolong the crisis.
- **Get out of abusive situations.** If you're currently in a situation where you're being abused, get out of it. (If you have an abusive partner, see "Recognizing Bad Relationships," page 234.)
- **Sit tight and ride out the storm.** Your decision-making capability is limited right now. Except for getting out of abusive situations, the emergency stage is usually not a good time for making major life changes.
- **Remind yourself that you're brave.** This is a challenging, scary, difficult period. You don't have to do anything but live through it.
- **Remember to breathe.** Stay as connected to your body as you can. (See "Exercises for Connecting with Your Body," page 214.)
- **Develop a belief in something greater than yourself.** Spirituality can give you inspiration and strength.
- **This too shall pass.** Your experience tomorrow, or next week, or next year will not be the same as it is right now. (Pay special attention to "Why It's Been Worth It," page 168.)

HEALING CRISES OVER TIME

Although you won't experience the same intensity of crisis once the emergency stage is over, you may go through other crisis periods in the course of your healing. Though these times can be agonizing, we like to call them healing crises, because they offer an opportunity for deep growth.

Some women have experienced so much trauma in their lives that they go through an emergency stage that lasts several years, with only short breaks in intensity. Even though they may be making excellent changes in their current lives, they still feel suicidal, self-destructive, or obsessed with abuse much of the time. If this is the case for you, get all the support you can, and know it won't last forever.

WHAT GAVE ME HOPE

"I had this vision one day of me at the end of the tunnel, and I could look out and I could see the blue sky. I was standing on this very thin ledge, not holding on to anything, just balancing there, and I had my arms spread out and I was going to fly."

"I was a nun in a contemplative order. Because I had lived that lifestyle, I knew that things took a long time. I was geared to an interior life. I knew that the process of becoming holy, of knowing God, was very slow. Day by day, I just knew I was growing closer to God. And I felt the same thing applied to dealing with the incest. I just trusted that something was happening, that there was a hidden growth going on."

"When I'm sure I'm about to be locked up as a crazy woman, the thing that gives me hope is remembering what my therapist kept saying to me, over and over: 'This is part of the change process.' I held on to that when there was really nothing else to hold on to: 'Oh, this is a recognized part of the change process.'"

"My friend Patricia gave me hope. She would basically talk me into wanting to live. She would tell me all the wonderful things there were about life in general, and I would believe her, because I loved her and I cared about her, and I knew she cared about me."

"My sister inspires me through her struggle. She had it a lot worse than I did. She went through absolute Nazi horror, and she is struggling to live. It's an amazing thing to see what people can live through, and still want to live."

"Reading gave me a lot of inspiration. I fell in love with the beauty of the human spirit through reading literature."

"Knowing another survivor who's been in a successful relationship for seven years gave me a lot of hope."

"My own inner strength gave me hope. I just won't quit. Period."

"Music. Spirituals have really helped me. Nina Simone. 'Ooooh child, things are gonna get easier. Ooooh, child, things'll get brighter.' 'The Need to Be Me' by Esther Satterfield."

REMEMBERING

I've looked the memories in the face and smelled their breath. They can't hurt me anymore.

For many survivors, remembering is the first step in healing. To begin with, you may have to remember that you *were* abused at all. Second come specific memories. (If you think you were abused but don't have any memory of it, see "But I Don't Have Any Memories," page 81.) The third kind of remembering is the recovery of the feelings you had at the time the abuse took place. Many women have always remembered the physical details of what happened but have forgotten the emotions that went with it. One survivor explained, "I could rattle off the facts of my abuse like a grocery list, but remembering the fear and terror and pain was another matter entirely."

Remembering is different for every sur-vivor. If, as a young woman, you turned your abuser in to the police and testified against him in court, there's not much chance you forgot. Likewise, if you had to raise your abuser's child, or abort it, you've probably always remembered. Or the abuse may have been so present in the daily texture of your life that there was no way to forget.

One woman who'd kept a vivid image of what had happened to her said she some-times wished she *had* forgotten: "I wish I could have gotten shock treatments like my mother. She had forgotten huge segments of her life, and I used to envy her." On the other hand, this woman said she was glad she'd always known just how bad things were: "At least I knew why I was weird! Knowing what had happened allowed me to work on the damn problem."

You may not have forgotten entirely, but coped by having selective memories.

> I always knew that we had an incestuous relationship. I remember the first time I heard the word "incest," when I was seventeen. I hadn't known there was a word for it. I always remembered my father grabbing my breasts and kissing me.
>
> I told my therapist, "I remember every miserable thing that happened to me." It seemed like I remembered so much, how could there be more? I didn't remember anything *but* abuse. But I didn't remember being raped, even though I knew I had been. I categorically told my therapist, "I don't want to remember being raped." We talked about the fact that I didn't want to remember that for months. Yet I knew my father had been my first lover.

There is no right or wrong when it comes to remembering. You may have multiple memories. Or you may just have one. Years of abuse are sometimes telescoped into a single recollection. When you begin to remember, you might have new images every day for weeks on end. Or you may experience your memories in clumps, three or four of them coming in a matter of days, then not again for months. Sometimes survivors remember one abuser, or a specific kind of abuse, only to remember, years later, a second abuser or a different form of abuse.

There are many women who show signs of having been abused without having any memories. You may have only a vague feeling that something happened but be unable to remember what it was. There are reasons for this, and to understand them, we have to first look at the way early memories are stored.

ABOUT MEMORIES

The process of storing memories is complex. We store different experiences in the right and left halves of our brain. The left brain stores sequential, logical, language-oriented experience; the right stores perceptual, spatial experiences. When we try to retrieve right-brain information through left-brain techniques, such as logic and language, we sometimes hit a blank. There are some experiences that we are simply not going to remember in an orderly, precise way.

If you were abused when you were preverbal, or just as you were learning to talk, you had no way of making sense of what was happening to you. Babies don't know the difference between touching someone's penis and touching someone's leg. If a penis is put in their mouth, they will suck it, much as they would a breast or a bottle. Young children are aware of sensations but cannot come up with a name or a concept—like "sexual abuse"—for what is being done to them.

Another thing that makes remembering difficult is the simple fact that you are trying to remember details of something that happened a long time ago. If you ask friends who weren't abused, you will find that most of them also don't remember a great number of details from their childhood. It is even more difficult to remember the times when we were hurt, humiliated, or otherwise violated.

If the abuse happened only once, or if it was an abuse that is hard to name (inappropriate boundaries, lewd looks, subtler forms of abuse), it can be even harder to remember. For others, the constancy of the abuse prevents detailed naming. As one survivor put it, "Do you remember every time you sat down to eat? What you had for dinner the Tuesday you turned six? I remember the flavor. It was a constant, like eating. It was always there."

WHAT REMEMBERING IS LIKE

Recovering occluded memories (those blocked from the surface) is not like remembering with the conscious mind. Often the memories are vague and dreamlike, as if they're being seen from far away.

The actual rape memories for me are like from the end of a tunnel. That's because I literally left my body at the scene. So I remember it from that perspective—there's some physical distance between me and what's going on. Those memories aren't as sharp in focus. It's like they happened in another dimension.

Other times, memories come in bits and pieces.

I'd be driving home from my therapist's office, and I'd start having flashes of things—just segments, like bloody sheets, or taking a bath, or throwing away my nightgown. For a long time, I remembered all the things around being raped, but not the rape itself.

If memories come to you in fragments, you may find it hard to place them in any kind of chronological order. You may not know exactly when the abuse began, how old you were, or when and why it stopped. The process of understanding the fragments is a lot like putting together a jigsaw puzzle or being a detective.

Part of me felt like I was on the trail of a murder mystery, and I was going to solve it. I really enjoyed following all the clues. "Okay, I was looking at the clock. It was mid-afternoon. Why was it mid-afternoon? Where could my mother have been? Oh, I bet she was at . . ." Tracing down the clues to find out exactly what had happened was actually fun.

Ella is a survivor who remembered in snatches. To make sense of her memories, she began to examine some of her own strange ways of coping. She started to analyze certain compulsive behaviors, like staring at the light fixture whenever she was making love:

I'd be making love and would think, "Why would somebody lay here, when they're supposed to be having a pleasurable experience, and concentrate on a light fixture?" I remember every single lighting fixture in every single house we ever lived in! Why have I always been so obsessed with light under doors, and the interruption of light? That's a crazy thing for an adult woman to be obsessive about—that someone walks past and cracks the light. What's that about?

What it was about was watching to see if her

father's footsteps stopped outside her door at night. If they stopped, that meant he'd come in and molest her. Once Ella started to pay attention to these kinds of details, the memories started to fit in place.

FLASHBACKS

In a flashback, you reexperience the original abuse. Flashbacks may be accompanied by the feelings you felt at the time, or they may be stark and detached, like watching a movie about somebody else's life.

Frequently flashbacks are visual: "I saw this penis coming toward me," or "I couldn't see his face, just the big black belt he always wore." First-time visual memories can be very dramatic:

My husband was beginning to initiate some lovemaking. I had a flash in my mind. The closest way I can describe it is that it was much like viewing slides in a slide show, when the slide goes by too fast, but slow enough to give you some part of the image. It was someone jamming their fingers up my vagina. It was very vivid, and enough of the feelings came sneaking in that I knew it wasn't a fantasy. There was an element of it that made me stop and take notice. I lay there and let it replay a couple of times.

I felt confused. I was aware that it was something that happened to me. I even had a recollection of the pain. I scrambled around in my mind for an explanation. "Was that a rough lover I had?" Immediately I knew that wasn't the case. So I went back into the flash again. Each time I went back, I tried to open it up to see a little more. I didn't see his face, but I could sense an essence of my father.

Sometimes visual memories are more complete. A survivor who's had them both ways explained the difference:

A flashback is like a slide compared to a film. It's the difference between getting one shot or one look into a room and getting the expanded version. A full memory is more like panning over the whole scene, with all the details, sound, feeling, and visuals rolled into one.

But not everyone is visual. One woman was upset that she couldn't get any pictures. Her father had held her at knifepoint in the car, face down in the dark, and raped her. She had never seen anything. But she had heard him. And when she began to write the scene in Spanish, her native language, it all came back to her—his threats, his brutality, his violation.

REGRESSION

Another way to regain memory is through regression. Under the guidance of a trustworthy therapist, it is possible to go back to earlier times. Or you may find yourself going back on such a journey on your own, with only the prompting of your own unconscious.

Most of the regressions I experienced felt almost like going on a ride. They'd last maybe three or four hours at a time. One of the most vivid physical regressions I went through was late one evening, when Barbara and I were talking about her going to visit a friend. All of a sudden, I felt like I was being sucked down a drain. And then I felt like a real baby. I started crying and clinging and saying, "You can't go! You have to stay with me!" And I began to talk in a five-year-old's voice, using words and concepts that a five-year-old might use.

All of a sudden I thought I was just going to throw up. I ran to the bathroom, and then I really started to sob. I saw lots of scenes from my childhood. Times I felt rejected flashed by me, almost in slides.

Barb held me, and kind of coached me through it. "It's okay. You can get through this." Having her just sit there and listen really helped me. I just kept crying, and described to Barbara all these slides that were going by. After about twenty minutes, I fell into the deepest sleep I'd had for months. The next morning when I woke up, I felt a million pounds lighter.

SENSE MEMORY

Often it is a particular touch, smell, or sound that triggers a memory. You might remember when you return to the town, to the house, to the room, where the abuse took place. Or when you smell a certain aftershave the abuser wore.

Thirty-five-year-old Ella says, "It's all real tactile, sensory things that have brought memories back. Textures. Sounds. The smell of my father's house. The smell of vodka on somebody."

Ella had a magic purple quilt when she was a little girl. Her grandmother made it for her. It was supposed to keep her safe—nothing bad could happen to her as long as she was under it. The quilt had been lost for many years, but when Ella finally got it back, at twenty-one, it triggered a whole series of memories.

Touch can also reopen memories. Women have had images come up while they were being massaged. You may freeze up and see pictures when you're making love. Your lover breathes in your ear just as your abuser once did, and it all comes spilling back:

Sometimes when we're making love, I feel like my head just starts to float away somewhere. I feel like I literally split off at my shoulders, and I get very lightheaded and dizzy. It's as if someone was blowing a fan down on top of my head. There's a lot of movement down past my hair. It's like rising up out of my head. I get really disoriented.

The other thing I experience is a lot of splitting right at the hips. My legs get very heavy and really solid. They just feel like dead weight, like logs. No energy is passing through them. Then I get real sick to my stomach, just violently ill. I find the minute I get nauseous, whatever it is is very close to me. And if I pay attention to it, I can see it, and move on.

THE BODY REMEMBERS WHAT THE MIND CHOOSES TO FORGET

It is also possible to remember only feelings. Memories are stored in our bodies, and it is possible to physically reexperience the terror of the abuse. Your body may clutch tight, or you may feel the screams you could not scream as a child. Or you may feel that you are suffocating and cannot breathe.

> I would get body memories that would have no pictures to them at all. I would just start screaming and feel that something was coming out of my body that I had no control over. And I would usually get them right after making love or in the middle of making love, or right in the middle of a fight. When my passion was aroused in some way, I would remember in my body, although I wouldn't have a conscious picture, just this screaming coming out of me.

WAYS TO REMEMBER

Memories come up under many different circumstances. You might remember because you're finally in a relationship that feels safe. Or because you've just been through a divorce and everything in your life is unraveling. Women often remember childhood abuse when they are raped or attacked in adult life.

Memories don't always surface in such dramatic ways. While talking with her friend, one woman suddenly heard herself saying something she didn't realize she knew. "It's as though I always knew it," she explained. "It's just that I hadn't thought about it in twenty or thirty years. Up until that moment, I'd forgotten."

You may remember seemingly out of the blue. Or because you're having persistent nightmares that reach up through sleep to tell you:

> I'd always had a dream about my brother assaulting me. It was a foggy dream, and I had it over and over again. I'd wake up thinking it was really disgusting because I was enjoying it in the dream. I'd think, "You're sick. Why are you having this dream? Is that what you want?" I'd give myself all those kinds of guilt messages, 'cause it was still a dream. It wasn't history yet.
>
> Then, six months ago, I was sitting in a training meeting for working with sexual assault prevention. I don't even remember what the trainer said, but all of a sudden, I realized that it wasn't a dream, and that it had really happened. I can't tell you anything about the rest of the meeting. I was just in shock.

The fact that this woman remembered in the middle of a training session for sexual assault is significant. As the media focus on sexual abuse has increased, more and more women have had their memories triggered.

MEDIA COVERAGE OF SEXUAL ABUSE

Jennierose, who remembered in her mid-forties, was sitting with her lover one night, watching a TV program about sexual offenders in prison. The therapist running the group encouraged the offenders to get very emotional, at which time they'd remember the traumatic events in their own childhoods.

In the middle of the program, Jennierose turned to her lover and said, "I wish there was a therapist like that I could go to, because I know there's something I'm not re-membering." As soon as she said that, Jennie-rose had a vision of the first time her father sodomized her, when she was four and a half and her mother had gone to the hospital to have another baby. "It was a totally detailed vision, to the point of seeing the rose-colored curtains blowing in the window."

Sobbing, Jennierose said to her lover, "I think I'm making something up." Her lover

---

While Making Love
by Laura Davis

It was a sunny Sunday morning. We had not made love for a long time. We lay in bed, curled together like spoons. I was half-asleep, half-awake, feeling her warm weight curve into mine, her knees fitting smoothly against mine. Her musky breath touched me, warm and familiar on my neck, her fingertips gently searching my back, a question: "Can it be now? I want you."

I turned to face her, to study the green-gold eyes I loved. To wonder at this miracle woman who had crashed through all my defenses and disarmed me. She had made it all the way in and I trusted her. Finally, at twenty-eight, I felt safe in love. Before, I'd been a loner, too busy achiev-ing, too busy living in my head, afraid of loving, a terror I could not name keeping me distant, just out of reach. There'd been other lovers, surely, others whom I dis-missed when they got too close, others who skirted my edges. But she was the first who'd reached all the way through those walls. She was the one I'd dreamed of but never thought possible, the one whose soft presence beside me still surprised and awed me these slow weekend mornings. I was happy, happier than I'd ever been.

So to answer the question of her searching fingers, I looked up and smiled at her, inviting her caresses, and reached to stroke her face. She pressed her belly up against mine, and I felt the sudden jolt of passion flare skin to skin. "I love this woman," I thought. "And we have our whole lives to share it."

She was kissing me now, teasing and slow, waiting for me to answer, for me to rise, for me to catch the rush, like winds in a sail, to fly with her. "So far, so good," I thought, my tongue answering, respond-ing, my body firm against hers, passion ris-ing.

There was a gleam in her eyes. She'd been waiting for this for a long, long time. "I want you," she said, her fingers reach-ing in, her body on fire against me. "I want you."

And then I felt it. Subtle, unmistakable. Painfully familiar. A small spark of terror and then the screen. An impermeable wall suddenly cast between us, my body cut loose, my mind floating free. I tried to call myself back, but already it was too late. I was gone.

"Well, there's not enough eggs for waffles," I thought. "But there are those leftover baked potatoes. And they'd make great home fries." I closed my eyes, tried again to reel myself in. "C'mon, Laura. You want to be here. You want to do this. Get back in your body. C'mon! This is the simply said, "Look at yourself! Look at yourself! Tell me you're making it up." And Jennierose couldn't. She knew she was telling the truth.

This kind of memory is common. Often women become very uncomfortable (nauseated, dizzy, unable to concentrate, emotional) when they hear another survivor's story and realize that what's being described happened to them too.

---

woman you love!"

But it didn't work. My mind was already far above my body, spinning, dancing intricate loops. I felt totally out of control. My body lay on the bed beneath, still going through the motions. God, how I hated this! The old grief, this lack of presence, surged through me.

I slowed down my caresses, pulled my mouth away. I grew quiet, solitary. Looked back at her face, drawn tight and hard with disappointment. "I'm sorry, honey," I said after a moment. "I just can't." She looked stung, tears frozen in her eyes. We'd come so close.

This was not the first time I'd "disappeared." Nor the second. This was old, familiar territory, a vast chasm spreading between us, wider and wider the closer we got.

"Where the hell do you go?" she screamed at me then, months of patience suddenly giving way. "Where the hell are you? Just what is wrong with you anyway?"

Then silence. Her words reverberating, burrowing in, digging deep into my center. I felt them choking me. Nothing else was real. I didn't know where I was, who I was looking at. Her face wavered before me. I couldn't breathe. I stopped seeing. Stopped doing anything but feeling those questions probing deeper and deeper inside.

I must have looked stricken because her face softened then, and she held me, her eyes deep with concern and tender with love. "Breathe, honey," she said. "Go ahead and breathe."

That's all I remember. I know there were moments passing, quiet pensive moments. Something was happening to me. I could feel it—a tiny bubble of truth rising up from deep inside, a knowing coming from an unnamed core, the kind of knowing that pierces through years of fog and cannot be denied.

I started sobbing. Deep, wracking sobs that scared me and confused me, leaving me helpless and hurting, a child in pain. I had never cried like this. What was happening to me? Someone had hurt me very badly.

She stroked my forehead, peppered it with kisses. "Sweetheart, what is it?"

More sobs, more shaking. A terror, a truth, a knowledge too awful to utter, was finally breaking free. I did not recognize the words until they spilled from my lips. I knew I was going to say something, but I did not know what it would be.

"I was molested," I finally said, a tiny child's voice at last managing those three small words. As I heard them cut through the quiet of the sunny morning air, I knew that they were true. "I was molested."

WHEN YOU BREAK AN ADDICTION

Many survivors remember their abuse once they get sober, quit drugs, or stop eating compulsively. These and other addictions can effectively block any recollection of the abuse, but once you stop, the memories often surface. Anna Stevens explains:

At the point I decided to put down drinking, I had to start feeling. The connection to the abuse was almost immediate. And I've watched other people come to AA and do the same thing. They have just enough time to get through the initial shakes, and you watch them start to go through the memories. And you know what's coming, but they don't.

(For more of Anna's story, see page 387.)

WHEN YOU BECOME A MOTHER

Mothers often remember their own abuse when they see their children's vulnerability, or when their children reach the age they were when their own abuse began. Sometimes they remember because their child is being abused. Dana was court-ordered to go for therapy when her three-year-old daughter, Christy, was molested. Dana first remembered when she unconsciously substituted her own name for her daughter's:

I was in therapy talking about Christy, and instead of saying "Christy," I said "I." And I didn't even catch it. My therapist did. She had always suspected that I was abused too, but she hadn't said anything to me.

She told me what I had said, and I said, "I did? I said 'I?'" I hadn't even heard myself. It was really eerie.

What came out was that I was really dealing with Christy's molestation on a level of my own. The things that I was outraged at and that hurt me the most were things that had happened to me, not things that had happened to Christy. Part of the reason I fell apart and so much came back to me when I found out about Christy was because my husband was doing the same things to her that my father had done with me.

AFTER A SIGNIFICANT DEATH

Many women are too scared to remember while their abusers are still alive. One woman said, "I couldn't afford to remember until both my parents were dead, until there was nobody left to hurt me." A forty-seven-year-old woman first remembered a year and a half after her mother died: "Then I could no longer hurt my mother by telling her."

FEELING THE FEELINGS

Although some remembering is emotionally detached, when you remember with feeling, the helplessness, terror, and physical pain can be as real as any actual experience. You may feel as if you are being crushed, ripped open, or suffocated. Sexual arousal may also accompany your memories, and this may horrify you, but arousal is a natural response to sexual stimulation. There is no reason to be ashamed.

You might remember feeling close and happy, wrapped in a special kind of love. Disgust and horror are not the only way to feel when you have memories. There is no *right* way to feel, but you must feel, even if it sends you reeling:

When I first remembered, I shut down emotionally right away. I climbed all the way up into my mind and forgot about the gut level. That's how I protected myself. For a long time it was just an intellectual exercise. "Oh, that's why I have trouble with men and authority. That's why I might not have remembered much about growing up." It took nine months after I first remembered for the feelings to start bubbling up.

I found myself slipping into the feelings I'd had during the abuse, that hadn't been safe to feel at the time. The first was this tremendous isolation. From there, I moved into absolute terror. I got in touch with how frightening the world is. It was the worst of the fear finally coming up. I felt like it was right at the top of my neck all the time, just ready to come out in a scream.

I was right on the edge. I had an encounter with my boss, who said that my performance had been poor. I finally told him what had happened, which was really heavy—telling some male authority figure that you remembered incest in your family. He is a kind and caring person. The best he could do was back off and leave me alone.

I was then carrying around all this external pressure—my job was in jeopardy, my life was falling apart, and I was having all these feelings I didn't know what to do with. In order to keep myself in control, I started compulsively eating. Finally I decided I didn't want to go through this stuff by myself anymore. I got myself into therapy.

Having to experience the feelings is one of the roughest parts of remembering. "It pisses me off that I have to survive it twice, only this time with feelings," one woman said. "This time it's worse. I'm not so effective at dissociating anymore."

Another woman said, "I started off very butch [tough] about remembering. I kicked into my overachiever thing. I was going to lick this thing. I believed getting the pictures was what was important. I got a ton of memories, all on the intellectual level. It was kind of like I was going to 'do' incest, just like I might take up typing."

It was only after a year of therapy that this woman began to realize that *she* was the one who'd been abused. "I finally realized, I finally *felt*, that this was something that had happened to me, and that it had been damaging. I had to realize that just getting the memories was not going to make it go away. *This was about me!*"

LETTING MEMORIES IN

Few survivors feel they have control over their memories. Most feel the memories have control of them, that they do not choose the time and place a new memory will emerge. You may be able to fight them off for a time, but the price—headaches, nightmares, exhaustion—is not worth staving off what is inevitable.

Not everyone will know a memory is

coming, but many survivors do get warnings, a certain feeling or series of feelings, that clue them in. Your stomach may get tight. You may sleep poorly, have frightening dreams. Or you may be warned in other ways:

> I always know when they're coming. I get very tense. I get very scared. I get snappy at things that ordinarily wouldn't make me angry. I get sad. Usually it's anger and anxiety and fear that come first. And I have a choice. It's a real conscious choice. It's either I want it or I don't want it. And I said "I don't want it" a lot. And when I did that, I would just get sicker and sicker. I'd get more depressed. I'd get angry irrationally.
>
> Now I don't say I don't want it. It's not worth it. My body seems to need to release it. The more I heal, the more I see these memories are literally stored in my body, and they've got to get out. Otherwise I'm going to carry them forever.

REMEMBERING OVER TIME

Often when you've resolved one group of memories, another will make its way to the surface.

> The more I worked on the abuse, the more I remembered. First I remembered my brother, and then my grandfather. About six months after that I remembered my father. And then about a year later, I remembered my mother. I remembered the "easiest" first and the "hardest" last. Even though it was traumatic for me to realize that everyone in my family abused me, there was something reassuring about it. For a long time I'd felt worse than the initial memories should have made me feel, so remembering the rest of the abuse was actually one of the most grounding things to happen. My life suddenly made sense.

The impact new memories have will shift over time. One woman who has been getting new memories for the past ten years says remembering has become harder over time:

> My first flood of memories came when I was twenty-five. The memories I get now are like fine-tuning—more details, more textures. Even though there was more of a feeling of shock and catharsis at first, remembering is harder now. I believe them now. It hurts more. I have the emotions to feel the impact. I can see how it's affected my life.

Laura also says new memories are harder:

> Just when I felt that my life was getting back to normal and I could put the incest aside, I had another flashback that was much more violent than the earlier pictures I'd seen. I was furious. I wanted to be finished. I didn't want to be starting in with incest again! And my resistance made the remembering a lot more difficult.

Other survivors say memories have gotten easier to handle:

IF YOU THINK A MEMORY IS ON ITS WAY:

- **Find a place where you will be safe.** If you're at work, try to get home. Go to the safe place in your house (see "Create a Safe Spot," page 203), or go to a close friend's house.

- **Call a support person.** You may want to be with a supportive partner, friend, support group member, or counselor before, during, or after your memory. Or you may prefer being alone.

- **Don't fight it.** The best thing to do is to relax and let the memory come. Don't use drugs, alcohol, or food to push it back down.

- **Remember, it's just a memory.** What you're experiencing is a memory of abuse that happened a long time ago.

Your abuser is not really hurting you in the present, even if it feels that way. Reliving a memory is part of your healing, not an extension of the abuse.

- **Expect yourself to have a reaction.** Recovering memories is a painful, draining experience. It may take you a while to recover. It's best to give yourself that time and not expect to run off and do something else right away.

- **Comfort yourself.** Having a memory is a very vulnerable experience. Do some special things to take care of yourself (for suggestions, see "Nurture Yourself: The Teddy Bear's Picnic," page 187).

- **Tell at least one other person.** Even though you may prefer to be alone when you have a new memory, it's important that you tell someone else about it. You suffered alone as a child. You don't have to do it again.

As I've come to terms with the fact that I was abused, new pictures, new incidents, don't have the same impact. The battle of believing it happened is not one I have to fight each time another piece falls into place. Once I had a framework to fit new memories into, my recovery time got much faster. While my first memories overwhelmed me for weeks, now I might only cry for ten minutes or feel depressed for an hour. It's not that I don't have new memories. It's just that they don't devastate me.

And new memories don't take anything away from the healing you've already done. Paradoxically, *you are already healing from the effects of the things you have yet to remember.*

"BUT I DON'T HAVE ANY MEMORIES"

If you don't remember your abuse, you are not alone. Many women don't have memories, and some never get memories. This doesn't mean they weren't abused.

If you don't have any memory of it, it can be hard to believe the abuse really happened. You may feel insecure about trusting your intuition and want "proof" of your abuse. This is a very natural desire, but it is not always one that can be met. The unconscious has its own way of unfolding that does not always meet your demands or your timetable.

One thirty-eight-year-old survivor described her relationship with her father as "emotionally incestuous." She has never had specific memories of any physical contact between them, and for a long time she was haunted by the fact that she couldn't come up with solid data. Over time, though, she's come to terms with her lack of memories. Her story is a good model if you don't have specific pictures to draw from:

Do I want to know if something physical happened between my father and me? Really, I think you have to be strong enough to know. I think that our minds are wonderful in the way they protect us, and I think that when I'm strong enough to know, I'll know.

I obsessed for about a year on trying to remember, and then I got tired of sitting around talking about what I couldn't remember. I thought, "All right, let's act as if." It's like you come home and your home has been robbed, and everything has been thrown in the middle of the room, and the window is open and the curtain is blowing in the wind, and the cat is gone. You know somebody robbed you, but you're never going to know who. So what are you going to do? Sit there and try to figure it out while your stuff lies around? No, you start to clean it up.

You put bars on the windows. You assume somebody was there. Somebody could come along and say, "Now how do you know someone was there?" You don't know.

That's how I acted. I had the symptoms. Every incest group I went to I completely empathized. It rang bells all the time. I felt like there was something I just couldn't get to, that I couldn't remember yet. And my healing was blocked there.

Part of my wanting to get specific memories was guilt that I could be accusing this man of something so heinous, and what if he didn't do it? How horrible for me to accuse him! That's why I wanted the memories. I wanted to be sure. Societally, women have always been accused of crying rape.

But I had to ask myself, "Why would I be feeling all of this? Why would I be feeling all this anxiety if something didn't happen?" If the specifics are not available to you, then go with what you've got.

I'm left with the damage. And that's why I relate to that story of the burglar. I'm owning the damage. I want to get better. I've been very ill as a result of the damage, and at some point I realized, "I'm thirty-eight years old. What am I going to do—wait twenty more years for a memory?" I'd rather get better.

And then maybe the stronger I am, the more the memories will come back. Maybe I'm putting the cart before the horse. Maybe I've remembered as much as I'm able to remember without breaking down. I don't want to go insane. I want to be out in the world. Maybe I should go with that sense of protection. There is a survivor in here and she's pretty smart. So I'm going with the circumstantial evidence, and I'm working on healing myself. I go to these incest groups, and I tell people, "I don't have any pictures," and then I go on and talk all about my father, and nobody ever says, "You don't belong here."

WRITING EXERCISE: WHAT HAPPENED TO YOU

(See the basic method for writing exercises on page 28.)

Write about your experience of being sexually abused as a child.

Many women have found it very difficult to tell people that they were sexually abused. When they do tell, it is often in very generalized terms: "I was molested by my brother," "I was raped when I was ten." Rarely do you share the details, partly because it's hard to tell even the general facts and partly because you want to spare the listeners. You don't want to impose.

But the tight statement "My stepfather abused me" is not the way you live with the abuse, not the way you experience flashbacks. That's not indicative of the creepy feelings you get when something triggers your memory. What you remember is the way the light fell on the stairway, the pajamas you were wearing, the smell of liquor on his breath, the feel of the gravel between your shoulder blades when you were thrown down, the terrifying chuckle, the sound of the

TV downstairs. When you write, include as many of these sensory details as you can.

If your abuse covers too much time and too many abusers to write it all in half an hour, just write what you can. Don't worry about which experience to start with. Begin with what feels most accessible or what you feel you most need to deal with. This is an exercise you can do over and over again.

If you don't remember what happened to you, write about what you *do* remember. Re-create the context in which the abuse happened, even if you don't remember the specifics of the abuse yet. Describe where you lived as a child. What was going on in your family, in your neighborhood, in your life? Often when women think they don't remember, they actually remember quite a lot. But since the picture isn't in sequence and isn't totally filled in, they don't feel they have permission to call what they know "remembering." Start with what you have. When you utilize that fully, you usually get more.

If you come to things that feel too difficult to say, too painful or humiliating, try to write them anyway. You don't have to share them with anyone if you don't want to, but in order to heal you must be honest with yourself. If there's something you feel you absolutely can't write then at least write that there's something you can't or won't write. That way you leave a marker for yourself, you acknowledge that there's a difficult place.

If you go off on tangents, don't pull yourself back too abruptly. Sometimes what may look irrelevant leads us to something more essential. Although you want to stay with the subject, do so with loose reins.

There is no one right way to do this exercise. Your writing may be linear, telling your story in chronological order. It may be a wash of feelings and sensations. Or it may be vague, weaving together scattered bits and pieces. As with all the writing exercises, try not to judge or censor. Don't feel that you should conform to any standard, and don't compare your writing with others'. This is an opportunity to uncover and heal, not to perform or to meet anyone's expectations—not even your own.

I Give Thanks for the Sky
by Teresa Strong

Teresa Strong's poetic response to this exercise is vivid and deeply moving. We hope it inspires you to tell your own story.

It's morning twilight, gray world, dreamworld, non-world time. I'm asleep, or at least I think I am. I'm dreaming, or maybe I'm crazy like my grandmother. I'm sleeping in the back room and hear my grandfather (and know he's *not* really my grandfather) coming in. He sits down beside the bed I used to sleep in—the one my niece sleeps in now. (Get her *OUT* of the fucking bed. It should be burned and chopped and destroyed. No one should sleep in that bed.)

He sits down beside the bed and starts easing me from sleep by rubbing his hand over me on top of the covers (the whole world is asleep), and under the covers and under my nightgown and over and all around me. And his touch is soft and he strokes and I don't know what is going on but it feels like a charge, like Life going through me. And it feels good to be touched and sometimes I pretend to be asleep and sometimes I am asleep and he just keeps touching and stroking and gliding and then somewhere in the tingling and feeling like Life going through me flashes *DANGER!*

DANGER! DANGER! STOP! And that's when he starts moving faster and he's not stroking or touching anymore. He's grabbing and rubbing and holding me down and leaning over me. And all I see are cold steel balls where his eyes used to be. And he's over me and all I can see from the corner of my eye is the sky and a leaf. I hold on to them.

That's the sky. I know that's sky. That's a piece of the sky, and that's a leaf. I know that's a leaf. And I'm clinging to the sky with my eye and he's whispering in my ear. "Oh Honey, see how much you like this and the best is yet to come."

I hear his zipper unzip. My body is jerking and writhing under him. *I* say it's because I'm trying to get away and he's almost giggling (these are the only times I see him smile big smiles), telling me how much I love this. His touch isn't a human touch anymore. He just presses and grabs. And then his penis is in front of my face and I know I'm either dreaming, crazy, or about to die, and my only hope is to hold on to the sky. And I do.

That's the sky and that's a leaf and he shoves his penis in my mouth. I die looking at the sky and he pushes and shoves and it feels like the roof of my mouth has to split open soon. And it feels like he's all the way down my throat. I can't breathe! I can't breathe! I need to throw up! *WHERE* is the sky? *WHERE* is the leaf? I can't see anything. I'm going to be sick. I want to *DIE*. I leave my body. I hide in my forehead and then in the sky. My throat is burning. He comes half in my throat, half in my face. I gasp for breath. He holds my jaw shut and I lose sight of the sky. I *HAVE* to see the sky—it's my only hope of getting out of here alive.

Sometimes he wipes my face clean and sometimes he forces me to eat it. Sometimes he grins and sometimes he strokes for a long time. Sometimes I completely lose sight of the sky and pass out. And when I wake up to the sounds of breakfast being prepared, the world is ordinary and fine.

As time goes on he doesn't bother to stroke or hold or touch me. I'm not even there. But each time before he leaves, he leans down, his nose brushing against my ear, and whispers, "Just remember, Honey, nothing happened." And being eager to please, I remember perfectly.

Once I ask my mother to let me sleep in a different room and she refuses because I'm now four and a big girl. My grandfather's story changes. Sometimes he tells me that if I tell, everyone will know I'm crazy and I'll be sent away. But, unlike my grandmother, he'll make sure I never come back. He also tells me that because I like this so much (and here he'll stroke me again like he hasn't for a long time and I do like the touch), if anyone finds out I'll really be in trouble because only whores/bad girls/crazy people like being touched like this. And besides, he tells me, we come to his home every year on my father's vacation.

So when early morning comes I pretend to be asleep as long as I can until he shakes me awake. And when I can't do that I look for the sky. And I keep the secrets that I like being touched and that I'm crazy. I fool people by getting good grades so no one knows I'm crazy. And I don't let anyone touch me, so they don't know I like it. And I hold on to the sky.

BELIEVING IT HAPPENED

Up until three months ago, I didn't *really* believe it happened: "It was hypnosis." "I only imagined it." I was acting as if it really happened. I'd go to an incest survivor's group. I'd freely tell people. But when I was alone, I'd say, "Of course it didn't *really* happen."

To heal from child sexual abuse you must believe that you were a victim, that the abuse really did take place. This is often difficult for survivors. When you've spent your life denying the reality of your abuse, when you don't want it to be true, or when your family repeatedly calls you crazy or a liar, it can be hard to remain firm in the knowledge that you were abused.

On the other hand, you may have no trouble believing it happened. You may even have corroboration. A sister or brother who remembers. A mother who said, "But honey, we had to stay with him." Physical scars from a rape at age four. A doctor's report. Court testimony. An abuser who says, "Yes, I did it." A neighbor who remembers. Another child you told.

What cemented it for me was when I told my mother what I remembered. I watched her face go blank, like she was in shock, and then she said, "That's your old room on the farm in Kentucky."

But most survivors don't have access to proof that they were abused, and few get support or validation from family members. Yet even if your memories are incomplete, even if your family insists nothing ever happened, you still must believe yourself. Even if what you experienced feels too extreme to be possible or too mild to be abuse, even if you think, "I must have made it up," or "No one could have done that to a child," you have to come to terms with the fact that someone did do those things to you. This is something you will have to acknowledge again and again.

THE ROLE OF DENIAL

Survivors often go to great lengths to deny their memories. One woman convinced herself it was all a dream. Another dismissed her memories by saying, "Oh, it's just a past life." When Laura was getting her first pictures of the actual abuse, she did not want to believe what she saw:

> I did not want to believe with a passion. Even as part of me recognized the truth, another part fought to deny what I had seen. There were times when I would rather have viewed myself as crazy than acknowledge what had happened to me.
>
> I had come from a wonderful family. *I* couldn't have been raped as a child. *I* couldn't have been molested by the grandfather I had revered and loved. I remembered all the wonderful things he did. That he had abused me was out of the question! It couldn't be!

This type of denial might seem surprising, but in reality, it is a necessary stage in dealing with traumatic pain. Denial gives you a respite when you cannot bear to align yourself with that small, wounded child for another minute. It allows you to go to work, to make breakfast for your kids. It is a survival skill that enables you to set a pace you can handle.

Often in the beginning stages, belief in your memories comes and goes. One woman explains:

> It's like being in a fog and the clouds going away. I'd have a memory. I'd relive the experience. Then I'd know it was true. "That was real. I don't want it to be true. But it happened." Then as soon as I said that, I'd deny it: "But I love my father. He couldn't have done that." But there'd be these little things inside that would say, "But what about the mysterious bladder infections I had when I was eight? He never could look me in the eye when I was in the hospital."

A dramatic example of this touch-and-go belief in memories occurred in one of Ellen's workshops. During a writing exercise, one woman wrote about the abuse she experienced when she was preverbal. When she read it aloud to the group, she experienced a complete regression, sobbing, stuttering, and shaking as she relived the experience. Everyone in the group was deeply moved.

Later the same day, the same women asked, "Do you think I really could have been abused? Maybe I was just acting." Another woman in the group turned to her and said, "Could you have acted joy and happiness as convincingly? If you're such a great actress, why do you only act out the same scene again and again?"

There Are Things
by Lisa Schweig

I. Facts and Figures

There are facts and figures
Dates and times
True statements
There are things I know.

   I know what I was wearing
   I know what I wasn't wearing
   I know where I was
   I know who was with me

   I know his body over me
   I know his hand on my breast
   I know his hand going down
   I know there is more

   I know I felt scared
   I know I curled up
   I know I tried hard
   I know I said no.

II. Confusion and Doubt

There is confusion and doubt
Frustration and denial
Questioning
There are things I don't know.

   I don't know why
   or how
   it really
   happened.

   I don't know when
   it started
   where
   he stopped

   I don't know who
   he is
   if
   I love him.

It is natural that you have periodic doubts of your experience. But that's because accepting memories is painful, not because you weren't abused.

LOOK AT YOUR LIFE

One practical way to validate your abuse is to look at your life. If you see the effects of abuse and then, as you begin the healing process, you see your behavior change, even slightly, you can trust that your belief is sound.

The hardest part was accepting and believing that it really happened. Being in the group really helped. I was able to see other people who have gone through sexual abuse, and my symptoms were similar. I have all the classic symptoms of sexual abuse—feeling suicidal, running away, a high pain tolerance, spacing out, not being able to succeed at anything, denial, always being isolated.

First Light
by Aurora Levins Morales

This is an excerpt from a longer, unfinished piece. The character, a nine-year-old girl, has just been raped by her uncle.

She lay on the narrow bed in the very early morning light and felt herself dying. She kept herself very still until she could feel nothing at all, and then she knew the process was complete. She was dead. Now, she knew, came the washing of the corpse, and this one needed it. The monster that had killed her had left blood on her. It was a strange thing, being killed in your own bed like that, in such an ordinary place. Nothing looked different, but it was all unfamiliar. Like the kind of bad dream where after you wake up, for a few minutes the clothes draped over the chair still look like a wolf and you're afraid to move.

Only she couldn't remember waking up after this dream. The events were seamless. She had paid close attention, but the only waking she remembered was when the door opened and the monster came in her room.

So it must be real. As she thought this, she felt the cold in her body deepen. Because what if they insisted it was a dream? Insisted she was still alive? What if they made her walk and talk and go to school and eat, when really she was dead? What if they told her it was just pretend?

Suddenly, small and clear, like a picture on a very tiny far-away television screen, she remembered the afternoon with her aunt Luisa. They had been playing that she was a wicked witch and her aunt was the evil creature who tagged along. In the middle of the game her aunt got tired and said she wasn't an evil creature at all.

Disappointed that the game was ending so soon, she had insisted, "You *are*, you *are*, you *really* are!" Aunt Luisa had made her sit down on the floor for a serious talk, and her face—long and stretched tight around the eyes and mouth—had scared her.

"It's okay to play and make up stories, but you mustn't believe in what you make up. You have to know the difference between real and pretend. Otherwise people think you're crazy." Then she whispered, "And maybe they'd be right!"

Now her aunt was in the hospital and all anyone would say was that she didn't feel well.

So if this was just a dream and she couldn't tell the difference, then maybe she was crazy. But even if she wasn't, even if the monster was real, what if no one believed her? They would think she was crazy anyway, and put her in a loony bin. She imagined a loony bin. It had smooth white sides like the bin her mother kept onions in, and the crazy people were dropped in with tweezers and lay in a heap on the bottom of it. She would hate that. It would be much better to pretend, to go along with them and act alive.

The first thing was to wash. When you washed a dead person, later people went to look at them and said "She looks just like herself," "She looks like she's only sleeping." She would pretend she was only sleeping from now on, and she would look like herself.

It was growing lighter now. She could see the blood on her thigh, but none of it was on the bed yet. She got up quietly and went to the bathroom, closing the door gently so as not to wake up her grandmother. Using wet toilet paper she began to wash herself between the legs, and being dead, it hardly hurt at all.

Another thing that helped me believe it was watching my own behavior patterns change. Like my paranoia going away. I used to think the Mafia was out to get me, and that someone was going to set fire to a place I was in. When I remembered the incest, I realized those were threats that my father had made. He used to lock me in the cedar closet and sodomize me. Then he'd threaten to set fire to it. He said if I ever told anyone, the Mafia would come and get me. As soon as I made those connections, my paranoia went away.

YOU NEED VALIDATION

Emily, who was abused by her parents as a very young child, struggled for a long time against believing it happened. Although she suffered from a multitude of emotional effects, she could not reconcile her memories with her parents' behavior in the present. When confronted with the abuse, her parents denied everything and her father offered to see a counselor, take a lie detector test, anything, to prove his innocence.

Every time Emily spoke to her parents she became ill—the conflict between what she knew inside and what they presented was too great. She was easily convinced that she was a terrible person for making up such lies. It was only when Emily broke off all communication with her family and established a consistent relationship with a skilled therapist who believed her that she stopped doubting herself and got on with her recovery.

Talking to people who believe you and validate your experience is essential.

I would talk with my therapist about what people had done to me in my family. And she would say to me, "That's abuse. That's terrible that that happened to you." And I was shocked, because I thought I'd had a normal childhood. I only knew it was abuse because other people would mirror it back to me. I would walk around saying, "My family abused me." I had to say it a lot to really believe it. My first year and a half was spent just accepting the fact that I had been abused.

Believing It Mattered: Vicki's Story

Many women believe their abuse doesn't count because it happened only once. But as the following story shows, all abuse is harmful.

There was always a creepy feeling in my house of my father being really inappropriate. He'd just be too affectionate, too close. He was always kissing me too long. It got worse when I was a teenager. He had a more difficult time containing himself. My girlfriends felt weird around him and he was really hostile to my boyfriends.

My father only molested me once, when I was twelve years old. I was asleep in bed. He came into my room and lay down next to me. He put his hand down my pajamas and started playing with my vagina. It woke me up. I turned away from him. I pretended I was turning over in my sleep. He must have gotten frightened that I would wake up, and he left. I remember watching his shadow outside the door. He never did it again.

Before he molested me, I felt very free in my body. I felt wonderful. I was coming into the height of puberty. I was outgoing and friendly. I had boyfriends. Everything was awakening. And my first intimate sexual experience was with my father. He was the first man to ever touch my genitals.

It was very upsetting and confusing to me. I loved my father. We had a really strong relationship. After he molested me, I went into a deep depression. I shut off communicating with the outside world. It was like this veil just came down, and that was it. It took me until I was twenty-two to even realize something was wrong. I've had to find out what my real personality was underneath.

I never forgot what happened. It sort of went underground. I didn't think about it a whole lot, but it's had long-lasting effects. I've had a really difficult time getting close to my lovers. I need a disproportionate amount of control in relationships.

I've been estranged from my father for the last five years, ever since I confronted him. Our relationship has basically fallen apart.

I never compared what happened to me to what other people went through because I really felt the hell inside myself. I knew it was wreaking havoc in my life and in the lives of my lovers. You don't have to have it happen over and over to know "This is really terrible." It doesn't take much for a child to feel the devastation of a parent crossing over those boundaries.

If I was talking to someone and she said, "Oh well, he just fondled me a little bit. It's not such a big deal," I'd ask, "When you connect with another human being in a deep way, how does it make you feel? Does it make you feel scared? Like closing down? Or like being completely one with that person?" Really check it out with yourself. In the deepest part of you, how are you connecting with people? Then reassess if you were affected.

It counts if it keeps you from being close to another person. It counts if it's devastated your life, if you're missing a part of yourself. Even if it only happened once, it counts.

BELIEVING DOESN'T HAPPEN ALL AT ONCE

Even once you know the facts are true, you may still, at a deep emotional level, have trouble believing it happened. Believing doesn't usually happen all at once—it's a gradual awakening.

At first, I had regular doubts that the abuse had happened at all. Once I became more steady, I still thought of it as something that had happened to someone very far away from me. Over time, I've been able to incorporate it more into the texture of my life. I include it when I tell people about my life. I talk about it freely, much as I would the fact that my family went to museums a lot when I was a kid. It's no longer a shameful secret, separate from the rest of who I am. I used to feel I had this good childhood and then off to the side was this horrible, shameful abuse. But now I know there was only one child and she lived through it all.

BREAKING SILENCE

What would happen if one woman told the truth about her life? The world would split open.

—Muriel Rukeyser, from "Kathe Kollwitz"

An essential part of healing from child sexual abuse is telling the truth about your life. The sexual molestation of children, and the shame that results, thrive in an atmosphere of silence. Breaking that silence is a powerful healing tool. Yet it is something many survivors find difficult.

I feel very lonely and isolated. I've always had so much to say, and I've never said it. What's hindered me the most is being so skilled at being silent. Incest has had so much to do with being silenced and silencing myself.

HOW YOU WERE SILENCED

The first time you tried to talk about your abuse, you may still have been a child. Under ideal circumstances, you would have been believed, protected, and assured that the abuse wasn't your fault. You would have been given age-appropriate counseling and placed in a support group with other children. If the abuser was a family member, he would have been the one sent away, not you.

Unfortunately, this was probably not the response you got. More likely, you were threatened, blamed, or called a liar. You were accused of "asking for it" or were called "a little whore." You may have been warned not to tell during the abuse itself: "It would kill your mother if she knew," or "I'll kill you if you tell."

Sometimes telling led to further abuse. One child confided in her best friend. That girl told her father, who asked for the details. He then took both girls into the garage and did to them all the things he'd just heard about.

Telling frequently ignites the wrath of the abuser. Eleven-year-old Carey was abused by both her mother and her stepfather.

When I was eleven, I went horseback riding with my best girlfriend. I told my girlfriend what I was doing with my stepfather. She told her mother, who called my mother. When I got home, my mother came tearing out of the house, crazy angry. She grabbed me and pulled me off my horse. Kicking me and hitting me, she dragged me into the house, up the steps, across the porch, into my bedroom. She threw me on the bed, screaming at me about telling stories.

I was sobbing and saying, "They're not stories, they're true, and you know they're true." And she started to choke me. My stepfather was standing right behind her, watching, with no expression on his face.

I couldn't breathe. I believe she would have killed me. It was the third time she'd tried. Finally he pulled her off, saying, "You know nobody's going to believe her. Nobody believes anything she says."

If your case was taken to court, you may have been subjected to brutal testimony procedures, grilled by insensitive defense attorneys, or repeatedly forced to face your abuser.*

---

* Recently some states have begun to amend the legal codes to meet the special needs of child witnesses. These changes are slow in coming, but pioneering programs have been introduced. In some jurisdictions, judges no longer wear formal robes or sit on an elevated platform. Instead everyone sits around a table at eye level with the child. More support people and family members are allowed in the courtroom. Some courts appoint a special child advocate to wait with the child before and after the court appearance, to make sure the child does not see the offender beforehand, and to be a supportive friend to the child.

Washington state has actual children's courtrooms. Children sit on the floor with toys and the judge sits on the floor with them, taking their testimony. The room is equipped with a one-way mirror and the defendant is on the other side, so the child never has to face him.

Videotaped testimony is used throughout the country, even where it is not yet admissible evidence in court.

Videotapes of a child's testimony are used to confront offenders, and are often enough to elicit a guilty plea.

There are proposals in various states for a "hearsay law" which would enable a second party, such as the child's therapist, to testify on behalf of the child. Such a system is used in Israel, where children never appear in court in incest cases. A youth counselor is assigned by the police department to get the child's statement, in accordance with legal code, and that person then testifies for the child.

The bias against children's testimony is slowly changing. In order for offenders to be convicted, it has to be. Generally these are crimes without evidence. There are no pictures of bruises or broken bones. In most cases, the child's statement is the only evidence. While some states still discredit children as witnesses, others are allowing younger and younger children to testify. In California, a three-year-old was recently qualified as a credible witness.

If your mother divorced your father because he was abusing you, you may have felt guilty for breaking up the marriage, for separating your family, or for ruining a "happy home."

Children not slapped with an actively cruel response are often met with devastating silence or told never to speak of it again. Families often go on as if nothing happened, never mentioning it. In that case, children get the message that their experience is too horrible for words. And, by implication, that *they* are too horrible.

In this way, children learn there is no one they can trust, that sharing leads not to help but to harm or neglect, that it's not safe to tell the truth. In other words, they learn shame, secrecy, and silence.

HOW CHILDREN TELL

Children do not generally say "My brother molested me six times," but in their own way, all children "tell" that they've been abused. They tell in vague terms: "I don't like Mrs. Johnson." "I don't want to go to Boy Scouts anymore." For a child, "Don't make me go Poppa's house anymore" is a very clear message.

If children don't tell with words, they often tell through behavior. They wet their beds. They steal from a parent's wallet. They are terrified to go to sleep, and wake up screaming from nightmares. They regress to more babyish behavior. They don't want to be left alone. They develop asthma. They stop eating. They have trouble in school. They cry hysterically every time a particular babysitter comes over. They demonstrate a precocious interest in sex. They act seductively to get things they want.

Sometimes older children or teenagers act out by disobeying or getting into trouble with authorities. They become depressed, take drugs, or engage in self-destructive behavior. They are trying to get someone to pay attention, but their behavior is usually misinterpreted. They are labeled "bad" or "stupid." These messages make them feel even more hopeless. "Perhaps they're right," the kid thinks. "I am no good. No wonder he does that to me."

Perceptive parents notice changes and respond. They listen, no matter how their children express themselves. But until recently most abused children had no one who would listen.* No one wanted to know. Stuck in an abusive situation, often with an unrealistic sense of responsibility, they carried this secret burden alone.

If you believe you didn't tell, look again. In your own way, you reached out for help—and were denied.

TELLING: IT TAKES A LEAP OF FAITH

It's not only children who have been met with insulting or insensitive responses when they tried to talk about their abuse. Adult

---

* As parents and professionals become more aware of the need for compassionate responses when children are abused, this is changing. Hopefully survivors years from now will find this statement false. They will have received prompt, skilled, and sympathetic help and so will have much less compounded trauma to heal from.

survivors have also been blamed, ridiculed, or shunned. Yet in spite of these negative experiences from the past, it is necessary to take a leap of faith—and tell.

Telling is transformative. When you let someone know what you have lived through and that person hears you with respect and genuine caring, you begin a process of change essential to healing.

Catherine was in a therapy group when she first told about her abuse:

I had to get up and talk about what my parents had done to me, and why it was hard for me to grow up in my family. I remember being in the group and crying, and saying, "I can't tell this to you. My parents are going to get me if I say this to you!" It was horrible. People encouraged me to tell my story, and I finally did.

When it was over I went home and laid in my bed, and literally waited to die. I had never told anybody before. I knew my parents would find out that I had told on them, and would get me.

And that's when I decided I was going to become a person who could talk, instead of being a person who had to keep secrets.

In workshops, when a woman tells her story the effects are often dramatic. She no longer feels so different or alone. She knows she is understood because she has been listening to other survivors' stories and she understands them. She learns that she is important, worthwhile, and lovable because she feels the compassion of the other women as they listen and respond to her. She feels authentic because she allows herself to feel her real feelings. She experiences release because there is relief in the telling.

When I talked about the incest with my counselor, it stayed almost as big a secret as when I hadn't told anyone. Going to group and speaking to all

---

WHY TELLING IS TRANSFORMATIVE

- You move through the shame and secrecy that keeps you isolated.
- You move through denial and acknowledge the truth of your abuse.
- You make it possible to get understanding and help.
- You get more in touch with your feelings.
- You get a chance to see your experience (and yourself) through the compassionate eyes of a supporter.
- You make space in relationships for the kind of intimacy that comes from honesty.
- You establish yourself as a person in the present who is dealing with the abuse in her past.
- You join a courageous community of women who are no longer willing to suffer in silence.
- You help end child sexual abuse by breaking the silence in which it thrives.
- You become a model for other survivors.
- You (eventually) feel proud and strong.

BREAKING THE SILENCE: ABUSE BY WOMEN

Although the majority of sexual abuse is committed by heterosexual men, women do abuse children. Both girls and boys have been abused by their mothers, aunts, grandmothers, or other women. *

Since much of the incest literature has focused on father-daughter incest, or solely on abuse with a male perpetrator, those survivors who were abused by women have felt even more isolated than those abused by men.

At an incest art gathering in Los Angeles in 1980, one woman played a videotape in which she talked about the incest she'd experienced with her mother. The response she got was one of shock and disbelief.

---

* The Safer Society Press has published a summary of data about female sexual abusers by Faye Honey Knopp and Lois B. Lackey (The Safer Society Program, Shoreham Depot Road, Orwell, VT 05760).

A woman who'd written a major book about incest stood up in the audience and said, "There is no incest between mothers and daughters." So I walked away thinking, "I must be crazy."

This unwillingness to acknowledge women as offenders has slowly started to break down. Support groups for survivors abused by women are beginning, but many women still find themselves discounted:

I find that when I tell my story, a lot of people are uncomfortable. People have all these squirmy reactions. It's almost as if they don't quite believe it. I can't just tell my story—I have to tell my story and then explain it.

People like to think in categories. So when you talk about women as sexual abusers, it blows a lot of myths: Women aren't sexual. Women are gentle. Women are passive. How could a woman do that to a child?

But people need to hear it. They need to hear, "I'm an incest survivor, and it was my *mother*." Women do abuse, and if it's not put out there, the healing can't happen.

Most of the issues explored in this book apply equally to all survivors, but there are some unique problems faced by survivors of abuse by women. Although women sometimes abuse in overtly sexual or violent ways, their abuse is typically more subtle and less forceful. Women's abuse is often masked in cuddling and daily caretaking. The violation is often fuzzier, less clear-cut than a penis in a vagina. But it is no less devastating.

Since children frequently bond most closely with their mothers, abuse by mothers, in particular, can leave a child with a severe lack of boundaries between herself and her offender.

For a while I didn't know where my mother left off and I began. I thought she had a psychic hold on me. I was convinced she knew every thought I had. It was like she was in my body, and she was evil. I felt I was possessed, that I was going to be taken over. I've had a real fear that if I look at all that stuff that I don't like about myself, it would be my mother inside of me. And I've had to do a lot of growing over the last few years to know that she's not inside me anymore.

Other women have had a hard time maturing, watching their bodies grow similar to their mothers'.

For a long, long time, I didn't call myself a woman. When I left home at eighteen, I continued to call myself a girl because I couldn't stomach the associations with "woman," which meant being sexual. My mother was a woman, but I was a girl. If being a woman meant being like her, that's not what I wanted. It took a long time for me to get rid of that self-hate.

It is essential not to discount the pain and betrayal experienced by survivors of abuse by women. Every survivor deserves to heal. (For more on healing from abuse by a mother, see Anna Stevens' story on page 387.)

those people was important. It was a real coming out.

After telling in a group, you may feel as though being a survivor, with all its difficulties, is not all bad. As one woman said, "We're a beautiful, courageous bunch of women—and I'm proud to be one."

THE LEVELS OF TELLING

There are many levels of telling, ranging from the first time you dare to broach this subject to when you have told so many times and in so many ways that you can talk about it naturally, as just another part of your life. Each time you tell is a different experience. Telling your therapist or your support group, telling your partner or a new lover, telling a friend, telling publicly, telling in writing, will all feel different.

You may tell with detachment, with sadness, with anger, or occasionally even with humor. Participants in a recent summer I Never Told Anyone group nicknamed the workshop "Incest Camp," and one woman sent everyone T-shirts with "I.C. Survivor" printed across the front.

Jude Brister, a co-editor of I Never Told Anyone, said that each time she talked about her abuse, it put more distance between herself and the pain. The more she talked about it, the less she identified herself as a victim. She saw herself instead as a strong, capable adult.

Ella, another survivor who has told her experiences many times, described her process in detail:

For me there were at least three different levels of telling. The first was telling the story and not feeling anything. Telling it as a third-party story. Saying "I" but not really meaning it happened to me. At that point I still didn't really believe it happened. And part of that telling was that I was really angry. It was a way to get back at them. Like "I'm going to tell on you." It's kind of like "I couldn't get anybody mad at you then, but watch this!"

Then there was a really painful, scared level of telling. The tone of my voice changed and I looked like I was seven years old. My language was more simple. And it hurt. That's the place I discovered my feelings. And usually people got sad when they heard it that way. They felt sorry for me. The people I told that way included my therapist, my close friend, people in caretaker positions, paid or unpaid. It included the people in my support group. I told not like a victim, but like a little kid that hurt.

The last way I've told has to do with stepping back and seeing the bigger picture. I looked at family dynamics and got the rest of the story. I saw what happened and why it happened. I put the abuse through a sieve and was able to see parts of it I couldn't see when I was only hurt or angry.

So I went from anger to pain to a fixing. In Hebrew there's a word, tikun, that means a fixing, a healing. That way of telling was a tikun.

CHOOSING SOMEONE TO TELL

If you are in counseling or a support group where you feel safe,* that's an excellent place to begin to talk about your abuse. Telling for the first time can feel scary, and it helps to be in a context where you know someone will listen compassionately.

Telling your partner, lover, or close friends is also important. You need to let the people around you know why you are sometimes sad, angry, upset, busy, needing to be alone. Your friends need to understand why you may not trust them readily. Your lover needs to know why you may have difficulty with sex, why you withdraw or cling. There is a lot of work involved in building healthy relationships, and you need the people in your life as allies. Although it is not necessary —or even appropriate—to tell every single person you meet, it is important that you share with the people you want to be close to.

I don't run around telling every soul I meet that I'm an incest victim, because I don't want that to be my definition, but I went through a period of time when it was just about like that. That was the first thing I would tell people, almost anybody. "Did you know I was an incest victim?" "Oh really, thank you for sharing that." It's like any movement, whether it's Black power or gay

rights, you need time to try that identity on and claim it. I needed to do that, but that need has faded over time. Now I just do what I feel like doing. If I feel like telling someone, I do. If I don't, I don't.

For some women, telling goes even further. They see it as a political choice, a necessity. Dorianne Laux, who runs workshops on sexual abuse for teenagers and has read her poetry about incest extensively, explains:

So many women still feel they have to hide the fact that they were molested. I can just see it in their bodies, that they're real frightened that somebody might find out. Well, I don't like that. I don't have to be frightened that somebody's going to find out.

I always use my first and last name when I talk about incest. It's a political statement for me. I don't have anything to be ashamed of. I don't have to be anonymous. Even though it could affect my life in some way, it shouldn't. It should affect *his* life.

And the whole idea of the secret is perpetuated when I keep my name out of it. Incest doesn't need to be hidden. It needs the exact opposite. People need to come out and say, "My name is so-and-so, this happened to me, and I'm angry about it."

Also, I'm a fairly well-adjusted person, and I make a good role model for the young people I work with. So speaking out and saying who I am is real important to me.

* If you don't feel safe enough with your counselor or support group to talk about these issues, read "Healing Resources," on page 458, to determine whether your counselor is safe and it's just hard for you to trust, or whether you would do well to seek a different counselor.

HOW TO TELL

Talking about your abuse with a skilled counselor or supportive group of survivors needs no planning. They should be able to hear you however you get the words out. But if you are telling friends or family for the first time, it's best to make the circumstances as favorable as possible. (This applies only to telling family members you expect to be supportive. If you're planning to tell unsympathetic or unpredictable family members, read "Disclosures and Confrontations" on page 133. That's a whole different kind of telling.)

You can maximize your support by choosing wisely. When you're considering talking to someone, ask yourself the following questions:

- Does this person care for and respect me?
- Does this person have my well-being in mind?
- Is this someone I've been able to discuss feelings with before?
- Do I trust this person?
- Do I feel safe with this person?

If you can answer yes to all of these questions, you're choosing someone who's likely to be supportive.

Tell your friend (lover, partner, cousin) that there's something personal and vulnerable that you want to share and ask if this is a good time to talk. Suggest that it if isn't, you could make it another time. By asking, you ensure that your friend doesn't need to leave for work in five minutes. You also give that person a chance to either postpone the talk or prepare to listen.

If there are certain responses that you want or don't want, say so. You may want your friend to listen but not to give a lot of advice. You may want to be asked questions, or you may want to be listened to silently. You may want to be held or you may not want to be touched at all. Often people want to support you but don't know how (or how to ask). A good friend will welcome your guidance.

And if you want what you say to be kept confidential, say so. Although it is important to break silence, do so at your own pace, with people *you* choose.

WEEDING

Listening to the truth of someone's life is a privilege and an honor. When you tell someone your history, they should receive it as such. But because this is not always the case, you need to be prepared for possible negative responses.

Some people may be threatened. Some will go blank or be shocked. These people may be reminded of their own abuse. If they have not yet recovered their memories, all their defenses may ring in alarm, trying to protect them from their own remembering. Some people will be horrified. Some may not even believe you initially. Others may be incredibly rude. One woman waited until after she had had three children to finally tell her husband about the incest. His response: "You mean I wasn't the first one?"

One survivor was reluctant to tell: "I have been afraid of people's reactions. People like victims. There's an animal part in people, and they get excited, and they'll just jump on you." Other people have been titillated by the stories of survivors and have asked for "details." In a society where the sexual abuse of children has been eroticized, this is not surprising.

Although you will meet up with some of these hostile, insensitive, or insulting responses, it is still important to tell. There is a weeding out that goes on in relationships when you start to share who you really are, how you genuinely feel. You may find that some relationships cannot stand this challenge and you will grieve for them, along with your other losses. Or you may choose to continue the relationship on a more superficial level rather than abandoning it altogether.

Although it is likely that you will get some unsatisfying responses, it is also likely that you will get some supportive, sympathetic ones, as Laura described:

When I first remembered my abuse, I was overwhelmed. I stopped calling my friends and when they called me, I was distant and preoccupied. Karen, my closest friend, was hurt and angry. She was about to write me off totally. Finally, I told her about the abuse. Once she knew what was going on, she was wonderful. She became my most devoted supporter.

It is important that you have some relationships in which you can be your whole self —with your history, with your pain and anger—and the only way to create those is to share honestly about yourself. When you are met in that honesty, then you feel real intimacy.

One Hundred and Fifty-Seven Ways to Tell My Incest Story
by Emily Levy

Tell it in Spanish
In Sign Language.
Tell it as a poem
As a play
As a letter to President Reagan.
Tell it as if my life depended on it.

I was not molested as a child.
I feared, when I was three years old, that a man would come into my room in the middle of the night and Get me. Where did that idea come from?
I wonder why I hate my father so much. The explanations I've developed don't add up to the amount of anger and hatred I feel.

There's a vague possibility I was molested as a child.

Tell it as a court case
As a congressional debate
As if the power of children were respected.
Tell it as domestic terrorism
As a national sport.
Tell it as a jump-rope game:

A my name is Annie
He stuck it up my Anus
Now I am Angry
And I want Action.

B my name is Betty
The penis was my Brother's
I wrote a Book
'Cuz I want to get him Back.

C my name is Carla
He said he'd give me Candy
I told my Cousin
And her Dad got Caught.

D my name is Doris
I was still in Diapers . . .

Tell it as graffiti
As a religious service.
Tell it as a classified ad.

*Why is it that when I see Dad I make sure to
    wear a long scarf that covers my chest?
There's no way he could have molested me.
    I'd remember it. I have a great memory.
    Everybody in my family says so.
Why did I suddenly start hating him when I
    was eleven years old?
I think my father might have molested me
    when I was a child.*

Tell it as a TV commercial
As a science experiment
As a country western song.
Tell it as ancient history
As science fiction.
Tell it in your sleep:

> This time I decided to get him instead of
> letting him get me. I jerked him off
> angrily, scratching his cock with my
> fingernails, digging them into his flesh as
> deep as I could. I kept going at it, trying
> to make him ejaculate. Then I realized it
> would be meaner to stop. As soon as I
> stopped, my mother was there again.

Tell it as a bedtime story
As a bumper sticker.
Tell it as if we liked it.

*When I was young, I used to say, "Don't touch
    me, I'm alive!" Why did I make up that
    expression?*

Tell it as justification for nuclear war
As justification for never having another war.
Tell it as a greeting card:

To A Beloved Niece—

On this day I think of you
A girl with virtue always true
A sweeter thing I ne'er did see
No wonder Pop molested thee.

Your rosy breast and dangling tongue
What heaven in a girl so young!
Your beauty now is crowned with luck
His love shown by a family fuck.

One wish for you, now, if I may:
Happy Molestation Day!

Tell it as a gossip column
As a last will and testament
As an exhibit at Ripley's Believe It Or Not.

*Am I making this up as an excuse to hate him?
    If I falsely accused him, I'd never forgive
    myself.*

Tell it as a soap opera
As a telephone answering-machine
    message.
Tell it as a board game:

> "Snake eyes. Damn it, I rolled snake
eyes."

"Ha, ha. You get molested by your twin brother. Your nightmare quotient goes up 60%, your therapy sentence up three years, and your sexuality goes into the shop for repairs."
"Hey, give me that marker! I can put my own sexuality in the shop!"
"OK. My turn now. Three. One, two, three. All right! 'Doctor Feminist'!"
"Pick a card."
" 'You go to a three-day workshop where you cry, talk about why you cried, and talk about why you talked about why you cried. Take six months of therapy off your sentence.' All right!"
"How come you get all the good ones? My turn."

Tell it as a "How To" book
As a newscast
As instructions on the box it came in.

Why do the muscles in my vagina tighten when I hear his name?

Tell it as a fairy tale
As a magic trick.
Tell it as of this moment:

Kissing your lips is like walking into a lush garden. I watch each emotion bud within your dark eyes.

My palms engulf your breasts, your fingernails cruise across my belly. We rock until you lie on top of me. You press your knee against my cunt, whisper I want you Baby, and suddenly you become him. You are pinning me down, holding me so tight I cannot breathe. You are pushing your prick into me, insisting I want it. I wrestle with your body and with the voice inside my head saying Calm down. This is different: you choose to be here.

Hey, where are you, you ask. What happened. My eyes clearly describe to you the fear my mouth cannot speak. You sigh and hold me gently. Finally I cry.

Tell it as a healing ritual
As an epitaph
As discovered and interpreted seven
    generations from now.

Maybe my family named me The One Who
    Remembers so they could believe that
    anything that I don't remember didn't
    happen.

Tell it as a map of the world
    As if I were still forbidden to speak the
    words.

My father molested me when I was a child.

Tell it so it will never happen again.

UNDERSTANDING THAT IT WASN'T YOUR FAULT

I know I was only five years old, but I was an extremely intelligent five-year-old. I should have been able to figure out a way to escape.

Victims often believe they are to blame for being sexually abused. Many adult survivors continue to hold this belief. Although large numbers of children and adolescents are abused, it is never the fault of any of them. Yet there are many reasons why survivors assume that blame.

Some survivors were told explicitly that it was their fault. The abuser said: "You're a bad, nasty, dirty girl. That's why I'm doing this." "You really want this to happen. I know you do." "You're such a sexy little girl. I just can't help myself."

You were punished when someone did find out. If you said anything, you may have been told you made up horrible lies. Or the subject was never discussed, giving you the message that it was too terrible to talk about.

Your religion may have told you that you were a sinner, unclean, damned to hell. You may have become convinced you were unlovable, even to God. One woman said: "That little incested girl inside of me is still waiting for the lightning to strike because I told people what happened to me. If I say, 'I think it was my Dad,' I'll burn up in hell-fire."

One small child was even begged by her abuser to stop him. He kept telling her how wrong it was and that she must not let him do it ever again—and then he'd force her once more.

I felt I was really evil. It's almost like those child-devil movies, like Damian. Inside this innocent little child is this evil seed. I used to think that just my presence made people feel bad and made bad things happen. I used to think that if only I did something, then everything would change. If only I got straight A's, then my Dad would stop touching me. I felt I could control things by my behavior. No one around me seemed to be controlling anything. I still have this really warped sense of what I can do with my presence or my actions.

There are also less obvious reasons why survivors blame themselves. It is a stark and terrifying realization for a child to see how vulnerable and powerless she actually is. Thinking that you were bad, that you had some influence on how you were treated, gave a sense of control, though illusory. And perceiving yourself as bad allowed for the future possibility that you could become good, and thus things could improve.

In truth, nothing you did caused the abuse; nothing within your power could ever have stopped it. Your world was an unsafe place where adults were untrustworthy and out of control, where your well-being and sometimes your very life was in danger. This perspective, though realistic, is more distressing for many children than thinking that they were bad and somehow responsible for the abuse. For if there is no hope that the people whose job is to love and protect you would do so, where could you turn?

Recognizing that you were not to blame means accepting the fact that the people you loved did not have your best interests at heart. In one workshop, a woman blamed herself because at the age of twelve she said no, and her father stopped. "Why couldn't I have done that right away, at four, when he started?" she chastised herself. "I *did* have the power to stop him."

Another woman answered her: "I said no and my father never stopped. I fought and kicked and screamed no. But abusers don't stop because you say no. They stop when they're ready to stop. By the time you were twelve your father was ready to stop. Maybe he only liked small children. You had less control than you think."

Women blame themselves because they took money, gifts, or special privileges. But if you were able to get some small thing back, you should instead give yourself credit. One woman in a workshop was given a bicycle by her abuser. On it she was able to ride away from her house, out to the woods, and there feel the safety of the trees. She blamed herself for having taken the bicycle. Instead, she should be commended for taking what she could get in that wasteland.

BUT I WANTED TO BE CLOSE

Many survivors hold particularly shameful feelings if they needed attention and affection and did not fight off sexual advances because of those needs. Or if they sought out that affection. The closeness may have felt good to you. You may have adored your abuser. You may have loved feeling like Grandpa's special little girl. Women say, "I'm the one who asked for a back rub," or "I kept going back,"or "I climbed into bed with him."

But you were not wrong. Every child needs attention. Every child needs affection. If these are not offered in healthy, nonsexual ways, children will take them in whatever ways they can, because they are essential needs.

BUT IT FELT GOOD

Although some women felt only pain or numbness when they were abused, others experienced sensual or sexual pleasure, arousal, and orgasm. Even though your experience of abuse may have been confusing, frightening, or devastating, you may also have felt some degree of pleasurable feelings. For many, this aspect of the abuse is one of the most difficult.

Some of it felt good, and ugh! It's still hard for me to talk about it. When I think back on some of the times I was close to my mother in a sexual way, where I was getting turned on, there's a lot of shame there. It feels real yucko! It feels really embarrassing.

Another woman was gang-raped as a teenager and had an orgasm. "For a long time I thought it was a cruel joke that God had made my body that way. I forgot what had happened because of the shame of having liked it." When she first remembered the rape, this woman spent a night frantically skimming *Voices in the Night* cover to cover to see if anyone else had had an orgasm while being abused.* She urgently needed to know that she wasn't the only one.

---

* Toni McNaron and Yarrow Morgan, eds. (see the "Sexual Abuse" section of the Bibliography).

It is important to recognize that it is natural to have had sexual feelings, and that even if you had sexual responses to the abuse and those responses felt good, it still doesn't mean that you were responsible in any way.

Our bodies are created to respond to stimulation. When we are touched sexually, our whole physiology is designed to give us pleasure. These are natural bodily responses over which we do not always have control. When we eat a sandwich, our stomachs digest the sandwich. We can't stop our stomachs from digesting the sandwich. In a similar way, when we're stimulated sexually, we can't always stop our bodies from responding.

The girl or woman who is sexually abused and experiences orgasm does not want to be abused. The fact that she responds sexually is not a statement that sexual pleasure is bad. And—very important—it is not a betrayal of her body. Her body did what bodies are supposed to do. You were betrayed not by your body, but by the adults who abused you. For Saphyre, it's taken a lot of self-love to overcome the shame:

I had to realize I didn't get off because I liked it, but because I have a woman's body that is made to experience passion. My body responded to touch. That was all. And they had no right to mess with that. That anger helped me get over the shame.

BUT I WAS OLDER

When children are abused, their capacity to say no and set limits is severely damaged. So even if the abuse continued into your adult years, you are still not to blame. There is no magic age when you suddenly become a responsible, cooperative partner in sexual abuse. Even if your father is still having sex with you when you are thirty, it is not your fault. You may be an adult in age, but you are still responding from the perspective of a small, powerless child.

Mary spent her childhood being regularly abused by her stepfather and brothers. When she was twenty-one she went on a weekend trip with her twenty-two-year-old brother and some of his friends. The two were asked to share a room. "I spent the night sleeping on the bathroom floor, because my brother would not leave me alone. He begged to make love with me. He kept grabbing at me. Finally I locked myself in the bathroom."

For a long time, Mary felt guilty about what had happened. He was her brother. He was only a year older than she was. She was an adult and should have known better. She should never have agreed to go on the trip in the first place. It was all her fault.

It wasn't until Mary went to therapy that she began to accept the real facts of the matter. "What happened when I was twenty-one was exactly the same thing as being eight years old and having to take a bath with my father. I just hadn't been trained to say no."

If your boundaries have always been violated, then it is unfair to expect yourself to be able to set them all of a sudden. You don't become assertive and powerful just because you grow up and leave home. No matter what age you are, no matter what relationship you have with the abuser, if someone with more power is pressuring you into a sexual relationship, then you are being abused.

IT'S NEVER YOUR FAULT

It is unfair to expect children to be able to protect themselves. Children do a lot of testing. They test limits. They test attitudes. This is their job. They develop a sense of what the world is all about through this testing. And it is *always* the responsibility of the adult to behave with respect toward children.

Even if a sixteen-year-old girl walks into her living room naked and throws herself on her father, he is still not justified in touching her sexually. A responsible father would say, "There seems to be a problem here." He would tell her to put clothes on; he'd discuss it with her, get professional help if necessary. Regardless of age or circumstance, there is never an excuse for sexual abuse. It is abso-lutely the responsibility of the adult not to be sexual with children.

As a child, you did not have the skills or power to protect yourself. Today at least there are child assault prevention programs in schools, which teach children to be "safe, strong, and free." (For more information on these programs, see the footnote on page 281.) Now many parents are teaching their children that they have the right to say no. But it is only recently that children have been provided with even these few basic tools. No woman we know was told, as a child, that she had the right to control her body. Even those of you who did try to resist or fight back often encountered increased coercion.

Bubba Esther
by Ruth Whitman

She was still upset,
she wanted to tell me,
she kept remembering
his terrible hands:

> how she came, a young girl
> of seventeen, a freckled
> fairskinned Jew from Kovno
> to Hamburg with her uncle
> and stayed in an old house
> and waited while he bought
> the steamship tickets
> so they could sail to America
>
> and how he came into her room
> sat down on the bed, touched
> her waist, took her by the
> breast, said for a kiss
> she could have her ticket,
> her skirts were rumpled, her
> petticoat torn, his teeth were
> broken, his breath full of
> onions, she was ashamed

still ashamed, lying
eighty years later
in the hospital bed,
trying to tell me,
trembling, weeping with anger

OVERCOMING SHAME

A key sign of healing is that your shame becomes less. Instead of looking at somebody's watch while you tell them what happened, you can look at their face. And then eventually you can look in their eyes and tell them, without feeling they can see what a creep you are. You can just look at someone, tell them, and say, "And I'm okay" without having to ask, "Right? I am okay, aren't I?"

There are many ways to overcome shame. The most powerful is simply talking about your abuse. Shame exists in an environment of secrecy. When you begin to freely speak the truth about your life, your sense of shame will diminish.

You know how they say, "Speak the truth and the truth shall set you free." Well that's how it really is. I'm not in a cage anymore. I have no bars. The best part is there are no more secrets. And it's the secrets that kill you. It's not the poison and the hate that kill you; it's keeping secrets. Because you live in fear that someone will find out. Secrets destroy people, and they destroy them unnecessarily. It's like being reborn when you shed the secret, because you have no more fear.

JOIN A SURVIVORS GROUP

Being in a group with other survivors can be a powerful way to vanquish shame. When you hear other women talk about their abuse and are not disgusted, and when you see those same women listen to your story with respect, you begin to see yourself as a proud survivor rather than as a conspiring victim. As one woman said, "When your counselor says, 'It wasn't your fault,' that's one thing. But when you have eight people saying it to you, it's a lot more powerful."

SPEAK OUT IN PUBLIC

Speaking publicly—doing outreach to other survivors, working on child assault or rape prevention programs—is a powerful way to transform shame into a feeling of personal effectiveness and power. For Jennie-rose, who'd been a prostitute and a thief in her twenties, speaking out was a way to let go of shame, once and for all:

> After I'd been working with the incest for a while, I felt the need to help other people. I did it by going out talking to kids in school, and talking to professional training groups. One of the training programs I did was for police officers. All these years, I'd been sure that people still thought that I was a prostitute. And that was twenty years ago! I stood up before all those cops and I said, "I'm not a thief. And I'm not a prostitute." It was one of the most rewarding moments of my whole life. I faced the enemy.

LOOK TO THE CHILDREN

Spending time with children can provide you with convincing evidence that the abuse wasn't your fault. Children help you remember how small and powerless you actually were. One mother said:

> Watching my daughter grow up gave me a sense of "How could anyone do that to a kid?" that I couldn't get just in relation to myself. I had been able to rationalize the mistreatment of kids for a long time. But when I saw how little power she had, how small she was when I put her to bed, I got a real picture of how small and vulnerable *I* had been. I got it in my heart that abuse was not okay. And that I had not been responsible for what had happened to me. I started to forgive myself.

At the workshops she does for teenagers on child sexual abuse, this woman passes around a picture of herself at three years old. "I tell them, 'This is the child that my father was having sex with, the one with the rubber pants and the little lace-up shoes.' I always show that picture to let the kids know it wasn't my fault."

Even if you don't have children of your own, you can still find opportunities to observe children. The next time you're near a schoolyard or at a mall where kids hang out, look around for kids who are the age you were when your abuse began. Watch the way they interact. Listen to the pitch of their voices. Look at their actual size. Do you honestly think one of those children deserves to be abused?

If you still believe the abuse was your fault, you have lost touch with the simplicity of a child's longing to share love. One woman told the following story:

> When my daughter was about six, we were riding in the car on our way to visit friends and she told me she wanted to be my lover. I knew her concept of lover was somewhat fuzzy, but she had enough idea to feel she wanted that. I responded gently that it wasn't possible.

She quickly added, "I know I'm too small, but when I'm grown up."

"No," I explained. "Even when you grow up, I'll still be your Mom and you'll still be my daughter. We have a special relationship that will never change. We can never be lovers, but we will always love each other in our own special way."

"Yes," she assented, "that will never change." Then, as we got out of the car she turned to me. "Mom, don't say anything to them about what we talked about, okay?"

I took her hand as we walked to the house. "Of course not."

This is the innocent love that abusers exploit.

THE CHILD WITHIN

When I first heard people talk about forgiving the child within, I raised my left eyebrow and thought, "California." There was no little girl inside of me. And if there was one, she was too weak and helpless for me to want to know her. She was the one who'd gotten me into this. She was a troublemaker and I wanted nothing to do with her.

Many survivors have a difficult time with the concept of the child within, even though forgiving that child is an essential part of healing. Too often women blame her, hate her, or ignore her completely. Survivors hate themselves for having been small, for having needed affection, for having "let themselves" be abused.

You may feel split, caught in a real schism. There is the "you" that's out in the "real" world, and then there's the child inside you who is still a frightened victim: "I felt like all my successes had been one big fake, be-

cause I ignored the little child who never got over it, and who lives her life in humiliation and pain because of it." This survivor pictured herself as a successful career woman, carrying a briefcase and walking out the door to work. Beside her she'd imagine a little child whining over and over, "You can't go to work! You have to stay home and take care of me."

For a long time the briefcase-carrying woman could only respond in one way: "I can't stand being around you. I hate your guts, and I don't want to sit and look at your sad little face all day!"

Yet as long as you ignore that child's frozen pain, you won't feel whole.

Coming to terms with the little girl was really hard. I had to see all along that I'd had the enemy in the wrong place. And when I started to see what she had to deal with, and how well she did, I began to see how amazing it was that she survived whole. It took me a long time to accept and love her, but I finally was able to start cutting her some slack.

WHY IT'S HARD

It is helpful to know why it's so difficult to open yourself up to the little girl. To begin with, your survival depended on covering up her vulnerability. Even acknowledging the fact that you once *were* a child can be very threatening. It means remembering a time when you did not have the power to protect yourself. It means remembering your shame, your vulnerability, and your pain. It means acknowledging that the abuse really happened to you.

One woman had a terrible time accepting the fact that the incest wasn't something she'd conjured up in her adulthood. Even after years of therapy, this woman, like many survivors, couldn't remember being a child at all. It wasn't until her therapist asked her to bring in pictures of herself at various ages that she began to realize that she was the same person as that child who'd been molested. "See," her therapist would say, pointing to the photos, "*this is you*. This is

something that happened to you. Do you see that this child is only *this* tall? Can you see that this child is you?"

Survivors who are mothers often say that seeing their own children's vulnerability is what enabled them to connect with the child within. Laura's reconnection to the inner child came about in a similar way:

I have always loved children, but for months after I remembered the incest, it was too painful to be around them. I'd see them playing or running down the streets, little girls flipping up their skirts and showing white cotton panties, and I'd cringe inside. "They're too vulnerable," I'd think. "They're too little."

I spent Halloween at my friend's house, just a few months after I had my first memories. I'd fled the trick-or-treaters in my neighborhood. It still hurt too much to see those innocent little faces. They'd say, "Trick or treat," and all I could think was, "Who's going to ruin you?" Every child seemed like a target.

The doorbell rang. My friend asked me to get it. I opened the door to a mother and a little girl. The girl was dressed as an angel, in a flowing white dress with gold trim. She had straight blond hair cut in a pageboy. Set on her head was a halo made of aluminum foil and a bent wire hanger. I asked her how old she was. "Five and a half!" she answered proudly.

I couldn't take my eyes off her. She looked exactly like I had when I was her age. It was like looking in a mirror back twenty-five years. I just stared at her, until her mother put a protective arm around her shoulder, and glared at me. I gave the girl a Snickers bar and turned away. I shut the door slowly and sat down in the living room, dazed.

All I could think was, "That's how small I was! I was that little when he forced himself on me. How could he have done that?" I felt tears of outrage and grief. I had been innocent! There was nothing I could have done to protect myself. None of it had been my fault. "I was only a child," I screamed into the empty living room, the sudden reality of what a child of five is flooding through me.

MAKING CONTACT

Not having that little girl in your life means you have lost something. You have not had access to her softness, to her sense of trust and wonder. When you hate the child within, you're hating a part of yourself. It is only in taking care of her that you can really learn to take care of yourself. And although you may start with feelings of mistrust and ambivalence, part of healing is accepting her as a part of you.

I had to make a real commitment to the child inside myself. I had to say, "What do you need today? What can I do to make you feel safe? No, I'm not going to just tell you to go away." I had to make a literal commitment to do that. I had to say, "Okay, you need for me not to talk to so many people about what's going on." Or, "Okay, today you need for me to take five minutes at lunchtime to talk to you."

It was really wonderful, because suddenly I felt a real loyalty to this child. I began to feel that I wanted her to be a part of me. I wanted to help her feel all right. And I had never felt that before. What I had felt was, "Get this fucking brat out of my way, and let me get on with my life!"

Feeling that I had the ability to parent her was amazing. I had always said that I would never have children because I didn't want to do to them what my parents had done to me. So the fact that I could develop parenting skills toward myself was real important.

Coming into an intimate relationship with the child means hearing the depth of her pain, facing her terror, comforting her in the night. This will not be easy. But embracing the child inside is not all painful. It also means giving yourself extra pampering. Julie Mines gave herself birthday parties:

When I turned twenty-five, I began a countdown to thirty, anticipating an approximate five-year healing time. Starting with my "fifth" birthday, I have been counting down to my first. I celebrated my "fifth" over children's stories and chocolate cake. Friday I'll be celebrating my "third" birthday with the women in my life who help me heal. I'm going to build a tent out of bed sheets and we'll sit inside and read stories by flashlight. There will be glow-in-the-dark stars on the tent ceiling too. Oh, I love being little!

Another woman set up whole playrooms for the injured children who lived inside her.

Getting to Know the Child
by Eleanor

When I communicated how dependent I feel on being fat to keep me safe from men, my therapist asked me to imagine what it would take for the little girl inside of me to feel safe. When I closed my eyes, I saw myself as a young girl walking down the road, with a machine gun, a shoulder sash full of bullets, a couple of grenades, and a knife in my cowgirl boots. My therapist noted that my child believes she has to take care of herself, whereas it is my job to become the kind of adult who can protect her from harm. That way she won't have to do it herself with excessive body weight and other defenses.

In a later fantasy, I approached the little girl to tell her that I would keep her safe. She was playing in a sandbox with toy soldiers and tanks. She had on khaki shorts, a T-shirt, and an army helmet. She never looked at me. In utter sarcasm, she said, "Yeah, right." But she believed me. When she knew that I knew she believed me, she said, "But don't think this means I'm going to put on a dress or be nice to company." I told her not to worry, she doesn't have to do anything to get my protection.

Later the same day, she let me see tiny glimpses of her, sometimes tough, sometimes vulnerable, soft, feminine, pretty, scared. Once when I approached her she was in her jeans and T-shirt, with a camouflage army cap on. Long, soft tendrils of her beautiful hair had escaped her hat and were falling along her back and shoulders. I asked her if there was anything I could do for her.

Without a moment's delay she answered, "Well, you *could* stop stuffing me with food!"

"What do you mean?" I asked, shocked. "It's you who demand all that stuff."

She made a loud smack with her tongue. "*Somebody* has to be the adult around here, you know. Just because I ask you for it doesn't mean you have to give it to me. You don't let your son eat all that junk, no matter how he acts to try to get it. Don't you love me as much as you love him? What's the matter with you anyway?"

I am so delighted with her. She's intimidating too, though. I told her that I'd think about what she's saying, but that I don't have any magic solutions and she's going to have to be patient while I learn to parent her. She seems satisfied with that. She doesn't trust adults, but she thinks I'm a lot better than most grown-ups. She likes me. Maybe not full-out, but she does like me. She has seen me parent my son and she trusts me to proceed with integrity. I'm educable, she has decided.

She's such a smart, alive, spunky little thing. If she thinks I can do it, I can do it. She's an excellent judge of character. I'm hopeful. I have a new chance. I begin now.

She created safe places for each one, complete with age-appropriate toys, stuffed animals, postcards sent and received, drawings, and lots of affirmations.

You can draw pictures or play hide-and-seek in twilight. One woman got her husband to read her children's books every night before going to sleep. Another sat down before she went to bed and wrote a letter to the child within. "I'd tell her all these nice things. And then I'd get up and read it in the morning."

Your job is to give that child pleasure and to listen to the stories she has to tell. As one survivor, Gizelle, explained:

> I began to listen to her and honor her, to do nice things for her. I needed to be her mother. That awakened my own healing energy. And I began to respond to that child: whether she needed to wear soft clothes, or eat an ice cream cone, or watch *I Love Lucy*, or sit out in the flowers. She knew what she needed to heal.
>
> And this I'm discovering more and more. She will guide me. She's the one who's been wounded. She knows if she needs to be held. There may be times she just needs to have her hair brushed. She *knows* and I do as much as I can. I hold myself. I stroke myself. Or I rock. I comfort the child.

(For more of Gizelle's story, see page 446.)

WRITING EXERCISE: THE CHILD WITHIN

(See the basic method for writing exercises, page 28.)

This is a chance to talk to the child within. If you're capable of loving and comforting the child within, if you can let your adult self express the compassion you have for this child, write to her now and let her know. You can write a letter directly to her. Or you can engage in a written dialogue with her, first writing as the adult, and then as the child responding.

If you don't feel any allegiance, tenderness, or connection with the child yet, start with how you honestly feel. You can't write "I love you, I'll take care of you" if that's a lie. Start with: "I'm willing to sit down and write to you even though I'm not quite sure you exist," or "I don't sympathize with you yet," or even, "I hate you. You got me into this mess to begin with." Any point of contact is a start. You can't have a loving relationship until you make contact. Take the first step.

If you feel totally alienated from the child in you, imagine another child the age you were during your abuse. Try writing to her instead.

This is a good exercise to do more than once, particularly if you're not starting from a place of compassion. Eventually you'll be able to tell the child she's not to blame, that she's innocent, and that you'll protect her.

TRUSTING YOURSELF

What I've had to tell myself again and again is "Trust yourself." When my body tells me to stop, I stop. When my body tells me to go, I go. I used to push myself beyond my limits, and I'd always get sick. Now I've learned to listen so I don't have to go to that point. I trust myself because I'm my own greatest healer. Even the best therapist can't help me heal unless I listen to my body.

When children are abused, their perceptions become threatening to them. To acknowledge that the neighbor who pushed you on the swings and gave you birthday presents was also the man who made you suck his penis was unbearable. To admit that your father, who went to work to support you and stayed up late to make you a dollhouse, had a scary smile on his face when he touched your genitals was too terrifying. So you pretended they weren't doing these things or that these things were really all right. The lengths to which children go to distort their perceptions are striking.

When my father would come into my room at night, I would think, "That's not my father. That's an alien being." I'd look at these people doing these things to me and think, "Invaders have taken over their bodies." And these invaders were doing things to me. The original was still out there somewhere and why wouldn't they come back? I'd think, "Daddy, why did you let those aliens take your body over?"

If the significant adults in your life told you that your experiences didn't really happen, or that they happened in ways radically different from the way you perceived them, you probably became confused and distressed, unsure what was real.

A father can touch his daughter's breast and explain it away by saying, "I'm just tucking you in." A daughter can tell her mother that her stepfather touched her in a funny way. The mother can respond, "Oh, honey, that was just a dream."

Family members aren't the only ones to perpetuate this invalidation. Many young girls try to tell teachers, counselors, ministers, or other adults, only to be told, "You must be mistaken. Your Uncle Jimmy is a deacon in the church." Survivors have gone to therapists for help and been told, "You should be over that by now," or "It was just your brother; all kids do that."

It can also be terrifying to trust your inner voice if you're afraid of what it will tell you. One survivor explained: "My greatest fear is that if I listen to my insides, I will become crazy like my Mom. She's often said to me, 'You have the same kind of powers I do.' So the message is if I listen to my insides, I will really become off the wall. If I listen to my inner voice, I will drift into my own inner world, which is really crazy."

Although you may find it difficult to have faith in your own perceptions, it is possible to develop the capacity to trust your inner voice.

THE INNER VOICE

Within all of us, there is an inner voice that can tell us how we feel. If it's been covered over, or if you are not practiced at listening to that voice, it may be very small, just a pipsqueak. Yet it is there. And the more you listen and act on it, the stronger and clearer that voice will grow.

In child assault prevention programs, children are taught to identify the voice inside that warns them that something isn't right. They refer to this voice, intuition, as the *uh-oh* feeling. With encouragement, children easily recognize this feeling as danger—uh-oh, something's wrong here.

The uh-oh feeling is the one that tells you if you're in danger on the street. It tells you to cross the street and walk the other way. It's the sixth sense that warns you that something is about to happen.

Everyone experiences her inner voice differently. You may have bad dreams. You may get headaches. You may become exhausted. You may have a sudden urge to binge on crackers. Or you may notice you've cleaned the house twice in two days. The important thing is not what you experience, but that you recognize it as a message.

Ellen discovered a few years ago that every time she was about to make a poor decision for herself, she'd get a tight, anxious feeling in her stomach:

Looking back, I could see that that simple physical warning had been there throughout my life, but I'd never before given it a hearing. I'd never stopped and said, hey, what is this squeamish feeling in my stomach telling me? Once I began to listen and to respect this feeling, I began making much better decisions for myself. Now, whenever I feel it, I stop what I'm doing and take a minute to trace where the feeling originated. This information has been immensely valuable.

For more on getting in touch with your inner voice, see "Feelings," page 191.

GRIEVING AND MOURNING

Sometimes I think I'm going to die from the sadness. Not that anyone ever died from crying for two hours, but it sure feels like it.

As a survivor of child sexual abuse, you have a lot to grieve for. You must grieve for the loss of your feelings. You must grieve for your abandonment. You must grieve for the past and grieve for the present, for the damage you now have to heal, for the time it takes, for the money it costs, for the relationships ruined, the pleasure missed. You grieve for the opportunities lost while you were too busy coping.

And sometimes the losses are extremely personal:

I don't remember ever being a virgin. It wasn't fair. Everybody else got to be one. It has always really hurt me. I still have a real anger that that was taken away. Nobody asked. It was just gone. I didn't have that to give. I know that's just "The American Dream," but I heard that dream the same as any other woman did. Whether it's important now or not, it was to me.

If you maintained the fantasy that your childhood was "happy," then you have to grieve for the childhood you thought you had. If your abuser was a parent, or if you weren't protected or listened to, you must give up the idea that your parents had your best interests at heart. Part of grieving is replacing the unconditional love you held for your family as a child with a realistic assessment. Your childhood may have been completely awful. On the other hand, there may have been a lot of good times mixed in with the abuse. If you have any loving feelings toward your abuser, you must reconcile that love with the fact that he abused you.

You may have to grieve over the fact that you don't have an extended family for your children, that you'll never receive an inheritance, that you don't have family roots.

You must also grieve for the shattered image of a world that is just, where children are cared for, where people respect each other. You grieve for your lost innocence, your belief that it's safe to trust. And sometimes, you must even grieve for a part of you that didn't make it:

> I went down to see the children inside me. The first one I noticed just sat on the curb in my abdomen. She'd sit there with her head in her hand, looking very sad, or she'd be jumping up and down, being manic. Then there was one in my heart who would sit in a room behind a door. She'd open the door and peek out, and then shut the door, 'cause she got scared. Then there was the one who was dead. I'd been waiting for her to wake up. And one day I was lying in bed crying, and I said, "Okay, it's time for you to wake up," but she was dead. I sobbed and mourned that a part of me had died. The part of me that had really wanted to believe in the good of the family and the good of everyone just died.

Some survivors grieve not just for themselves, but for the abuse that was done to the people who abused them, for the generations of victims continuing to perpetuate abuse. A woman who was abused by her mother explains:

> There was a lot of grief, lots of tears realizing I didn't have the kind of family I thought everybody else had. It really hurt. It still hurts. It comes in waves. Those kinds of tears go real deep. It's a sadness for what I didn't have; it's also a sadness for my mother. It hurts that she's so sick. It hurts that she never realized her beauty, and still doesn't. Because she had so much self-hate, she had to abuse me. For a long time I was angry about that, but then there was a stage of grieving for her because she *is* beautiful, she is loving; it's just that her sick side is overwhelming to her.

BURIED GRIEF

Buried grief poisons, limiting your capacity for joy, for spontaneity, for life. An essential part of healing from traumatic experiences is to express and share your feelings. When you were young, you could not do this. To fully feel the agony, the terror, the fury, without any support would have been too devastating to bear. And so you suppressed those feelings. But you have not gotten rid of them.

To release these painful feelings and to move forward in your life, it is necessary, paradoxically, to go back and to relive the experiences you had as a child—to grieve, this time with the support of a caring person and with the support of your adult self.

What you need to heal is not fancy or esoteric. It is remarkably simple, though for many survivors it has been hard to find. All you need is the safety and support that enable you to go back to the source of your pain, to feel the feelings you had to repress, to be heard, to be comforted, and to learn to comfort yourself.

And in this way, a transformation takes place. Once you have fully felt a feeling, known it and lived in it, shared it, acted it, given it full expression, the feeling begins to transform. The way to move beyond the grief and pain is to experience them fully, to honor them, to express them with someone else, thus assimilating what happened to you as a child into your adult life.

ABOUT GRIEF

You may feel foolish crying over events that happened so long ago. But grief waits for expression. When you do not allow yourself to honor grief, it festers. It can limit your vitality, make you sick, decrease your capacity for love.

Grief has its own rhythms. You can't say, "Okay, I'm going to grieve now." Rather you must allow room for those feelings when they arise. Grief needs space. You can only really grieve when you give yourself the time, security, and permission to grieve.

After I had been in therapy for several months my whole self began to respond to that environment, within which I could allow my feelings. There were weeks I entered the building, went up the stairs, checked in with the receptionist, all with a smile on my face and cheerfulness in my step. Then I'd enter the office, my therapist would close the door, and before she'd even get to her chair, I'd be crying. Deep within me I held those feelings, waiting until I knew there would be time and compassion.

THE ROLE OF RITUAL

In order not to stifle your feelings of grief, take this period of mourning as seriously as if someone close to you had died. One survivor, whose abusive parents were still very much alive, spent many months dressed in black, telling everyone her parents had died. Another woman wrote a eulogy for her abuser, imagining herself at his grave, telling everyone exactly what she would remember him for. A third held a wake. Rituals such as these can be powerful channels for grief.

I wrote a divorce decree from my mother, because I kept having these dreams of wanting to cut the umbilical cord and her not letting me. I just couldn't figure out how to separate from her. We weren't talking. We weren't seeing each other, but I was still feeling too connected.

You may not be inclined to ritual or ceremony. You may simply cry a lot. As one woman put it: "I hadn't cried in years. It's only recently that that's been restored. I'm not sure I'm happy about it. It's like Niagara Falls at times."

However you grieve, allow yourself to release the emotions you have struggled all your life to smother. Grieving can be a great relief.

Own Your Own Pain
for Alana and Irma

by Patricia Roth Schwartz

Own your own pain.
Why not? It's yours.

You've hawked it, pushed it, pimped it—
     now,
Your body, breathing, life, guts, luster,
     sweetness, softness,
Pays the price.

So own your own pain. Why not?

You've eaten it for breakfast,
Sung it to sleep at night,
Rinsed it out in the basin,
Watched it rise with the bread.

So—take it, turn it,
Let it slither,
Into blood-beat, breast-bone, cell-song,
     skin.

Give it a name.
What you possess
Cannot possess you.

WRITING EXERCISE: GRIEVING

*(See the basic method for writing exercises
on page 28.)*

Write about what you lost, what was
taken, what was destroyed. Write about the
extent of the damage. Write about the things
you need to grieve for. This is a chance to
give voice to your pain, and to write about
how you feel about your loss.

ANGER—
THE BACKBONE
OF HEALING

When I'm angry, it's because I know I'm worth being angry about.
—Shama, 25-year-old survivor

Few women have wholeheartedly embraced anger as a positive healing force. Traditionally women have been taught to be nice, conciliatory, understanding, polite. Angry women are labeled man-haters, castraters, bitches. Even in new-age psychotherapy circles, anger is usually seen as a stage to work through or as something toxic to eliminate. And most religious or spiritual ideologies encourage us to forgive and love. As a result, many survivors have suppressed their anger, turning it inward.

I'm albino and I get severe sunburn whenever I'm exposed to the sun. As a kid, I'd get really pissed about what was happening at home. But you weren't allowed to get angry at my house. So rather than say anything, I'd purposefully go out on a sunny day without a hat or any other protection. I'd come home blistered and with a fever.

Other survivors have been angry their whole lives. They grew up in families or circumstances so pitted against each other that they learned early to fight for survival. Anger was a continual armoring for battle. And sometimes the line between anger and violence blurred, and it became a destructive force.

I saw men and women angry and rageful when I was growing up. Both of

122

my parents, and other relatives too. I remember my mom slapping the shit out of this woman in the bar because the woman said, "We don't allow dirty Mexicans in this bar." But then my parents would turn it on each other, and on us. Anger, violence, and self-defense are all mixed up for me.

But anger doesn't have to be suppressed or destructive. Instead, it can be both a healthy response to violation and a transformative, powerful energy.

DENYING AND TWISTING ANGER

Anger is a natural response to abuse. You were probably not able to experience, express, and act on your outrage when you were abused. You may not even have known you had a right to feel outraged. Rather than be angry at the person or people who abused you, you probably did some combination of denying and twisting your anger.

One way survivors cut themselves off from their anger is to become so immersed in the perspective of the abuser that they lose connection with themselves and their own feelings. This approach is enthusiastically endorsed by most of society. Many people find it easier to sympathize with the abuser than to stand up as a staunch advocate for the victim. This is particularly true once time has passed and the abuser is an older man and the child a grown woman. People will feel sorry for him, perceive even weak attempts toward reconciliation on his part as major efforts, and blame the survivor if she continues to be angry.

But if you are unable to focus your rage at the abuser, it will go somewhere else. Many survivors turn it on themselves, leading to depression and self-destruction. You may have wanted to hurt or kill yourself. You may feel yourself to be essentially bad, criticize yourself unrelentingly, and devalue yourself. Or you might stuff your anger with food, drown it with alcohol, stifle it with drugs, make yourself ill. As Adrienne Rich writes: "Most women have not even been able to touch this anger, except to drive it inward like a rusted nail."*

Having been taught to blame yourself, you stay angry at the child within—the child who was vulnerable, who was injured, who was unable to protect herself, who needed affection and attention, who experienced sexual arousal or orgasm. But this child did nothing wrong. She does not deserve your anger.

LASHING OUT

Many survivors have also turned their anger against partners and lovers, friends, co-workers, and children, lashing out at those who (usually) mean no harm. You may find yourself pushing your child against the wall or punching your lover when you get mad.

I had a lot of physically abusive relationships. I didn't know how not to fight. My first impulse when I got angry

---

* Adrienne Rich, "Disloyal to Civilization," in *Lies, Secrets, and Silence* (New York: W. W. Norton, 1979), p. 309.

was this [she smacks one hand hard on the other], because that's what I saw growing up. Whenever I started to get upset with someone, I would literally feel the adrenaline running up and down my arms. My muscles would get really tight, my fists would clench, and I would break out into a sweat. I'd be ready to smack the person around. I'd want to fight.

If violence has been part of your life and you find yourself expressing your anger in abusive ways, you need to get help right away. It's okay to be angry, but it's not okay to be violent. (For help, see "Controlling Abusive Anger," page 200.)

If you don't physically fight, you may pick verbal fights or look for things to criticize. You mean to tell your son to do his homework and you find yourself yelling or calling him names. Your husband forgets to put oil in the car and you tell him he's a stupid idiot. Even though it isn't violent, verbal abuse is destructive.

DIRECTING YOUR ANGER WHERE IT BELONGS

It is time to direct your anger accurately and appropriately at those who violated you. You must release yourself from responsibility for what was done to you and place the responsibility—and your anger—clearly on the abuser.

I had a hard time directing the anger at my Dad. My therapist would say, "Well, how did you feel when your Dad picked you up and threw you against the wall?"

And I'd say, "Well, I pretty much felt like he was an asshole."

And my therapist would say, "Hmmm."

One time, after years of therapy, when he asked me something about my father, I was holding this pencil, and I just threw it across the room and said, "That bastard!"

It was the first time I was ever clearly angry at him. Sure, I'd been mad at my Dad. But it was directed in all the wrong directions. And this was the first time in all those years that I was just mad at him, period, without laughing about it, without being sarcastic or defensive. Just full on, "That shit!"

GETTING IN TOUCH WITH YOUR ANGER

If you're willing to get angry and the anger just doesn't seem to come, there are many ways to get in touch with it. A little like priming the pump, you can do things that will get your anger started. Then, once you get the hang of it, it'll begin to flow on its own.

It's often easier to get angry for someone else's pain than for your own. That's fine for a beginning. Imagine a child you love being treated the way you were treated. Read the writings of other survivors in anthologies and feminist journals. You can listen to their stories at conferences, workshops, and in small support groups. You can look at the expressions of grief on their faces and be touched.

WORKING THROUGH MOTHER BLAME

Although our culture usually criticizes women for being angry, it does not hesitate to direct anger toward women. Women, and specifically mothers, are frequently designated as the recipients for whatever anger needs a target. This is sometimes evident in the extreme, as when a mother is blamed for the father's abuse of their child.

Fathers have habitually blamed their wives for the fact that they abused their daughters. Many psychologists and sociologists have endorsed this position as well. They cite the wife's failure to meet the husband's needs for nurturing or sex. They refer to her drinking, illness, working nights, or being otherwise unavailable. "And so," the father pleads, holding up his hands in a gesture of helplessness, "I turned to my daughter."

This is preposterous. It is never anyone else's fault when a man abuses a child. Regardless of how inadequate a mother may have been, no behavior on her part is license for any man to sexually abuse a child. It's time to stop blaming women for what men have done.

Some survivors perpetuate this blame of mothers, remaining far angrier at their mothers than they are at their abusers. There are logical reasons for this: Society supports it. Blaming mothers is more acceptable because on the whole, we are more threatened by men than by women. As a group, men wield more clout in our society—they're bigger, richer, more assertive, more apt to be violent. Many of us have personally felt the sting of their indiscriminate power. So when it comes to expressing anger, or even just feeling it, we're usually more comfortable pointing it at a woman. And there's a precedent: most survivors have been angry at themselves for a long time.

At the same time, you do have a right to be angry at your mother. Mothers of abused children are often fearful, self-protective, and denying. If your mother did not listen when you tried to tell her, did not leave an abusive or alcoholic man, did not offer the warmth, attention, or understanding that you needed, you have a right to hold her responsible.

Although some women direct all their anger at their mothers, others are afraid to get angry at them at all. You may identify so much with your mother's oppression that you minimize or negate your own. You may feel allied with her as women in a patriarchal society and think that acknowledging your anger would threaten that bond. But if your mother didn't protect you, looked the other way, set you up, or blamed you, you are inevitably carrying some feelings of anger. It is necessary to experience, validate, and express those feelings. This is not only your right; it is essential for your healing.

However, unless your mother was your abuser, you must not direct *all* of you. anger toward her. The abuser deserves his share. Besides, as you allow yourself to know the genuine depth and range of your anger, you will find there's enough to go around.

You can hear their fury and be incited. Know that any time you cry or get angry for someone else, it taps your own grief and anger as well.

Getting into an angry posture also helps. Physically taking an angry stance, making menacing gestures and facial expressions, invites genuine anger to rise. One woman, who described herself as much more prone to feeling hurt than angry, was quietly weeping during a therapy session. As she relates:

My therapist scooted her chair toward me so that her knees almost touched mine. Then she put out her hands, palms facing me, and instructed me to put my palms against hers. "Push," she said. "Push against me." I pushed against her palms and she pushed back. As I pushed harder, she met me with equal pressure. It took all my strength to maintain. Within seconds I was angry. The tears were long gone. I was mad! And it felt powerful.

Therapy and support groups can be ideal places for stirring up anger:

I felt incredible anger, but I never allowed anger my whole life. It was really a difficult thing to let out. One day my therapist got up out of her chair, and she said, "Your father's in that chair." And she handed me a rolled-up towel and she said, "I want you to hit your father."

It took me a long time to psych myself into doing that, but once I started, I couldn't stop. I pounded and screamed until I couldn't move anymore. It was such a relief.

That was an important turning point for me. After that, I did a lot of pounding on beds and screaming and writing angry letters to my dead father. I even worked with a punching bag.

Another way to get in touch with your anger is to role-play a situation that made you angry in the past. A therapist, friend, or group member can play the part of the person with whom you are angry. You describe the body language, gestures, and words that made you angry originally, and then you recreate the scene. This time you can respond with your genuine anger, and experience release and relief.

In order for this kind of exercise to be safe, the people involved have to be trustworthy and able to handle strong feelings. There must be guidelines for the expression of anger—for example, no hurting people, no hurting yourself. Also there should be an agreement that you can stop whenever you've had enough.

If you prefer to work with your anger alone, there are a number of writing exercises that can rouse your ire. Make a list of all the ways you're still affected by the abuse. If you do this in detail, you can hardly avoid at least some anger. You can also write a letter to your abuser. Try beginning with "I hate you."

Eva Smith arranged a satisfying outlet for her anger (for more of her story, see page 367):

I had a friend who made ceramic things, and if they were cracked or whatever, he'd set them aside for me. I'd come around at midnight. I'd go around the back and throw them against the fence. It was a miracle no one called the police because I'd be out there throwing stuff.

Piggybacking your anger at your abuser to more accessible anger is a good, sneaky way to bring it past your internal censors. If international issues like apartheid in South Africa easily inflame you, let yourself get worked up over those problems, and then, when you're really angry, remind yourself that the mentality that allows whites to torture blacks is the same mentality that allowed your abuser to vent his twisted, uncontrolled needs, fear, and ruthlessness on you. You can slide your own trauma in with the rest of the ills of the world, and you'll find yourself finally angry.

FEAR OF ANGER

Many survivors are afraid of getting angry because their past experiences with anger were negative. As one survivor put it, "I don't get the difference between anger and violence yet. When I hear loud noises, I think they're coming after me." In your family, you may have witnessed anger that was destructive and out of control. But your own anger need not be either. You can channel your anger in ways that you feel good about and respect.

Even women with no history of violence are often afraid that if they allow themselves to feel anger, they're liable to hurt or kill someone.

I know the anger is there. I'm too scared to let myself experience it. I'm scared that I won't be gentle with myself. That I'll turn the anger on myself.

And I'm so used to watching other people hurt people. I don't want to be a perpetrator. I don't know how to discharge my anger in a way that's safe.

It is extremely rare for women to violently act out their anger toward the people who abused them as children. And for women with no history of violence, the fear that you might hurt someone with your anger is usually unrealistic.

Anger is a feeling, and feelings themselves do not violate anyone. It's important to make the distinction between the experience of feeling angry and the expression of that anger. When you acknowledge your anger, then you have the freedom to choose if and how you want to express it. Anger does not have to be an uncontrolled, uncontrollable phenomenon. As you welcome your anger and become familiar with it, you can direct it to meet your needs—like an experienced rider controlling a powerful horse.

ANGER AND LOVE

Another aspect of anger that is often misunderstood, and thus keeps women from releasing their dammed emotion, is the relationship between anger and love. Anger and love are not incompatible. Most of us have been angry, at one time or another, with everyone we love and live closely with. Yet when you've been abused by someone close to you, with whom you've shared good experiences, it can be difficult to admit your anger for fear that it will eradicate the positive aspects of that relationship or of your childhood.

But getting angry doesn't negate anything you want to retain of your history. What's good can still remain in your memory as something from which you've benefited.* You forfeit nothing of your past by getting angry, except your illusion of the abuser as innocent.

Often survivors are afraid of getting angry because they think it will consume them. They sense that their anger is deep and fear that if they tap it, they'll be submerged in anger forever, becoming bitter and hostile. But anger obsesses only when it is repressed and misplaced. When you meet your anger openly—naming it, knowing it, directing it appropriately—you are liberated.

I'D LIKE TO KILL HIM

At one point or another, many survivors have strong feelings of wanting to get back at the people who hurt them so terribly. You may dream of murder or castration. It can be pleasurable to fantasize such scenes in vivid detail. Wanting revenge is a natural impulse, a sane response. Let yourself imagine it to your heart's content. Giving yourself permission to visualize revenge can be satisfying indeed.

---

* It is fine, of course, if you do not love your abuser. This should be obvious, but because many women carry a sense of responsibility for loving everyone, it is necessary to reinforce again and again your right not to love your abuser—even if he bought your food, taught you to ride a bike, read you bedtime stories.

If you start to think about acting on your fantasies, you need to consider how your actions would affect your own future. It's not wise to seek violent revenge in this society; you'd most likely perpetuate your own victimization.

What I say to myself is, "Wait a minute. I don't want to go to prison. I don't want the cops to come." I grew up with the cops coming. I don't want to go back to jail for being violent.

You also have to decide if you want to perpetuate abusive behavior further or if you want to break the cycle. As Soledad put it, "I've learned to respect human life." (For more of her story, see page 373.)

There are nonviolent means of retribution you can seek. Suing your abuser and turning him in to the authorities are just two of the avenues open. One woman threatened her abuser with the following telegram:

YOU HAVE WONDERED WHY I DON'T WANT TO BE IN TOUCH WITH YOU ANYMORE. NOW I KNOW WHY, AND I HAVE PEOPLE WATCHING YOU. IF YOU EVER MOLEST ANOTHER LITTLE GIRL, EVEN LOOK AT HER IN THE WRONG WAY, I WILL TAKE YOU TO COURT AND WIN.
BARBARA LITTLEFORD

YOUR MESSAGE WAS DELIVERED BY TELEPHONE AT 2:19 PM PST ON 1/21 AND WAS ACCEPTED BY JACK.

THANK YOU FOR USING OUR SERVICE.
WESTERN UNION

Another woman, abused by her grandfather, went to his deathbed and, in front of all the other relatives, angrily confronted him right there in the hospital.

Some survivors feel revenge is something that's not in their hands. One woman, a devout Christian, said simply, "God will take care of him. It's not my job." Another woman said she couldn't do anything to her father that was worse than what he was doing to himself. He was dying of testicular cancer.

And sometimes the best revenge is living well.

THE POWER OF ANGER: THREE STORIES

Barbara Hamilton, a sixty-five-year-old survivor who is writing a book about her abuse and her healing, describes the first time she really got in touch with her anger.

I went racing back and got a hold of my therapist before she left. I started to rage and the whole mental health department of Napa heard me, because I raised the roof. Everything came up. All the obscenities and everything were connected. The male assaults of me and my kids all went together. I had been intellectually angry at my father before, but this time I just blew. I just screamed my fury all over the place. I threw my glasses against the wall. I was just beside myself. I can't say that it felt good, but it was a turning point. It was so clear where the rage was coming from. It was the beginning of me not blaming myself.

If you've suppressed your anger for many years, it can be explosive. But even torrential anger doesn't have to be dangerous. Esther Barclay was able to trust her anger with striking results:

As I regained more memories, I moved through terror to a period of

---

POSITIVE EXPRESSIONS OF ANGER

Whether you express your anger directly to the abuser or you work with it yourself, it's essential that you give it some outlet. You can:

- Speak out.
- Write letters (either to send or purely for the chance to get your feelings out).
- Pound on the bed with a tennis racket.
- Break old dishes.
- Scream (get a friend to scream with you).

- Create an anger ritual (burn an effigy on the beach).
- Take a course in martial arts.
- Visualize punching and kicking the abuser when you do aerobics.
- Organize a survivors' march.
- Volunteer at a recycling center and smash glass.
- Dance an anger dance.

The list is endless. You can be creative with your anger. And ultimately, you can heal with anger.

such intense anger toward my parents that I fairly radiated. . . . One night I was awakened by a loud screaming. At that moment just preceding full consciousness I was aware that I was the person screaming and that it was coming from the soles of my feet. As I became fully awake, I put my arms around myself and sobbed with relief. I did not know where this was leading, but soon after an especially heavy counseling session in which I worked intensely on anger toward my father, two things were apparent: (1) my vision changed; colors were bright and clear in a way unusual to me, and (2) for several days my back and legs were sore and tender in a way that can best be described as an enormous taproot being pulled out with all the little branches following.

And Edith Horning's experience clearly illustrates the dramatic healing effects of anger:

I had my therapist on one side of me, and a man I was very close to on the other. My therapist had me imagine I was in the balcony of a movie theater, and that quite far away my father was up on a tiny movie screen. I did this scenario where I imagined him coming closer, getting larger and larger, and as he did, the people on either side of me encouraged me to stop him, to do whatever I had to do to make him powerless. They encouraged me to say no. It took me two or three tries before I could get the nerve to shout. Suddenly I got this tremendous surge of feeling from inside. I screamed, "No! You get back!

Just stop it!" And in my mind, I could see my father getting smaller and smaller and smaller. And I pounded on him until he was really tiny, just a shrimp.

That's when my father stopped being more powerful than I was. That's when I stopped protecting my mother or father. I no longer felt sorry for them. They made choices as they went along, just like I have. And when you make the choices, you pay the price. I did. They are. And that's the way it is.

SUPPORTIVE ANGER

In the introduction to *I Never Told Anyone*, Ellen wrote about her experience as a child being protected by her mother's anger when a deliveryman tried to molest her: *

My mother got furious at him. Then she fired him. She cared about me. Not the delivery man. She didn't tell me to take his feelings or his bad past experiences into consideration. She didn't care if he had trouble getting another job. She cared about me. I internalized the message that I was important, worthy of protection, worthy of her outrage.

Even if you are not yet in solid contact with your own anger, you may welcome a show of supportive anger. Although counselors are traditionally trained not to show

---

* Ellen Bass and Louise Thornton, eds. (see the "Sexual Abuse" section of the Bibliography).

more emotion than their clients, and parents are warned not to "overreact" when their children are abused, someone else's anger can help you experience your own. Women say things like, "It's still too scary for me to get angry at him myself, but it feels good to see you get so angry." Ellen has seen this frequently:

Anger fuels my work. The women with whom I've been privileged to work have felt the power of my fury and it has been a shelter, a spark, a breath of fresh air, a model, an exciting if scary possibility, an affirmation.

Similarly, one woman's anger can clear the path for another. At a workshop, one survivor, Patricia, was rationalizing her father's abusiveness. Another woman kept quiet for a long time and then burst through in a passionate torrent, saying that she couldn't understand how anyone could not be angry, that she was so angry, all the time so angry, that she felt alone in the intensity of her anger. Rather than being overwhelmed or feeling criticized by this outburst, Patricia rushed across the room and took the hands of the outraged woman. She said that by overstepping the normal bounds of tidy, well-contained anger, this woman gave her permission to reach her own hidden anger. Patricia was grateful, receiving that strong anger as a valuable gift.

ANGER AS AN ORDINARY PART OF LIFE

As you become more familiar with experiencing and expressing your anger, it can become a part of everyday life. When it's not so pent up, it stops being a dangerous monster and takes its place as one of many feelings.

I'm learning that I can let people know when I'm angry without it being this terrible traumatic thing. I can say, "No, that upsets me," without feeling like the world is going to end.

Anger can be so safe that even children aren't scared by it. In Ellen's family, they have an enormous stuffed frog that a friend bought for two dollars at a garage sale:

When one of us gets really angry, we stomp all over it. Even as a very small child, my daughter would explain, "It's okay to beat up Big Frog because he's not alive. It doesn't really hurt him." And at times when I was crabby she would encourage me: "Go get Big Frog, Mom. You can yell all you want. There's nobody here but me and you, and I don't mind."

ANGER INTO ACTION

Our task, of course, is to transmute the anger that is affliction into the anger that is determination to bring about change. I think in fact that one could give that as a definition of revolution.
—Barbara Deming, "On Anger"*

* Barbara Deming, "On Anger," In *We Are All Part of One Another: A Barbara Deming Reader*, edited by Jane Meyerding (Philadelphia: New Society Publishers, 1984), p. 213.

In Ellen's story about her mother protecting her from the deliveryman, her mother experienced her anger, expressed her anger, and then acted on her anger. She fired the deliveryman. She threatened to tell his wife if he ever spoke to Ellen again. She demonstrated her power to take action. This part is critical.

One woman in her late thirties described her realization that action is necessary:

In the early seventies, when I began participating in growth and therapy workshops, we were encouraged to express our anger. I had, it became apparent, plenty to express. I ranted, broke chairs, pounded pillows, slammed doors, screamed and raged for a number of years. I had married a man with whom I was incompatible and we both expressed great quantities of anger toward each other, often in emotionally abusive ways. Yet none of this helped me feel better.

It took a long time for me to realize that experiencing my anger and expressing my anger were not enough. The last critical step, acting on my anger, was missing. Finally I gained the courage and clarity to act. I left my marriage and was no longer filled with rage.

Action, using the anger as a motivating force, is a critical part of healing. If you listen to what your anger is telling you, if you allow it to be a guide, then it becomes a valuable resource moving you toward positive change.

Women's anger has inspired them to cut ties with abusers, never again to have to endure pinches, inappropriate jokes, and drunken advances while they try to chew their Thanksgiving turkey. Women's anger has catalyzed them to quit jobs with domineering bosses, to divorce battering husbands, and to break addictions to drugs and alcohol. Focusing anger precisely—onto the abuser and away from yourself—clears the way for self-acceptance, self-nurturance, and positive action in the world.

DISCLOSURES AND CONFRONTATIONS

If you feel you need to talk to your mother about it, if you feel you need to confront your molester, do it. Because the next thing you know, that person's going to be dead, and you're going to be wishing for the rest of your life that you had. It's those unvoiced cries that haunt you forever.

Everyone has a right to tell the truth about her life. Although most survivors have been taught to keep their abuse a secret, this silence has been in the best interests only of the abusers, not the survivors. Nor does it protect the children who still have contact with the abuser.

Many survivors have a compelling desire to speak out. Yet whenever you consider breaking the taboo of secrecy, you are apt to feel fear and confusion. You may question your right to tell or criticize your motives. In order to understand the strength of these feelings, you must remember that you are emerging from a context of severe cultural and personal repression. You are challenging the secrecy that is the foundation of abusive family structures. You are taking revolutionary steps toward self-respect and respect for all children. You are exercising your power.

There are many motives for wanting to confront or disclose. You may want validation that these things actually happened, perhaps from a sibling who experienced abuse or witnessed yours. You may want factual information to help piece together your memories. You may want to make the abuser, nonprotecting parents, or others feel the impact of what happened to you. You may want to see them suffer. You may want revenge. You may want to break the silence. You may want financial reparations or payment for your therapy. You may want to warn others that there are children still at risk. (*And they are.* We have heard countless stories of survivors who didn't think the abuser would hurt anyone but them, only to find he had also molested their own children, nieces, nephews.) You may want to explore whether it is possible to establish an honest relationship, to get support. If you choose to speak out, it is probably for several purposes, some more attainable than others.

There is no right course of action in disclosures and confrontations. There is no right time to tell, no right way to tell, and no right decision whether to tell. It is very important not to be pressured into confronting. Although some stages in the healing process are absolutely necessary, confronting abusers and telling family members are not.

Be clear that whatever you do, you are doing it for yourself. Consider your decision thoroughly, and whatever your choice, carry it out in a way that will best allow you to assert your own rights to honesty and visibility.

MAKING THE DECISION

There are some questions you can ask yourself to help you make up your mind:

- Whom exactly do I want to talk to? Why?
- What do I hope to gain from this confrontation? Are my expectations realistic?
- What are my motives for confronting or disclosing?

- Is there anyone who can give me the information I need?
- What do I stand to gain? To lose?
- Would I be risking something I still want from my family? A job in the family business? An inheritance?
- Could I live with the possibility of being excluded from family gatherings?
- Am I willing to take the risk of losing contact with other family members with whom I want to stay connected?
- Am I stable and centered enough to risk being called crazy?
- Could I maintain my own reality in the face of total denial?
- Can I withstand the anger I am likely to face?
- Could I handle no reaction at all?
- Do I have a solid enough support system to back me up before, during, and after the confrontation?
- Can I realistically imagine both the worst and the best outcomes that might result?
- Could I live with either one?
- Have I prepared for the confrontation?

THE WORLD DOESN'T FALL APART

If you decide not to disclose, make sure it's not because of shame or because you still think it's more important to protect the abuser or the family than to take care of yourself. There are some good reasons not to tell, but shame and protecting a sick family system are not among them (see "If You Don't Confront" on page 142).

Celia is a poet. As she began to write about the incest and to go public with her work, she was terrified. She was convinced that her words would destroy her family.

Like many abused children, she had grown up with an unrealistic sense of her own power. "I had this ridiculous feeling that any little thing that I said or did could blow the whole world apart and destroy all its inhabitants. What I had to realize was that my family stayed intact through all those years of incest. Me opening my mouth and talking about it now was not going to break those bonds."

When Celia finally began to read her work in public, her mother was afraid that Celia would end their relationship. But Celia chose to keep visiting her family. "In doing so," Celia said, "I was saying to my mother, 'I don't have to only hate you. I don't have to only love you. I can do both.' I was setting an example that these things can be talked about and the world doesn't fall apart."

NOW HE'LL FINALLY LOVE ME, I JUST KNOW HE WILL

In thinking about confronting or disclosing, you need to be realistic about the kinds of responses you might get. If someone has abused you in the past, it is unlikely that person will suddenly become sensitive to your needs. Although you may get some sympathetic, supportive responses, the disclosure of abuse usually disrupts a family system of denial. Often family members find the exposure so threatening that they turn the survivor into a scapegoat, denying her experiences, minimizing them, or blaming her. One survivor who told her mother that she had been abused by her father received a letter back from her mother saying that, although it was hard, she forgave *her* (the survivor) for having sex with her father!

Another woman, whose grandfather violently attacked her while she was playing cops and robbers in the basement, told her mother about the abuse. Her mother retorted, "You wanted it. What else would you have been doing playing in the basement? You must have been looking for sex."

This kind of extreme defensive reaction is common. What you must remember is that if your mother didn't protect you from your older brothers or your uncle when they abused you, it is unlikely that she will be understanding when you talk to her now.

Often other members of your family also have been abused and have either repressed it entirely or want to avoid feeling the pain around it. Unearthing these feelings can be so threatening, or can imply such changes, that the family will reject the survivor altogether rather than deal with her. Therefore it is essential that you approach any confrontation focused on yourself, what *you* want or need to say, how *you* want to handle the situation, rather than on any response you may hope to get.

You should never proceed naively expecting that finally, now that you are telling, you will get everything you didn't get as a child. Or that if you tell in the "right" way, you'll get the support and love you're entitled to. Yet many survivors hope, secretly or openly, for just such a response. You need to be very clear about this so that you don't set yourself up for another betrayal. When you confront the abuser or disclose your abuse, you are deciding to give up the illusions in order to determine reality. You must be willing to relinquish the idea that your family has your best interests at heart.

If (as happens rarely) your nonprotecting parent, other relative, or even the abuser can genuinely hear you, extend understanding, and be willing to support you, then you have the real benefit of that relationship.

It Brought Us Closer Together: Vicki's Story

The way I told my mother that my father had abused me was during a therapy session I arranged with her therapist. I'd set it up that way because she was the hardest person for me to tell. I called her up and said, "Mom, I have something really important I want to talk with you about. Is it okay if I fly down and go to your therapist with you? It would probably be a lot easier."

Her first reaction was, "Are you okay?"

And I said, "Yeah, I'm okay." She told me to go ahead and call her therapist. So I did. I told her therapist what I wanted to do and we set up an appointment two weeks later. I talked to my mother a few times during that period. She never once said, "Tell me what it is! You're driving me crazy." But she was terrified.

I flew down and she picked me up at the airport. In the car, on our way to the session, she said, "I want to ask you two questions. Are you dying of some terrible disease?" I thought my heart would break. Her second question was, "Are you in very deep trouble?"

I said, "Neither one of those."

She said, "I feel better now."

When I finally told her that my father had abused me, her reaction was what I'd always wanted the whole time I was growing up. She looked at me and said, "I'm so sorry." She reached toward me and just held me, like a mother holds a child who's been hurt. It wasn't thought out. It was genuine. She just came toward me with raw emotion. Twenty years flashed in front of me. I said, "My God, why did I wait so long to tell her?" She was totally sympathetic.

She had no denial whatsoever. And it wasn't until halfway through the session that she started in on what a bad mother she must have been. Then she got fiercely angry at my father. She wanted to go over to his house and shoot his brains out. She wanted to kill him. I loved it.

Telling her has brought us much closer together. We're much more honest with each other now.

CONFRONTING OUTSIDE THE FAMILY

If the person who abused you was not a close family member, you may find it easier to enter the confrontation purely for yourself, not longing for reconciliation. Your family may find it less threatening to be supportive as well. Obviously it will be easier for a mother to hear that a neighbor or a teacher abused her daughter, than it will be to hear that her husband, father, or son did the abusing.

But whatever your situation, it is important not to minimize the effects the process can have on you. One woman, who'd been abused by her teacher, found herself shaking and unable to sleep all night just from looking up the man's name in the phone book and finding him listed. Breaking the taboo of silence is never something to take lightly. It can shake your whole world.

PREPARING FOR A CONFRONTATION

Although it is impossible to predict the response you will get, the odds are that it won't be satisfying, compassionate, or responsible. If it is, that's terrific. But it can't be counted on. Instead you must say what you have to say for yourself and assess how you feel about the confrontation in terms of what *you* did, not the reaction you get.

It is important that you prepare yourself for defensive and aggressive reactions. As a child you were violated without any adequate way to shield yourself. Now you do not have to be so vulnerable.

There are many ways to protect yourself. You may want to talk to family members individually rather than all together. You also may want to talk to some family members and not others. You may want to begin with one person at a time, starting with those most likely to be allies. Respect your own inner timing.

However, once you begin to tell, you have set the ball rolling. Although you may tell someone and ask them not to tell others, they may not honor your wishes or follow your guidelines. In dealing with families in which there has not been adequate respect, don't underestimate the betrayal you may experience.

WAIT UNTIL YOU'RE CLEAR

Usually it's a good idea to work through some of your own feelings before you talk with family members who may not be sympathetic. If you're still doubting that it could have happened, unsure that it was really all that bad, still believe it was your fault, then it's not the best time to try to deal with people who are likely to challenge or attack you.

If your memories of the abuse are still fuzzy, it is important to realize that you may be grilled for details. Laura received a letter from one of her relatives, full of demands for proof:

> Rape and incest are among the most heinous of all crimes and he does not become guilty on the basis of 25-year-old flashbacks. . . . These are very serious charges and you had better present some factual evidence to back it up.

Of course such demands for proof are unreasonable. You are not responsible for proving that you were abused. However, you need to assess whether you feel solid enough to withstand such attacks. It helps if you seek out people who can support you rather than undermine you at this stage. In this way you build your own foundation first.

PUT YOUR OWN NEEDS FIRST

In preparing for a confrontation or disclosure, it's important to remember that, except for the protection of children, confrontations are for you. Take the time to prepare. The terms are yours: you set the boundaries, you pick the timing, you choose the turf.

After a long silence, Louise made contact with her father. She confronted him about his abuse, and they began a painful correspondence. After a year or so, it became clear that he was not able to communicate through letters, that if Louise wanted a satisfying confrontation, she'd have to do it in person.

When Louise told her husband about this, he suggested she talk to her father with a mediator or a therapist present. Louise responded, "But I don't know if there's anybody down there who could do that."

Her husband almost hit the roof. "Down there?" he exclaimed. "You'd actually think of going down there? Why would you leave your whole support system behind and go there? Let him come here."

"Oh," Louise replied. "I didn't think of that."

Like Louise, many survivors have trouble figuring out how to take care of themselves. But when you're considering a confrontation, it's essential to put your own needs first. Where and when the confrontation takes place is of primary importance.

Preparation for an actual confrontation can be as important as the event itself. You can role-play possible scenarios in therapy or with supportive friends. Practice saying the things you want to say and responding to different reactions. You can write out the things you want to get across and memorize the essential points. That way, if you get nervous, you'll be able to remember what you wanted to say.

Talk about what it is that you want. What do you want to say? What do you want to achieve? Assess what is definitely possible (I want to tell my mother that my father raped me), what is unpredictable (I want her to listen to me; I want her to care about my feelings), and what is probably fantasy (I want to feel totally taken care of by her; I want her to divorce him; I want her to support me in suing for damages).

Look at several possible outcomes, some of them unsupportive or hostile. Imagine the worst reaction you could get. Can you live with that?

When one woman was preparing to tell her mother that her father had abused her, she was afraid her mother wouldn't be able to handle it:

I knew she wouldn't attack me or reject me, but I was afraid she'd stop eating and sleeping, get sick, have a heart attack, and die. My therapist asked me to consider whether I could live with that, her death. That was a difficult session, but what I came to was that I would not have been the cause of my mother's death. That if she got sick and died, that would be her choice. There were many other ways that she could respond to the information that I'd been abused, and if she chose death that was beyond my responsibility. I would be deeply distressed, of course; it would be hard to keep from shouldering the blame. I would feel terrible not to have her alive, but I would not die myself. I would recover. That would be my choice.

As it turned out, this woman's mother did not get sick or die. But in order for the daughter to speak her truth, she needed to confront the worst and know she could handle it.

STAY CENTERED

Dealing with abusers or close family friends can flip you into childhood insecurities. You can begin to doubt your own reality. Therefore it is important that you provide yourself with ample support when you approach abusers or family members. You need people who can offer a contemporary mirror, who can remind you of who you are now and affirm that your reality makes sense.

Another practical aid in staying centered is to keep a record of your interactions. If you write letters, keep copies; record phone call or make notes after the conversations; during visits, keep a daily log. If you're going for a visit, bring things with you that remind you of your current life: photographs, your pillow, a favorite memento or a present given to you by a friend. You can also call home for reality checks while you're away. Or better yet, take a friend with you as a witness. Be careful about whom you pick to do this. Choose someone who won't get drawn in by your family. (Another family member is usually not the best choice.) Be clear with that person about your expectations. Make sure they can come through for you.

THE CONFRONTATION

In confrontations, say what you want to say and ask for what you want. You may not get it, but you can at least have the satisfaction of knowing that you spoke up for yourself. If there are things you want, say so. You may want an apology, an acknowledgment of responsibility, an admission that what you say is true, an expression of willingness to make reparations or payment, or a change in your present relationship (such as, don't hug or kiss me anymore). You may want the abuser to read certain books about sexual abuse or to go into therapy. Chances are the abuser will not make major psychological changes as the result of a confrontation, so it's usually more effective to ask for specific behaviors rather than changes in attitude. And it's eas-

ier to see whether you're getting what you've asked for if you've been concrete.

There are many ways to confront or disclose. You can do it in person, over the phone, through a letter, in a telegram, or through an emissary. Twenty years ago, a woman went to her grandfather's funeral and told each person at the grave site what he had done to her. In Santa Cruz, California, volunteers from Women Against Rape go with rape survivors to confront the rapist in his workplace. There they are, ten or twenty women surrounding a man, giving tangible support to the survivor, as she names what he has done to her. This makes for a dramatic and effective confrontation.

One survivor told us the story of a woman who exposed her brother on his wedding day. She wrote down exactly what he'd done to her and made copies. Standing in the receiving line, she handed everyone a sealed envelope, saying, "These are some of my feelings about the wedding. Please read it when you get home."

The initial confrontation is not the time to discuss the issues, to listen to your abuser's side of the story, or to wait around to deal with everyone's reactions. Go in, say what you need to say, and get out. Make it quick. If you want to have a dialogue, do it another time.

BUT HE'LL COME AND GET ME

You may fear that your abuser will further hurt you if you speak out or confront him. One woman was sure her father would appear on her front steps and try to kill her. In actuality, he hid from her after that, avoiding her totally. *He* was scared of *her*. You may not realize it, but you hold a lot of power when you choose to disclose and confront.

Of course there are some instances where there is danger. In those cases it is essential that you take measures for your safety. You need to set up adequate protection for yourself so that the confrontation does not lead to further assault. For example, you may want to meet only in a public place, not give out your present address or phone number, or have witnesses along. You may even choose not to confront at all because the person is too violent or unpredictable.

AFTERWARD

The aftermath of a confrontation can feel horrible, great, or anything in between. Women often fear that a disclosure will cause a cataclysm: their mother will go insane, their father will kill himself, their aunt will divorce their uncle, the principal will fire the teacher. In fact, what may happen is very little. Whole families or systems may pretend nothing was ever said. You expected an earthquake and got a shiver.

Or you may get a sympathetic response initially, and then, when the implications sink

PROTECTING OTHER CHILDREN

Many women were molested by abusers who work professionally with children—teachers and counselors. A growing number of these survivors have confronted their abusers and alerted the schools or institutions where the abuse took place, in order to protect other children.

Whether the abuser is a person who works with children, a neighbor with access to children, or a family member, protecting children in the present and future is an important consideration. Child sexual abuse thrives in a climate where people let the past be past and hope for the best. As adults we all have a responsibility to children—to confront abusers, to warn parents of children the abuser has access to, to alert supervisors in camps and schools, to let children know that we will listen if they need to talk.

Sometimes it is difficult to weigh your own needs to be silent or to go at a slower pace against the pressing need to protect children presently at risk. Just as you are opening up to your own pain, feeling overwhelmed with your own experience, you remember a niece or a grandson.

I'd had no contact with my father for fifteen years when my sister called up, finally furious about what he'd done to her. He'd molested both of us since early childhood, and she'd been forgiving ever since. In the course of that conversation, she told me our half-sister was leaving her daughter with him for babysitting. We realized that he might be molesting this little girl, and discussed calling our half-sister to warn her. At first my sister was worried that we'd be calling for the wrong reason—because we wanted revenge. I said, "So what if we are vengeful? He took his revenge out on us for years. Besides, in, all support may be withdrawn. You may get a negative initial response, but as time goes on, your family may come to terms with what you are telling them and become more supportive. Sometimes one family member will support you and another will reject you. Alicia wrote to her parents and told them her uncle had abused her:

My mother wrote me back, accusing me of being spiteful. It was a handwritten letter, and she must have used the word "abuse" twelve times in two pages. It was over and over again, how *I* was abusing *her*. It was clear that *she* wanted to be the abused child in this interaction.

My father, on the other hand, was wonderful. And this was his brother we were talking about. When he first got my letter, he sent me a note. He said, "I don't feel defensive for Steve. What I feel is for the little girl, and I just want to pat her on the head and say, 'There, there.' It was just the perfect response. There was no question at all that he believed me. I know I was really lucky.

I went to visit them a couple of months after I sent the letter. He and I were alone in the car together, and at

---

we have to protect this child."

So we called our half-sister and told her that our father had molested us and other foster kids for years, and that we were concerned for her daughter's safety. She took it all in very calmly and thanked us for telling her. We felt frightened and empowered at the same time. Mostly we felt we had done something for that little girl that had never been done for us —we told, we protected, we valued her safety over the secret.

Although it is not good to sacrifice yourself to save others, children need and deserve protection. Deciding what to do in this kind of situation requires taking into account all the factors:

- How immediate is the risk to the children?

- How much time do I need to prepare myself?
- Are there ways I can inform the children's parents before I'm ready to confront the abuser?
- Is there a step I can take now, knowing that more is required later?

There may be more options than you think. You can call Child Protective Services and anonymously report abuse. You can talk to the child's teachers or the family doctor. One woman thought her brother was abusing his children. She sent them child abuse prevention books that encouraged telling. Another woman knew that her neighbor's children were being abused by their paternal grandfather. Instead of talking to the father, who she knew would be defensive and possibly hostile, she chose to talk to his wife. Since she was not a blood relation, she was more receptive.

one point he said, "Can I ask you something about the incest?"

And I said, "Yeah." I expected him to ask me factual things.

All he wanted to know was, "Are you going to be okay? Is there an end point in sight?"

It was so moving. He didn't care about his brother. He didn't say, "Are you sure?" He just wanted to know I was going to be okay, and then he wanted to know how he could help. He offered to help me pin down factual stuff. He said he'd find out when my uncle was and wasn't in the country, to help me get external timetables. My dad actually sat down and helped me figure out how and when it could have happened.

All he said to me about my mother was, "We feel very differently about this. Don't assume we have the same reaction."

(For more of Alicia's story, see page 410.)

Confrontations and disclosures can be difficult, frightening, painful, and demanding. Yet they are also opportunities to express your feelings directly, to break the twisted pact of secrecy, to assert your own needs and boundaries, to overcome your fears, and to act for yourself. All these are potent steps in working through the victimization of abuse.

Whatever the consequences, it's common to feel some sense of relief mixed in with your other emotions. There is no longer a secret in the air. There is no longer hiding. If you don't want to trim the Christmas tree, share Chinese New Year, or attend a cousin's wedding because you don't want to be near the abuser, you don't have to lie about it.

After the confrontation or disclosure, you will need to decide what kind of contact, if any, you want to continue, either with the abuser or with others. You may choose never to see your abuser again. You might want to try to rebuild shattered relationships. (See "Families of Origin," on page 289, for more suggestions.)

IF YOU DON'T CONFRONT

Choosing not to confront your abuser or your family is a reasonable option if the choice is made from strength rather than fear. Sometimes women have felt pressured by other survivors who've done particularly painful confrontations: "We went through it. You can go through it too." This kind of peer pressure is damaging. You are not "more healed" if you confront than if you don't.

There are many reasons for not confronting. You may be in actual danger. You might not have enough support to back you up. You might not want to take on the additional stress. You may not feel firm enough in your own sense of reality. You may not be ready to risk a total break with your family. Your parents may be paying your tuition at school, and you can't yet afford to be economically self-sufficient. Or perhaps you just don't want to be discounted, or once again told that you're crazy.

The thing about confronting my abuser is that I don't think it would be very satisfying. He's a real reality manipulator. He's been married a whole bunch of times, and each time he gets a divorce, he justifies it by saying how crazy his wife is, using all this medical terminology. I decided I didn't want to hear that crap turned on me.

It hasn't felt like there'd be a whole lot of satisfaction talking to most of my family. If I'm not going to get validation, it doesn't make sense to put energy into talking to people who are probably going to dump a lot of junk on me. I decided to talk only to the people in my family who were either going to give me additional information or give me validation.

Whatever your reasons, if you're not ready for a confrontation, or if it's not right for you, don't feel obligated to do one. You can heal without it.

WHAT IF HE'S DEAD OR GONE?

You may not have the option of confronting your abuser or disclosing to family members. If your abuser was a stranger or someone you no longer know, you may be disappointed that you don't have the opportunity to confront him. If your abuser is dead, you may be furious that there's no chance for reconciliation. At the same time, you may feel tremendous relief that you don't have to go through the ordeal you see other survivors face, that you don't have to carry around the hope that someday (if you're good enough, wait long enough, pray enough) things will change.

If your abuser has died, you may be glad he is dead. This is a perfectly reasonable feeling to have. One woman said she couldn't wait for her father to die so she could spit on his grave. Another said:

I went through periods where I knew my father was lucky he was already dead because if he was alive I would have killed him. I would have beaten him to a pulp. He would have been eighty-something years old and I would have demolished him. I can imagine him denying the whole thing, me flying into a rage, and not even having the awareness of what I was doing until I did it, and ending up behind bars.

This woman probably would not have actually killed her father, but it felt good to think about it. Imagining the confrontation gave her a place to direct her anger, a way to feel powerful. Her father's death hadn't stopped her from actively engaging in resolving her own feelings. It only meant she didn't have the option of meeting him directly.

The fact that your abuser or other significant people are no longer around doesn't mean you can't (and won't need to) resolve your relationships with them. Although you can't interact face to face, you still need to deal with your own unresolved feelings.

YOU CAN STILL LET GO

Even without a direct confrontation, you can experience the satisfaction and catharsis of a confrontation. There are many symbolic ways to face your abuser or sever your ties. You can write him a letter and not mail it (see the exercises at the end of this chapter for suggestions). You can write a poem or draw a picture about your abuse and publish it in a survivors' newsletter. You can donate money to an organization that helps survivors. You can design your own ritual.

One time I buried my uncle and sent him out to sea. It was a ritual Indians do. I chanted and I cried about it. I put him and all the things he had done to me into this litter box and visualized him going away. I took a picture of him and burned it.

There is also a lot you can do in a workshop or therapy setting. Psychodrama is a particularly useful tool for acting out confrontations. In a psychodrama, you choose people to act out certain people in your life. You tell them what the person is like and what they might say, so they can respond to you in character. Then you set and enact a scene with them. Psychodrama can often be quite realistic, and it is a dramatic and powerful tool for resolution when real-life confrontations are impossible.

Doing It: Catherine's Story

Catherine is a twenty-eight-year-old West Coast radio producer. She grew up in a rural midwestern town, the child of alcoholic parents. Her father was a doctor, her mother a psychiatric nurse. Catherine was abused by her father from early childhood, and began to recover her memories a year before she did this confrontation.

I was beginning to want to tell one of my parents. My mother called one weekend. She said she'd been worried about me, that she knew I'd been depressed. She was concerned that I had been avoiding the family. She asked me what was wrong.

I had just gotten out of bed, and I thought, "Well, I might as well do it now."

So I just said, "I'm an incest victim, and I think it was Dad." Then I said to myself, "Oh my God! Why did you say that? You're half asleep! What have you gotten yourself into?"

I could hear my Mom choking on the other end of the phone. It was awful. She cried while I told her the story. I cried also.

At first she was very comforting. The first thing she said was, "I believe you 100 percent. You were a trustworthy child. Mothers usually side with the fathers in this kind of thing, and I'm not going to do that."

A couple of days later, I got a letter in which she asked me how she could possibly go on living with him. Her attitude began to shift from that point on. And now she denies it even happened.

TALKING TO MY FATHER

I had specifically asked her not to tell my father. I said I wanted to be able to tell him in my own time. But she told him everything and he called up a week later, extremely angry, demanding, "What's this incest shit you're talking about?"

And at that moment, I decided to tell him the whole story and we spent the next two hours on the phone, screaming at each other about whether or not it had been him, why I hadn't said anything before, and why I hadn't been able to remember. He said it was just like me to accuse him. He said he'd never touched me in my life. He demanded that I come up with proof and that I meet with him. I said I didn't know whether I wanted to meet with him at this time, and that when I did, it would be on my time and on my turf. Turning him down and maintaining my own power was really really hard. I'm proud I did it.

I hung up. The whole time I'd been on the phone, I had successfully maintained my position—that this had been done to me, that I was hurt, that I was angry, that there was no excuse for it. I had cried to him and I had given him the facts. I kept both my intellect and my feelings intact. And the truth of that was real powerful.

FAMILY THERAPY

I asked my mother and father to do a family therapy session with me. I met with them for two hours. We both drove about a hundred miles to get there. There was a very tense scene while we waited for my therapist to get there, a lot of suspicious glances between us.

Once we got in the session, my therapist introduced the topic. She said we were here to talk about my feelings about having been abused. She said we had to walk a fine line between honesty and kindness and if we were to err, we would err on the side of honesty. She said the session would dwell on the bad things that had happened, but that didn't mean there hadn't been good in our family life.

Then she turned it over to me. My goal was to show my parents how hurt I was, to cry in front of them, and to tell them what had happened. It was hard for me to let myself be vulnerable to people who I felt had a lot of hatred for me.

My worst fear was that my parents were going to come off being the sweetest, nicest, most rational people, who never could have abused anyone, and that my therapist would know what a liar I was. Within five minutes they played out their whole relationship right in front of her—yelling, screaming, running all their usual numbers. It was a relief to have

someone else see what had gone on my whole life.

The thing that changed for me the most since that family session was my level of hope that they would ever change. It dropped dramatically to about minus ten. Part of the session, I think, was to destroy the hope that maybe they really weren't the people who had done this to me.

Listening to them, and watching them during the session, I saw how abusive they were. And that perception has certainly changed how I went about dealing with them. It helped me to focus on my own work, not to drag them into it, because they certainly weren't out to help me.

WHY I'M GLAD I DID IT

I'm really glad I told my parents. It was one of the most unpleasant things I've ever done in my life. But the freedom of telling the truth to the people who abused you is really amazing. It feels rotten before you do it, it feels rotten while you're doing it, and it feels rotten after you've done it, but at least it's not hanging over your head anymore.

I would like to tell people who are considering doing a confrontation about the attitude I took in my family session which really helped me, and which was absolutely terrifying for me. I would recommend it for anyone who is afraid they might waffle and not say everything that they have to say. Just think that they're going to die the minute you end the session. I pictured them dead, and me still alive, living a miserable life, wringing my hands, saying, "Why?" Oh, why didn't I tell them?" It really helped me to be bold and to say the worst, and to say it in a way that didn't protect them.

WHAT WAS THE HARDEST AND SCARIEST?

Laura says: Every time I sat down to write another section of this book, I found myself thinking about the topic at hand and saying, "That was the hardest part of dealing with the abuse." Believing it happened was the hardest. No, reliving memories was the hardest. But then again, dealing with my family was really the hardest. The truth is, the hardest stage was whichever one I was currently in.

WHAT DID OTHER SURVIVORS THINK WAS HARDEST?

"The hardest part was going back to therapy every week."

"The collective wrath and the collective lie of my family has been the hardest thing to deal with. I see them as an embodiment, kind of as a big shadow hanging over me, telling me I'm making a big deal out of nothing."

"The hardest thing was accepting the fact that someone I loved and cherished—my father—could have violated me so deeply. That and the fact that he died three years ago, and I will never be able to go up to his face and say, 'Why did you do this to me?' "

"The hardest thing is still having this confrontation thing with my father hanging over my head."

"Dealing with my mother, dealing with her absolute refusal to hear about it."

"The hardest part was getting in touch with my feelings, allowing myself to feel sad and to cry."

"That he was *still* interfering with my body was very, very hard. That years after he had ever touched me, I still couldn't feel things, that I still couldn't make love and feel safe, that it didn't stop when he stopped touching me."

"Letting myself feel the absolute isolation, how absolutely lonely I had been, to remember how frightening the world had been."

"Patience has been the hardest thing for me."

"The hardest part for me still is being involved in an intimate one-on-one relationship with a man. It just doesn't go easy for me, and it has nothing to do with the man. It is something I do all by myself."

"Sex—because there's only so much

you can do on your own. Then you need another person to cooperate."

"The hardest part of my healing process has been trying to end it."

WHAT WAS THE SCARIEST?

"The scariest part for me was that I had to do this all by myself, that no matter how many people expressed their caring for me, or told me I'd get over it, I had to be the one to do the work. And to face that has been almost more than I could bear."

"The scariest thing has been intimacy. It's terrifying."

"The scariest part was when it actually happened. Nothing in the healing compared to that."

"The scariest part was that I might remember I was a whore, that I'd find out that it really had been my fault. And if I had been bad, then I would have to die."

"The scariest part was wanting to hurt myself or kill myself."

"It scared me when I thought that therapy was an endless process and that I wasn't making any progress."

"The scariest part is the panic. It's like you're dissolving and there's nothing to hold on to. There's just this terror and there's an incredible impulse to do something and there's nothing to do."

"Telling."

"The scariest thing was talking about my psychosis and giving up my medicine, being able to give trust one more chance."

"The scariest thing has been not fogging over. Committing to being present has been very scary."

"Telling a male authority figure 'No, I'm not going to do that' was really scary."

"The scariest part has been resigning myself to the fact that my mother loves my father and has chosen him, and that I've lost her."

"The scariest part is that I might be crazy like my mother."

"The scariest point was when I didn't know whether I was going to make it or not, when I felt I'd rather die than know anymore, or feel anymore, or even have it be true. I really felt he could succeed in killing me."

"It's a circular answer, but the scariest thing is facing my fears."

WRITING A CONFRONTATION

Sandra Butler, the author of *Conspiracy of Silence*, does trainings for therapists and leads workshops for survivors, using writing as a tool. In her Writing As Healing workshops, Sandra uses a powerful series of exercises to help survivors get in touch with their feelings. These can also be an excellent vehicle for preparing for a confrontation.

She asks participants to choose a significant person from their childhood about whom they have unresolved feelings. "Now," Sandra continues, "write everything that has been unsaid in the relationship. The person can't interrupt or threaten you, but must simply sit and listen. Just say everything—the rage, the disappointment, the betrayal, the sadness, the loss. Start with the sentence 'There are some very important things you need to hear.' "

After ten to fifteen minutes of writing time, Sandra interrupts and says, "Now write as you imagine the other person would respond. Get under their skin and speak as you think they would. Let them respond just as powerfully to what you've said."

After another ten minutes, Sandra interrupts again and says, "Now, return to your own perspective and set some ground rules for any further communication. Begin with the sentence 'While I never imagined that this conversation would resolve a lifetime of history between us, I need to set some basic ground rules. There are a few things we need to get straight.' "

Ten minutes later, she stops the writing again. "From this point on," Sandra instructs, "keep going back and forth in the two voices until you feel the interaction is finished, staying as dramatic and powerful as you can."

WRITING EXERCISE: DISCLOSURES AND CONFRONTATIONS

(See the basic method for writing exercises, page 28.)

Write a letter to your abuser. Do not be reasonable. This is not a letter to send, although you can send it when you're done, or you can modify it and send a variation. Write it as if you weren't sending it so you can say exactly what you want to say without having to think about possible repercussions. Be as angry and hurt and blunt as you want. Let it be a cleansing.

You can write this letter more than once. You may have had more than one abuser. Your feelings about your abuser may change over time. You may want to write to a nonprotective parent or other person as well.

FORGIVENESS?

I'll never forgive my father. It would be a lot different if he had come to me at any point in time and said, "I'm sorry for what I've done. I've hurt you terribly. I'm going to get myself in therapy. I'm going to work this out." But he's never done anything like that.

He'd have to work awfully hard to get me to forgive him. He'd have to work as hard as I've worked from the time I was seventeen until now and he doesn't have enough time left in his life. He's going to die soon. So the chances of me forgiving my father are real slim.

When talking about the stages in the healing process, the question is inevitably raised: What about forgiveness? The only necessity as far as healing is concerned is forgiving *yourself*. Developing compassion and forgiveness for your abuser, or for the members of your family who did not protect you, is *not* a required part of the healing process. It is not something to hope for or shoot for. It is not the final goal.

Although there is a need for you to come eventually to some resolution—to make peace with your past and move on—whether or not this resolution encompasses forgiveness is a personal matter. You may never reach an attitude of forgiveness, and that's perfectly all right.

Forgiveness? I have my doubts. Acceptance, maybe, but not forgiveness.

Acceptance of who he was and what happened to me. Because there's no way of changing that. But I can't forgive him. He robbed me of twenty years of my life.

Many women try desperately to forgive. Survivors have often said how stuck they feel. They despair for their complete healing, because they can't foresee forgiving the person who abused them. But, as Ellen says in her workshops, "Why should you? First they steal everything else from you and then they want forgiveness too? Let them get their own. You've given enough."

WHAT IS FORGIVENESS AND WHO BENEFITS FROM IT?

To find out exactly what forgiveness is, we looked in the dictionary and found these definitions: (a) to cease to feel resentment against an offender; (b) to give up claim to requital from an offender; to grant relief from payment.

There are, then, two elements in what we call forgiveness. One is that you give up your anger and no longer hold the abuser to blame; you excuse them for what they did to you. The other element is that you no longer try to get some kind of compensation from the abuser. You give up trying to get financial compensation, a statement of guilt, an apology, respect, love, understanding—anything. Separating these two aspects of forgiveness makes it possible to clarify what is and what is not necessary in order to heal from sexual abuse.

It is true that eventually you must give up trying to get something back from the abuser. This process need not be hurried. It is appropriate and courageous to fight back in any way you choose. However, at some point, trying to get from abusers what they aren't going to give keeps you trapped. There comes a time when what you feel about the abuser is less important than what you feel about yourself, your current life, and your future. The abuser is not your primary concern. You say, "*I* am my primary concern. Whether the abuser rots or not, I'm going on with my own life." You recognize that many of your current problems stem from past abuse, but you also recognize that you have the power to make satisfying changes.

This stance is not incompatible with anger. And none of this pardons or excuses the abuser.

When a friend inadvertently hurts our feelings and apologizes, we forgive her. We no longer blame her. The relationship is mended. We are reconciled and we continue with trust and respect, without residual anger between us. This kind of forgiveness—giving up anger and pardoning the abuser, restoring a relationship of trust—is not necessary in order to heal from the trauma of being sexually abused as a child. You are not more moral or courageous if you forgive.

"OH, HONEY, JUST FORGIVE AND FORGET"

It is insulting to suggest to any survivor that she should forgive the person who abused her. This advice minimizes and denies the validity of her feelings. Yet the issue of forgiveness is one that will be pressed on you again and again by people who are uncomfortable with your rage or want to have you back under their control. While you don't have to stay angry forever, you should not let anyone talk you into trading in your anger for the "higher good" of forgiveness.

If you have strong religious ties, particularly Christian ones, you may feel it is your sacred duty to forgive.* This just isn't true. If there is such a thing as divine forgiveness, it's God's job, not yours. If feelings of compassion and forgiveness rise naturally and spontaneously during the course of healing yourself, fine. They can be a powerful part of your healing, but not if they're forced into being because you think you should feel them.

Trying to forgive is a futile short-circuit of the healing process. Trying to speed things along so you can "get to the forgiveness" is one of the fastest ways to undercut yourself. No one forgives by trying. If forgiveness of others is to be part of your healing (and it does not have to be), it will take place only when you've gone through all the stages of remembering, grief, anger, and moving on. It is not the grand prize. It is only a by-product. And it's not even a very important one.

Healing depends a lot on being able to forgive yourself, not on being

* For an excellent analysis of the role Christian forgiveness plays in healing from child sexual abuse, read *Sexual Violence: The Unmentionable Sin* by Marie Fortune. The author combines a theological perspective with a feminist analysis of sexual violence. (See the "Sexual Abuse" section of the Bibliography.)

able to forgive your molester. I don't think any time spent trying to forgive your molester is worthwhile time spent. You don't try to forgive Hitler. You don't sit around and work on that. There are a lot of other things to be doing with a life.

Forgiveness of yourself is what's important and when you start to feel that forgiveness, it just naturally extends itself to other people in the world. You start to get an understanding of what humanity is all about. You become able to see when somebody does something right. You can respond to a humane, loving act. And that's what forgiveness is really about.

AND WHAT IF COMPASSION SNEAKS UP ON ME?

If it does, let it. Experiencing compassion for another human being feels good. Often it rises out of the fact that you are feeling compassionate toward yourself, or because you have begun to view a particular family member in a different way.

Sometimes I feel forgiveness toward my brother because he was just as mixed up as I was. He really cared for me a lot.

One woman came to forgive her nonprotective mother as she gained more perspective on her mother's position in the family.

My mother was no more empowered than any of us. She was very much the victim. There's a picture that stays in my mind of my mother standing in the hallway with all of us kids when my father was in the bathroom, beating one of my brothers, and we're all crying and saying "Daddy, Daddy! Daddy!" And my mother's saying "Don, don't! Oh, Don, don't!" And she's right there crying with us. And to me she was as much a part of the helplessness as we were. I really believe she did the best she could do. It wasn't very good but it was the best she could do.

Laura had a similar experience as a result of doing a creative exercise:*

I was at a two-week writing workshop. One of the assignments was to take an incident in my family history that I could never really find out about, and to make up the story of what really happened, based on the few facts I did have. I wrote the story of my mother's childhood.

I had very little to start with—I knew she'd been the smart one in an immigrant family, the one sent to the door when people came over and had to be answered in English. I knew she'd been ashamed of her home, that she'd escaped into the world of the movies, a nickel a shot, at the Roxy. I knew my grandfather had been her father, that she'd had to live with him every day. And I'd seen a photograph of her. I knew how she looked, a scared, shy little waif. I created the rest.

It was an amazing exercise. It allowed me to start thinking about my mother as more than just my mother, as a woman with a whole life before I was ever conceived, and a whole life afterwards. I started to understand, from her point of view, why she'd responded to me the way she had. The pieces started to fit together. I felt compassion for her and I liked it.

This attitude of compassion is something that happens naturally, often when you least expect it. One woman who was abused by all four members of her family swore she would never forgive them. She'd written them off and gone on with her own life. Months later, she had an impulse to go to temple for Yom Kippur, the Jewish Day of Atonement. Yom Kippur is the one day of the year when Jews let go of the wrongs they have done and the wrongs others have done to them. Without trying to, or expecting to, this woman suddenly started sobbing and much to her surprise found herself not only deeply forgiving herself but forgiving her family as well. "From that day on my life was mine. For the first time in my life I had an experience of being separated from them." This woman's experience of forgiveness transformed her, but it wasn't something she set out to do.

Women who have naturally come to feel compassion or forgiveness often have a new sense of freedom:

After the grieving and the anger and the loss, somehow came forgiveness. It's not okay what she did, I can't excuse her, but I forgive her from my

---

* This exercise can be an effective healing tool in other ways as well. See "Writing Exercise: Reconstructing Family History," on page 154.

heart. I've let go of the anger and by doing that I'm not carrying it on my back as much. I can walk straighter. Forgiving her is a way of healing myself.

****

One of the things I find is that a lot of the intensity in my feelings is gone since I've forgiven him. I don't wake up feeling like if I had his picture I'd throw daggers at it. In fact, I have been able to see him in dreams again after not being able to visualize his face for years. I was able to say "Your face no longer scares me. Your name no longer puts me in fear."

If you do come to feel forgiveness, the important thing is that forgiveness *has* to be for you. You cannot absolve someone else for what they have done in their life. If abusers are to heal, it will only be because they've acknowledged what they've done, made reparations, worked through their own pain, and forgiven *themselves*.

Not all survivors will feel compassion for abusers and family members. Depending on what someone has done, it may not even be appropriate.

I don't forgive him. He was an adult. He is ultimately responsible. I can't forgive anyone who does anything like that to a child, particularly anybody that did it to me. If someone tried to do that to my kids, I would flat out kill them. He deserves to die a lonely, miserable man. Let it die with him. I'd be glad to see it kill him. It's not going to kill me.

BUT THEY HAD A BAD CHILDHOOD

Laura remembers her mother coming home from her job as a social worker and telling stories about all the crazy, misguided people she worked with:

She'd take us to Burger Chef, and over the french fries she'd tell us a particularly juicy story about a sixteen-year-old murderer or a fifteen-year-year-old rapist. We'd always look up from our Cokes and ask the same question: "But why, Mom? Why would somebody do something like that?" My mother's answer never varied. She'd pick up her double cheeseburger and say, "They had a bad childhood."

While it's true that many abusers were abused as children and that sexual abuse ravages generation after generation, those facts alone are not enough to forgive the horrible things adults have done to children. Many women have been abused, and the vast majority of them have not become abusers. Regardless of childhood pain, there is no excuse for abusing children.

Bastard. He took my soul, and I don't give a shit that it might have happened to him. It happened to me, and I didn't do it to my kids! That excuse is bullshit. It's pure shit.

****

I would never in a million years forgive my father. He had a choice. He made a choice. I've had choices in my life that were just as difficult. Sometimes I've failed. But for the most part I try very hard not to. And I don't think he tried one bit. I think he gave in every single time to his impulses.

FORGIVING YOURSELF

The only forgiveness that is essential is for yourself. You must forgive yourself for having needed, for having been small. You must forgive yourself for coping the best you could. As one woman said, "I've had to forgive my genitals for responding. I've had to forgive myself for not being able to second-guess my father and avoid the abuse."

You must forgive yourself for the limitations you've lived with as an adult. You must forgive yourself for repeating your victimization, for not knowing how to protect your own children, or for abusing others. You must forgive yourself for needing time to heal now, and you must give yourself, as generously as you can, all your compassion and understanding, so you can direct your attention and energy toward your own healing. *This* forgiveness is what's essential.

WRITING EXERCISE: RECONSTRUCTING FAMILY HISTORY

Irena Klepfisz, author of Keeper of Accounts and a gifted teacher, developed an exercise that enables you to piece together things you can't possible know about your history or the history of your family. This form of "remembering," which she calls "imaginative reconstruction," can be a valuable tool in coming to terms with people and patterns in your family. Although you write about things you couldn't realistically know, the result often seems chillingly realistic:

Take an event in your family history that you can never actually find out about. It could be your father's childhood or the circumstances in your mother's life that kept her from protecting you. Using all the details you do know, create your own story. Ground the experience or event in as much knowledge as you have and then let yourself imagine what actually might have happened.

SPIRITUALITY

There was some voice in me that just said, "You'll get there." And I took hope and courage from the voice inside of me. Somehow, I felt sure there was a process, that there was a reason for all of this, and that I was going to get to the end of it. And I believe that was my spirituality.

Finding the spiritual part of yourself can be an important aspect of your healing process. This has long been recognized in the twelve-step programs (Alcoholics Anonymous, Al-Anon, and others, which have helped millions of people overcome their addictions). Yet the very word "spirituality" turns a lot of people off. You may imagine people with shaved heads, forced processions to church, the hypocrisy of piety in an abuser who molested you. You may think of stiffness and formality. Like many survivors, you may have lost your faith.

I was in a very conservative religious group for twenty years. For a long time I thought Jesus could heal me. When I was thirty-eight, I went to hypnotherapy as a last resort to cure the intense migraines I was having. That's when I started remembering the sexual abuse. And the first thing I thought was, "What kind of God have I been believing in?"

A little girl had been beaten and raped and no God did anything about it. I got real angry. So I went to my minister and he gave me this cock-and-bull story about how God wasn't responsible. It was all man's badness. He told me I shouldn't be angry at God.

The more I remembered, the more I realized that God didn't care for me at all. If He didn't care for me, He wasn't who I thought He was. And who was He?

It's been an incredible loss. The spiritual side of me, which had been nurtured all my life, doesn't have a place to go. It's been very painful. I lost my sense of roots, my sense of purpose. All my friends in the church rejected me. I haven't been able to find a God I can believe in.

A healing spirituality is the opposite of this alienation. It's a passion for life, a feeling of connection, of being a part of the life around you. Many people experience this in nature, watching the ocean roll in, looking out over a vast prairie, walking in the desert. When you are truly intimate with another human being, when you are uplifted through singing, when you look at a child and feel wonder, you are in touch with something bigger than yourself. There is a life force that makes things grow, that makes thunderstorms and mountain ranges and perfect avocados. The fact that you can create a baby and give it birth, watch it roll over, then sit up, and then crawl, is a miracle of life. There's a part of everything living that wants to become itself—the tadpole into the frog, the chrysalis into the butterfly, a damaged human being into a whole one. And that's spirituality: staying in touch with the part of you that is choosing to heal, that wants to be healthy, integrated, fully alive. The little part of you that is already whole can lead the rest of you through the healing process. It's the inner voice that you learn to trust again.

A BREAK IN THE CLOUDS

Laura once spent a couple of years in Ketchikan, Alaska, the rain capital of North America, where annual precipitation averages thirteen feet a year. "It was always raining. We were on an island and it was gray and stormy and overcast all the time. I'd forget what the sun even felt like. But every time I flew out of there, I'd have the most incredible experience. The plane would take off. As usual, it would be raining. But seconds later, we'd break through the cloud cover into the most brilliant sunlight. It had always been there. It's just that I couldn't see it from the ground."

It's the same with healing. That person you want to become is already with you; you just can't always see her. If you stay focused on how far you have to go, rather than turning around to see how far you've already come, you stay caught in the storm and forget that the sun is just overhead. You lose your sense of perspective. Getting in touch with the stillness inside is a way to gain it back, a way to remember that you are more than just the abused child crying out in pain. It's not that you transcend your abuse or get rid of the "bad" parts of yourself—rather you enlarge yourself to include everything. You start to see a self separate from the struggle.

KEEPING THE FAITH

One way to lose perspective is by focusing exclusively on your problems, your process, and your pain. While a certain amount of obsessing is inevitable, and in fact sometimes helpful, beyond a certain point it can be self-defeating. Obsession often comes from a lack of conviction that you've already set the healing process in motion through your own hard work and determination. You think you have to be vigilant at every moment. But that doesn't work.

If you have an injury and you press on the wound, insisting that it heal *now,* it will not heal. But if you take care of it and then direct your attention somewhere else, healing naturally takes place.

Breakthroughs often happen that way. You work and you work, and then suddenly, when you stop trying, you grow. But letting go takes faith. You have to trust your capacity to heal yourself. And each time you do, you move forward just a little farther. You gain confidence that you're going to be all right.

If you have an established religious path, faith will probably play a strong part in your healing. Mary, a survivor who spent several years as a nun, told the following story: "I had this picture of Jesus. And I used it like you'd use a candle, to center me to pray. And I looked at this picture, and I said, 'It's too much! No more. You have to make this stop. My heart cannot bear any more pain. They say you don't push a person beyond, but I'm telling you, this is it. This is as much as I can bear.' And somehow that particular moment of anguish passed, and I felt less burdened."

But no matter how much faith you have, it's not going to work for you unless you roll up your sleeves and do your share. Having a relationship with God doesn't mean He—or She—does all the work. Mary explains: "I really believe I received the grace of God to do this work and to stick with it. I've always believed I've been blessed with a strong mind to survive what I survived. I chose to go back to therapy week after week. I chose the grace.

I could have not gone back and just said, I'd rather suffer this quiet way I've always suffered. But then I had the grace to choose. I'll give God 65 percent and my guts 35 percent."

Whether you have a fixed concept of a God, believe there is a life spirit coursing through us all, or simply trust your own intuition, having faith in something more powerful and constant than your shifting emotions and ideas can be a great comfort to you as you heal.

FINDING OUT WHAT YOU ALREADY KNOW

When you're about to make a decision and a friend says, "Sleep on it," what they're really saying is, let the implications settle down past your conscious mind. And it often works. We go to sleep unresolved about what to do, and we wake up with a clear idea about the course of action to take.

Getting in touch with the spiritual part of yourself is a way to find that clarity, a way to back off from trying, a way to take a mini-vacation. It's a way to find a place of stillness, of calm inside, a neutral corner in which you can stay centered and watch the rest of the action. This enables you to see what's essential, to let other things fall away.

There's comfort in that space. It's the quiet place that can come right before sleep, the peaceful stillness you sometimes feel when you wake, before all the thoughts of the day crowd in. It can be soothing, a place to lay down your burdens for a moment. A place you can go for reassurance before diving into the fight once more. Like an oasis. A

Remember the Moon Survives
For Pamela

by Barbara Kingsolver

Remember the moon survives,
draws herself out crescent-thin,
a curved woman. Untouchable,
she bends around the shadow
that pushes itself against her, and she

waits. Remember how you waited
when the nights bled their darkness out
like ink, to blacken the days beyond,
to blind the morning's one eye.
This is how you learned to draw
your life out like the moon,
curled like a fetus around the

shadow. Curled in your bed,
the little hopeful flowers of your knees
pressed against the wall
and its mockery of paint,
always the little-girl colors
on the stones of the ordinary prison:
the house where you are someone's
daughter, sister, someone's flesh, someone's

blood. The Lamb and Mary
have left you to float in this darkness
like a soup bone. You watch
the cannibal feast from a hidden place
and pray to be rid of your offering.
The sun is all you wait for,
the light, guardian saint of all the children
who lie like death on the wake
of the household crime. You stop
your heart like a clock: these hours
are not your own. You hide
your life away, the lucky coin
tucked quickly in the shoe
from the burglar, when he

comes. Because he will, as sure
as shoes. This is the one

with all the keys to where you live,
the one you can't escape, and while
your heart is stopped, he takes things.
It will take years

to learn: why you hold back sleep
from the mouth that opens in the dark,
why you will not feed it with
the dreams you sealed up tight
in a cave of tears; why
the black widow still visits you,
squeezes her venom out in droplets,
stringing them like garnets
down your abdomen,
the terrifying jewelry of a woman
you wore inside, a child robbed

in the dark. Finally you know this.
You have sliced your numbness open
with the blades of your own eyes.
From your years of watching
you have grown the pupils of a cat, to see
in the dark. And these eyes are
your blessing. They will always know
the poison from the jewels that are both
embedded in your flesh.
They will always know the darkness
that is one of your names by now,
but not the one you answer to.
You are the one who knows, behind
the rising, falling tide
of shadow, the moon is always

whole. You take in silver
through your eyes, and hammer it
as taut as poems in steel
into the fine bright crescent of your life:
the sickle,
the fetus,
the surviving moon.

place of nourishment, of regeneration—what a baby feels at its mother's breast, what it feels like to be held and comforted when you're scared.

TAPPING THE LOVE

All survivors healing from sexual abuse have a tremendous need for love and support. Many women feel that they're always working at a deficit, trying to make up for the love and security they missed out on as children. A spiritual connection can be a way to connect with a deep source of love.

I think, like most incest survivors, I have kind of a bottomless pit of need inside me. I no longer believe human beings alone can fill it. Nobody can give that sort of thing. If there's a source of love in the universe that can fill that, it's not another person.

"I don't have to say the hole will never be filled," one survivor explained. "Love doesn't only come from the two people who raised me. I can parent me. Other people can love me. God can love me."

With this love comes a feeling of belonging, a sense of safety, a deeper experience of faith in your capacity to heal. And this love is not people-oriented. It's based on a relationship within yourself that no one can take away.

SPIRITUALITY IS NOT ESCAPE

The whole point of getting in touch with your spirituality is to enhance your healing, not to escape it. Spirituality is not a shortcut through any of the stages of the healing process. It's not an alternative to feeling your anger, to working through the pain, to fully acknowledging the damage done. Rather it should be an enrichment to healing, a source from which you can draw comfort and inspiration.

Certain religions, cults, and spiritual practices encourage you to avoid emotions, particularly anger. They stress forgiveness and are not likely to support you in confronting your abuser. These attitudes do not promote healing. If you are involved in a practice that denies your needs as a survivor in an active healing process, you are not helping yourself.

A PERSONAL THING

A spiritual connection is a very personal thing. You may feel it's all hogwash and want nothing to do with it. You might have a vague sense of longing for something you can't quite identify. Or you may have a precise discipline to practice. You may feel at peace in nature or you may feel inspired by your weekly support group. The important thing is that no one can tell you how to do it right. Your experience of spirituality will be unique.

I like to think this is my last day on earth. If this was my last breath, what would be important to me? I think of the song "Gracias a la Vida," which is about the simple things in life. That song says, "Thank you for the alphabet. Thank you for words. Thanks for being able to hear music. Thanks for being able to see." Taking time each day to notice the simple things I have to be grateful for has been one of the most healing things for me. Let today be enough. For peace of mind, I have to stop all my doing and be content with the simple things.

RESOLUTION AND MOVING ON

I feel like I'm home free. I still have a lot of work to do, but I know it can be done. I know what the tools are and I know how to use them. When I talk about the incest now, a lot of it is about the healing and the success and the joy.

—Saphyre

Jean Williams, an incest survivor and the adult child of an alcoholic, has worked on healing from child sexual abuse for many years. Recently she had an experience that dramatically shifted her focus:

I went to live in Mexico for a few months, and I really learned a lot by living in another culture. When I came back here my mail was full of circulars and fliers about human growth workshops and self-improvement programs. And I thought, "My God! I don't want to improve myself anymore. I don't want to go to therapy anymore. I'm good enough the way I am! For eleven years, I've been improving myself. It's time to realize *I'm already there*." I want to do things because I enjoy them, not because I'm going to fix myself in some way. I *am* healed. I'm whole. I'm ready to go.

Moving on is a tricky business for survivors. It cannot be rushed. It cannot be pressured from the outside. And there will be pressure. From the moment you first speak up, people will tell you to forget it, to "let the past be the past." But moving on to please someone else will not help you.

Most survivors reach points in their healing where they want to "move on" simply because recovery is such a painful process. When you're motivated by the fact that you don't want to face your rage, your parents, your abusers, or your vulnerability, moving on is an escape, not a liberation.

Authentic moving on is a natural result of going through each step of the healing process. It comes slowly and sometimes takes you by surprise.

> Knowing I'm not against the wall means I can get up in the morning, look in the mirror, and not have to say, "Oh God, incest again!" It's being able to brush my teeth and get through half my breakfast before I remember. Or I went to a movie and laughed through the whole thing, and didn't think about abuse one time.

STABILIZING

Resolution comes when your feelings and perspectives begin to stabilize. The emotional roller coaster evens out. You no longer doubt what happened to you. You see that your life is more than just a reaction to abuse.

> You can look at my life and say there've been some real tragedies, and there have been, but there've also been some exquisitely beautiful times. To me those far outweigh the others.

One survivor, whose childhood had good times mixed in with the abuse, sat down with a calculator and figured out the number of minutes she actually remembered being abused as a child. She multiplied this number by five, figuring there was probably a lot she'd forgotten. Then she took that total and compared it to the total number of minutes in her childhood. The nonabused hours far outweighed the abusive ones. "It helped me realize that there were other, more positive forces that had shaped me as a child. I had other things I could draw on."

Moving on means affirming the strengths you've developed. You recognize your own resiliency and drive to be healthy. You stand up for what you know to be true. You face your demons and come out alive. And finally, you make the changes you can, letting go of the things that aren't in your power to change.

RESOLVING RELATIONSHIPS WITH ABUSERS AND FAMILY

Resolving relationships with the people who abused you, didn't protect you, or don't support you now is essential to moving on. You come to your own sense of clarity in what you think and feel about each of these people.

As long as you continued to hope they would change, apologize, or understand you, you lived in a fantasy. Now you stop basing your life on that hope. When you stop longing for rescue from unlikely sources, you open the way to realistic richness in your life.

When you come to a place of resolution with your family or your abuser, the effect is often enormous. It's as though all the energy you'd been funneling into that old longing is suddenly released and you are catapulted into the present. Your identification with the abuse and its effects is greatly diminished and you are freed to enjoy a new and much more satisfying relationship with yourself and with the world.

It's taken me a long time to integrate the fact that people who were supposed to love me and care about me could have molested me and made my life miserable, and then deny that to my face. To try to squeeze that reality into the happy American home scene that's in my head has been very hard.

But it's worth it because it's a quantum shift in my perception of the universe. It's put me back on the track of creating my own life. As long as I held on to those fantasies and ideas that never were and never will be, it really limited me. As long as where I came from was clouded, it was very hard for me to take steps in another direction. If I hadn't come to terms with the reality of my family, the only option I would have had was to repeat it all over again.

LETTING GO OF THE DAMAGE

There may be times in the healing process when sexual abuse is all you see, times when you lose touch with the fact that *you are investing all this time and energy in healing so you can move on to something else in life.* There may even be a part of you that doesn't want to get through it.

Survivors often complain about how long it takes to heal, but there is an identity in being a committed survivor of sexual abuse. That identity has been closely linked to your survival, and it can be hard to give up.

A lot of people get stuck in that rage and that hatred and that fear. But I realized I didn't have to hang on to it. I started to think of it like a big wad of mucus that I had to cough up. I decided, "Okay, I've had enough of walking around like I'd like to brutalize everyone who looks at me wrong. I don't have to feel like that anymore." Then I thought, "How would I like to feel?"

I wanted to feel safe in the world. I wanted to feel powerful. And so I focused on what was working in my life, in the ways I was taking power in real-life situations.

I stopped sitting there picking open wounds, saying, "If I only pick deep enough, I can see some real blood and gore here." I started to function like I didn't have to carry around that baggage anymore. There was a point where I simply stopped carrying the bags.

Every now and then the porter brings it up to me and says, "Here's your baggage, ma'am." And I open it up and go through it again. And then I say, "I've seen enough of you for now. I want to go on with my life again." And life feels much better. It's a tremendous relief to stop suffering all the time.

And it's not a question of denial. It was an organic change. It wasn't like there was a road sign that said, "Leaving Guilt. Entering New Zone of Healing."

It was almost like looking in a mirror after you get out of the shower, and it's all fogged over, and as the moisture begins to dry up, you see more of yourself. Things just got clearer.

I began to relate more to the person who I was becoming, rather than the person I had been. When I leave that baggage over to one side and step into that new self, I recognize her. She's not a facade. She's real. She's the person I was before I ever got abused.

REASSURING THE CHILD

One thing that can make moving on difficult is the feeling that you are somehow betraying the child who was injured. If you have had to struggle to get in touch with your childhood pain, you may be surprised by a reluctance to let it go. Evie Malcolm explains:

Emotionally, for me, and I'm not defending this, letting go of the damage would mean abandoning that eleven-year-old girl who's still alive in me, who nobody was there for, who wasn't listened to. If I get better, if the bruise heals, then there's going to be no sign of it, and it'll be as if she never got heard. And that would be an incredible disloyalty, a betrayal of that little girl.

So I'm trying to get myself healed and over the symptoms of the damage without denying that it happened. This is the intellectual "me" talking. This is not the eleven-year-old girl. She doesn't want to let go. It's an emotional feeling. And emotions are very powerful. You can have all the right intellectual thoughts, and emotionally you can be very childlike. And the fearful child in

me doesn't want to be forgotten. So I have to reassure her that my getting better doesn't mean I'm abandoning her or denying her pain.

(For more of Evie's story, see page 381.)

There is no need to leave the child behind. Rather, by healing, you are creating a safe, healthy place where she can thrive.

INTEGRATION

A big part of moving on is integration. You see yourself as whole, not compartmentalized—your body, your sexuality, your feelings, and your intellect as interconnected parts of a whole. You start to accept the gray, the fuzzy in-between places that make us all human.

The last thing someone from our kind of family can do is learn to accept paradox. It's not black and white. It's not all neat. It's not all going to work out perfect. Learning to hold paradox is a real sign of healing to me. It's been very hard for me to accept that I'll still feel bad. I thought when you were healed everything felt good, but it's not true. You still feel shitty, though not all the time. I wanted to select certain things—humor, warmth, love, fun—I didn't want to feel scared, angry, or any "negative feelings." But they're all part of being human.

Integration means gaining perspective on growth over a lifetime. Susan King found a wonderful image for her healing journey:

I think of a Russian nesting doll my sister had. It fascinated me. A brightly painted wooden doll. I could twist her apart at the waist, and there was another smaller doll inside her. And another inside that, and another, down to a tiny diapered baby. And each Susan inside me has other little Susans inside her, and I am, at this moment, inside a wiser gray-haired Susan that is yet to be. Like the Russian doll, I am round—and complete.

LETTING GO OF CRISIS

It's easy to get used to the tangible anguish and turmoil of healing. Being in constant crisis means that you don't have to look at the changes you need to make in your life. Those survivors who are accustomed to crisis know just how hard giving it up can be.

Reconciliation
by Cheryl Marie Wade

Thirty-seven years of denying my father's sexual abuse has taken a toll: massive deterioration of all my joint tissue. I use an electric wheelchair for mobility and my almost boneless fingers are as fragile as a cat-mauled wing. The medical establishment calls this rheumatoid arthritis. I call it my body's eloquent expression of my incest story.

I wheel my chair through Mojave sands
until I sink
There I sit
sun baking my spongy bones
so brittle
that when I stand
instead of feeling shin
push into ankle
ankle press
into heel
heel slam into a shoe of nails
my pelvic bones
snap
and I fall
slow motion
onto the warm
warm grains

I am bleached
white
nothing but a heap
of white sprigs
He comes
with his little girl
Holding her hand
he guides
her eyes to the lizard
a flicker of iridescent pink
but her interest is the white twig
at her feet
She bends and with a small
perfect hand
lifts what once had been
my aching finger
Look Daddy
a treasure
He leans down to admire her find
She puts it in the pocket of his plaid shirt
and the two of them walk on
My skull
opens wide
swallows the desert
and sings hosanna to the dry dry air.

I'm an intensity junkie. I feel a let-down whenever I come to the end of a particular cycle of intensity. What am I going to cry and throw scenes about now? What am I going to obsess about now? What is going to lend my life that particular tinge of stormy skies and wuthering heights?

I see it as almost a chemical addiction. I became addicted to my own sense of drama and adrenaline. Letting go of the need for intensity has been a process of slowly weaning myself. I've gotten to a point where I've actually experienced bits of just plain contentment, and I notice it, and I enjoy it.

Letting go of stress and turmoil as compelling forces in your life is a major milestone in your healing. You may be excited, proud of yourself. Yet after the initial victory, you may also feel hollowed out inside. You have cleared space so that new things can grow, but at the same time you may enter an unsettling limbo, just you with no trappings, ground zero.

It may take some time before you begin to get the first inklings of who you are becoming. Those empty in-between times can be scary, but you will regain your bearings. You will come through, in fact, more solid than you've ever felt before.

LIFE IN THE PRESENT

When you let go of the need for crisis, you make room for the rich and varied texture of ordinary living. You discover new, less stressful sources of excitement—challenging work projects, creative ventures, or greater risks in intimacy.

Part of moving on is learning to balance the excitement in your life with quiet, peaceful times. With practice, you can find contentment in small things—listening to music, cooking dinner, taking walks. From a calm place, you can assess what you want and take steps to get there.

If you don't yet know what you want in your life, this is a time to explore possibilities. Make a list of things you've dreamed of doing or becoming. This kind of self-discovery is something no one can take away from you. It is more rewarding than any crisis. And as you leave the effects of the past behind, the future becomes open possibility.

I lived a hard life on the streets. I was in and out of mental institutions. I don't know what's going to happen now. So much has changed, and I'm seeing myself differently. I am forty-seven years old, and there are not a lot of options at forty-seven like there are at fifteen. But I'm not closing any doors. I'm opening up a lot of doors in fact.

HOW HEALED DO I HAVE TO BE?

Healing is not about eternal struggle, the kind where you push the boulder up the hill, only to have it roll back down on top of you. There is a point when you will stop feeling like a victim, either of the abuse or of healing itself.

Recently Ellen was talking to a young woman who has been in therapy for the past two years, actively working on her healing. Because the work was so demanding, she cut back on many other activities early in the process in order to devote her full energies to healing. Gradually, as she became able to handle both the healing work and more commitments, she added school, a part-time job, and a lover to her life.

Now this woman had the opportunity to move to another city, join her lover there, and enter a school program that she very much wanted to be in. "But," she said to Ellen, "I think maybe I should wait until I'm all better. I'm not finished with therapy. How healed do I have to be to do what I want?"

Ellen laughed and told her to go. Part of healing is doing what you want to do, those things that will give you both fulfillment and pleasure. You don't have to wait.

THERE IS NO END OF THE LINE

There is no such thing as absolute healing. You never erase your history. The abuse happened. It affected you in profound ways. That will never change. But you *can* reach a place of resolution.

I don't know if I will ever be completely healed. It's like there was a wound and it healed over, but it was still infected in there. It needed to be lanced and cleaned out so that good healthy scar tissue could grow over it. I knew that once that scar tissue grew, it wouldn't be very pleasant to look at, but it wouldn't hurt anymore. It would be raised, and you would know it was there, but you could touch it and it wouldn't be painful. And I think that's

how it is. I have scars, but they don't hurt. They're cleaned out now.

That doesn't mean every scar is. I'm sure there are still some I will discover as the years go by. That's one thing you can say about people like us, there's always going to be something that comes up. I don't think I will ever be completely healed, because it really cut to the core of my trust in the world. I don't believe in complete transcendence. I think people are too complex for that.

You need to accept the fact that the healing process will continue throughout your life. One woman spent years resisting and hating herself every time the incest resurfaced in a new way:

Finally, I had to realize it was part of me. It's not something I can get rid of. The way I work with it will change, but I think it will always be there. And I think I have to get to the point where I love it, because then it's really loving me wholly. If I'm going to really love myself totally, then I had to love all of me, and this is part of who I am.

Many survivors make the decision to heal out of pain, shame, and terror, and at the outset the work frequently feels like a burden. But by the time you reach the stage of resolution and moving on, you come to an appreciation of the deep healing you have done. You recognize that healing has brought you more than just the alleviation of pain. You may, in fact, see your healing as the beginning of lifelong growth. As one survivor put it, "I have no intention of stopping. I fully intend to grow until I die."

WHY IT'S BEEN WORTH IT

"I feel like Rip Van Winkle sometimes, like I'm just waking up. Things like crying—I find myself crying now. I had given it up when I was eight. Or laughing. Giggling. Roughhousing with my kids and having it be safe. Playing. Getting angry at somebody I love. Telling the truth. Feeling something in the moment it's actually happening, instead of five minutes later, five years later, always *later*. Taking risks I never would have taken before. Just kind of waking up. It's a silly metaphor, but it's what flowers do. They just come out."

"Solitude has become important to me. I used to feel terribly lonely. I don't have to be lonely anymore."

"I'm not afraid of people like I used to be. I have a phone list that's incredible, and I really talk to these people. A lot of the barriers I've always put up between myself and other people are gone."

"These are the ways I've turned things that have damaged me into things that work. They're survival tools, and I've sharpened them up to use in real life. I'm proud of them."

"I feel life more intensely. Pain, but good things too. I can take a walk in the park and be really upset, and I can still see how beautiful everything is."

"I feel more peaceful. I feel like I'm normal now. Like I don't have to carry around this burden anymore."

"I'm thriving as opposed to surviving. There's all the difference in the world in how I look at life. I like myself so much better. And I'm happy most of the time. I'm more completely myself almost all the time. In fact, I am myself all the time."

A BROADER COMMITMENT

As you heal, as you feel more nourished, balanced, and whole, you will find that you have energy available to direct in creative and life-affirming pursuits. No longer struggling just to cope day-to-day, you can begin to make an impact in the world.

What really amazes me is that survivors can be out in the world completely functional using maybe 20 percent of their capacity. Can you imagine what we'll be able to do when we let the other 80 percent out? If we were able to recover, stop the abuse, and heal everyone, the world we live in would be so phenomenal.

If you think of all the ways in which you have been stunted, all the energy you have consumed simply to keep hanging on by your fingernails, all that you might have created or accomplished or simply enjoyed had you not had to stagger under the burden of abuse, you may have a formidable list.

If you multiply that times the number of other women similarly struggling—not only now, but back through the decades and centuries—the result is awesome.

Now, imagine all women healed—and all that energy no longer used for mere survival but made available for creativity, nurturing relationships, freeing political prisoners, ending the arms race. The effect on the world would be monumental.

We have never in recorded history lived in a time when women were, as a whole, empowered. We can only begin to imagine the riches.

HEALING MOVES OUT FROM THE CENTER

Your first allegiance must always be to yourself. If you race out to do good deeds without attending to your own needs, it's easy to create more problems than you solve. Women have been expected to sacrifice themselves while they help everybody else for too long.

It's a little like using oxygen masks on an airplane. If you're traveling with small children, the flight attendants tell you to secure your own mask first, and then to assist the child. Your initial reaction might be to help your child first, but if you pass out while trying to help your child, no one survives. When you ensure your own stability first, then you can help others, and everyone can be safe.

Although your responsibility toward healing begins with yourself, it does not stop there. Child sexual abuse originates from the same fear, hatred, deprivation, selfishness, and ignorance that lead people to abuse and assault in other ways. These attitudes are woven into the very fabric of our society and oppress on a large scale. We get nuclear waste, inhuman conditions for migrant farm workers, the rampages of the Ku Klux Klan.

Part of your healing is the healing of the earth. If you don't make it a priority, there is little hope for the world. By and large, it is not the abusers who are going to write letters to our government, imploring them to stop funding slaughter in El Salvador. It's not the mothers who are too terrified to hear your pain who are going to fight for changes in the legal system to make it easier for children to testify. And how many pedophiles care about toxic waste?

It is you—who know something about both justice and injustice, about abuse and respect, about suffering and about healing—who have the clarity, courage, and compassion to contribute to the quality, and the very continuation, of life.

PART THREE

CHANGING

PATTERNS

THE PROCESS
OF CHANGE

For a long time I felt like damaged goods. I was obsessed with the question "What is wrong with me?" But I just kept doing the work. A part of me knew that I was not locked into anything. My cells replace themselves completely every seven years. How could I still be damaged goods? Of course I could change.

—Saphyre

When you first remember your abuse or acknowledge its effects, you may feel tremendous relief. Finally there is a reason for your problems. There is someone, and something, to blame. But eventually you realize that things are not that simple—or fair. As one survivor said: "My grandfather was dead and gone and I was still alive with the same problems I'd always had. I had to face the fact that if I wanted a different life, I was going to have to do something about it."

One woman went to ten years of incest-related therapy before she realized she was the one responsible for changing her own life:

I had to go from dealing with the incest an hour a week in therapy to dealing with it in my real life. I realized I had to stop talking at forty dollars an hour and start doing. It's a lot cheaper to fix yourself on your own time than to depend on an hour a week to get better. I could talk therapy with anyone who had the lingo, but I had to realize I wasn't taking care of myself in real life.

I decided to change my life and take responsibility for what was happening to me. I started asking myself questions like "What did I do to immobilize myself? Why did I stay in an abusive relationship?"

And then I started taking care of my own life. I *changed* my relationship. I *changed* my job. I *changed* my home. I started taking care of business! I filed a suit against my ex-lover for assault. I got money back that I had loaned out. I fought a custody battle against my ex-husband. I started getting angry. I started to cry. I've really changed. I *look* different. I *sound* different. I changed my life intentionally.

HOW TO CHANGE

The basic steps to making changes are:

- **Become aware of the behavior you want to change.**
- **Examine the reasons you developed that behavior to begin with.** When do you first remember feeling or acting that way? What was going on then? Try to understand why you needed that behavior.
- **Have compassion for what you've done in the past.** Even if you didn't make the wisest, healthiest choices, you took the options you saw at the time. And now you're making better choices. Focus on that.
- **Find new ways to meet your needs.** Although every change doesn't expose an unmet need, many do. By taking such needs seriously and finding new ways to

meet them, you make it possible to maintain the change.
- **Get support.** The environment in which you live—the people you see—affects your ability to make changes. People who are working to grow and change in their own lives will support you with encouragement and by example. People who are living out the patterns you're trying to break will continually suck you back in. Respect the power of influence.
- **Make several tries.** Although sometimes you can soar, usually making changes is a plodding process that doesn't look very heroic or exciting. Yet those everyday steps lead to real change and a more rewarding life.
- **Be persistent.** Most of the changes we make in our lives require repetition. If not smoking *one* cigarette were sufficient, it wouldn't be so hard to quit smoking.

OBSTACLES TO CHANGE

We do not change in a vacuum. Your new choices have repercussions on those around you. Your determination to change can be threatening to them because it means they will have to change too. Even though it's change for the better, people don't always willingly make the commitment to healthier living.

A forty-six-year-old survivor described the way her second husband responded when she got into therapy: "I made change after change after change. John was terrified. What happened to the woman he married? I looked like a little widow lady with three kids. All of a sudden, I wasn't. I was this woman who was just taking off."

Change requires support and community. If you do not get it from the people closest to you, seek it elsewhere, whether through new friends, a counselor, or a group of other survivors.

ACKNOWLEDGING FEAR

It helps to name your fears. Naming things gives them less of a hold. One woman, who suffered from continual depression and immobility, made a list of what she would have to face in life if she actually healed. Her list was extensive. She'd have to face the possibility of success—or failure—in her career. She'd have to risk greater intimacy with her lover. She'd have to stop blaming her family for her problems and would have to give up their image of her (that she was a loser). She'd lose her identity as a sick person, as a victim. She'd have to learn to deal with her real feelings instead of masking them with hopelessness and anxiety. She'd have to attract people on her own merits, not because they felt sorry for her. When she looked over her list, she could see why she was afraid.

FEAR DOESN'T HAVE TO STOP YOU

Often fear accompanies the unfamiliar and exciting leaps we take in life. It's the feeling that makes your knees shake the first time you sing in public, when you confront the person who abused you, or when you apply for a job you really want. When you do something new and challenging, you need that energy. It's adrenaline. Often women feel this kind of fear when they are taking absolutely the right steps for themselves.

Fear doesn't have to stop you. Even if you're afraid, you can still go ahead and make the changes you want. You just do it anyway. You do it afraid. You do it nervously, awkwardly. You shake or sweat. You are not graceful or composed, but you do it.

THE PATTERN FIGHTS BACK

A pattern is any habitual way of behaving. By its nature it is deeply entrenched, set by repetition, and brings a familiar result. Even if that result is not, ultimately, what you want, its predictability is part of its grip. Patterns usually start unconsciously as a way of coping when your options are limited. They serve you, but at a cost.

Patterns have a life of their own, and their will to live is very strong. They fight back with a vengeance when faced with annihilation. Once you recognize a pattern and make the commitment to break it, it often escalates. Laura remembers:

I decided I wanted to be more present in my life, that I no longer wanted to space out every time a strong feeling surfaced. But the pattern fought back with a frenzy. Things got much worse than they had ever been. I was spaced out all the time. Then just when I thought I couldn't stand it anymore, that I would never, ever get through it, it broke. I'd earned the scary miracle of being able to stay present.

Another woman, who'd had a whole series of abusive intimate relationships, worked toward changing this pattern. But just as the pattern was about to give way, she said, "I had a three-week affair in which I replayed every screwed-up relationship I ever had. I went through all my patterns in real rapid motion. It was like a Charlie Chaplin movie."

It's important that you don't give up at this critical point. It's likely the "I can't stand it anymore" feeling means you're close to the change you're working so hard to achieve.

A LITTLE SELF-LOVE GOES A LONG WAY

Be kind to yourself. Be patient. Babies do not go from crawling to walking in a single day. We are not impatient or angry when they totter and fall. In fact, we delight in their first forays, even when they end in a plop.

Forgiving yourself when you backslide, being gentle with yourself, may be a pattern-breaker in itself. One survivor related how her attitude toward herself has softened over time:

When I slip into an old pattern, I see it almost as if I'm putting on a pair of shoes that don't fit anymore. I've put them on again, and here I am trying to tap-dance, and it's not working. At first I'd whip myself: "Why did you put those stupid shoes on again?" I'd get really despondent that I'd never change.

As I've gotten further along in my healing, I've been able to be gentler with myself: "Oh God, I slipped again." I'll congratulate myself on recognizing it so quickly, and then I'll ask myself, "What happened this time to trigger it?" Instead of beating myself up, I tell myself I'll take care of myself the next time and I figure out ways to do that.

GIVE YOURSELF CREDIT

Often people are acutely aware of how difficult something is before they do it. You are scared, you vacillate, you collect all your strength and courage, and somehow you manage to do what you set out to do. Then, as soon as it's over, you jump in with "Okay, what's next?" Or worse, you frown at yourself and say, "I don't know why I had to make such a big deal out of that. It wasn't much."

It was much. And you need to acknowledge that.

One woman, who was in counseling with Ellen, was upset with herself for being in a relationship with a man she really didn't care for. Afraid she'd never find anyone else who wanted her, afraid to be lonely, she hung in. Now and then she'd try to work up her courage to break off with him, but each time she'd waver and stay. Finally, after many months, she ended the relationship. That week in counseling she talked about other things for most of the session and then mentioned that she had broken up with this man. In the same sentence she went on to say that she was feeling bad about herself because she was still ambivalent and wondered if she should go back.

"Wait," Ellen interrupted. "You broke up with him?"

"Yes, but I don't feel strong about it. I've—"

Ellen interrupted again. "But you broke up. Even if you decide at some time that you want to go back, you still did this thing that you really wanted to do and were very afraid to do. You did it! You don't even give it a sentence of its own."

Finally this woman slowed down enough to experience her achievement. She was willing to hear that many people feel unsettled when they act in unfamiliar ways, even if those ways are in their best interests.

CELEBRATE

When you accomplish a goal, when you make a change you have worked hard to make, celebrate. A celebration can be anything that feels right to you, from raucous to serious. Eat lobster, buy a lovely card and mail it to yourself. Have a ritual. Light a candle. Do what's special for you.

WRITING EXERCISE: CHANGING PATTERNS

(See the basic method for writing exercises on page 28.)

1. Take some time to assess how far you've come in your healing. Are you at the beginning, or have you made some progress? What have you accomplished already? What do you have to be proud of? What obstacles have you broken through? What small (and large) successes have you achieved? Give yourself credit. In detail.

2. You've already done a lot of work—and there's still more to do. What are your goals for your healing now? What are some ways you may be able to work toward these goals? Write about the things you still need to do to move ahead in your personal life.

These can be general, such as "I need to be more compassionate with myself," or as specific as "I need to burn the picture of my abuser that still hangs in my living room."

Change
by Ellen Bass

This is where I yank the old roots
from my chest, like the tomatoes
we let grow until December, stalks
thick as saplings.

This is the moment when the ancient fears
race like thoroughbreds, asking for more
and more rein. And I, the driver,
for some reason they know nothing of
strain to hold them back.

Terror grips me like a virus
and I sweat, fevered,
trying to burn it out.

This fear is invisible. All you can see
is a woman going about her ordinary day,
drinking tea, taking herself to the movies,
reading in bed. If victorious
I will look exactly the same.

Yet I am hoisting a car from mud ruts
half a century deep. I am hacking
a clearing through the fallen slash
of my heart. Without laser precision,
with only the primitive knife of need, I cut
and splice the circuitry of my brain.
I change.

SELF-ESTEEM AND PERSONAL POWER

I remember saying in fits of depression, "You think I'm a good person, but I'm not. I'm a bad person." Deep inside, under all this cheerleader, straight-A bullshit, there is this little kernel, this bad seed, that's forced me to become perfect on the outside. Beause if I keep pretending that I'm good, it will make up for the awful person I really am.

Self-esteem is a basic issue for women. Because our culture devalues women, we often fight feelings of inadequacy or struggle with self-doubt. For survivors, these issues are heightened. You were damaged early. Something was broken at a core level. The reality that you were precious, that you deserved love, that you were capable, that you were okay just the way you were, was denied you as a child. You weren't given a chance to feel good about yourself. Instead, you were abused. You were left feeling dirty, somehow at fault. And the ways you were forced to

cope may have left you feeling even worse about yourself, more ashamed.

You may experience low self-esteem as a constant feeling of worthlessness, a nagging voice that tells you you didn't do enough, you didn't do it right, you don't deserve it. Or your feelings about yourself may fluctuate. You may feel good about yourself most of the time, self-critical feelings lying dormant until you have some kind of setback—a loss, a period of change, an argument with someone you love. Then you suddenly lose touch with the good things about yourself. The self-love you've nurtured so carefully seems out of reach, unattainable.

Feelings of self-hate can erupt seemingly out of the blue. A small interaction can trigger a whole avalanche of self-doubt and uncertainty. You get one problem wrong on a college exam and you say to yourself, "I'm a stupid idiot. I'll never amount to anything." You stop dating someone because you decide that person isn't good for you, and instead of feeling proud of yourself for setting limits, you feel abandoned, sure you'll never love again. Even though you are taking care of yourself, you somehow end up feeling wrong —again.

Self-esteem is experienced in the moment, and your sense of yourself will fluctuate as you move through the healing process. When you're first recovering memories, struggling to accept the truth of what happened to you, or dealing with your abuser, you may feel worse than you felt before. Often feelings of shame, powerlessness, and self-hate are bottled up with the memories, and as the memories come through, these feelings do too.

Yet healing isn't just about pain. It's about learning to love yourself. As you move from feeling like a victim to being a proud survivor, you will have glimmers of hope, pride, satisfaction. Those are natural by-products of healing.

This whole book is about improving your self-esteem. Whether you are contacting the child within, discovering your anger, working on sex, or grieving for your past, you will be forging a more gentle, loving relationship with yourself. This chapter will give you some specific tools that can help you feel better about yourself along the way—on your own, in relation to others, and in the work you do.

INTERNALIZED MESSAGES

When you were abused, it's likely that you were told, directly or indirectly, that the abuse was your fault. You may have been told you were bad or stupid. You may have been humiliated or called a liar. Many survivors were told that they would never amount to anything. You may still be receiving this message. One survivor whose poem was published in a local newspaper sent a copy of it to her mother. Her mother replied, "It was just beginner's luck. You'll never write another one."

Another woman, elected homecoming queen in high school, had such a distorted image of herself that she was convinced her friends had chosen her only because they pitied her.

Even if you weren't given such messages directly, the very fact that you were abused taught you that you were powerless, alone, not worthy of protection or love. If you were ignored or neglected, your basic value was denied. You learned you were undeserving, unable to have an impact in the world.

When our own worth is negated often enough, we begin to believe there's something wrong with us. As a result of these childhood messages, you may believe you're only good for sex, that you're unlovable, that nothing you do matters, or even that you don't deserve to live. As Ellen says, "Survivors were programmed to self-destruct. You learned to put yourself down so effectively that the abusers don't even have to be around any more to do it. They can go off and play golf while you do yourself in."

This self-destructiveness often is at war with the positive, sustaining self-concept you are trying to build.

I have often felt like two different people. Wednesday I was going to buy a gun to kill myself. The gun store closed at 6:00. We had a sales meeting at work, which I didn't go to because I figured it was going to take me a half hour to get to the store from downtown.

All day I'd been going through this bullshit with the gun, but I'd also made this list of things that make me feel good. And then on my way to the store, I decided I didn't really want to buy the gun. So I bought a teddy bear instead. I made an appointment for a massage. And I bought myself a ticket to a show I really wanted to see.

A lot of times there's two people operating. There's this person inside who's really striving to be healthy. And then there's this other person who's been beaten so much, she just takes up where my father left off.

CHANGING INTERNALIZED MESSAGES

At the beginning of your healing, you may be experiencing negative messages constantly. But as time goes by and your basic self-image starts to shift, these messages will come less frequently. They will stand out more distinctly against a background of basically liking yourself.

While you may think such thoughts come without cause, the fact is that they are always sparked by something. Each time you feel bad about yourself, try to isolate the thought or event that set off the feeling. At first this won't be easy, but with practice you will be able to ask yourself a few quick questions to identify the source:

- When did I start feeling this way?
- Did I have a disturbing conversation with someone? Receive a disturbing phone call or letter?
- Did something scare me or make me angry?
- Is there a reason I'm feeling particularly vulnerable right now?
- When did I stop feeling good about myself?

Once you find the event or thought that started this feeling, ask yourself, "Is this feeling familiar?" Search back to find the first time you felt that way, the first time you were told that particular lie. What was the context? Who told you you were selfish? Who implied you were in the way? When did you decide it was you who was bad?

Allow yourself to feel the pain of the child you once were. Allow your compassion for her, your anger at those who hurt her, and any other feelings to rise. Recognizing and expressing these feelings helps to release the grip of negative internalized messages.

As you identify the lies you were told about yourself, you can get rid of them. One woman, who called the voices in her head "the committee," set about killing them off, one at a time:

Whenever I start to feel bad about myself, I say, "Okay. Who is that talking? Who on the committee is saying, 'You're no good. You can't do that?' Is it Daddy? Is that Mommy? Is that the scared kid? Is that the hurt kid? Is that Grandmom Jean?"

When all the committee members are sitting in my head making it so that I can't see and I can't feel, I need to identify and silence their voices. I iso-

THE MOST COMMON ONE-LINERS

I hate myself.

"I felt like I had an oil slick oozing goo inside me. I knew I was filled with something evil, and that evil rubbed off on everyone I came into contact with. So I didn't let anybody really get near me."

I don't deserve it.

"Struggle is my middle name. The basic pleasures other people enjoy—companionship, relaxation, fun—have always seemed out of reach to me. Underneath all my flirting and bravado, I don't believe anyone will ever love me. I know I'm really meant to be alone."

I can't do it.

"When I was a little kid I was expected to be the adult. I had to cook, keep up the house at some maintenance level. I was left in charge as early as nine, ten years old. And how good can a kid be at keeping together a household? I was always blowing it. They were always criticizing me. Now, I don't even try. What's the point? I can't do anything right."

It has to be perfect.

"In my family they were generous with failures, but they were very stingy with acknowledging success. So when someone says, "You did a really great job," I say, "Yeah, but look up there, there's a flaw." It's hard for me to see the good. I still see the wrinkle in the left-hand corner."

Whatever I do, it'll never be enough.

"I know I'm smart. I know I have a lot of skills. If I say I'll do a job, I have no doubt I'll get it done—and probably in half the time it would take someone else. My problem is that I don't feel I deserve anything for it. Why should I get money or recognition or stability? Everything I do, great as it is, is only making up for what happened when I was a kid. My achievements only bring me up to zero."

It's not worth trying.

"I've always had a real lack of ambition. I have a terrific business mind and I always use it for someone else's advantage instead of my own. Why? I've never looked for anything more than to just get by. I never wanted more than survival. I never wanted to be more than normal. And there's so much more to life than that."

What I want doesn't count.

"I was brought up as the receptacle. There were four people living in my house and every one of them abused me. All I learned was to accept abuse. I was never in my body long enough to know: Did I want to write? Did I want to draw? Did I want to play? I never learned to know what I wanted to do. So later, whatever came along job-wise, I took."

late the committee member and kick 'em out. I say, "Stop. Get out! This is my head! *I* get to decide. You don't have control over me! *Get out!*"

Just paying attention and discovering the roots of your negative thoughts will dramatically interrupt your tendency to feel lousy about yourself. By seeking the origins of these negative images, you are acknowledging that they did indeed come from somewhere. You are affirming that you don't feel this way because it's true, but because you were conditioned to feel that way.

After rejecting the lie, replace it with the truth about yourself. If you think you don't deserve love, say to yourself, "I am a beautiful, deserving human being. Just because I'm breathing, I deserve love. Just because I'm human. I don't have to do anything." This is the truth. If you don't believe it yet, say it anyway. In time, you will believe it. (See "Affirmations and Visualizations," on page 184).

Sometimes, especially in the beginning, a friend's perspective can really help. Laura worked out a unique system with her best friend:

Whenever one of us says something self-hating, that doesn't reflect our healthiest, most adult self, the other one lovingly interrupts the conversation with our secret code word, "Tomato!" If I start to say "Oh, it'll never work out. I couldn't possibly do that," she yells out, "Tomato! Tomato!" until I give it up and start laughing. If I'm having a really bad day, she'll explain to me, like you would to a child, *why* my tomato statement isn't true. Then she replaces it with the truth as she sees it: "Laura, you're a powerful woman, my best

friend. Of course you can do it." Having a friend like her really helps.

SETTING LIMITS AND BOUNDARIES

The capacity to set limits is essential to feeling good about yourself. Many survivors have not known how to define their own time, to protect their bodies, to put themselves first, to say no.

I've always given my time over to whoever asked for it because I didn't think it was mine to deal with. When I was little, if anybody wanted anything from me, they took it. I have poor boundaries. It makes me ridiculously easy to get along with. I'll do anything anyone asks me to do. If you do that, everybody likes you. And it's very important for me to be liked.

Although learning to say no is a difficult challenge, it is a relief to be able to stop doing what you don't want to. By setting limits, you protect yourself and give yourself freedom at the same time. As you say no to other people, you start to say yes to yourself.

But saying no isn't easy. As women, we've been taught to please others, to put their needs first.

I went to a workshop on dating. We were paired up and told to ask each other out on an imaginary date. Those of us being asked were instructed to say no. We were supposed to turn down the invitation. But when the women reported back to the group, a surprising number had said yes anyway. One even offered to cook dinner.

If you can't imagine saying no, set up some practice situations. Get a friend to role-play with you. Try a scene in which you are asked—or told—to do something you don't want to do. Then say no. Pay attention to the feelings that come up, but say no anyway. If you find yourself thinking "I just can't say no," ask yourself why not. What would happen if you said no? Do you think you or the other person couldn't handle it? If so, why? Talk about your feelings, and then say no anyway. Try reversing roles. Listen to the way your friend says no. Try out her style.

Then watch for situations in your life in which you want to say no. Start with what's easiest and build up to the harder ones. When a friend wants you to go out to lunch but you've set aside time to play the piano (and playing is what you *really* want to do), say no. When your six-year-old tells you to get her the milk, tell her she's capable of getting it herself, and that you're sure she can do a good job of it.

If you've never (or hardly ever) said no, your first attempts may feel awkward or even rude. When you feel you don't have the right to say no, or when you're new at it, you may add cumbersome explanations or refuse more strongly than necessary. Yet saying no doesn't have to be loud or hostile (although it can be if you want it to). As you feel more secure in your right to say no, you'll be able to do so with a simple statement: "No, I don't want to." "No thanks." "No, I'd rather not."

If you've been taking care of other people and saying yes all your life, you may encounter some angry resistance when you start to say no. People may say you were nicer before. They may say you're being selfish, that

Autobiography in Five Short Chapters
by Portia Nelson

I

I walk down the street.
    There is a deep hole in the sidewalk.
    I fall in
    I am lost . . . I am helpless
        It isn't my fault.
It takes forever to find a way out.

II

I walk down the same street,
    There is a deep hole in the sidewalk.
    I pretend I don't see it.
    I fall in again.
I can't believe I am in the same place.
        But it isn't my fault.
It still takes a long time to get out.

III

I walk down the same street
    There is a deep hole in the sidewalk.
    I see it is there.
    I still fall in . . . it's a habit.
        My eyes are open.
        I know where I am.
It is my fault.
I get out immediately.

IV

I walk down the same street.
    There is a deep hole in the sidewalk.
    I walk around it.

V

I walk down another street.

they prefer the "old" you. On the other hand, you might find that your honesty and clarity is respected by friends who are glad that you are finally taking care of yourself.

Although it's sometimes scary to say no, the rewards are worth it. You feel safer because you are protecting yourself from situations you don't want to be in. You get more of what you want, more of the time. You don't feel like a victim. You experience more confidence, power, and self-respect. Your self-esteem will rise.

CREATING A POSITIVE SELF-IMAGE

LIVE FOR YOURSELF

We all have the right to make choices that we believe will bring us satisfaction. We have the right to determine our own values, lifestyle, and priorities. If you are still trying to please others, if you are still hoping for someone else's approval, then you will never be smart enough, thin enough, successful enough.

Try approaching your life from your center rather than from external considerations. Try putting aside your father's expectations. Stop comparing yourself to your best friend. Think about what you like to do, whom you like to spend time with, what you find worthwhile.

Approach these changes gradually. Thinking for yourself and making your own decisions can be terrifying. Letting go of other people's expectations can leave you feeling empty for a time. And yet, seeing yourself as an independent adult who can stand up for your own choices frees you to accept yourself as you are. As you begin to trust your decisions and pursue your own goals, your self-respect will naturally increase.

DO THINGS YOU'RE PROUD OF

It's impossible to feel good about yourself if you are doing things that you aren't proud of. If you are gambling compulsively, not spending enough time with your children, or avoiding therapy, you're not going to feel good about yourself. To improve your self-esteem, it's essential that you stop doing things you don't feel proud of and start doing things you can respect and admire.

AFFIRMATIONS AND VISUALIZATIONS

Many women have found affirmations to be helpful in creating a positive self-image. You can say things like "I am a worthwhile, deserving person," "I like myself," "I am lovable," "I can trust my perceptions." By repeating these daily—out loud or in writing—you consistently affirm your positive qualities.

Some women prefer to phrase the affirmation to reflect what they hope to become, even if they don't fully feel that way yet. For example, you may want to feel powerful and effective in your life. At present, perhaps you feel more powerful than you used to, but still not all that powerful. By making the affirmation "I am powerful and effective," you create an image of yourself as you will be, and in doing so, you bring about what you wish for.

Visualizing how you want to be is another effective way to move toward your goal. You can imagine different scenes that show you as a more capable, powerful person: you may be brilliantly arguing a case in front of a jury, receiving your black belt in karate, or simply walking along the street with your back straight and your head held high. You can visualize yourself in a healthy relationship or even having fun. You can imagine whole scenarios. One woman who felt as if she was dirty, as if she was covered with shit, imagined scraping off all the shit and throwing it back at her abuser. Afterward, she reported feeling great.

ACCENTUATE THE POSITIVE

If you're used to seeing yourself as ineffective or worthless, you may not notice the wonderful things about yourself. Try making a list of all the things you do well. Include everything. "I make perfect fried eggs. I can whistle on pitch. I'm good at untying knots." Make another list of the things you like about yourself: "I like that I'm a good listener. I like my feet. I like my stubborn determination." Read your lists to yourself when you're feeling self-critical. Find an appreciative friend and read the lists aloud. Or ask friends what they like about you. Listen and take notes.

It's important to acknowledge both small and large changes. Eva, a survivor and former battered wife, was inspired when she saw how much her self-image had changed:

I used to feel like nothing I said counted, that people wouldn't listen to me. I didn't like myself. I think I went out of my way to find things that happened in my life that reinforced the things my ex-husband said about me, that I believed about myself. It took a long time for me to acquire the characteristic of being my own woman, of not letting other people dominate me and dominate my ideas.

All those things have changed tremendously. I'm more confident about who I am now. There were parts of me I liked when I was young. Now I've reclaimed them. I have a certain boldness. I was the boldest woman I knew. There was a time when I was afraid of what people would say, and now I don't give a damn. I'm gonna be who I am and if other people can't hang it, that's their tough luck.

(For more of Eva's story, see page 367.)

FIND A TASK

If you find that you're sinking into the quicksand of self-hatred and desperation, it can help to get planted in the present by taking on some manageable task that you can handle competently. You might want to clean house, cook a pot of soup, or plant some flowers. Ellen says that when she feels miserable, accomplishing something helps:

I often go to my desk and answer mail, pay bills, clear the mass of papers that accumulate. Throwing things out always helps. And doing dishes—the warm water and the clarity of the task. After doing such routine tasks, I may not feel great, but at least I can feel good that I got something done.

TAKE BREAKS

When you're immersed in working through the trauma of sexual abuse, it's easy to feel that all you are is a person who has been sexually abused. You're in therapy, going to survivors' meetings, crying, raging, struggling with your partner, breaking addictions, reading, talking, and dreaming sexual abuse.

Although a time of intense involvement is often inevitable, as well as useful, it helps if you stop and appreciate how far you've come. When you feel that you haven't healed, that you still have the same basic problems, you need to remind yourself this is only a partial assessment. In reality, the severity of your problems may have lessened, and the way you handle them may be radically different.

Taking breaks can help you see that you are more than a reaction to abuse. Acknowledging the other parts of your life affirms that you are a complex, multifaceted person and that abuse issues, even if they loom over much or even most of your life, still do not gobble up every bit of it.

SELF-ESTEEM IN RELATIONSHIPS

An important part of creating a healthy self-image is being with people who mirror you positively, who believe in your strengths, your goodness, your capacity to manage your own life.

It's necessary to structure your life so that you are in contact with people who respect you, who understand and take you seriously. This is what you did not have as a child, and what you need now in order to construct healthy feelings of self-worth.

It's important to stop being with people who make you feel bad about yourself, whether it's your husband or lover, the neighbor who always takes advantage of you, someone in your original family, or your abuser. In their place, plant and nourish relationships with people who respect you and understand you.

Those who appreciate you can be friends or even just acquaintances. They can be counselors, co-workers, teachers, family, other survivors, members of a support group.

Consider yourself valuable enough to be discriminating about whom you relate to. Although you are not always in a position to cut off contact completely with people who don't respect you (for example, a teacher in a required course), weed out the ones who put you down as much as possible. Then you will hear positive things about yourself. Listen. Take it in.

I am hearing from people around me that I'm a courageous person, and that often surprises me. I don't feel that what I'm doing takes guts, just that I've *had* to do it. Hearing people say I'm courageous has made me take another look at it.

Ellen has grown to like one of her clients very much. Recently, when this woman was feeling bad about not having a lover or many close friends, Ellen reassured her that as she began to feel better about herself, she would connect more deeply with others. "You're a likable person," Ellen told her. "I like you."

The woman continued talking as though

NURTURE YOURSELF: THE TEDDY BEAR'S PICNIC

There are a million ways to nurture yourself. Choose things that make you feel good and do them often. This is not optional. It's an essential part of feeling good. Once a day, at least, do something nice for yourself.

"I love sushi. So I go out and have sushi."

"I love movies and I love to buy books. So I do a lot of both."

"I go away on the weekends to places I like."

"I set aside times in my week when I plan to come home and *not* think about incest. Or I go out with a friend and we agree not to talk about it."

"I go to a lot of hot tubs and get massages."

"I've been exercising more."

"I surround myself with people with whom I can discuss the whole of my life, that I don't have to keep any secrets from. I worked very hard to get the secret out of my life. I need to be able to talk about it with the people in my life as easily as I can ask them what kind of coffee they want."

"I'm in a support group. I have close contact with the other group members. We talk every other day. And when one of us is feeling real bad, like wanting to hurt herself or something, we call. We support each other a real lot."

"I have affirmations all over my room. They say things like: 'I do not deserve to be hurt.' 'There's nothing wrong with my body.' 'I love myself.' 'I am gentle and patient with myself.' 'I am good.' 'I forgive myself.' "

"When I come out of a heavy therapy session, no matter what it feels like, I always buy myself flowers."

"I eat a good breakfast. I try to look after myself with food. It's the least I can do."

"I write."

"I make myself a big cup of tea and curl up with a book. Or I take a really hot bath with some nice bath oil, and stay in there with a book till the water gets cold."

"I've gotten clothes that are far more colorful and flattering. I went out last year and bought myself this absolutely gorgeous emerald green dress that was very fashionable. I look very good in it, and that was a real gift for myself. That was a real step for me, not to just buy it because it was on sale."

"Working in my garden is a wonderful healing metaphor for me. I'd never done anything like that before. When we bought our house, the garden was totally overgrown. I went out with pruning shears and cut back twenty loads of debris we took to the dump. Each time I turned over a shovelful of dirt or planted something new, it felt like I was doing that for myself."

"I try to get into nature and walk and hike and ski as often as I can."

188 / CHANGING PATTERNS

Ellen hadn't said anything. "Did you hear me say 'I like you'?" Ellen asked.

The woman looked at Ellen quizzically. "No."

"Well, let's try it again," Ellen said. "I like you."

"You're different. I pay you to like me," the woman protested.

"No," Ellen responded. "You pay me to help you, to support you in your healing, to care about who you become. You can't pay me to like you. I just happen to feel that way."

The woman looked at Ellen again and nodded, taking it in just a little.

At first, the simple genuine appreciation of who you are can be so unfamiliar that you don't even notice it. Train yourself to hear the positive things people reflect back to you. They shouldn't go to waste.

THE NURTURING PARENT EXERCISE

In her book *Solving Women's Problems*, Hogie Wyckoff* presents a group exercise called "The Nurturing Parent," in which women write on a big sheet of paper what they would like their ideal nurturing parent to say to them: "I love you." "You're beautiful." "I like you just the way you are." "I'm proud of you." They use crayons and their "other" hand (the left if you're right-handed, and vice versa) to write the sentences, so they are more childlike. When their lists are finished, each woman gets up and reads these things aloud in the way she would like to hear them: warmly, lovingly, slowly, tenderly. Next, each person gives her list to a partner, who cuddles her in her lap and reads the list

over and over to her in a nurturing way. Then the partners switch.

This is a beautiful way to experience some of the nurturing you need. You can do this in groups. You can also do it with a trusted partner, friend, or counselor.

A Name of My Own: Rachel Bat Or

Some women have changed their names in order to establish their own definition of themselves. This is an ancient way that many cultures have used to mark major transformations. Rachel Bat Or, who gathered her friends together to share in a naming ceremony, experienced empowerment and renewal both from the name change and from creating the ritual.

I changed my name. It was the most healing thing I've ever done for myself. My old name was Ruthann Theodore. And I never liked it. I wanted a name that reflected who I really was. Picking "Rachel" was easy. That was my grandmother's name, my name in Hebrew, the name I should have gotten. Then a friend of mine, who speaks Hebrew, said Bat Or meant "daughter of the light," and that felt right. The light, and by that I mean my inner enlightenment, has kept me alive and has gotten me to heal myself. And I wanted to be someone's daughter. I felt like I had lost my parents. And that was very sad to me. So I changed my name to Rachel Bat Or.

I invited nine friends, women who I've known over the last nine years. Together we were a minyan.†

---

* See the "Sexual Abuse" section of the Bibliography.

---

† In Jewish tradition, a *minyan* is the minimum number of men required to hold religious services.

The first thing we did was cast a circle. We turned to each direction and invited the spirits of that direction to join us. The person facing each direction just sat where she was and said, "Welcome the spirits of the east." The east is air and dawn and springtime, the beginnings. And then each person said how I reminded them of that direction and what was in me that was strong in the same way. South is fire, noontime, summertime. It's the real burst of energy. The west is water, emotions, twilight, and autumn. It's the beginning of the ending, when things are calming down. And the north is very dark, and the earth, and the night and winter. It's the place we settle into when we take things into ourselves, the place of death and rebirth.

We read "The Sisters of Rachel," which I had written:

And the sisters of Rachel gathered around her to celebrate the naming. Long had she waited for this moment. Dreamed of it. Planned it. Sometimes doubted it would ever happen. Each sister stood and one by one spoke aloud to Rachel and the other sisters. And when they spoke, their true feelings emerged.

Rachel, you have worked hard for this moment. You have been valiant and now you shall be rewarded.

Rachel, you have survived years of not being able to feel who you are. Today you allow yourself to feel.

Rachel, you have taken care of others for many years and helped them grow. Now it is your time to be cared for, to be nurtured.

Rachel, you have not permitted the joy and pain of love to reach you. It is time

to feel that love flowing out of and into yourself.

Rachel, you have often thought of death as a reason to live. You now know that life is the only way to live.

Rachel, you have often been alone. From today on, we will be with you. You will carry our love, nurturance, feelings, life. We acknowledge and witness your valiant struggle to survive and applaud its success.

Rachel, you are now whole again.

It was very powerful to have everybody facing me, reading one of these sentences. And then the friend who helped me find the name read the Hebrew prayer used when girls are named. In English, it was:

Sustain this woman for herself,
for her friends, her lover, and
for her son;
And her name shall be called
in Israel
Rachel Bat Or.
Let us rejoice in this beautiful
and strong woman.

And then I read "I am Rachel, daughter of the light":

I am Rachel, daughter of the light.
I renounce my mother's claim to my being.
But I am not alone or motherless.
I have the light to nurture and comfort me in times of distress.
I look to the light for the answers to my dilemmas and I trust that the light will never lead me astray.
Within the light I am able to express strength and weakness; love and hatred; fear and comfort; spontaneity and rigidity;

thoughtfulness and rashness; patience
and impatience.
All of my dualities are acknowledged and
honored.
There is no part of me that is not holy in the
light.
I am Rachel, daughter of the light.

After that we all talked about our
names. Everyone had some feelings about
her name. Either she had changed it, or she
had thought about changing it, or she really
loved it.

Finally, I asked everyone to write my
old name on a piece of paper and to throw it
into a moving body of water. I didn't want to
destroy the name, but I didn't want it. I
wanted to pass it on. Then we opened the
circle and had a party.

When everyone left I really felt that I
had a new name. I'd been struggling beforehand with "What did the name mean to me?
Was I really worthy of it?" But after the ritual, I felt my sisters had given me that name
and it was truly mine now.

FEELINGS

Four survivors when asked about feelings:

"Feelings? What feelings? Are they in this room with us?"
"What did you say? Huh? I didn't quite hear you right."
"Mostly I have feelings with my head."
"I think one feeling a day is all I can handle."

We have feelings all the time, whether we're aware of them or not. Feelings arise in response to whatever is happening in our lives. A threat makes us fearful. When someone injures us, we feel hurt and angry. When we are safe and our needs are met, we feel content. These are natural responses. We may not always have the ability to recognize and understand our feelings, but they are there.

For a long time, I thought I didn't feel. I had ignored my own internal cues for so long that I was sure I didn't have any feelings to be in touch with. I thought of feelings as some mystical thing I had to concoct, rather than as an already functioning part of me I had to uncover. Any feelings I did have were something separate from me that I had to hurry up and get over, so I could shift back into the safety of neutral— being numb and in control.

When you were a child, your feelings of love and trust were betrayed. Your pain,

191

rage, and fear were too great for you to experience them fully and continue to function, so you suppressed your feelings in order to survive.

Certain feelings just went under. I stopped having them at a really young age. I stopped having physical sensations. You could beat me and it literally didn't hurt. By the time I was thirteen, I no longer felt angry. And once I stopped feeling anger, I never felt love either. What I lived with most was boredom, which is really not a feeling but a lack of feeling. All the highs and lows were taken out.

But we all need feelings. They are useful messages from which we gain insight and the ability to make wise choices. Feelings, even painful ones, are allies, telling us what's going on inside and, often, how to respond to the situations in our lives.

FEELINGS ARE A PACKAGE DEAL

When you open up to your feelings, you don't get to pick and choose. They're a package deal. One of Ellen's clients was abused by her father over the course of many years. When she and Ellen began working together, she said she felt numb; she wanted to have feelings. After a few months she was crying through every session, crying at home, crying when she went out with friends. One day she came in, started crying, and then laughed, "Well, I sure got what I asked for."

Yes. She was feeling. And the way feelings work is that you can't feel selectively. When you decide to feel, you feel what there is to feel. For this woman, there was a great deal of pain and sadness. And after that, a lot of anger. And some fear. But slipped in among these difficult feelings were pride, hope, pleasure, self-respect, and a growing contentment.

To feel, you have to be open to the full spectrum of feelings.

When I first started to grapple with the concept of feeling—and in the beginning it *was* only a concept—I ranked all the possible emotions in two lists: good feelings and bad feelings. Every time I had a feeling, I'd think, "Is this a bad feeling or a good feeling? Is this a feeling I can allow myself to have?" Then I'd either feel it or suppress it. It's been hard for me to accept that there is no right or wrong to feeling.

The more you can accept your feelings without judgment, the easier it will be for you to experience them, work with them, and learn from them.

GETTING IN TOUCH WITH FEELINGS
YOU FEEL IN YOUR BODY

Getting in touch with feelings requires that you live inside your body and pay attention to the sensations that are there. Feelings are just that—things that you feel in your body: tightening in your throat, trembling, clutching in your stomach, shortness of breath, moistness behind your eyes, moistness between your legs, warmth in your chest, tingling in your hands, fullness in your heart.

If you have ignored your body for a long time, tuning in to these sensations may seem strange and unfamiliar. Or you may be able to objectively report the sensations you feel in your body but not know what they mean.

When children are very small they don't have the conceptual ability to say "I feel scared." They say, "I feel yucky in my stomach." When adults give that sensation a name, the child learns to connect the feeling with the emotion.

If no one paid attention to what you felt and you never learned to name your feelings, you will be starting at the beginning, teaching yourself to read the messages your body gives you. (For a powerful example, see Krishnabai's story, on page 425.)

PAY ATTENTION

All of us feel in different ways, with different levels of intensity. Getting to know your feelings is part of getting to know yourself as a unique person.

Many survivors have spent their lives racing to stay just one step ahead of their feelings. Slow down enough to ask yourself, "How do I feel?" Whenever you notice yourself gliding on automatic pilot, stop and check in with your body. Are you in your body? What sensations are going on? What might those sensations be telling you?

Pay attention to your behavior also. If you are acting inappropriately, slamming around the kitchen or crying at something small, you may be having a feeling you haven't yet acknowledged. Laura remembers:

When I first started to pay attention to my feelings, the thing I felt most often was the sensation that I was lost in a dense fog. Or I'd be overwhelmed by things like boredom, confusion, desperation, hopelessness, or anxiety. What I gradually learned was that these were not actually emotions, but lids I kept on my emotions. As soon as I'd have a glimmer of the raw feeling, I'd throw a big thick blanket over it to cover it up. If I scratched beneath the boredom, there was usually anger. Anxiety covered up terror. Hopelessness and depression were rage turned inward. And so on.

If you have habitually covered your feelings, this may take place so quickly and automatically that you don't even have a chance to feel the initial emotion. When you begin to feel happy, you slide into anxiety. When you're angry, you immediately hate yourself. These patterns are different for everyone, but if you are overwhelmed by states such as depression, confusion, or guilt, there's probably a specific emotion, triggered by a specific event, underneath.

Sometimes it's a thought pattern that intercedes when you start to feel something. If you catch yourself in an old line of thinking that makes you feel bad about yourself, it probably has a feeling underneath. Thoughts like "I'll never change" or "People don't like me" usually indicate buried feelings. As a child you couldn't afford to say "I hate my father; I want to kill him," so you hated yourself instead, finding a hundred reasons why you were bad, why the abuse was your fault.

EXERCISES FOR GETTING IN TOUCH WITH YOUR FEELINGS

CREATIVITY

All the creative arts can help you connect with your feelings. Put on music and move with your feelings. Sing the blues. Cut words and pictures out of magazines and make a collage. You do not have to be an accomplished artist, dancer, or musician to express your feelings in these ways. This isn't about performance—it's about expressing yourself.

Draw Your Feelings

Amy Pine, a creative-arts therapist in Santa Cruz, California, suggests trying to draw a feeling you have. Use color, shape, texture, degree of pressure, use of space, as well as literal pictures to help you express this feeling. Stick figures are also fine. Then draw the way you want to feel. Share these drawings with someone. What do they represent? What do you notice when you look at them? Then draw a third picture that takes elements of the first through a transition that brings it to the second. What had to happen to connect them? How did you do it? Is there any correlation with what you might do in your life?

USE YOUR MIND

If you can't readily identify a feeling, your intellect can sometimes help. Say to yourself, "My lover just left me and I don't feel anything. What would someone else be feeling in this situation? What have I learned from books, movies, and friends about the feelings that might be common in this circumstance? Could it be relief? Anger? Grief? Could that be what this knot in my throat is about?"

The next two exercises, from *Learning to Live Without Violence* by Daniel Sonkin and Michael Durphy, can be helpful in beginning to identify feelings.

By this time it's like a rut in an unpaved road. Hundreds of cars drive on a dirt road. Each car travels the same path, until it becomes automatic for the tires to follow the tracks. The same is true for thoughts. If you've had a lifetime of practice diverting the first glimmer of anger into "I'm bad," you need to explore the feelings underneath that habit, consciously changing the track. (For more on changing negative thought patterns, see "Internalized Messages" on page 179.)

HONORING FEELINGS

When you first become aware of the simple, pure emotions that move through you, all you have to do is be aware: "I'm feeling a feeling." If you're sad, let yourself feel sad—without worrying, without panicking, without needing to take any action. It's okay just to feel sad. Your feelings aren't dangerous. And most people find that once they get

FEELING vs. THINKING

People commonly confuse feelings with thinking or observation. For example:

"I feel it was unfair."

"I feel you are going to leave me."

These statements are "I feel-thinking" statements rather than "I feel-emotion" statements. A good test for whether a statement is an "I feel-thinking" statement is to replace "I feel" with "I think." If it makes sense, then it is probably more of a thinking statement or observation than a feeling statement. If we change the above "I feel-thinking" statements to "I feel-emotion" statements, they might read:

"I feel hurt by what you did."

"I feel afraid that you might leave me."

WHAT ARE FEELINGS?

The following is a list of feeling words. Say them out loud. Try out different tones of voice for each word, or say it louder or softer. Pay attention to your feelings as you say each word. What sensations does it stir up? How does your body feel? Do some words fit you, but not others? Write in any other words that especially describe you. When you are finished, underline the three words that you respond to most strongly.

excited	frustrated	hurt	_____
tender	frightened	jealous	_____
sad	contented	loving	_____
lonely	depressed	elated	_____
edgy	timid	happy	_____

started, feeling isn't as bad as they feared it would be.

The more I felt, the easier it got. Feeling became less and less scary. Even though I lost my capacity to just put things aside and I felt a lot of pain, my main feeling was one of relief. I found that the fear of feeling and the stress of suppressing my feelings were more painful than the feelings themselves.

Some of the feelings—especially the old ones I had to relive—were just as awful as I thought they'd be, but they didn't last forever.

Feelings exist in and of themselves, but when you're not used to them, having an emotion you can't tie to a concrete event can be frightening.

Whenever I have a strong feeling,

I think, "There has to be a reason I'm feeling this way." And when I do figure it out, I'm incredibly relieved. "Oh! So that's what made me so angry." It's less scary for me to have feelings when I can understand them.

It is reassuring to understand why you feel a certain way or where that feeling originates, but that's not always possible. Even if you don't figure it out, the feeling still counts.

Valuing and believing your feelings takes time. But eventually you will stop seeing feelings as something separate from yourself.

I've integrated emotions into my life. I no longer have to take time out to feel. If I'm walking down the street and I feel sad, I can start crying. I don't have to wait until I get home and plan the time to do it. My emotions are a part of who I am, they're not split off from my body. I don't have to make a date to feel my emotions anymore.

It's the nature of feelings to ebb and flow, to change. You can be furious one hour, sad the next, full of love an hour later. Pain turns into rage, and rage into relief. If feelings are not jammed up, they shift with a natural rhythm that matches your experience in the world. Paradoxically, the best way to get rid of a feeling is to feel it fully. When you accept and express a feeling, it often transforms.

It's like a fire hose. When it's plugged up, the internal pressure is explosive; water bursts forth in a torrent. But when the water is flowing and the pressure is even, the water rushes steadily out through the hose and does its job.

When you're working with long-denied feelings, the transitions won't happen as quickly as they will with contemporary feelings, but all feelings, once released, eventually change.

GET SUPPORT FOR FEELING

If your feelings were denied or criticized in childhood, it may take a while before you feel safe enough to express your feelings. Many women first experience this safety with a counselor.

One day my therapist said to me, "I won't leave you no matter what you do." Before the session was over I got angry at her for the first time.

Being with people who respect your feelings and who are in touch with their own can also speed the learning process. Through feedback, example, and tenderness, you can learn to connect with your own emotions.

At first I didn't know how to have feelings by myself. I'd be numb until I saw my lover, my therapist, or a really good friend. They would draw me out, help me figure out what I was feeling. When they held or talked to me, I would squeak out a few tears or have a quiet moment of anger. I needed comforting and permission from someone else to be able to feel.

Although it's good to have loving, supportive people around when you start to connect with your feelings, over time you'll feel safe enough to open up by yourself. In your mind or out loud you can tell yourself the comforting things others have told you: "It's okay to cry." "You have a right to your anger." By calling on the part of yourself that is able to nurture you, to stand up for you, you provide a wise and kind mother for the frightened, hurt, or angry child within. You can stroke your own hair, rock yourself in a rocker, make yourself a cup of warm milk and honey, or set out pillows to punch. You become your own catalyst, midwife, permission-giver.

COMMUNICATING YOUR FEELINGS

Once you start to feel your feelings, you still may have a hard time expressing them:

My facial expressions didn't match what I said. I was always grinning. I might be down in the dumps, three feet depressed, but I kept smiling no matter what, so the outside world wouldn't know how much pain I was in, couldn't guess my secret. That way, they wouldn't fuck with me.

Or as Laura recalls:

All my life I've had this problem. I'd be overwhelmed with feeling and no one would believe me because it didn't show. A big expression of heartfelt grief for me would be several tears rolling down my cheeks. I'd be suicidal, sure I was going crazy, and my friends would maybe think I had a little something bothering me—a flea bite maybe? For a long time I thought something was wrong with me, that I had to become

dramatic in the way I expressed my feelings before they counted. I wasn't really angry unless I tore up phone books with my bare hands. Being happy without ecstatic leaps in the air didn't count.

There's no single way to show emotion. Everyone has her own individual style. But it's important to be able to express what you feel in a way that's satisfying and that communicates.

Certain ways of communicating feelings increase the likelihood that you will be heard. If you say, "I'm upset. When you are late and you haven't called, I worry. Please call me next time," you'll probably get a better response than if you say, "You're the most thoughtless person I've ever met. You never care about my feelings."

Timing is important too. If you have something to say that's important or vulnerable, don't undermine yourself by picking a time that is not conducive to real listening. Give yourself—and your friend—the benefit of a fair start.

DEVELOPING DISCRIMINATION

In an ideal world, you could express your real feelings anywhere, any time. Since we don't live in such a world, you need to make a balanced decision each time you consider whether to express your feelings. Balanced decisions take into account feelings, intellect, and judgment.

Getting angry at a police officer who pulls you over for a ticket isn't strategically sound. If you want to be intimate with someone, you have to express your feelings. But not all relationships are intimate.

EMOTIONAL RELEASE WORK

Recognizing and expressing contemporary feelings is often easier than getting in touch with buried feelings from childhood. Yet part of the healing process entails going back and feeling those feelings. (See "Grieving and Mourning," page 118.)

One useful tool for clearing out old feelings is emotional release work. Because memories and feelings are stored in the body, working through feelings physically can provide a powerful adjunct to talking. With proper safeguards and a responsible helping person to support you, emotional release work is a powerful and active way to get rid of emotional baggage.

Some therapies such as bioenergetics, rebirthing, primal therapy, and psychodrama include cathartic emotional release. Because this kind of work is active and intense (and sometimes takes people back in time to the original abuse), it is important to have the supervision of an experienced support person who is comfortable with the expression of deep pain.

EMOTIONAL RELEASE EXERCISES*

For anger: With a support person present, take a tennis racket and whack it against a mattress or piled-up cushions. Use sound and words if you feel them. Let them out. You can start with your full strength or start easy and work up to it. The support person

---

* These exercises were contributed by Amy Pine.

LEARNING TO LIVE WITHOUT VIOLENCE

An excellent book, Learning to Live Without Violence by Daniel Jay Sonkin and Michael Durphy, gives sound, practical guidelines for changing abusive patterns of expressing anger. Although it is directed toward men, it is useful for women as well. (See the "Sexual Abuse" section of the Bibliography.)

RECOGNIZING YOUR OWN ANGER

There is a difference between anger and violence. Anger is an emotion and violence is one of the behaviors that can express that emotion. Many people do not know when they are angry until they reach the explosion point. Learning to identify your own anger cues will help you control your violence. (You can modify these questions to learn to identify other emotions as well, such as sadness or fear.)

Body Signals

- How does your body feel when you are angry? (Sad? Afraid? Happy?)
- Are the muscles tense in your neck, arms, legs, face?
- Do you sweat or get cold?
- Do you breathe deeper, faster, lighter, slower?

- Do you get a headache? A stomach ache?

Behavioral Signs

How do you behave when you're feeling angry? Do you:
- Get mean? Blame others?
- Act extra nice?
- Start laughing?
- Become sarcastic?
- Withdraw?
- Break commitments? Arrive late or leave early?
- Have difficulty eating or sleeping? Eat or sleep more?

TIME-OUTS

Time-outs are a basic tool for controlling violence. They provide a structure that allows you to break abusive patterns. Time-outs not only stop the violence, they also help to rebuild trust. The rules are simple:

- **When you feel yourself beginning to get angry, say, "I'm beginning to feel angry. I need to take time out."** In this way, you communicate directly. You take responsibility for your own feelings and assure the other person you're committed to avoiding violence.

- **Leave for an hour.**

- **Don't drink, take drugs, or drive.**

- **Do something physical.** Take a walk, go for a run, or ride a bike. Exercise will help discharge some of the tension in your body.

- **Come back in an hour (no more, no less).** If you live up to your agreement, it will build trust.

- **Check in and ask the person you were angry with if they want to discuss the situation.** If you both agree, talk about what made you angry and why you needed the time out. If it's still hard to discuss, come back to it later.

ALCOHOL AND DRUGS

Alcohol and drugs do not cause violence. However, if you already have a problem with violence, they can make it worse. Alcohol and many drugs suppress feelings. You may be less aware that you are getting angry, and thus less able to take a time-out or direct your anger appropriately. Your ability to control violent impulses may also be lessened. If alcohol and drugs are a problem in your life, it is essential that you deal with your addiction if you want to stop your violent behavior.

can encourage you and cheer you on, as well as talk over your feelings with you afterward.

For grief: If you feel like crying but are stuck, allow your breath to help you connect your feelings with their expression. Exaggerate the breathing pattern—for example, long exhales, shaky inhales, adding sounds if you can. If tears do not come, it's still okay. Notice the feelings, thoughts, and sensations you do have.

For tension: Use your body. Wrestle with a friend. Chop wood. Swim.

FEAR OF FEELING

Many survivors fear that if they open up their feelings, they'll suddenly go out of control.

I was terrified of my anger. I knew that if I didn't laugh about what had happened to me, I'd go stark raving mad and kill everybody who was in my way.

Although you may indeed be very angry or very sad for a long time, those feelings don't have to be overwhelming.

As I've allowed myself to feel a little at a time, I learned that the valve to feelings was neither totally open nor totally shut—totally overwhelming or totally suppressed. I could feel bad without wanting to kill myself. I could be scared without being terrified. There was a whole range of gradations. Once I stopped trying to rein my emotions in, I had more control than I thought.

When you've repressed feelings for a long time, it's natural to be wary. But just because you have strong feelings doesn't mean you'll be unable to control yourself. Pounding pillows furiously does not mean you've gone berserk. In fact, actively expressing intense feelings in a safe, structured way makes it less likely that you'll explode. Very few murderers kill their victims after coming out of a pillow-pounding session with their counselor or support group.

CONTROLLING ABUSIVE ANGER

If you find yourself slapping your children, yelling at your co-workers, furious at your partner for the small trespasses of daily life, you're probably misdirecting your anger. Although it may be anger triggered in the present that is appropriate to the current situation, you may also be tapping into the wells of old rage from childhood. When the two blur, you tend to react in ways that are out of proportion to what's going on now.

As soon as you become aware that your feelings do not fit the present, take a break. Excuse yourself from the situation and try to separate the old from the new. If this is difficult, it will help to do some emotional release work so you have the opportunity to express your old rage in an active and focused way. (This is true for other feelings as well, such as feeling rejected, abandoned, or hurt.)

Violence is a way to assert power over others. It's effective in the short run but at too great a cost. You cannot heal from the effects of child sexual abuse while continuing to perpetrate abuse on others. If you're in a situation where you are battering or being battered, or if you find yourself repeatedly fighting or in dangerous situations, you need to stop now and get help.

PANIC

Panic is what you feel when you get scared by your own emotions and don't have the skills to calm yourself down. Or when you're trying like mad to suppress feelings or memories. Although panic sometimes seems to come out of the blue, there is always a trigger. Often it is a reminder of your abuse that you aren't consciously aware of.

Randi Taylor panicked whenever she stopped at a red light. The feeling of being boxed in and unable to move reminded her of the trapped feeling she had when she was being molested. (For more of Randi's story, see page 405.)

In a panic attack you are usually not aware of these connections. You simply feel out of control. Your heart is racing, your body feels as if it's going to explode, you want to run. Even your vision may change. You fear you're going crazy. And not understanding what is going on only makes things worse.

Laura had her first anxiety attack when she was twenty years old:

I was scared. I was scared about being scared, and the whole thing kept snowballing out of control. I was getting more and more terrified by the minute and I didn't know how to find the release valve. Somehow I had the sense to call my best friend. I remember telling her on the phone, "I feel like either I'll realize God, go insane, or kill myself." She gave me a priceless and simple piece of advice. It got me through that attack of panic and many other tight situations in the years that followed. "Breathe, Laura," she said. "Just breathe."

If you start to feel panicky, breathe. Sit with the feeling. Often women think they have to do something quickly to get away from the scared feeling, but this frenzy to escape can escalate your fear rather than relieve it. Don't rush into action. Instead, reassure yourself that this is just a feeling, powerful though it may be.

Acting out of panic makes for poor choices. Putting your hand through a glass window, driving too fast, screaming at your boss, can have long-term negative consequences.

You need to call on your judgment (what you know to be true when you're not scared) to guide you. Expressing feelings when you're extremely frightened can free you from that fear, but only if you're in a setting that's safe. A therapy group is a good place to get in touch with deeply buried feelings. Driving home isn't. You could probably drive safely while feeling some sadness or even yelling into the night, but not if you're reliving the terror of being raped. If you decide it isn't a good time to express or act on your feelings, take steps to calm yourself down.

CALMING DOWN

The most effective way to deal with panic is to catch it early. Once the panic spirals out of control, it's more difficult to stop, but at least you can keep yourself focused in a positive direction so you don't hurt yourself or others.

The important thing in calming down is to do whatever works for you, even if it seems silly or embarrassing. Through trial and error, you can develop a list of things that help. Try including comfort for as many of the senses as possible (feeling, hearing, sight, taste, smell). Actually write a list and keep it handy. You don't think as clearly or creatively when you're in a panic. If it's all written out, you only have to pick up your list, start at the top, and work your way down.

A sample list could look like this:

THINGS TO DO WHEN I'M DESPERATE

1. Breathe.
2. Get my teddy bear.
3. Put on a relaxation tape.
4. Get in my rocking chair.
5. Call Natalie. 555-9887.
6. Call Vicki if Natalie's not home. 555-6632. Keep calling down my list of support people. [Put their names and numbers here.]
7. Stroke the cat.
8. Take a hot bath.
9. Write a hundred times: "I'm safe. I love myself. Others love me," or "It's safe for me to relax now."
10. Run around the block three times.
11. Listen to soothing music.
12. Pray.
13. Breathe.
14. Yell into my pillow.
15. Watch an old movie on TV or read a mystery novel.
16. Eat Kraft macaroni and cheese.
17. Start again at the top.

DON'T KILL YOURSELF

I've been very suicidal in the process of remembering, to the point where I've had to say to myself, "You will not go to certain places because you couldn't resist the urge." I felt like the last things in my life that were important and gave me strength had been devastated. So there wasn't anything to look forward to. It's only been in the last few months that I've started to make plans again. Which means I've decided I want to live.

Sometimes you feel so bad, you want to die. The pain is so great, your feelings of self-loathing so strong, the fear so intense, that you really don't want to live. These are your authentic feelings and it is important not to deny them. It is also essential not to act on them. It's okay to feel as devastated as you feel. It's just not okay to hurt yourself. *

We have lost far too many women already. Far too many victims—both adults and children—have lacked adequate support and, out of despair, have killed them-

---

* Many of the women whose stories appear in "Courageous Women" have felt suicidal at some point in their healing. Their words can reassure you that it's worth staying alive.

Your list will be different, but number 1 on everybody's list should be breathing. Counting breaths or focusing on breathing in and out is a good way to calm down. Try breathing out for twice as long as you breathe selves. We can't afford to lose more. We can't afford to lose you. You deserve to live.

Reread the chapter on anger. You have been taught to turn that anger inward. When you feel so bad that you want to die, there's anger inside that you need to refocus toward the person or people who hurt you so badly as a child. As you get in touch with that anger, your self-hatred will dissipate. You will want to sustain your life, not destroy it.

All this takes time. In the meantime, don't kill yourself. Get help. If the first help isn't helpful, get other help. Don't give up. When you feel bad enough to want to die, it's hard to imagine that you could ever feel any other way. But you can. And will. As one survivor wrote in her journal:

I HATE LIFE! I hate myself! I hate what I do to myself. I want to crawl into the dark earth and cover myself up. I hate that I need to remember! That I need to go through the abuse over and over again in order to let it go and find life. Why should I want to live again? How do I know it won't just be more pain? How can anyone expect me to continue working towards something so unknown and intangible?

And yet I do. There is something inside me that must have incredible strength, because it has survived three major suicide attempts and lots of disillusioned and desperate times. And it's still there, keeping me going, making me work, urging me to remember and fight the guilt, to get angry, to cry, to feel, and share . . . and share . . . and share! Pushing me on toward that unknown which they call life.

If you start feeling suicidal or compelled to hurt yourself, get help right away. Make an agreement to call a counselor or a friend if you feel you can't control your actions. Call your local suicide prevention hotline. (Find the number *before* you need it).

The feelings will pass. You may think the feelings will consume you, will be absolutely unbearable. But you can learn to wait them out. It's like a difficult childbirth. The laboring woman thinks she can't handle another contraction, but she does. And then it passes.

Each time you are able to bear the pain of your feelings without hurting yourself, each time you are able to keep safe, to reach out for help, to befriend yourself through the anguish, you have built up a little more of the warrior spirit. You have fought the brainwashing of the abusers and won the battle. You have not let them destroy you.

in. With less oxygen flooding your system, you naturally calm down. (See the belly breathing, grounding, and relaxation exercises on pages 214–215.)

CREATE A SAFE SPOT

It's a good idea to create a safe spot in your house, a place you can go when you're scared. Make an agreement with yourself that as long as you're in that spot, you won't hurt yourself or anyone else—you'll be safe. And make an agreement that if you start to feel out of control and afraid of what you might do, you'll go to that spot and stay there, breathing one breath at a time until the feeling passes.

Your safe spot might be a window seat on the stairway, your bed, or a favorite reading chair. Or it might be a hiding place where no one can find you. One woman spent the night sleeping in her closet on top of her shoes, something she'd done as a small child to comfort herself in a house where no place was safe.

Take your own nurturing seriously, no matter how odd it may look. When all else fails, Laura's been known to head for bed with her teddy bear and a baby bottle full of warm milk.

CHANGE YOUR ENVIRONMENT

Consciously changing your environment can sometimes snap you out of panic. This can be as simple as leaving your bedroom and walking into the kitchen to make tea. Or you can leave your house and take a walk down the block. If you're out in nature, looking up at the stars or trees can give you a sense of perspective.

Sometimes the things that upset you are sensory reminders of past abuse. The smell of a certain cologne, the tone of someone's voice, the sound of corduroy rubbing together, can trigger real anxiety.

One day I was in the kitchen, getting more and more depressed. I started trying to calm myself down, telling myself, "Okay, you're doing fine. This'll pass. It always does." That didn't help at all. I'm beginning to know how

to take care of myself, so I just went back to the basics. I reminded myself to breathe, asked myself when I'd eaten, started cutting up vegetables for dinner —and felt worse. Finally I noticed that the light in the kitchen was really dim. I turned on an overhead light and felt better right away. That kind of dim light always makes me feel terrible. It reminds me of the house I grew up in.

By becoming aware of these cues, you will be better equipped to take care of yourself when you encounter them.

REACH OUT

Sometimes it's hardest to reach out when you need it the most, but give yourself a loving push to break out of your isolation. If you're with a trustworthy person, you can ask for a hug or to be held. If you're alone, call someone. It's a good idea to arrange this beforehand. When you're in that panicky place, you sometimes feel alienated, unsure why anyone would want to know you, let alone help you. If you're in a support group or in therapy, arrange to call a group member or your therapist. Make a contract with a friend that you'll call each other when you're in need. This may be the last thing you feel like doing, but remind yourself that you made the agreement for just this kind of circumstance, that it really is a good idea (even if you can't remember why), and then pick up the phone and dial.

SOME THINGS TO AVOID

Almost anything that works is fair game in dealing with panic, but there are a few things you should avoid.

- Don't enter stressful or dangerous situations.
- Stay off the road.
- Don't drink or abuse drugs.
- Avoid making important decisions.
- Don't hurt yourself or anyone else.

AFTER YOU COME DOWN

When you're on the other side of an attack of panic, self-hatred, or despair, relax and rest a bit. Such emotional intensity is exhausting and you need to replenish your energy. When you feel balanced again, try to determine what triggered it.

- What was the last thing you remember before you felt overwhelmed?
- Where were you? Who were you with?
- Was there anything disturbing that happened to you in the last day or two? (An upset at work? With a friend? A lover? Did you get a disturbing phone call? Piece of mail?)
- Was there a glimmer of any other kind of feeling before you lost touch with yourself? Is this something you've felt before?
- Are you under any unusual stresses? Time pressures? Money pressures?
- Were there thoughts in your mind that you quickly pushed away because they were uncomfortable? Were they old, familiar ones?
- Do any of these things remind you of your abuse in any way?

Sometimes questions like these can help you find the roots. It may take a series of episodes with similar dynamics before you are able to pinpoint the source, but it's worth the work. This kind of analysis can help you avoid getting swept up in the same cycle the next time. (For in-depth examples of how two survivors dealt with panic, read Evie Malcolm's and Randi Taylor's stories in the "Courageous Women" section.)

POSITIVE FEELINGS CAN BE SCARY TOO

Over time, your positive feelings will increase. Happiness, excitement, satisfaction, love, security, and hope will appear more frequently. Although these are "good" feelings, you may not be comfortable with them at first.

For many survivors, positive feelings are scary. As a child, happiness often signaled a disaster about to occur. If you were playing with your friends when your uncle called you in and molested you, if you were sleeping peacefully when your father abused you, if you were having Sunday dinner at your grandparents' when you were taken by surprise and humiliated, you learned that happiness was not to be trusted. Or if you pretended to be happy when you were suffering inside, happiness may feel like a sham to you still.

Even the idea that you might, at some time, feel good can be threatening. One woman said she dared not hope. As a child she hoped day after day that her father might come home cheerful, might be nice to her, might stop abusing her. And day after day, she was disappointed. Finally, out of self-preservation, she gave up hope.

Sometimes peacefulness and contentment are the most disconcerting feelings of all. Calm may be so totally unfamiliar that you don't know how to relax and enjoy it. Unexpected good feelings can be hard to come to terms with.

I'd been unhappy all my life. When I remembered the incest, I finally knew why, but I was *still* unhappy. Healing was a terrifying and painful experience and my life was as full of struggle and heartache as it had always been. Several years after I started therapy, I began to feel happy. I was stunned. I hadn't realized that the point of all this work on myself was to feel good. I thought it was just one more struggle in a long line of struggles. It took a while before I got used to the idea that my life had changed, that I felt happy, that I was actually content.

Learning to tolerate feeling good is one of the nicest parts of healing. Once you get started, you may find that you want to do it a lot. Take all the opportunities that come your way. A quiet moment drinking tea in the morning. Reading your child a bedtime story. A totally engrossing movie. A call from a friend just to say hello. An omelette that turned out perfect. Notice these things. Take the risk of admitting that you feel good—first for a moment, then for longer.

Being liked, loved, and appreciated has felt threatening for many survivors. Visibility is a kind of exposure. Appreciation can bring up feelings of shame. The contrast between someone's high opinion of you and your own self-hatred can be wrenching. And feeling positive about yourself—feeling worthy, deserving, and proud—may seem fantastically out of reach. But again, these feelings are so pleasant that you'll find it's worth getting used to them.

When someone pays you a compliment, try saying "Thank you" instead of immediately rattling off a list of your faults. If you receive a present, say "This makes me feel really good." If you get a raise, say "I like being acknowledged for my work."

Although you've experienced a lot of pain in your life, you have a multitude of opportunities for experiencing wonderful feelings as well. Take them. You deserve to feel good.

YOUR BODY

If someone said, "What do you feel in your arm?" I would have had no idea what they were even talking about. If I touched it, I felt my arm with my hand. But I couldn't get inside of it. I could only touch the skin from the outside. I couldn't have felt my heart beating. I couldn't experience anything from inside my body, because *I* wasn't inside my body.

—Rachel Bat Or

When you talk about your experience of abuse, when you share your feelings verbally, you are doing important releasing. But to fully heal, this release must happen in your body as well. The way you breathe, the way you eat, the way you feel, in fact your entire relationship to your body was affected by the abuse. You were abused on many levels, and healing must take place on many levels as well.

Children initially learn about themselves and the world through their bodies. Hunger, fear, love, acceptance, rejection, support, nurturing, terror, pride, mastery, humiliation, anger—all of what you know as emotion —began with sensation and movement on the body level. As a child, your body was the means by which you learned about trust, intimacy, protection, and nourishment. But when you were abused, you learned that the world was not a safe place where your needs would be met.

When children experience the world as unsafe, they do things to adapt. All the prob-

207

lems survivors experience with their bodies —splitting, numbing, addictions, and self-mutilation, to name a few—began as attempts to survive.

You cut off from your body for good reasons, but now you need to heal that separation. You need to move from estrangement from your body to integration, to move from self-hate and rejection of your body to self-love and acceptance.

FROM HATING YOUR BODY TO LOVING YOUR BODY

Sexual abuse was done to you through your body. Since many survivors blame their bodies for responding, for being attractive, for being womanly, for being small, for being large, for being vulnerable, for being susceptible to stimulation and pleasure, even for feeling anything, learning to love your body is a major element of healing.*

THE ONE-INCH EXERCISE

Sandra Butler, who leads Writing As Healing workshops for incest survivors in San Francisco, has a wonderful exercise for beginning to accept and nurture your body:

---

* It's not just survivors who have trouble loving their bodies. Most women have been taught to hate themselves. For help in this area, we recommend *Transforming Body Image* by Marcia Germaine Hutchinson. See the "Your Body" section in the Bibliography for more information.

the one-inch exercise. If switching from self-hatred to self-love seems impossible to you, begin one inch at a time. Think about one inch of your body that you feel is quite lovely. It doesn't need to be a sexual part, but simply one inch you feel good about. It may be your throat, your knee, the skin behind your ear. Find a small part of your body that you can love. For the next week, pay attention to that part of your body. Stroke it. Buy it gifts—perhaps a bit of satin fabric or a jar of oil. The following week, expand that inch to an adjacent inch and do the same thing. Repeat this process, slowly increasing the reclaimed territory of your body, inch by precious inch.

AFFIRMATIONS

Try writing a sentence that feels both true and positive about you and your body. You can begin with ones most easy to embrace and then move to harder ones as you gain confidence. Some examples:

"My body is strong and healthy and serves me well."

"I appreciate my legs for taking me wherever I want to go."

"My hands are competent and can do many things, like hold my baby, type, make egg rolls, dig in my garden. I am grateful for such good hands."

"I am radiant. My loving spirit shines through my face."

"I have a well-shaped head. My short hair looks good on me."

You can say these affirmations to yourself, write them in your journal, tape them to the wall, or slip them into your wallet.

LOOK IN THE MIRROR

Another way to counteract the distorted messages you received is to look in the mirror —and really look. Take a little time for yourself when you won't be interrupted. Look at your face and also at your body. Don't look in order to criticize. Look simply in order to be introduced, to make the acquaintance of your body, to see this body in which you live. This time look with *your* eyes, not through the eyes of the abuser, the society, the lover, the mother, the judge. Look as if you were an artist, a painter. Look to see, not to judge. Do this five minutes a day and then write about the experience.

DRAW YOURSELF

Another way to reconceive your image of your body is to draw it. Artemis is an artist (her story is on page 431). While she was remembering her abuse, she drew an extensive series of self-portraits. "At first, the agony was drawn all over them, but bit by bit, they became softer. In the beginning, the lines were hard and black and angular, but then I would force myself to sit in front of a mirror and draw my own body nude, and try to draw it with all the sensual softness of a female body. I would use charcoal, which is very soft, and I'd keep drawing until I could draw my body very soft and very sensuous. And I learned to love my body through that."

NURTURE YOURSELF

Treating your body with care is another way to love yourself. Relax in baths, soak in hot tubs, or take saunas. Build a sweat lodge. Use bath oil, body lotion, powder.

Just paying attention to your body while you wash can make a difference. One woman began to feel more sensual this way. "My therapist suggested that when I take a shower in the morning, not to treat myself like I'm scrubbing the kitchen table—that I take some pleasure in my body, to feel the curves of my body with the soap and the water."

You can buy yourself warm socks, cozy pajamas, flannel sheets, silk underwear— whatever feels good. You can also wear things that are soothing to areas of your body that have been especially traumatized. One woman, who survived being strangled, felt particularly tense and vulnerable in her neck. Wearing soft, lovely scarves was a way she took care of herself. She liked the feeling of the extra warmth and gentle protection.

FROM SPLITTING TO BEING IN YOUR BODY

One of the common ways children deal with the unbearable experience of being sexually abused is to flee from the experience, to split.* Most survivors have experienced this at least to some degree. In its milder form, you live exclusively on the mental level, in your thoughts, and aren't fully present. At its most extreme, you literally leave your body. This feat, which some yogis work for decades to achieve, comes naturally to chil-

---

* See the footnote on page 42.

dren during severe trauma. They cannot physically run away, so they leave their bodies. Many adult survivors still do this whenever they feel scared.

> I do feel a good part of the time that I'm not present in my body. It's as if inside, from my neck down, it's hollow, and there's this ladder, and depending on how things are going, I'm climbing up the ladder, and this little person that is me is sitting in my head, looking out through my eyes.

Many survivors describe splitting as a sensation of floating above themselves, looking down at their bodies from the ceiling:

> It's like I'd actually rise up out of my body. I could feel myself sitting in a chair, and I could feel myself floating up out of my body. That's exactly what it is, like being suspended in midair. I know that my body is in the chair, but the rest of me is out of my body.

Others go somewhere they can't identify: "I can't tell you what happens when I leave my body because I'm not there."

You may consciously choose to split, but sometimes splitting happens spontaneously when you don't want it to—when you're in the middle of a serious conversation, for example, or making love.

TO STAY IN YOUR BODY

- **Remember to breathe.** Often when we're scared, we stop breathing. The simplest and most basic way to stay in your body, or to return once you've split, is to breathe.
- **Pay attention to when you split.** What's going on? What's the last thing that hap-

pened before you split? What feelings arose that were threatening?

- **Be willing to feel.** Listen to your fears and your needs. Be gentle and responsive to yourself. This makes it safer and more possible to stay present.
- **Make the commitment not to split unconsciously.** Make every effort to notice when you're splitting, and consciously decide whether you want to do so or not.
- **Reach out.** Splitting is a lonely, solitary condition. Telling someone what's going on can bring you back. Make an agreement with your close friends that they will notice when your attention seems to wander, and will ask you what's happening.

FROM NUMBNESS TO FEELING

Numbness is another way not to feel. During the trauma of sexual abuse, children often numb themselves, just as surgery patients are anesthetized to avoid excruciating pain. Like splitting, numbing physical sensations was a sensible and effective defense at the time. You blocked out pain, as well as conflicting sensations of arousal. But numbing no longer serves your needs.

To experience more feeling in your body, start paying more attention to physical sensations. Watching your breathing is a good place to start. Just allowing yourself to feel the breath entering and leaving your body, to feel the air through your nostrils, to feel your chest and abdomen expand and contract, to feel the small sensory components of breathing, can bring your body back to life.

Extend this awareness of detail to any common activity: walking, brushing your teeth, petting the cat, drinking a glass of water. Starting with the less threatening physical experiences, you can pay attention to how your body feels. You can register cold and hot, texture, thirst, taste, pressure, tingling, the pumping of your heart.

NURTURING TOUCH

Self-massage is a wonderful way to become aware of body feelings, to release tension, and just to feel good. Try giving yourself a foot or neck massage.

You can also seek safe, nonsexual touch from others. Everyone needs touch. You can talk forever, but some wounds are in a place more primal than words. You need circumstances that are safe enough to allow you to begin to let go of your protective numbness.

You can receive safe touching with friends who are comfortable holding or stroking you in nonsexual ways, with a counselor who is at ease with touching, or with members of a support group or workshop who agree to share safe, nurturing touch.

If you haven't received a massage by a sensitive, skilled practitioner, this can be a powerful way to wake up your body. Be sure to find someone who is trustworthy so that there's no chance of inappropriate touch or reabuse.

If you tell your masseuse that you are healing from child sexual abuse, you may feel more free to cry, to stop the massage, or just to breathe into your feelings. You can set limits, saying you don't want to be touched in a certain way or in a certain place. Although it may feel awkward at first, stating your needs directly is a mature way to take care of yourself.

Massage sometimes releases intense feelings. Some women have felt overwhelmed either during or after a massage, especially if they aren't accustomed to the vulnerability of being touched deeply. If you're planning a massage for the first time, you may want to start with a foot massage or just neck and shoulders. You may also want to arrange a session with your counselor or a supportive friend shortly afterward, so you will have a chance to talk about your feelings.

If you start to go numb when you are touching yourself, or when someone else is touching you, stop and try to isolate your thoughts or feelings at the moment the numbness started. Talk about your feelings or write them down. It's important not to continue the touching while you are numb. That's what happened during the abuse, and it won't help to repeat that same pattern.

FROM IGNORING YOUR BODY TO LISTENING TO YOUR BODY

Many survivors have decided that their bodies are more trouble than they're worth and have chosen to ignore them. Ignoring body needs includes working when you're sick, failing to put on a sweater when you're cold, or waiting to pee until you've finished just one more task.

This kind of negligence can have serious consequences. A former deputy sheriff, who had to retire early because of a back injury, describes the events that led up to her disability:

I never was in touch with my body. The reason I ended up having back surgery is because I completely ignored serious symptoms for six months.

I had a doctor. I had medical coverage. There was nothing keeping me from the doctor except that I didn't want it to be true, because I had something else I wanted to do at that time, and as far as I was concerned, my back was betraying me. I wanted to go to school and I wanted to graduate. And I did.

It wasn't until years later that I realized I believed my body had betrayed me by having pleasurable feelings when my brothers were abusing me. Therefore I hated my body, and if it did anything I didn't want it to do, like be hungry at an inappropriate time, or be in pain at a time that was inconvenient to me, I would simply ignore it. And I did that to the point of nerve damage in my leg and a ruptured disk.

Our bodies are a great source of wisdom. Listening to body messages is not only critical for maintaining physical health, it is also necessary for being in touch with your feelings and your needs. Our bodies are our essential connection to life.

To listen to your body, you have to be willing to feel. Although sometimes this means being willing to feel fear or pain, it also means being willing to take the time to feel good. If you're used to ignoring your body, this can be a radical, yet pleasant change.

I always took a shower the very last thing at night before sleep. Showers for me are a total pleasure. Unless something very serious is bothering me, I feel relaxed afterwards. But even if I needed a shower earlier in the day, even if I was tense, chilled, or irritable, I wouldn't take one until I had done all my work.

One evening around seven o'clock I decided to take a shower even though I still had a lot of homework to do that night. I showered, put on pajamas and a robe, made myself a cup of tea, and sat down to study. It was so pleasant. I was warm, relaxed, and productive. Feeling good wasn't incompatible with working. And feeling good didn't always have to come last on my list.

EXERCISE

Our bodies are designed for motion. You don't have to be a marathon runner or an Olympic swimmer to enjoy moving. Even simple walking is good exercise. Moving stimulates your circulation, massages your internal organs, stretches and strengthens your muscles, and energizes you. Exercise is also a great way to discharge tension, work through emotional blocks, release anger, and gain self-esteem. As Jayne Habe relates:

I swam again today. It feels so good to be back in the water, to be pushing my body to get strength. I look at it as being in training for my life.

If you're not accustomed to exercising, choose an activity you think you might enjoy, and start with just a little. It's more inviting to start small and work up than it is to set unreasonable goals, strain muscles, exhaust yourself, and give up. Exercise is not another ordeal to be endured. Rather it is a healthy part of living in your body.

INSOMNIA

Insomnia is common for many people under stress, and survivors are certainly under enough stress. Added to that, many survivors were abused when they slept, as they were falling asleep, or in their beds. Many have nightmares or recover terrifying memories in sleep.

If you suffer from insomnia, there are ways you can help yourself:

- Drink warm milk or chamomile tea before going to bed.
- Take a warm bath before bed.
- Exercise early in the day, rather than in the evening.
- Don't do upsetting things right before bed.
- Don't go to bed before you're tired.
- Give yourself thirty minutes early in the day as your worry time. Write down your obsessions in a room other than your bedroom.
- Put on quiet, soothing music or relaxation tapes, or turn on the television very low. Visualize sleepy, relaxing things.
- Make the environment feel safer. Put locks on your windows. Hang pictures of your friends on the wall next to your bed.
- If masturbation or sex is not anxiety-filled for you, it may help you relax.

If all these fail and you still can't sleep, don't fight it. Don't get mad at yourself, tell yourself how badly you need your sleep, or remind yourself of all you have to do the next day. Decide that lying quietly and listening to soft music will at least rest your body and that you won't die by missing a few nights' sleep. Or get up, put on a bathrobe, and read a book you really like (or something really bor-

ing). Write in your journal. Draw a picture. Call someone in another time zone. Do your income tax. Sew your child a Halloween costume. The night can be a quiet, special time just for you.

Insomnia is a result of stress, and it can lead to further stress. The important thing is to respond to it in ways that soothe and nurture you, even if you're not sleeping. In time, as you heal, you'll sleep more easily.

FROM PHYSICAL ILLNESS TO A HEALTHIER BODY

Some survivors were abused in ways that have left them with physical illnesses. For others, the ways they coped led to illness. Migraines, environmental illnesses, pelvic disorders and problems with sexual organs, asthma, arthritis, and many other illnesses can result from early trauma and stress.* Sometimes an area of your body that was injured will develop problems later—such as pain in your jaw if you were orally raped. You may also experience more subtle problems such as chronic tiredness, low resistance, susceptibility to colds and flu.

However, illness does not necessarily stem from abuse. People who were not sexually abused develop arthritis, and environmental illness is increasing dramatically because of the increase in toxic pollution. Some schools of alternative healing "blame the victim" by insisting that any physical ill-

---

* Read Gizelle's story on page 446 for a dramatic example.

EXERCISES FOR CONNECTING WITH YOUR BODY

Some of the exercises in this section require a partner. Others can be done alone.*

BELLY BREATHING

Belly breathing is a great thing to do when you panic—when you're scared that you may stop breathing altogether, or close to it. Your breath becomes shallow, uneven, and catches high up in your chest. To belly breathe, lie on your back and place one hand on your stomach, one hand on your chest. If the hand on your chest is the one moving up and down, you're breathing from your chest. Practice sending your breath deeper into your belly, until the hand on your stomach begins to rise and fall. Consciously blow the air out of your mouth, and let your belly refill with air.

RELAXATION EXERCISES

I. Lie on your back, or in any other comfortable position. Make sure your clothing isn't constricting you in any way. Take off your shoes; undo your belt. Take a few deep slow breaths and release the air. Starting at your feet, focus your attention there and feel any tension in your feet. With

your next natural exhalation, let the tension go, and let your feet relax. Next, move to your ankles. Notice any tension there. As you exhale, release any tightness. Continue the same exercise, working your way up your body—feet, ankles, calves, thighs, buttocks, genitals, stomach, chest, back, shoulders, arms, hands, neck, face, head —until your body becomes more and more relaxed. This is wonderful just before sleep.

II. Find a comfortable position, sitting with your feet on the floor or standing. Turn your attention to your breathing, watching the inhale, the exhale, and the space in between. Don't force any change in your breathing, just watch it. Feel your body expand away from the center and release back toward the center. In time, allow your breath to deepen, moving deeper down into your abdomen. Let your belly be soft. Take in good things as you breathe in (hope, self-love, courage) and let go of things you don't want as you breathe out (fear, tension, self-criticism). Do this for five or ten minutes.

GROUNDING EXERCISES

I. Imagine that you are a tree sending your roots deep into the earth. Imagine these roots reaching down through your legs, through the bottom of your feet, into the earth, all the way to its center, where they're firmly planted.

II. Walking, especially without shoes (weather and terrain permitting), can be very grounding and centering. The beach and the woods are both good places. Your neighborhood is also fine if it's safe.

---

* Most of the exercises in this section were contributed by Amy Pine, a creative-arts therapist in Santa Cruz, California. We would like to thank her for helping to identify and conceptualize material throughout this chapter.

Breathe deeply and feel your contact with the ground. See what is around you. You can decide ahead of time how long you want to walk, and experiment with the pace.

III. Stand facing a partner and place your hands together, palm to palm. At a signal "go," push against each other as hard as you can. Take turns trying to back each other up to the end of the room (or yard). (Make sure there are no obstacles behind you.) Either person can stop the exercise if he or she feels uncomfortable. Afterward, check your body and see what you notice. Discuss your reactions. Try the same exercise back-to-back. This is not a competitive exercise. It should be done in a spirit of support, the goal being for each person to feel solid and grounded. This can also be a good exercise for getting back into your body.

TO GET BACK IN YOUR BODY

I. Sit or stand with your feet solidly planted on the floor. Make eye contact with a partner and really see her. Don't space out. Squeeze your partner's hands if your attention starts to waver. Simply be there together, with the partner mirroring (following and imitating) your breathing pattern as it changes. Talk about how you feel as you do this exercise. Notice any changes.

II. Explore the full range of movement in your joints. Beginning with your fingers, wrists, and elbows, moving to your shoulders, spine, hips, knees, and so forth, move through the joints in your body.

CONNECTING WITH BODY SENSATIONS

I. Begin a movement journal. Pick a body part and spend five to ten minutes allowing that part to move in any way it wants. The rest of your body may join in, but keep your primary focus on your chosen part. There is no right or wrong way to do this—the movement can be very small, almost still, and silent. It can also be large or connected to a sound. You can choose a toe, a hand, wrist, eyes, mouth, or pelvis—any part. Give your attention to what the movement feels like or has to say to you. After five or ten minutes, write down what happened for you. Share your writing with a trusted person.

II. Choose a theme that is relevant in your life—being open/closed, strong/weak, hiding/reaching out, depression/elation, centered/off-centered. Ask a partner to sit with you as a witness while you explore this theme through movement. You don't have to be a dancer—everyone moves. Afterward, talk about it together, sharing your feelings and observations. (The witness should be careful not to interpret the mover's experience.)

III. Give your body parts a voice; let them talk. A partner can ask questions in order to get more information and explore with you. For instance, the stomach might say, "I'm all knotted up. I've been tense for the past week. I'm sick of everything!" Your friend might ask, "What are you sick of?" Allow the stomach to answer. If you don't know for sure, guess. Give yourself permission to improvise. See what comes out.

ness is a result of some emotional attitude, and claim that if the patient would only work through the emotions, she would no longer be sick. This is simplistic and damaging.

Yet there sometimes is an emotional component to illness. If you are suffering from an illness that you suspect has its roots in your abuse, becoming aware of its origins gives you a chance to work with those aspects. Although traditional doctors are sometimes skeptical about the emotional component of illness, too many people have experienced a direct correlation to ignore the potential benefits of emotional work on physical healing.

There are many alternative means of healing available today, many of which work well on both the physical and emotional levels. Acupuncture, chiropractic, homeopathy, massage, meditation, and visualization all can be valuable. If you are under the care of a physician, you may want to discuss some of these possibilities. Doctors are becoming increasingly open to the benefits of less conventional treatments. Sometimes you can design a treatment plan in which you utilize both traditional and nontraditional methods.

FROM ADDICTION TO FREEDOM

Addictions are ways to escape, to find relief, to protect yourself, to gain control, to feel better. Addictions can also destroy your body, cut you off from your feelings, tear down your self-esteem, interfere with relationships, and sometimes kill you. To break an addiction, you must *want* to change. You must be honest about the extent of the problem, identify the purpose it serves, and see it as both a survival tool and a self-destructive pattern. Then get help and break the habit.

ALCOHOLISM AND DRUG USE

Many survivors are addicted to alcohol or drugs. Drugs and alcohol are temporarily effective ways to numb feelings, suppress memories, and escape from pain. Yet healing requires that you experience your feelings and look clearly at your life. *You can't do this if you're addicted to alcohol or drugs. To heal from child sexual abuse, you will have to break your addictions.*

Even if you are not addicted, you may still be using drugs or alcohol as a way to avoid feelings. This too will block your healing.

Breaking addictions is very difficult to do in isolation. Alcoholics Anonymous and Narcotics Anonymous have been tremendously effective in helping people break their addictions to alcohol and drugs. Depending on how far your addiction has progressed, you might also need the help of a residential treatment program.

If you are the child of alcoholic parents (as many survivors are), meetings for Adult Children of Alcoholics can help you identify patterns common to alcoholic families. If you are the partner of an alcoholic (or addict), Al-Anon can offer valuable support. For more on these and other twelve-step programs, see "Healing Resources," page 458.

QUITTING SMOKING

Quitting smoking is not a requirement for healing from child sexual abuse, but it can be a potent way to affirm your own power and choose to have a healthier body. Since smoking suppresses feelings, quitting is a good way to get more in touch with yourself. It's also a very tangible goal. So much about healing from sexual abuse is not concrete. Quitting smoking has visible results that can do wonders for both your body and your self-esteem.

It is difficult to break more than one addiction at a time. So if you are dependent on both alcohol (or drugs) and tobacco, tackle the alcohol and drugs first. They interfere directly with your healing in a way smoking does not. But do consider quitting cigarettes as one more way to choose life and health.

EATING DIFFICULTIES

Before we begin to talk about problems with eating, it is essential to say that there is no ideal size or shape for a woman's body. Some of us are tall, some are short; some are angular, some are rounded; some are small, some are large; some are firm, some are soft. And none of these qualities are better or worse in themselves.

Our culture sends out a strong message that women should look a certain way. That way has numerous characteristics, ranging from light-colored skin to long eyelashes, and one of its most relentless characteristics is thinness. The mass media today praise thinness and condemn large women. This is oppressive to anyone who isn't slim. We don't want to perpetuate that standard.* What we are talking about are problems *with eating— how we eat or don't eat, and what that means to us. We are not talking about body size.*

---

* We recommend *Shadows on a Tightrope* by Lisa Schoenfielder and Barb Wieser, a powerful anthology from the Fat Liberation movement. See the "Your Body" section of the Bibliography.

COMPULSIVE EATING

Survivors eat compulsively for many reasons. Some women binge in order to numb their feelings. While they are totally involved with eating, shoveling spoonful after spoonful of ice cream into their mouths, other pains, fears, and hungers recede. Compulsive eating is an escape. Although you may hate yourself in an hour, you get relief in the moment.

If you are hurting, eating compulsively may be the only way you know to nurture yourself. You need to be held, you need time alone, you need more fulfilling work. But you're not accustomed to recognizing these needs and responding to them, so you eat. You give yourself food as a substitute for other needs.

Some women overeat for protection. Our culture perpetuates the myth that if you are large, you'll be safer, because you'll be less sexually desirable and will therefore avoid sexual advances or assault. Although this is not true, many women feel less vulnerable when they are large. Children are small. When you were a child you were abused, and so now you feel more substantial in a large body. You feel more visible, sure that you take up space. Or, conversely, you may feel more invisible, less likely to attract attention.

Although body size is not necessarily related to how or how much you eat—many women are naturally large or small regardless of their eating patterns—some women purposefully eat large quantities of food to make themselves larger. One survivor decided in her late teens that the only way to avoid sexual abuse was to get fat. She didn't like sweets very much, but she forced herself to eat them—and everything else—until she got to be a size that she thought was large enough to be unattractive.

Look at why you eat the way you do. What does it give you? What needs does it meet? Don't condemn yourself for having tried to meet those needs through food. Instead, begin to honor them in healthier ways.

If you eat in order to be larger so that you'll feel safe or have more power in the world, think of other ways you might gain that same protection or power. If you eat to avoid unwanted advances, it's essential to learn to say no. "No" is simple and direct. Practice saying it frequently. In most situations, a firm "no" will protect you at least as well as eating, and usually better.

ANOREXIA AND BULIMIA

Anorexia and bulimia thrive in our culture, which exalts thinness and despises fat. Girls and women internalize this attitude and are terrified of being large. Sexual abuse then compounds the problem.

Many girls who have been sexually abused begin to suffer from anorexia when they go through puberty. They falsely believe that if they don't grow breasts, develop full hips, become curvy, they won't be attractive, and then no one will force them into being sexual. For these girls, it's understandable that it would be especially frightening to become a woman. They think, if this is what happens to children, how much worse will it be as a woman?

Anorexia, like compulsive eating, is an attempt to protect yourself, to assert control. By strictly controlling what you do and don't take into your body, you are trying to regain the power that was taken from you as a child.

Not eating, or eating too little to sustain health, is also a way of saying no to life. If life has given you abuse, fear, pain, and humili-

ation, this attitude is understandable. With anorexia, you are not instantly killing yourself, but you eat only enough not to die. And sometimes not even that.

Bulimia is a pattern of eating and throwing up, or binging and throwing up. You may have begun this pattern because you didn't want to gain weight, or you may have felt a compulsion to vomit that you've never understood.

Bulimia, like anorexia, is an attempt to control what happens to your body. Throwing up is a way of saying no. As children, many survivors had fingers, penises, and objects shoved into their body openings. You may have had a penis shoved into your mouth. You may have gagged or vomited. If you're still vomiting, you may be trying to get those things out of your body.

RESOURCES FOR ANOREXIA AND BULIMIA

American Anorexia/Bulimia Association
133 Cedar Lane
Teaneck, NJ 07666
(201) 836-1800

ANAD
National Association of Anorexia Nervosa & Associated Disorders
P.O. Box 7
Highland Park, IL 60035
(312) 831-3438

ANRED
Anorexia Nervosa & Related Eating Disorders
P.O. Box 5102
Eugene, OR 97405
(503) 344-1144

The problem, of course, is that food is actually nourishing to you. And repetitive throwing-up robs your body of important nutrients, as well as damaging your teeth and digestive system. Ultimately, it can kill you. It is essential that you establish the ability to say no in other ways.

In a workshop for survivors who also had eating problems, Ellen helped one woman make a dramatic breakthrough in her struggles with bulimia:

> After one survivor read her writing, some painful and humiliating memories began to surface. She felt a strong urge to vomit. If this had been a woman who rarely vomited, I would have grabbed a bowl and told her to feel free. Vomiting, if we do it *very* rarely, can be a cathartic release. But since this woman was bulimic, vomiting would have been just one more repetition of a self-destructive behavior. Instead, I encouraged her to get that penis out of her mouth another way. She was terrified and shaking, recoiling into a small childlike bundle. But with encouragement, she gradually sat up and began to say no. Bit by bit she got louder, until she was pounding the pillow in front of her with passionate force, screaming. "NO! Get that out of me! You can't put anything in me that I don't want! NO. NO. NO!" She screamed and pounded to exhaustion and then leaned back. Sweating, trembling, and smiling, she looked at us and said, "That felt a lot better than throwing up."

Anorexia and bulimia are dangerous, life-threatening patterns. If you're caught in either one, you need immediate skilled help so that you can sustain your body while you heal your emotions and your spirit.

FROM SELF-MUTILATION TO SELF-CARE

Many survivors have hurt themselves physically—carving into their bodies with knives, burning themselves with cigarettes, or repeatedly injuring themselves. It is natural that survivors struggle with self-abuse. As children they were indoctrinated to abuse, and now they continue the pattern themselves, never having known other choices.

Self-mutilation provides an intense feeling of relief and release that many survivors crave. It is also an attempt at control, a type of punishment, a means of expressing anger, and a way to have feelings. Self-abuse is a way to re-create the abusive situation, producing a familiar result.

One woman suffered from severe nighttime attacks of terror and vaginal pain. When she could stand it no longer, she would insert objects into her vagina and hurt herself. Immediately afterward, she would feel relief and fall asleep.

At first glance this might seem incomprehensible, but like other coping mechanisms, it had its own intrinsic logic. When this woman was a child, she went to bed every night terrified that this would be one of the nights when her father would abuse her. She would lie sleepless until he did come in—and torture her by putting objects in her vagina or by burning her. Only after he had left could she sleep, knowing that her agony was over for that night.

This woman had no explanation for her actions. She only knew that after the pain came relief and sleep, states of being she was able to achieve no other way. Once she began to understand the connection to her childhood abuse, she took the first steps in stopping this self-destructive compulsion.

Self-mutilation is not always obvious. One survivor hid it under the guise of accidents:

> One of the only ways for me to get attention and be taken care of was to be sick or injured. I intentionally injured myself playing sports. Later, when I worked as a contractor, I'd slice my hand. Because of my work, there was always a reason for the injuries. I was not a wrist slasher. One thing about me, I'm subtle to the max. But these things were clearly intentional.

Self-mutilation is a source of great shame and humiliation. But it is important to talk about it because, like child sexual abuse, self-abuse grows worse in a climate of secrecy.

To stop self-abuse, you need to get help. A skilled counselor can provide essential support. It's no longer necessary to hurt yourself. You deserve kindness both from others and from yourself.

> To keep from cutting myself, I write affirmations. I do it right on my wrist. I'll write things like "I love myself," "I will not hurt myself," "I am good," "It's okay to be in pain. It's okay to say it." There was a while I'd change it every day. And then I tell people about what I want to do. I tell my group members. I tell my therapist.

One survivor went so far as to write loving messages all over her body. As a child she had carved "help" into her arm. Now, wanting to make peace with her body, she gently wrote love notes to all her body parts.

Once you decide that hurting yourself is no longer an option, you need to find healthier ways to gain that feeling of release. Physical activity and emotional release work can both be effective alternatives (see "Emotional Release Work" on page 198).

Stopping a pattern of self-mutilation requires that you express feelings directly. If you are angry, refocus your anger where it belongs—at the person or people who abused you (see "Anger—The Backbone of Healing" on page 122). If you hurt yourself when you get scared, practice responding to feelings of terror in a different way (see "Panic" on page 201).

SELF-DEFENSE: FROM VICTIM TO VICTOR

All women are targets of violence. Even if you use good judgment, have solid self-defense skills, and firmly believe you have the right to protect yourself, you are not immune to assault. For survivors, the risks are even greater.

A high percentage of women who were sexually abused as children have been revictimized in adulthood through assault, rape, and battering.* When this happens, the adult

---

* Many of these women have no memory of their childhood abuse when they are attacked as adults. Often the adult victimization brings up a woman's first memories of the earlier abuse.

survivor frequently blames herself or feels she somehow deserved it. This is completely false. The reasons so many survivors experience violence as adults is that they were trained to be victims. The effects of childhood abuse leave them especially vulnerable to attack.

If you are unable to identify your own feelings or gauge other people's intentions, you may not recognize danger. If you space out, you may be oblivious to warning signals. And if you freeze when you're frightened, it will be harder to act appropriately. More generally, if you have been indoctrinated to believe that you deserve abuse, if you expect to be a victim, it's less likely that you'll be able to defend yourself.

In order to feel comfortable and relaxed in your body, you need to know that you can protect yourself. Usually the ability to say no firmly and to move out of a threatening situation is enough to keep you safe. But sometimes an assailant will not be repelled by words alone. Then you need to use additional self-defense skills to keep you from further violation—shouting, yelling, kicking, hitting, making use of your wits and intuition.* Women in this society are not encouraged to be fierce on their own behalf. But you have the right and responsibility to take care of yourself.

There are many forms of self-defense that are helpful in increasing your determination to fight back against assault and in gaining the confidence to do so.† Many rapists and assailants will be frightened away by a vigorous show of opposition, even if your skills are less than perfect.

Of course, there will always be situations in which you can't fight back successfully, or in which you judge it more dangerous to do so. But if you have basic self-defense training, if you feel powerful and entitled, you can protect yourself much more of the time.

MODEL MUGGING

One practical and effective self-defense program is called Model Mugging.‡ Model Mugging was developed by martial artist Matt Thomas after the brutal rape of one of his female black belt karate students. Although this woman had won many awards for karate, she was unable to defend herself from rape because she had never learned to fight from the ground.

Model Mugging is a fifteen- to twenty-hour course in which women do not just practice self-defense techniques; they use full-force defenses in simulated rape situations. The course is team-taught by both a woman instructor and a man who is specifically trained to be a "model mugger." The mugger dresses in extensive protective gear. He attacks each woman in turn in a realistic

---

* Read *Her Wits About Her* edited by Denise Caignon and Gail Groves, and *Stopping Rape* by Pauline Bart and Patricia O'Brien. Both are described in the "Self-Defense" section of the Bibliography.

† Py Bateman has done pioneering work in the field of feminist self-defense. Her excellent journal, *Sexual Coercion & Assault: Issues and Perspectives*, surveys recent literature, provides abstracts of current research, and offers insightful articles on self-defense and sexual assault. For more information, see the "Self-Defense" section of the Bibliography.

‡ There are Model Mugging chapters in many cities. For information call 1-900-KICK outside California or (818) 997-3306 inside California. Or write IMPACT/Model Mugging, 13550 Roscoe Blvd., Van Nuys, CA 91624.

scenario—approaching her with obscene and insulting comments at a bus stop, waking her from a sound sleep while she is lying on the floor, physically attacking her. He continues his attack until the woman delivers a knockout blow (one that would knock out someone not dressed in protective gear).

Coached by the instructor, students actually experience fighting back against the model mugger. Their bodies learn the feeling of delivering a knockout blow. For most women, it is the first time in their lives they have used their full force to fight.*

---

* Not only is self-defense important for adults, but children can gain a tremendous empowerment by learning skills to protect themselves. KIDPOWER is a nonprofit organization that provides self-defense programs for children. For more information, contact KIDPOWER, P.O. Box 1212, Santa Cruz, CA 95061, (408) 426-4407.

Model Mugging is an intense, exhilarating, and effective way to move toward further safety and empowerment. Survivors who have participated in the course often reexperience the fear and pain of their old victimization. The difference this time is that they are the victors. With the support of the instructor and the other students, they win. They knock out the assailant and walk away to cheers and applause.

Whether you take advantage of a Model Mugging program or learn other forms of self-defense, learning to protect yourself is an important component of taking back your power. And age, health, or disabilities don't necessarily have to stop you. There was a story in the newspaper recently of an eighty-year-old woman in a wheelchair who scared a young rapist so with her spirited defense that he jumped out the window.

INTIMACY

I have beautiful things and people in my present. I have beginning friendships with women who understand from inside what I'm going through, unlike the friends I had a few years ago. I have a lover who supports me in my healing, who is not afraid or enraged to see me, and sometimes be with me, in the hellish place I must go in my deeper remembering. I do not have to lie to them. I do not have to keep up appearances for them, I do not have to regain perspective (their perspective). I am not alone.

—Ely Fuller

Intimacy is a bonding between two people based on trust, respect, love, and the ability to share deeply. You can have intimate relationships with lovers, partners, friends, or family members. Through these relationships you experience the give-and-take of caring.

Most survivors have problems with trust. If handling things alone and taking care of yourself was what you had to do as a child, it may feel unfamiliar and scary to be in a close, committed relationship. Many survivors describe intimacy as suffocating or invasive. They feel claustrophobic when someone gets close. Learning to tolerate intimacy, to feel safe with deep sharing, is a challenge.

One survivor, Saphyre, had no love in her life for many years:

I had nobody who cared about me,

nobody who touched me, or who I touched emotionally. I didn't know how to be emotional. I'd go into total anxiety if there was a hint of connection with anybody. It's hard to explain how severe that is. It's really a critical problem. People die from it. I think "shy" has got to be the biggest euphemism for pain.

On the other hand, you may cling to those you love, unable to tolerate a healthy level of independence. Or you may find yourself too absorbed in your own problems to pay attention to anyone else.

I needed relationships with people who would allow me to be close when I needed to be close, and in another world when I needed that. Since I needed to be close a lot less of the time than I needed to be in my own world, I never got what I needed. I ached for it. I can remember feeling like I would do anything in the world to have the kind of friend who would just put their arms around me and hold me and love me and care, without me having to give anything back. Some nights I would cry all night long, just wishing for that.

You may not know how to give or receive nurturing. Physical closeness may be threatening or confusing to you. You may be able to establish intimacy with friends but not with lovers. You may sexualize every friendship or run away when sex enters the picture. Or a certain level of intimacy may be okay, but when you start to get more involved or the relationship starts to feel like family, you panic.

You may sabotage relationships or repeatedly test them to the breaking point. You may find yourself alienated, lonely, or trapped in relationships where your basic needs are not being met. You may not be able to say no, to set boundaries and limits. You may have no idea what a healthy relationship is like.

These may seem like insurmountable problems, but it is possible to teach yourself the necessary skills to have good, supportive loving in your life. The capacity for intimacy lives inside you. As a child, you started out with a perfect sense of trust and closeness. It was stolen from you.

Healing is the process of getting it back.

A WORKING RELATIONSHIP

Intimacy isn't something you can do alone. By its very nature, it assumes a relationship. And a relationship means risk. The other half of any relationship is a person you can't control. But being hurt or disappointed by someone you love can never be as devastating as it was when you were a child. If your trust is broken, it will hurt, but such a breach need no longer annihilate you. You can recover. You are building a more complete self to fall back on.

In order to develop a working relationship, you don't have to marry someone or be lovers. You can learn a tremendous amount about intimacy in the context of a close friendship.

If you are already in a partnership or friendship you consider intimate, assess the quality of that relationship. Ask yourself the following questions:

- Do I respect this person?
- Does this person respect me?
- Is this a person I can communicate with?
- Do we work through conflicts well?
- Do we both compromise?
- Is there give-and-take?
- Can I be honest? Can I show my real feelings?
- Do we both take responsibility for the relationship's successes and problems?
- Could I talk to this person about the effect child sexual abuse is having on our relationship?
- Is there room for me to grow and change in this relationship?
- Am I able to reach my own goals within this relationship?
- Is this person supportive of the kind of changes I am trying to make?
- Is this person willing to help me?

If you can answer most of these questions with a yes, it's likely you have a solid working relationship. If you aren't sure of the answers, either the relationship is very new or you're not asking enough of the relationship to know what is or isn't available to you. If you answered mostly no's, you should seriously consider changing or ending the relationship (see "Recognizing Bad Relationships," page 234).

THE IMPACT OF CHANGE ON RELATIONSHIPS

When one person changes in a relationship or a family, the whole equilibrium shifts.

Although sometimes people appreciate the changes you make, upsetting the status quo usually causes reactions designed to keep things as they were:

> As I got more in touch with my needs and my rights, I got more assertive. And of course, I brought it all right home to my relationship. Like with anything, when we get a new skill or a new tool we almost bludgeon people with it until we're comfortable enough to back off and relax. So I said, "I'm not going to whimper through life. I'm going to start having some expectations of my own."
>
> And my partner said, "I liked you better before you were in therapy. You used to want to please me all the time. I don't get my way now, and I don't like it."
>
> I got very assertive and she got very angry. Her feeling was "Okay, take care of yourself, but this is ridiculous!" And my feeling was that I was barely taking care of myself.

As you heal, you will change and your loved ones will be challenged to change along with you if you are to create healthy, meaningful relationships. This is often stressful, but if both of you are committed to growing personally, you will be more likely to see changes as positive and to welcome—or at least tolerate—them.

> My lover has had to change a lot for our relationship to work. But mostly they've been changes he wanted to make anyway. He knew he needed to be more independent, less desperate about sex, less tense in general. The fact that I needed him to be that way just pushed

him to move a little faster than he would have done otherwise.

Your changes make demands on the people close to you, but when they are changes toward health and fulfillment, ultimately they can enhance your relationship, as well as your individual lives.

CALCULATED RISKS

Learning to be intimate isn't comfortable. As one woman said, "I kept myself safe, but I also kept myself alone." Becoming intimate means peeling back the layers of protection to let someone in. It means going to the place where you're comfortable, and then taking one step more. One step, not twenty.

Instead of spilling out all your innermost thoughts, say "I'm frightened" one time. Instead of moving in with your lover, try spending the weekend together. It's the little steps that have staying power.

There's no fixed goal. Intimacy is experienced in the moment as part of a changing, fluid relationship. Learning to be intimate is a slow process, involving mistakes, small successes, and backsliding.

To break through to a deeper level of intimacy, you need to be willing to take calculated risks. A calculated risk is different from a blind leap. With a blind leap, you shut your eyes and lunge forward, hoping that things will work out magically. You start an affair with a married man, positive he'll leave his wife. You get pregnant, hoping a baby will save a faltering relationship. You tell a friend your deepest secrets a week after you've met. Blind leaps rarely pay off.

Calculated risks are different. With a calculated risk, you weigh your chances and step out onto the ice only when you're relatively sure it's solid. With intimacy, nothing is 100 percent sure, but with forethought and a responsive partner, you maximize your chances for communication, increased closeness, and satisfaction.

LEARNING TO TRUST

Survivors tend to see trust as an absolute, either not trusting at all or trusting completely. You may bounce between the two, not trusting until you are so desperate for contact that you throw your trust at the first likely target. Since most people can't handle that kind of desperation, you end up disappointed or abandoned, thus proving your original beliefs—that people aren't trustworthy, that you aren't lovable, that love isn't worth it.

Before you can trust anyone, you have to trust yourself (see "Trusting Yourself," page 116). If you know you can take care of yourself, you won't need to blindly fling your trust out in the hope that someone will take care of you. That kind of absolute love is what a child feels for its parents. It's not what two mature adults feel for each other.

I've come up against the issue of trust again and again. The more I love myself, the more that allows me to love someone else. And the loving is getting stronger than the fear.

In a healthy relationship, you vary your level of trust according to what's actually happening between you and the other person.

You experience gradations of trust, periodically assessing whether your needs are getting met, whether you're growing in the ways you want to grow. And if you see that the relationship warrants it, you open up more. Trust accrues over time. It's earned.

EXPERIMENT WITH TRUST

As you come to trust yourself, you build a foundation for trusting someone else. You can always go back to not trusting if you want to, but at least give it a try. The basic premise of this experiment, whether you believe it yet or not, is that under some circumstances, and with some people, trust is safe. Given that, try trusting in small doses.

Choose simple situations that give you a good chance of success. Instead of saying "I trust that you never betray me in any way," ask your partner to make dinner for you on a night you work late. Trust a woman in your support group to hold you in a nonsexual way for five minutes. Or call a friend when you're feeling sad and ask if she'll spend a little time with you.

Say that you are experimenting with trust and that this is important to you. Then, if they come through for you, let that affect your world view. Let it enter in on the tally. Maybe trusting is not as dangerous as it was when you were a child.

If the experiment fails and you are let down, try to analyze what happened. This is a learning experience. Ask yourself:

- Whom did I pick to trust?
- How long did I know the person?
- Did we have good communication?
- What kind of thing did I trust the person with?

- Did I explain what I was doing, letting them know it was very important to me?
- Did I make my expectations clear?
- Were there any elements in the interchange that paralleled my original abuse?

Use the answers to these questions to learn about when it is and isn't appropriate to trust. Then try again. Jerilyn Munyon is one survivor who learned to trust through trial and error:

I didn't know how to trust—not others, not myself, not the world. I always thought trust was something you either had or you didn't, like a talent. It took me a while to figure out that trust is a skill, a skill that even I could learn. I really didn't know what trust felt like or how to get it, but I did know I wanted and needed it. For a long time I either couldn't trust or I'd trust the wrong person, or the right person for the wrong thing.

Eventually, as I found out more about myself and accepted myself more, took more responsibility for myself, I began to see that I could actually make choices that would affect the outcome of situations. I hadn't known there were right—or at least better—times, people, and places for trusting. I had learned from my conditioning that I had to take everything that came along, good or bad. That was a lie. It was true when I was three and had no choice, but now I was in my thirties and for the first time, I really began to take my life in hand and make some choices. At first they were pretty mixed, but as time has passed I find that my choices get better.

TESTING

It's healthy to do some testing in a new relationship, but many survivors carry this to extremes. You may taunt your partner, waiting to see if he hits you. You may sleep with your lover's best friend to see if she'll get disgusted and leave. One woman never shows up for the first three dates. If someone makes it to the fourth date, she'll begin to consider that person a potential friend.

In the early months of the relationship I'm in now, I can't think of anything I didn't do to test Malcolm. After three years it's just starting to ease up, because he's stuck it through. He's passed the major tests.

It's legitimate to test people to see if you should trust them or if they can meet your needs, but if you find yourself excessively testing your friends or lovers, you may be reenacting the familiar betrayals of your childhood. If you set up tests that no one could possibly pass, then you're not testing. You're saying goodbye.

Instead, try designing tests that are fair: "I'm going to wait and see if you really take care of the kids two afternoons a week like you promised," or "I need to see if you stay open with me if I tell you what I'm going through."

Discuss your needs with your friends and lovers to make sure that you've set up reasonable assessment points.

CONFUSING THE PAST WITH THE PRESENT

You may have a partner or friend who genuinely loves and respects you, but you don't experience it that way because you expect relationships to be abusive.

I was very frightened of being abused again. And it didn't take much for me to think someone was being abusive, either. Until you get clear, you judge men from the standpoint of what you've learned in life, right? My experience was that 95 percent of men are abusers. So all I had to figure out was, "How do they do their abuse? Is it physical, mental, or emotional?"

Of course if someone *is* abusing you, you need to get out of that situation (see "Recognizing Bad Relationships" on page 234). But if you only *think* you're being abused, you must learn to make the distinction between the people who care about you now and your abuser.

One way to break this identification is to create reality checks for yourself:

- My father never listened to what was important to me. Bill usually listens.
- My mother always said things were going to change and nothing ever did. With Maureen, although we've still got a way to go, our relationship *has* changed.
- My friend John has straight brown hair and wears sloppy clothes. My uncle's hair was black and curly and he always dressed immaculately.

Reinforce these distinctions so that you can stay aware that the people in your life today are not your abuser.

DON'T COME NEAR ME

It is common for survivors to keep distance between themselves and the people they love. If you feel threatened by closeness, you pull away. You tear the other person down because you're scared and want a reason to leave. Or you stay present in body, while your mind is whirring a million miles away.

I knew I was going to get a divorce. No matter how hard I tried, this just wasn't going to work. I didn't want to be close to him, period. I just wanted out. And that statement, "I just wanted out," is a direct result of the child abuse. The way I kept myself safe all through my childhood was by getting out. I got out of the house. I got out of the bedroom. I got out of the basement. I spent half my childhood in the orchards, up a tree, over with the horses, anywhere that was out, away from people. I only felt safe when I was alone. There was no safety with people. Not ever.

Sometimes creating distance is a good thing to do. It's important to be able to separate from someone you're close to, so you can nurture other aspects of your life and keep your relationship in perspective. Being close, and then returning to yourself, and then being close again is a natural cycle in a healthy relationship. But if you withdraw every time you feel uncomfortable, it's a problem.

Notice when and why you pull back, and in each situation assess whether it's what you really want to be doing, whether it's appropriate, or whether it's a carryover from childhood that is no longer useful. If you decide you do want to be more separate, practice moving away in healthy ways. Picking a fight or having a secret affair is not a good way to create separation.

If you decide what you really want is to be close and not to withdraw, you will have to force yourself to reach out, even if your natural habit is to retract. Instead of saying "I'm leaving you; this will never work," say "I'm scared; let's talk." Tell your friend "I'm having a hard time," instead of not calling for weeks at a time. The key to greater intimacy is honestly expressing what's going on, instead of covering your panic and running away.

And if you need to build in a cushion of safety, strike little bargains with yourself—"I'll let myself be close tonight, but tomorrow night is just for me to be by myself."

If the distancing you do is in your head, the triggers may be harder to pinpoint. Try to watch where and when your thoughts stray. Enlist the help of the people close to you. Ask them to watch for the telltale signs —a lack of focus in your eyes, a drop in your voice, the sneaking feeling they get that you're just not around anymore. If you're caught, or if you catch yourself, stop and look at the reasons why you withdrew when you did (see "Spacing Out" page 45).

FEAR OF LOVE

If the people who said they loved you abused or neglected you, it can feel terrifying to love again.

I had a hard time telling anyone I loved them. My father, you see, was always gentle and loving to me. He always told me, "I love you. I love you in a way I can't love your mother." He'd say that to me while he was doing these horrible things to me. So I've had real fears of saying "I love you."

Commitment or love with a family feeling can be scarier still. The child in you still equates commitment with being locked into a situation where there's no escape. So as you get closer, you may become paralyzed by all your old defenses and memories.

When my therapist started telling me that she loved me, I hated her for it. I screamed at her. I wouldn't talk to her. For her to tell me she loved me meant that she was going to leave me or abuse me. That was all that I could believe about it. It wasn't until she kept sitting there, week after week, saying "But I love you" with this complete open heart that I stopped being so terrified and let it in.

Try talking to those close to you about what love and commitment mean to them. And if the word "love" sticks in your throat, try saying how you feel in your own words: "I am so glad I know you." "You make me feel special." "I get happy just thinking of you." One woman who refused to use the word "love" told her new lover, "I'm in serious like with you."

Love is a terribly misused word.* Eileen, a workshop participant, began to feel hopeful when she discovered there was more to love than she had experienced as a child:

I felt a lot of sadness when I realized that "love" was not what I was getting when I was a kid. The funny part is that the awareness comes as a tremendous relief. It gives me the opportunity to say, "Well, if that wasn't love, maybe it's not love that I'm terrified of." Hence the new beginning . . .

STATIC CLING

Our culture sanctions an image of women as dependent, unable to take care of themselves, and incomplete without a relationship. In addition to this societal conditioning, you may not have gotten the nurturing you needed in childhood. Or you may have been smothered, not allowed to separate from your family in appropriate ways. Now you find yourself clinging, afraid to be alone.

Overcoming this state of unhealthy dependency is much the same process a two-year-old goes through in learning to play independently. The toddler will spend a few minutes with a toy and then run back to the living room to make sure her mother is still there. Once reassured by a pat or a smile, she

---

* See "But Honey, I Love You," page 300.

ventures out again, until a few minutes later she needs to see her mother again. Learning to feel secure while spending time alone requires much the same thing: practice, positive reinforcement, and more practice.

Take time alone in small increments, doing things you actively enjoy. Ask your friend or partner to say encouraging things: "I'll still be here when you get back" or "I'm proud of you." Planning ahead is a big help too. You can arrange to have dinner with your husband after spending the day alone. Expand your sources of nourishment to non-people sources: pets, nature, creativity. If you spread out the ways you take care of yourself, you will be less dependent on any one person.

MERGING

Merging is a state of extreme dependency. Not having a strong enough sense of your own identity, you confuse your thoughts, feelings, and needs with those of others, until it's hard to tell where you stop and they begin.

My former husband and I were so desperate for intimacy that we totally fell into each other's lives. We capitalized on the things we genuinely had in common and denied our real differences. We wore the same kinds of clothes, went on the same health food diets, and read the same books. We used to make a joke that you could tell us apart because I was the one in the green sweater.

If you are lonely or afraid to be alone, this kind of closeness is seductive. It's also unhealthy. A strong relationship is made up of two individuals sharing together. For that you need an independent self.

WALK ALL OVER ME, WHY DON'T YOU?

Survivors often have trouble setting limits in relationships, because they didn't learn about healthy boundaries as children. You may do all the giving. Or you may feel you don't have the right to say no. But if you are one half of a relationship, you deserve to do half the decision-making and to exercise half the power.

In balanced relationships both people contribute to making it work. You don't have to be all-giving to merit love. Total self-sacrifice is not a virtue.

If you haven't had much practice setting limits, start with something small: "I don't want you to call me after 11:00 p.m. because my roommates are sleeping." Or, "If you use up the milk, please replace it."

Once you've had a little practice, go on to something bigger. If you've been expected to cook the family dinner every night and you no longer want sole responsibility for that job, make an announcement: "I will no longer be cooking on Tuesdays and Thursdays." Talk it over with your partner and children and help them come to terms with their new responsibilities. If they won't cooperate, you can still say no.

The fact that someone doesn't like a limit you set doesn't mean you have to back down. When 5:00 p.m. on Tuesday rolls around, head up to your room with an apple and a good book. And if you don't want to hear complaints from the kitchen, a walk in the park might be nice.

Your family may grumble. They might even make a lot of noise, but they won't starve. Your oldest boy might even find out he likes to cook. And you might find that you like setting limits a lot.

DEALING WITH CONFLICT

Conflict is threatening to many women, and especially to survivors. If you grew up in an environment where conflicts exploded into violence or where they were suppressed entirely, you may feel at a loss when it comes to dealing with conflict in a healthy way. Instead you may freeze, withdraw, or try to manipulate the situation to meet your needs without a direct confrontation. You may be afraid that if you assert yourself, you'll be abandoned. You may fear getting hurt or hurting someone else. Or you may escalate the disagreement until you say or do things you really don't mean.

But conflict is normal—and inevitable. It's a basic part of intimacy. As Ellen's mother says, "If two people always agree, one of them is superfluous."

Talking directly, with respect for both yourself and the other person, is a healthy way to air problems. Try to share your feelings as soon as you recognize them so you don't store up a backlog of resentments and disappointments. Say how you feel and what you want. Then listen to your friend or partner without interrupting.

To keep a conflict from spiraling out of control, you can agree beforehand on some basic guidelines, such as no violence and no name-calling. You can agree to stick with the present issue and not trash the relationship as a whole. Ground rules like these can help you feel safer.

Until now, I've had trouble sharing when it had to do with anger. I think, in a sense, anger is the ultimate intimacy. If you can feel safe enough to express anger with a significant person in your life, then you've got a real measure of intimacy. My relationship now is the first one where I've felt free to do that.

Not all conflicts involve anger. Sometimes you simply see things differently or have different desires and need to work out a compromise that's acceptable to both of you. Either way, it's important to hear each other's perspective. If this isn't happening naturally, set a timer so that each of you can talk for five minutes while the other really listens. Or try reversing roles—pretend that you're the other person and say what you think he or she is feeling.

In most situations there's at least one— and usually more—solution that could meet both people's needs. It's not necessary to back down from what's important to you or to invalidate your friend's or partner's needs. Negotiating respectfully and successfully is a skill you can learn.* And as you resolve conflicts in ways you feel good about, you build trust.

---

* There are a number of excellent books on nonviolent conflict resolution and successful negotiation. We recommend *Getting to YES: Negotiating Agreement Without Giving In* by Roger Fisher and William Ury of the Harvard Negotiation Project (New York: Penguin Books, 1986).

GIVING AND RECEIVING

There are two sides to intimacy: giving and receiving. You may have a hard time with one or with both. The way to learn either is to practice. If you have been unable to give, start by giving someone what's easiest for you—perhaps a compliment or a favorite food. Ask the person to acknowledge and thank you for what you've done. Recognition goes a long way in reinforcing behavior.

As time goes on, work up to giving things that are harder. You may find it relatively easy to give on your own terms—what you want to give, when you want to give it. Children often pick out presents, for instance, that reflect their own interests rather than the interests of the recipient. But as an adult, you need to work toward being able to give people what *they* need, when *they* need it. Your lover may want to be accompanied to an important event, not cooked for. Your friend might need to talk to you even though you want to treat him to the movies. This doesn't mean you can't say no, only that you become capable of stepping out of yourself to meet the other person halfway.

Receiving feels wonderful once you get used to it. But first you must acknowledge how scary it is to be open. If, as a child, you were left to fend for yourself or there were strings attached to getting what you needed, you learned that nurturing was either unavailable or unsafe. But now, receiving doesn't have to mean owing something back.

Start asking for at least one thing you want every day. It can be as small as "Would you make me some tea?" or "Can you drop this off to the Sales Department on your way out?"

Tell the people close to you that you're learning to ask for what you want, that you're learning to receive. You never know—your partner might spontaneously put love notes in your lunch bag. Your daughter might pick a flower for you on her way home from school.

In healthy relationships, there is a balance to giving and receiving. If you've always leaned heavily one way, you will need to focus more on the other aspect, but eventually, as you feel safer, both giving and receiving will develop a relaxed natural rhythm.

IN TIMES OF CRISIS

During certain crucial periods when healing from child sexual abuse demands all your attention, you may be unable to give anything. You may be so self-absorbed that you become temporarily unable to meet (or even pay attention to) the needs of your family and friends.

This kind of self-absorption is a natural side effect of engrossing emotional work, but you can't immerse yourself in it all the time and expect to maintain intimate relationships. You need to make an effort to keep relationships reciprocal.

If you can't give quality attention, at least apologize. Acknowledge that you can't do more just yet, but that you intend to be more present and available as soon as you can. Express your appreciation for your friend's loyalty in continuing to love you even when you can't give much back. Then see if there's something small you *can* give. Perhaps you can do your lover's laundry even while you're obsessed with your own thoughts. If you can't give fully, give what you can.

This doesn't mean you should fake it.

There may be legitimate times when you absolutely can't give anything. If this is the case, acknowledge your limitations and take responsibility for them, instead of putting down the other person for having needs.

Generally, the deeper a foundation you have with someone, the more the relationship is able to withstand trying times. (See "For Partners," page 321, for more on working through hard times.) Sometimes a healing crisis actually helps a relationship grow in depth and commitment. But even if you have a solid relationship, the demands of healing will still be hard on your partner and friends.

RECOGNIZING BAD RELATIONSHIPS

We all have the tendency to repeat childhood patterns. For survivors, this often means leaving a family situation that was unsupportive, distant, or abusive only to get involved with a partner who embodies those same qualities.

I'd be talking to a man I was in a relationship with and suddenly I'd hear him talking to me like my father or acting like my ex-husband, who abused me. It wouldn't be obvious until a month or two into the relationship, but then one thing would happen and it would all click into place. I picked men like my father over and over again.

When women are in bad relationships, they frequently try not to notice, and hope things will change. Or they think that because nothing overtly abusive is going on, the relationship is okay. But relationships that lack life, inhibit trust, or are simply boring are unfulfilling too. If your partner is unwilling to relate to you as a courageous, vulnerable, strong woman, then you must question the nature of that relationship.

IS MY RELATIONSHIP ABUSIVE?

Because many survivors grew up in homes where abuse was the norm, they often have a hard time identifying and acknowledging abuse in their adult lives. In *Getting Free*, Ginny NiCarthy gives some guidelines for recognizing abusive relationships.* Has your partner done any of these things to you?

PHYSICAL ABUSE

- pushed or shoved you
- held you to keep you from leaving, or locked you out of the house
- slapped, bit, kicked, or choked you
- hit or punched you
- thrown objects at you
- abandoned you in dangerous places
- refused to help when you were sick, injured, or pregnant
- subjected you to reckless driving or kept you from driving
- raped you
- threatened or hurt you with a weapon

SEXUAL ABUSE

- made demeaning remarks about women

---

* See the "Battering" section of the Bibliography.

If you have a partner who belittles you, a husband who hits you, or a friend who doesn't respect your values, you can't count on them to change. Everyone changes—that's a fact of life—but you can't expect them to change in any particular direction or at any particular pace. The only thing you can do to change a relationship is to change yourself.

You can act. You can develop alternative

- treated women as sex objects
- been jealously angry
- insisted you dress in a more sexual way than you wanted
- minimized the importance of your feelings about sex
- criticized you sexually
- insisted on unwanted touching
- withheld sex and affection
- called you names like "whore" or "frigid"
- forced you to strip when you didn't want to
- publicly shown interest in other women
- had affairs with other women after agreeing to monogamy
- forced sex
- forced particular unwanted sex acts
- forced sex after beating
- committed sadistic sexual acts

EMOTIONAL ABUSE

- ignored your feelings
- ridiculed or insulted women as a group
- insulted your valued beliefs, religion, race, heritage, or class
- withheld approval or affection as a punishment
- criticized you, called you names, shouted at you
- insulted your family or friends

- humiliated you
- refused to socialize with you
- kept you from working, controlled your money, made all decisions
- refused to work or share money
- taken car keys or money away
- regularly threatened to leave or told you to leave
- threatened to hurt you or your family
- punished the children when he (or she) was angry at you
- threatened to kidnap the children if you left him
- abused pets to hurt you
- manipulated you with lies and contradictions

Although some items are clearly more dangerous than others, almost all of them are potentially dangerous, and all show a lack of respect and an effort to intimidate and control you. One problem with accepting a certain level of abuse is that there's a tendency for the abusive person to interpret it as permission to escalate the assaults into more dangerous and frequent acts. You're the only one who can decide how much is too much and what you're ready to do about it, but it's important to recognize what's being done to you and to know that you don't have to take it.

support networks. You can forgive yourself for not knowing better in the past, and start saying no in the present. If you make all the changes you can and still aren't getting your needs met, consider leaving the relationship.* It is better not to be in a relationship at all than it is to be in one that continues to link closeness to betrayal, abandonment, and violation. (For information on leaving an abusive relationship when children are involved, see "Children and Parenting" page 270.)

SEPARATING

Separating from an unsatisfying relationship can be very difficult. Many women are so attached to their partners that the relationship is more an addiction than a freely chosen partnership. In her book, *Choice-Making,* Sharon Wegscheider-Cruse defines this state of co-dependency as "a condition of chronic dependency, a state that keeps us from self-fulfillment and personal freedom.†

Breaking this kind of addiction can be frightening. But there is more and more help available for women who are reclaiming their autonomy and self-worth. Al-Anon, the organization for spouses of alcoholics, recognizes that women can be co-dependent even if their spouses don't drink. And there is an entire growth movement based on twelve-step programs to support co-dependent women in making changes.‡ Robin Norwood's book, *Women Who Love Too Much,* is a good resource.

Sometimes the process of weeding out people who are no longer good for you is spurred by a decision you make about changing your lifestyle. If part of your recovery from sexual abuse involves getting sober, for instance, you will have to leave your old drinking buddies behind. Or if you have a friend who tells you you're lying every time you talk about sexual abuse, you may need to end that friendship.

All these changes can be hard. You may feel lonely or lost. Even if you know you are making room for something better, there's still loss—the loss of the familiar, the loss of the good qualities in the people you leave behind. This can be a painful and awkward time for you, a kind of limbo when you have let go of the old but have not yet grabbed hold of the new.

When I feel lonely, I find that several things help me—telling someone how I'm feeling, knowing that the feelings will pass, and remembering a parable an old friend told me once: it's only when you have an empty cup that it can get filled with fresh, life-giving water.

YOU DESERVE TO HAVE ENRICHING RELATIONSHIPS

If you've previously chosen relationships for the wrong reasons, it's possible to break

---

* Seal Press has published an excellent series of step-by-step guidebooks for women on getting out of abusive relationships. We recommend them highly. (See the "Battering" section of the Bibliography for more information.)

† For more information on co-dependency see the "Co-Dependency" section of the Bibliography.

‡ See "Healing Resources," page 458, for information.

that pattern. For instance, if you find your-self repeatedly attracted to older, authoritative men who remind you of your abuser, and you know from past experience that you feel powerless with that kind of person, turn away and look elsewhere. However, some-times you know what you *don't* want, but don't yet know what you *do* want. A woman in her mid-fifties said:

> I realize I need to know more about men. I really don't know much about them. My father was so distant and so abusive. My uncles were distant. My husband was distant. And I didn't get along with my son, naturally. I don't have any models from my past of what it's like to be warm and friendly with a nice man. So I've been working on de-veloping that. And it's funny, my per-ception of men is changing—they're seeming nicer all of a sudden!

You may feel you have no choice about the people you get involved with.

> I believed if someone was nice to me, or wanted me, I had to comply. It was a miracle that someone wanted me at all! So what if he didn't respect me or even like me? I might never have an-other chance. At the time, I couldn't af-ford to say no.

As your self-esteem increases, it will seem natural that other people will like and love you. You will realize that you can say no to some people and actively choose others.

Try looking at new relationships as places to practice intimacy. We have all been conditioned to judge relationships on the basis of their length—a good relationship is one that lasts forever and everything else is a failure. But relationships can be worthwhile even if they are short or don't give you every-thing you need. If a relationship seems to provide a context in which you can practice communication, trust, and the give-and-take of caring, then you have a healthy basis for growth and intimacy.

ARE WE HAVING FUN YET?

A women's band in Santa Cruz sings a song about relationships that has as the chorus:

> Work on it, work on it,
> I don't wanna work on it.*

Whenever they play it in concert, the audi-ence roars. We can all recognize the feeling of having worked at relationships to the point of overkill.

If you add to that the work of healing from child sexual abuse—memories and con-frontation, rage and grief—and then throw in the laundry, the kids, and earning a living, life can be overwhelming. When you're run-ning on empty, trying to catch up, fun is the first thing to go. But that's a mistake.

If you see your partner only when you crawl into bed, exhausted, at the end of the day, you're both liable to forget what brought you together to begin with. If you talk only about sexual abuse when you see your friend Carol, Carol may stop calling. And even if

---

* From "Work On It" by Wicked Stance.

you're fortunate enough to have friends and lovers who stick by you, you'll be missing out on fun times together.

If healthy relationships are important to you, structure your life to allow for quality time with the people you love. Laura did this quite successfully with a friend who is also a survivor:

When we first met, we'd get together and spend the whole evening talking about heavy, depressing things. After a few months, it wasn't so exciting to see each other. So we decided to make a change. We made a contract to do something fun once a month. Last month I took her on the carousel in Golden Gate Park. This month we're going bowling.

Fun is not an optional part of the healing process. It's one of its chief rewards.

SEX

Q: "Have you ever made love while working on incest issues?"
A: "Well, I have . . . and I haven't!"

The perspective on sexuality that is presented here applies to both lesbian and heterosexual women. Although there are some differences in the difficulties these groups face, they are far outweighed by the similarities. (If you're not sure about your sexual preference or want more information, see "On Being a Lesbian and a Survivor" at the end of this chapter.)

We use the word "lover" in this chapter to describe any sexual partner. This includes someone you are casually dating, someone you are deeply committed or married to, and any relationship in between. Healing takes place on many levels, and whether you are celibate, dating, in a short-term relationship, or in a committed partnership, you can heal sexually.

(If you are the partner of a survivor, see "For Partners," page 321.)

Survivors are not alone in needing to heal sexually. Our culture leaves little room for any woman to develop a healthy, integrated sexuality. Almost from birth, girls are given mixed messages about their sexuality. They are alternately told to hide it, deny it, repress it, use it, or give it away. The media flaunt sex constantly as a means of power, seduction, and exchange. As a result, most women grow up with conflicts around sex. For women who were abused, these problems are compounded.

Survivors face a wide spectrum of sexual

239

difficulties, all of which are natural and reasonable results of being abused (see page 37). For some women, these problems connect directly to the abuse. If your softball coach pinched your breasts in the locker room after every game, you may not want your lover touching your breasts today. If your stepfather violently raped you, you might experience pain in your vagina today, or you might be scared of intercourse.

Your problems may not be tied to specific abuse. You may feel an overall terror whenever you're in a sexual situation. You may try to meet all your needs through sex. Or you may find yourself unable to stay present when you make love. There is nothing crazy about you if you have these problems. Your sexual problems, like the abuse itself, were forced upon you. Fortunately, it is possible to experience your sexuality in a dramatically different way.

> For a long time I felt like a sexual failure, like I was damaged beyond repair. Yet something in me wouldn't give up. And it just amazes me. Problems that seemed insurmountable five years ago, I can hardly relate to anymore. I haven't had a flashback in years. And now I regularly initiate sex. I can actually say I like sex. No, in fact, I love it. I'm not afraid of my passion anymore. It's an exciting part of my relationship.

Reclaiming your sexuality is slow and painstaking work. As you allow yourself to remember and open up to repressed feelings, you may find that making love is even harder than before. You may question your wisdom in trying to heal, wondering if it wouldn't have been better to just stick with your old ways of getting by. But you deserve more.

YOU DESERVE TO FEEL GOOD

Experiences of sexual pleasure and intimacy often raise conflicting feelings:

> I'm afraid of feeling too much pleasure in my body. Do I really deserve it? I'm afraid if I feel that much, I'll burst open, that my body can't contain that much pleasure. It can contain that much pain, but can it contain that much pleasure?

Although many survivors experienced only pain or numbness when they were abused, others felt sexual arousal or orgasm. Because these good feelings were entwined with fear, confusion, shame, and betrayal, they grew up feeling that sexual pleasure was bad. As one woman said, "It hasn't been until recently that I even thought of putting the words 'sex' and 'pleasure' together."

Some survivors do not feel any pleasurable sensations when they make love. Others have orgasms but feel tremendous guilt about enjoying sex. And some feel conflict or distress: "Pleasure doesn't feel like pleasure to me. I want to throw up every time I have an orgasm. I feel disgusted, and all I can think about is my uncle."

It was a terrible violation that your body's natural responses were exploited. However, sexual pleasure in itself is not bad, not intrinsically connected to your abuse. And now, as an adult, it's safe to feel good. You can make choices about where, when, how, and with whom you want to be sexual, and within those choices, you can give yourself permission to feel pleasure. Sexual feelings are not inherently dangerous or destructive. Like fire, their qualities and effects depend very much on who is using them and to what purpose.

TIME OUT FROM SEX

Taking a break from sex is not necessary for every woman, but it can be a clarifying beginning. If you experience fear, disgust, or a lack of desire for sex, or if you have been unable to say no to sex, this is a wonderful opportunity to set your own boundaries and to get to know your body without the pressure of sex. If you have been sexual in addictive or abusive ways, taking a break from sex offers a chance to examine and change your behavior. It is up to you to say how long this time of celibacy should last. You may want to take a year or years. Or a month may feel sufficient.

LEARN TO SAY NO

Around the age of two, children learn to say no. They practice it all the time. They are asserting themselves, making it clear that although some things are okay with them, not everything is, and they are going to make sure they have some say about it. Toddlers often say no to almost everything. This is healthy. Unless you can say no clearly and effectively, yes is meaningless and cannot give you full satisfaction.

To heal sexually you must learn to say no to unwanted sex. It is important to make a commitment to yourself that you will never again grit your teeth and endure it when you really don't want sex. Every time you have sex when you genuinely don't want to, you add another layer of abuse, repeat the pattern of victimization, and thus delay your healing.

THERE'S MORE TO LIFE THAN SEX

One woman said she not only wanted to say no to sex with lovers, she wanted to say no to sex with herself. She established a hands-off policy that applied even to touching herself, recognizing that she needed a break from any kind of sexual stimulation.

Many survivors were given the message that they were useful only for sex. All your other qualities and skills, your needs and aspirations, were minimized while sex was emphasized. By allowing sex to recede for a time, by saying no to the pressure of it, the problems of it, and even the pleasure of it, you can begin to recognize that there is more to life, and to your worth, than sex.

If you are in a relationship, an extended period of celibacy can cause a lot of strain. You may need to consider compromises in order to include your lover's needs. But it is important not to deny your own needs in the process. If you absolutely need more time without sex and you push yourself to begin sex when it's not right for you, it won't do your relationship much good in the long run and it will certainly not help your healing.

START WITH YOURSELF

When you are ready and you want to begin the process of experiencing yourself sexually, start slowly and with awareness. Many women find that they are their own best lovers in these early stages. As one woman said, "If I can't have sex with myself, there's no point trying to do it with anybody else."

If you've never been comfortable touching yourself, you're not alone. Most of us have been told that touching ourselves is wrong, dirty, and shameful. Although you are supposed to enjoy it when your lover touches you, you are not supposed to touch yourself.

This attitude is not in your best interests. Who has more right to your body than you?

Many survivors carry disgust for their bodies. Some were told directly that they, or their genitals, were disgusting. One woman hates her right hand because her grandfather forced her to masturbate him with that hand. For others the whole experience of abuse was so disgusting that everything connected with it still carries that feeling.

But your body is not disgusting. It is rich and marvelous. And it belongs to you.

MAKING LOVE TO YOURSELF

The way you masturbate is very important.* Many survivors have approached masturbation, like sex, from a disconnected place. One woman explained: "Using my vibrator doesn't have anything to do with sex or intimacy. It has to do with tension and it's about release. It doesn't take that long. If I turn it on high it takes even less time."

Another woman said she would start out with a good warm feeling, be unable to come

---

* We recommend *Sex for One* by Betty Dodson, a wonderful sex-positive guide to masturbation. See the "Sex" section of the Bibliography.

to orgasm, and keep frantically masturbating just to have a climax. "It's as if I become the rapist. I don't even enjoy it anymore. It's the angry, compulsive part of myself."

If you avoid touching yourself altogether, or if your past experience with masturbation is quick stimulation and release, take some time to be with yourself in a relaxed, attentive way. (You might first try the exercise on page 214.) Run a hot bath, light candles, listen to Nina Simone. Put clean sheets on the bed, light incense, place fresh flowers in your bedroom, take your time. Maybe you'd like to smooth oil or lotion on your body. Feel your skin, your muscles. Don't start out by touching yourself genitally. Begin by holding hands with yourself. Stroke your arm. See what kind of touch feels good to you, what you like. Many women have gone through sex numb or in a panic, never taking time to notice how touch actually feels. Maybe on the first date with yourself you'll only touch one shoulder. That's fine. There's no rush. Make another date. Touch the other shoulder.

Over time you can allow yourself more and more feelings, more sensation. Perhaps you will feel sexual arousal, perhaps not. Whatever you feel is fine. When you're ready, but not too quickly, you can touch your breasts, your vulva, your clitoris, your vagina. The object here is not to do it fast and be done. The object is not orgasm. It's to feel your feelings, to give yourself pleasure, to know your body. Stop any time you want to. Notice when you want to stop, what makes you uncomfortable. Stay aware. Stay in your body.

If you find yourself spacing out—thinking about what you're going to wear tomorrow, splitting from your body—stop. Slow down, back up, breathe back into your body.

Do whatever it takes to reconnect with yourself. Sex is about connection—in this case, your connection with yourself.

I consciously try to connect my whole body. I have this meditation I do, even in the middle of making love. I imagine my body filling up with fluid or light. I imagine it coming all the way up from my feet and washing over me. Somehow that circular thing helps me feel like I'm all in one piece.

FLASHBACKS

If you have flashbacks to the original abuse while touching yourself, don't panic. Flashbacks can be an opportunity to understand your experience as a child and can yield valuable information and insight. They can give you a chance to release long-held feelings. (For more on flashbacks, see "Remembering," page 70, and "Flashbacks with a Partner," page 249.)

If you get too upset, open your eyes and ground yourself in the present. Tell yourself that touching yourself here and now is not abuse even though it may bring back memories of abuse. Tell yourself that touching yourself in a loving way is your right, that you deserve touch, you deserve pleasure. It is neither harmful nor shameful nor wrong. This is fine. This is healing. And you deserve it.

ORGASMS

For women who have difficulty having orgasms, it can be helpful to take some time deliberately avoiding orgasms when you make love to yourself. For a week or two you might decide to masturbate as often as you want, but rather than having orgasms (or trying to), allow the sexual energy to build and then contain it, holding it in your body. If you get close to an orgasm, back off a little, lessen the stimulation, let the energy subside. In this kind of lovemaking there's no prescribed time to end. You stop when you want to.

Touching yourself without striving for an orgasm can be a tremendous relief. There's no longer any pressure to "achieve" orgasm. There's nothing to strive for, nowhere to rush to, no "trying." Instead, there's a spaciousness to experience whatever feelings arise, to become aware of the gradations of arousal as you feel them, to stay in the moment, to experience pleasure, and to get to know your own responses as they are, rather than as you think they should be. This kind of exploration can clear some of the obstacles to experiencing orgasms. It can also be very exciting. (This is effective with a partner too. In that case, neither of you has an orgasm.)

While the point of this exercise is to take the pressure off, you may instead feel it's putting pressure on. One woman had a hard time not having an orgasm, because having an orgasm as a child signaled the end of that particular episode of abuse. "For me, sex without an orgasm is incredibly threatening because the sex becomes endless. I panic when there's no clear end in sight."

If you've never had an orgasm, there are some excellent suggestions for becoming orgasmic in the books on sex in the Bibliography. If you've never tried a vibrator, we suggest you get your hands on one (see page 479 for mail-order sources).

Some women say that their orgasms have changed as they worked out their sexual abuse issues. Old blockages were loosened and stored emotions were released, allowing room for a fuller body experience. One woman found that doing emotional release work changed her orgasms from tight pin-pointed bursts to a much more powerful whole-body sensation.

MAKING LOVE WITH A PARTNER

How long you explore your sexuality alone is up to you. No one can tell you how much time you need. Listen to your body and your feelings to know if you feel ready or pushed. If you have a lover and have taken a break from sex, it is essential that you don't start again solely because you feel pressured, want to avoid conflict, or are afraid your lover will leave you. Making love for the wrong reasons will backfire on both you and your relationship.

WHAT'S YOUR MOTIVATION?*

Be honest with yourself about your reasons for wanting to work on sexuality at this time. You might make a list of the things you want to change about your sexuality. Then make a list of the reasons you're willing to do so. In one column list the reasons you want to change for yourself, and in another, the reasons you want to change for your lover's sake.

---

* This concept is drawn from the work of JoAnn Loulan, author of *Lesbian Sex* (see the "Sexuality" section of the Bibliography).

Although it's often hard for survivors to separate their own needs and desires from those of others, it's essential that you have your own reasons for beginning to make love. Such reasons might be: "I feel that I'm missing out on an important part of life," "I want to feel pleasure," "I don't want my past to rule me," "I want to experience an intimate sexual relationship."

Lasting changes are made only when we have a deep desire to change within ourselves. At first you may be motivated by your acute awareness of your lover's impatience or your fear of losing the relationship, but eventually you must come to see sexual healing as something you're doing for yourself. If you force yourself to be sexual before you're actually ready, it's likely you'll experience struggle and disappointment, but little growth.

When my memories first came up, I turned off sexually right away. I told my lover I wanted to take a few months off from sex. He refused. I didn't want to lose him, so I backed down. We struggled over sex for six more months. He got more and more angry. I withdrew more and more. Finally we broke up over it. Those last six months were devastating. If I'd followed my own intuition and just held firm to my no, the relationship might have ended, but I wouldn't have felt like such a hopeless failure.

If it becomes clear that you're not ready to tackle your sexuality, and you're doing it solely because of the outside pressures, then this isn't the right time for you to focus on sexual healing. As a child you engaged in sex because someone else wanted you to. It is essential that you break this pattern. Sex is for you first, and there is no sense forcing yourself through a deep and painful process of change if you don't want it for yourself. It's okay if you're not ready yet. Someday you will be. Focus on other aspects of your healing now. There is more to life than sex.

WHAT IS SEX, ANYWAY?

Making love while healing from child sexual abuse will probably not fit the description in a popular romance novel: You fall into your lover's arms, your clothes magically drop away, you have no need to talk about fears or discomforts, and you come together in a burst of spontaneous passion.

Before you start sharing sex with a partner, it's important to reconceive lovemaking. Too often sex is seen as a series of events that takes place in a prescribed order. Survivors often go through the motions either not feeling at all, not liking what they do feel, or absolutely panic-stricken. You (and your lover) must give up the idea that sex is a series of events: first you kiss, then you touch, then you get genital, then you have orgasms, then you go to sleep. Instead, try looking at sex as an experience in loving, loving both yourself and another person—sex as an experience of honesty, pleasure, and intimacy. It starts, it changes, eventually it's over. But other than that, anything can happen.

IF YOU'RE STARTING A NEW RELATIONSHIP

Most sexual healing requires at least a minimal level of commitment between you and your lover. Finding a sensitive, under-standing lover is difficult for many women, not just for survivors. If you feel frustrated or impatient, you are not alone.

You may feel burdened at the beginning of a new relationship by your problems with sex. One woman said it was actually harder to start new relationships the further along she got in her healing:

The more aware I am of the problems I face sexually, the less confident I feel with someone new. In the old days, when I was out of my body, things were much easier. If I was scared or disconnected, I never knew about it and neither did my lovers. Now I can't fake it anymore. Even though I'm more healed, the ways I'm damaged are a lot more visible. Couples who've been together for years have a hard time with this stuff. How can I expect a new person to deal with it? Sometimes I feel like I'm giving my relationships a death sentence before I even start.

It's important to remember that everyone comes into a new relationship carrying unresolved problems. No one is perfect. While it's true that you might have a difficult time having an orgasm or you might experience flashbacks, bear in mind that your lover might have a hard time with other things, like initiating sex or talking about feelings. Everyone has difficulties they need to work out.

If you feel too damaged to be in a sexual relationship, work on your fears with someone besides your new lover, so you don't drag the relationship down unnecessarily. Focus on your strengths. The person who is falling in love with you is noticing your good qualities. Pay attention. Those qualities are just as much a part of you as your problems.

Going slow can help if you're afraid your problems with sex will overwhelm a new lover. If you make love right away and then shut down sexually, there won't be much basis for sticking it out. But if you get to know each other first, without sex, you will have a basis of friendship that can sustain you through a rocky period later on.

Couples often use immediate sexual closeness as a way to obscure the fact that they are starting a relationship with someone they barely know. Opening up to a new person can be terrifying. Passionate sex creates a comforting illusion of safety. But sex alone is not a lasting or substantial basis for intimacy. The fact that you need to go slow may seem to be a hindrance now, but actually it can be an asset. When you're forced to develop trust and closeness before leaping into sex, it gives you and your lover the opportunity to build a solid foundation.

Try some old-fashioned courtship. Go out for a few dates where you only stare at each other with lingering looks. Let the excitement (and the trust) build. When you're ready to touch each other, start with some hand-holding, a few goodnight kisses, or even some heavy petting before jumping into genital sex. And when you're ready to make love, acknowledge that you're ready. Savor every moment.

One couple even designed a lovemaking ritual. They knew they were going to make love, but they took the time to acknowledge the rising passion between them. They talked about their feelings for each other, about their hopes and expectations for the relationship. They lit candles and proceeded very slowly, honoring the specialness and vulnerability of the moment. In doing so, they were able to ease each other's fears, build trust, and celebrate the beauty of coming together.

COMMUNICATE

Talking to a New Lover. With the proliferation of highly contagious and sometimes life-threatening sexually transmitted diseases, it is absolutely essential that you talk with a new lover before having sex. Although these conversations are awkward and difficult, there is an up side: they open the door for talking frankly about sex. You can slide a little information about sexual abuse right in there next to the herpes.

Be direct and straightforward when you talk to a new lover. Keep it simple. Give your lover an idea what he or she can expect from you sexually. If you're scared or uncertain or want to go slow, say so. Explain your limits. If you've made a commitment to yourself never to make love when you don't want to, or to stop when you have a flashback, say so. Tell your lover what you need. Give as much information as is necessary so that you don't feel alienated or that you need to fake it.

Women have said, "But I don't know him/her well enough to talk about things like that." If you don't know your lover well enough to talk, consider getting acquainted first. As one survivor said:

> You shouldn't be sexual with someone that you can't talk to, because that's a pattern. If you're in a relationship where you can't say no, then you're sleeping with Daddy.

At the same time, don't overwhelm your lover with more history or detail than is appropriate. Don't make things sound horrendous if they're not. Remember to say that you're actively healing, and that things will change over time. Set the basis for talking if problems come up.

Your dialogue can be a two-way street. The fact that you are being open gives your lover a valuable opportunity to talk about his or her sexual fears, needs, and wants. Honest communication may not burden your lover at all; it may be a welcome relief from the assumption that satisfying sexual intimacy should just magically happen.

Talking in an Established Relationship. If you haven't told your lover what you really experience when you make love, he or she may be stunned when you first start talking. If you admit you've been faking it, don't feel desire, or are often disgusted by sex, your lover is likely to take it personally. He or she may think you've fallen out of love, feel responsible for your sexual problems, be furious that you never said anything before, or fight to deny what you're saying so that things can remain the same.

Although you risk a negative reaction in being honest, you also stand the chance of gaining your strongest supporter. Lovers often feel relieved, having sensed all along that something was wrong. They may grieve for your pain and become allies in your healing. Honestly confronting problems deepens intimacy.

Whatever your lover's reaction (and it may shift over time), healing requires that you stop pretending and tell the truth about your experience.

Lay the Groundwork First. Whether you are talking to a new or an old lover, there are certain things you can do to make difficult conversations about sex easier:

- Think about what you want to say ahead of time.
- Practice. Role-play the situation with your counselor or a friend. Imagine your lover's reaction. Keep practicing until you can say what you want to say with grace.
- Work with your own feelings. Deal with your own fears outside of the relationship so you don't overwhelm your lover.
- Talk out of bed. You're both less vulnerable with your clothes on. It's easier to listen and talk on more neutral ground.
- Pick the time carefully. Don't initiate this conversation when your lover is on the way to work or otherwise preoccupied.
- Don't talk as a way to push your lover away. The goal of this conversation is to make you closer.
- And remember, you're worth it. You deserve loving support, an ally in your healing.

Pillow Talk. Communication doesn't always have to be heavy or serious. You can talk sweet talk, make jokes and laugh, or just share your feelings as you're going along.

One day about a month ago, Nancy was hugging me and being very affectionate, and she said, "This is how I feel when I am making love to you." Her words gave me a completely new sense of lovemaking. Something clicked in me, and I said, like a child, "Say it again." She did. Laughing and delighted, I said, "Say it again and again so it won't disappear."

A few nights later, we were making love and I asked her to repeat those words. She did, which was very moving to me. For the rest of the lovemaking, she expressed her feelings a lot, instead of stressing how turned on she was, which is what she had done in the past. I felt much more connected to my body and my feelings and to her, and the lovemaking was wonderful. I was able to stay in the present without having a flashback, and without fear.

Even if you don't have a specific problem to discuss, talking is a way to feel close and reassured.

I've always needed to talk, to hear a voice during lovemaking, but I think men can get thrown by this. I'd sometimes ask for a glass of juice or an extra blanket, just to make contact.

You may have felt uncomfortable asking to talk directly, but the need to connect is a real and valid one. Talking is another way of making love.

TAKE YOUR TIME

In exploring sexually with a lover, it's important to remember that you can stop anytime. You must allow yourself the freedom to do only what feels good, to go slowly enough so that you can feel, and to take breaks, just as you did with yourself.

If you get scared, tell your lover you're scared. This gives your lover the chance to slow down and connect with you, to offer comfort, to talk, to learn more about what scared you. At that point you might be ready to continue making love or you might want to get up and do something else.

If your lover does anything that makes you uncomfortable, say so. If you start to make connections between the way you respond now and what happened to you as a child, let your lover know. These realizations are an essential part of healing.

I always pee a little when I am very aroused. One time when this happened, I suddenly realized that when my brother molested me, peeing was my only line of defense. I used to think it might save me from making love. When I remembered all of this, I had to say to my lover, "I need to stop." And then we talked about it.

Often there are some sexual acts that feel okay, but others that don't; some places you're comfortable being touched and some that you're not. Tell your lover. Just because you say yes to one thing doesn't mean you're saying yes to everything possible. And just because you say yes once doesn't mean you have to say yes every time.

Talk. Share. Experience the level of closeness and touch that you can handle now. You can feel good with someone even if you don't sail through sex, even if you don't "finish." There *is* no finish, no goal except intimacy, honesty, and pleasure.

SPACING OUT

To me, making love is a duet in solos. It's nice that someone's there with me, but I'm not there with them. I'm there as an observer. I'm there all by myself, and I don't like it, and it's scary. I have a flight reaction: "I *have* to get out of here." And the more someone likes me, the more they're turned on to me, the more scared I get and the faster I'm out of my body. I start looking up and making patterns out of the cracks on the ceiling.

I would make love with my husband and be totally detached. I'd look over his shoulder and watch the football game: "Oh, it looks like they made another ten yards." I'd find as many ways as I could to space out during The Act. I'd look out the window and think, "God, aren't you done *yet?*" I don't remember much about it. I just wasn't there. And the thing I find incredible is that I so rarely got caught, that I could be in this relationship and I'd be the only one who knew I wasn't there. *Don't they know I'm gone? Can't you even see that I'm not here anymore?*

If you find yourself spacing out or splitting while you're making love, stop or slow down. Talk to your lover. Look your lover in the eyes. Say your lover's name. One woman kept a jar of potpourri on her night table and stopped to smell it when she felt herself drifting. That strong sensory jolt helped her stay present.

But don't keep going through the motions while you are disconnected from your feelings. Even though you may be scared, awkward, or embarrassed, come back. Give yourself –and your lover— the respect of honest communication.

FLASHBACKS WITH A PARTNER

I had flashbacks making love. Frequently. One time the light was a certain way in the room. My lover got up to go to the bathroom. I looked up and she was standing in the doorway. I knew it was her. But what I saw was my father standing in the doorway watching my brother molest me. It didn't matter that I knew it was my lover. It *was* my father. It *was* my brother.

If you find yourself bombarded by flashbacks, talking helps. One woman and her husband developed the code word "ghosts," which she would say whenever she had a flashback. This would alert him that they were no longer in present time and he could then respond appropriately.

What is appropriate will vary. Sometimes you may want your lover to leave you alone, so you can stay with the flashback and open it up, so you can gain information about the past. Other times, you will choose to stay in the present. At those times, you can say to your lover, "I want to stay here, with you. I don't want to go back to the past. Help me stay here. Talk to me. Call my name. Remind me who you are."

One woman had a lover who helped her stay in the present just by saying, "Open your eyes, Edith. Open your eyes." When she opened her eyes, she saw him, saw her own room, and was able to slip into the present, away from the flashbacks.

You have a right to feel good in your present experience, even if it means regular reality checks to remind yourself that the abuser is no longer in your bed. Even if you start off with, "Sex? Uh-oh," you can talk to yourself and say, "No. Now sex is fun. This is James. This is not my cousin."

BE CREATIVE

In a relationship in which one person is actively healing from sexual abuse, sex is rarely something that just goes on conventionally. By talking with your lover, you can explore possibilities that will work for both of you. There may be times when your lover wants to make love and you don't. You have the right to say no. But you can't simply say no every time.

If you do not want to make love, you might be willing to suggest alternatives: a massage, kissing and cuddling, a walk holding hands, sharing a bath, an intimate talk. Although these don't meet the specific desire for sex, they can fulfill the longing for closeness and intimacy. Many lovers will appreciate being able to share in *some* way, rather than being totally shut out. You may find yourself appreciating the closeness as well, once you know the touching is within safe, nonsexual boundaries. Often when survivors say no to sex, they are so enmeshed in their own guilt that they push their lovers further away. Finding other ways to be close is an opportunity to build intimacy and trust instead.

Variations on mutually involved sex can help ease the process of working through sexual difficulties. Sometimes you may not want to be touched sexually—you don't want that stimulation or intrusion. But you may be comfortable touching your lover. Or you may not want to touch your lover, but you would be open to being touched. Other times you may not want to give or receive, but would feel fine about holding your lover while he or she masturbates:

When I finally remembered the incest, it was as if this tidal wave hit me. I really didn't want to be touched. But I'd struggled so hard to get to a point where I was a little bit free sexually that I didn't want to stop. So I decided even though I didn't want to be touched, even though I didn't want to have sex, I wanted to find a new way to make love, so my lover's needs could get met, so that I could have my needs met, so we could still be intimate, and so I could still feel safe.

We explored that. We found safe ways to make love. Sometimes I didn't want to do anything. I needed to write, or to cry, or just to be quiet. Sometimes I didn't even want to be hugged while working on incest, but that wasn't too often.

What you want or don't want sexually will vary. Perhaps you could enjoy watching your lover, or talking to your lover on the phone, saying provocative things. Or sending a letter describing a lovely sexual fantasy you'd like to enjoy together someday. If you expand your preconceptions a bit, you'll find that more is possible than you thought:

We're the vibrator queens. They're great. I don't think it requires intense intimacy to have an orgasm. Sometimes you don't want to make love, you just want to have an orgasm. We've had a lot of fun. We've had dueling vibrators.

Being sexual in a couple doesn't mean you have to do it with them. Often what will happen is that she'll just hold me and I'll buzz off. I didn't know that you got to do that with someone else there. And it's great. It's terrific. It works.

TRY A LITTLE TEENAGE SEX

Sometimes survivors find they are blocked at a certain age sexually, as if they haven't been able to grow up beyond a particular stage. When you were abused, you either had sexuality thrust upon you before you were ready or you were exploited in the process of coming into your sexuality. If adult sexuality still feels overwhelming, it can be helpful to give yourself the opportunity to redo your sexual awakening, this time at your own pace.

Try proceeding slowly and from your own inner promptings. Don't kiss until you feel the desire to kiss in your lips. Don't pull someone closer until your body yearns for that. As Kyos tells us, the results can be quite nice:

I started a sexual relationship with a friend who is a survivor. When we touch, there's space for me to explore, to learn about touch. It's okay for me to be whoever I am, and for her to be whoever she is. It's like reclaiming the child on a sexual level. I learn by doing.

Whatever I feel when she touches me is the important thing, not how it matches some sexual idea. We're not there to get off on each other. We're there because we love each other. If I start sobbing right before I come, that's okay. If I suddenly get angry, that's okay. If I have a flashback, that's okay. It doesn't matter. It's in the safety to stay in the present moment with whatever is happening that the healing takes place.

Sexuality is not a problem anymore. It's an exciting process. We're exploring our passion together. Once I realized that my sexuality was my power, I was able to embrace it. I'm looking forward to a lot of fun practice for the rest of my life.

(For more of Kyos's story, see page 394.)

YOUR LOVER CAN BE YOUR ROLE MODEL

If sex is an exciting, rich part of life for your lover, free of conflicts and problems, you can hold this not as a threat to your limitations, but as a vision of what sex can be.

Making love was special for her. She wanted to know how to please me. She had so much patience. It was new. People really feel this way about sex? My God! I'd never seen anyone that passionate. I watched her for a year and a half. Eventually I decided I wanted to learn to be that free. That's what it was —freedom. So I slowly started to say, "It's okay."

She would do or say something, and I'd say, "Oh, that's nasty!"

And she'd say, "That's not nasty. It's a lie. Who told you that?"

I'd say, "Yeah, it's not nasty," but in my mind I was still saying, "That's nasty!"

Eventually I got to the point where I could say, "Well, maybe it's not *that* nasty." I started to relax.

SEE YOURSELVES AS ALLIES

Lovers can become allies, united in solving a difficult and painful problem, rather than adversaries blaming themselves or each other. When your needs and the needs of your lover differ, it does not mean that either of you is wrong or to blame. It is helpful if you can see yourselves as caring partners facing a mutual challenge.

Working It Out with My Lover: Catherine's Story

A lot of times what I wanted to do sexually and what I could do were light-years apart. I wanted to maintain a pleasant, fun, playful sexual relationship with Barbara. At the same time, our lovemaking became tense, nearly impossible, and finally impossible. It became burdened with so much meaning. If she didn't get off, I couldn't just chalk it up to one time and see that it wasn't so important. It was "Because I'm an incest victim, you don't like making love to me anymore." *Everything* was my fault. I blamed myself for all our sexual problems. I was hyperaware of every little change in our usual routine.

She had to reassure me constantly. I needed her to validate my decision to look at incest material, that it was worth going through a period of changed sexuality in order for me to be able to integrate what had happened in my life. She needed patience and more patience.

I needed a lot of affection that wasn't sexual. I needed a lot of verbal expressions of love so all the pressure wasn't sexual. I needed to know she didn't love me only because I fulfilled her sexual needs. I needed to know she wanted the person inside the body, not just my body. I needed reassurance that I was still the person she wanted to be with. I needed to know she wasn't eager for me to get over it.

We decided that if sex felt bad to either one of us, we would stop. I felt, "Phew! Now I don't have to do that anymore." I started saying no all the time. Barbara got furious: "You're *always* saying no! You're always the one that doesn't want it! What am I doing wrong? I'm sick of you going through your goddamn incest stuff! I'm not your Dad! I'm not your Mom! I'm not the people who hurt you!" That would just make it worse. I'd feel like I was a terrible person.

That started to turn around when I said, "Look, it's not my fault. I know you're angry. I'm angry too. I want there to be sexuality. Yes, you're angry. But go deal with it somewhere else. And if you can't take it, leave!" We had to start from scratch, rebuilding our sexual relationship from zero. It's scary. But we're doing it. And it's been worth it.

MAKING ROOM FOR DESIRE

There is no set amount of sexual desire that is "normal." Some people have sexual feelings many times in a day, others once a week, once a month, or once a year. And everyone experiences changes in their level of desire. These fluctuations can result from stress, accompany feelings of grief or depression, or coincide with major life changes (sobriety, the death of someone close to you, moving in with a lover). Such shifts are a natural part of life.

Survivors often experience a lack of desire as a direct result of their abuse. Your lack of desire might be a defense against unwanted sex, a sign of sexual fear, a symptom of being disconnected from your body, or a reaction to the fact that you see desire as dangerous.

I've never had a sexual desire. It's amazing that someone can have screwed as often as I have, and as many as I have, and in as many places as I have, and had no desire. People ask, "Well, why did you do it?" I did it to get rid of them. I thought it was appropriate to sleep with your husband. I had a multitude of reasons, and one of them was never because I wanted to.

You may never have had a chance to feel your own desire. When children are forced to be sexual at an early age, their natural sexual feelings don't have a chance to emerge. This pattern often continues into adulthood.

When I began to get in touch with the earliest abuse, I could no longer feel desire of my own, only desire called up by the needs and desires of someone else, in this case my lover. This was so terrifying that I would space out, feel pain, or fear, or just not want to make love in the first place. I wanted loving and affectionate and sometimes sensual closeness, but I wanted these to have their own integrity, and not just be a prelude to sex.

As a child, you experienced the desire of your abuser as being out of control. You were forced to comply with your abuser's needs. Desire was a weapon used against you. And so today you may be threatened by your own desire, afraid it too may be abusive.

I got to a point where I allowed myself to get very turned on when I was making love. I was being very aggressive and in touch with my passion. I was on top of my lover, and all of a sudden I had this creepy feeling that I'd become the abuser. I just froze and turned off right away. The next thing I knew,

I started having flashbacks of being raped as a child. It was horrible. I didn't have a sexual feeling for months afterward.

The fact that you have flashbacks or painful feelings while making love may eliminate your desire for sex. People want to have sex because it makes them feel good, connected, and whole. If sex for you dredges up pain, grief, and anguish, it makes sense that you experience a lack of desire.

If you never (or rarely) experience sexual desire, taking a break from sex can give you room to see if those feelings emerge naturally when you are not having to perform for somebody else (see "Time Out from Sex," page 241). One woman who'd opted for a period of celibacy said she was feeling sexual desire for the first time in her life, but added that the feelings began to arise in an embarrassing way:

Recently, I've just started to have sexual feelings like "God, I'd really like to make love with my therapist." God, am I attracted to her! I've told her. We talk about it. She's the keynote speaker in my sexual fantasies.

BROADEN YOUR CONCEPT OF DESIRE

JoAnn Loulan, author of *Lesbian Sex,* has creatively reshaped traditional concepts of desire in a way that is enlightening for all women.* Loulan says desire can be felt on an

---

* See the "Sexuality" section of the Bibliography.

intellectual, emotional, or physical level. Intellectual desire is a decision that you want to make love. Emotional desire is wanting to make love with someone because you feel close to them. And physical desire is a specific feeling in your body that says you want to make love. These three types of desire can exist together or separately. All three are valid.

Loulan suggests making a list of things that the culture defines as desire (being turned on by your lover's naked body, wanting sex whenever you can get it, and so on). Then make a list of what desire is for you. Compare the two. It's likely there'll be differences. That's because the cultural stereotype doesn't have much to do with people's real feelings. What's important for you to focus on is your own internal experience of desire.

If you let go of the expectations you have for yourself and broaden your concept of desire, you may find that you have more sexual feelings than you thought.

> Sex for me used to be what I did when I went into the bedroom with my husband. Now everything can be a turn-on. Like ice cream. I'm not talking about wanting sex ten times a day. It's how I respond to things, visually and tactilely. I'm much more in touch with my senses now. Life is so much more of a turn-on now.

WILLINGNESS

One of the most pervasive myths about sexuality is that you have to feel desire or excitement to enjoy making love. Loulan exploded this myth in her revised version of the female sexual response cycle. Previous models of women's sexual response cycle (Masters and Johnson, Helen Singer Kaplan) cite either desire or excitement as the necessary starting point for sex.

In Loulan's model, the sexual response cycle begins with neither of these. It begins with the willingness to have sex. Willingness simply means that you are willing to enter into the sexual realm with yourself or another person and to be open to what you might find there. Willingness is an attitude. It doesn't commit you to anything more than beginning.

The concept of willingness as a legitimate entry point for sexual activity makes sex much more accessible to women who don't experience desire. It means you can have sex even if you're not feeling physical longing, emotional excitement, or desire of any kind. This is a radical and liberating approach to female sexuality.

The reasons you are willing may vary. You might be willing because you want the pleasure sex brings, because you know you will enjoy it once you get started, because you want to work on sexual issues with your lover, or because you want to practice making love to yourself.

For many women, the idea of willingness is a tremendous relief. Instead of asking yourself "Do I want sex?" or "What's wrong with me that I don't feel desire?" you can ask instead "Am I willing to begin?" The concept of willingness gives you the permission to explore sexually from exactly where you are. Instead of trying to generate desire out of nowhere, you can simply say, "Yes, I'm willing to try."

EXPANDED PLEASURE

In Loulan's model, willingness leads to any of the other stages in the sexual cycle—

shutting down, desire, excitement, engorgement, orgasm, or the final stage, pleasure. In this view of women's sexual response, pleasure is not dependent on orgasm, physical excitement, or arousal. Rather, it is a unique experience determined solely by the woman involved.

You may experience pleasure because you took the time to touch yourself in a loving way, because you were willing to engage in sexual activity after a long period of celibacy, or because you took good care of yourself when memories of your abuse came up. All these are reasons to feel good about sex. If you expand the acceptable reasons for getting into sex and widen your expectations of what you can get out of it, your pleasurable experiences will increase considerably.

SEXUAL FEAR

Many survivors are afraid of sex:

I'm fifty-three and I've never married. I have close friends, but as soon as somebody wants to be sexual with me, I get absolutely terrified. I've had sex twice in my life, not counting my uncle. The first time the guy couldn't penetrate me. With the second guy, I felt disgusting and dirty and couldn't wait for it to end. I never wanted to see him again. I feel really, really angry—not about the rape, but about my life! I'm fifty-three years old and I don't even know what it's like to have somebody be intimate with me, to have sex that I love.

As an abused child, your sexual feelings were wired directly into fear. Every time you felt aroused, you also felt afraid. Now you can't become aroused without fear. Or you might be terrified of the painful feelings that come up whenever you make love.

It seems to me that the memories are stored at the same level the passion is. If I don't make love, I don't connect with them. But whenever I open myself to feelings of passion, the memories are right there. It's a little like opening Pandora's box.

You might be afraid of being hurt or hurting someone else.

There's some kind of connection between passion and anger for me. As soon as I start feeling passionate, somehow anger gets involved, and I get afraid of being aggressive in a hurtful way. So often when I start feeling passionate, I shut right down, because I'm afraid of hurting my partner.

Or you may not want anyone that close to you, because you fear you'll be suffocated or overwhelmed by such intimacy. You may be afraid of losing control, losing touch with yourself or your own boundaries.

These fears are the natural result of being abused, and there are ways to work with them:

- **Go slow.** Back off to whatever is more comfortable.
- **Find a place in the middle.** Many survivors fluctuate between extremes—shutting down totally or trying for complete sexual abandon.
- **Stay in the present.** Pay attention to the sensation of touch.

- **Listen to your fear.** What is it trying to tell you? Is there something unsafe in your current environment? Or is it the kind of buried fear you want to push through?
- **Find ways other than sex to connect deeply to yourself.** If you start to confront painful feelings and memories in other settings (like therapy), sex will no longer be the only access point for connecting deeply with yourself, and you will gradually break the connection between passion, letting go, intensity, and abuse.
- **Check in with your lover.** If you're afraid you're being abusive when you have strong sexual feelings, ask your lover if he or she feels abused. (Your lover probably likes your passion.)
- **Push yourself a little.** If you want to make love and you're afraid, push yourself a little. Stay in touch with yourself and your partner. Communicate like crazy. Be prepared for a lot of feelings. Don't expect simple sex.
- **Stop if you need to.** Sometimes the gap between what you *want* to experience and what you *are* experiencing gets too wide. If your terror is too great, take a break. Find another way to be close.

UGH, GENITALS!

If you were abused by a man, you may find male genitals scary or repulsive, as Gizelle did:

When I start making love again, I have a feeling it's going to be difficult. You know, in my fantasies, when I imagine having a lover, I'm making love to him and everything is going along beautifully until he takes out his penis.

And then I vomit all over the floor. Literally, in my fantasy, I vomit all over the floor!

So whoever I'm with is going to have to have an understanding of that and a secure enough sense of his own maleness that he isn't going to take it personally. He's going to have to be someone who can help me very gently work through my sexuality.

(For more of Gizelle's story, see page 446.)

It may help to set aside a quiet time, perhaps just to look at your lover's body.

I find playing doctor really helps: "Oh look, it curves to the left," or "I wonder what'll happen if I touch it this way." When I look at his penis when it's not erect, it's small and soft, not so much like a weapon ruling him and me.

Try giving your lover a whole body massage, genitals included. This is not as a prelude to sex, but rather an opportunity for you to feel and explore his genitals in a safe way—a chance to realize that although his genitals are constructed in the same way as the genitals that violated you as a child, they are *not* those same genitals and will not violate you now. If your lover becomes sexually aroused, back off from touching, talk about your feelings, and continue to share in this exploration, which can help you to diffuse your fear in a safe, controlled way.

If your lover is a woman, you can get to know her body just as you have been getting to know your own. If you were abused by a woman, the same process applies. Become familiar with your lover's body. Learn about it, demystify it.

I HAVE TO LOVE THEM TOO?

Although many survivors manifest difficulties sexually, the more basic issue is often trust. As one survivor put it, "It's difficult to talk about sex without talking about intimacy. That's one of the problems."

I've always had the physical and the emotional separate, so I can always fuck men. I like to call it that because I like to call things what they are. I always knew I wasn't making love to them.

If you were abused by someone you loved and trusted, sex, love, trust, and betrayal became linked in profound ways. Many women have been able to maintain sexual relationships with some satisfaction until they fell deeply in love. Then the bottom dropped out and their fear rose like crazy. Sex was okay when they kept their feelings out of it. But sex with deep feeling brought back all the ancient pain. It was too much like the original abuse.

The image I have of my husband is that he reached through some sort of window in my life and pulled me out. He was being nonjudgmental. He was loving me unconditionally. Here was love coming at me without any expectations. We were really good friends. We got along well. I liked his temperament.

After we met, I went into a two-month anxiety attack. My stomach was always in knots. The closer we got emotionally and the more vulnerable we were to each other, the less I could be present when we were making love. There were points when the sexuality was very present, but then we were communicating less. I felt that if I gave all of myself over, I'd lose myself and I wouldn't be able to get me back. So I kept parts of myself inaccessible.

Some women have not even remembered the abuse until they were in a loving, trusting relationship. They needed that much security to allow themselves the memories.

I met my husband eight months after my father died. I'd never had a constructive, positive relationship before. He was someone I'd really been waiting for. And it was about a year later that I had my first memory.

Understanding these patterns is essential. Then you can stop breaking up as soon as relationships become meaningful. You can see your difficulties as signs that this is, indeed, an important relationship in which you feel deeply, a special opportunity to restore your trust and inner security.

CONTROL: "WE HAVE TO DO IT MY WAY"

One common element among survivors is the need to control the sexual experience, sometimes to the extent of controlling every detail. You may feel comfortable only if you are in certain positions, if the lights are on, if you initiate, if it's morning, if it's *not* morning, and so on. Although this is limiting and sometimes difficult for your lover, it is essential for you. You need to set your limits. You need to be in an environment in which you can feel secure enough to relax. In short, you need control.

> Sex is the act of being out of control. It's wonderful, but it terrifies me to give up control. It's the approach that stops me. I have to stop and think, "Do I want this to be happening? Or is it because someone is approaching me and I'm letting it happen?" If I initiate it's much easier. Then I'm the one feeling sexual, I *know* I'm feeling sexual, and I'm pretty sure I'm not being molested.

Recognizing and fulfilling your need for control, without criticizing yourself, gives you power.

> It was very threatening for me just to have a male reaching out and touching me. The fact that someone was coming to me wanting something was hard. Our therapist suggested that he ask my permission before he touch me. We did that for a while, and then it felt less like an attack. It allowed me to make the differentiation: "This isn't my father coming after me. This is my husband."

As you feel more able to be both sexual and protected, you will find that some of the elements you once needed to control absolutely are no longer as critical.

YOU'RE NOT IN THIS ALONE

While there may be short periods when you need to exercise total control over sex, ultimately you have to engage in some give-and-take with your lover.

> One day, our therapist asked Roger, "How do you feel when Karen's not responding to you, when she's closed off?" And he started talking about being flat-out terrified. To hear him talk about being terrified that our relationship was going to end made me stop and realize that I wasn't the only one who was going through terrible, awful feelings. Here was another human being, who I loved very deeply, who was bleeding, and some of that was a wound I had inflicted by being so wrapped up in myself.

While there may be essential stages in your healing when you are oblivious to the needs and feelings of anyone but yourself, the fact is that your pain—and your healing—affects everyone close to you. Nowhere is this more apparent than in the realm of sexuality. Lovers are often confused, hurt, frustrated, and furious with the sexual changes survivors go through. They may be enraged at having to deal with sex in such a conscious way. They may take your sexual problems personally. Or they may pressure you, threatening to leave the relationship.

> All along my lover has felt rejected by my sexual fears, rejected and angry. Her anger has become a steady bass, louder and more relentless and ready to lash out, to which my burgeoning sexual self-awareness became a weak treble. She asks too frequently, "How long will it be? *Promise* me it will be better soon. I don't see why you can't be better now. You don't know what you are missing. You don't understand what I am going through." In the face of these questions, I felt less like making love.

She got angrier. Now I don't feel like making love at all. Two nights ago she told me she wants a nonmonogamous relationship, she wants to look for someone else.

While you'd probably like an all-giving, totally understanding, completely patient lover while healing sexually, this is not realistic. Even the most supportive lover has personal feelings and needs. Although you can't force yourself to be sexual, you do have to make room for your lover's feelings, as fully as you possibly can. This is essential if you want the relationship to survive.

- **Be willing to listen.** Although your lover should have other people to talk to, you need to hear his or her frustrations and anger at least some of the time.
- **Validate your lover's feelings.** Your lover has a right to have needs, to be hurt, angry, or frustrated. You would too, if the situation were reversed.
- **Put yourself in your lover's shoes.** If you can't imagine being upset about not having sex, think of something important to you —like communication—and imagine how you'd feel if your lover wouldn't talk to you, and wasn't sure when he or she might feel like it.
- **Don't condemn your lover for wanting sex.** The fact that right now you see sex as a problem or a threat doesn't mean it is. Your lover's desire is a healthy, vital part of life.
- **Don't blame your lover.** This is all the abuser's fault, remember?
- **Be as consistent as you can.** At times this may be impossible, but it helps if you keep your limits as clear and consistent as possible, so your lover doesn't feel like a puppet on a string.

- **Communicate.** Let your lover know what's going on.
- **Let your lover know you're committed to changes over time.** Say it a lot. Reassure your lover that you want your sexual life to change.
- **Say the good things.** If you'd like to be able to make love, if you find your lover attractive, say so—frequently.
- **Give as much as you possibly can.** Then stretch just a little bit more. If you can't give sex, then give something as close to sex as you can.
- **Take breaks from dealing with sex.** Don't forget—there's more to life, and to your relationship, than sex.

SEXUAL ADDICTION

While most survivors' sexual difficulties have to do with not wanting sex, others experience another range of problems: wanting sex all the time and trying to use sex to meet all needs, including nonsexual ones.

After my divorce, I was really into frantic fucking. I think that what I felt was some kind of release, some feeling of being held or comforted. But it was so fleeting I had to keep doing it over and over again.

When you want closeness, intimacy, or communication, when you want to feel you are loved and worthwhile and cared for, when you're unhappy, disappointed, or angry, you ask for sex instead. It makes sense that survivors who received all their attention and affection sexually as children now sexualize even nonsexual needs.

Anyone who ever loved me had a sexual relationship with me. So if you didn't make a pass at me, you didn't love me.

Abusers used sex irresponsibly to avoid their real feelings and needs. And a lot of survivors have learned that lesson all too well.

I've noticed that whenever I felt lonely or scared or had a need to connect with my husband, I would immediately interpret it as a sexual need, even though it was clearly an emotional need. I wanted to be made love to all the time. I was very seductive, trying to get sex I really didn't want at all. I would feel real stormy and out of control and freaked out if I couldn't get it. It felt like a powerful way to behave, but it really came from a distorted sense of my own desires.

Sexual addiction, like other addictions, can be broken. Begin by paying attention to how you feel when you want sex. Ask yourself if the need or longing you feel is a desire for sex specifically, or whether it might be one or more other needs that you habitually try to meet through sex. Try to assess exactly what you want. Is it closeness, intimacy, relaxation, approval, validation, power, the gratification of pleasing someone, distraction from worries or problems, security, good feelings in your body?

In *Getting Free*,* Ginny NiCarthy breaks sexuality down into five components: affection, sensuality, eroticism, intimacy, and romance. Of the five, eroticism (which she defines as "orgasm and the explicitly sexual arousal and tension associated with it") is the only need that can't be approached in ways other than sex itself.

If your pattern is to try to fill a wide variety of needs sexually, it will be difficult, but rewarding, to try other approaches. Sometimes just cuddling will actually give you more of what you want than sex. Sometimes an honest talk is more satisfying. Sometimes you'll feel better swimming, dancing, going to a concert, or painting a picture. The idea here isn't to stop enjoying sex, but to broaden your repertoire of ways to meet your needs, thereby giving you more freedom and more creativity.

It is also a clear message to yourself that you are more than just a sexual being. Although sex can be a wonderful and amazing aspect of life, it is only one aspect. You are a whole person, of many aspects, and you deserve to have access to them all. †

REPEATING THE ABUSE

Many survivors have repeated their victimization. Some have married abusive lovers or had sex with many lovers in contexts that ranged from dangerous to humiliating to dull. Survivors have allowed others unlimited access to their bodies, and have been hurt again and again.

---

* See the "Battering" section of the Bibliography for more information.

---

† If your addiction to sex is not something you're able to break on your own, consider joining Sex and Love Addicts Anonymous, a self-help organization based on the Alcoholics Anonymous twelve-step model. (See "Healing Resources," page 458, for more information.)

PROSTITUTION

Over a million women in the United States earn all or part of their income by working as prostitutes. Many of these women were victims of sexual abuse.

Prostitution was another way of becoming a victim. At the time, I was doing it because it was the only way I could see to earn a living and support my babies. I was too young to be emancipated. I wasn't getting public assistance. I had kids who needed diapers and food, and prostitution was the only way I could think to get it.

When survivors become prostitutes, strippers, or topless dancers, they are repeating an abusive pattern.* You may feel sex is all you're good for. You may reason that now you'll get paid for what was once stolen from you. But once again, you find yourself in a role where your value is solely sexual and in which you are sexual, not basically for your own gratification, but for someone else's.

After I left my second husband and my children, I came to California and

---

* Many prostitutes have organized politically to gain the protections they need so desperately in their work. Groups such as C.O.Y.O.T.E. (Call Off Your Old Tired Ethics) have worked hard to make prostitution a reputable, safe profession. While some prostitutes see their work as positive and nonvictimizing, for women with a history of child sexual abuse, prostitution is inevitably going to repeat aspects of the abuse.

W.H.I.S.P.E.R. (Women Hurt In Systems of Prostitution Engaged in Revolt) is a newsletter written by and for prostitutes or former prostitutes. For subscription information, see the "Violence Against Women" section of the Bibliography.

within three weeks hooked up with a very violent pimp who turned me out on the streets. I was twenty-four at the time. I was a prostitute for five years. They were very abusive years. I ran away from my first pimp, but I couldn't run away from the street. When I look back, it's hard for me to understand how I did that to myself. *I didn't know I didn't have to.* It was too close to my childhood.

Women say they're on the streets by choice, but it's not really a choice; *it's their only option.* I'd been set up for it. My father was abusive and he would pay me for sex. He would give me something afterwards that I wanted, something he hadn't let me have before. He taught me, "That's all you deserve. That's all you're good for." Being out on the streets was just a continuation of the same pattern.

If you are currently working as a prostitute, there are areas in which you can actively move forward in your healing. However, your sexual healing will be severely limited until you stop.

VIOLENCE AND SEX

For many women who were abused in violent circumstances, the connection between sex and violence is strong.

When I was little, my mother would start yelling and screaming and throwing things from one end of the room to the other. And what that usually meant was that I could count on my father being in my room later. So there was a connection established between violent scenes and sex. And that's been repetitive in my adult life. It's the "break up to make up" syndrome. Sex is always better after a fight. That feels really familiar. I know when I was beat up by my last lover, one of the things that really frightened me was that when I was on the floor and she was kicking me, I flashed back on my mother. I had no idea who was hitting me. My lover pulled me up by the hair, and I knew at that very moment that it could only end in two ways. One was me taking the door to the right, which was outside. Or I could take the door to the left, which was to the bedroom.

Changing this pattern is essential to creating a healthy sexuality. If you are in a relationship where violence and sex are linked, you will need to break the connection between the two. Or you may need to leave the relationship altogether. If the combination of sex and violence is exciting to you, it will require systematic work to change your orientation. (See "A Truly Chosen Sexuality," page 263.)

ABUSE AND FANTASIES

Many survivors can feel sexual arousal or have orgasms only if sex incorporates some aspect of abuse. One woman could climax only if she imagined her father's face. Another only if she imagined being bound or raped. Another only if she was stimulated in the way her neighbor stimulated her as a child. Another only if she fantasized being the abuser herself. Many masturbate while reading incest literature.

For weeks on end I compulsively read about incest—*If I Should Die Before I Wake* in one hand and my vibrator in the other.

Most women feel ashamed to admit they have such feelings or fantasies. A fifty-six-year-old psychotherapist, who was tortured with enemas when she was a child, explains:

I felt grossed out by my own sexuality. At times I've felt that my sexuality was grotesque and that it was sick and that it would land me in the hospital. When other people bring up the grosser details of their sexual abuse, I'm fascinated. Everything else just pales and I go right straight to it like a starving dog.

I have tremendous sado-masochistic fantasies which are just beginning to come out after seven and a half years of therapy. That's because of the intense shame. I have hospital fantasies, concentration camp fantasies, slicing people's bodies up fantasies. So naturally I had to keep my sexuality, my life energy, bottled up, because I felt so ashamed and terrified of where that stuff would take me.

When the fantasies first came up in therapy, I experienced a lot of destructive rage at myself. I wanted to kill myself. I was so horrified that those were the things that turned me on. I just wonder if that isn't really the hard core, the pivot of this whole thing—the shame and horror and utter self-despair about being turned on by terribly abusive, sadistic situations.

If abuse and sadism turn you on, you

aren't to blame. You did not create these fantasies out of nothing. They were forced on you just as intrusively as those hands, penises, and leers were forced on you during the original abuse.

The context in which we first experience sex affects us deeply. Often there is a kind of imprinting in which whatever is going on at the time becomes woven together. So if you experienced violation, humiliation, and fear at the same time as you experienced arousal and pleasurable genital feelings, these elements twisted together, leaving you with emotional and physical legacies that link pleasure with pain, love with humiliation, desire with an imbalance of power. Shame, secrecy, danger, and the forbidden feel thrilling.

SM

Some women have acted out these linkages in sado-masochistic (SM) scenarios, claiming the right to feel sexual excitement and release by whatever means works. Advocates of SM argue that in mutually consensual SM, one can experiment with power. But for women who are working to heal beyond their conditioning to abuse, participating in SM—sex that involves pain, humiliation, or a situation in which one person wields power over the other—makes no sense. It would be like an alcoholic trying to heal from alcoholism by drinking only in special environments created for that purpose.

Saphyre, who was involved in SM for a while, says it felt to her like a self-betrayal:

At the time I thought SM was opening me up to my sexuality, but in retrospect I can see it wasn't. People talk a lot of propaganda about SM. I believed a lot of the rhetoric. Looking back, it was counterproductive to healing. It contributed to me *not* dealing with my sexuality because I didn't have to stay with what I was feeling in the moment. I was playing a role.

People say SM is about taking risks and having trust. It wasn't a risk to me, being a bottom. I'd already been there in real life. I'd already been at someone's mercy in reality. How could playing a game be a risk? What's a risk for me is being in the moment with what I'm feeling when someone touches me. That's a risk for me. That's what takes a lot of trust. Not SM. I think SM is a way of avoiding sexuality.

I don't think SM is ever confined to the bedroom. In my relationship, it went from being a game that was fun to a game that trapped us. It's got to affect the rest of the relationship. When you're doing SM, you're practicing how to treat your lover like shit. How can that be healing?

Whether you're into SM or you're not into SM, you can still get into society's game—one kind of sex is good and the other kind of sex is bad. I'm going for something that's different: being in the present moment when someone touches me, accepting my own passion without having to role-play to do it.

A TRULY CHOSEN SEXUALITY

You can release yourself from the linkage of pain, humiliation, and sexual excitement. It is possible to change your conditioning, to disconnect those associations, to create an authentic, truly chosen sexuality that embodies passion and excitement.

- **Make the commitment that you want to change.** Saying "I don't want to do this anymore" is a powerful beginning.
- **Back up your commitment with action.** Stop engaging in sex that is abusive in any way.
- **Start with yourself.** Work with your fantasies as Saphyre did (see below).
- **Practice staying present in the moment.** Allow yourself to actually feel your feelings without using fantasies to take you somewhere else. Remember, there is no goal.
- **Talk honestly about your experience.** Even though it's difficult to talk about these things, it is essential to do so if you are to overcome your shame and move on. Talk to your therapist, a trusted friend, and your lover.

Changing the Tapes: Saphyre's Story

When Saphyre started working on incest, her only way of getting turned on was through rape and SM fantasies. She decided she wanted to get rid of them.

I don't believe we're born with our sexuality that way. I knew I had to start from a place of not feeling guilty about the fantasies, in the same way that I stopped feeling guilty about the incest. They were both coming from the same place. Letting go of the guilt was really important. But I wanted to take it further than that. I wanted to stop having them.

I started masturbating more, paying attention to exactly what the core feeling was that made me come. The characters could change, the costumes could change, but what was the core feeling? It was "I'm totally overcome by passion. I'll do anything you want." It was the only way I knew how to deal with my passion. I couldn't afford to take responsibility for it without being overpowered.

I kept working with those fantasies until I could really identify that feeling. The next step was learning to isolate the orgasm, the passion, the intensity, from the fantasy. I had to undo the programming. It was hard to separate the two. I didn't have any support. I was doing this in isolation. I didn't know what the outcome would be, and I wasn't even sure of what I was doing, but I wasn't about to wait till someone came along and told me what to do. I had the belief that I could change.

It helped for me to feel that I *deserved* to have passionate feelings, and that they didn't have to be linked to those fantasies. I came to the point where I really understood that they weren't *my* fantasies. They'd been imposed on me through the abuse. And gradually, I began to be able to have orgasms without thinking about the SM, without picturing my father doing something to me.

Once I separated the fantasy from the feeling, I'd consciously impose other powerful images on that feeling—like seeing a waterfall. If they can put SM on you, you can put waterfalls there instead. I reprogrammed myself. Instead of having to say "I'll do anything you want," I would see a waterfall and have the same intensity of feeling.

The Gift of Water
By Jeanne Marie Vaughn

This sexual fantasy began as a conscious attempt to replace old negative images with new nurturing and healing ones. I picked the thing that absolutely gave me the most pleasure, and that was water. My favorite place to have sex with myself is in the bathtub. This piece unfolded as I took the positive aspects of what worked for me and tried to reinforce them. The excerpt that follows is a portion of a short story which I wrote for myself. More than just a sexual fantasy, it has become a meditation.

I am in a rowboat in the middle of the ocean. It is early morning. The water is a brilliant turquoise blue. There is a calm which pervades the day and I comfort in the slight rocking motions of the boat. I am seated bare-chested in the small craft, wearing a loosely wrapped cloth garment around my waist. I feel the salt in the air, on my skin, in my mouth. A breeze gently scatters a strand of hair across my face. My nostrils widen as I fill my lungs with the salt sea air.

I notice the rhythm of my muscles rowing, the slap of the oars. The sun is warm on my nipples, the length of my back, my shoulders. Small beads of sweat begin to form under my arms and then roll slowly, teasingly, down my sides. My lungs swell with the exertion and I rejoice in the light, the sound, the smell of the morning.

I am nearing the island. I have come here before and I will come here again. It is a place to which women return over and over.

I gather up the fabric of my sarong, tying it between my legs, and step into the water, pulling the boat behind me onto the shore. I head into the jungle. The air is humid and hot, the aroma of the vegetation thick and heady. Barefoot, I wonder momentarily if I need to watch for thorns on the trail. The earth itself answers me— the path is well trodden. Here I am safe.

I continue on for a while and then emerge into a clearing. Before me is a small grotto encircled by a pool. Overhead a thin stream of water flows from a bamboo tube to a solitary point below; it spills over an ancient slab of stone partly submerged in the water. This is an altar, a place of offering, and I have come to offer myself.

Dropping my garment on the moss, I wade into the pool and position my body on the stone. As I continue breathing, I lower myself until I am reclining on the stone. It is warm and rounded on my back, molded over the centuries by the bodies of the women who have lain here in this spot.

Slowly I spread my legs, opening myself up, positioning myself under the stream of water which falls down, caressing my vulva. I feel the heat, the fire of life, creep into my solar plexus, spreading warmly into my thighs and buttocks. The water laps at my clitoris like waves nibbling and rolling against the shore. I take in the water as it mingles with the light of the sun; they fill me completely, cleansing, healing, empowering. I surge and swell with these gifts of water and light.

TAKE A BREAK AND LIGHTEN UP

Sometimes as you work to change sexually, the process seems grim. You're fed up with "trying to do it." Words like "spontaneity" and "enjoyment" sound foreign. This is when it helps if you can dig out your sense of humor and lighten up.

Sometimes we take on this real hardworking approach to making love, so sincere and serious and lacking in spontaneity. We focus in a very narrow way. We don't laugh. We don't tickle. We don't play. It's very cut-and-dried. And that can be terribly boring and frustrating. What we're trying to do now is consciously lessen that, to be more playful in bed, to just have fun.

SEXUAL HEALING OVER TIME

Sexual healing takes a long time, but gradually it happens. What you experience sexually today is not what you'll experience a year or two years from now. What seems like a terrible problem now may be just a minor annoyance later on. Or sex may get easier for a time, and then hard again, when you hit a deeper layer.

Sex also has a lot to do with the level of intimacy in your relationship, the dynamics in the relationship, even the particular lover you have. Adrienne has had several lovers since she started working on sexual abuse issues, and her experience has been dramatically different with each one:

Before I met Alan, I'd had lots of lovers. The sex wasn't fantastic, but I enjoyed myself, and it was never a big issue. But Alan was the first man I really fell for, and somehow the combination of love and sex did me in. I started to have a hard time with sex, and since sex was really important to Alan, he got more and more upset. He pressured me a lot and the pressure just shut me down entirely. It got so bad, we broke up. I felt like a failure.

After Alan, I was afraid to get involved with anyone. I felt like I wasn't good enough, that something was really wrong with me. But then I met Lance, and after being friends for a while, we became lovers. I'd warned him about my problems, but he didn't seem to care. Lance was a wonderful lover and never pressured me, and the sex was great between us. He gave me lots of room to explore and let me control the whole thing. I did a lot of healing with him, and left the relationship feeling good about my sexuality.

I thought I had this sex thing licked then, so when I got involved with John, I didn't even tell him. We got into it hot and heavy, and I opened up to feelings of passion I'd never allowed before, and then, boom! Two months later I started having new memories. And sex was the furthest thing from my mind. It was bad. I thought I was finished with all this stuff. But there it was again. At least I didn't hate myself this time. I had a better idea of what to do.

Your experience of sex can change within a single relationship as well. With a new lover, there's often a passionate rush that obscures problems. But as the relationship settles, sexual issues may need attention again. As you risk more emotional intimacy, you may start to shut down sexually. Or you may find that as your trust grows and deepens, you heal on a deep body level, surpassing even your own expectations.

Because it takes a long time to heal sexually, you may wonder whether you're making progress. But even though the process has ups and downs, you are headed in the right direction. If you are putting steady, consistent effort into developing a fulfilling sexuality, have patience, accept where you are, and trust your capacity to heal.

I've had to learn to accept myself. I know I've had experiences that maybe made me a little different, and that might have made my sexual appetite more, might have made my sexual appetite less, it might have made my sexual appetite different, but so what! It's me! Let me enjoy who I am! I feel that within every woman there are a thousand and one women, and it's okay to let each one of them out. The partner will just have to deal. That's all there is to it. Sexuality is not just about getting up and humping every night. It's about exploring who you are and not being afraid of that.

Although sex was used against you in bitter ways, you can reclaim your sexuality and shape it to reflect your own deepest values.

Sex can be a powerful surge toward creation, like writing a song or choreographing a dance. All of these require absolute attention and presence; all have that great intensity; all bring something new into existence. If you choose to share that opening with a lover, it's a risk, a thrill, and a deep affirmation of trust. You affirm vitality, joy, connection. Your passion becomes a passion for life.

Even without a lover, reclaiming your sexuality is worth it. One older survivor went through a long period of struggle before she realized why:

I don't expect I'll ever be in that kind of relationship again. And just thinking about having a sexual feeling makes me practically want to kill myself. But there's a way I've been looking at it recently—that sex is a part of life, part of being alive. It's a kind of life energy. And even if all I ever do is just feel the feelings in my own body, even if I never act on them, it's still worth it. Can you understand? It's like saying yes to life, yes to being alive.

ON BEING A LESBIAN AND A SURVIVOR

I've heard forever and ever, "Oh, you're a dyke because your Daddy did this to you." It's a comment that makes me mad. It's a way that people take choices away from me. Maybe if I was a murderer, you could say that was connected to the incest. If there was going to be a correlation, it would be between the incest and my capacity for violence or hatred, not with my capacity for love.

If you are a lesbian, what you are trying to heal from is the destructive effects of having been sexually abused, not the fact that you're a lesbian. This should be obvious, but some survivors still believe that there is something wrong with them that caused them to be lesbian—that if they hadn't been damaged sexually, they'd be heterosexual. And that it's better to be heterosexual.

I had believed that I was a lesbian because I had been so badly abused by my father. I thought maybe it was a point of being stuck in my emotional growth. I thought that until I met a lesbian who came from a happy home, who had never been abused in any way. She was well balanced. Her family accepted that she was a lesbian. She never had any problems with it, and that's when I realized my lesbianism didn't have to have a cause. It's got nothing to do with what happened to me.

It is true that being abused by men has influenced some women to relate sexually and emotionally to women rather than men. However, no one becomes a lesbian solely because she was abused by a man. After all, many heterosexual women were abused by men, and they continue to choose men as their mates and sexual partners. If abuse were the determining factor in sexual preference, the lesbian population would be far greater than it is now.

I'm a lesbian because I love women, not because I hate men. I'm not a separatist. I have a male child who I think is terrific. There are men in my life I care a great deal for. I'm not a man-hater. In fact, I think heterosexual women have a lot more reason to hate men than I do.

Being a lesbian is a perfectly healthy way to be, not another effect of the abuse you need to overcome. One workshop participant commented wryly on this search for the pathological reasons behind lesbianism: "If I'm a lesbian because I was abused, at least something good came out of it."

If You're Not Sure

If you're not sure about your sexual preference, give yourself some time for things to settle. It's okay not to know, or to be in transition.

If you haven't been in touch with yourself sexually—because you've been splitting, pretending, or not very conscious—it may take some time to find out what your true responses are. Try to tolerate the ambiguity of not having a set sexual orientation for a while.

Sexual preference is a continuum. A small percentage of people are exclusively heterosexual or homosexual. Most are somewhere in the middle. Some lesbians say they were born that way; others that it was a choice they made. Women explore their attraction and love for other women at many times in their lives—in adolescence, in early adulthood, after years of marriage, after menopause. The decision is up to you.

However, if you hope becoming a lesbian will magically solve all your problems with sex and intimacy, this isn't the case. While becoming a lesbian may make things possible for you that weren't possible before, it's not a panacea.

If you are rethinking your sexual preference, consider what you want in an intimate relationship. Whom do you seem to get that from? See what it's like to relate to individual people. Stay open to how you feel moment by moment. Gradually you'll get an indication.

If you think you might be a lesbian but the idea scares or disturbs you, what you're feeling is natural. It's common to have doubts and questions in the coming-out process. Try reading about lesbians who are comfortable with themselves. Read coming-out stories.* Talk to people you know to be unbiased, who will support you in whatever choice you make.

The most important thing is to take your time. Don't pressure yourself. It's better not to label yourself prematurely. And if you don't want to, you don't have to label yourself at all.

If You're Not Comfortable Being a Lesbian

You may not be comfortable being lesbian because it's a sexual identity, and you're not comfortable with sex. You feel that being a lesbian puts more emphasis on the sexual part of you than you want. But there is more to being a lesbian than

---

* See the Bibliography for suggestions.

sex. There's music, art, politics. There's a culture, a supportive community. There's an emotional, philosophical, and spiritual connection to women.

The context of your life can also make you uncomfortable about being a lesbian. Are you in the closet, surrounded by homophobic people (people who are afraid of lesbians and gay men)? Do you have role models—lesbians who are comfortable and relaxed in their sexual identity? Are there places you can go where it's safe to be visible as a lesbian? Hold hands with your lover? Feel that you're not the only one?

If you're uncomfortable, it may be because you feel you can't afford to be open with anyone around you. While this is stressful for any lesbian, it can be particularly painful for survivors. The secrecy, isolation, shame, and fear of exposure are very close to the feelings you had when you were abused. So if being a lesbian is the second secret you've had to keep, it can bring up unresolved feelings of terror, isolaton, or pain.

Even if you don't come out publicly, there are things you can do to counteract your isolation, no matter where you are. Subscribe to lesbian journals and magazines. Get on the mailing list for women's music festivals and conferences (see the "Lesbians" section of the Bibliography for resources). Reach out. You're not alone. For many women, their lesbian identity is a strong, positive anchor in their lives:

When I first started dealing with the abuse, I questioned everything. I mean *everything*. The only thing I was sure of was my choice to be a lesbian. That felt like the one healthy, sane thing about me. It was a relief to have something that felt solid!

CHILDREN AND PARENTING

My kids gave me hope. My kids would laugh, be crazy and stupid, and pull me out of it: "Okay, back to the future." Feeling totally responsible for these kids has really been an incentive to get better. I wouldn't have made it without them. I wanted them to have a responsible adult taking care of them, to be able to say, "This is where it stops. This is the end of it."

Not only biological parents have nurturing family relationships with children. We use "parent" throughout this chapter to include stepparents, gay parents, adoptive parents, foster parents, extended families, and friends who are "chosen" family.

Being around children can be an inspiring and challenging part of healing. Children can teach you that the abuse wasn't your fault. They can help you get in touch with the child within. They can motivate you to heal, to keep on keeping on. They offer you an opportunity to have a positive experience of family life. But children also bring up unresolved feelings. They can restimulate memories, put you face-to-face with the ways you're like your parents, or remind you of your own vulnerability.

CHOOSING TO HAVE CHILDREN— OR NOT

For many women, motherhood is not a choice. Yet increasingly, women are consciously deciding whether or not to have children. For survivors, this choice sometimes relates to their own healing.

One survivor, who is trying to get pregnant, says: "I think having a child is going to be really healing in itself. I'll be able to interrupt the cycle."

Another has made a definite decision not to have children:

Here I'd been meandering around my entire life in a gray fog and only living half a life, and the idea of stopping my life to have a child, now that I'd finally come back to life, was more than I could bear. It's too exciting being alive now. So my husband had a vasectomy.

And another isn't ready yet, but may be in the future:

If I did have kids I'd want to make sure it was many more years into my healing process. I don't feel capable of giving enough love and attention. I'm wrapped up in trying to nurture my own child. I already have a child, and it's me.

You may find that your feelings change as you move through the healing process. Coming to terms with your own childhood can radically alter your perspective. You may have always wanted children, but come to realize that what you were really longing for was the healing of your own childhood pain.

Or you may have been afraid of kids, only to find that now you enjoy them.

CHILDREN AS TEACHERS

One of the most delightful parts of being a parent is the way children are always trying to snag you into playing.

The real reason I decided to have kids now is that I get to have fun! I never had that in my own childhood.

Many survivors never really had a childhood. You were expected to assume adult responsiblities or to meet unreasonable demands. Even when you were allowed to play, you may not have felt very playful, carrying your secret burden. But now you get a second chance at fun. You can romp in the park, swing on the swings, dress up for Halloween.

For thirty-five-year-old Ella, having children has been a integral part of her healing process:

I nurture them and I get it back. They love me, and you can't coerce that out of a kid. You can coerce sex out of kids, but you can't coerce something as pure as love. That's what keeps me going all the time. I look at my kids and know that I really *am* a survivor. Being able to parent gives me a perspective on how well I really am. Just the way they are shows me that I'm okay. It makes me feel that I'm a real winner. I can have anything I want. I can do absolutely anything. Being around them shows me that all the time.

Children challenge you to grow. Steps that you may hesitate to take on your own behalf, you will sometimes take for your child.

I have to learn how to do it first, so I can say, "See, watch Mommy. Mommy's strong. She can do it. You're strong. You can do it too." Things like expressing anger. Things like letting myself cry. Talking about someone hurting my feelings. Learning to reach out for comfort. I used to keep it all inside, and so did Christy. But we're changing now. Both of us.

Some women who were abused, neglected, or poorly parented have comfortable relationships with children and face basically the same problems that anyone faces in trying to be a good parent. For other survivors, the difficulties are more formidable. They have problems setting appropriate boundaries, or they repeat aspects of the inadequate or abusive parenting they experienced as children. As parents, they often feel confused, resentful, or overwhelmed.

The best way to learn parenting skills is through example. If you had supportive parents yourself, good parenting tends to come more naturally. But even if your parents weren't good role models, you can still learn to be the kind of parent you want to be.

LEARNING TO PARENT

When Ellen had her first child, she had no idea how hard it would be:

The lack of sleep, the twenty-four-hour-a-dayness of it, the shift of putting another person's needs before my own, just stunned me. And no one was applauding me. I'd gotten enormous recognition for publishing a few books of poems. People thought that was such a great feat. But writing poems is easy compared to being a mother. Yet the world just went on as if it were no big thing. Immediately I felt a kinship to parents everywhere. And the injustice that our work is so discounted.

Parenting is one of the most complex and demanding jobs anyone can undertake. Under the best circumstances, it's hard. If you have to teach yourself from scratch, it's even harder.

I wasn't sure of myself and what I was doing with my boys. I didn't have a memory of the right things to use as a base in my parenting. The base I had was of the wrong things, the things not to do. So I couldn't go with what I *felt* was right; I had to do what I *thought* was right. I had to be awake all the time to make sure I didn't hurt my kids. I had to be very aware.

Though demanding, this awareness has its advantages. Our culture doesn't give much thought to the ways we interact with children, often assuming that raising children just happens naturally. Survivors who approach parenting with a commitment to pay attention are able to make clear choices instead of working out of unconscious patterning.

CHILDREN AND PARENTING / 273

I parent my kids very intentionally. I knew what kinds of things kids needed, that I didn't get—things like good touching, good physical contact, talking to them like real people—but I didn't know how to provide them. I had to teach myself to do those things. I watched how a couple of good families worked. I did a lot of reading. I actively fantasized about what a good family would be like. Initially it was awkward, but now it feels natural.

If you're unsure of yourself, you can join a parents' support group, take Parent Effectiveness Training,* read books, or talk to a friend whose parenting you respect.

Making mistakes and trying out new approaches is a natural part of parenting. As your children grow, you grow too. While it's not easy, learning to become a good parent —in your own estimation—is a rich and rewarding experience:

Parenting is something I conquered. At first I thought I would be a wonderful parent and that I could undo all the wrongs my parents had done to me. And then I realized that was an absolute farce. And I was able to really pull out and say to myself, "You can do it. It's not going to be as easy as you thought it was, but you can just plod through it, day after day, and have little tiny victories along the way." That's real affirming to me as a human being, that

I was able to do a right thing. I committed to it, and I was actually able to carry it through.

FACING YOUR STRENGTHS AND WEAKNESSES

Honestly facing your strengths and weaknesses is essential. No one is a perfect parent. The goal isn't perfection. It's a healthy, growing relationship.

Ask yourself:

- What works? How do I feel successful as a parent?
- What am I proud of?
- Do I feel inadequate in any way? How?
- What would I like to change in my relationship with my kids?
- Are there areas where I feel confused? What are they?
- Are there patterns with my kids that remind me of my family of origin? Are there things that push my old buttons?
- Where do I feel stuck?
- When do I feel out of control?
- Am I able to protect my children adequately?
- How do my partner and I work out our differences about parenting?
- Do I have a support system of other parents I can talk to?

It's very difficult to be objective about your relationship with your children. You may feel defensive ("I'm doing the best I can"), or you may feel that any criticism of your children reflects badly on you.

---

* For information on classes in your area, write to P.E.T. Information, Effectiveness Training Associates, 110 South Euclid Avenue, Pasadena, CA 91101. Also see the "Parenting" section of the Bibliography.

My best friend told me I was letting my son walk all over me. "He's spoiled," she said. "The way you let him talk to you!" I was devastated. I was aware that my son did have kind of a snotty tone of voice recently, but I didn't know what to do about it. And he's a really sweet kid. Didn't she know that?

If someone points out a problem in your parenting, try not to get too defensive. Instead, ask yourself if you think there's truth to what they're saying. If not, disregard their opinion. But if their criticism resonates with your own inner feeling that there's something wrong, then it's time to make changes that will benefit both you and your children.

When my daughter was five, we lived in a very small house, and the way it was set up, she had to walk through my bedroom to get from her room to the rest of the house. I thought it was important for kids to have privacy, so I gave her the room with the door. Anytime she had to go to the bathroom in the night, she passed right by my bed. The rooms were so small she had practically to crawl over my bed. So she crawled in instead—and went back to sleep.

I had a new lover at the time and she stayed over with me a lot. Finally, she got fed up. She got angry. I had no idea why. She explained that I should have *my* privacy. That she wanted privacy with me. That she didn't want my daughter always climbing into the bed.

At first I was furious. How dare she come and criticize my mothering? But by morning I recognized that she was right. It was time for my daughter to get out of my bed. And for me to have the room with the door. That night I rearranged the furniture.

OPEN COMMUNICATION

Honest communication is an important part of any healthy relationship. Sharing your thoughts and feelings and listening to the thoughts and feelings of your children builds an environment of trust, safety, and intimacy.

I don't lie to my kids. We talk about what's really happening. And in my family, we never talked about what was real. Never.

Even painful or frightening subjects need to be talked about. A few years ago, Ellen was asked to speak at a conference about being a parent in the nuclear age:

As I was getting ready to leave, my daughter asked me where I was going. I told her and asked if there was anything she thought I should tell the parents. I said, "They'll want to know if they should talk to their children about bombs. They may be worried that they'll scare them if they do. What do you think?" Without hesitation, Sara answered, "Tell them, 'Talk to your children or they won't talk to you.'"

This sound advice applies to all the difficult issues in our lives. As a survivor, you know too well the danger and pain that silence carries.

TALKING TO CHILDREN ABOUT YOUR ABUSE

Children are very perceptive. If you are angry, distracted, or in crisis, they will sense it. Pretending nothing is wrong will only make them feel crazy and confused. Without facts, children draw their own conclusions, generally assuming that they are the cause of the problem. Let your children know they're not to blame.

In telling children about your own abuse, talk to them in ways that are appropriate to their age. They do not need detailed descriptions. Instead, make a general statement that reassures them and speaks to *their* needs: "I was hurt by my father when I was a little girl. That's why I've been going to so many meetings and crying a lot. I want you to know that if I seem sad, it doesn't have anything to do with you. I'm getting help now so I can feel better."

If your children want to know more, they will ask. For example, if a six-year-old asks, "How were you hurt?" you can respond with a little more information, such as, "When I was a little girl, my father made me touch his penis. That scared me a lot." If a fourteen-year-old asks, "What did Uncle Bobby do that was so awful?" you can say, "He raped me and beat me."

Answer questions honestly, always providing just the information they need at the time instead of overwhelming them with aspects of the abuse they might not want to hear or be able to deal with.

If you're not comfortable answering certain questions, communicate that in a respectful way, such as, "I'm not ready to talk about it more now, but I really did want to tell you a little about how I've been feeling, so you won't think my upset has anything to do with you. As I become more comfortable with my feelings, I'll answer more of your questions."

If your children are adults, it's still important to talk. A mother of five grown children describes the impact of her disclosure on her family:

I told my kids about the incest when I was working at the rape crisis center. My kids were surprised and supportive and then mixed up in their feelings toward their grandfather. "I can't believe he did that." Or, "He's real nice to me." And they've continued to be mixed in their feelings toward him.

Two of my daughters live in the same town as him and he takes them out to breakfast. They know all about the incest. They say, "Granddaddy's been good to us. We don't like what he did, but we're willing to see him." So they visit him, and at the same time they've been understanding about why I don't.

How much they want to talk is different for each of them. My son won't talk about any of it now. But my other kids do. I try not to impose on them. If they're not ready, I back off and respect that, and we connect however we can. I treasure my relationships with each of them more now.

If your children say they don't want to hear any more about your abuse or your healing, don't force it. Perhaps it will take some time for them to assimilate the fact that you were abused. This doesn't mean you should censor every word when they're around. But don't expect them to support you or to be sympathetic listeners. It's enough that you tell them the basics and then take your cues from them.

As with all important issues, abuse and its effects aren't things you can bring up once and be done with. Talking with your children is an ongoing process, part of creating a family environment of openness and sharing.

Incest is no longer a secret in our family. I'm committed to having as real a relationship with my kids as I can, to deal with as much of this with them as they're willing to at any point in time. Incest is not the only secret that needs to be talked about. In most families, a lot of things are treated as secrets. I've talked to them about the incest, their Dad's alcoholism, the breakup of my marriage, my lesbianism, all of it.

SETTING BOUNDARIES

If your own boundaries were violated as a child, you may have difficulty maintaining appropriate boundaries with your children now, or you may be confused about what is appropriate.

When I had my children, I experienced real bonding for the first time— a physical, sexual, emotional bond with these babies. It was just overpowering and I was scared to death that I was going to engulf them. For years it frightened me.

EMOTIONAL BOUNDARIES

Clear emotional boundaries enable you to experience yourself as separate from your children. You realize that they don't think and feel as you do, nor should they. Their interests and needs are different from yours and don't necessarily reflect on you. Assuming your own individuality and allowing your children theirs is respectful and healthy, though not always easy.

I believe in dressing for comfort. I always wear casual clothes. My daughter, on the other hand, is extremely finicky about what she wears. She loves ruffles and bows and is very dainty. She hates getting dirty and takes forever getting dressed. Sometimes I get impatient or wish she'd go out and play in a puddle or two, but that's not who she is.

Children have a right to their own ideas and beliefs. They have a right to time alone, solitary thoughts, and private places. Parents who establish their own right to privacy often find their children imitating this behavior. Your three-year-old may go to his room for "alone time" with his teddy bear, or he may ask you to knock before entering his room. If your children don't have their own rooms, they may find a place in the house or yard where they feel especially comfortable. Respect their need for solitude—to read, to be involved in their own projects, even just to daydream.

It's not appropriate to use your children as confidants or to look to them for sympathy or advice. Your emotional intimacy with them should be to meet *their* needs, not yours. If you're unsure about your emotional boundaries with your children, pay attention to their responses. If your children are pushing you away, let them move out from you a little more. Be available if they want to come close, but don't hold them to you.

SEXUAL BOUNDARIES

Parents often have sensual feelings toward their children. Caretaking, especially of small children, is very physical and it's not unusual for mothers to feel an occasional sexual response. If these feelings are neither consistent nor compelling, they are probably within a normal range. If, however, sexual desire for your children is strong or persistent, get help for yourself immediately.

Don't act on these feelings. And don't talk about them with your child. If you do, you will be sexually abusing your child.

Be aware that children often test limits, sexually as well as in other areas. They experiment with boundaries regarding intimacy, closeness, and physical affection. They might try to touch you in sexual areas or try to get you to touch them. If your child is testing you in these ways, set limits firmly while staying affectionate.

When my son was eight he kept trying to French-kiss me. I guess he saw me kissing my lover and was interested. Also, on TV there's plenty of all that and it's made to look pretty exciting. I had to tell him over and over that he couldn't do that with me. I said I knew he was really curious and wanted to try it out but that he'd have to wait until he was a little older and then experiment with kids his age. He was incredibly persistent until finally I insisted he stop asking. He even cried and begged, "If you let me do it just once, I promise I'll never ask again." I told him absolutely no, but said he could ask for something else—he could have three wishes. He asked for a roll of scotch tape, a lullaby at bedtime, and Play-doh.

This story illustrates the innocence of a child's "sexual desires," and underlines the need to be clear about what is and isn't appropriate physical contact between parent and child.

FEAR OF BEING ABUSIVE

Some survivors go through a period of discomfort around children, when they fear they will act inappropriately or be unable to set proper limits.

I have to be constantly aware of my boundaries. Whenever I'm being physical and and affectionate with a little kid, I have to think, "Is this okay? Am I crossing over his boundaries? Is this getting into anything sexual?"

If you've been abused and had your own boundaries violated, these are natural fears. You may, in fact, have had abusive thoughts or feelings. But once you are actively engaged in healing, it is extremely unlikely that you will *start* abusing children *if you haven't already done so.* (If you have been abusive to children, read "If You've Been Abusive" on page 285.) If you continue to be afraid, see a counselor to determine if there's a danger or if you're just scared. Being scared is okay. And common. Acting out isn't.

HEALTHY TOUCH

Children have a right to say no to touch, even if it's yours. Let your children know that their bodies are their own and that no one should touch them without permission. Unless you're sure your child wants a hug, ask, "Can I give you a hug right now?" Or say,

"Tell Uncle Fred goodnight," instead of "Give Uncle Fred a kiss." These are ways of giving a child control. Affection should meet their needs, not the needs of the adults around them.

On the other hand, don't be so cautious that you deny children their basic need for human contact.

I don't touch people, and I don't like being touched. When it came to my kids, I had to make a conscious decision that they were going to get the benefit of the physical contact that I didn't get. Once I decided they would, I had to say, "Okay, who's going to do it?" And it looked like it had to be me. So that became part of my healing, having these babies and touching them.

As you learn to nurture yourself, you will find you are better able to give to your

---

STRONG ENOUGH TO BE GENTLE

Essential to ending child sexual abuse is raising children in ways that will influence them to value each human life—including their own. In a society that glorifies violence, perpetuates prejudice, and reinforces rigid sex-role stereotyping, this is a staggering job. Through the media, advertising, and general cultural conditioning, boys are encouraged to be tough and insensitive and girls to be passive and compliant. Both are taught to bury painful feelings and ignore genuine needs. As parents, we struggle to instill value and attitudes in our children that will help them be both strong and sensitive, respectful of themselves and of others.

Pray For The People
For Evy

by Denise Low

My sons ignite Chanukah candles
one, two, three, four flames
and our friend recites Hebrew blessings.
Black solstice night cloaks the windows.

Flickering light ends this hard year.
We still see
    the Cheyenne people at Sand Creek
    the Jews of the Holocaust
    the murdered Cambodians
and our friend beside us
    raped by her insane father
    all through her growing years
    and bullied and beaten.

Somehow the candles are a healing.
Her voice rises over my sons,
over their slender, fragile bodies.
Soon they will grow and thicken into men
sure and strong enough to be gentle.
The first word we taught them,
while touching the cats, was "gentle."

May they live this next year as children.

May this Chanukah heal us all.

children. As you begin to trust your capacity to set appropriate boundaries, you will feel more comfortable giving them the warm, safe touching they need. And you'll be able to experience the pleasure of being close too.

Sometimes at night when I'm reading to my daughter before bed or kissing her goodnight, I'm so touched by how good she feels. Snuggled up soft against me, with that sweet child smell. I love the physical closeness of mothering.

PROTECTING YOUR CHILDREN

If a survivor hasn't remembered her abuse or acknowledged its effects, she may not be able to recognize signs that her children are in danger or may not be able to respond effectively. One woman, who'd forgotten her own abuse, described an incident that happened to her daughter when she was six:

A young man in church started paying attention to her and of course she ate it up. He'd come over to the house and ask to take her out on rides. They'd go to his house and he'd take pictures of her. We always let her go with him. This went on every day. Then we'd see the pictures. She'd be up a tree, her dress pulled up, her panties exposed, in a very seductive pose. I'd feel uncomfortable looking at the pictures, *but my husband and I knew absolutely nothing about child molesting.*

It wasn't until a friend called to say he was doing it with her daughter, too, that we went to a deacon in the church to put a stop to it. He put us in touch with a psychologist who said, "The man's a child molester. Get your kids away from him." I did, and that was many years ago, but to this day I cannot talk to my daughter about it. I'm afraid something happened, that I didn't protect her. That would be an almost unbearable burden.

When survivors are forced to confront the fact that their children are being abused, they sometimes freeze and are unable to act.

When I heard that my brother had molested one of my girls, I blanked out. I was a total zombie. It was like I was back in bed as a nine-year-old. It was like trying to run in a dream. I could hear myself saying, "He did? Isn't that terrible?" My daughter was screaming at me, "You've got to do something!" And I didn't know what to do. All I knew how to do was avoid.

Situations don't have to be blatantly abusive for your child to need protection. You may let your child play at a friend's house where there's inadequate supervision. You may not take action when your child has an overly harsh music teacher, a neglectful baby-sitter, or a problem at preschool.

I'm disturbed to realize that I've been passing victimization along to our daughters by failing to resolve an unpleasant child-care situation. They're not being hit or molested, but they're not treated with love and respect. The message I'm giving them is that I won't (am afraid? don't know how to?) protect them. It has forced me to forgive my parents, because I see how easy it is to become immobilized, to hope a situation isn't really bad or that it will just go away.

As a victim the thing I've been trained to fear most is confrontation. I'm beginning to grasp why we need to confront our abusers and those who failed to protect us. I need to confront my nameless fear, my fear of standing up for myself and for those I love most. Yet here is a situation where I have a chance to confront, to experience growth and healing, and I'm still hiding my head, wishing the problem would magically disappear.

It's essential to do your own emotional healing so that blocked memories or fears don't obscure your vision or keep you from acting on your child's behalf. As difficult as it is to break lifelong patterns of ignoring, denying, and hiding, this is what is required of us as parents. And as with all growth, the rewards exceed the challenge. Not only are your children protected, but you emerge a more courageous, capable person.

OVERPROTECTION

Overprotection is an exaggeration of the healthy desire to keep children safe. If you're afraid, especially if you're unaware of the source of your fears, it's easy to become obsessive.

I always scrutinized anyone I left my children with. If just a hair was out of place, I wanted to know about it. I wouldn't leave my kids if I could help it. I never let my husband bathe my kids. I didn't think then that I didn't trust him, but I clearly didn't. All this was before I remembered anything. I never knew why I took all those precautions. I just did.

You may try to keep your children safe by limiting their activities, but children should have the mobility and freedom appropriate for their age. You need to overcome your fears, not pass them on.

I remember going through this thing about my daughter wearing shorts and trying not to let her do that. Luckily I have this friend who is like my brother, and he told me how unreal I was being about this whole thing. He said, "Now we know you have a certain amount of things that bother you. Do you want to give her a trip about her own sexuality because you won't let her wear those shorts?" He's really helped me keep on track with my children on little things like that.

If you're uncertain about the limits you're setting, talk with other parents. Getting feedback from others is a useful way to gauge if you're being overprotective.

Although wanting to protect your children is a valid desire, you need to distinguish what you can protect them from and what you can't. No matter how careful you are, you cannot regulate every aspect of your child's life. Children spend time in situations and with people you cannot control. For this reason, it is essential that you teach your children to protect themselves. Children need to be educated and empowered. You must prepare them as best you can, take a deep breath, and let them go.

TEACHING CHILDREN TO PROTECT THEMSELVES

Parents sometimes hesitate to talk to their children about sexual abuse because they don't want to frighten them. But in reality, children are aware of danger. With the extensive coverage of sexual abuse in the media and the faces of missing children appearing daily on milk cartons, children are already afraid. And fear does not make powerful children. You were scared when you were a child, and fear did not save you from being abused.

Teaching children personal safety skills so they can protect themselves will replace their fear with self-confidence. Some excellent books and programs are described under "Safe, Strong, and Free" in the Bibliography.*

---

* CAP, the Child Assault Prevention Project, is a national model for school and community prevention efforts. Using role-plays and guided group discussion, facilitators train children to recognize potentially dangerous situations and to make effective choices. Based on a philosophy of empowering children and supporting their autonomy, rather than limiting their activities, CAP teaches children protection strategies such as self-assertion, self-defense, peer support, adult support, and reporting to an authority.

ETR Associates (Education, Training, Research) offers numerous books for children, parents, and teachers about preventing sexual abuse, as well as curricula appropriate for various age groups. ETR also conducts training programs to enable school districts to develop sexual abuse prevention education programs for adolescents. For more information about CAP or ETR or to order their publications, see the "Safe, Strong, and Free" section of the Bibliography.

Children need to know that they have choices, that they can say no, and that they are capable of protecting themselves in a variety of ways.

When my daughter was little, I told her that she should tell me if she ever felt funny about the way anyone talked to her or touched her, and that she had a right to her own body. I told her no one should ever touch her body in a way that was uncomfortable, even her mom or dad.

And she did have an incident happen to her. She and a girlfriend were playing outside, and a man offered them some candy and asked them to get into the car. As it turned out, they both ran in the house and told me. Later the police came. They identified the man, and he was indeed a child molester they'd been looking for for a couple of months. So they were instrumental in getting him caught and sent to jail.

I made sure they were very proud of what they had done, of how strong and brave they had been. I told them they had saved a lot of other kids, and that they were the heroines of the block. My daughter still talks about it, about how she did the right thing. She helps other kids now. She's very strong.

DEALING WITH YOUR FAMILY OF ORIGIN OR YOUR ABUSER

If you were abused by one of your relatives, you may wonder if you have a right to deny your children access to your family. If your children already have an established relationship with your father, for instance, you may not want to spoil their image of Grandpa. Or you may feel it's okay to take your children to visit the abuser as long as you don't leave them alone. But maintaining family ties for the sake of tradition does not help your children. You do not owe the molester an opportunity to have a relationship with your child, just as you do not owe your child the opportunity to bond with a child molester. Let the abuse have the repercussions it merits.

In the rare case when an abuser has sought therapy and has truly transformed his life, *carefully supervised* visits may be an option.

It's your responsibility to make decisions about your child's relationships with your abuser or family of origin (see "Families of Origin," page 289). If you do decide to break ties, this can be very painful. As one woman said, "I don't have grandparents for my children. I ache for an extended family."

If you discontinue your children's visits with their grandparents (or if they never visited in the first place), tell your children why. Tell in a way that is appropriate for their age, but do tell. Maintaining an illusion about the abuse protects the abuser and reinforces secrecy as a family pattern.

And if your relatives are unsuitable as a healthy extended family, consider surrogates —friends who can be loving companions and role models for your children.

YOU'RE THE PARENT NOW

In visiting members of your family who haven't been abusive, you may still encounter behaviors that aren't acceptable to you. Your relatives may want to give your children more sweets or money than you want them to have. They may tell your children not to cry, force them to eat everything on their plates, ridicule them, or slap them.

If these are the same behaviors that you experienced as a child, your initial reaction may be to respond in the same way you did then. If you froze, withdrew, or complied, denying your real feelings, it will be important to remind yourself that you're the parent now. You get to set the rules for yourself and for your children. It's your responsibility to take control and use your appropriate power.

IF YOUR CHILD IS BEING ABUSED

If your child tells you he or she has been abused, believe it. (For information on how children tell, see page 94.) Children do not lie about sexual abuse. If you suspect that your partner, the person who abused you, other family members, or your child's caretakers are being abusive, take action immediately. Countless women have been sure they were the only ones to be abused, only to find out years later that their own children, or grandchildren, or even great-grandchildren had become victims as well.

Barbara Hamilton was in her late fifties, at the start of her own healing process, when she discovered that there had been extensive abuse in her family:

My own healing came to a screeching halt when I heard about my daughters. The pain of that whole thing, I don't know how to describe it. I just felt

YOUR CHILDREN SHOULD KNOW

This information is taken from *Your Children Should Know* by Flora Colao and Tamar Hosansky, an excellent resource for teaching children how to recognize and escape from dangerous situations, how to protect themselves from assault and abuse, and how to feel both safe and empowered.

In order to teach children the skills to protect themselves, it's necessary to talk frankly. Personal safety strategies can be presented in the same manner as fire and traffic safety—with straightforward, practical information and explanations.

Self-defense is anything that enables children to escape dangerous situations. It can be crossing the street if being followed; not answering questions over the telephone; refusing to open the door to a stranger; saying no; screaming and yelling; making a scene; calling for help; running away; talking calmly to an attacker; pretending to cooperate with an attacker; or physically resisting an assault. It is a state of mind and body that allows children to feel comfortable and secure. It's the belief that their own safety is more important than the feelings of the assailant. And it's the knowledge that they're in control of their own well-being.

Children need to be given rights over their bodies and feelings in order to prevent abuse effectively. The following rights are crucial.

A CHILD'S BILL OF PERSONAL SAFETY RIGHTS

1. The right to trust one's instincts and funny feelings.
2. The right to privacy.
3. The right to say no to unwanted touch or affection.
4. The right to question adult authority and to say no to adult demands and requests.
5. The right to lie and not answer questions.
6. The right to refuse gifts.
7. The right to be rude or unhelpful.
8. The right to run, scream, and make a scene.
9. The right to bite, hit, or kick.
10. The right to ask for help.

When introducing these rights to children, be simple and concrete, using language they can understand. Encourage children to think for themselves by using imaginative or what-if games, role-playing, fantasies, or incidents from your own childhood. Always acknowledge the children's contribution, thus helping them to develop the ability to do spontaneous problem solving in unexpected situations.

so much worse about them than I did about me. That's the trap you're in as a mother. I felt flattened by the news. It just knocked me out. I didn't have the *umph* left to deal with my own abuse.

These men, starting with my father, were stealing my childhood, and were stealing my children's childhood, and were stealing everything about us, even our memories. I felt like there was some big force trying to obliterate us from the earth. It was all one great big river of male abuse. We were all just tumbling down the rapids together and there was no possible way I could separate myself from them, because they were littler, and they were going to drown sooner.

Even though it is devastating to find out that your children are being abused, *it is essential that you muster the strength to protect them.** Take your son out of day care. Stop visiting your father. Don't let your brother baby-sit anymore. Don't think the abuse was an isolated incident that won't happen again. It will.

Your family is in crisis and you must break the silence to get help. Call Child Help, the National Child Abuse Hotline (1-800-422-4453). They can refer you to support services. Call your local women's shelter. Call a supportive neighbor or friend. Report the abuse to Child Protective Services. (They are listed in the state or federal listings of your

phone book.) While reporting the abuse may be frightening and traumatic for you, it is important for your child, for your family, and even for the offender.

The job of the people to whom you report is to stop the abuse and keep it from recurring. Reporting will serve to protect other children. It will make a clear statement to the child that he or she is not to blame and deserves protection, and that the abuser will be held accountable. Also, reporting the case and having it go to court is often the only way the offender will get into treatment.

GETTING AWAY FROM THE ABUSER

I remember when I was a kid saying, "I'll never be like my mother. I'll never let those things happen to my kid. I'll stand up to my husband." But in retrospect, I can see that I was doing exactly the same thing. I thought I had broken away from all of them, that nothing was ever going to happen like it had to them. Yet it did. I was so blind. I married someone exactly like my father. He battered me and molested our daughter.

If you're living with a molester, the only responsible option is to have the molester leave the home, or to leave yourself with the child. *Children should not have to live with an abuser.*

Leaving can be terrifying. It goes against all the social pressure that says the family must stay together. You also may be in desperate financial straits. But economic dependency and fear do not justify sacrificing your children.

Some organizations that deal with incest

---

* *The Mother's Book: How to Survive the Incest of Your Child* by Carolyn M. Byerly is an excellent resource. (See the "Safe, Strong, and Free" section of the Bibliography.)

encourage reunification of the family as a goal. This can be very dangerous. Reuniting the family is acceptable only if it is truly in the child's best interests, and this is rare. Abusers do not become safe caretakers of children after a few counseling sessions and a little group therapy. It is far better for a child to live in a difficult—or even dire—economic situation with one nurturing, protective parent than to live with an abuser. (See "Recognizing Bad Relationships" on page 234 and the "Battering" section of the Bibliography for practical help in leaving an abusive situation.)

Breaking the Chain: Dana's Story

Dana, the daughter of a survivor, the mother of a survivor, and a survivor herself, took her ex-husband to court in Indiana after he molested their daughter, Christy. She talks about the resistance she met in her family and the isolation she felt when she took action to break the cycle of repeated abuse. (For more of Dana's story, see page 293.)

My mother-in-law and I were in court one day and she said, "Dana, why are you making such a big deal out of this?" And I said, "Do you know what he's done?" "Look," she said, "Jack slapped me around and he slapped the kids around and I'm okay." She refused to connect the fact that her son was doing it to his wife and to his child with the fact that she had allowed it to happen to her and her children.

Then when I was having dinner with my grandmother, my mother's mother, I was trying to get her to tell me more about when I was little. And she said, "Why do you have to bring up these things? Does it really make a difference?"

And I said, "It really does make a difference." And then I asked about what happened in her family when she was young. She said, "Well, my mother and father fought a lot. My mother was always antagonizing my father and he would have to hit her to make her stop. She really brought it on herself."

Those are the two women who are the matriarchs in the families that came together and created Christy. There's so much complacency. No one is willing to look at the fact that abuse formed the way we behave now, the way we react in relationships, the way we treat our children, and the messages we give our children about their self-worth. No wonder it's going on generation after generation.

And I can't believe that I'm the only one in these two families that include my grandmother, who had nine children, and my mother-in-law, who was one of eleven children, and my father-in-law, who was one of eleven children, who is saying anything. Of all those people and all those people's children and grandchildren, I'm the only one who's saying, "Hey, you think maybe we have a problem here?" It makes me feel incredibly alone. But someone had to stop the cycle. And I did.

IF YOU'VE BEEN ABUSIVE

When I was fourteen I was baby sitting for a little girl who was around two. I was diapering her, and she was lying there with her legs spread, and I felt furious with her for how vulnerable she was. "You can't do that! You can't be a little girl in the world like that!" And what I ended up doing was touching her vagina and putting my finger inside. I did it for a minute or two, and I was furious at her the whole time. I hated her for being vulnerable. And I had this warped feeling that I was protecting her. "You can't go around being this vulnerable, so I'm going to do something to make you less vulnerable. That way, when the *real* child molesters come along, you won't be hurt by it."

I had the assumption this happened to every little girl, and that didn't stop me from hurting a child. I had to smash the vulnerability I saw in her. It frightened me. It was that simple.

Although a vast majority of abusers are heterosexual men, women do abuse children —emotionally, sexually, and physically. When a woman's abuse remains buried, there is a chance that she will repeat the pattern.

My earliest memory of my mother is her trying to drown me when she was washing my hair. She was holding my head under the faucet, crying, saying, "I can't love you. I'm sorry. I can't love you." I have no reason to believe I received any warmth or comfort from her as an infant. She was always drunk and beat me all the time. When I was eighteen she told me she'd never loved me. My grandmother said my mother openly hated me while I was in her womb.

I got pregnant at seventeen to get away from home. I had a baby boy and settled down with my husband to raise him. Less than a year later, I got pregnant again. This time it was a daughter. And I hated her while she was in my womb. I didn't want her. I was desperately ill the whole pregnancy. I vomited all nine months. I kept trying to miscarry.

She was born and I still didn't like her. I just knew I couldn't love her. I never held her close. I wouldn't care for her. She cried constantly. I started abusing her right away. I'd take my daughter and slam her down on the sofa. The rage was uncontrollable. I never made the connection to what my mother had done to me. At that point, I hadn't even remembered it. And all the time I was abusing her, I was being a great mother to my son.

Admitting that you have abused a child is terrifying. This is why abusers almost always deny it. Yet, if you have abused a child, it is imperative that you acknowledge the seriousness of your actions, get yourself into counseling right away, and take responsibility for the implications of what you've done. If the child is still under your care, it's important to get that child into therapy with someone trained to work with abused children. Don't assume the abuse won't have a lasting effect. You have only to look at your own life to know that abuse keeps affecting you until you deal with it. Good early intervention can help children heal now and save them from carrying damaging effects into their adult lives.

IF YOU'RE FEELING SHAKY

If you haven't abused a child but feel that you're on the verge—either sexually, physically, or emotionally—get help right away.

One day when I was taking Jerri to her baby-sitter's, she started crying that she didn't want to go. I was already late for work. She was screaming and throwing a fit. I finally got so angry, I picked up her box of crayons and threw them at her. She was absolutely terrified.

I took her to the baby-sitter and when I was about a minute away I turned back, got her, sat down with her on the step and said, "What I just did was really terrible and no mother should ever treat her daughter like that." I told her I knew I'd been mean to her for a long time, and that I was going to get help so I wouldn't do it anymore.

I got in touch with a family counselor who would see Jerri alone for play therapy and then would see the two of us together. It really helped our relationship a lot. The pressure was let out.

Many communities have groups for stressed parents. Ending your isolation can dramatically improve your capacity to cope. Don't be ashamed to ask for help. Admitting your need and dealing with your problem is an honorable way to protect your child and take care of yourself.

If you still feel you can't control yourself with your children, consider placing them in a temporary safe home away from you. Leaving them may be necessary for their safety or for your healing. Living in a nurturing environment without you is better for your children than living in an abusive or neglectful one with you. Wrenching as it is, sending a child to live with a safe relative or even with warm strangers in a foster care situation is sometimes the most responsible thing to do. Protecting children has to come first. As Jennierose relates:

I left my children with my second husband when they were four and a half and eleven months old. I couldn't have taken care of them. I was extremely disturbed. Looking back, I now know why I left them when I did. Because four and a half was when the worst part of my life started. And a few days before I decided to leave, I found myself hitting my son for the first time. I was pounding on his back and I knew that I could really injure him, like my parents had injured me, if I stayed. So really, I left because I loved them and didn't want to damage them, and I would have damaged them.

IT'S NOT TOO LATE

Children challenge us to change and grow—no matter how old we are, no matter what mistakes have been made. For years after Jennierose left her children, she was full of guilt. She repeatedly tried to find them, but every time she came close, their father and stepmother moved. Finally her children came to her:

When my eldest son was eighteen, he came looking for me. He stayed for a week. And then my younger son, who was fourteen, came and stayed for a couple of weeks.

We had years when we weren't in contact, but in the last few years we've gotten really close. My older son asked me to tell him my life history: "I just want to know about you." And I wrote him a whole series of letters. I told him everything. Since then we've developed a real closeness, because I don't have to protect what I say. They know who I am.

I've asked them if they were angry that I left them. Both of them said they were, but they're not anymore, because they understand. There was no way I could have cared for them. I left to protect them.

Their stepmother has since died. I'm grateful to her for raising my children, but her death has made it more possible for me to be their mother again. Since my first granddaughter was born, I've stayed in close contact with both my sons, and that's been really wonderful. I have my children.

Even when children are grown, you still have an impact on their lives. The opportunity to be nurturing and supportive, to be an inspiring role model, and to contribute to your children's healing continues. And for some survivors, healing the pain with their children is a part of coming to a resolution with their own abuse:

I'm standing in the middle between the generations. I can't face my parents and heal it that way. Maybe I can turn to my children and heal it in the other direction. That would be making an end to it.

FAMILIES OF ORIGIN

I saw this picture. I was standing in the sunlight and my family and ex-husband's family were all back in this dark cave. They were crowded in there, and I was in the sunlight with fresh air all around me. They wanted me to come back in and I wouldn't do it. I'd finally made it out into the sunshine and I wasn't going back. And I had no sense that they were going to come out either. I knew for the first time that I didn't have to make them come out, that I didn't have to save them.

If you were abused within your family or if your family is generally unsupportive, critical, or withholding, continued relations can be very difficult. Sometimes survivors receive genuine support and understanding from members of their families, but this is unusual.* Most survivors look back from their own changed perspective at families who are still caught in the patterns that existed when they were children. And as they step out of the family system, they are confronted with the possibility that there will no longer be a place for them.

Before I told my family about the incest, I believed they would always offer me unconditional love and nurturing. Afterwards, I had to tear down

* For an example of how family members can support each other in healing, read Michelle and Artemis's story on page 431.

those false assumptions and replace them with reality.

Giving up the little girl's longing for security and protection was excruciating. Stepping outside of the shared beliefs of my family system and insisting on the truth was terrifying. I felt like a speck of dust floating all alone in a big empty universe.

It's common for survivors to have one or more family members who support them and others who deny everything.

My brother has completely supported me. He always has. He's the one person who's been consistent in my whole family. He's been very compassionate toward me. He's told me he loves me, and that he knows my parents have always treated me badly. He says he's sorry about that. And he's offered me a place to stay if I ever need one.

My sister, on the other hand, has completely cut me out of her life. She doesn't want to talk to me. She thinks I'm nasty and I've ruined both my parents' lives by bringing this up. She says it never could have happened and that I'm crazy to say it did.

In a situation like this, it's particularly important not to consider your family as a conglomerate. You can decide to keep a strong connection with one or a few relatives and not the rest.

ASSESSING YOUR RELATIONSHIPS WITH FAMILY MEMBERS

It is up to you to decide how you want to relate to your family. It is not a requirement of healing that you work toward reconciliation. Nor is it always necessary to stop seeing your family altogether. One course of action is not more courageous than the other. You can choose either end of the spectrum or anywhere in the middle, as long as your choice is based on what is genuinely in your best interests.

Look realistically at your relationship with each member of your family. Ask yourself:

- Do we have any contact now? Why? When? Is it because I want to, or is it out of obligation? Who initiates the contact?
- Have I told this person what happened to me? Does he or she acknowledge it? Is he or she supportive of my healing?
- How do I feel when we talk?
- Do I take more drugs, drink more alcohol, or eat too much or too little when we're together?
- Does this person criticize me, insult me, hurt my feelings, or show a lack of interest in my life?
- How do I feel after a visit? Depressed? Angry? Like I'm crazy? Nurtured and supported? Relaxed? Basically okay, but not great?
- What do I get from this relationship?

Look at the dynamics that exist between family members and at the role you play in the system. Is it comfortable, or is it something you want to change? If yours was an incestuous family, is incest still going on? Just because you grew up and left home doesn't mean the incest has ended for you. Maybe your uncle doesn't come to your bed anymore, but if he comments on your figure and asks if you've "had any" lately, that kind of intrusion is still sexual abuse.

Contact with your family can throw you back into the reality you knew as a child, almost as though you'd traveled through a time warp. You know you're a thirty-five-year-old adult, but when you go home for the holidays you start feeling like a powerless, frightened child. You may still be terrified of your abuser, when in reality he's a weak, seventy-year-old man. You may be plagued by nightmares or revert back to patterns of coping you abandoned long ago.

One woman was so upset by seeing her parents that she became suicidally depressed, got involved in car accidents, and was unable to function for weeks afterward. If you are shattered by the experience of being with your family, it is probably time to stop torturing yourself.

As you assess your relationship with your family, tally the good and the bad. What are the rewards? What is the price you pay? Look at what you want from each relationship. Are your expectations realistic?

If you let her, the child within will often choose to continue a destructive relationship solely in the hope that one day things might get better. In order not to revictimize yourself, it is wiser to appraise your family with the distance and honesty only your adult self can provide.

SETTING THE GROUND RULES

You have a right to set ground rules. This means deciding if, when, and how you want to see the people in your family. Many survivors feel that if they open the channels at all, they have to open them all the way. When you were a child you had two options —to trust or not trust. Your options are broader now. If you choose to stay in contact with your family, you don't have to do so in any prescribed way, or in the way you've done in the past.

> The first time I didn't send my mother a Mother's Day card, I thought for sure the sky would open up and God would strike me dead. Yet I couldn't maintain the facade. So I didn't send the card, and God didn't come to get me.

It can be a good idea to send family members a letter outlining the guidelines they must respect if you are to see them. You can choose to discuss certain things and not others. You can say that you want contact with them only when you initiate it. You can tell your mother that you want to see her, but only if the visit doesn't include your father. Or you can share information with your sister and ask her not to pass it on through the grapevine. There is no guarantee that these requests will be honored, but you have a right to ask, and then make choices based on the outcome.

There are many ways to set limits. You can get an unlisted phone number. You can insist that family members don't drop in without calling. Or you can not visit in person at all, limiting contact to phone calls or let-

I'M SAYING NO, MOMMA

by Laura Davis

ESTRANGE: 1. turning away in feeling, becoming distant or unfriendly; 2. to remove from customary environment or associations; 3. to arouse enmity or indifference when there had formerly been love, affection or friendliness; synonym, to wean.

WEAN: 1. to accustom (a child or young animal) to loss of mother's milk; 2. to detach affection from something long followed or desired. WEAN implies separation from something having a strong hold on one.

—Webster's Dictionary

Paul calls from Miami. He says I should forgive you and let go. Not hold a grudge.

Dotsy sends a postcard from Idaho: Your Mom is worried about you.

Dad says you called him, cross-continental, to ask if I'd had a nervous breakdown; seems there was no other way you could explain my letter. After all, how could a daughter in her right mind say she didn't want a relationship with her mother? How could your good little girl say no, not now, I'm not ready for you in my life?

I'll tell you how, Momma, I'll tell you how. Brick by careful brick, that's how, Momma. I've built this wall between us with careful, conscious precision. It is thick, my wall. Thick and nontransparent. I stand behind it and you cannot reach me. Its walls are smooth, Momma, flattened by ancient anger; its walls are caked with memory, bound with pitch, thick, black, and alive.

I stand back, separate from you for the first time ever, and inspect my work. What is the nature of this space I've created? What are its dimensions? What are its depths? How far can I travel inside before I come back round full face to you? What does it mean to be estranged? To take space? To create distance? What does it mean to set a boundary? To say no?

I'm saying no, Momma. I decide I like my wall.

It is not a wall of denial, of stasis, of immobility. It is a wall that grants permission. Behind its firm thick boundaries, there is movement. I stretch. I reach. I remember. What was given. What was denied. What never was there to begin with. What was good and whole and right. The lies that

ters. The important thing is that you say no to any interaction that doesn't feel good to you.

Setting Limits: Leila's Story

My mother used to call me up at two in the morning and tell me she had just taken a bottle of pills and was going to die. I'd run over and call an ambulance and get her to the hospital. I did this on a monthly basis because I felt sorry for her. I knew what she'd been through. But I couldn't do it anymore.

One night I said, "This is the last time I'm ever coming here to make you throw up. If you decide you want to commit suicide, it's your decision. I'm going to have nothing were told.

For twenty-eight years, I never shared my pain with you. Only my successes, only how good life was, only the happy times. Never the sadness or fear or anger. I've been trying to make up for being different, Momma. Trying to win your love, your respect, your blessing. But I'm not trying now, Momma. I'm starting to let go.

You see, I've got this wall. They call it estrangement. I call it freedom. Behind its thick surface, I can feel and do and be, and I don't have to show you anything. I know I'm not the daughter you wanted, Momma. I've always known that. But with my wall close around me, I can see you're not the mother I wanted either, all-knowing, all-giving, all-protective. From behind my wall I can see things as they are, find my courage, and grieve for what's been lost. From behind this wall, tall and smooth and straight, I can stop striving for what I'll never have, and find room again for you in my heart.

And when I'm done, I can take it down, my wall. Brick by careful brick. So I can see you clear.

They call it estrangement. I call it loving.

to do with it. You can call me, but I won't come."

Before that, there had been this semblance of connectedness: "Gee, we're all women and we went through this together. Aren't men fucked? We have to stick together." It was real hard to give that up, because I needed to feel she was my ally. But I had to make the break. And you know what? She stopped attempting suicide. From that moment on, my life improved dramatically. I could almost see it in the daily things I did. I could bake bread better. Because I was relying on myself. I had a certain kind of faith in myself that I hadn't had before.

You've Got Two Choices: Dana's Story

Dana is a survivor whose mother and daughter were both molested. For more of her story, see page 285.

When my daughter, Christy, was five years old, she started asking, "Why did Daddy do these bad things to me? Nobody else has this kind of daddy." I explained that other people do have that kind of daddy, and that in fact, my own daddy did those kinds of things to me when I was little.

Soon after, Christy was visiting my mother. With a five-year-old's candor, she turned to her grandma and said, "My mommy said that her daddy did those same things to her that my daddy did to me."

To which her grandmother promptly replied, "What? *No!* Your mommy and her daddy never did any of those things! Oh no! *No!* Your mother's daddy loved her and he would have *never* done any of those bad things to her. You must be mistaken."

The next morning Christy reported the conversation to me. Angry and hurt, she said, "Your mommy said that your daddy didn't do those things."

I immediately called my mother: "Look, you've got two choices. You can either come back here and tell Christy the truth or you can just not see us anymore, because that's exactly the kind of lying that's gotten us into this situation. That's why it happened to you, that's why it happened to me, and that's why it happened to Christy. And I'll be damned if it's going to happen again."

My mother and I were both shocked by what I'd done. I'd never talked to her that way before. But that night my mother came over. We went out for tacos and while I went up to order the food, she talked to Christy. She said that sometimes when you remember things that really hurt a lot, it's easier just to pretend they didn't happen. And she said she was sorry she lied.

REPERCUSSIONS

Setting these kinds of limits may make you feel shaky and guilty. You are rejecting the status quo and insisting on what you need. It may be the first time you have ever said no to your family. It may be the first time anyone in your family has said no. If this is the case, you will probably be met with resistance. You may be called selfish or told you are wrecking lives because you "have an ax to grind."

Worst of all, you may find that your family cannot respect your needs, and you must choose between them and your own integrity. Standing up for yourself means running the risk of finding that you can't afford a relationship with your family anymore.

You deserve respect, support, and acknowledgment. You do not gain by remaining part of a family system that undermines your well-being. In fact, many survivors have

I'm Glad I Did: Edith's Story

Edith Horning is a forty-seven-year-old personnel director who lives on a farm and raises horses. She's the mother of three grown children, and has made many changes in the way she's related to her own parents about the incest she experienced as a child.

I love my parents. And they love me. They love me the best they can. I happen to be a lot more fortunate than both my parents, in that my capacity for loving is far greater than theirs. They just don't have it.

For a long time I had more anger at my mother than I did toward my father. I felt the same way a lot of women do—you somehow always forgive the man because he's "weaker" and "can't help himself." But I expected my mother to be much stronger and to protect me.

As I got older and became a mother myself, I found out how little an ability to protect I had. I changed my feelings and became more compassionate toward my mother.

In the last couple of years, she has finally begun to acknowledge that there was incest. She's started to remember little pieces. A few years ago, she totally denied that it had ever happened. I told her, "You didn't listen to me any more this time than you did when I was nine."

And she said, "You never told me. You've never spoken to me about this."

And I said, "When I was nine years old, I came to you and said, 'Mom, Dad's coming into my bedroom, and he pulled down my pajamas.' And you said, 'How did you know it was a man?' And I said, 'Because I felt his whiskers on my leg.' And you said, 'No. That's a dream.' And mother, that was no dream. I was nine and I remember."

She said, "No, you never talked to me about this."

That was in November. In January, she called me on the phone and she said, "I remembered something. I remembered holding you by the hand and walking out of the house and walking all the way down the road, and getting clear down past the end of the corner, and realizing I had nowhere to go. And so I turned around and walked you back home again."

I said, "I'm glad to see that you can remember these things. Now you understand how I felt. Now you understand how it happened. You can't blame yourself. You just do the best you can at the time, Mom. When you're trapped, you're trapped." I really heard her. I could very easily see just how powerless my mother had been.

When I decided to go on television to talk about the incest, I went to my parents and told them. I didn't ask their permission. I just told them so they'd be aware of it. I told them I was going to be using my own name. And my mother said, "Aren't you going to turn your face or anything?"

And I said, "No, I'm not going to turn my face! What's the matter with you?"

"Well, people will *know*!"

"That's right. They sure will."

"Well, what will they think of me?" That was the first thing my Mom said. "What will people think of me?"

"They'll think you made a mistake, probably."

"Well, I don't know how you can do this."

And I said, "It won't be easy, but I'm going to do it."

When I told my father I was going on TV, he couldn't even get close to me, he was so scared. It just terrifies my father that I'm not weak anymore. Once it registered with him that I had taken charge, my dad became scared to death of me. All because I didn't ask him. I told him what I was going to do. I watched him get little. But I think it also registered that I wasn't out to beat him, to destroy him. I said, "Dad, this is going to be hard for you. It's going to be hard for me. But I don't want it to continue. If I can talk to people and I can stop one person, it's worth it."

When I went on TV I wasn't concerned with protecting my family. Why should I be? They never protected me. What the hell did they need protection for? They're all adults.

My kids knew. They weren't embarrassed for me. In fact they encouraged me to do it. I talked to the man who owns the business I work for and told him what I was going to do. And he said, "Edie, if you throw out a net and you catch one little fish, it's worth it. Do it!"

And I did. And I'm glad I did.

made great strides in healing by cutting the cord.

But you do not have to make radical changes all at once. You have choices every step of the way. This is a process of testing and trying, evaluating and reevaluating. You can judge the success of any particular strategy or shift what you do as circumstances change. The essential thing is to stay aware that you have the right to make changes, to choose, and to set limits.

DEALING WITH THE ABUSER

The same issues that need to be considered in relating to your family of origin are also important in relating to former abusers.* Of course, you may not want any relationship at all. The abuser may have been a stranger or someone with whom you don't feel a connection. There may be a physical danger. The abuser may be a person you hate or simply someone you don't respect enough to warrant working on a relationship.

But even if the abuser has been through treatment and owned up to everything, it still doesn't mean that you should have contact if you don't want to. It is not your responsibility to be part of the abuser's healing process or life. If you do want a relationship, the possi-

bility of building a healthy one will depend on how much the abuser is able or willing to change, to acknowledge responsibility, or to contribute to your healing.

Setting appropriate guidelines is absolutely essential if you choose to continue a relationship with a former abuser. You must be explicitly clear about what is and isn't acceptable. Unless the abuser has gone through a major transformation, you may need to specify things like the fact that it's not okay to make dirty jokes or to comment on someone's cleavage. You may want to avoid any physical contact, including hello hugs, goodbye kisses, or slaps on the back.

Inappropriate intimacy with the abuser can be harmful to you. One woman, who was a massage therapist, gave her ailing father a massage. The physical contact was devastating to her, and she was distressed for days afterward.

Setting these boundaries and sticking to them is not easy, but it is crucial.

The incest hasn't stopped, even now. It has stopped actively because I've stopped it. But her incestuous behavior hasn't stopped. She still will call me and say, "Suzanne, why don't you just come home for a week, and lie in my bed with me, and let me smoosh you like I used to." And I say, "Mom, that's what you have Dad for. I'm not here for that." I just cut it. Or if she kisses me on the lips, I stop it. But she'll still say, "What's wrong with that?" And I say, "It does not feel good to me." That's all I say. I've learned not to put myself on the defensive with her.

---

* For information on confronting abusers and taking punitive action, see "Disclosures and Confrontations" on page 133. If you're interested in taking legal action against your perpetrator, read "Mary Williams: Attorney for Adult Survivors" on page 307.

VISITS

Visiting your family should not be taken lightly. It's work, not a vacation. Stop doing it for the wrong reasons: because it's expected, because you have to prove you can do it, because you're supposed to, because one member of your family wants you to work things out with another, because you want some time off to relax.

If you do visit your family, it should be because you have made a decision that visiting is in your best interests. You should know why you're doing it. And you should prepare yourself thoroughly.

Ask yourself:

- Why do I want to visit?
- What do I hope to get out of it?
- Are my expectations realistic?
- Is this the right time for me to go? Is this what I need at this point in my healing process?
- How do I usually feel during and after a visit? Do I have reason to believe I'll feel the same or different this time?

When you do visit, make it on your own terms. You can visit at non-holiday times instead of the more loaded traditional ones. You can opt to stay in a motel instead of sleeping at your parents' house, or stop by for an afternoon instead of a week. You can bring a friend along for support. Or plan a visit on neutral turf or at your own home.

Visits are an opportunity to dig for facts, to unearth forgotten memories, to discover more about your history, to compare your memories with those of others, and to collaborate on putting together the whole picture. Sometimes a visit home is a chance to rebuild a broken relationship. Other times it is a validation that, yes, it really was (and still is) as bad as you remembered it. This kind of information is painful and you may not visit again as a result, but it is useful fuel for the healing process.

HOLIDAYS

Traditionally, holidays are times for extended families to come together and celebrate. In addition to whatever personal desires you have to enjoy the holidays with your family, there is enormous cultural pressure to do so. If your relationship with your family is strained, or if you are not seeing them at all, you may feel the loss acutely at holidays (the same can be true of birthdays or significant days of any kind). You may feel lonely and sad. You may be jealous that your friends are visiting their families and you're not. If you don't have close friends to be with, you may feel unloved and alone. You may even feel suicidal. You may be drawn to spend time with your family even though you have an intuition that it's not in your best interests.

You may be tempted to slide into patterns that put you in a compromised position. Be extra careful to protect yourself. All the guidelines for dealing with your family apply to holiday times as well. You are not required to give presents, send cards, visit, or do anything else that doesn't feel right for you. You still have the right—and responsibility—to make conscious choices. A good rule of thumb is not to do anything during holidays that you wouldn't be comfortable doing other times.

FOR ABUSERS: GUIDELINES FOR INTERACTING RESPECTFULLY WITH SURVIVORS

TO THE SURVIVOR:

Many survivors choose to break off all contact with their abusers. But some try to mend the rift. While this rarely results in a healthy relationship, the process of trying to come to resolution with the abuser can be a useful one for the survivor. If you are interacting with the abuser, you may want to set the following guidelines as a basis for your communication.

TO THE ABUSER:

Most abusers do not genuinely try to be helpful to survivors. Sometimes they make no pretense of trying to be helpful; other times they do things that make a show of being helpful, but which in actuality are not. Often their actions are tainted, so that they perpetuate the original dynamics in which the abuse occurred—the misuse of power. The abuse may no longer be sexual, but it's still abuse.

One abuser agreed to pay for his daughter's counseling after she threatened him with legal prosecution. Although he contracted to pay monthly, he was repeatedly overdue, sometimes as much as five months. This caused his daughter embarrassment as well as fear that if he didn't pay, she'd be forced to stop therapy. As a student, she could not pay for herself. Yet her father prided himself on his generosity and expected gratitude.

Looking as if you're helping is not the same as helping. If you really want to help, don't fool yourself. And don't try to fool the survivor. Follow these guidelines in your interactions:

Let the survivor control the relationship. She should choose if, when, and how much she wants to interact. Respect her limits, her boundaries, her pacing. Expect to comply with her needs, rather than asserting your own. For example, if she wants to meet with you, ask her where she would feel most comfortable. Be willing to travel, if necessary. Be willing to take off time from work, if needed.

Honor the survivor's need for distance. If she wants no contact, do not try to see her. If she wants only contact initiated by her, or only contact by letters or only under certain conditions, accept these with the attitude that they are necessary and reasonable.

Honor the survivor's anger. She not only has the right to be angry at you, but it is essential that she be angry at you. She has reason to be. Don't minimize or criticize her anger. Listen. Absorb what she has to say.

Acknowledge full responsibility for what you did and its effects. Make it clear that you know the abuse was entirely your fault. It was not something that happened between you, but rather something you did to her. Make it clear that you know that the effects of the abuse, the problems she continues to suffer from, are your responsibility.

Don't make any excuses. There are none.

Say you're sorry. Say that what you did was wrong.

Make a commitment that you will never act inappropriately again. Obviously this means not sexually abusing the survivor or anyone else. But it means not acting inappropriately in subtle ways as well. It means not telling jokes about sex to the survivor, not admiring her figure, not commenting on her sexuality (or anyone else's in her presence). It means not prolonging physical contact, such as kisses or hugs. If she chooses not to have any physical contact with you, respect that. Be scrupulously careful in your behavior, not only with the survivor, but with all people. Educate yourself about what is and what is not appropriate behavior. Stay aware.

Never use the survivor as a support person in your own struggles. You need your own support system to deal with this issue. If the survivor asks questions about what happened or asks for explanations, answer with the relevant information, but be aware that the survivor is not there to help you. You are there to help her. Don't shift the focus to your problems, past or present.

Go to therapy or into treatment yourself. This is the place to attend to your needs, your problems, your struggles. Find a knowledgeable counselor; join a support group where you will be challenged to confront yourself, not just patted on the back. Make the changes neces-sary to become a respectful, trustworthy person.

Ask the survivor if and how you can be of help. This could include being available to talk about the abuse, if or when she wants to, acknowledging your responsibility to other family members, or providing financial support for therapy.

If the effects of the abuse have limited the survivor's educational or vocational opportunities, she may ask you to make financial reparations. Many women find it extremely difficult to do the emotional work necessary for healing while working full time. In these circumstances, she may ask you to provide financial support for a time.

Do what she asks. Do it even if you don't want to. Do it even if you don't think you can. You're responding to a crisis you created long ago. Find a way.

Don't expect that you can make up for what you did. You can't. There's no way to effect justice. But this is *not* an excuse for not doing any of these things.

Don't expect the survivor to forgive you. If there is any forgiveness to be done, you must, through your own healing work, eventually forgive yourself.

You may or may not be able to heal your relationship with the survivor. That will depend both on your willingness and ability to change and on her decision whether a relationship with you is in her best interests, change or no change. And you must respect her decision. But if you act in accordance with these guidelines, you will definitely help the survivor in her healing.

It's okay to feel your grief. You don't have to pretend to be having fun when you're not.

The first holiday after I stopped seeing my family was Thanksgiving. I went to a dinner at the house of an acquaintance and tried to act like I was having a good time, but I ached inside. When Christmas approached I knew I didn't want to do that again. I decided that I just wasn't going to do Christmas. I was in graduate school and I had an enormous amount of work due in January, so I decided to just ignore Christmas and work straight through the day. It turned out much better for me. I felt peaceful and productive.

If you no longer celebrate holidays with your family of origin (or even if you do sometimes), begin traditions of your own. Think back to your childhood. Were there holidays you especially liked? Are there parts of those holidays that you could incorporate into your own traditions? Are there ways you've seen other people celebrate that you'd like to try? Holidays are rituals in which we affirm our values and our relationships. Although most people follow customs established by their families, religion, or culture, it's possible for you to modify these or to create new ones with people of your own choosing.

Passover has always been an important holiday for me. My grandfather, the patriarch of the family, presided over seders. He also molested me. I stopped going to family seders because I couldn't stand the idea of all my relatives sitting around talking about what a great man he was. So I make my own seders instead.

I always invite the same close friends. We eat the traditional foods—matzoh, hard-boiled eggs, bitter herbs—and sing the traditional songs, but instead of using the customary service, we write our own each year. Since Passover commemorates the Jews' struggle for freedom, each of us talks about what the struggle for freedom means to us today. For me as a survivor, escaping from bondage has taken on a whole new meaning. Combining the old and the new feels liberating, which is what Passover is all about.

BUT HONEY, I LOVE YOU

When a relative who has abused you, not protected you, not believed you, or still doesn't support you in a wholehearted way says, "I love you," you are apt to feel confused and disturbed.

It infuriated me that she could sit there, smile sweetly, and say, "Honey, I love you." That was her answer to everything—"But honey, I love you," in this weak, little sad voice.

You may sense that there is strong feeling behind those words, but also that there are strings attached. "Love" in your family may mean keeping silent or being bound by obligations you longer want to meet. Many survivors were even abused in the name of love.

Genuine love is a commitment to act in someone's best interests.

When my mother tells me how much she loves me, and how sorry she is, I don't want to believe it. If I believe she *does* love me, then I have to make sense of the fact that she allowed such a terrible thing to happen to someone she loved. Even though I know, for her, that's love, I know that's not really love. When you love somebody, you'd kill for them. You do whatever's necessary. And she didn't do that. Her love is not the kind of love I can believe in. She doesn't have the instincts of the lioness for her cubs, and that's the kind of primal love I need.

This fierce, clear love isn't available to many survivors from their families. Instead you may be offered love that is smothering, manipulative, controlling, or desperate. Love that doesn't take into account your needs is not really worthwhile. And love that requires you to compromise your integrity, your values, or your healing isn't, ultimately, love.

Yet it can be terrifying to say no to any kind of love. You want it. The need for kinship and closeness is a basic human need. Even the songs tell you "All you need is love." If the love your family has to offer is the only kind of love you've ever known, it can be hard to trust that something better will take its place. When there is some real caring mixed in with the distorted need, it can be even more difficult to turn their love down. But when you start saying no to the kind of love that drains you, you open yourself to recognizing and receiving nourishing love.

DON'T BUY THE BULLSHIT

Family members often lack understanding or compassion for the work you are doing. Their outright accusations or naive blunders can be terrible. Sometimes the insidious nature of a relative who is trying to be supportive, but slips in a little jab now and then, can be harder to deal with than clear-cut rejection.

With practice, you can recognize and reject these barbs immediately, before the first strains of self-doubt and confusion set in. To help, we have compiled a list of some of the worst (and most common) one-liners used on survivors by their families.

If you hear one of these, don't believe it. It doesn't matter that your mother says she has your best interests at heart, or that your grandmother has always given you good advice before. Their responses are most likely based on the fact that they are uncomfortable with what you are doing and want you to stop.

These stock lines don't have anything to do with reality, but you're bound to hear at least a few of them. When you do, remember, you're not alone. You read them here first.

- "It happened a long time ago. Why don't you leave it behind you and go on? Stop living in the past."
- "Now what *exactly* did he do?"
- "Your father [uncle, brother, grandfather] would never do such a thing."
- "You've always been crazy. Now you've gone and made this up."
- "You're just jumping on the incest bandwagon."
- "What do you expect me to do about it now?"
- "We only call those experiences to us that we need to grow."
- "It must be karma from a past life."
- "You must have been a very sexy little girl."
- "How did you bring this on yourself?"

- "Are you going to hold on to this forever?"
- "Now honey, it wasn't that bad."
- "It only happened once. What's the big deal?"
- "But he didn't penetrate you, did he?"
- "But didn't you enjoy it?"
- "Why didn't you stop it?"
- "Why didn't you tell me?"
- "I don't believe it. A mother could never do that to her child."
- "Give your brother a chance. He really misses you."
- "Forgive and forget."
- "You must be a lesbian because your mother molested you."
- "You must be a lesbian because your father molested you."

Develop an instant bullshit deflector. When one of these comes your way, scoop it up and throw it back. Tell the person you never want to hear that particular bit of advice again.

GIVE IT TIME

When you first tell a relative that you were abused, it may be a shock. But sometimes a lukewarm reception will change to real support if you give people time to work through their initial feelings. If you don't write them off immediately, they may become your allies later on.

If it's not shock or denial, sometimes it's simply ignorance that keeps family members from being supportive. Someone who says, "But it happened twenty years ago. What difference could it make now?" may be totally unaware of the long-term effects of sexual abuse. While it's not your job to educate your relatives, providing a little information may turn a skeptic into a supporter. You might want to give them this book to read. Then, if they're still antagonistic, you'll know it's not because of a lack of information.

Sometimes people who cannot deal with your sexual abuse undergo major changes when the issue surfaces in their own lives. One survivor told her cousin that she'd been molested by their grandfather. The cousin abruptly broke off the relationship:

She left me when I needed her most. I was furious. I felt abandoned and betrayed. We had no contact for many months, when I received a letter from her explaining that she hadn't been able to listen because she had been molested by him too. She said she was sorry and we met for lunch. Over Chinese food, she was ready to hear about everything that had happened to me—and about how angry I had been with her for leaving. She talked about her own fears and pain. And we recemented our bond more solidly than ever.

DON'T HARBOR UNREALISTIC HOPES

If you want to work out a relationship with someone in your family, it's a good idea to assess the odds. If your father has denied that he abused you for many years, there's little chance that he will significantly alter his outlook. As one woman put it, "He's seventy-two years old. I'm forty-six. I haven't gotten a response from my father in forty years. Why should he start now?"

On the other hand, it's not accurate to say that people never change. Anything is possible. It's like the lottery—we could all win a million dollars. But if you quit your job and start planning to spend the rest of your life on a South Sea island, you're foolish. The odds are simply against it.

SEPARATIONS

Separations can be a part of developing healthier relationships. With certain people in your family, there may have been nurturing as well as abuse or complicity in abuse. As you move along in your healing, you may want to reconnect with the positive aspects of the relationship that are still there. A period of separation can help you to sort out the good from the bad and determine exactly what, if anything, is salvageable. It can also help you to replace the child's longing with the realistic vision of the adult.

Separating from someone in your family should be based on your need to heal in a controlled environment, rather than on hope for a particular outcome. Although you may someday reconcile, it's self-defeating to separate and at the same time carry around a deep longing for the day when your relationship will transform. You control only your end of any relationship. Although you may want a healthy bond, the other person may not be willing or able to reciprocate. Expecting someone to change to meet your needs is an exercise in frustration and futility.

If you decide to make a separation for the sake of your own healing, you will have to let go, grieve, and move on. If you want to reconcile at some point in the future, you can try from your own willingness, knowing there are no guarantees. And if you decide that a permanent separation allows you to live a saner life, that's a responsible decision.

GIVING UP THE FANTASY

Painful as it is to cut off contact with family members, it can be even more painful to give up the fantasy of what your family could have been. In reality, your needs may never have been met, but the child inside has sustained a hope that maybe, maybe someday, your family would come through for you. One woman, the daughter of an abusive, alcoholic father, hadn't seen or talked to him in years when she got word that he was dying: "I was furious because I could no longer hope that he would love me."

Giving Up the Fantasy: Laura's Story

After a six-month estrangement, my mother came to visit me. I sat across from her and read her a letter I had written in her voice. It was the letter I wished I'd received from her during this heart-wrenching period.

Dearest Laurie:

I received your letter today. I'm so sorry you are in so much pain. It has been very difficult for me to believe what you've told me—until now—because I did not want to face the fact that my father could have hurt you that way. Frankly, for me denial has been the easiest way to deal with the unpleasant things in life. But now that I see how deeply this has affected you, I realize that I must step past my own denial and support you. I believe what you have told me. What my father did to you was an atrocity. No wonder it has so deeply affected your life. I know sometimes it must seem like it would have been better never to have remembered at all, but now that you have, you at least can put to rest some of the deep questions you've had about your life.

Laurie, I am so sorry it happened to you. I am sorry I didn't see it, sorry I didn't stop it, and I am sorry you are living with it still. My biggest regret is that I didn't protect you, but you have to remember, Laurie, such things were not even thought of then.

Unfortunately for both of us, nothing can be done about that now. Yet here we are in the present, two adult women. As your mother, I want to give you whatever love and nurturing I can to help you get through this thing. I'm not saying this to rush you. I know it will take time for you to heal from the effect this has had on your life. You've lived with this secret festering inside of you for more than twenty years, and that's got to have taken its toll. I want you to know, Laurie, that you have my full support for as long as it takes for us to lick this thing. He's not going to win, Laurie. You're not going to let him and neither am I. Whatever I can do for you, just let me know.

I also want to tell you that this last year has been one of the hardest years of my life. It has been hell for me to come to accept this about my father, to shatter the picture I had so carefully constructed of the man who raised me.

At times I hated you for bringing this horror into my life, but now I realize that it's not your fault—it's his. He's the one who did this to us. Now that I understand that,

I've been able to let go of my anger and put myself in your shoes a little more. I never thought the day would come when I would say this to you, but I'm actually glad you told me. You've given me a chance to give you the kind of love and support I wish I could have given you then, when you couldn't fight back for yourself.

Laurie, I think you are incredibly brave to do this work. I am proud of you. Your willingness to face the truth of your life is an inspiration to me. I only hope I can face my own life with as much grit and determination. For a while, Laurie, I was convinced that this incest thing would tear us apart and destroy all love between us. But now I know it is only with this kind of truth that we can forge the kind of healthy mother-daughter relationship that we have both always wanted. I truly believe this healing can bring us together.

All my love,
Mom

I had to stop many times as I read, I was crying so hard. When I finished, there was a long silence in the room. Then my mother turned to me and said she couldn't give that to me.

She said, "It's like the Laurie I love so much and want to comfort is sitting right there. And there's this other horrible monster next to her, who's making these accusations about my father."

I told her, "They're just one person, Mom. They're all me. It's a package deal. It's taken me over a year to accept and love that monster and I can't afford to split her off from me anymore, not even for you."

That exchange said it pretty clearly. I was not going to get what I wanted from my mother. She was not going to get what she wanted from me. I had to live my own life.

MAKING THE BREAK

I have no grandparents for my children. My mother is alive. My father is alive. I have grandparents who are alive, and they won't see me. I have aunts and uncles in the same town who won't see me. My sister won't see me. And it's all because of the incest. I ache for an extended family.

It is painful to make a break with your family, but it is even more painful to keep waiting for a miracle.

One thirty-six-year-old survivor spent years trying to have decent visits with her mother. Each time the visit would fail, she'd berate herself: "Why can't I work it out with my mother?" Then she'd try again, always bolstered up with phone numbers of friends she could call for support. Again the visit would fail.

Finally she decided to stop seeing her mother: "I was sick of repeatedly putting myself in a situation in which I needed back-up reinforcements just to get through. I thought, Why am I doing this to myself? And I decided to give myself a break. I started doing more of what I liked to do, instead of always picking the hardest thing and forcing myself to do it."

This woman stopped torturing herself when she accepted the reality of her situation. "The best relationship I have with my mother is through letters. We write nice letters to each other. We cannot be in the same room, but at least I have a mother in letters."

Another survivor, who was molested by her older brothers, had made plans to visit her sister:

I wrote to my sister and I asked if I could have a party at her house when I came to visit. She said sure, send me a list of the people you want me to invite. So I did. She wrote back and said, "I don't think you should invite Mother because the last time you two were together, it was very uncomfortable for me. And I think you should invite the boys." My brothers! She knows exactly what I'm going through. She said, "There isn't a time they don't ask after you. They love you so much. And I don't think you should invite your friends. They can see you anytime." It was crazy. So I wrote her back and said, "At your suggestion, I have rethought the whole visit. I am going to the country instead."

One survivor, after years of going back and forth, finally came to the conclusion that she had "evolved past" her family altogether. "I have no family," she said. "They're still relating in that old destructive way, and I don't want anything to do with that. Life is too short."

The main factor in the decisions of these women was the respect they had for themselves. Like them, you can be kind to yourself and take whatever course of action will give you the most peace.

MARKING THE OCCASION

When you experience a major loss, a ritual can help you integrate the change and move on. Giving up your family, and the anguish that causes, deserves recognition.

One woman wrote up a divorce decree,

officially terminating her relationship with her parents. Other women have changed their names, casting off any identification with the abuser. One survivor, who was sick of everyone reminding her how much she had loved her father, wrote a will specifying that she did not want her body to be buried in the family plot next to him.

Another woman, who was abused by her mother, created a mother-separation ritual:

As Mother's Day approached, I began to feel depressed and anxious, as if I was sinking into a deep hole. I knew I had to do something. I called the women in my incest support group for a ritual.

They brought candles, wine, and small gifts, tokens of their love for me. I cut a slit in a dress my mother had given me, in the Jewish tradition, a sign of mourning. I had a photo from childhood of me sitting on my mother's lap and I cut us apart with scissors.

Doing the ritual was a powerful marker. Things were not magically different afterwards, but at least I knew what I was shooting for.

Other rituals could include going to the desert, holding a wake, throwing a party, writing a "Dear John" letter. Pick something that has personal significance for you, that will acknowledge and honor your feelings and your decision.

COMING TO RESOLUTION

Resolving things with your family is never completely over. Although it can get much easier, you rarely become invulnerable. If you feel insecure, if your life circumstances change, if you forget the reasons you've set certain limits and consequently break them, you may experience another round of pain. But as time goes on, you will be affected less and you will make your way back to solid ground faster.

If your original family is not a source of enrichment in your life, put your energy into cultivating what you want from sources that can actually yield. Although you may have only one mother, one father, one sister, or one Aunt Bea, you can create an alternative family of your own choosing in the present. Look to your friends, the members of your incest group, your partner, or your children. Although they will not replace what you have lost, they can offer abundant opportunities for nurturing, closeness, and comfort. This is what makes a healthy family.

WRITING EXERCISE: YOUR FAMILY NOW

(See the basic method for writing exercises on page 28.)

What is satisfactory for you in relating to your family of origin now? What do you like? Who are your supporters? Whom do you enjoy being with? What do you get from your contact with them? What are the advantages in being with your family?

What isn't okay for you? What is destructive, irritating, infuriating, frightening, painful? Who are your adversaries? Whom do you feel bad being with? What are the disadvantages of being with your family?

MARY WILLIAMS: ATTORNEY FOR ADULT SURVIVORS

In 1982 a thirty-four-year-old woman approached Mary R. Williams to see if it was possible to sue her father for molesting her as a child. Williams took the case and since then has represented many other adult survivors in suing their perpetrators. All of the cases have been settled out of court.

Williams practices in California. Although the laws vary from state to state, suits have been filed on behalf of adult survivors in New York, Wisconsin, Vermont, Minnesota, and Massachusetts.

By the time my first client came to me, she had already gone to other lawyers who had told her that the statute of limitations (a specified time limit for filing legal actions) had run out. They said there was no way she could file a personal injury lawsuit for abuse that happened when she was a child, but I thought there would be a way to argue around the statute of limitations, since she had repressed the abuse for so many years.

The California statute of limitations for personal injuries states that you have one year from the date of the injury to file a lawsuit. For any injuries that occur when you are a minor, you have one year from the date you turn eighteen, which is the age of majority. But like most states, California has a delayed discovery exception to the statute of limitations for personal injury. If you have an injury such as asbestosis, the injury occurs when you're exposed to the asbestos, but you don't know that. It's a hidden injury. It may take ten or fifteen years to develop symptoms, and even longer to discover the cause of those symptoms.

Under this doctrine, if your injury is incurred without your knowledge, develops in a hidden way, and only manifests later, the statute of limitations doesn't start to run until you have become aware of the injury and its probable cause.

In cases for adult survivors of childhood sexual abuse, I've argued that delayed discovery should apply because the psychological effects of incest cause the victim to repress and deny what is happening, to develop internalized guilt and shame, and to keep it a secret. Those dynamics continue to operate long after the abuse stops, and prevent the person, even after she's turned eighteen and can legally sue, from being able to understand that she'd been injured by what happened.

California recently enacted a new three-year statute of limitations specifically for civil actions based on childhood sexual abuse where the abuse was committed by a family or household member. Under this statute, victims would have until their twenty-first birthday to bring suit for the abuse.

Although the new law does not specifically say that delayed discovery applies, it doesn't prohibit it. If delayed discovery is held to apply to the statute, then survivors would have three years from the date of discovery (which could be when they started therapy) to file suit.* This would be

Box continues on page 308.

---

* In November 1987, the Wisconsin Court of Appeals ruled that delayed discovery can apply in these cases (Hammer v. Hammer, District #1, 86-2039). G. Jane Kaftan was the attorney in this case (see "Lawyers Handling Cases for Adult Survivors," page 311).

a major breakthrough for survivors, because one year from the date of discovery is not enough time for many survivors to make the decision to sue. The process of discovering memories and trying to heal is terrifying and painful. It can be very difficult to think about suing, much less to have the state of mind required to stand up to the demands of the litigation process.

When survivors come to me, I ask them to consider several things if they're thinking of filing a suit. I ask if they are prepared to go through the slowness and frustration of the litigation process, which may take two years or more and may be filled with legal maneuvers that seem irrelevant and a waste of time. I ask them to think about how they'd feel if they lost the case. Would they be so devastated that it would be a real threat to their emotional health and recovery? I also ask clients to think about what they really want to get out of it, what their expectations are. I try to help them look at the prospects realistically so they can decide whether they want to follow through.

In my experience, most survivors aren't thinking primarily about the money they might get. Their main motive is a desire to get the abuser to take responsibility for what he did. They want him to have to face up to it, and they feel the court system will do that.

Unfortunately, a lawsuit is not a great vehicle for getting someone to take responsibility for something. What lawsuits are best able to do is get money. A lawsuit is not likely to make the defendant feel differently or apologize from his heart. Once you file a lawsuit, the defendant is going to fight it. He'll deny it and try to undercut your case. However, being sued for this kind of abuse does have a strong impact on the abuser, who is often more afraid of public exposure than anything else.

The abuser will not be directly confronted by the lawsuit, except at his deposition (oral testimony given out of court but under oath) or at the trial. The expectation that there's going to be some kind of emotional resolution is a false one, but a lawsuit does allow the survivor to go into the legal system and face this person as an adult, as an equal, as another citizen who now has power of her own.

It is often a cathartic experience for victims to talk about the abuse, to say things that have been said to only a few people, and to say them in an adversarial situation where they're sitting across the table from someone who is being paid to cross-examine them. It's really an experience of standing up for yourself and saying the truth.

One of the best parts for most of my clients is being able to watch the defendant give his deposition. Often he doesn't come across as well as she does. The defendant is lying, so he's got a fundamentally weak position, and that often comes across in the way he testifies. Seeing that the abuser is in fact weak, not convincing, and unable to stand up as well as she is to this process can be tremendously healing to the person whose memory of the abuser is that he could do anything, that he controlled the world she lived in.

Two sisters I represented gave depositions that were very powerful releases for them. One sister had dreams afterwards in which she finally stood up to her abuser. A couple of months later, they came to watch their abuser give his deposition. He was shaking all over and his testimony was totally unbelievable. It was revolutionary for them. They no longer needed to be afraid of this man who had occupied such a terrifying place in their minds for years.

GETTING MONEY

Monetary compensation, even if it cannot undo the damage, is a form of justice, of being vindicated by society while the abuser is blamed and punished. Money is also helpful in a practical way, to pay for therapy and perhaps provide educational and economic opportunities that had been lost.

The range of settlements varies widely, depending on the potential sources of recovery and the relative strengths and weaknesses of the case. I have had settlements ranging from $20,000 to nearly $100,000.* Money is typically awarded in these cases for therapy costs and for potential income lost due to emotional stress or lack of educational opportunities.

If the defendant has money, we try to collect from him. But more typically settlements are paid by the abuser's homeowner's insurance policy.

Homeowner's liability insurance protects the homeowner for damages he might cause by his own negligence.† In California, insurance contracts are interpreted very broadly by the courts. The meaning of an act of negligence for the purposes of insurance is not that you did something that you didn't intend to do, but that you didn't intend to cause harm by it. Cases of assault and battery have been covered under this personal liability coverage, so I argued that incest cases should also be covered by the homeowner's policy.‡

I have argued that the person who is perpetrating this kind of sexual abuse does not think that he is causing harm and therefore insurance coverage should be available. Even if they admit they abused their kids, most offenders never get to the point of acknowledging that what they did was harmful or bad. This doesn't excuse their behavior or make their abuse less criminal, but it can mean some financial compensation for the survivor.

At first I had a very hard time with this because abusers should be held responsible and society should not excuse them in any way. However, if insurance coverage

Box continues on page 310.

---

* As issues about delayed discovery and insurance coverage are resolved, average settlement amounts will probably rise.

† If the abuse happened in a car, sometimes automobile insurance can be used in the same way.

‡ There hasn't been a definitive decision regarding the liability of insurance companies in these cases. But the threat they might be held liable if the case went to court has been strong enough for some companies to offer settlement money. Insurance companies are now changing policies to close this loophole, but that won't affect adult survivors suing today.

is not available at all, many deserving cases will never get to court, because no attorney will take on a case where there is no possibility of getting paid.

AFTER THE CASE IS SETTLED

In my experience, nearly every client who has undertaken this kind of suit has experienced growth, therapeutic strengthening, and an increased sense of personal power and self-esteem as a result of the litigation.

At the same time, there's often a feeling of letdown and disappointment. Frequently we've prepared for the possibility of a trial, and when the case is settled out of court, all you're left with is a check which comes in the mail a month later. And if the case does go to court, the decision will probably be appealed. With lawsuits, even if you win, you seldom win clearly and overwhelmingly, nor do you get everything you're entitled to. The process is always a compromise.

Another thing that can happen after a lawsuit is that the survivor suddenly has to deal with all the feelings that came up during the lawsuit, which she couldn't afford to feel fully while it was going on. Even though the lawsuit was resolved in her favor, the effects of the abuse haven't necessarily disappeared or become any easier. The emotional reconstruction still has to be done.

But again, a lot of my clients also feel a tremendous sense of relief and victory. They get strong by suing. They step out of the fantasy that it didn't happen or that

their parents really loved and cared for them in a healthy way. It produces a beneficial separation that can be a rite of passage for the survivor.

Critics say it's bad for survivors to sue because it means cutting ties with their families, but I can't think of anyone who's come to me who has any healthy tie left to her abuser. If there was something there they could use to work with, they wouldn't be coming to see me. Many of my clients have tried writing letters, going to other relatives, or confronting the abuser. So it's not suing that breaks the ties. They were already severed, destroyed by the offender a long time ago. The lawsuit is just the final result of that.

And family relationships are not severed in every case. Many of my clients have at least one ally in their family who believes and supports them. And occasionally, relationships with siblings or mothers actually become stronger as a result of the lawsuit.

Ultimately, it's educational for society as a whole for these cases to come into the courts. The legal system is so important to the American consciousness. If you can take it to court, there's a way in which you symbolically get vindicated that doesn't happen in any other way. If victims of sexual abuse use the court system, then people can no longer accept abuse and not talk about it. Abusers can no longer count on not being confronted. And society cannot just sweep it under the rug.

LAWYERS HANDLING CASES FOR ADULT SURVIVORS

The following lawyers are knowledgable about both the legal and the emotional issues involved:

Mary Williams
1727 Martin Luther King Jr. Way, Suite 107
Oakland, CA 94612
(415) 893-7120

Alan Rosenfeld*
P.O. Box 35
Marshfield, VT 05658
(802) 426-3846

Michael S. Morey
Holmes, DeFranq and Schulte, P.C.
811 SW Front, Suite 500
Portland, OR 97204
(503) 223-4131

Kevin P. McBride
Brett G. Pearce
Strong & Hanni
Sixth Floor, Boston Building
Salt Lake City, UT 84111
(801) 532-7080

Stephen J. Fortunato, Jr.
Fortunato Law Offices
West Exchange Center, Suite 305
260 West Exchange Street
Providence, RI 02903
(401) 351-7722

Tom Brown
Brown and Scruggs
120 Mission Street
Santa Cruz, CA 95062
(408) 429-1434

William Boggs
P.O. Box 7881
Missoula, MT 59807
(406) 728-3088

Elizabeth Kelly Ebitz
15 Columbia Street
P.O. Box 641
Bangor, ME 04401
(207) 947-8666

G. Jane Kaftan
822 Jordan Road
DePere, WI 54115
(414) 336-5222

Shari Karney
16055 Ventura Blvd., Suite 1020
Encino, CA 91436
(818) 995-6966

Gregg Meyers
Finkel, Georgaklis, Goldberg,
Sheftman & Korn
192 East Bay Street, Suite 300
Charleston, SC 29402

---

* Alan Rosenfeld represents protecting parents in custody and visitation cases.

PART FOUR

FOR SUPPORTERS
OF SURVIVORS

THE BASICS

Being a close supporter of a woman actively healing from child sexual abuse can be a challenge. While being part of a deep healing process holds the potential for tremendous growth and intimacy, it can also leave you feeling conflicted, overwhelmed, or resentful. You may be frightened or confused, unsure what to do, how to feel, or what to expect. These are natural and appropriate responses to a complex and trying human situation.

This is a time when it's important for you to take care of yourself. It's essential that you honor your own needs. If the survivor wants more than you are able to give, admit your limits. Encourage her to call on other resources. Take some breaks. Get help for yourself. Dealing with such raw pain is difficult, and you need a place where you can express your own fears and frustrations.

If you find yourself feeling extremely defensive or upset when the survivor talks about her abuse, you may be reacting from experiences you've repressed from your own past. This is very common. One person's pain frequently brings up hurts for another. Seek support in dealing with your own unresolved feelings. You are important too.

All intimate relationships—friends, couples, or family—have a lot in common. "For Partners" (page 321) offers specific suggestions that will help even if you're not in a partnered relationship with the survivor.

HOW TO HELP

When a survivor tells you that she was sexually abused as a child, she is entrusting you with a part of her life that is painful,

315

For Neil, Because You Asked
by Krishnabai

Stress, long my enemy,
visits me often
wearing long, full skirts
which harbour her children.
They creep out
when my back is turned.
They try to overtake me.

The eldest, Fear
is strong and cruel.
He jumps on my back,
arms around my throat
shrieks horrors in my ears,
and on fast feet I jump
out the window,
scream down the street
into the dark
horizon of night,
and only much later do I return
ragged, weeping, alone.

Here's how to care for me
when I'm with Fear:
move softly as approaching
a luna moth,
have gentle, calm eyes,
stay centered from my panic,
and, if we ever
reach this place of safety—
just hold me.

frightening, and vulnerable. These guidelines can help you honor that trust and assist her healing:

- **Believe the survivor.** Even if she sometimes doubts herself, even if her memories are vague, even if what she tells you sounds too extreme, believe her. Women don't make up stories of abuse. Let her know that you are open to hearing anything she wishes to share, and that although it's painful and upsetting, you are willing to enter those difficult places with her and to receive her words with respect.

- **Join with the survivor in validating the damage.** All abuse is harmful. Even if it's not violent, overtly physical, or repeated, all abuse has serious consequences. There is no positive or neutral experience of sexual abuse.

- **Be clear that abuse is never the child's fault.** No child seduces an abuser. Children ask for affection and attention, not for sexual abuse. Even if a child responds sexually, even if she wasn't forced or didn't protest, it is still never the child's fault. It is always the responsibility of the adult not to be sexual with a child.

- **Educate yourself about sexual abuse and the healing process.** If you have a basic idea of what the survivor is going through, it will help you to be supportive. See the Bibliography for suggested reading.

- **Don't sympathize with the abuser.** The survivor needs your absolute loyalty.

- **Validate the survivor's feelings: her anger, pain, and fear.** These are natural, healthy responses. She needs to feel them, express them, and be heard.

- **Express your compassion.** If you have feelings of outrage, compassion, pain for her pain, do share them. There is probably nothing more comforting than a genuine human response. Just make sure your feelings don't overwhelm hers.

- **Respect the time and space it takes to heal.** Healing is a slow process that can't be hurried.

- **Encourage the survivor to get support.** In addition to offering your own caring, encourage her to reach out to others. (See "Healing Resources," page 458.)
- **Get help if the survivor is suicidal.** Most survivors are not suicidal, but sometimes the pain of childhood abuse is so devastating that women want to kill themselves. If you are close to a survivor who is suicidal, get help immediately. (See "Dealing with Suicide," page 331.)

- **Accept that there will very likely be major changes in your relationship with the survivor as she heals.** She is changing, and as she does, you may need to change in response.
- **Resist seeing the survivor as a victim.** Continue to see her as a strong, courageous woman who is reclaiming her own life.

FOR FAMILY MEMBERS

Child sexual abuse is a difficult thing to face. When a survivor tells you that she was abused, you will have many strong feelings. You may feel guilty, enraged, appalled, or devastated. You may feel threatened or trapped. You may not believe the survivor. You may feel attacked or blamed. You may feel deep compassion and sorrow for her pain. Or you may feel confused, hopeless, or even completely numb. If the abuser is (or was) a family member, the image you have of your family will be shaken. If the perpetrator is your husband, son, brother, or father, someone within your immediate family circle, you will be faced with agonizing choices. You may have to make critical decisions about separation, divorce, family loyalty. Your life will be thrown into turmoil.

Although it is distressing to give up your image of your family, this is a crucial opportunity for everyone to face unhealthy pat-terns. If child sexual abuse is not dealt with, it often repeats itself generation after generation. It is a serious problem that affects the whole family, not just the survivor.

PARENTS WHO DIDN'T ABUSE

Although it is a terrible thing for a parent to realize that she (or he) has not protected a child, your opportunities to be a good parent are not over. When your daughter tells you that she was abused, or when she begins to work on her healing, you have an opportunity to be helpful. Don't allow yourself to be overwhelmed by guilt or regret for what you didn't do before. Your feelings need recognition and expression—and for that reason you should seek support for

318

yourself—but don't lose sight of the chance to be an understanding parent to your adult child in the present. Your compassion, courage, and willingness to change are extremely valuable.

If the survivor feels you didn't protect her, she may be very angry at you. Although no one is ever responsible for someone else abusing a child, children have the right to expect to be protected by their parents and other caretakers.

If you are a mother, be aware that our society is more comfortable with anger directed at women than at men. Although a mother is responsible for failing to notice that her child is being abused or for not protecting her, she is not responsible for the abuse itself. The person who abuses the child is always to blame for that. (See Working Through Mother Blame," on page 125.)

Accept the responsibility for not protecting your daughter. Apologize. Tell her you wish you had been awake enough to see what was going on, strong enough to recognize it, courageous enough to stand up for her. And then take her side now. Acknowledge her feelings rather than defending yourself or the abuser. Stand up for her now.

It's a good idea for you to get counseling to sort out your own complex feelings. Both individual counseling and a group with other parents in your situation can be helpful.*

There are also a number of worthwhile books for parents of children who have been abused. Although they are written for the parents of young or adolescent children,

---

* See "Healing Resources," page 458, for guidelines on screening for a therapist. Although you may not be a survivor yourself, you will still want to see someone sensitive to the subject of child sexual abuse.

much of what they suggest will be pertinent to your adult daughter. Check the Bibliography for suggestions.

SIBLINGS

If your sister was abused by a relative, or if there were other abusive elements in your home (alcoholism, battering, neglect), you were affected by the same family dynamics. You too grew up in a family in which there was betrayal, secrecy, pain, and fear. One way or another, you suffered.

If you weren't sexually abused yourself, you may feel guilty. You may criticize yourself for not having protected your sister. It's common for those who escape abuse to blame themselves. Those who live through situations in which others are hurt or killed often feel guilt, question "Why me?" and struggle both emotionally and spiritually to come to terms with the injustice of tragedy. Whatever your feelings, you will need support. This is a stressful time for everyone.

If you were abused but have not dealt with your feelings, you may be threatened or angry when your sister speaks out, forcing you to face your own abuse. Don't criticize her for wanting to deal with this. Don't abandon her. Instead, get help for yourself. Find a counselor who is knowledgeable about sexual abuse. Your are a survivor too. You too deserve more than coping and band-aids. You deserve to heal.

Since many children cope with abuse by repressing it, it is possible that you have been abused yourself and have not yet recovered the memories. If you find yourself particularly anxious, angry, or upset when your sister brings up this issue, be open to the possibility that it may have happened to you.

Whether you were abused or not, you both grew up in the same family, and by talking together you can lend each other invaluable help. You may have a memory she needs. She may be able to fill in a piece of your puzzle. The functioning of many families is so distorted, so painful, so confusing, that survivors often find it hard to trust their memories. You can confirm for each other that things were as bad as they seemed. And that neither of you is crazy. For a survivor to have even *one* member of her family who validates her reality is invaluable. You are in a position to give a great gift, and the gain for you can be the healing of your own childhood wounds.*

---

* For a good example of what supportive siblings can do for each other's healing, see "Michelle and Artemis" on page 431.

FOR PARTNERS

Unless you have your own psychological house in order, relating to a survivor opens up old wounds and challenges every facet of the way you live. My feelings toward Barb run the whole gamut from "What did I do to deserve a relationship with a screwed-up person like you?" to "If we can hang on and lick this, my life will be rich beyond measure."

—Phil Temples, husband of a survivor

The information in this chapter pertains to all couples—married and unmarried, heterosexual and lesbian. Although there are significant differences in cultural conditioning, power dynamics, and role expectations between heterosexual and lesbian couples, these differences are far outweighed by the common problems all couples face when one or both partners are survivors.

This chapter addresses the partners of survivors, but many of the suggestions will be equally useful to other family members and to the survivors themselves.

Being the partner of someone actively healing from child sexual abuse has both problems and rewards, although the problems are often more obvious than the rewards.

Survivors commonly have difficulties with trust, intimacy, and sex, all of which have a direct impact on your relationship. Often, at least for a time, the survivor's problems and healing dominate your time together. Depending on the stage of the healing process the survivor is in, she may be angry, depressed, or totally preoccupied. She may be self-destructive or suicidal. (If the survivor is suicidal, see "Dealing with Suicide" on page 331.) She may have a great need for maintaining control in her life. Sometimes the abusive patterns from her original family are acted out with you or your children.

As a partner, you may not understand what is going on. You may feel inadequate because you can't fix things, guilty if you aren't 100 percent supportive. You may be isolated, with no one to talk to. Partners often feel frustrated at the amount of time healing takes. Sometimes you will have to continue to deal with the survivor's abusive family members. Other times, your own family history will be reawakened, accompanied by painful emotions. And all the while, your own needs may not be getting met.

If both you and your partner are survivors, your relationship can be affected in complex ways. Depending on how far along you are in the healing process, you may be able to offer each other tremendous support, reassurance, and understanding. On the other hand, you can intensify each other's struggles, trigger memories and old patterns, and otherwise get entangled in painful dynamics.

Since so many women have been abused, lesbian couples often find themselves in this situation. So do an increasing number of heterosexual couples, as more men are beginning to identify their childhood abuse. If both you and your partner are survivors, you

WHERE ARE YOU NOW?

- You suspect your partner is a survivor but isn't aware of it yet.
- Your partner has just recognized that she's a survivor. She's starting to have memories, and you're totally bewildered.
- Your partner admits she was abused, but says it has nothing to do with your relationship or her life today. You think differently, but she refuses to discuss it.
- You understand that the survivor has a problem but don't think it has any connection with you. Up until now you may have thought it was all her responsibility. Now you're starting to wonder.
- Both you and the survivor have been working on these issues for a few years. You have good communication and a basic handle on these issues, but want help in dealing with a few problem areas.
- You want help with sex.
- You're just getting involved with someone who hands you this book and says she thinks you should look it over.
- You're on the verge of splitting up. This is your last resort.
- Your partner is suicidal. Your life is falling apart. Everything's in chaos. You don't know what to do.
- You've just separated from a woman who is a survivor and you want to understand why you broke up.

have both liabilities and opportunities. Be especially patient and compassionate with yourselves and each other, and consider couples counseling with an experienced therapist.

THE BENEFITS

There are powerful positive elements to being in a close relationship with someone healing from childhood sexual abuse, but sometimes these may be hard to see. At a workshop for partners of survivors, Ellen suggested that the participants write about the ways they could benefit from being in a relationship with a survivor—what were the opportunities for them? One man sat through the fifteen minutes allotted for this exercise, looking perplexed. At the end he said, "I'm really confused. I came here to learn how to help my wife with her problems and now I'm supposed to be finding my opportunities!?"

It may seem crazy to look for what is positive for you, personally, in a situation that causes you—and the survivor—a lot of pain and stress. But there are valuable aspects to being the partner of a survivor.

Being with someone actively engaged in the healing process means that you are in a growing relationship, not a stagnant one.

People unconsciously pick a mate where your meeting point is where you both need to grow, and that's definitely true for us. Around this issue of sexuality is where we're both wounded and we're both the most deaf to each other. There's no way I would dredge through my own shit as deep as I have if I didn't have to relate to Karen. If we each didn't have this problem, we wouldn't each be confronting our own shadow.

One partner found that her own problem area was learning to be separate:

She's good at autonomy. She knows how to take care of herself. She's not so good at intimacy. I'm good at intimacy. Give me a person and I'll merge. Being with her, I've had to learn to be independent.

Another partner grew in his capacity to express feelings:

As I look back over the last six months, I realize the tremendous personal growth we've both undergone. I've always lagged a bit behind in the communications department. But I'm now expressing feelings and allowing myself to experience emotions that never before would have been possible. At the height of an argument I can now recognize when I'm no longer mad, but instead very sad—and then I can cry.

If you haven't been used to thinking about your own feelings, your own fears, or the ways you were influenced by your childhood, you may initially feel uncomfortable with such a major focus on self-exploration. But even if this is unfamiliar to you, the emphasis on growth can provide you with valuable opportunities. And working together can bring you closer to your partner, build your foundation more solidly.

When we've come through the

rocky points, we were able to look at each other with pride and say "We did it!" It was a sense of mutual accomplishment. That's been a real special thing in our relationship.

Taking part in a deep healing process is a miracle and an inspiration. Although it's demanding, it is also a privilege. There are rewards both in the giving and in the receiving.

DON'T TAKE IT PERSONALLY

Intimacy is paradoxical in relationships with survivors, especially if they were abused by someone they were close to. Their love and trust were met with betrayal. Now, the more intimate a relationship becomes, the more it feels like "family," the scarier it is for the survivor. If you're unaware of this dynamic, the whole thing can look crazy.

Some survivors have had more superficial relationships in the past and have handled them relatively well. They may have managed short-term relationships, or even long-term ones, before they began to deal actively with the abuse. They kept their coping mechanisms intact and though some depth was sacrificed, things functioned.

If the two of you really love each other and yet the relationship is rocky, this does not mean that something is wrong. It's more likely to mean there's something very right—so right, in fact, that she's threatened. If both of you know that it is frightening for her to get close—and for good reason—then it's less likely you'll be diverted into dwelling on rejection, fighting, or breaking up.

Survivors always tell their partners,

"Don't take it personally." This is extremely difficult because so much of it *is* personal.

A lot of my fears sexually have always had to do with rejection. I'm a very threatening size and part of me has internalized those threatening pictures as who I am: "Okay, I'm a real monster." I began to believe that all the things that are frightening and injurious about maleness were embodied in me. Having Karen withdraw brought all those feelings right to the surface.

If the survivor withdraws, is angry, is sad, needs time alone, doesn't want to make love, all this affects you personally. And yet it is true that her behavior does not necessarily reflect her feelings for you or for your relationship. In reality, your partner is either repeating coping behaviors from years before you ever met her, or she is doing what she needs to do to heal. It often has very little to do with you.

Maintaining a balance between sharing wholeheartedly in the process and keeping an appropriate sense of independence and separateness is one of the challenges of supporting a woman who is actively healing from child sexual abuse. Throughout, you will be trying to encourage her, nurture yourself, and create healthy patterns for a relationship that will serve you not only during this crisis, but throughout life.

OVERCOMING SHAME

One man at a workshop for partners asked Ellen, "Could you talk about shame?"

So Ellen went on at length about survivors' shame for having been abused, for having experienced sexual arousal, for having needed attention, for the ways in which they coped. When she finally stopped, the partner looked at her blankly. "Am I getting to what you want?" Ellen asked.

"No," he said. "I mean the kind I felt today when I was coming to this workshop and I had to tell my co-workers where I was going. I didn't tell them. I made up something."

Yes. You may be ashamed too. You're not supposed to have problems. Your sex life is supposed to be terrific, your relationship perfect. You're not supposed to need counseling, workshops, or help.

Partners, as well as survivors, find obstacles that keep them from reaching out for support—or even from just being honest about where they're going. And shame is a major one. But you have nothing to be ashamed of. There is nothing shameful about loving a woman who is working to heal from trauma. There is nothing shameful about experiencing the problems that result from such abuse. There is nothing shameful about your own pain, anger, or fear.

GETTING SUPPORT

Just as survivors need support through the healing process, you need support as well. Some of this can come from the survivor, but the demands on her own healing are often too great for her to have a lot of energy left over to support you. Nor should you expect it. As one survivor put it: "If someone has a heart attack, you don't go into the hospital and go on and on about how upset *you* are about *their* heart attack. You talk about it with other people, and you act confident while you're with that person about their ability to heal. You have to approach survivors the same way."

Yet you need someone to listen to your pain, your fears, your frustrations, and your confusion. You need compassion too.

For the partner, it's bewildering. There's no information. There's no way to cope with what seems like rejection. I would not have been able to do it, as dedicated as I was to making this relationship work, without knowledge of what was happening. I had a friend who was an incest survivor too. Talking to her about her feelings helped me understand what the impact of abuse can be.

It is essential that you have time when it's safe to express your feelings bluntly. You need to air your anger, your frustration, your despair. Sometimes you need to just stomp around and yell, "I can't take it anymore!" The survivor needs to hear these feelings from you too, but she probably doesn't need to hear them as frequently as you need to express them.

- **Talk to a counselor.** Couples counseling or individual therapy can provide you with essential support.
- **Seek out friends who are good listeners.** Before you do this, clarify with your partner the specifics of what you can share and with whom. But within these guidelines, share. It's not healthy to be isolated with your feelings.
- **Find other partners of survivors.** Other

partners can be a tremendous source of comfort and support. If there are workshops specifically for partners in your area, that's great. If not, your partner may know other survivors who have partners. Try calling a local counseling center for leads. If you're already in counseling, ask your counselor about starting a group for partners.

There still aren't many resources for partners, but it's worth the effort to build a support network. The chance to talk and to listen can be an incredible relief. As one man put it, "You think there's something wrong with you—that you're too demanding, too impatient—and then you hear everybody else feels that too. It's like the burden drops. You can stop thinking of yourself as a rapist just because you want sex. You can stop feeling so bad about yourself."

CO-DEPENDENCY

Although any caring person feels the pain of a loved one, excessive identification with the survivor's pain is not healthy. Some partners are more comfortable attending to the survivor's problems than to their own. If you played the caretaker role in your original family, you may be doing so now out of habit.

It is recognized that partners of alcoholics can be addicted as well—not to alcohol, but to the alcoholics in their lives, to the consuming caretaking that shields them from facing their own issues. The same can hold true for partners of survivors.

If this has been your pattern, it will be a difficult but necessary change in perspective to make a distinction between your partner's feelings, wants, or needs and your own.* Do whatever it takes to get some time alone for yourself, to get to know yourself separately from your partner and her problems. (For more on co-dependency, see "Separating" on page 236.)

DO THINGS THAT MAKE YOU FEEL GOOD

Many, if not most, people look to their partners for their primary emotional contact and companionship. But while your partner is immersed in her own healing, she may not have the time, energy, ability, or desire to meet your needs. It's essential that as the partner of a survivor and also as an autonomous person, you not be totally dependent on your lover and your family for all your nurturance.

Start to make meaningful connections with people outside your relationship, and find fulfilling activities that are your own. Think about the things that make you feel good, and do these things regularly. If you have previously relied on shared experiences for pleasure, you may have to change your patterns in order to avoid feeling deprived and annoyed.

One partner said that she and her lover had always gone backpacking together, but recently her lover was so involved with other survivors and support groups that she didn't want to go away with her. The partner was

---

* Al-Anon, the support group for partners of alcoholics, can be a useful resource. Many partners have benefited from attending Al-Anon meetings, even if alcohol wasn't directly involved in their relationship.

disappointed, but decided to go backpacking with a friend. Although she missed her lover and felt some sadness that they weren't together, she was a lot happier backpacking with her friend than she would have been sitting home idle and lonely.

Ellen is the partner of a survivor and has gained by learning to take pleasure alone:

> Personally, I have a tendency toward workaholism. Evenings that I spend with my lover, I put on the telephone answering machine, close the door to my study, and relax. But if she is out or wants to be alone, I gravitate toward my desk and "get a little work done." Recently I realized what an unsatisfactory setup this is. It means that if she's unavailable, I am deprived not only of her company but also of a good time.
>
> In the past few months, I've been giving myself permission to relax in the evening when I'm alone. I can listen to the radio, embroider, or take myself to the movies. I can read a novel in bed. All things I rarely have time for during the busy days. I've found I like being home alone, listening to my sleeping daughter breathe in the next room, inviting the cat to my lap for petting. When I go to sleep, I feel nourished, whole, good about myself and my life.

BECOMING ALLIES

One of the important realities to keep in mind is that your partner did not create the difficulties you are both facing.

I've never blamed her for making the relationship difficult because of the incest. That seemed like such an obvious trap. It would just be terribly rude for me to think that. She didn't do it. It was her father who did it. Not her. She didn't have this little qualifications list when we got together. Neither of us knew this was coming. To me, it's just part of growing and trusting and opening doors, and that was what was behind one of them. That was just part of the package.

Although the abuse happened to the survivor, it affects your life and becomes your concern as well. Many partners get angry when they realize they have to deal with abuse, but they may be reluctant to express that anger. Ellen says this was true in her relationship:

> When my lover and I were in the midst of difficulties, she continually encouraged me to tell her when I was angry. "Don't store it up," she insisted. "I want to know when you're angry."
>
> But it was hard for me to express my anger. I wanted to be perfectly understanding, perfectly supportive. After all, wasn't I an expert in the healing process? Didn't I support hundreds of other women through it? How could I be angry at my own lover?
>
> But of course I *was* angry. I was both angry and supportive. I was a whole person, with many varied responses. And they were all valid and all needed expression, not just the understanding ones.

It's essential that throughout your struggles with all these issues, you communicate your feelings frankly and respectfully. Both you and your partner have valid feelings and needs. Neither of you is wrong or to blame. If you can see yourselves as allies with a common problem, rather than as adversaries in combat, it becomes possible to find ways to reconcile your differing needs.

COMMUNICATION

Communication is essential for a healthy relationship. It's important when things are going well, and it's critical when you face major difficulties. You need to tell your partner how you feel, what you think, what's going on inside you. And you need to hear the same from her. Communication is the basis for understanding, compassion, and creative problem solving.

On Communication: Roger

We got into this situation where the communication between us was getting more and more closed. Karen had been seeing a therapist for some time. She'd come back from therapy and I'd ask her how it went, and she'd say, "It's too painful to deal with. It's too much work. I don't want to talk about it." That keyed me into my stuff about feeling rejected: if she couldn't trust me, then I must really be a monster.

I needed her to communicate with me

more. I needed her to pay more attention to what I needed. I needed just as much support and nurturing as I gave. I finally came to a point where I exploded. We call it the dynamite incident. I said to her, "General information isn't enough for me. I need you to tell me what you're going through. And you have to deal with what's happening to me too! I want communication and I'm not going to settle for no!" I knew I had to break through. It really caused fireworks because Karen felt threatened, but I couldn't keep letting the gap widen.

Things did change after that. We started talking more. And since then, I feel much more hopeful. I have some idea where she is and where she's going, and where we are in the process.

LEARNING TO ASK

Even with a good support system and other friends to talk with, there will be times when you want and need attention from your partner, and no one else will do. You may want time together, reassurance that you're loved, or help with some problem of your own. Whatever it is, you need to ask.

For many partners this is difficult. You may be afraid of making demands. You may feel the survivor is too fragile. But stating a need is not the same as making a demand. Stating your needs directly is the most effective way to communicate. But as one man explains, it's not always easy:

My habitual way of asking was to complain: "You haven't told me you loved me for ages," or "It's been four days since you've even wanted to make love. Monday night you were at class. Tuesday you went to the movies. . . ." Immediately my wife became defensive. She wanted to protect herself, not open up.

It felt too vulnerable for me to say, "I really need to be close to you," or "I'd like it if you'd rub my back," or "I've been feeling insecure. Would you tell me that you love me?" Coming forward with criticism was easier for me than exposing my simple need.

Even though you can't always get what you want, you increase your odds by asking clearly in a nonthreatening way. If, for example, you're not getting the attention you want, you might ask your partner to set aside one night a week to be with you—an evening to *not* talk about sexual abuse, to just have a relaxed time together. The rest of the week, you won't expect her to really be with you. If she feels able, she may agree. If not, you can ask if an hour might be possible or even ten minutes. The bottom line might be, "Are you able to give *anything* at this point?" Although at some critical times the answer may be no, it's likely that most of the time she will be able to agree to some minimal togetherness.

Some partners have struggled along for months or even years without ever finding out what the survivor could give. It may feel risky to ask exactly what you can and can't expect. Talking about it frankly—negotiating—can also feel strangely businesslike or cold. And you may be afraid of rejection. But the survivor may be relieved to hear clearly and uncritically what you need. And unless you talk together, you can't work out a solution.

As a bonus, sometimes just talking about a difficulty goes a long way toward dissolving it.

SETTING LIMITS

If you're committed to supporting your partner, that doesn't mean you're required to be available for every crisis or to take care of every need. There are limits to everything and you need to be responsive to your own. When you try to give beyond your capacity, there's usually a backlash of resentment that undercuts the value of what you've given. It's far better to admit honestly that you can't be there, to tell her that you love her and have faith in her, and to go on with your own life.

It's not realistic to expect yourself to be able to handle everything just because the survivor is healing from a major trauma. A relationship, even when one person is in crisis, involves two people, and you can't obscure yourself totally without damage to both of you.

You may not want to hear every detail of her healing process. Or you might not want to hear every detail, every time. One woman said, "She had some horrible things happen to her and sometimes I don't even want to know." This partner felt guilty for feeling that way, but no one is superhuman. You do your best, and then you have the right to say no, just as she does.

Everyone has different limits. Don't wait until you're over yours before you speak up. If you do, you're apt to be resentful, and it will make your communication less effective. Instead, speak up when you're approaching your limits.

DEALING WITH HER PAIN, GRIEF, AND DEPRESSION

Recovering from child sexual abuse entails feeling the pain and grief of early wounding. For some survivors, a generalized depression blankets everything. This can be very difficult for partners. As one partner put it, "It's hard to witness so much pain and be so helpless."

People tend to think they have to *do* something to help a person get over pain, but often there's not a lot you can do. Some of that pain is inevitable. Some of it is her work to transform. Your place is not to make it better—your place is to be a loving partner through hard times.

- **Listen.** Sit with her and let her talk.
- **Try to understand.** Be as compassionate as you can.
- **Ask her what she needs.** Offer extra comfort.
- **Don't ignore it.** Make room for her feelings.
- **Don't try to smooth it over and make it better.**
- **Reassure her.** Tell her it's okay to feel her feelings.
- **Get help yourself if you start feeling shaky.**
- **Be patient.**
- **Lighten her load when you can.** Take on extra housekeeping duties. Do more child care. Cook her a hot meal.

In doing these things, you not only help the survivor, but you give her a gift that may be new to her—the experience of a healthy, nurturing relationship.

CRISIS PERIODS

For many survivors, there is a time when pain eclipses every other feeling. These crisis periods often come when a survivor gets her first memories, initially faces the long-term effects of her abuse, or confronts the people who hurt her. If your partner is in a crisis stage of her healing, you will have your hands full. (See "The Emergency Stage" on page 65.) She may be unable to function, unable to meet any of your needs and few of her own.

It is extremely stressful to love someone who is in deep pain. Even if you're good at taking care of yourself, being with someone who's anguished has to affect you. On top of that, the survivor may be angry. She may blame you or pick fights with you. You may feel overwhelmed by the extras duties you've had to take on—reassuring your children, paying for therapy, covering for her financially if she can't work. And you may be frightened, unsure of what to do.

At one workshop, a man described his conflict and guilt as he was torn between taking care of his wife and taking care of his child: "It'll be in the middle of a Saturday afternoon and my wife will be totally hysterical. I want to comfort her, but our four-year-old daughter is there and she's affected by all of this. So I take my daughter out—to a shopping mall or something—but I feel so guilty. I'm not there supporting my wife. But I can't just leave the child."

Everyone in the group hastened to assure this man that he was doing the right thing. He was taking care of his child and giving his wife space to experience her feelings. Anyone who cares for the child of a distressed mother is supporting that mother. The partner was reassured that he wasn't abandoning his wife, but their lives were still in tumult. "It can happen any time, any day," he said.

"I know what you mean," another man said. "When I walk into the house I never know what I'll find. It's totally unpredictable."

And another: "I thought I had a reasonable relationship with a reasonable person."

The important thing to remember is that such a crisis will not last forever. It is part of her healing process. The best thing for you to do is make sure you both have help and find ways to take care of yourself.

DEALING WITH SUICIDE

If the survivor is talking about suicide, has attempted suicide, is taking large quantities of drugs or alcohol, is mutilating or injuring herself, or is driving recklessly, her life is in danger. Do not try to deal with this alone. Get help.

Call suicide prevention. Make sure you have the phone numbers of the survivor's therapist and support group members. Call them. If the survivor is isolated, take an active role in helping her find skilled support. Have her make a no-suicide agreement. Tell her you want her to contact you or her therapist before she tries to kill herself.

While it's impossible stop a person from killing herself if she is determined to do so, these measures can help sustain the survivor through a time of acute despair.

(For more on preventing suicide, see "Don't Kill Yourself," pages 202–203.)

CONTROL

Survivors often have difficulty compromising or relinquishing control. It may seem to you that the survivor needs to control everything: when and if you make love, how you should raise the children, even down to details of everyday life—when and where you go out to eat, which movie to see, where to hang a picture on the wall. Sometimes this control will be obvious. Other times it will be less clear-cut—such as maintaining control through moodiness or preoccupation.

What you are up against is a survival mechanism that has been absolutely essential to her. By now it is a firmly entrenched habit. If you want to work toward balancing the control in your relationship, start by appreciating how fundamental her need for control is. She grew up being abused by an adult who was out of control. Now she feels it is crucial to maintain control over her life. It's only when the survivor knows that you understand the depth of her need for control that she will be able, gradually, to give it up.

Expect changes to go slowly, but do express your needs. For example, you can make it clear that you need something to change, but don't expect to set all the terms. If you want to spend more time with your partner, try saying "I need to spend more time with you. How can we do that?" instead of "You've got to quit your aerobics class. You're spending too many nights away from home."

When your partner is being particularly controlling, it may also help to ask if she wants to talk about what's going on. If she's feeling powerless in another area of her life, if something is frightening her, or if there's a crisis, her need for control may flare up. Often it helps just to recognize and talk about her fears.

TRUST

When children are sexually abused, their capacity to trust is shattered. Now this trust has to be consciously rebuilt. You can't just say "Trust me, come on and trust me already" and expect your partner to leap into the land of the trusting. If she could do it that easily, she would have done it already. To make the shift from not trusting to trusting, she must go step by step. (Read "Learning to Trust" on page 226.)

At the same time, *you* need to be conscious of the ways in which you are or are not trustworthy. Be scrupulously honest: In what ways can she trust you safely? In what ways are you careless or untrustworthy? Inconsiderate or scared? Is there an arena in which you feel confident that you can absolutely be trusted, where you can commit yourself to come through no matter what? For example, if you're supposed to be on time, would you be willing to get there an hour early rather than be five minutes late?

To establish trust, you must work together. Try making a specific offer: "I'll water your plants while you're on vacation. You can tell me in detail just what each plant requires and I'll do it carefully." Or, "Please trust me that if I offer to give you a massage, I won't try to seduce you into sex." Or, "I'd like to make a commitment to you to cook dinner on Mondays and Wednesdays since those are the days you work late. It won't always be a big deal, but there'll be something ready by the time you get home." You can add, "I really am reliable about this. Please risk it and trust me."

If you do come through, that will make an impression. And if you do this over and over, you will definitely build trust.

WILL THE REAL ABUSER PLEASE STAND UP?

It is common for survivors to see the person they're relating to as the abuser. Various things can trigger this identification: a similar gesture, an increase in closeness, sexual passion, anger. If you start to feel that the survivor isn't relating to you anymore, but rather to the abuser from her past, you need to stop and check. Ask her "What's happening? Did something scare you? Are you reminded of something?" Or more simply, "Where are you?"

Getting to know what the issues are, naming them, and tracing them back to their source will help differentiate the present from the past. One partner, Phil, describes a unique way he was able to do this for his wife:

> For a long time Barb had asked me to grow a beard. She kept telling me how attractive it would look. I wasn't very keen about the prospects of a scraggly-looking face, but I started growing it.
>
> About six months later, I told Barb I was thinking of whacking it off. She suddenly burst into tears. She told me that the hair on my face allowed her to maintain a reality check during certain times when flashbacks of her father molesting her interfered with our lovemaking (Barb's father was always clean-shaven).
>
> I don't believe Barb fully understood the importance of my having a beard until that conversation. Certainly I didn't. And keeping my hair took on a totally different perspective for me. I now take a certain delight in experi-

menting with various cuts and trims. More importantly, I've found yet another way I can be there for Barb.

This determination to distinguish her husband, whom she loved and wanted to make love with, from her father, who had molested her, appeared in a guise neither of them consciously recognized at first.

IF THE SHOE FITS

At one workshop for partners, Ellen explained that survivors often identified their partner with the abuser, and one man said that yes, that was happening in his relationship. Ellen went on to talk about not taking it personally and supporting the survivor in differentiating between the two, but she failed to mention the fact that sometimes partners *are* abusive.

About a year after that workshop, the survivor who was married to this partner told Ellen that every time she had tried to get him to see that he was being abusive, he referred back to Ellen's statement that survivors often identify their partners with their abuser. And that became his excuse for not changing. Eventually, though, he was able to hear her and did join a group of men who batter. Their relationship improved dramatically after that.

This man, like many others, was not blatantly violent. But in subtle ways his behavior was threatening, and the power he wielded was destructive to their relationship.

Especially in heterosexual relationships, a power differential is built into the fabric of the relationship. A certain amount of condescension toward or power over women is accepted as normal in our society. Even if you're not an overtly abusive man, it may be a real challenge to develop more equal power dynamics in your family, but it's essential if your relationship is to thrive.

Although they are generally more egalitarian, lesbian relationships are not immune to violence or threatening behavior. If there is any abuse in your relationship, you and your partner need help right away.*

HER FAMILY

Survivors usually have complicated feelings about their families. The mother who didn't protect her also tucked her in at night and sang lullabies to her. The brother who raped her was a victim of their parent's abuse too. It's natural for her feelings to be complex and difficult to sort out. And they may change more than once over the course of her healing.

Your feelings may be complicated too. You may feel loyalty or love for her family. If the abuser is someone you've respected, you may find it hard to see him now as the perpetrator of a terrible violation. You may not want to believe it's true. Or you may want the survivor to forgive the abuser or other relatives. You may want relations to go on as they always have.

But this is not possible. It is essential, in fact, that you do not in any way defend the abuser for past or present actions. It is up to

---

* *Naming the Violence* by Kerry Lobel is an excellent resource. See the "Battering" section of the Bibliography.

the survivor, and the survivor alone, to determine what kind of relationship she wants to have with the abuser, with the people who didn't protect her, or with anyone in her family who doesn't respect her healing now.

If you feel an allegiance to the abuser, you need a place to talk about your feelings. But the survivor is not the one to whom you should turn for this help. She should not have to convince you that the abuser is to blame, or that she has a right to be angry.

If, on the other hand, you're so raging mad that you want to kill the abuser, it may be difficult to allow the survivor the room to sort through her own mixed feelings. Although it's essential that she not minimize what was done to her, it frequently takes some time for women to tap into their fury.

Sometimes partners of survivors feel that they shouldn't get angry at abusers or family members, especially if the survivor isn't angry yet. But your anger can be a helpful catalyst in awakening her own. She needs to hear that she has a right to her anger, that it's safe to be angry, and that you're angry that she was hurt.

Although it's important not to overwhelm her with your own reactions, your anger is appropriate, justified, and ultimately in her best interests. If she tells you that she doesn't want to hear it, respect her request, but find other people to talk to. You wouldn't be angry if you didn't care about her. It's part of love.

FAMILY VISITS AND ONGOING RELATIONSHIPS

Sometimes it's hard to understand why the survivor would want to continue a relationship with people who abused or neglected her. Yet ultimately it is her decision whether she wants any relationship with her family—and if so, what kind.

You, however, get to decide what your involvement will be. You don't have to subject yourself to humiliation, pretense, or danger. If the survivor wants you to continue to attend Friday night dinners at the home of the parent who abused her, if she wants you to pretend nothing happened, embrace them, and talk pleasantries, and if all this makes you incapable of digesting your chicken, you can decline. If the survivor wants the brother who abused her to visit for the weekend, you can negotiate the arrangement: he can visit during the day but sleep in a motel; you want it to be the weekend your children are at the Girl Scout sleep-out, or he can come, but you want to be free to speak your mind frankly.

If, however, the survivor wants to sever relations with the abuser or her family, you will have to go along with that decision even if it's not your preference. To continue to relate on friendly terms with someone who abused your partner, or who is buying into the family facade of denying or minimizing the abuse, is a betrayal in itself.

ACTIVE SUPPORT

There are many things you can do to actively support the survivor in dealing with her family. One partner reads the letters that come from her lover's relatives. She passes on any important information and then throws out the letter. That way the survivor doesn't have any unwanted contact. Another woman took this a step further, intercepting calls from her lover's father:

My lover was abused by her father. It had been many years since she had talked to him when he called one day while she was at work. He said he'd call back that evening. She was upset, felt invaded, and didn't want to talk to him. I wanted to answer the phone, but I was afraid she might see that as butting in

---

Conversation with My Lover's Father

Carol Anne Dwight wrote the following confrontational letter to her lover's dead abuser as a way to discharge her own anger:

Lloyd Edwards,

I want to talk to you for a moment. Could we step over there?

No. We don't need to go to another room. This is fine, thanks. I'm concerned about Rhonda, your daughter.

Lloyd Edwards, *you raped my lover* when she was eight years old.

You covered it up very thoroughly. You lied. You lied to Rhonda. You lied to the doctors. And you refused to discuss the matter later. You trivialized a major childhood trauma, an event that destroyed Rhonda's chance for a secure childhood and safe launch into the adult world. You stole all those years and happiness from her. And you had the unmitigated *gall* to disown her for behaviors we now know to be symptomatic of childhood sexual abuse, behaviors you actually caused.

Lloyd Edwards, you are responsible for all of that. You are responsible for her drug use. You are responsible for her prostitution. You are responsible for her difficulties with sex and intimacy. You denied her a childhood, ruined a large segment of her adult life, and made things harder for me too. That's right. I as lover/life partner inherit some of the "fallout" from your acts.

No, I'm not finished yet. I'm afraid that you'll have to endure more insults, Mr. Rapist.

I hate you for having interfered in my lover's ability to trust me. I hate you for having hurt her, violated her, lied to her when she was utterly vulnerable. Most of all I hate you for being dead, beyond my reach or the reach of the law. How dare you escape this judgment!! Off scot-free, never to be exposed, humiliated, to atone, apologize, explain. How dare you be dead!

I hate you for the guilt I feel, trying desperately sometimes to avoid hurting Rhonda. I hate you for how careful I must be when I wish to be sensual/sexual with my lover. I hate you for making it so hard for me to persuade her to take care of herself. I hate you for making my burden so heavy in this relationship.

There is no forgiveness or pity from me. None of the good things you did will in any way compensate for the rape of Rhonda. The fact that you, too, may have been molested as a child will not lighten my judgment. Perhaps, if you were alive now, Rhonda would accept your apology, explanation, restitution, love—that would be her choice. If it were up to me, though, I'd prosecute.

Okay, I'm through now. But remember that Rhonda isn't finished. *She* may have something further to discuss.

and usurping her power. But I took the risk and asked, figuring the worst that could happen is that I'd look pushy.

As it turned out, she was grateful. It was the first time in her life that anyone asked to protect her, the first time anyone came forward without her having to drag it out of them. She was grateful and I felt good to be able to do it.

Phil regularly composes letters to his wife's parents and relatives. Then he mails them:

One of my coping mechanisms for my anger and frustration is writing confrontational letters to Barb's parents and other relatives. In fact, I have spent hours and hours in front of the word processor with a letter—polishing every insignificant word and phrase.

If there's a way you'd like to offer active support, first ask the survivor, so she can tell you if your suggestion would be helpful. If it's not what she wants, you don't have to feel hurt or rejected. You're a caring person who is willing to try, and she'll probably appreciate your intentions.

SEXUALITY

Beginning the Journey: Ellen

"I don't want you ever again to make love with me when you don't want to. I don't want you ever to pretend," I told my lover earnestly. We had been together for over a year. She was a survivor, and I knew that making love when she didn't want to was damaging.

She started to shake. "I don't think I can do that," she said, her voice almost a cry. "It's too hard. I don't think you could handle it either."

"I know it's essential that you say no when you want to say no. That you're honest with yourself and with me."

She looked straight into my eyes. "You don't know what you're asking for," she said.

I didn't.

But even if I had, I would have told her the same thing. Only more soberly, with less optimistic enthusiasm in my voice, for the mutual journey we've taken has been painful, demanding, and difficult. It's also been worth it.

PROBLEMS WITH SEX

For most couples in which one or both partners are healing from child sexual abuse, sex is particularly difficult. Since the means by which the survivor was abused were sexual, it makes sense that this would be an area charged with conflict.

It will help you to be allied with the survivor if you understand the process of healing sexually. Many survivors have been split sexually—what they felt inside didn't match the way they acted on the outside. To heal, the survivor must stop doing anything she doesn't genuinely feel.

Healing sexually takes conscious time and attention. It requires stopping, slowing down, and reexamining everything, so that the survivor has time to integrate the feelings, memories, and associations that emerge.

This will probably have a radical effect on your sex life. The survivor may want no sex. She may want sex only under very controlled circumstances. She may want only certain sexual activities. She may want only to touch you and not be touched herself, or vice versa. She may want sex only if she initiates, only if you massage each other first, only if you have time to talk before or afterward. Sometimes it may seem to you that she wants sex only if the moon is new, it's snowing, *and* the kids are at summer camp.

The survivor may have difficulty staying present when you make love. One partner explained, "We'll be kissing and making out and then I get this eerie feeling that I'm all alone." She may have flashbacks to her original abuse. She may have to stop suddenly. She may go numb or have no desire whatsoever. If your partner has had orgasms, she may stop having them. Or she may cry hysterically when she comes, as she connects with powerful feelings of rage, horror, or sadness. She may become afraid of or disgusted by sex. Or she may vacillate. As one partner put it, "I feel like this oven getting turned on and off, but I don't know which way to turn."

Frustration: Roger's Story

There was a long time when we shuffled around to find out what was safe sexually. Karen set the standards. She began orchestrating what our lovemaking would involve, and I went along with that because I wanted to support the growth she needed.

It felt to me like there was this stone wall with this one little box in it where we could make love according to certain rules. Then, and only then, was it okay. For a while it felt real hopeless. The box kept getting smaller and smaller. It was very difficult for me to be patient when I had no idea whether she was in the first 10 percent or the last 10 percent of working this out. I felt like she was saying, "I'm going to work on this stuff. You're just going to have to forget all about sex until I'm done. I'll call you and tell you when I'm through." I knew it could take years. It felt like it could take forever.

It seemed like my only options were either to shut down or to leave. I didn't want to leave. And the problem with shutting down was this: She finally gets through her stuff and there I would be, all shut down, and how do you break through the ice then?

In the beginning I just stuffed down my needs and said, "I'll wait my turn," but then I realized I had always put someone else in front of me, and my turn never came. I finally got to the point where I realized I couldn't keep sitting around patiently waiting, slam my dick into a drawer until she was through, and just forget it.

COMMUNICATION IS THE BEST FOREPLAY

When couples first admit that they have sexual difficulties, they often see only two options when sex isn't going well: pretend and continue to make love, or be honest and stop. Once the survivor is committed to honesty, she stops. At this point the partner is usually hurt or angry, and withdraws more or less. The survivor is left feeling guilty and alone in addition to whatever was bothering her in the first place.

This is a time for communication. Talk to each other. Ask questions. What's happening that is upsetting her? When did she go numb? When did she get scared? Did she have a flashback? But don't barrage her with questions. The survivor may not be ready to talk right away. She may need time to stay quiet with her feelings. She may want to wait a day or two. Or she may want to spill everything out immediately. The important thing is that the two of you figure out a way to discuss what happened.

One partner described the process with her lover, Jesse, this way:

> Eventually Jesse told me that she didn't want me to just turn away if she didn't want to make love, or if she spaced out while we were making love. She asked me to talk to her, to help her identify her feelings and to express them. We discovered that this communication right on the spot really helped.
>
> Jesse began to identify her feelings more precisely. Rather than say "I'm not sure if I want to make love," she'd say "I feel very closed right now. I'm afraid to open up and let you in." Often she discovered that it wasn't so much the sex that scared her, but the intimacy, the trusting.

If the survivor hasn't explained what she wants from you, ask. If she doesn't know, experiment together. For every survivor, what is frightening will be somewhat different. By communicating, you can explore the threatening aspects and find ways to move through them.

CREATIVE INTIMACY

Many of us are accustomed to getting our needs for intimacy met through sex. Sex is the only way we really feel loved. When sex is not an option, we're stymied. Yet there are times when simple holding or tender words can bring comfort and closeness. Soothing, rather than forced passion, may be more appropriate when you are ragged from a difficult day or are overly tired. As you begin to explore a variety of avenues for intimacy, you will feel less compulsive, freer, and more satisfied.

Look at the needs you meet through sex. We all need intimacy, touch, validation, companionship, affection, nurturing, pleasure, intensity, love, passion, release. See which of these needs you can meet in other ways.

If Not Sex, How About . . . : Ellen's Story

When my lover began to say no to sex on a regular basis, I quickly realized that it wasn't okay with me for her to simply say no, turn over, and go to sleep. I wanted *something*, even if I couldn't have sex. And the closer to sex the better. If she didn't want us to make love together, then maybe she could hold me while I made love to myself. If she couldn't do that, I wanted her to take a bath with me. If that was too threatening, maybe she could give me a massage. And if that was too much, then maybe we could go for a walk and hold hands. And so on.

Also I didn't want to have to ask for it. Asking and having her say no was difficult enough. I wanted the next move to be hers.

"I want you to offer me something," I told her, "anything you feel you can give. You can say 'No, I don't want to make love, but I'd like to kiss a little,' or 'No, but I love you very much,' or 'No, but I'll rub your back.' "

This was hard for her. When she said no she felt guilty. It was difficult to offer something else, and to her, the offerings felt pitifully small compared to actually having sex, which is what she knew I really wanted. Often when she said no, she was in her own turmoil—which was why she said no in the first place—and she resented having to deal with my feelings at all. Now I was asking her to give even when she didn't really want to, to stay aware that there were two of us in this relationship.

It didn't develop smoothly, but my lover gradually learned to offer something when she didn't want to make love. One morning after a particularly bad night she said, "Would you like me to make you breakfast?" I really didn't want her lousy breakfast. I wanted sex. But she had offered something, as much as she was capable of at the time. I knew she was sincere. "Yes," I said. And we ate omelettes together while Tina Turner sang "Let's Stay Together" on the radio. We both cried. And I learned that there were ways to be close, to feel nurtured and loved, that weren't sexual.

OKAY, I'VE DONE ALL THAT

Some needs simply can't be met in non-sexual ways. Some of what you want is sex, making love, that specific combination of you and your lover coming together with all your body parts engaged. Foot rubs aren't going to do it. You're frustrated and angry. Okay. Allow yourself to be frustrated and angry.

It's important to be clear about what you need even if you're not getting it at the time. Don't pretend to yourself that you're satisfied if you're not. Don't be dishonest with yourself about what you want or need. One partner, whose wife hadn't yet remembered her abuse, tells the following story:

There was a time early on in my marriage when my wife wanted to be permanently celibate, like Gandhi. Because I didn't know myself very well, I decided that if she wanted to be celibate, I would accept that. The way I put it to myself was that I loved *her,* that she was more important to me than the nature of our relationship.

This was very noble. It was also a complete failure. I was hurt, angry, and frustrated with myself and with her. It would have been far better if I could have been honest with both of us and said that although I loved her, I didn't want a celibate marriage. But I didn't know then that I was entitled to want or to need.

Your partner is trying to learn about herself, to learn what she does and doesn't want. This is an excellent time to explore for yourself what *you* need in a relationship. Keep in mind your image of the satisfying relationship you're working toward, even if you can't realize it in the present.

Healing sexually is usually a slow process, but as one partner said, "Going slow is a lot faster than not going at all."

MUTUAL HEALING

Few of us feel totally healthy, joyous, integrated, and free. As one survivor advised partners: "Be really up-front about your own damage. However you learned about sex as a child in this society, you're damaged. Explore it honestly."

Both survivors and partners have the opportunity to heal sexually.

The quality of my own experience of sexuality has improved dramatically since my lover and I began to work together on her healing. I can't ever just go through the motions anymore. Both of us are more present than ever. The sexual inhibitions and tense, blocked places I used to experience are much less present because I have had to become aware of myself. I've had to face my own fears and vulnerabilities. So, although I've assisted her, she's assisted me as well. Even speaking selfishly, it's been more than worth it.

DO I WANT TO BE IN THIS RELATIONSHIP?

Be realistic about your commitment to the relationship. Are you willing to hang in through some rough times? For how long? Is your bond strong enough to withstand the problems you're having?

If someone came to me and said, "I just found out my partner's dealing with incest. What should I do?" I'd say, "Seriously evaluate your relationship and how much you're willing to put out when you may not get much back in return. After that, make sure your partner gets professional help, and consider therapy for yourself too. It'll bring up a lot for you. But first, evaluate the relationship, because it's hell. You've got to be strong. You've got to be patient. You're going to get angry."

***

During the period where I felt a widening chasm, a lot of what I went on was just faith and commitment: "I promised to hang in with this no matter what, and damn it, I'm going to make it work." Our wedding vows said we would be together "through all the changes of our lives." I often remembered those exact words. Either I was going to eat those words, or I was going to back them up.

***

If someone had shown me the job description for being the partner of an incest survivor, I never would have signed up for the job.

Even if you are married or in a committed partnership, you still have a right to make choices about staying in the relationship. You can make the choice that you will stay no matter what. Or you can choose to reassess an earlier commitment. But if you feel trapped, your resentment is likely to poison the relationship.

She Has to Put Her Healing First: Ellen

There was a time when I was impatient for my lover to make changes in our sexual relationship. I wanted her to want me passionately. We weren't making love as often as I wanted, and I told her that I wouldn't mind the droughts if there were *some* times that we really made love a lot. She looked at me as if I was denser than she'd thought, and explained, not entirely without patience, "Ellen, if there were *some* times when I could make love a lot, there'd probably be a *lot* of times. The problem is that I can't yet feel that. I want to. But I can't leap from here to there. I have to go step by step."

I remember this talk clearly. We were sitting on the couch, facing each other. I finally realized that she was doing the best she could, she was going as fast as she could. She was in therapy. She was working on this stuff. She wasn't just fooling around.

"I want to change as much as you want me to," she continued. "More. You can always leave and get another lover. I've only got myself. I *have* to change. But I can't fake it anymore. I have to put my healing first even if it means losing you, which I very much don't want to do."

This was an important moment, because it set the priorities straight. She was right. She was on this healing journey and it was up to me whether or not I came along.

In that same talk she told me she could understand that I might not want to stay. "I wouldn't blame you," she said.

It was true. I didn't have to be with her. I could find another lover. If it was hard for me to stay, that made sense. It wasn't because I was a weak, lousy, or disloyal person. I was choosing to be part of a situation which was genuinely difficult, which everyone wouldn't choose, and which, after that talk, I felt appreciated for. Through my lover's understanding that I might want to leave, I felt I was given absolute freedom to choose. Not surprisingly, this drew us closer together, and I continually made the choice to stay.

ACKNOWLEDGING DOUBT

Most partners go through periods when they wonder whether they are doing the right thing, doubt their capacity to help the survivor, or question their overall commitment to the relationship. You may wonder if the survivor will heal or if the relationship will stabilize. Partners often question their capacity to deal with the deep pain that accompanies healing. One partner spoke of her lover's journals: "She says if I knew what was in those notebooks, I'd leave her. Sometimes I wonder myself."

You may worry that you're repeating a self-destructive pattern of your own. This might mean staying in a situation where your needs aren't getting met, staying in crisis, or concentrating on someone else's problems instead of your own. One partner, the child of an alcoholic, said, "I just don't think it's healthy for me to be waiting around for someone to change. That's what my childhood was all about."

When you have doubts, it's important to accept them and to talk about them. While it's good to let the survivor know what you're thinking, it's also important not to burden her excessively. Find other people to talk to.

Partners often feel guilty if they think of leaving. At one partners' workshop, a woman told Ellen, "I want to leave but I feel like I shouldn't. She's trying so hard."

Ellen replied, "Just because someone is trying doesn't mean you have to make a commitment to go on the journey with her. You can leave and wish her well. The only good reason to do this is because you really want to. It doesn't help her if you stay only because she needs somebody. Just because someone loves you or needs you doesn't mean you have to be there."

You're not necessarily a better person if you stay. You're not selfish or cruel if you decide to leave. The essential thing is to be honest. It's very useful to be honest with someone who's been abused, even if the truth is blunt and miserable. Most survivors have had to deal with too many lies already.

Admitting what you can handle, the extent of your commitment, is essential. It gives you both the best chance of growing together through this challenge. And if it becomes clear that you are not able or willing to meet each other's needs well enough to stay together, you then can separate in a way that's respectful, even with its pain.

SEPARATING

Sometimes you have both tried your best and it still isn't working out. Your needs are incompatible. You're fighting all the time. You keep going around on the same loops and you're stuck.

It's natural to feel stuck temporarily. No couples glide through the healing process smoothly. But if the bitter times are outweighing the progress, and if you feel that you're in each other's way more than you're being helpful friends, then you may want to consider a separation.

Separations need not be permanent. A separation of a week, a month, six months, or a year can sometimes give you both the room you need and actually prevent the need for permanent separation. Although separations are usually painful, at least in part, there is often a good deal of relief as well. Both people get the opportunity to try to meet their own needs and live their own lives without tripping over each other.

Separations, like most major decisions, work best when there is mutual agreement. Leaving the survivor in the middle of a crisis is not going to be beneficial for her. If she's just recovering memories, inundated with flashbacks, and terrified of being alone, she's not going to appreciate your rational words in favor of time apart. But if you both agree that you've tried everything else and it's time to try a separation, that can be a positive step, not only for each of you individually but for the relationship as well.

If you don't want to separate but need some way to acknowledge that the relationship is in crisis, an amended living-together contract can help. You might come up with an agreement like this: "For the next four months, we'll live together but we will be like two ships that pass in the night. That way you'll have space to heal, and I won't be hanging on your every step. This is different from our regular relationship."

PERMANENT SEPARATIONS

Working through the difficulties of healing from child sexual abuse sometimes causes more stress than a relationship can bear. A new relationship may not have enough foundation to hold up under the pressure. The coping patterns of both people may have dovetailed for so long that there's no way to sort them out. And one or both of you may have changed to the point where you no longer want to be together. Although a permanent separation or divorce is painful, staying together when you truly can't support each other, can't grow, and can't make peace is worse for both of you.

IF YOU STAY

There are no guarantees about the length of time healing will take for any survivor. But if your partner is actively working —and you are too—you can be assured that things will change. The problems you're confronting now won't be exactly the same as the ones you'll be dealing with six months or a year from now. You are not in a static situation. There will be transformation. Of course, she's not going to be perfectly healed at some specific moment in time. But then again, neither are you.

It's difficult to be patient when you're under stress. You're trying to work, raise kids, cope with her problems, cope with your own, change, and keep it all together without going crazy. But she needs to pace her own healing. You can encourage, but you can't rush her. You can say what you need and negotiate what's possible, but sometimes you're just going to have to wait.

And of course it helps to take breaks. One husband of a survivor said, "I'd be happy if I never heard the word 'growth' again." If you feel like this, it's time for a break. The survivor may not need one, but you do. Take a weekend off and go fishing. Buy a record that makes you feel like dancing, then play it a lot. Enjoy yourself. Don't grow.

IT'S WORTH IT

Moving together through the tight places, learning about each other's fears and insecurities, becoming more sensitive to each other and ourselves, is a lifelong process. If you consider this a long-term partnership, a few years of struggle is worth it.

It feels to me right now that what's coming through on the other side is a much more fulfilling and exciting relationship than the one we started with. It's made us close. I mean, you don't get close living in a bowl of cherries. It's coming through stuff together that makes the bond stronger. When you're not dealing with it, it seems like a mountain. In reality, it comes down to a smaller scale when you take it apart and work with it. In retrospect, it really is not a very long process. I mean, what's a couple of years?

And as one partner makes clear, things do change.

Being sexually abused isn't that unusual. The shocking thing is that it's so common that it almost isn't an appropriate way to delineate people anymore. What's important isn't that it happened to her, it's how she's dealt with it in her life. She's not a victim anymore. She's a survivor. I'm coming to her years after she's delved into all this. She's a well woman. I'm happy with her just the way she is.

ALL THAT IS FINE AND STRONG BETWEEN YOU

When there are serious problems, it's easy to concentrate so much on the difficulties that you lose sight of all that is fine and strong between you. Make time to enjoy what you really like in your relationship right now. Affirm those aspects to each other. In the midst of all this growth and change, remember to celebrate what you've got.

In the meantime, expect her to be powerful. Don't think of her as a victim. Don't see her as weak, sick, or permanently damaged. Instead, hold the attitude that she's a whole human being going through some difficult struggles. See her as courageous and determined. Concentrate on her strength and her spirit.*

---

* This concept was taken from workshop facilitators Miriam Smolover and Meryl Lieberman.

Reflecting the survivor's strengths back to her is a gift you can give throughout the healing process. Even if it's a time when she doesn't want your direct help, even if you're separated by distance or differing feelings, you can always hold in your mind the image of her as a healthy, vibrant person.

Healing from child sexual abuse is a heroic feat. She deserves your respect, confidence, and admiration.

FOR COUNSELORS

If you have twenty clients and a good percentage of them are women, you're going to be working with some survivors—whether you're aware of it or not. I don't see how you can be a therapist today, in this country, and not be in the field. I didn't consciously choose to work with survivors.

—Patricia Pavlat, therapist

These guidelines are geared toward counselors—psychiatrists, clinical psychologists, marriage and family therapists, and social workers—who have survivors as clients. However, religious counselors, doctors, nurses, other medical workers, teachers, and other professional supporters will find them useful too.

Believe healing is possible. In order to work with survivors of child sexual abuse, you must have the conviction that survivors can heal. Hold a vision of your clients as strong survivors, as women who can heal and thrive, as people capable of creating joyous, satisfying lives for themselves.

Be willing to witness great pain. Working with sexually abused clients requires that you be witness to deep and wrenching pain. Over time, you can and must develop your own ways to process that pain in order not to be consumed by it.

Be willing to believe the unbelievable. Working with survivors puts you face to face with the sickest, most twisted things human beings do to each other. Adults rape and sadistically torture babies and children. This reality is one you have to come to terms with when you work with survivors.

Many survivors have lived in terrible isolation, thinking their secrets were too horrible to be told. Therefore it's imperative that you be willing to hear and believe the worst, no matter how disturbing.

Examine your own attitudes. Working with child sexual abuse forces you to face your preconceptions about sexual abuse, your personal philosophy or religion, your attitudes about good and evil, your own areas of sexual confusion and pain, your feelings about men, about women, about heterosexuality and homosexuality, about breaking taboos, speaking out, and being visible. In order to work effectively, you need to be clear about your own perspective so you don't inadvertently impose your views on your clients.

Explore your own history and fears regarding sexual abuse. If you were abused, work with a skilled counselor to be sure that you have resolved your own issues well enough to support your clients without confusing your problems with theirs. If you are in the midst of confronting your own abuse, consider taking a break from your practice with survivors. At a minimum, get experienced supervision to keep clear.

If you were not sexually abused as a child, explore those experiences in your history that come closest. This can include emotional humiliation, physical abuse, secrecy in your family, other childhood betrayals, adult experiences of rape or abuse. Your reactions and feelings about these experiences form a personal base from which you understand your clients.

She's the expert. When children are abused, their power is taken away. It's essential not to duplicate that dynamic in the counseling setting. The client is the expert in her own healing. Ask her what is helpful to her and what isn't. Let her set the pace. Encourage her to make her own decisions along the way. Assure her that you don't want her to do anything she doesn't want to do and that you're open to feedback at any time.

Validate her needs. Survivors are usually pretty accurate about what they need. If there are times when you can't offer a client what she needs, do acknowledge that her needs are valid. For example, you can say something like "I know you need the safety of talking to a woman right now. I can't be a woman, but I'll listen as best as I can and if you find you need to change counselors, I'll help you find a woman who can really support you." Refrain from discounting the survivor or judging her to be wrong about herself.

Your gender may be important to the client. Often survivors need to work with women counselors, and sometimes they want to work specifically with a male counselor, depending on their history and the issues they are ready to tackle. The need to choose a counselor based on gender is valid, and survivors shouldn't be criticized for this choice.

Support your clients in seeking appropriate help. It is often useful for survivors to work from various angles at once. For example, a client might be in one-to-one therapy, attend a survivors' support group, and receive regular massages. Many survivors grew up in families that operated on a basis of scarcity and exclusivity—if the child received love and attention from one parent, she couldn't get it from the other. Encourage your clients to seek and receive support from all healthy sources.

Group work is extremely helpful in combatting feelings of isolation and shame. Research the groups available in your area and suggest these to your clients. If there isn't one, consider organizing one with another counselor.

Believe the survivor. You must believe that your client was sexually abused, even if she sometimes doubts it herself. Doubting is part of the process of coming to terms with abuse. Your client needs you to stay steady in the belief that she was abused. Joining a client in doubt would be like joining a suicidal client in her belief that suicide is the best way out.

If a client is unsure that she was abused but thinks she might have been, work as though she was. So far, among the hundreds of women we've talked to and the hundreds more we've heard about, not one has suspected she might have been abused, explored it, and determined that she wasn't. Unfortunately, a feeling that you might have been abused usually leads to stronger feelings and eventual confirmation.

No one fantasizes abuse. Neither children nor women make up stories that they were abused because they were attracted to their fathers or other adults. The Oedipal theory as used in this way is false and damaging to women.

There are several thorough examinations of the way in which Freud constructed the Oedipal theory as a cover-up for the truth of child sexual abuse. Both Florence Rush, in *The Best Kept Secret: Sexual Abuse of Children,* and Jeffrey Masson, in *The Assault on Truth: Freud's Suppression of the Seduction*

Theory, document Freud's discovery that large numbers of his women clients had been sexually abused in childhood and that this was the cause of much mental illness.* They go on to present the information, from Freud's own letters and other writings, that he had reason to believe that incest had taken place in his own family. Not only were these radical discoveries too threatening for Freud's colleagues, but he shrank from the implications himself. He disavowed the seduction theory, his original discovery that sexual abuse was at the root of hysteria. In its place he substituted the Oedipal theory, thus turning the reality of abuse into a child's fantasy. There was no evidence to support his switch; Freud was simply unwilling to believe that so many fathers—possibly including his own—could abuse their children. Freud's new theory was obviously more palatable to society and to the patriarchal profession in which he worked. And it comfortably allowed him to avoid confronting the painful truth of abuse in his own family.

Don't say or imply that the client is to blame for the abuse. No child is *ever* to blame. Yet at one time or another, most women believe that the abuse was their fault. Teach them otherwise. One survivor said, "People kept telling me it wasn't my fault, it wasn't my fault. But they never told me *why* it wasn't my fault."

---

* Both books are found under "Sexual Abuse" in the Bibliography. Although Jeffrey Masson's work received great media response for exposing the fallacies in the Oedipal theory, Florence Rush was the pioneer. Her article "Freud and the Sexual Abuse of Children" appeared in 1977 in the first issue of *Chrysalis,* a feminist journal.

Educate yourself about child sexual abuse so that you have a clear conceptual framework from which to explain why she wasn't to blame, and why she thinks she was. Help her understand why she couldn't say no effectively. Help her see that her expectations of herself were unrealistic.

If your client experienced pleasure, help her let go of the shame. Sometimes children experience arousal, pleasure, or orgasm when they are sexually abused. This is often the most difficult, shameful aspect for survivors to come to terms with. Explain to your client that this is a common, natural response. Make it clear that this doesn't mean she wanted to be abused or was at fault in any way.

Incest is a criminal act with a victim. Some therapists mistakenly analyze any dysfunction in a family from the perspective that each member plays a part in keeping the situation going, and thus each holds a part of the responsibility. The stereotype is that the mother is drunk, working at night, or not sexually responsive to her husband. The father and daughter turn to each other to meet their needs. And for the father, this includes sexual needs.

Although there is nothing positive about alcoholic or neglectful mothering, neither is a mandate for incest. If family members have been irresponsible in their protection of the child, this is not an excuse for sexually abusing that child. And whatever the child does, she is *never* responsible. The abuser carries sole responsibility for the abuse. (See Working Through "Mother Blame," page 125.)

Don't minimize the abuse. Ellen conducted a seminar at a social service agency in which one social worker said: "When I deal with the parents of an abused child, I encourage them to keep things in perspective. I ask them, wouldn't you rather your daughter was molested than lost an arm or leg? After all, worse things could happen." Unfortunately, this kind of minimizing is not unusual. Be clear that all sexual abuse is damaging.

Don't spend time trying to understand the abuser. Most survivors have already spent too much time trying to understand the abuser. It's time to take back all that energy and keep the focus on the survivor. If you have a brief insight about the abuser, that is acceptable. For example, "He sounds like someone who is incapable of hearing your feelings, even now." But stay concentrated on the survivor's experience—her needs, her healing.

Never say or imply that the client should forgive the abuser. Forgiveness is not essential for healing. This fact is disturbing to many counselors, ministers, and the public at large. But it is absolutely true. *If you hold the belief that survivors must forgive the abuser in order to heal, you should not be working with survivors.**

Check to see if the survivor has a drug or alcohol problem. In order to work effectively, survivors must confront these addictions.

---

* For an excellent analysis of the role Christian forgiveness plays in healing from child sexual abuse, read *Sexual Violence: The Unmentionable Sin* by Marie Fortune. This book combines a theological perspective with a feminist analysis of sexual violence. For more details, see the "Sexual Abuse" section of the Bibliography.

Validate your client's coping behaviors. Even while supporting healthy changes, help her see the context in which she developed these ways of coping, their usefulness and necessity. Honor the ways in which she coped through the process of change.

Present a healthy perspective on what should be available to a child. Many survivors have a distorted idea about how children should be treated, about what a child should be provided with. They lived on crumbs so long that they believe crumbs are all anyone has a right to expect. It's important to help your client see that she had a right to much more, and that she has a right to be angry that she didn't get it.

Validate anger as a sane, healthy response to abuse, not as something to be rushed through. Don't be afraid of your client's anger. Encourage her to feel it, express it, and use it effectively.

Support clients in speaking out. This may include confronting abusers, disclosing to family members, taking legal action, or becoming an advocate for abused children. Although no one should be pushed to do any of these things, if a client wants to speak out, support her. Never imply that she wants to confront her parents only in order to hurt them or that she should consider their feelings. Nor should you project onto her your own fears about speaking out and taking a stand.

However, be sure your client is ready to handle the confrontation. If she isn't, help her to prepare thoroughly. And if possible, be available to facilitate confrontations or meetings between clients and abusers or other relatives.

Help build the survivor's support system. Becky Shuster, a Boston-based therapist, encourages clients to bring in partners, parents, close friends, or anyone who is a relevant support person in the survivor's life. The sessions are structured to give people permission to express the support they genuinely feel. There's also an opportunity to talk about what's kept them from unconditionally supporting the survivor. Just one session like this can help build a good foundation of support.

Don't say or imply that anyone's sexual preference is a result of sexual abuse. People prefer sexual partners of the same or of a different gender for a multitude of reasons. Sometimes past abuse is one of a complex of reasons, but reducing sexual preference to a consequence of abuse is simplistic and disrespectful to lesbian clients. This belief is usually based on homophobia and on the false assumption that one would not be a lesbian unless there had been trauma. (See "On Being a Lesbian and a Survivor," page 268.)

UNCOVERING THE ABUSE

Do not ignore the topic of sexual abuse. Many women have spent years in counseling but never talked about their abuse because they were never encouraged to do so. Intake forms should routinely include questions about sexual abuse.

Recognize the symptoms of early sexual abuse. If sexual abuse isn't the presenting problem but your client has eating disorders, an addiction to drugs or alcohol, suicidal feelings, or sexual problems, these may be symptoms of sexual abuse.

Be alert to hints from a client that she has been abused and wants to talk about it. Although everyone works at her own speed and it's important not to push, it's also important not to be too cautious. Ellen says counselors often ask for advice on how to bring up the topic of sexual abuse:

> Although this is a good question, frequently I sense it stems from a fear of touching such painful wounds. Respect for the pain is essential, but your own fear is not helpful. Although counselors should not push a client to work with issues she is not ready to confront, excessive caution gives the message that these things are too dangerous to talk about.
>
> When you work with someone you think may have been abused, ask outright, "Were you sexually abused as a child?" This is a simple and straightforward way to find out what you're dealing with. It's also a clear message to your clients that you are available to work with the issue of sexual abuse.
>
> If you sense that asking in this way would be too threatening or that your client may not yet be able to identify her experience as abuse, you can ask, "Did anyone ever touch you in ways you did not want when you were a child?"

If your client has already disclosed, ask questions. Ask for details. Make it clear that you're willing to hear the worst. It is difficult for survivors to talk about their abuse in detail. It is painful for them, and they hesitate to put someone else through the pain of listening. Usually when women talk about their abuse, they make generic statements such as, "I was raped by my uncle." But talking about the experience in detail, as it actually was, is an essential part of healing. And feeling that someone really wants to know is an important part of ending the isolation so many survivors feel.

Ask about other abuse and earlier abuse. Often a client will talk about one abuser, or one incident of abuse, but there will be others, perhaps even more disturbing, that she hesitates to disclose. Or there may be experiences that she has not yet remembered. Sometimes women remember the less threatening abuse first. It can take longer to remember abuse by a close family member, such as a father or mother, or to remember more violent abuse. Stay aware that the abuse you're working with may not be all there is. If you offer that possibility to clients, it will make it easier for them to remember and to disclose other abuse.

The following questions can be useful:

- Was that the worst that happened?
- Was that the first time anything like that happened?
- Did anyone else ever abuse you?
- Was anyone else in the room? Did anyone watch or take pictures?
- Have you ever been violated or raped as an adult?

If your client says she wasn't abused but you suspect that she was, ask again later. Children often repress memories of sexual abuse, and your questions may be the trigger that reveals those memories, either now or later. "No, I wasn't" may mean "No, I don't remember yet." (Read "Remembering," page 70, for more on occluded memories.)

If a client brings up the abuse once and then stops talking about it, bring it up again. Don't assume she's completely worked it out by mentioning it once or twice. If she says she's already dealt with it, know that there may be deeper layers.

Encourage her to feel. If there's no emotion connected with her telling, she may still lack integration. It's not enough for clients to "remember" in a detached way. To heal, survivors need to integrate the memories and the feelings.

Be creative. If the survivor can't say she was abused in words, be innovative and patient. Suggest that she draw with crayons, sculpt with clay, or position her body in ways that reflect her feelings.

One survivor, who began to recover memories right before her fiftieth birthday, was not able to talk at all for the first few sessions with her therapist. The therapist encouraged her to move her body, to dance her feelings, and this she was able to do, all the time silent. Then, when she was finally ready to start talking, she was unable to face her therapist. So they sat back-to-back for several more sessions until she felt safe enough to combine talking with seeing and being seen.

Don't have sex with clients. *NEVER have any sexual contact with a client during the course of counseling or after it's over.* It's distressing that this should even have to be emphasized, but many, many women have been terribly damaged by sexual relationships with their counselors. It's a way of replicating the original abuse, of breaching the trust the survivor has worked so hard to establish. This is one area in which the survivor's desires do not accu-

rately reflect what's necessary in a healing relationship.

Even after therapy is terminated, it is extremely damaging to engage in a sexual relationship with your client. This is a transgression of appropriate boundaries which is far too similar to the original sexual abuse to be justified under *any* circumstances.

Safe Touch. Nonsexual nurturing touch can be an important part of counseling *if, and only if, it's controlled by the client.* In Ellen's workshops, she tells participants that she is available for safe touch:

I tell the women I work with that I will hug or hold them if they want me to. I also state explicitly that I will never be sexual with them, that when I hug them it will be totally safe and there will never be any sexual innuendos. Although sometimes women look at me like I'm crazy—"Who thought you *would* be sexual?"—others have thanked me for that clarity. And many times after a hug or after holding a woman, she will tell me how important it is to her to be able to receive that safe touching. Sometimes that hug is the very first time in that woman's life that she has been able to receive nurturing touch free of sexuality. Many of the women I work with are starved for safe touch.

If you're not comfortable, don't touch. Touching with mixed messages is much worse than no touching at all. But don't imply that the client is wrong for wanting touch.

THE POWER OF LOVE

The guidelines presented in this chapter are essential for working effectively with survivors of child sexual abuse, but they will all ring hollow unless you add love.

Not only does the adult woman need your sincere caring, but the child within her is also hungry for heartfelt nurturing. Jayne Habe learned this from her own experience:

> You know, all I ever really need to grow is love. So simple but so hard.
>
> I really believe that the child within me needs to be loved by others—like a good parent loves—before she will know she is entitled to life. Sure I have to love myself, but if I could do it alone I wouldn't be spending all these years in therapy or have such a strong need for that kind of connection. My need is so great it's scary, but I can't get the little girl back alone.

Don't be afraid to love your clients. Keep appropriate boundaries, of course, but open your heart. Ellen says:

> When I look at a survivor with love, I can watch the response in her eyes. There is a sequence—and sometimes a mixture—of disbelief, hope, relief, gratitude, elation, peacefulness, and a surge of love in return.

So many women have never had the experience of being both safe and loved. It's love that makes us feel special, precious. All the techniques, all the methods, are really just tools to channel the love. It's the love that heals.

TAKING CARE OF YOURSELF

Working with survivors of child sexual abuse isn't easy. It is difficult to hear the stories, to share in the pain, to carry the responsibilities of helping. Because of this, some counselors choose one extreme or the other —they armor themselves to such an extent that they are not present for their clients, or they absorb all the pain like a sponge and quickly collapse. Neither works. It is important to be open and protected at the same time. This is what you want for your clients and what you need for yourself.

Protecting Myself: Ellen

When I first began facilitating I Never Told Anyone workshops, I felt exhilarated and deeply satisfied at the end, but I also felt poisoned. The stories of the women I worked with haunted my dreams, barged into my lovemaking, lodged in my body. I did not know how to let them go.

The first couple of years, I often was left with tumultuous feelings. Afterwards I cried, raged, and pounded pillows. It is impossible to be a feeling person and not be outraged and anguished by what survivors have had to endure. I knew it was essential for me to make room for the expression of these feelings. Just as we encourage this in our clients, we must give ourselves the same permission.

Friends told me I had to learn how to protect myself, and so I tried. I practiced staying in touch with my own boundaries. I learned to stay aware of the outline of my body, myself as separate from the woman I listened to, held in my arms. I remembered to breathe. With each exhale I released the pain down through my body and into the earth. I let their stories move through me, like a stream. As I inhaled, I felt myself receive the energy of the universe, the life spirit. I've learned to protect and renew myself so that I tire less quickly and absorb much less pain.

LETTING GO

Everyone must find a way to let go. It is too draining to carry around the pain of all your clients. That kind of merging isn't healthy for them or for you.

One woman, the director of a battered women's shelter, said when she left work and drove home, she pictured all the problems, people, and pain streaming behind the car blowing out into the wind. By the time she got to her house in the country, it was all gone.

Ellen has developed her own personal ritual for letting go of a workshop when it's over:

Immediately, I shower or bathe. I experience the water washing everything away. One by one I think of each woman from the workshop, skim over what she did and said, where she still has to go, my feelings for her, my concerns for her, my wishes for her, and then I release her to her own continuing healing, to her own life. I let go. This process is very quick, just long

enough to picture her in my mind, make contact, and release.

If I find I can't release someone easily, I analyze what's still holding me. Sometimes there's something for me to learn, sometimes I need to reassure myself that she will be okay, that I cannot do more. Once in a while, I realize I need to say something further to her, and make a mental note to do that.

At the end, I rinse with clean water, dry and put on clean clothes, brush my teeth, and I'm done. It's rare now that I can't release my feelings through this ritual cleansing.

Some of the best letting go can be play. One therapist, Rose Z. Moonwater, explains:

I have to take time off, get away, to play as intensely as I work. When I don't do that, I start to feel that the whole world is like the stories I'm hearing. I walk down the street and I see pain in each person's face. It's like I'm only tuned in on one channel. And that's why I need to have fun, to laugh and act goofy, be out in nature and with other people in a joyous, light and easy way.

Take care of yourself. If all you can offer to clients as a model for health is the harried, burned-out social worker, that's not much inspiration. Not only do you deserve to feel good, you need to create a vital, balanced life for yourself if you intend to assist your clients in their quest for such a life.

PART FIVE
COURAGEOUS
WOMEN

AN INTRODUCTION

The fifteen stories in this section highlight particular aspects of the healing process. They represent a broad range of experience, and you will probably see parts of your own life reflected in them. We hope you will find at least one woman with whom you can identify.

The stories are not finished, because the lives are not finished. Each represents one fixed moment in time—the day the interview took place. Often when we sent copies of the interviews back to the survivors, they'd say, "But that's not me. So much has happened since then!" Like all of us, these women have continued to grow.

Take your time reading these stories. Give yourself a chance to digest each one, rather than reading them all at once. Let yourself feel. They are meant to be an inspiration, a touchstone, a reminder that healing is truly possible.

NAMES OR PSEUDONYMS: THE RIGHT TO CHOOSE

It's such a disappointment not to be able to use my own name. I've earned the right to own my words, my journey. I feel angry at the situation, denied what is mine by birthright—my name connected with my truth. Strange, so much of the journey has been a "naming" of shadows. And now I must place my own name back in the shadows . . .

—Gizelle

About half the women who share their stories here chose to use pseudonyms to maintain their privacy. After careful consideration, they decided it wasn't in their best interests to publicly come forward as survivors. For these women, using pseudonyms was a way to protect themselves and safeguard their healing.

The other women wanted to use their own names. They saw identifying themselves as a way to end the secrecy and shame that burden survivors of child sexual abuse. They also wanted, quite simply, to tell their story honestly—to name themselves, their abuser, the place where they lived, the facts of their lives. They'd lived with enough lies already.

As authors, we were committed to respecting each woman's decision. We wanted each woman's participation to be an empowering experience for her. However, we learned that it was not legally possible for a publisher to print a survivor's story with actual names and places if the abuser (and possibly other family members) was alive and identifiable.

This situation perpetuates the very hiding and silence that we are working to end. To tell women that they can't speak up, name their abuse and their abusers, and tell their stories in their own names without fear adds to the already formidable obstacles that women must overcome to break the silence.

We talked with the women who wanted to use their own names and together decided that we'd rather use the stories with pseudonyms and changes in identifying details than not include them at all. We all felt their value to survivors was so great that it was worth compromise, but we want to make clear that this is yet another violation of the rights of survivors. As with many of the laws and legal procedures regarding child sexual abuse, this operates once again to protect the abusers rather than the abused. And like the others, it must be changed.

JUDY GOLD

There's nothing as wonderful as starting to heal, waking up in the morning and knowing that nobody can hurt you if you don't let them.

Judy Gold is forty-five years old.* She is a musician and lives with her husband, Howard, in an upper-middle-class, predominantly Jewish suburb of New York. Howard is a businessman and works for his father-in-law in the garment industry. Judy and Howard have been married for twenty-five years and have four children, the eldest of whom is nineteen.

Of her childhood, Judy says: "My father's sister died in an insane asylum and I was named for her. I was always told I was going to end up just like her—bad and crazy. We were upper middle class. My mother was addicted to prescription

drugs. She was always hazy. Before she married my father, she had been a published author. It's too bad because she could have had a successful life and it ended up being a real zero. She's dead now.

"My father was a very violent man. He was like Dr. Jekyll and Mr. Hyde. He was loving toward us whenever our family was portrayed to the outside world. He used to march us out every Sunday night to a fancy restaurant for dinner. It was like Make Way for Ducklings. *But what went on before we got into the car was a horror show.*

"The world loved him. He set up scholarships; he helped build the local temple. He's given buildings to universities and hospitals. So no one would ever suspect what went on in that house.

"The only time I can remember him being loving was when he was in my bed. He would batter

---

* Judy Gold chose to use a pseudonym.

me at night and after he'd beat me up, he'd make me take his shoes off and kiss him goodnight. And then in the morning he'd climb in my bed and molest me. There was never any intercourse, but there was everything else.

"My first memories of being abused are tied in to my sister's birth, when I was six. The beatings continued till I went away to college, but the incest stopped when I was about twelve, when my baby sister turned six. That's always made me wonder if he moved on to her.

"Even though the actual abuse stopped when I reached puberty, the sexual innuendos never stopped. He's just sleazy, horrible. You wouldn't want to meet him. Yet, as I say, the whole world loves him."

How did the incest affect me? I've never really been in touch with me or my feelings. I was always real tough. If I ran fast enough and far enough, then I wouldn't have to think. I did a lot of drinking, a lot of drugs, a lot of fast living. I would drive at high speeds. I would think nothing of walking out at three in the morning in a deserted area. It was almost like I was tempting fate.

I had learned to tune out when my father beat me as a child. I never physically felt any pain. I used to say, "You'll never make me cry." And I never did. I allowed myself to feel anger, but never sadness or pain. It's what saved me, but it got out of control, the living out of my body. Spacing out was a very common thing for me. It wasn't until about a year and a half ago that I stopped doing that. I would be sitting talking to you, and I wouldn't be in my body. I used to say, "I turn into foam rubber." Everything went numb. My whole body would tingle, like your fingers going to sleep. Or my hearing would go off.

A dread that something bad was waiting for me has followed me most of my life. I have a morbid fear of the dark. I will never close my eyes in the shower. There are parts of my own house I am just beginning to go into.

THERE WAS ALWAYS A WALL AROUND ME

I could go anywhere and make friends, but I allowed people to get only so close. The minute you got closer, I turned you off. I felt I was filled with something evil, and that evil rubbed off on anyone I came into contact with.

Then I met Howard, who was my knight in shining armor. I was twenty-three. He was going to save me from all this craziness. Howard is the antithesis of my father. My survivor self knew I could not get into a relationship that would be a repeat of what I'd had with my father. Yet I know I've tried to goad him. I would test him. I'd say, "Go on, I know you want to hit me." And he never did. When I look back, I marvel at the composure he had.

Howard put such order into my life. And I really believed he was going to save me from the insane asylum. That's how the relationship began. Of course, things have changed. Things are much more realistic. As I began to work on this stuff, I was strong enough to say to Howard, "You know, I'm never again going to hold you accountable for my failures, but I'm never going to give you credit for my successes either." That was the beginning of the eroding of the white knight.

My sexuality has definitely been affected by the incest. I was uncomfortable having sex, but I never knew why. Every time Howard and I had sex in our marriage, I would wake him up and tell him I was sure someone was breaking into our house. And afterwards, I would get up out of bed, go to the kitchen and eat, and make like it had never happened: "Who me? Have sex?" And the strange thing is *I enjoyed the sex!* It was hard to get started, but once I got into it, I really enjoyed it. There were parts of the incest I enjoyed too, and that has been a really heavy trip for me. I mean, my body responded. It had to. But I'm not so quick to forgive that part of me.

I've never been able to have sex in the morning, obviously. Howard wouldn't dare touch me in the morning. We've had a lot of fights, mostly over sex. As much as I loved him and looked at him like he was going to save me, I never trusted him.

It was also very hard for me to hold my kids. They suffered because of what happened to me. I was not a nurturing mother. People see me as a wonderful mother. They marvel at how laid back I am in my parenting, but what they don't understand is that I was afraid to get close to those kids because I felt that I would infect them. So what they interpreted as giving my children independence was me being scared to death of them. I was scared to touch them.

If you asked people, they would tell you I was the most self-assured, self-confident, commanding, imposing woman. Once I started therapy, I would always complain, "I don't know who I am. People tell me I'm one thing, but I feel like I'm another." They see me as someone who has her whole life in order, because I never talked to anybody about what I really felt.

COME ON, ASK ME

When I stopped smoking, I gained thirty pounds in four months. Somebody gave me the name of this therapist who did hypnosis for overeating. I really believe that there are no accidents. I think I ate myself up to those thirty pounds for the purpose of seeking therapy. It was right there on the surface, waiting to come out.

I was almost provocative in the kinds of things I said to my therapist, like "Oh, you should know my family." In other words, "Ask me. Come on. I'll tell you if you ask me."

What was going to be five sessions has now become over four years. A couple of months into the therapy, he asked me to tell him about my father. I said he used to beat me up. And he said, "What else did he do to you?" And I said, "Nothing." And he said, again, "What else did he do to you?" And I said, "Oh, well, he crawled into my bed." And he said, "What else?" And I kept insisting there was nothing. And then he just asked me point-blank, "Did he ever touch you?" That started the whole thing. I finally admitted, "Yes, he touched me."

When we started using hypnosis, I got to the first memory. Then I started to remember incidents without the hypnosis. I got to the point where I could remember my father's precise smell. It took me two years to clearly remember what had happened.

The one thing that brought it all into focus—and it was the hardest thing—was a memory that I had always wet my pants. I used to hide all these sticky underpants in my closet as a little girl. And now I know I didn't pee in my pants at all. My father had ejaculated on me when I had them on, and I had saved all those underpants on the floor of my closet. My grandmother found piles of them in the closet and she showed them to my mother, who accused me of wetting my pants. I told her I hadn't done it, but she wouldn't believe me. She punished me for denying it, and he beat me for lying later the same night. As I pieced this together in therapy, I realized she had to have known the difference between urine and semen. It was the the worst memory I had. But it made it all very real.

My mother's death freed me up to remember all of this. I remember when my mother was dying, I talked about the beatings. I said, "Why didn't you stop him? How could you allow him to do those things to us?" And her answer was "What could I do?"

I had always adored my mother because she was so talented. And I felt such pity for her. But when I realized that she had known what was going on, I hated her. I even went to her grave and stomped on it. I was screaming at her. They could have locked me up then if they had seen me.

After I got through all the anger, I realized that she really was helpless. I'm sure that she had been a victim herself. And she sacrificed me so that she could live.

IF FOR NO OTHER REASON THAN SPITE, I FORCED MYSELF TO GET BETTER

When I first started remembering, I was very scattered. I was totally depressed. I gained a tremendous amount of weight. I didn't go out of the house. I became very solitary. I couldn't stop crying for a long time. I was making up for forty years of not crying. I could have been hospitalized at points. It was an effort to get out of bed in the morning. It was an effort to decide what to put on. I would go through periods of that and then periods of feverish activity. I would play the piano for hours on end, and then I wouldn't sit down at it again for months.

I didn't want anyone touching me. There was no sex. I had a tremendous amount of back pain. The psoriasis I'd always had got worse.

But the worst part was the terrible despair. I just felt like I was down in the sewer and I was never going to see daylight again. And I kept saying, "Why did I do this? Why did I open up Pandora's box?" I cursed myself because I could see no end in sight. I remember saying to my therapist, "Am I ever going to smile again?"

I felt like I was being battered from the inside. It was like a parade of demons, only the parade never stopped. I'd no sooner put one to bed than another one would come out to haunt me. There were a lot of nightmares, and I was always being chased by an unknown male.

I felt so close to crazy, but I kept saying to myself, "Are you going to let him win out? How can you let that prophecy come true?" If for no other reason than spite, I forced myself to get better. I was hell-bent on surviving, if only to show him that I was going to outlast him.

If I was to name one particular reason I got through it, it would be the anger. I was angry at myself first, for having delved into the subject. What did I need it for? I was angry at myself for having put on so much weight, for doing all those drugs. And then suddenly the anger starting being directed where it should have gone all along. And that anger—at him—is what fueled me to get well. When I would be raging, my therapist would say to me, "Hold on to that anger. That's your best friend." And he was right.

Then I had to grieve. That came toward the end of the process. I grieved for that little girl who never was. I never had a childhood, and I think that's what I mourned more than anything. For the longest time, I never understood what my therapist meant when he said, "Get in touch with the little girl. Feel her. Forgive her."

It took me a long time to understand that I hadn't done anything to cause the molestation. The little girl was not to blame. Even if I had lain there spread-eagled, naked, he was the adult, and I was the child, and not accountable. I finally believe that now. I've been able to forgive her.

I FOUND OUT I WASN'T ALONE

Along the way, there were little tiny victories that got me through the next day: like getting up, like getting out of bed, like saying "I'm going to go to an exercise class today." It was a victory to be able to make dinner for my family, to be able to be out there in the market with people.

Another thing that helped me was reading articles, books, anything I could get my hands on. I watched every program about incest. I kept saying, "It's got to get better, because other people have lived through this and survived." It helped to know I was not alone.

I have a very dear friend from my college days who I've kept in touch with all these years. She knew I was in therapy for eating, and she could see that I was gaining weight. About a year into my therapy we went out to lunch, and she said to me, "I

have to ask you a question. Were you ever sexually abused? You don't have to answer if you don't want to. I'm asking you because I was, and you sound just like me."

You could have knocked me over. I couldn't even get the word "yes" out. I just nodded my head and started sobbing. And that has been one of the greatest sources of healing for me.

IT'S *OUR* PROBLEM, HOWARD

It was two years into my therapy before I told Howard what was going on. I never told him before because I thought he would be repulsed by me. It never occurred to me that he might be angry with my father instead. Until that point, I'd just said to him, "I'm dealing with some very heavy issues, and I just don't feel free to discuss them with you." I let him know I was in trouble, but I wasn't going to tell him why. It was a nightmare. The fact that we're still married is amazing.

In order to tell Howard, I had to get drunk and drugged and angry. I just spit it all out: "Oh, yeah, let me tell you something. . . ." He was numb. He never said a word. I picked something up and I threw it at him. And I said, "Damn you, you give me a reaction. Do you hate me? Do you think I'm terrible? Do you think I'm dirty?" I was filling in the blanks. Everything I thought he should think of me, I told him.

He admits now that for a whole year he never really integrated the information. I don't think he believed a lot of it. He'd seen my father get violent, so he believed that part. But he didn't want to talk about the incest. I think he operated on the premise "If I don't talk about it, then it doesn't exist."

But I would force him to talk about it. I said, "Didn't you ever wonder why I always fooled around for hours to avoid coming to bed? Didn't you ever wonder why you couldn't touch me in the morning?"

I remember one time Howard said to me something about "my problem." And I said to him, "You don't understand. The minute I told you about this, it became *our* problem." It took him a long time to realize it was a problem we shared now. It was very hard for him. It still is. And it's doubly hard because he works with my father.

Once we started to talk about it, we talked all the time. I would sometimes say, "I can't talk about it anymore." Or, "Let's promise that on Tuesday and Thursday night we won't discuss it." We actually had to make appointments *not* to talk about it. Your brain can only absorb so much.

I still have battles with Howard over the incest because he is embarrassed by it. He would say things like "Be careful who you tell." And I would say, "Look, I don't care who knows. As long as I'm the one who tells them." And he would say, "You better be careful who you tell. Some people would love to get some dirt on you." He's ashamed. He'd rather I kept it a secret.

Howard is thrilled about the changes in me—that I'm off the drugs and off the cigarettes—but it's hard for him to give up control. He's been used to having the control in our relationship. And now he's had to give a lot of it up. He's given up all control in terms of sex.

Now it's when *I* want it and that's been very hard for him, but he's been wonderful about it. I've finally been honest. A lot of these problems came up because I was so dishonest. Now I can say to him, "I don't want you to touch me." I don't have to hang out in the bathroom for half an hour or get busy doing something. I used to say my greatest creative time was at night. That was just so I didn't have to go to bed.

I am just starting to realize that I am a very sexual human being. It's such a nice feeling to know that after I have sex I can go to sleep. I don't have to go in that kitchen and eat and pretend that it didn't happen, that it was somebody else in that bedroom responding.

It's taken a lot of hard work for us to stay together. There have been some real rough times. My way of dealing with most problems was to run away from them. And in a marriage, you just can't do that. Gradually we've learned to deal with problems right when they happen. And that's making us closer than ever.

I WANTED TO GET MY FATHER OUT OF MY LIFE

I'd thought about it for a year. My father was in the hospital. Fittingly, he had something wrong with his pecker. I thought, "Maybe they'll cut it off."

We went to visit him. He had on one of those hospital gowns with the back cut out. He purposely stood up and exposed himself to me. Then he said, "Judy darling, would you help me with this?" Finally at one point I said, "For Christ's sake, can't you put a bathrobe on?" He just lay in the bed and said, "Judy darling, would you pull the sheet up for me?" And I said, "Pull your own damn sheet up," and I walked out. That was the beginning of the end.

When Howard saw this, he couldn't believe it. He said, "If I ever doubted you, I never will again."

But still, it wasn't easy getting my father out of my life. My husband was in business with him. And I was still scared of him. I made a list of all the times I had to have contact with him, whether it was by phone or in person. And I thought, "What is one thing I could cut out? Is it maybe calling him on his birthday? Could I not have him come to my house for Thanksgiving dinner?" Well, I couldn't do that the first year, but I didn't call him on New Year's Eve to wish him a Happy New Year.

Every time I was able to cross something off the list, I'd feel terrific. The first time I didn't call him on his birthday, I cannot tell you my sense of elation. But it was very hard. I lived in fear that that phone was going to ring and he was going to yell, "Why didn't you call me on my birthday?"

I would rehearse—"If he does call me, what am I going to say?" I had the whole thing planned. At first I'd pretend it was a bad connection and yell into the phone, "HELLO? HELLO? It must be a bad connection. Call back." And then I'd take the phone off the hook and pretend the phone was out of order. Or I'd drop the phone if I heard his voice. I had lists of things I could do next to each phone. Doing that gave me courage. I would act it out with Howard. He would play my father, and I would practice what to say. I wrote out scripts and carried them in my wallet.

And finally my father did call, and he said, "What is going on between us? You never call me back. Do you have any intentions of calling me back?" And I said, "No." That was the end of it. I never said why.

Then his wife called and asked what was going on. She said, "He's so upset. He doesn't understand. Is it because he took you out of temple when you were nine years old and made you go home?" Can you believe this?

And I said, "You know, I'm not prepared to discuss this with you right now." She kept saying, "What did he ever do?" And I just repeated, "I have no intention of discussing this with you. Now if you want to talk about something else, I'd be more than happy to talk to you. But otherwise, we have nothing more to say to one another." And that was the end of it.

Do you know how long it took me to rehearse that? But when I could do it, what a victory! When I got him out of my life, the rest of the healing just fell into place. That was the moment when I knew that I really was in control of my life.

I'LL NEVER FORGIVE HIM

I have such venomous hate. I pray to God that he comes down with some terrible disease. I'd like him to get AIDS. That or Alzheimer's.

I can't wait for his funeral. You can bet I'm going to be the first one at that coffin to make sure he's really dead. I've even rehearsed what I'm going to say to people at the funeral when they say how wonderful he was: "I'm glad you have good memories of him. Isn't it nice that some people have nice memories of him." Things like that.

I always tell my children, "Don't ever hate. It's not worth having that kind of poison." But this hatred affects me in a positive way. Every time I think of how much I hate him, it gives me the strength to say, "You're never going to beat me." My hatred has helped me get well.

Maybe someday I'll look at him as a defenseless old man and think nothing. I doubt that. I'm not sure I want to get to that point.

IT WAS TIME TO REBUILD

Over time, I've come to accept what happened to me. I don't think there's any more to remember. And even if there is, so what? It can't be any worse than what I've already remembered. So what am I going to remember, one more night?

The incest happened. I can't change that. But I have the rest of my life ahead of me. I'm not going to live the way I lived the first forty years, because they weren't fun-filled years. But I don't have to. And that's what I've worked so hard for. I can change.

There was a point where I felt like I had gotten all the poison out and it was time to rebuild. It was a different pain. Now the healing has to do with dealing with my life: What do I do from here on in? How do I set things up that I'm not so rigid in what I expect from myself?

I finally know that I'm a nice person. I'm not that sleazy, slimy black goo I thought I was. It's nice to look in the mirror and say, "You're not ugly. You're not crazy."

And I like myself. I never liked myself before. I always thought that what they'd told me was true, that I was bad. But I wasn't bad. I was screaming for help and nobody heard.

A YEAR AND A HALF LATER

A year and a half after this interview, I was diagnosed with cancer. Getting sick really put everything in perspective. I believe I got the cancer because of all the years of stress, of shoving this down. Keeping the secret took its toll. The human body is like a stuff bag. If you keep shoving things in, you start to rip at the seams.

Cancer is the ultimate test of survival. I've had unbelievable support from my husband and kids. They just held me. That became a very important part of my healing. I learned what safe hugs are all about. It was important for me to keep fighting. I underwent radiation and chemotherapy. Compared to what I survived all those years, this was a piece of cake. Last month the doctor told me the cancer was entirely gone.

I am a survivor, and I'm going to live to dance on my father's grave.

EVA SMITH

You get tired of dealing with incest all the time. There's an ending point to everything. There's an ending point to life. Why can't there be an ending point to dealing with this shit?

Eva Smith is a black woman in her early thirties who lives in California.* She is a therapist and an artist. She lives with her two teenage children. "I share this information with you as a gift of healing for other women. I am truly living my life now, after just surviving for so many years."

Between the ages of three and eight, I was molested by my great-uncle. From nine to fifteen, my stepfather molested me. I grew up just trying to live from day to day and survive, wishing the whole thing would

be over and stop. I used to pray my stepfather would get struck by lightning. I wasn't above making a pact with the devil to get rid of him. *Anything.* And anything happened. I got pregnant.

I had always been a fat child. When I was thirteen, I weighed 188 pounds. And then I lost weight. So when I got pregnant, everybody just thought I was getting fat again. I'll never forget—I was going into my junior year in high school and my mother and I went shopping for clothes, and my mother came into the dressing room with me. She really was looking at me and she was saying, "You look different." And I said, "I'm just getting fat again." And she said,

---

* Eva Smith chose to use a pseudonym.

367

"I'm taking you to the doctor." That was in September and considering that my son was born in November, I must have been at least seven months pregnant, but all this was brand new to me.

When the doctor told my mother I was pregnant, she asked me who the father was, and I told her. She confronted my stepfather and he claimed that he knew nothing about it. Within a week we left him and went down South.

When I first realized I was pregnant, I attempted suicide. It was a hard time for me. *I* knew I needed therapy. I wish somebody else had realized it at the time!

My mother told me I didn't have to keep the child, that I could put it up for adoption or that she would raise it as her own. I chose to keep that child because it was the first thing that was ever mine.

I created a cover story about who the father was. I said he was some boy I'd been going with. I had to deal with a lot of put-downs from people, you know, cause I was fifteen and having this baby.

Because of all the things that happened to me, there was this question that used to haunt me, you know, "Why me?" Those were the years I call my trauma years. And I went out of the trauma years into being a battered wife.

I got married at seventeen. I was already pregnant with my daughter. My husband and I were the same age. I told my husband about my stepfather and that he was my son's father. If only I knew then what I know now! I would have never told him. Because he got jealous. Every time we argued, he'd bring that up. I was different kinds of whores and sluts and this and that.

We were into it before we ever got married. We used to argue once a week when we were going together, but not real physical kind of stuff. But after we were married, he had the license. You know, they pronounce you man and *wife*, not man and *woman*. To my way of thinking it gives men a free ticket to do whatever they want. So the battering started and increased till I couldn't take it anymore.

I left him after he'd taken a branch off a tree and beat me with it, but then I came back and went through what I call my three months of hell. I was making $1.79 an hour. I was paying all the bills, I paid the rent. I was buying all the food, all the clothes, even renting him a television. I got off work at 4:30. I was expected to catch the bus at 4:35, hit downtown at 5:00, change buses, and walk in the door at 5:20. If I walked in the door at 5:30, I got my ass kicked.

So in essence, he held my children hostage. He did lots of sadistic things to me during that time. I was on a large dose of Librium. My nerves were so bad, I was going through bouts of temporary blindness.

I was twenty then, and I tried to kill myself. I had gotten my prescription filled. I came home and I took about half the bottle. He found the bottle and he woke me up 'cause I was going off to la-la land. And he got me up and went and got my son, who was about four then. He sprayed Raid in his hair, then he took a lighter and held it over his head and said, "If you don't wake up, I'm gonna light his hair." I mean I was going through it. We didn't have a phone or anything. There's that isolation thing.

I decided to kill him.

It was a question of survival. I knew we couldn't live together without one of us killing the other. So I was going to kill him. We had this argument on a Monday and I had planned that Friday that when I got paid,

I'd pay the rent, the water bill, buy a gun, go home, walk in the door, scream, and kill him. Even now, I can say with conviction I was going to kill him.

And this woman who was like my second mother said, "You don't want that on your conscience the rest of your life." So I turned him over to the military because he'd gone AWOL. They took him to jail. I took my children to safety and moved out of the house in four days. I started divorce proceedings immediately.

When I got rid of my husband, all that weird stuff went away. I didn't have to take Librium any more. The blindness went away. The shaking went away. All of that went away.

So by the time I was twenty-one, I had been married, divorced, and had two children. When I moved to California, I had seven suitcases, two kids, and one hundred dollars. And Lord, I've come a long way from there.

I HAVE TOLD MY SON

My son will be eighteen this fall, and when he was thirteen, I told him who his father was. He had been asking questions on a regular basis. He wanted to know who he was, where did he come from, what was he about.

When he was younger, I'd told him my cover story—that his father was a teenager I had sex with. That was okay then, but as he got older, when he'd ask questions about his father, there'd be a hush in the whole room or people would change the subject. So he got the feeling there was this secret, and there were a number of people who were in on the secret, and he wasn't one of them.

There's no father listed on his birth certificate, so there was always this air of mystery. And at thirteen he just asked me in a much more straightforward way than he ever asked me before, so I told him.

Ahmal, the man I was involved with at that time, who was a father figure for my children, and I got together and discussed it very thoroughly. And then the three of us went into my bedroom. My son was trying to be grown up, wanting to have a cigarette. Everybody was cool, you know. I think it's important to say how I told it to him because I didn't make it a real heavy-duty kind of thing.

I'm a storyteller, and I just told it like you'd tell any kind of story to a child. I had parts in it that made him laugh. I told it in a way that wasn't condemning about my stepfather, because no matter how much pain he had brought into my life, the bottom line to this whole thing was this: this man was my son's biological father and whatever I told him was going to mold a certain part of him for the rest of his life. So it was important to me to not make my stepfather an ogre, to tell my son about it in such a way that he would not become as devastated as I was by it. Your children are more important than anything that may hurt you or the hate that you feel.

And so I dredged up every good memory about my stepfather that I could find. I really worked at making him very human. I talked about his shortcomings and the good things about him. I talked about his smile, 'cause he had a wonderful smile. I didn't go into the sexual abuse real heavy because that was not the important thing at that point. I talked about what he did to me and how young I was. I put a little drama in, 'cause there was plenty of drama in what happened, but I didn't make it a great big thing. And I talked about what it was like being pregnant with him. How I felt. I was fifteen. How that felt.

My son's first reaction was, "Wow, all of that happened to me!" And Ahmal said, "Hey, blood, check this out. None of that happened to you. It happened to your mother." And so my son had to deal with that. He had to weigh how this affected who he was as a person. He had to make sure he was never that type of male himself. It was a very difficult time for him. And it was a very, very hard time for me because he was trying to punish me for who his father was.

Slowly it has healed for my son. Now it's just a fact of being. I don't think he resents me for it. If anything, I think maybe he loves me a little more. He was a spirit that had to come here and that was the way he came.

IT'S MADE ME MORE COURAGEOUS AS A PARENT

Because of the things that happened to me, I was very open with my children about sex. I've always told them the truth. My children did not grow up talking about dick and pussy. They grew up talking about penis and vagina, you know, and had a very clear understanding about what sex was all about. I didn't want them to be in the dark about what happens when you stick a penis in a vagina.

My son was talking to this woman and he said, "My momma would beat me to death if I hit a woman." Oh good, he knows. He's going to have to have a certain amount of respect toward women. That's how he's been raised.

I USED TO CALL MYSELF THE THIRTY-TO-NINETY-DAY WONDER

I was only involved in relationships that lasted thirty-to-ninety days. On the ninety-first day the relationship would be over, you could give it up. And this went on for many, many years, until I met Ahmal, who was willing to really put in some time.

After I'd been involved with him for ninety days, I began to end the relationship. On the ninety-first day I was suddenly pissed off and acting different. And he said, "Okay, what's going on? I woke up this morning and you've changed, you know. What's happening?" I can remember saying to him, "Hey! After ninety days I don't know what to do! We're into the ninety-sixth day and I don't know how to relate to you." And you know, we worked to stay together. And I give him a lot of credit for that.

He was a very compassionate man. I could come home from group and share what I had done and what had come up for me and he wouldn't browbeat me about it. If he felt there was something more that I needed to explore, he'd help bring that out for me.

But I think when you go through sexual abuse you almost become a bottomless pit—this is what he used to say—of need. And that's what he became upset with, became frustrated with. After a year we broke up and that was a part of it. He's still very close to me, though. He's still an integral part of my life and the lives of my children.

What's important to me now is to be in a relationship with someone who has a certain amount of tenderness and compassion toward me, you know. I am a very strong sister. I admit it. But by the same token, I got this other little part that's kind of, you know, soft, and you know, like lace, and most people don't see it. Most men don't see it. So when I meet a man who sees that, I'm very drawn to him.

"OKAY, BODY, FEEL!"

I have always enjoyed my sexuality. But there have been these "little" issues that come up from time to time.

I'd be out of my body and not even aware of it. Tactilely, I was very numb. I had one lover who used to pinch me all the time, just so I could feel. He recognized how numb I was.

When I began to make love or masturbate, these pictures from my past would come up and that was a trip. It was erotic and it wasn't. It was my orientation to sex, so it got me off, but I always felt bad. I had a lot of guilt and shame about it. So when I began to have sex and these scenes would begin to bleed through, it would make me numb out. I could be with somebody I really cared for and liked. I could be having a real good time, and all of a sudden I'd just numb out.

I'd never tell my partners what was going on. I'd just continue what I was doing and lay up there and say, "Okay, body, feel! Toes, I want you to feel. Let's feel in the toes now. Okay, let's bring it up to the ankles." I used to do this, you know. I'd bring the feeling up. "Okay, fingers, let's feel. That's the way. C'mon arms, we're feeling now!" I used to do this so that I could be able to have some kind of feeling.

Most of the time I did have orgasms, but how far I would let the orgasms go was another thing. I could feel sexual pleasure to a certain extent, but I was afraid that it would make me crazy, so I would feel a little bit and then I would cut if off—you know, put on the brakes. Then there would be no more feeling.

I've worked on it metaphysically. I took out those pictures and I destroyed them. As I eliminated the pictures, so went the guilt and the shame. And I'm *very* happy about that. It's a miracle that I am a sexually active woman today and that I enjoy sex as much as I do. And I *do!*

I NEEDED TO SCREAM AND HOLLER AND YELL

Confronting, dealing with, and releasing anger has been the hardest part of healing for me. In a survivors group that I was in, all this anger came up. I needed to scream and holler and yell, but I didn't feel safe in the group. So what happened was, I didn't express it.

You know how women talk about falling apart and crying all the time? They're going from crying to anger and all that. Well, I did that in three days. It came close to breaking me 'cause I'd never realized the depth of that anger. I realized why I'd never let myself feel it either, 'cause it was so debilitating. All I could feel was this raging. I probably could have torn up sheets with my fingers. And to go between this anger and this crying. I had to leave work because I was always breaking into tears. But I couldn't stay at home either.

I went to a movie. I watched the movie with tears just streaming down. In the theater I could be out of control and no one would pay attention to me. I felt like there were little pieces of me all over the theater. I called this man who was like a brother to me. He picked me up and took me to the beach. I lay down in the sand and cried. I made these mounds of sand and pounded them. My head was hurting terribly. I couldn't take it anymore. So he took me to the hospital and they gave me a shot, something to relax me. I was okay after that—physically.

My advice to someone working on this stuff is to find working therapy as opposed to talking therapy. Talking doesn't truly release it. That's why people can be in therapy for twenty years, you know—because they just talk about it. Express it and release. If you need to scream and holler, that's what you need to do. So do it.

A TRIP BACK HOME

Recently I made a trip back home, and a lot of that had to do with making peace with all of that old bull, 'cause that's where the original sexual abuse began. I went down to look at the house where it all began. The house isn't there anymore because it burned down. I went there and thought about some of the things that had happened to me there, and I was able to leave it and not feel that I had to carry it anymore, like "Hey, that was then!"

I went to complete one cycle and to begin a new cycle for myself—making peace and coming to terms with what that whole area means to me. Before, whenever I went into that area, I don't care how sunny it was, it was cloudy for me. One of the things that happened on this trip was that this was erased. All of that for me has been lifted and it's gone. It was really quite wonderful that I could be there and not be upset.

SOLEDAD

When it happened, I couldn't name it. And then when I got the words to be able to name it, I forgot. All I was left with was hatred for my father. For a long time, I thought that people were born hating their fathers.

Soledad is a twenty-eight-year-old Chicana who was severely abused by her father throughout her childhood.* For the past eleven years she has lived in Sonoma County, California. Today she is a high school counselor.

Soledad writes, "In this interview, I have spoken more of my biological parents (due to my feelings of betrayal and violation) than of my Tias and Tio, who were very much my parents, in the true sense of the word. Without them, I am convinced that my ultimate survival would not have been a reality, for I am certain that my life would have been beaten or suffocated out of me. To them I owe

my life. And because of them, I will struggle to keep it.

"I once read that we can give two things to children—one is a sense of roots and the other is a sense of wings. I now know my roots, my history. Now I am ready to fly towards the sun."

As was sometimes true for other women of color, it was particularly difficult for Soledad to entrust us—two white women—with her story. Because much of white America holds the stereotype that abuse happens only to "others," many women of color are reluctant to disclose their abuse for fear that it will reinforce already existing prejudices. Still others come from cultures that have a strong taboo against exposing "private" experiences.

---

* Soledad chose to use a pseudonym.

Pushing past these barriers to speak out is courageous.

Being Latina is real precious to me. However, part of the culture that I hate is the silence. As beautiful as our language is, we don't have words for this. Our history is passed orally, yet there's such silence in Latino families about this.

There was no talk of sex in the house, ever. It was all out on the streets. And how can you go to a woman you haven't been able to talk to about your damn period and tell her that her husband is raping you?

I think this kind of silence might be common, but I think it's especially true because my people feel so powerless in this culture, fearing authorities outside of the family. We had to stick together and protect each other from the system, and from the white people who control it. What other option did we have? We just had to keep it in. Admitting any problem would reflect badly on our whole culture.

And that's why it's still hard for me to talk about it. I don't want anyone to use this against people of color, because there are so many negative stereotypes of Latinos already. People are already more willing to trust white men than they are men of color. And I don't want to promote more mistrust of men of color. But this is how it happened for me and I feel I need to break the silence.

MY FATHER WAS LIKE A VOLCANIC ERUPTION

I was raised in an extended family in Los Angeles, in a hard-core ghetto. I'm the oldest of three kids. My dad worked on and off in factories. My mom worked in sweatshops until she became disabled. We not only lived in poverty, we *were* poverty.

I was beaten at least every other day for years. I hated that my parents beat us, but everybody around us got whipped, so that was just the way it was. At least when my mother beat us, we still had a feeling she loved us. And it hurt less.

My father was like a volcanic eruption. You wouldn't know when it was going to happen, but when it did, there was no stopping what was happening. He wore these steel-toed shoes for work, and he'd kick us everywhere, including the head. You could get arrested for kicking a dog like that.

When people smack you around the way my father did, it's hard to decide which is worse—that or the sexual abuse.

My father not only molested me, he molested all my cousins and all the girls in the neighborhood. The ones that I know, there are at least twenty-four. There are others I've thought about. People really trusted him with their kids. He was a great social manipulator and he knew how kids thought. It's amazing how one person can mess with so many kids.

From what I can tell, the sexual abuse with me started right when I was brought home from the hospital. I found out from another relative that for a long time he didn't even sleep with my mother. He slept with me when I was a little baby.

In the beginning there was a lot of fondling. He could be what you would call "gentle," but I would interpret that as being sneaky, because I knew that he could kill me too. If you already know that this man can kill you so easily, you're not going to say anything. And so I would just be frozen, with the feeling "Soon it will be over." But it got worse and worse.

The peak of it all was at about eight. That's when he first raped me. It was pretty regular after that, at least three times a week. It happened in a lot of different places. We lived in really small quarters. There was no privacy. So he'd tell me we had to go out for milk, or that we needed to go for a ride in the car. He really loved to take all the girls out for a ride. Most of this stuff happened in the car, a lot of it in the dark, so this left a blank for me because a lot of it I didn't see.

A lot of the raping happened from behind. When he abused me, he would talk to me in Spanish, threatening to cut my throat or cut my tongue out. So now, telling you my story in English is easier. Telling you in English keeps more emotional distance. I probably would be sobbing by now if I was describing what he had done in Spanish.

When I was thirteen the sexual abuse stopped. I had gotten more streetwise than ever, and he started to be fearful of me. He knew I was ready to die, that I would fight him to our graves if I had to.

I LIVED ON THE STREETS

I was very self-destructive in terms of drugs and fighting. I started taking drugs at nine. I started hustling. I did just about everything. I would do drugs and at the time I wouldn't even know what the hell it was that I was using. I didn't care. That went on until I was sixteen.

Fighting was an everyday occurrence on the streets. As we got bigger, the toys got more dangerous. I carried knives. I got into fights with people who carried knives. And some with guns. They would be tripping, too. You would never know if you would

come out of there alive. I thought this was just the way it was, and it was fine if I died with it.

Between what was happening to me at home with him and having to fight and live on the streets too, I always thought the only freedom would be to go to prison. Then I would be "free."

I always dealt with my life on an hour-by-hour basis. For a long time, I never did want to live. I'd be five and I'd think, "Maybe I won't live until I'm ten," and I would hope that that would be true. Or I'd get to be ten, and I'd think, "Okay, fifteen, max. That's as long as I'm going to live."

What other choices did I have? I grew up poor. I didn't know there were other worlds outside of this. I still have a hard time with the whole concept that you have control over your own destiny. Life was just the way it was, and the only way out of it was to kill myself or destroy myself or become like a vegetable. I never knew there was a way out.

I didn't have much self-esteem. Self-esteem wasn't a concept I learned till I went to college. With Chicanos, that can get confused with being pompous, and if you're being pompous, you're forgetting who you are and where you're from. I just didn't think too much about myself.

THERE WAS MORE TO LIFE THAN WHAT I KNEW

How I got out of that whole drug and fighting scene was that there was a teacher who took an interest in me when I was sixteen. I was always in and out of school and I was illiterate. And this woman did care about me. She thought that I had a good mind. She was scared of me, but she wanted to find out why I was the way I was. And I trusted her. I didn't tell her anything about the abuse, just that it was a bad situation at home. I think she knew what I was not telling her.

She started talking to me and just spending time with me. It mattered to her that I didn't destroy myself. And that made all the difference. There wasn't anyone before who had ever spent that kind of time with me.

Learning to read helped me see there was more to life than what I knew, and that in fact, this was not life. That was the beginning of my healing. It was the first time I thought that maybe I could survive without hustling. Maybe I could learn something from some magazine or some book and get some power from it. Get some options.

I was lucky. I got into an Upward Bound program. She helped me get into college. College was a real culture shock. I hadn't ever been around that many white people. I still couldn't read enough to understand the menus in the cafeteria. And I didn't know what any of the foods were. I not only didn't know what it was, I'd never heard the words "eggplant parmesan" before. But I stuck it out. I had to make it work for me.

I WAS BARELY KEEPING MYSELF ALIVE

Even though I succeeded in going to school and getting a job, I knew things weren't right inside. For a long time all I was doing was coming home and laying in my bed. Sometimes I'd turn the TV on, sometimes not. My dinner would be a bottle of Coke. Maybe I'd decide to have a real dinner, and I'd have a pint of ice cream. And that was my life. I'd never open these drapes, never would answer my phone. If anyone knocked on the door, I wouldn't even look to see who was there. I could care less who it was. I was barely keeping myself alive.

Because I wouldn't let anyone take care of me, I ate to comfort myself. I gained a lot of weight. I drank a lot. I remember one time in particular when I had no intention to fuck myself up, but that's just what I did. I drank shot after shot of tequila. I finished off half a bottle, and then I went for another. I think I would have died if my girlfriend hadn't found me on the floor and gotten help.

I never really believed that anyone loved me, so I felt kind of orphaned. I was self-sufficient. If I hadn't been, that would have been the end of me. It's prevented me from ever wanting anyone to take care of me. I will take care of myself and that's it. And if anyone needs to be taken care of, I will take care of them, but I will never let them take care of me. And that's kind of hard, 'cause I get sick too and I'll grow old.

I KNEW I WASN'T CRAZY AND THAT I NEEDED HELP

This whole thing got triggered by talking to a cousin of mine who had also been molested by my father. She called me up a year and a half ago and said, "Did you know that your dad molested my sisters?"

I said, "I never really thought about him that way. But it doesn't surprise me." I went to visit her to find out what had happened. We stayed up the whole night and the whole day to talk about it. It was painful, but I felt so vindicated the whole time. I knew I wasn't crazy. I knew there were reasons why I was destroying myself and why I hated him so much.

It was validating to know it happened to all of my cousins too. It's sad that it did. But if it had only just happened to me, I'd probably still be questioning it. If you're told you're crazy enough times, you really start to believe it.

From then on I couldn't stop thinking about what I knew. I started getting really obsessed. And I started to understand all these things. I started to wake up feeling powerful. I'd always had to carry a knife or be hustling to feel powerful before. All of a sudden, I had a belief in myself.

But at the same time, I got very depressed. It just seemed like one more heavy thing to cope with. It felt like another death. I needed help dealing with it. So I went to a Chicana therapist that I knew. I said, "God! I found this out. I talked to my cousin and then I remembered." I told her this had happened twenty years ago, that there were no kids around him now. Right while I was talking to her, she gets up and goes to the phone, and starts to call Child Protective Services.

Now that is my ultimate fear. First, I was just learning about this thing. And second of all, he has that fear about outside authorities, and if that car pulled up to his house, he would never live through that. And not that I especially wanted him to live, but I wouldn't want him to die in the hands of the system.

So she picked up the phone and she started saying, "Well, I have this situation here . . ." And I started saying, "What the hell are you doing? I swear to you there are no kids . . ."

And she said, "I need to talk to a supervisor." She just kept on. She asked how she was supposed to report this. And I was just shitting. Give me a break! What the hell are you fucking doing? I knew that they had to assess if there was someone in danger now.

What this person finally told her was that what she was reporting had happened twenty years ago, that there were no children in the home, and that they were overloaded and couldn't deal with situations that weren't definitely happening now.

That scared the shit out of me, but I still needed help. I couldn't handle what I was feeling. I had a definite picture in mind of the kind of person that could help me. I wanted a Chicana. I wanted a lesbian. I wanted this and that. I spent months and months looking, and I really couldn't find anyone who lived near me. And I didn't want to commute.

I could have been so damn picky that I never would have done it. That was my pattern. I would never have to be vulnerable and could just keep it in. And I couldn't do that anymore. Finally, I had to ask myself how much of this was my defenses in being scared to work on the molest issue. So finally I decided she had to be someone who had dealt with abuse. She couldn't be homophobic or racist, but I had to get started.

So finally I found this woman who's straight, middle class, white, but she's been good. She's been fucking good. I can't say a bad thing about her. I still wish I could have the other, but this is working for now.

I'M TRYING TO LEARN TO BE A LITTLE GIRL AGAIN

To be a healthy adult, I think you need to have been a child at one time. And I wasn't. I was always trying to be an adult. So now I'm an adult, and I'm trying to redo my childhood. It's totally reversed.

I'm trying to learn to be a little girl again. I have to find that softness that I lost or never was able to deal with. I have to cry those little girl tears. I have to feel what happened.

It's been painful. At first the only way I could relate to the little girl was by drawing pictures. Since I could always deal better with other people's problems than my own, she always came out looking really different from me. I'd think about the terrible things that had happened to her, and I would feel bad for the little girl in the picture, but I would separate her from me.

I've had to get under her skin, and that's when the process started getting hard. I've almost had to make myself regress. I've had to remember what it felt like to have a little body, to wear those little clothes.

I'VE HAD TO CHANGE PATTERNS AROUND SEX

I've always been more content being alone than with a lover, but I have had lovers since I was twelve, thirteen. I never felt I had the right to say, "No, I'm not interested in you. I don't want to be sexual with you." But they weren't relationships. They were just people to fill time with. I didn't know there was more to being a lover than just the sexual part.

It's always been important for me to control the whole sexual thing and to be really detached. I thought being soft was the same as being weak. When you're from the streets, you're just not vulnerable like that. You don't submit yourself to those feelings. At least you never let people know you have those feelings. I'd be hard and distant and cold, and now I can't even imagine why people wanted to be sexual and intimate with me.

A lot of times when I would have sex with someone and they would be coming, maybe they'd be making noise or breathing hard, I'd think to myself, "Oh, just get over it. How weak you are!" Because that's what I'd thought of my father.

I always made sure when I was sexual that I was really quiet. I was not having an orgasm because of anybody else. To me, having an orgasm was just like my body reacting to something. It had nothing to do with emotions. You know how you smack your knees to test how fast your reflexes are? Well, that's how I felt about sex. It's a crass way to describe it, but that's what coming was like for me. It was easy to be quiet. Some people call it being butch; I call it being really repressed. And that just came from that frozen little girl who was being molested and raped, waiting for it to be over soon.

The most important thing I've realized is that relationships can be different from how they have been for me. I'm really trying to turn that around, to let people in on an emotional level. I've been plenty in people's bodies, but not in their souls. I've finally been able to realize that just because you're being sexual with someone doesn't mean that you're being close with them.

I DIDN'T WANT TO HURT THE PEOPLE I LOVE

Another area that's been hard for me is dealing with my anger. Anger was always really easy access for me. It would come out like that! [She snaps her fingers.] But now that I have more information about *why* I'm angry, it's better. When I didn't have any information, the anger was explosive, just like my father's.

But I didn't want to hurt people I loved. I didn't even want to hurt people I didn't like. But it was hard to break that pattern. Whenever I started to have those feelings I'd stop and say, "I just want to beat the shit out of you right now!" It was hard to admit it. But it was a start. I'd be able to talk about the feelings of wanting to punch her out rather than doing it. It was a matter of starting to live my life watching what I did, because for a long time I hadn't ever watched any of it. Now I try to be more aware of where that behavior came from. I don't want to repeat what they did to me.

I think there's a lot of anger still pinned inside me, but I'm getting it out in better ways. I use my voice, and if the neighbors hear us, then fine. At least I'm not using my fists. I also have a couple of friends that I wrestle with. It's terrifying to be pinned, but it's an outlet for the rage. I've done weight lifting too. That really helped a lot.

I EXPECT TO CONFRONT MY FATHER BY THE END OF THE YEAR

Sometimes I think I'd like to confront him right in the middle of a party, right in front of all his friends. Other times I think I'll call him out to a park. I want to get it through his head that he really lost something and someone special. A lot of people who were really special. He lost the opportunity to even be a father to me and to my sister or to be a trusted uncle to my cousins. I want him to know he has no claims on me as a daughter.

I also want to tell him that he was the one who gave me reason to hate him, and that I do not love him. That I never loved him. And whether he loves me or not doesn't matter. If he does love me in his own sick way, he can just stick it somewhere else. And I also want to tell him that I think he is a really sick man. This thing he probably figured didn't hurt anybody, hurt plenty.

Some people don't deserve a chance. I'd like to put my hands around his neck and say, "Remember, you used to do this to me?" I really want that opportunity to deal with him in the way he deserves to be dealt with. I have fantasies of mutilating him in the ways he threatened to do to us, beating him in the ways he used to beat us. I'd like to cut off his little *huevos*. I've had offers from people who said they'd go with me. But I've learned to respect life more than he ever did.

I'VE COME OUT OF MY SHELL STRONGER THAN I'VE EVER BEEN

I feel lighter, like a real burden has come off me. I literally felt less pressure in my chest and in my shoulders. I felt like I'd been walking around with twenty pounds of cement on my chest all my life. If I had run away from the pain, I don't think I'd ever have been able to shed that weight. I would still be destroying myself in some way.

It's a small thing, but I never had plants

before. It's just my way of trying to keep something other than me alive. It gives me a lot of pleasure. I grew up where there weren't too many flowers, right in the middle of the damn city.

I got my first plant about six months ago. Now I have all sorts of flowers on my porch. I have big bushes with purple flowers. I have big round pots with different flowers in them. I wanted color around me.

It's real Latina, all these colors. It reminds me a lot of my aunts.

It's a reason to live, really. I was scared about it at first. But now I know I can nurture them and keep them healthy. I make sure they don't have bugs. After I've been so rough in my life, I can still take care of something so delicate. Even though I've been knocked around, I can still keep them alive.

EVIE MALCOLM

Face a fear, and the death of that fear is certain.

Evie Malcolm is thirty-eight years old.* She lives in Boston, works as a secretary, and lives with her partner of thirteen years, Faith. She has spent the last eight years recovering from agoraphobia, which resulted from her experiences being molested by strangers in New York City.

"When people hear my story they say, 'Oh that happens to everyone who grows up in New York. What's the big deal?' It's so common, they accept it. When I was in eighth grade, the teacher asked all the girls if it ever happened to them, and every single girl raised her hand. Were we given any advice on how to deal with it? Were we told we could yell or kick or even say "Stop"? No. It was totally expected and totally normalized. We learned that nothing could be done about it.

"But that doesn't make it tolerable for a child. That doesn't make it any less devastating. People say, 'That's just part of living in New York,' as though it's not bad if it happens to everyone. But the fact that it's so widespread makes it worse, not better."

I grew up in the suburbs of New York. My mother was a secretary who worked her way up to an administrative assistant position. My father is a businessman. They both grew up poor, leaving high school before they graduated, but they strove hard to be educated. Intelligence and scholastic ability were highly valued in my household. We were working class in reality, but rose through determination.

---

* Evie Malcolm chose to use a pseudonym.

My family was very old-fashioned. I was extremely protected. I was raised to be polite and respectful of authority. The abuse took place at a time when no young girl was encouraged to defend herself or be strong.

The first time, I was ten years old. I had taken my little brother to a children's matinee on a Saturday. A man sat down next to us, threw his coat on my lap, and started feeling me up. I said to my brother, "We've got to move." My brother complained, but we got up and switched seats. As soon as we were settled it happened again. I didn't know if it was someone else or the same man, but we got up again. The theater was crowded and I couldn't find any empty seats. By that time my brother was screaming. The usher told us we'd have to go back to our same seats or leave. So we left.

My brother screamed all the way home on the subway. I said, "I can't explain it, but when we get home, Mom and Dad will explain it to you." When we got home, I immediately told my parents. My mother turned away in disgust. My father started intellectualizing about the whole thing. They didn't do anything. They didn't explain it to my brother. They didn't say I was right to leave. They didn't offer to take us back to the movies the next day. I saw they were powerless against that man. And I learned I could never look to them for help. Somewhere inside I gave up.

Shortly after that, I passed the test to get into a public school for intellectually gifted girls. My new school started with seventh grade, so I was eleven when I began.

But I lived in Brooklyn and my new school was in Manhattan. And in order to get there I had to ride three different subways. And that's where the rest of the abuse happened. It started the second day of school, during rush hour. I got on the train. I sat across from an old man. He was staring at me. And then I realized that he was exposing himself and masturbating. I thought he was crazy and insane and I was afraid that he was going to kill me. In my mind, only a lunatic would do something like that.

For the next six years, that kind of incident and much more—the grabbing and being molested in a crowd, the being followed from car to car—kept happening to me. I was very tall for my age, five foot nine. Yet I was childlike in appearance—no makeup, plain and childish clothes. I made an easy target.

Something happened almost every day. It was inevitable. And then after it happens a few times, it doesn't matter whether it happens or whether it doesn't—you have to get back into the exact same situation, and you think about it happening all the time. I had to get on that train five days a week for six years.

Quite a few of the incidents are burned into my brain. I call it being raped standing up in a crowd. It was as much rape as if there'd been actual penetration. And sometimes they got awfully close. One man stood near me masturbating with a vacant look on his face. He was smiling and his penis was completely out of his pants. With his free hand he took my arm, linking it in his—like friends walking down the street together. Just then the train got stuck in the tunnel. I felt completely trapped. In my head I was screaming, "Oh God, get me out of here." My whole self went up into my head. I felt completely disembodied.

Have you ever heard of deer who get on the road and get blinded by the headlights and they stop, and stand there, and the car hits them? What, is the deer wrong?

That's what happened to me in the subway. I'd never seen these things before. I just thought, "Oh my God," and froze. And it ran over me like a two-ton truck.

I doubt it was ever the same person. There are a million nasty men in the subways of New York. The majority were well dressed, they were coming from good neighborhoods, they were carrying briefcases. It was never a black or Hispanic man or a man of any other race but white. It wasn't poor old bums. It was all so-called normal men on their way to work, who casually took advantage of the opportunity. It was just like "Here's this young flesh. Reach out and grab it." You can molest a child so easily.

I never told anyone. I knew it was useless to tell my parents. Besides, my mother would have taken me out of my school, and I wanted to keep going. It was a tremendous honor. And I had every right to go. And I love the kid that kept going to that school. She didn't let those fuckers stop her.

A FULL-BLOWN PANIC ATTACK

I graduated when I was seventeen. I left the city and for five years I didn't come back. When I did, I started riding the subway again, and I started having panic attacks. I'd go down to the platform to wait for the train, and as soon as the doors to the subway would open, I'd have a full-blown panic attack with all the physical symptoms —I'd feel like I was going to die.

It's the kind of terror anyone would experience if they were being kidnapped, if they were about to be murdered. I don't know how to make it strong enough that it's about the worst feeling you can have. Every

single body part feels threatened and the adrenaline is pumping in your body and you feel like a trapped rat. You want to run. You want to scream. You want to get out. And so I'd run out of the subway.

At that point I had no idea what was happening. I was twenty-two years old and I had no memory of what had happened to me as a kid riding the trains to school. It seemed like a panic that came out of the blue.

Over a period of years, I ended up not being able to ride the subways, then not being able to ride buses, then not being able to take cabs, then not being able to walk anywhere but to my college, ten blocks away. I could function at school and I could function at home, but I couldn't even go across the street for a cup of coffee.

Agoraphobia is like a mental cancer—it just extends into everything. At my worst, the panic attacks came on no matter what. I'd have several a day. And they're really debilitating. There's a lot of fatigue connected with agoraphobia. I was worried all the time. I developed a nervous bladder and a spastic colon. I have high blood pressure, and there's no history of that in my family. There isn't a part of my life it hasn't affected.

I WENT TO ALL KINDS OF THERAPISTS TO GET HELP

No one ever told me what was going on. No one ever told me I had agoraphobia. The therapists I went to didn't talk. You spill your guts and they never say anything. I just got worse and worse. I'd say, "I can't take trains anymore. Now I'm taking buses."

And then a year later, it was "Dr. Horowitz, I can't get on the bus anymore. I'm too frightened. What's happening?"

One doctor told me I was obsessive-compulsive and that he had a new medicine he wanted to give me for free, which means they don't know what it's going to do yet. I had to sign a release to take it. Not only couldn't I get out of my house on that medicine, I couldn't get off my couch. I was like a cucumber or a head of cauliflower. I got so depressed from that medication. I called Faith at work and I said, "You better come home. I'm thinking razor blades here. I don't want to kill myself, but it's all I can think of."

I finally self-diagnosed myself as agoraphobic after seeing a woman on the Tom Snyder show describe exactly what I experienced. I said, "Oh my God! That's me!" I called the station to get the number of one of the doctors who had been on the air with her. I ended up going to the Roosevelt clinic and getting help from some of the top people in New York.

I WASN'T ALONE

I went to phobic therapy three times a week for two and a half years. It was important for me to know there were other people suffering what I was suffering, that I wasn't alone. All my friends were phobics. Those women were very important to me. I worked on a phobic newsletter.

They teach you that fears don't come without thoughts. People usually say, "I was just in the supermarket and suddenly it hit me." It feels like it comes from nowhere, but there's always a trigger. It's your own thoughts. It's a command you're giving.

What you need to learn is, "What are the thoughts?" Then you can stop them. Then your body doesn't pump the adrenaline, your throat doesn't close up, your palms don't sweat, your legs don't get shaky, you don't feel like you're going to vomit.

I was lucky enough to hook up with a wonderful phobic therapist, who's called a "Helper." We did what's called contextual therapy. The purpose of contextual therapy is to get frightened, so you can feel the fear with another person who can help you reinterpret it and teach you to cope with it. You literally find the places where you're going to be afraid. If you're afraid of restaurants, you go to a restaurant.

You don't try to figure out why. You need to be able to function. If you can't get out of your house, a phobic therapist will come to your house, because obviously, how does the person get better if they can't get to the therapist's office?

My therapist's name was Sandy. We worked together for four years. She was completely fearless and warm. I owe most of my life to her.

Sandy got me out of my house again. She'd come over and walk out a little bit with me, walk me to the corner, go out to a restaurant. She asked me where I had the very worst panic attacks. I said, "On the subway." She said, "That's where we should start."

So we'd buy the tokens and go down there. We did it in small increments. It's sort of like someone who has a stroke and can't speak. They have the kind of therapist who teaches them how to speak again. Sandy taught me to be on the subway again.

At first we'd sit on the bench and watch the trains go by. That was all I could do. And she'd have me quantify the fear level from zero to ten. It would go up to an eight or nine, at which point my neck was stretched, my heart was pounding, I'd want to run. She would help me feel those feelings and not run. Then we'd get on the subway and ride one stop. And if I wanted to get out after one stop, I could. The important thing was for me to be in control.

When we got in a subway car and the doors shut—and that's a frightening moment for me—she would say, "Now what are you feeling?" And we would talk about it. Then she would say, "What are you thinking?" And I would say, "I'm not thinking anything. I'm just getting scared." And she would say again, "What are you thinking?" And it would be the same thing, over and over, until *I* could hear the thoughts. And the thoughts were saying, "You're trapped and you're going to die."

And she would say, "Look around. There are other people on the train. They're not trapped. You're not either. We can get off at the next stop. Whatever you want." She always restored the control to me, allowing me to break down in small pieces this huge problem of being unable to function in the world. Sandy made me feel there was no pressure or right timetable to get better. I was calling the shots. She was just there to help me.

And after an hour of working with her, I could come home just as proud from being able to ride the subway a couple of stops as someone who accomplished something at a high professional level at work. And I probably was using as much energy, intelligence, and commitment in what I was doing with Sandy as they did in their jobs.

THE GHOSTS OF THE MEN

After I'd worked with Sandy for a year and a half, I was able to get on the subways when I wasn't with her. On Thanksgiving that year, Faith and I were going to my parents' house for dinner. We had to ride the exact same route I had used when I was a kid coming home from school. When we got on the train, I had to ride in the first car, because my head was racing ahead to be on the other side of the tunnel. And she was saying, "Are you going to make it?" I was using every phobic technique they had taught me. I felt I was really driving that subway train with this incredibly powerful fear.

When we got to Brooklyn, the doors opened and I got off. I went up to a pillar, leaned against it, and I burst into tears. All of a sudden I was eleven years old. It wasn't a memory. It was a reexperiencing. The ghosts of all those men who molested me came around, and I sobbed and sobbed. Faith held me. I couldn't have cared less what people thought. It had taken a year and a half of healing for me to to have the strength to remember.

I'M VERY PROUD OF WHAT I'VE DONE

Remembering the molestation and connecting it to the agoraphobia didn't suddenly cure me, but it did allow me to know it wasn't all coming out of the blue. I don't think anyone develops agoraphobia for no reason. I mean you don't just develop a fear of pigeons for nothing. Something happened to you with pigeons. Agoraphobia is so complex, it's hard to figure out exactly where it started. but I think it often has to do with sexual abuse.

Phobias are coping mechanisms, and though they limited me, I found I was sad to give them up. The day I could get on the bus without any phobic feelings, I felt really weird. It's like when a refrigerator goes off and you realize it's always been on. It was disorienting, and it was a loss. But the gains were so much bigger.

All my symptoms have gotten less, but they haven't gone away entirely. I liken it to turning the volume down on a radio. If the radio is blasting, then you can't function. If you turn the radio down to a moderate level, you can still hear it, but you can function. There are times when that panicky feeling in me is very low and I can ignore it. Other times it's stronger but I can push myself to ignore it. And then there are times when it overwhelms me.

I'm rebuilding my confidence slowly. The damage that's done to you when you're a kid, I don't know how much you get over it. I'm strong in my conviction that I want to be cured, but I'm not looking for a miracle. At the same time, I don't want to see a therapist who says, "You have to live with this." Maybe I will have to live with some of it, but I want to break through those limits as much as I can. I've worked very hard to do that and I'm very proud of what I've done.

I FOUGHT BACK AND I FEEL GREAT ABOUT IT

There was a man who exposed himself to me, my mother, and my aunt in front of Korvette's in New York a couple of years ago at Christmastime. A Salvation Army Santa Claus was standing right next to us. My aunt and my mother were talking about where to go to lunch. I was looking around, and out of the corner of my eye I saw this guy's face, and I just knew this man was exposing himself. He had the same spacy, faraway look on his face that the molesters in the subway had. I thought, "I can't believe this. This guy's jerking off in the middle of a Christmas crowd, in front of Santa Claus, no less!"

The man was standing very close to me, and the look on his face was getting more and more urgent. He was beating off to beat the band. I had a shoulder bag, and it was heavy, and I swung it at him, hitting him really hard in the head. He started hopping and jumping everywhere, trying to protect himself from the blows and trying to zip up his pants and trying to run, all at the same time. I screamed at him and ran after him, and I said very loudly, very publicly to my mother and my aunt, "That man was exposing himself to us, right here in front of Santa Claus!"

There were very supportive. They said, "That's awful! Good for you for chasing him away!" Their response was wonderful. I didn't feel the shame or the humiliation I'd felt in the subway. Because this time, I fought back. And this time I wasn't alone.

ANNA STEVENS

Q: How did dealing with incest affect the rest of your life?
A: What rest of my life?

Anna Stevens was born in Taiwan.* A diplomat's daughter, she grew up in ports around the world. Her background is a cross between English and Irish. Anna's family was well off and kept up appearances. Her mother was an alcoholic and a pill addict—there is extensive alcoholism on both sides of the family. Anna has one brother.

Anna says: "Everything in my house was designed to keep conflict from surfacing. No one ever admitted my mother was crazy, of course. No one ever raised their voice. Nothing was discussed. Everything was shrouded in denial and secrecy."

Anna was physically abused by a nanny when she was three. Her mother sexually abused her repeatedly from the age of two until she was eleven. She masturbated Anna and used Anna's body to masturbate with. After her mother reached orgasm, she'd put Anna in a scalding bath or beat her. Anna learned to leave her body when the incest happened: "I watched it all through a kind of yellow fog.

"I forgot what happened to me as I grew up, but I hated my mother with a poisonous hatred. I was completely nauseated by my mother's smell. And as an adolescent, if she touched me, I'd throw up. The flip side of my physical revulsion was some kind of sexual feelings."

Anna now lives in New York City and works as a carpenter. She writes poetry and is working on a novel. She is twenty-six and has been in recovery for alcoholism for the last year and a half.

------

* Anna Stevens wanted to use her own name, but couldn't for legal reasons.

The bottom-line effect of the incest for me was trust and not-trust. I felt zip trust for anybody. When I reached a certain level of closeness, I'd have anxiety attacks so bad I couldn't breathe. But I'd also flip to the opposite extreme. I'd just throw my trust at people—because it became so intolerable not to trust. That got me into dangerous situations, including getting raped. I had no blueprint for knowing who or how to trust. I only knew the extremes.

It's only been in the last couple of years that I've even been able to admit I wanted human company. From the age of four, my strongest fantasy was to go live on a desert island by myself and to be absolutely self-sufficient. My basic attitude toward life had always been that I'd be happier alone. And if I was kindly permitting you to be in my life, I wanted you to know it was only on probation.

The ironic thing is, I tell people incredibly intimate things very quickly. It's an appearance of intimacy. I'd hear myself saying these "really honest things." But I said them so many times that they were just blunt instruments. The other person would react like I was taking them into my confidence, but I knew it was all fake. It was just an appearance of belonging to the human race.

I didn't have any self-esteem. I had a mixture of arrogance and fear. I always felt I was dirty. Part of me believed I must have asked for it. I had responded physically. I was sure people could see it on me.

Adolescence was particularly terrible. I was growing breasts and becoming like my mother. I felt puberty was a direct consequence of what had happened with her. It was as if she was pulling it out of me, making me like her. I loathed any resemblance between us. I remember when I was four-teen, looking in the mirror and seeing her face in my face, and wanting to tear the skin off my face. I felt an incredible sense of vulnerability and exposure. I disguised myself as best I could in men's clothes.

I was always acting out. I was a kleptomaniac. I stole from the time I was eleven until I was caught shoplifting booze when I was fifteen. When I was caught having a lesbian affair with a married teacher, I was expelled from boarding school.

I lied all the time. I didn't tell lies to get out of trouble. I told them to erase difference, because I felt so weird. I'd lie so I could make connections with people. It was a case of having to invent circumstances because my own truths weren't good enough.

AND THEN THERE WAS THE SPLITTING

I remember sitting on a stone step when I was twelve or thirteen and feeling this click, and then this voice in my head saying, "Oh, my mind's split!" One voice, the one that was sarcastic and snide and savage, went and sat in the left-hand corner of the ceiling. It sat there, and watched and sneered. It never felt anything, except maybe a sarcastic kind of anger. The other voice was an incoherent out-of-control scream. A lot of the time, she was preverbal. I knew she was there. She came out in nightmares. She felt incredibly guilty and ashamed. I would get drunk, and then I would be slashing my wrists. I tried to kill myself twice by the time I was eighteen.

I had to give up splitting because it was another out. Booze had been an out. The suicide attempts had been an out. I had to give up all of them. And each time I chose not to use those options any longer, it was the beginning of another growth cycle.

It's still very hard for me not to split. It's just starting to heal. I talk to the different people inside myself and write it down on paper. I can give those parts of me voices. And I've been able to talk about it. I talk to my lover, and I talk at AA and Sexual Abuse Anonymous meetings.* Talking and writing has really helped heal the split.

I STARTED DRINKING WHEN I WAS TWELVE

I was an alcoholic drinker from the start. I drank alone. I kept a supply of booze I didn't like, in case I ever ran out. When I was sixteen, I was told I was an alcoholic. I thought that was ridiculous. After all, I only drank like my parents. But really I did it more drastically. I drank not to feel, and then when that became intolerable, I'd drink to feel. I did that for thirteen years.

I was always as rigidly controlled about my drinking as I was about everything in my life. But you can't control alcoholism in the long run. By the end I had such an incredible thirst for alcohol, it had become the most important thing in my life. I was terribly lonely and frightened. The thing that had helped me to control things was finally out of control. So I had to stop.

I'd always been sure I'd be dead by the time I reached twenty-five. Instead, that's when I went to AA and got sober. Going to AA was terrifying. My specialness was being taken away. My specialness had been being

---

* Sexual Abuse Anonymous is a program for incest survivors, modeled on AA. Anna helped start that program in New York City.

crazy. But there was also this tremendous relief. I don't think about my drinking in terms of wasted time. Partly that's because I got in fairly young. I'm actually very grateful that I'm an alcoholic because it got me into AA and that's been the basis for real growth.

TRUTHS I DIDN'T KNOW YET

When I put down drinking, the connection to the abuse was almost immediate. There'd been this black hole I'd inhabited at various points in my childhood. Once I got sober, that image began to obsess me again. I started to paint it. I drew all these strange pictures of children being pulled back into the womb.

I had this recurring dream when I was a child. I had it again when I first got sober. It was of a happy family on a speedboat, smiling in the sun. They all had on bright new clothes. I wanted to scream and I wasn't able to. There was a monster that was coming up under the water. And everyone was immobilized with these smiles on their faces. Everybody knew that the monster was there, but nobody could react at all.

After a month I went to see a therapist. The third session, I went into that black hole and remembered being abused by my nanny. I saw someone pushing a hairbrush into my vagina. Then I became the three-year-old. It was terrifying.

I knew the memories were true because I was remembering in German, and that was what the woman spoke. I only spoke German until I was six. I was completely bilingual. Then I forgot it all. My therapist said, "What's she saying to you?" And I said, "I don't know. I can't translate it."

That was the beginning. My therapist asked me if I thought there might have been any incest. She said lots of people make up stories like this because it's safer to say it's somebody outside of the family. And I said, "No." What I kept thinking was, "Not my father. Not with my father." I had never heard anything about incest with your mother. A part of me knew it, but it seemed so outlandish. And I was very practiced at denial.

When I first starting having actual memories of incest with my mother, I had a hard time believing them. It was over a year before I believed that it was my mother who raped me. But increasingly, and mostly through my writing, so many involuntary things I'd always said and done just suddenly fit into place. It was like writing a story. You know things are right when they start falling into place. I *knew* this story was right. Everywhere I turned with it, something just went, "Yes. Uh-huh. Yes."

There were so many things that I thought were lies, and I couldn't understand why I kept telling them. I would think, "That's a lie. Why do you say that?" Things like telling people "I don't know who I lost my virginity to." I knew perfectly well the first boy I had fucked, but I kept saying this other thing. Everything I habitually said has a story inside of it. Part of me was always telling the truth. I realize now that some of the lies I told weren't lies, they were just truths I didn't know yet.

THERE WAS NOWHERE TO HIDE

When I talk to incest survivors who've been abused by men, I'm always relieved that the effects are the same. I need to talk to other women who've been abused by their mothers in order to see what the differences are. But there hasn't been much opportunity. I've come across little snippets, mostly by women who were abused by both parents.

I didn't want my mother to know anything about me. I had the feeling that if she knew me, she'd be able to dismantle me and turn me into someone else. I was fighting for my right to exist at all as a separate self. My gut feeling about my mother was that she had reached so far inside my body that there was nowhere to hide.

I also had to accept that I was turned on by my mother. I had wanted contact with her—even if it was sexual contact. For a long time I felt like a collaborator. It was very hard to untangle my need for closeness from "I wanted it. I deserved it. I seduced her." I tried to protect her by taking on the blame myself.

I have had to accept that my mother is a part of me. Because she violated me when I was that young, my boundaries got fucked. Literally, they got fucked.

Because she was my mother and not my father, I think the separation issue is stronger. Even though other survivors talk about being colonized by their fathers, or that they were his toy or his doll, or that they can't get the dirt off, I haven't heard many people talk about the feeling of actually *being* their abuser, or just having them inside you. And that, I think, is really tied up with it being my mother. I mean I get really nauseous if I think about being born, because being born has sexual connotations for me.

It brings up such wells of self-destructiveness. I feel her in my throat. I feel I have to give birth to her, which means giving birth to the anger. There's a scream inside

Poem for My Mother's Birthday

Athena was born from the head of Zeus
you will be birthed in my throat
no wonder it hurts

you'll be born from my throat in a scream   in a
puke   the passage shredded and raw   like eating
too fast   like needing to shit   muscles ache to
spit you out

Athena was born from the head of Zeus

my pores bleed tar   my walls seep blood
I can smell it on my fingers like I saw it on
my panties   white   the kind that leave elastic
lines   midriff high   I saw it one Christmas morning
mother   your fingers tore it from me

Athena was born from the head of Zeus

and you   child monster child   your smell
in the hall   in my room   on my bed   on my hand
on my tongue   I swallowed it all   night against
night   if I close my eyes

Athena was born from the head of Zeus

I am afraid to scream   afraid you'll come   afraid
you won't   and the wet wolf's breath in my face
her gray eyes   telling my lies

Athena was born from the head of Zeus

and you mama you   your bulging eyes   your
hanging head   the dribble   the chin   the gray green
stench of you in my bed at night   I'll wash you
in vomit   I'll powder you with tears   I'll
hurl you to the crowd and turn away my ears

Athena was born from the head of Zeus
the cap of his skull gliding aside

While I   I was born in the slit of you   violet
violent blood black scab   torn into air
while you   your hands tangled in arteries   your
limbs poking lumps in my breast   in my elastic skin
you will be birthed in my throat
no wonder it hurts

me that I've wanted to scream forever. Just saying that is making my skin crawl right now. I feel revolted.

INCEST WAS STAMPED IN EVERY YARD OF MY CLOTH

During the first stage of dealing with incest, I was in shock. I fought for a long time about how much it was inside everything. I'd scream, "Enough already! Why the fuck doesn't it just get fixed?"

Eventually I had to accept that incest was stamped in absolutely every yard of my cloth. I had to understand that it was a part of my life, not just something to fix and get over. What happened gave me strengths as well as incapacities, and I am learning from it. It was only when I reached that level of acceptance that I could be patient with myself.

The second stage was developing enough trust in myself and in other people to put down the survival mechanisms that didn't work any longer. That's about healing from the splitting. It's about not repeating the same patterns in relationships. It's about taking risks I wouldn't have taken before. It's not quite so backward looking. I also feel strongly that part of the second stage is beginning to reach out to other people, to pass the strength on. That's what saves me from hopelessness.

HEALING SEXUALLY

My pattern was to get intensely involved sexually with someone for a few months. Then the intimacy would have built up to the point where it started to bring up real problems. Then I would cut off. I would decide the sex was no good, and I would leave the relationship. It never occurred to me that you could negotiate a sexual relationship, that you could take it apart and change it. It was either there or it wasn't. And if it wasn't there, I left.

When I first got sober, I realized that since I wasn't going to get involved with anyone for a while, I was going to get sexually frustrated if I didn't deal with masturbation. I had always felt that my masturbation was very ugly, and so in limited doses, I started to allow myself to touch parts of my body and just feel them. That was very difficult because I felt safer with other people touching me than I did with myself. I did not trust my own hands not to hurt me. I would masturbate in a sensual way, and then, all of a sudden, I would start thinking, "I have to orgasm now. I have to orgasm now!" And I would rev into these old fantasies that actually bored me, that actually took away from the pleasure but helped me orgasm fast. It was a feeling that I had to orgasm fast or I would hurt myself.

There were certain things I didn't want to do because they had happened with my mother. I didn't want anything to do with oral sex. I detested the nice romantic practice of bathing after sex. And before I could change any of those things, I had to accept that it was okay to have limits: "It's okay. Not everybody in the world likes oral sex."

I had to be clear with anyone I slept with: "These are things that I don't like, and they are in the course of changing. I will let you know what's okay and what isn't. My commitment to you is that I will let you know if something is upsetting, so you don't have to worry about it. And if you do freak me out inadvertently, I won't hate you forever."

Then I had to pay attention to times when I really *did* want to do those things. Doing them once didn't mean I always had to do them. And there are a whole lot of behaviors I use now which let me know I am not with my mother anymore. I can't orgasm if I can't make noise, because I had to be silent with her. I always call out the name of the person I'm with when I orgasm, because I need to know it's them and not her.

It's difficult for me to feel sexual when my partner isn't. As soon as my desire makes someone else feel uneasy, I want to crawl right back in my shell. I'm sure that has to do with my fear of being abusive. Not that I'm going to throw them down and rape them, but simply that my desire for them is abusive. And that's pretty obvious in its origins.

Surprisingly, I'm fairly accepting of my sexuality. Sex is something that I enjoy. All the exploration I've done I figured out on my own. And I feel proud of that. My experience of masturbation has really changed. It's much more sensual. The orgasms have grown. They're no longer just like a sneeze.

YOU DON'T GRADUATE

Healing is not a finite thing. You don't graduate. It's been a lot of work. The beginning of the healing process was a sequence of choosing not to kill myself, then beginning to write and let things through, and then getting sober. Next I came to understand that I only got what I could handle. And that was the beginning of a spiritual connection, the feeling that I am on a path and that I am being looked after. All I have to do is be with whatever is happening in the moment.

KYOS
FEATHERDANCING

"What do you feel there is left for you to do?"
"Heal the earth. My mission in life is to heal the earth and all living things."
"Yeah, but is there anything left for you to do for your own healing?"
"That *is* for myself. I don't see my healing as separate from that."

Kyos Featherdancing is a thirty-four-year-old Native American woman, born and raised in a rural town in California's San Joaquin valley.* She now lives in the San Francisco Bay Area. Kyos works odd jobs as a landscaper and as a chef, but primarily she is a healer.

Her father was of the Caddo tribe, her mother a mixture of Choctaw and German. Kyos grew up poor. Her family picked cotton. Later her father became a welder and a plumber, and eventually he went to work for the nuclear industry. Kyos says, "He sold his soul and stopped being an Indian."

Kyos has two brothers and two sisters, all of whom were abused by her father.

The most sustaining influence in Kyos's childhood was her grandmother. From her Kyos learned the "old ways," which have remained the source of her survival and healing.

---

* Kyos Featherdancing is using her own name.

I THOUGHT IT WAS A GENTLE AND VERY LOVING RELATIONSHIP

From the time I was a baby until I was nine, I loved my father more than anything in the entire world. No one could say anything bad about him to me. His favorite thing was to suck my cunt when I was a baby. When I was three years old, I first remember him actually putting his prick into my vagina. That was something that we had between each other. He made me believe that every father did that with their daughter. So I believed that. And I became that. And I loved it, too.

My parents didn't let me go to other people's houses very much. I know now my father didn't want them knowing what he was doing. But when I was nine, I went to stay with a friend, and when it was time to go to bed, her father and mother tucked us in and gave us a kiss on the forehead and said, "Good night." I thought that was real strange. I kept wondering if anything else was going to happen. And finally I nudged my friend and said, "Hey, does your father come in and give you nookie?"

And she was like, "What? What are you talking about?" She told her parents about it, and they said we couldn't be friends anymore after that. That was the first time I realized not everybody had a father like that.

YOU DO WHAT YOU HAVE TO DO TO GET THROUGH IT

I became the woman my dad wanted me to be. I dressed how he told me to dress. I never went out of the house without makeup. I always shaved my legs. I shaved my underarms. I shaved my eyebrows and my legs around my cunt so I wouldn't look hairy. I shaved hair on my stomach. My dad taught me women were put here to be fucked by men, so that's the way I was. I began to be that to men in the neighborhood, to men in the streets, to the men in the office in that town. I had routes. I made money.

And my father sold me to his friends. I couldn't bring my friends to the house because they would end up in bed with him. He'd manipulate that somehow.

From nine to eighteen, I hated my father's guts and did every conniving thing I could think of, every conniving thing he taught me, and turned it around on him. I used his money. Made him buy me cars. Made him buy me good clothes. I got hooked on drugs, made him pay for it. I was strung out on junk by the time I was sixteen. I did speed. I dealt drugs to some of my teachers. I made grades that way. Some of them passed me to get rid of me. They didn't want to get hit or kicked in the balls. I was mean. No one could control me.

I hated myself completely. It was, "Okay, this is who you are. This is who he wants you to be. This is what you have to do, so just do it to get by." To me, that's what surviving is about. You do what you have to do to get through it until you can get out of it.

"YOU'RE GOING TO FIND OUT YOU HAVE A PATH"

When I was thirteen, I had an abortion. It was my father's child. He made it look like I was lying, and I was really angry. I started going to this Pentecostal church with my aunt. It was a place where I could go to scream and shout out my anger. She told me, "Give it all to the Lord." And that's what I did.

When I was fourteen or fifteen, I started hanging out with this black woman. She was my best friend. The woman took me in and mothered me like I'd never been mothered before. She'd take me down to the church and she'd jam on her piano. She gave me singing lessons, and the first thing she said to me was, "Sistah, you're gonna hafta open up your mouth and get ugly!" And from that point on, I just let it roar. I sang it out. Singing has been one of the most healing things for me. Singing and shouting and dancing in the spirit.

My father would forbid me to go to church. He was into all kinds of ugly spiritual things—black magic and all kinds of sorcery. That was one of the things that he put on me at a very young age. Different tribes do their own sorcery, their own ceremonials, but my dad used magic in very dark ways that are not to be done. I was into those things too, but I began breaking away from them.

My grandmother had taught me healing ways. She taught me a lot about my own self and about healing, about how to cook, how to clean. My grandmother lived the old ways. She had her blackberry bush. She did her rituals. She burned sage. She burned cedar. She had her path. I never forgot those ways. My dad forbade me to do them. He tried to keep me away from her. But she's alive in me. She always told me, "You're going to find out that you have a path and it's going to be different from who your father is." He tried to kill that, but he couldn't.

SOME HARD AND HEAVY THINGS CAME DOWN ON ME

I left home at eighteen. I'd run away before, but every time they'd pick me up and take me right back. I hung out with bikers and rowdies from the time I was twelve, and my father always made it look like I was the bad one and he was respectable. He had cousins and uncles that were pigs in that town and he did deals with one judge there. I learned real fast that he could get me locked up for a long time.

The day I turned eighteen, I split. It was about a month before I was going to graduate from high school. I was going to go to college and get into home eonomics. Being Indian, the government was going to pay for the whole thing. But a close friend of mine came home from Viet Nam and committed suicide and I couldn't go through with it. So I left with just the clothes on my back and an overnight change. I sold some dope and hitched to Chicago. I stayed in an all-night laundromat the first two weeks.

The next years were rowdy. I got into a biker's club. I was heavily into drugs. I didn't take a bath. I wore Levis for months on end. I was mean. Always drinking, always fighting, always in gang fights—*rowdy*.

After I left the bikers, I joined a Christian band. They were doing heroin addict programs and I ended up in a halfway house. Christians is the biggest way to get out of tight situations. I learned how to use it for my benefit. I got myself clean and stayed with the halfway house for quite a while. Then they sent me to do a street ministry in Boulder, Colorado. I was living with three other single Christian women. I fell in love with one of them and we got caught having an affair. I felt guilty and I started getting back on drugs again. And they kicked me out of the house.

I WANTED TO LOVE WOMEN

I moved to Denver to this boarding house. Ended up meeting all these lesbians, women who were into all kinds of healing. At that point, I was an alcoholic. I was back on drugs. I was just sick. I felt I was dying. I didn't want to be a Christian anymore, but I didn't know what direction to take.

I met this woman and we hitched to the Michigan Women's Music Festival. I'd never met so many healers in my life. I learned that being a lesbian is not just about sexuality. It has to do with healing power. It was the first time I was allowed to be a real woman, because churches do not allow this. I became aware of who I really was. Then I had a real clear picture of why my father wanted to destroy me. But it hadn't worked. I had survived.

YOUR HEART WILL NEVER LIE TO YOU

At that point I started healing on a different level than I had ever known before. I started cooking healthy foods. I was stretching. I was running. I was riding a ten-speed. I didn't do any more prescription drugs. I didn't do any more speed. I didn't do any more cocaine. I didn't go back to junk. For a while I kept drinking, then I quit. I had a lot of support. It was a good time for me. I was very impressed with the changes that I was making.

Then I met a woman who became my mentor. She taught me about group ther-

apy, primal screaming, and co-counseling. I added this to everything I knew from my grandmother, everything I had picked up from the earth.

This woman helped me to realize that I needed to have a relationship with myself before I could have a positive relationship with anyone else. So I became celibate for quite a long time, about nine years. I chose to be celibate because I didn't know how I wanted to be touched, or whether I wanted to be touched.

When I was younger I had relationships I would just call fucking relationships. I didn't know or care who I was fucking or who was fucking me. I had practiced this one pattern my whole life, that I had to be fucked in order to be loved. And that was a hard pattern to break.

I spent a lot of time alone, loving myself, touching myself in loving ways. I spent a lot of time hugging myself. Getting feelings back of sensuality rather than sexuality. Just lots of real comforting times with myself. Hot tubs. And sweating. I like to do sweat lodges with sage.

It was a time for my own personal therapy. I lived in the mountains for a while. I rented a room in the city for a while. I beat drums. I chanted. I wrote. I did anger work. I went to the woods and shouted and beat and screamed and cried and gave it to the wind. I did rituals for turning myself around and letting the earth heal me. I did rituals in the sun to burn the poisons out of me. I fasted. I drank spring water.

I had collected a lot of ideas about how to heal myself and I needed to be alone to do that healing. That time was really important. I learned how to have a relationship not only with myself, but also with the earth I love so dearly. When I need to be alone, I need to be alone with the earth. I get my energy and my answers from her.

I have everything I need to heal myself. That's what my grandmother taught me. She taught me how to follow my heart and my intuition. I have always had a vision of my grandmother's brown crinkly hand coming toward me to walk with me in that blackberry patch. She is my protector and has always been my protector. She taught me, "Trust your heart. Your heart will never lie to you."

That's one of the reasons I've never really been able to get therapy, because I don't believe therapists can give me the answers. I have everything I need to heal myself because no one knows my experience like I know it. I've turned myself around and nobody else could.

I DON'T NEED TO FORGIVE THAT BASTARD

A lot of people believe forgiveness is the ultimate healing. And to me, that's bullshit. The man doesn't deserve my forgiveness. *I* deserve my forgiveness. What I need to do is get right the fuck on with being right where I'm at with my anger. If you're looking to forgiveness as this goal, then you're still believing that lie that keeps you under control. That's what Christianity is about—keeping you under control.

And as far as freeing myself, I freed myself by saying, "Get out. I don't want you, and I will not be ruled by you, and I will not let you overwhelm my life."

I wrote this poem and sent it to my father:

To My Dad   *For Father's Day 1984*

To my Dad.
To the Daddy you never were.
Daddy, why?
Why didn't you teach me the ways of our
     people?
You only taught me how sucked in and
     limited you are,
and trapped in the white man's ways.
The earth is keeping me alive.
And you have chosen to die.
Didn't you realize,
Didn't you know that I would find out?
Did you think you could kill my powers?
My powers were louder than your white lies.
I have listened for a long time.
And I have heard.
Never been a child
Just born
Never been a child
Just fucked.
Didn't talk too much
Just watched a lot
Learned a whole lot.
Wild but tamed
Never been little
But I know how to play the game.
Mom always told me,
Your dad has needs
I can't meet them all
But you can, so be a good little girl,
he's been through a lot.
Anyway, you got it good.
My paleface mother
Stupid white woman.
Powerless bitch.
She gets what she wants by letting others
     shit on her.
It makes her feel like she's worth something,
and she's being a good wife.
Daddy sure loved her, according to her.

But Mom, what about all those other women
    in his life?
Oh, they're just friends of his, helpless
    women. He feels sorry for them,
And takes care of them. Most of them are
    widows.
Not to speak of me, my sisters, their friends
    and mine.
Great love, a father who takes care of every
    woman's needs.
Oh mighty fuck father fuck of best fuck of the
    world super stud
Save the Indian race, fuck the chief
Never satisfied
Had to fuck till it finally fell off.
Cancer, you say?
Are you satisfied?
Did you finally come Daddy?
I'm tired, leave me alone.

In rage and anger.
With hate,
Kyos

I don't have to get any revenge, because the way he's done his magic, he's brought it back on himself. He avoided the earth and who he is, so now he's dying. He's got cancer. They've cut half of his stomach out and his genitals. That's where it all started. And that's where it's all ending for him.

GIVING IT TO THE WIND

I sometimes wonder when the work is going to be finished. I don't think it ever really is. It doesn't overwhelm me as much as it used to. I used to cry and cry about it. It felt like everything inside of me was collapsing. I don't feel that way now. Some subjects about this, I'm just cried out. I've let it go and given it to the wind, and let the wind heal it.

I'm excited about my life now. I'm excited about the healing I'm going to do next, because it's going to be the ultimate freedom that I've been wanting—the healing of my spiritual life. I know now that I can truly be a healer and that what I've lived through doesn't have to hold me back. When it does, I can control it. I can tell it to leave me alone. I can spend time with it. Whatever I choose. It doesn't have to hinder my walk with the spirit.

LORRAINE WILLIAMS

Q: Was there any time in the process of healing that you lost hope that life was worth living?

A: Oh, about once a week.

Lorraine Williams is a twenty-two-year-old albino black woman.* She is legally blind, and her disability makes her extremely sensitive to the sun. Lorraine is a sociology student at a large eastern university.

Lorraine was the second child of five in an upper-class home. Her family was a religious one. Several of her relatives are ministers and missionaries.

Lorraine was abused by a brother and a cousin, though her primary abuser was her maternal grandfather. The incest with him started when

Lorraine was fourteen and lasted until she left home at eighteen.

On being abused as a teenager, Lorraine says, "Being fourteen or fifteen years old had nothing to do with it. I could have been three for all the power I had." At fifteen, Lorraine became pregnant with her grandfather's child and a quiet abortion was arranged. Everyone denied he was the father.

In the course of confronting her grandfather and talking to other relatives, Lorraine learned that he also had sexually abused her mother, a sister, and a niece.

I was twenty years old when I actively started to deal with the incest. The first year there was a lot of groundbreaking, actually

---

* Lorraine Williams wanted to use her own name, but couldn't for legal reasons.

facing and pinpointing instances, saying "Yes, I am an incest survivor." Before that time, those words did not exist. Yet deep down I knew: "This happened to you, Lorraine." Once I admitted that to myself, everything came caving in. Life was therapy. I couldn't focus on anything else. I felt like I was going insane. But after the first six months, I realized I would live. I still didn't want to deal with all of this, but I knew I had to.

I CONFRONTED MY GRANDFATHER

In the second six months, I confronted my grandfather. I didn't plan to confront him. I was going to visit my mother and I had taken my friend, Debra, with me. My brother picked us up at the train station and then proceeded to drive to my grandfather's house "to get a few things."

I felt really set up. Debra said, "I won't let that bastard touch you." When I saw him, I was instantly repulsed. He was up to his old tricks, guilt-tripping me for not visiting him. I stood there, listening quietly. All of a sudden I started screaming at him, "Who do you think you are? Who do you think you are, trying to make me feel guilty? *You*, of all people! You who hurt me, who abused me, who molested me? Don't you think that's sick? Don't you think you've done anything wrong?"

He just laughed. He said he hadn't done anything wrong, but that it had been, as he called it, his right to "educate his girls." This angered me even more, because I realized he was probably going to die thinking he'd done nothing wrong. He didn't deny it at all! He called it "educating his girls"!

MY MOTHER WAS THE MOST DIFFICULT PERSON TO CONFRONT

I wrote my mother a letter and was absolutely crazed on the day I knew she was going to receive it. I was so overwrought I got on the wrong bus.

The letter was direct. It said that my grandfather had molested me for years because she hadn't done anything about it. That I was in therapy now to recover. It was a very detailed letter with lots of different instances spelled out. I told her that she was a fool if she couldn't believe me. Why the hell would I be going through therapy if nothing had happened? And I said that she was partly responsible.

I had always been the good girl in my family, the one that didn't cause any trouble. This is not what a good girl does. So I was terrified. She had denied it when I was a teenager. She was his daughter. I didn't know how she was going to react. I could only go by how she reacted previously. So I unplugged my phone.

When I finally plugged the phone back in, she called right away. It was six in the morning. I knew it was her. I just picked up the phone and said, "Yes, mother?"

I think the letter really got to her. My sister disclosed to her too, so she was getting it from both of us. She was very sympathetic and she cried. She didn't get angry. I was prepared for her to be angry, and I was unprepared when she wasn't. She believed me. She said she was so sorry she hadn't believed me before. Then she told me he had molested her too. She was very angry with him. She actually wanted to go kill her father. I remember saying, "It's not worth it, Mama. He's already dead as far as we're concerned."

Since then, she's been a good ally when I've confronted other family members. She and I have done a lot of work getting to know each other.

I'M NOT BEING SILENT

My grandmother didn't believe anything had happened and said that I had an overactive imagination. And if anything *had* happened, I should be over it by now. My sister, who's also a survivor, doesn't talk about it. She won't see my grandfather and won't let her child see him, but she won't talk about it either. My brother, who molested me when I was younger, blames me and sides with my grandfather. He feels nothing wrong happened.

Last Thanksgiving, I went to Pennsylvania to visit my mother. The family has a week-long celebration every time there's a holiday. Different people in the family have different creative pursuits. Some dance, some sing, some play an instrument. I'm the writer. I was to bring up some of my writings and read them.

I have a very large family. There were thirty people there. Only two of them—my mother and my brother—knew anything at that point. So there were twenty-eight people who knew nothing. Included among them were two of his other daughters.

I thought I had brought only "safe" pieces, and then I realized I had brought very volatile pieces. One of these dealt with the incest. I wavered back and forth about whether I should read it. I really didn't know if I would until the actual moment I got up there. I pulled it out and was trying to decide. And then I realized that I had brought that story for the specific purpose of reading it. I just said to myself, "Yes. These people need to know he's not the angel they've painted wings on."

So I said, "There really isn't anything that I can tell you to preface this story, except that by the time I finish reading it you'll know why I wrote it." I was scared. I was shaking and sweaty on the inside, saying, "You really can't do this!" But on the outside, all appearances were intact. And I read it:

NOVEMBER
by Lorraine Williams

It was November, the month each year that Grandmother went away. She took a week off from the family to attend the annual church convention in Memphis. It was my job to stay at the house that she and my grandfather shared, to cook and clean. The two operated a board and care home for emotionally disturbed men.

The year that I was seventeen I especially resented having to stay at the house. I fussed, fumed, and fought, trying to find a way out. I tried endlessly to convince my mother that she should be the one to stay at the house. I mean, they were her parents. I did not want to be alone with my grandfather. Finally defeated, I gave in. I created what I thought was an elaborate plan. I'd make my younger brother, then eight, sleep in the bed with me. For him, it was a way to stay up late and watch TV. For me, it was a small act of defense.

. . .

My grandmother always departed at night, because she said the flights were cheaper. I sat on her bed as she packed the last few things in her overnight case. We sat and talked as we waited for her sister's arrival. She, too, was a missionary.

"You'll take care of everything, won't you?" Grandmother asked, as she stood adjusting her hat in the mirror.

"Of course," I told her. I wondered if she knew just how well things would be cared for.

"If anyone calls, tell them that I'll be back next Wednesday."

"But that's ten days!" I said in shock. Usually she was only gone for a week.

"Three more days won't kill you."

"No, I suppose it won't." Inside however, I was already dead.

. . .

That night, after I'd gone to bed, my body jolted awake, feeling another next to it. Immediately I knew it was him. I tried to pretend I was asleep as his hands invaded me, probing. Inside I felt nauseous, sick, repulsed.

"Get up and come into my room," he demanded. I ignored him, refused to move.

"Dammit, get up or I'll do it here." I didn't want my little brother to see anything, so I rose and did as he said.

I followed him into his bedroom, separate from that of my grandmother, slid into the bed, and went back to sleep. I hoped that he would feel sorry for waking me and thus leave me alone.

I awoke once again to his hand pawing my body, trying intently to gain access. I fought him by clamping my legs shut and wearing flannel pajamas, my only defenses. I didn't want to be there, didn't want any of it to be happening. Silently, I began to cry. Anger, agony, and shame filtered through me, lingering. He continued in an attempt to force an entrance. I crying, he pushing, me feeling totally helpless.

"Open your legs," he whispered angrily.

"No," I said, knowing already that I was powerless.

"Well then, I'll just take what I want."

. . .

He pushed against me, pumping hard and harder again. My skin felt as if it were being bludgeoned, beaten. His body slapped against my own, making it feel like it was being stoned. Heavy breathing filled the room as he panted and exclaimed obscenities. His moans and words filled my ears, though I attempted to block them.

"I'm coming, baby please, please never leave me," I heard.

My only thoughts were that it was almost over. The steamy, slick semen contaminated me. It burned the insides of my vagina, reaching, it felt, far into my uterus. My tears lay in a puddle on each side of my head.

. . .

I rose like a zombie as he rolled off of me, leaving the room quickly, quietly. I went straight to the bathroom adjacent to my room, sat on the toilet, and sobbed uncontrollably. I sat there, still like a mannequin, for an endless amount of time. Finally I turned on the water in the tub. I made it hot, steamy hot, as hot as I could bear. I needed to cleanse the infection from my system. I scrubbed and rubbed, making my white skin pink. Afterward, exhausted, I returned to bed. I changed the sheets, making the bed clean once more.

Sleep did not come. I lay there motionless, awake, afraid to return to slumber. I listened to my brother's breathing, deciding it was easier being a boy. I watched as dawn crept into the deep blue sky. Watching until my eyes closed in some deep sleep.

Time came for me to get up and prepare for school. I dressed carefully, finding soft clothes to hug my body, for it still hurt. I saw my image in the mirror, very pale. I knew it was going to be a bad day. I went downstairs to breakfast, my brother and my grandfather already there. Grandfather had a smile on his face that read, "'I got what I wanted from you. HA HA HA."

We said not a word to each other until I started to leave, when, as I was exiting the door, he said to me, "Have a good day."

* * *

I read the story. Everyone just sat there and didn't say anything. I looked up occasionally. Some of their faces were blank. Some were horrified. Others were just awed. There was dead silence.

I followed it with a light poem, and they all discussed the poem, but no one said a word about the story. Afterwards, various individuals came up to me. One of my aunts was angry at him. My other aunt was furious at me, saying I had written a bunch of lies: "My father couldn't have done anything like that. My father is a good person." I was the bad person. A couple of my male cousins and uncles were very angry at him and supportive of me. I was really shaken up.

And then during the course of my visit there, my twelve-year-old cousin told me that after I'd done the reading, she had had a dream that he had molested her too. She remembered everything and was very upset, very afraid to tell her mother. So I did it with her. The three of us sat down and talked. We all ended up sitting there crying together.

It was an overwhelming visit.

But I'm glad I told in the manner I did, because it destroyed their image of me as the good one, as the one who was always nice. Having that spot in the family meant I couldn't be me, couldn't be independent. And I feel better about myself.

We have to speak out and break the silence, especially in our own families. I know I have been able to heal because I'm not being silent.

RANDI TAYLOR

I never saw anyone like me in the incest books. I never saw anyone who said she had a good relationship with her father. All the perpetrators looked like angry, ugly, mean people, and yet my father appeared to be a loving, charming, wonderful man. I loved and adored him. He treasured me. That made the whole thing even more insidious. My story needs to be told because women need to know their experience counts. There's no such thing as mild abuse.

Randi Taylor is thirty years old.* She is single, lives alone, and works as a restaurant manager in Seattle. Randi was raised in an upper-middle-class family. Her parents were English, Scottish, and German. Randi's father was an accountant; her mother a housewife. She has two sisters and two brothers.

Randi's parents were very liberal. She called them by their first names. They were "cool." They knew their children were smoking pot but never reprimanded them. They kept a keg of beer in the garage so the kids could invite their friends over to drink. There were no limits, no boundaries.

Randi was always Daddy's girl. She idolized him. The molestation occurred when Randi was twelve to fourteen, just as she was going through puberty. It was always in the guise of playing games and laughing.

---

* Randi Taylor wanted to use her own name, but couldn't for legal reasons.

My father and I would do a lot of ruckus, fun things together. I'd pour a glass of water on his head, and he'd pour a glass of water on mine. We'd be tickling and wrestling and chasing each other around the house. A lot of times while he was tickling me, he'd reach his hand around and cup my breast. I'd always scream at him not to do that, but my screams would get mixed up with all the laughter and hilarity and screaming that was already going on. I'd tell him to stop, and he'd say, "Oh gee, did I slip? I didn't mean to." It was in the same tone as someone who just poured a glass of water on you and said, "Oops! I didn't mean to do that." He made a mockery of it.

Whenever we rode in the car, I'd sit in the middle of the front seat. When we went around a sharp turn, my father would elbow my boobs. He'd do it on purpose, always with an exaggerated gesture. My sisters and I had a name for it. We said my father was "boobing" me.

Then there was a routine we went through every morning. I'd get up to brush my teeth, and when I came back to my room, I'd have to search in my closet and under my bed, because my father would be hiding there, waiting for me to undress. I knew he wanted to see me naked, so I'd have to chase him out before I changed my clothes. I had to protect myself from this Peeping Tom who was my father, but it was made into a game. It was just part of the Taylor family morning routine.

At one point my father took up a sudden interest in photography, but the only thing he wanted to photograph were his daughters. He made me wear a thin T-shirt and he shined a light from behind my boobs. He wanted a picture of my boobs showing through a filmy T-shirt. That one never quite came out right, so he talked me into taking off my shirt. He promised he wouldn't photograph my breasts—only my chest and shoulders above my breasts. But they were definitely erotic photos.

While he was doing the photos, his hands would get shaky. His breath would be louder than normal. He would be excited. It was very scary for me to see him that way. Here was this man I adored and something happened to him. He was out of control and I never knew how far he would go.

One time my mother was going to be away all day. I was home sick from school. And in the middle of the day, my father came home from work. I was very frightened. I said, "What are you doing here?" He was joking and smiling and happy. "Oh, I thought I'd come home to see you. I knew you were here by yourself not feeling good. I thought I'd spend a little time with you."

He'd brought home some felt-tipped pens, and the game he had in mind was to decorate my breasts. He made me pull up my nightgown and he drew on my body. He made my two breasts into eyes, and then he drew a nose and mouth below it. His hands were shaking and his breath was really hot while he was doing that. And all the time, he was joking and teasing. It was horrible for me. Yet it was the one experience that allowed me to feel anger at him later on. All the rest of it, I said to myself, "Oh, he just slipped accidentally." But this was clearly thought out ahead of time. It was the only time he ever did anything that no one else saw him do. The rest of it was all out in the open.

Soon after, when I was fourteen, he complained that I was never home anymore, that I was always off with my friends. I turned to him with anger and said, "Why do you think I never spend time at home anymore? It's because I'm always afraid of what you're going to do to me." That stopped him cold and he didn't touch me again after that. But an atmosphere of sexual jokes and innuendos continued.

I DIDN'T KNOW HOW TO SAY NO

Before he molested me, I was a happy child, a normal child. But after it happened, I started seeking out friends from the other side of town. I hung out with guys with motorcycles, the kind of guys who drank a lot, who had tattoos and dropped out of school. We stole cars and went joy-riding. I had a boyfriend who was a year older than me. I got pregnant the first time we had sex, when I was thirteen. He dumped me, and I was afraid to tell my parents. I wore a lot of baggy clothes. It was the style at the time. I was six months pregnant before they figured it out. It shows how little parenting was going on.

My mother and I went shopping for a new bra because my breasts were swelling. When she saw me nude in the dressing room, she knew, but she didn't say anything to me. Instead she came home and told my father. That night when I was in bed, he came into my room and said my mother had told him I might have a problem. He asked if I was pregnant. I said I was. He asked me when I'd had my last period. I said six months ago. He was shocked. He told me my mother had known I was pregnant because my breasts had changed, that the nipples were larger and the brown area around the nipples had gotten bigger and browner. Then he said he wanted to see. I protested.

He said he wouldn't touch me, and then he insisted I pull up my shirt. He stared at my breasts for a few minutes, and then let me pull my shirt down. I felt invaded and ashamed.

My parents never got angry at me for the pregnancy. They asked me what I wanted to do. I said I just wanted to get rid of it. I flew to New York with my mother to some sleazy hospital for a saline abortion. They injected saline to kill the baby and then they gave me a drug to induce labor. It was extremely painful. I gave birth to the baby more than twenty-four hours later. I had no idea what was happening. I remember the water broke and I thought that was it. I yelled for the nurses and told them it was over. I had no idea there would actually be a baby, or that it would be so big. I only knew that the abortion would get rid of this problem.

The nurses had me give birth into a bedpan. It was only then that I realized it was a baby. It wasn't just a thing. Then they took it away. I never found out if it was a girl or boy.

My mother visited me a couple of times, but she only sat there crying. She was frightened and didn't nurture me at all. She hadn't brought enough cash and her main concern was that she might have to spend the night in the hospital waiting room. I ended up feeling guilty that I'd caused her all this pain. I felt like a horrible person. And once we got home, it was never mentioned again.

I now see how the pregnancy was a direct result of being molested. I didn't know how to say no. My boyfriend told me he had biological needs and that all the other boys were getting it, that if I didn't give it to him, he was going to have to go somewhere else.

And I didn't think enough of myself to let him go. Having had the experience of my father being sexually out of control made me believe that boys had this need that had to be filled. And of course I had to fill it.

SELF-ABUSE AND ANXIETY ATTACKS

As a teenager, I smoked a lot of pot and took a lot of acid. I went through a period in my early twenties of eating compulsively and making myself throw up. I finally quit overeating when I started doing cocaine. I no longer had any desire for food. The cocaine addiction only lasted a few months. I spent all kinds of money, and then I knew I had to stop. Then I started drinking too much.

But nothing worked to keep away the fear. I'd started having anxiety attacks when I was a teenager, but they got really bad when I was in my twenties. When I was twenty-four I had a nervous breakdown. I thought I was going crazy. I said to myself, "This is it. I'm over the edge. I need to be taken to the mental ward." I went to see a psychiatrist, but I couldn't afford to keep it up. Besides, it didn't seem to be helping.

The panic attacks kept increasing. They seemed to come from out of the blue. They were crippling. Adrenaline would rush through my whole system. My muscles would pump up, my arms would tighten, my whole body would start to sweat and shake. I'd feel like I was about to blank out. My vision would change. It's like looking at an overexposed photo. The world becomes this foreign place where everything is just white-washed.

The panic attacks happened most frequently when I was in the car. I'd be driving on the freeway and I'd feel like I was being forced to go faster than I wanted to go. When I had to pull up at a stop light, I'd feel completely trapped. I'd want to run the red light.

Sometimes I got the feeling that the sky was just too big. I wouldn't see it as blue sky but as infinity, as something that went on forever, that really had no boundaries. For me that had a lot to do with the lack of boundaries when I was growing up. I'd feel like I was going to be swallowed up by that vast, limitless sky. If I was walking in a field, I'd cover my head and crawl on the ground so I didn't float away into this limitless space. It was terrifying.

"IT WAS MOLESTATION"

One of my sisters is an alcoholic. When I was twenty-five, she got into AA. As part of her 12-step recovery program, she did an inventory of her life and had to tell someone about it. Part of her story dealt with our father. He'd never touched her when she was a teenager, aside from the photo sessions. But when she was twenty-two, they went on a trip together. They'd gotten drunk and had sex. Because of her age, my sister had always blamed herself.

When she talked about it in her inventory, the other person said, "My God, you were molested. That was incest. It wasn't your fault." My sister started reading books about incest, and then she came to me and said, "What Dad did to us was incest."

I said, "Maybe for you, but not for me. I love my father. He loves me. He never did anything to hurt me." But she gave me a bunch of books to read. And I started to think about it. I went back into counseling.

It took the longest time for me to

wholeheartedly believe that my experience counted. I felt like what happened to me was minor compared to what happened to other women. Molestation sounded like something horrible, and what happened to me didn't seem that horrible. My father just slipped once in a while.

I think it was the panic attacks—the fact that there was a direct result I could point to —that made me start to believe that he had done something wrong. They pushed me to break through that barrier of protecting my father, to face how terrified and angry I had been.

One day when I was driving, I started to panic. I was trying to talk myself down by saying "You don't have to scare yourself this way." And all of a sudden this thought popped into my brain: "You don't have to frighten yourself the way he frightened you the day he came home from work."

That's when I finally made the connection. I realized the phobias were the fears I had to suppress. It was like a suspense thriller, where the girl has trusted someone to protect her from the killer who's after her, and all of a sudden she finds out he is the killer. That's the kind of fear that was going on for me. My father, who was supposed to keep me safe from harm, *was* the harm.

I finally realized there had been damage done. For the first time in my life, I got angry at my father. He lost his hero status.

For a long time I stayed in the grief of having lost him. Looking at the reality of what happened meant losing the fond relationship I had with my father, and I wanted to hang on to that desperately.

AT FIRST I FELT SORRY FOR MY FATHER

My sister confronted my father a couple of years ago. She told him we were both in therapy. When she told me she'd talked to him, all I could think was "How is he going to handle it?" I felt sorry for him. I felt it was such a big burden for him to shoulder— that two of his daughters were in therapy. I thought the guilt would crush him. I'd taken care of my father's emotional needs for so long that it was hard for me to recognize that he was a sick person who did bad things.

My father's admitted to me that what he did was wrong. He knows there's nothing he can do to make it better, but says if there was, he'd do it. He says I'm still special to him, and that the only important thing is that I get better. For a while he called me quite regularly. I'd get angry at him over the phone and he'd apologize. But it wasn't really helping me. Finally I told him I didn't want to do that anymore. Just recently I wrote him a letter and said I didn't want to have contact with him for the time being. I was crying, but it felt terrific to write. It's hard because I don't know what kind of relationship I will have with my father when this is all over. I don't know what will be left. But at least I know I'm getting healthy.

ALICIA MENDOZA

I figure this thing is at least a camel, and that I'm over the first hump.

Alicia Mendoza is a thirty-one-year-old writer and teacher who lives in San Jose, California, with her husband, Joe.* They are newly married and are planning to have a child.

Alicia was born to a Venezuelan mother and a Jewish American father. She lived in Venezuela until she was thirteen, at which time her family moved to Minnesota, where her father had a university research position. Alicia has two younger brothers.

Alicia was physically abused by her mother. "She was an alcoholic, but I didn't realize it until I was nineteen, when she went to AA and quit. No one in the family had ever talked about her drink-

ing while I was growing up. We just called it 'Mama's temper.' "

At five, Alicia was sexually molested by her uncle Steve. "He was a medical student. He'd come home during the day and play doctor with me. Take my temperature vaginally. All kinds of innovative things like that." The abuse continued until she was nine, when he raped her in the middle of the night. After that it was more sporadic, and it stopped when her uncle moved to another city, when she was twelve.

Alicia grew up in a politically active leftist family, and she was a feminist and anti-war activist in her teens. She has been involved in many different progressive movements and organizations over the years. She sees her writing as an important part of that work.

Since early childhood, Alicia has written

---

* Alicia Mendoza chose to use a pseudonym.

poetry and stories. She has been published in magazines and anthologies, and has recently published a novel. She teaches literature and creative writing.

IT WAS SAFE TO REMEMBER IT AGAIN

The main way I coped with the incest was deciding not to remember it until it was safe. The main thing that made it safe was finally being in a relationship where I felt I could really count on my partner.

We were in couples therapy when I had my first flashback. I remembered the sensation of being molested, and I got a very clear image of the room. In fact, as the memory came back, I got more and more details of things in the room—there was a window here, and a dresser there, and always a person-size hole in the picture where my uncle should have been. He wasn't in the picture.

One of the objects I first remembered was the clock on the dresser. That was very significant in terms of letting the rest of the memory come through. For a couple of years, I'd had an inkling that something was there, because every time people started to talk about incest, my stomach would start churning. I think one of the reasons I held off remembering for as long as I did was that I was afraid that it might have been my father who molested me, and I have a very close relationship to him now. That was just too terrifying to face.

But when I saw the clock in that room, and saw what time it was, I knew I was waiting for my father to come home from work, so it couldn't have been him. And as soon as I realized my father couldn't have been in the room, it was safe to remember the rest of the incest. I had no attachment to protecting my uncle.

I kind of started with the margins of the memory and then worked my way in. More and more pieces kept fitting in. At first it was hard to believe them. I needed complete belief from the people around me, especially when I just had feelings and nothing to attach them to. Joe had to keep saying, "Trust your instincts. Trust your feelings. Trust your body. You're not making it up. These images are coming from somewhere."

I went to a workshop called "Healing from Hurts of Violence," and the leader said that there was a high correlation between children who wet their beds late and incest survivors. I wet my bed until I was twelve. And when I heard that, it was a piece of external evidence that opened up a new chunk of memories. Each time I got some confirmation that said "This might really be true, you know," another piece opened up.

As I dealt with the memories, there were repercussions in how I dealt with other parts of my life. I was able to face my mother's violence for the first time, because the underlying silence had been broken. Unlocking the incest unlocked other things too.

I COULDN'T TAKE A BREATH WITHOUT THINKING OF INCEST

Remembering the rape triggered the very worst period of the whole healing process. It felt like I was going to die. I couldn't take a breath without thinking about incest. In fact, it was a struggle to breathe a lot of the time. I had a few days where I just sat on the kitchen floor, rocking and holding myself. I don't think Joe really knew what to do.

There were times when I felt I would just start babbling. I made these subconscious connections when I was out on the street. *Everything* reminded me of incest. "Oh, look at that lamppost. Oh God—incest!" It was everywhere! The landscape was about incest. It took over my awareness all the time.

It felt like my body was inhabited by this thing that had happened in my childhood, that there wasn't a cell in my body that wasn't involved in it. The memories felt like they were invading me, in the same way my uncle had invaded my body. I spent a lot of time feeling like I was going to throw up. I was often out of my body. I'd feel like I was floating somewhere at the other end of the room. I couldn't feel anything below the neck. My brain was working, but my *legs?* "What legs?"

I had to keep reminding myself to sleep and eat. I had notes all over my house, saying, "When did you last eat? When did you last sleep?" I wasn't rigid about it. I just said, "To maintain basic health, I have to eat once a day and I have to go to bed at night. Even if I don't sleep, I have to lie down and rest every night."

The first few months after I remembered, I developed this pattern of waking up at four in the morning, every single morning. Four a.m. was the exact time he came in and raped me. I'd sit bolt upright in my bed every night, to the minute.

At the point when I was having a lot of flashbacks, I kept thinking I had the body of a nine-year-old child. I'd look at my body in the mirror and not recognize myself. Joe had to constantly remind me that I was not nine years old, but thirty, that I was in the present, that he was with me, and that he would never touch me against my will in any way. I needed constant reassurance. He had to say it over and over, like a broken record.

Right through the emergency stage, I felt dirty a lot. I got a bunch of vaginal infections. But I got through that pretty quick, because of the support I got from Joe. He would say, "You were a beautiful little girl. You are a beautiful woman now. Nothing he did to you could ever make you dirty." He just said things like that over and over again.

Gradually there was a shift in how I saw it. The temperature lowered, and I got past the point where it felt totally urgent to deal with it all the time. I started to be able to think about other things, to allow the incest to sit on the back burner.

I STARTED TO HAVE DREAMS WHERE I WAS TAKING POWER

I kept a record of all the dreams I had during that time. I had a dream where my uncle was sitting on a chair, and I went and sat on his lap. He got a hard-on, and then a little bit of semen dripped onto his pants. And I grabbed his pants and I said to Joe, who was standing right there, "Look! We have a stain!" And I rushed it to the lab. "Now we have proof!"

I had another dream about a doctor trying to molest me in his office. He said something terrible would happen if I told. And I told him that if he laid a finger on me, I was going to scream at the top of my lungs, scratch his eyes out, kick him in the balls, and tell absolutely everybody I knew. And the doctor collapsed in this powerless heap on the floor.

DEALING WITH INCEST HAS BROUGHT JOE AND ME CLOSER

Joe was tremendously willing to treat the whole subject as something he didn't know much about. He's really followed my lead. When I was intense about it, he'd be right there with me. When I wasn't talking about it as much, he'd back off and just check in with me about it periodically.

He was also willing to be experimental in helping me: "What would you like to do? Do you want to talk or not talk? Do you want me to touch you or not? Do you want me to hold you while certain feelings come up, or do you want me to leave you alone?"

He was doing co-counseling on his own, and we were in couples counseling together. I think that gave him the necessary support to talk about how it was affecting him.

Joe never doubted that I would get through it, and he kept expressing that. Somehow he was able to see past what was going on, to the potential for us if we worked together. He got real tired of it at various points along the way, but the long view enabled him to hang in through some pretty unpleasant times. It was a strain on the relationship, but it illuminated so many things. Things that were just annoying or frustrating to him about me before suddenly fit into a framework that made sense.

I know it's also brought things up for him—old hurts from his own childhood. It made him much more aware of the nuances of sexual power.

There were times in the process that I would forget he was Joe and react to him as "generic Man." He had never hurt me in any of those ways, but I would confuse his identity completely. We'd be lying in bed at night. I'd be trying to go to sleep, and I'd have to get up because I felt "I can't lie here with this male body. It's too terrifying."

That was really painful, because Joe was being tremendously supportive and loving through the whole thing. And the fact that he acted in such a contradictory way to what I expected was a real strong part of the healing process for me.

There was a point, right around the time we decided to get married, where I just decided that the relationship wasn't giving me anything I wanted, and that I should start from scratch with somebody else. It was terror about the intimacy. I had assumed that people wouldn't come through for me for so long. And here he was coming through for me, and what went along with that was a price tag of intimacy. I had to open up. I no longer had an excuse. There were no wrong actions on his part that I could blame for the lack of intimacy. So I had to let go of my defenses. I was absolutely terrified. And he stuck by me.

If I had to do it over again, I'd work on the incest more outside of the relationship. I didn't have a real strong support group to work with then. And I think it would have been better if he'd been in some kind of support group for partners. There was too much imbalance with him taking care of me. That's slowly started to shift, but I've been scared that if he wasn't taking care of me, he wouldn't want to be around me. And he's been scared that if I didn't need him, I wouldn't love him. Shifting that balance has been real tricky.

THE INCEST DID STRANGE THINGS TO MY SEXUALITY

I had a whole variety of problems. Because I didn't get much physical affection from my mother, I was very receptive to the physical cuddling from my uncle. Then when he violated me, I somehow made the connection that sex was the only way to get touched.

As an adult, I wanted to be made love to all the time. I would feel real stormy and out of control and freaked out if I couldn't get it. And at the same time, I didn't really want to make love to anyone else. I didn't want to bother. I didn't want to touch someone else. I particularly had trouble going anywhere near a penis. That's changed since I've been with Joe.

Another problem I had was that focusing any sort of special attention on sex made it impossible. Birthdays, anniversaries, any occasions that were supposed to be romantic would just ruin any chance for me to be sexual. I'd start fighting immediately. I'd sabotage it in any way I could. Or if we did try to make love, everything that was disturbing about sex would come up immediately. Something about it being romantic was just too huge a contradiction to what my initiation into sexuality was. All that pain would just surface in the face of it.

Also, when I was younger I had experienced sexual excitement with my uncle. As a result, I've felt there was something really shameless and animal-like about sexual pleasure. Like I was just an animal in heat whenever I had strong sexual feelings. With my uncle, I was constantly being put in a state of sexual arousal and then abandoned. I never had an orgasm. And as an adult I had a hard time having orgasms with a partner.

I'd always freeze up. Then I'd get angry at my partners for not being able to make me come. When it happened with Joe, he got really frustrated. So we went to couples counseling and got some basic information on touching one step at a time. It's only since I've worked on the incest that I've been able to have an orgasm while making love with someone else. I could by masturbating, but I'd never been willing to give someone else that much power over me before.

Once I started actively dealing with the incest, there were a lot of shifts in my sexuality. The way I moved down the street was different. I felt my body differently. I found myself acting real childlike when I was being sexual. Playing that out—talking in a little girl's voice, giggling a lot, wanting to play childhood games. My whole way of going for sexual contact changed.

I also had a lot of sexual dreams about my uncle, which I felt really guilty about. Sometimes in bed with Joe, I'd have flashbacks that horrified me. Other times they'd turn me on. Then I'd feel disgusted. I started having fantasies of going back as an adult and seducing my uncle. It was, "Hey, you think I was something when I was nine? You should see me now. I'm *hot* stuff. You better finish what you started, and this time, you better make it good!" It was a cross between wanting to confront him with the incest and wanting to initiate the whole thing myself, so that I would be the one in control. My feelings in these fantasies were very aggressive and hostile, and the images really turned me on. I felt fine on the inside about having them, but I didn't feel safe telling people.

I found myself getting turned on when I wrote about the incest. And I'd think, "God, this is really disgusting!" And when

I'd see girls who were the age I was when the abuse happened to me, I tended to imagine it happening to them. And sometimes that had a sexual charge too.

I found myself reacting to touch in different ways. Some touching that had been pleasurable felt like irritation. Specific gestures, expressions, or positions would put me into a nightmare state. My uncle used to cover my mouth with his hand. And if anyone got their hand anywhere near my mouth, even in the most playful way, I would panic. I only wanted to be held in a specific way. And if his arm went around my neck at all, I'd get violent.

Sometimes I'd continue to make love when that happened, but eventually I stopped doing that. That had more to do with Joe than it did with me. I wouldn't even have to say anything. He got real fine-tuned. There'd just be this little twitch in my body and he would pay really close attention. If I was shrinking away at all, he would stop and say, "You want to stop now?" in a cheerful "it's-fine-with-me-if-you-want-to-stop" voice. He was often the one to make the decision. I didn't have the strength to do it. I would just freeze and say to myself, "Well, I'll just close my eyes and then it will be over with soon," which is exactly what I did as a child. And Joe wouldn't let me get away with that.

My desire for sex would come and go, because I had the pattern of going after sex, and I also had the disgust. For a couple of weeks I just wouldn't want sex at all. And then I'd go in the other direction. I'd feel really urgent about making love. So we'd start making love, and I'd freeze up and say, "I can't do this." I went back and forth and back and forth for about six months.

One of the ways that affected the relationship was that Joe was really scared to make love to me. He was understandably wary, because half the time I'd run to the bathroom and start barfing, or suddenly push him away and start sobbing. It was nerve-wracking for him.

There was a point when it got real hard for him, when I didn't want to touch him. And because he'd been so understanding and respectful about my needs, I was able to see, "Oh, he's hurt because of this," instead of thinking, "He's angry. He wants to throw me down on the bed and rape me." When I saw he was being hurt, I was able to remember, "Oh, *this* is Joe. *That* was Steve. *This* one's my buddy." I wouldn't necessarily want to make love, but I was able to hold him or touch him in ways that would comfort him.

It was Joe's attitude that really helped me move through the feelings. I needed him to hang in there, to separate himself out enough not to take it personally when I was completely unpredictable around sex.

He also told me when he was upset. He managed to stay consistently supportive, but it was very hard on him. He was starting to wear thin with it at the point when I started to feel more comfortable.

All the work I've done has been really worth it to me. I feel I'm moving toward more and more power with my sexuality all the time.

HAVING A CHILD IS GOING TO BE HEALING

Another thing that's really shifted my feelings about sexuality has been thinking about having a child. It's the positive part of feeling like an animal. I've had feelings of power in my body since we started talking about it. And I think having a child is going to be really healing in itself. I expect it will be hard to watch my child being as vulnerable as I once was. I can even imagine wanting to be abusive myself, but I'm not afraid of acting those feelings out. I'm in such a supportive situation with people who talk so openly, I don't think I'll have anything to worry about.

ANNETTE

By working my steps and traditions, by living my program on a daily basis, the healing just comes naturally. I'm strong. I don't need anyone to do my thinking for me. I've been healing and growing for twenty-two years and I do the work with God.

Annette is sixty years old.* She is divorced and has three grown sons. Seven years ago, she founded Incest Survivors Anonymous, a national self-help organization built on the Alcoholics Anonymous model.

Annette grew up in an upper-middle-class town in the Midwest. Her father held the same managerial job for over thirty years. Both her parents were community leaders, active in church affairs. Secretly they were involved with a group that performed ritualized abuse according to a satanic calendar. Town leaders, businesspeople, and church

officials were all involved in this cult. From infancy, Annette was abused in rituals that included sexual abuse, torture, murder, pornography, and systematic brainwashing through drugs and electric shock: "I was what they called a 'breeder.' I was less than twelve years old. They overpowered me and got me pregnant and then they took my babies. They killed them right in front of me."

THEY COULDN'T GET MY SOUL

How did I get through it? I had a lot of little inside people. They call it multiple personalities. I call them "adaptables." When I was being tortured, each little kid would

417

come out and take it for as long as he or she could. When that kid couldn't take anymore, the next one would come out and take over. And the first one would go off to green pastures to play with baby Jesus. She wouldn't come back until the bad people left.

I completely blocked out the abuse. Some of the blocking came from the trauma. Some was because they set it up that way. They used hunger, pain, hypnosis, electric shock, isolation, and sleep deprivation to brainwash me. They programmed me to either die, kill myself, go crazy, or to grow up and go back to them. They were after my soul, but they couldn't get it. I never willingly participated. They had my body, but they couldn't get my soul.

None of the programming works today, but they haven't given up. Now they try to discredit me and my story.

JUST AN ORDINARY HOUSEWIFE

If you'd seen me, you would have thought I was just an ordinary housewife who never got too far away from her husband, her home, and her kids. I was a den mother. I went to church. I took the kids to Sunday school. But I never understood why I felt the way I did. I felt worthless, dirty, unable to go forward in life. I could help my kids and my husband, they were my life. I could never do anything as an outside career for myself. I kept making the same mistakes, going in circles.

I couldn't remember what people said to me. I'd forget whole stretches of time. Now I know I was losing time when I was slipping and sliding in those other personalities.

I was hooked on pills and alcohol by the time I was in my early twenties, although I was functioning. They used drugs on me when I was a little bitty baby. They gave me cocaine. They gave me paregoric. They got me started on alcohol and drugs. Finally in 1964 I went to Al-Anon, and in 1965 I went to Alcoholics Anonymous. But even after I quit the booze and legal prescriptions, I knew there was something else inside that needed to be healed. I didn't know what it was, and I had no idea how to get to it. But I was willing to pay the price of recovery.

I secretly feared I was born crazy. It never dawned on me that this was memory. I wasn't born crazy.

UNKNOWN TO ME I'D BEEN LIVING A LIE

I didn't remember anything about the abuse until I was forty-eight years old. That's when I remembered the incest. Seven or eight years after that, the ritual abuse started breaking through. I don't know how to explain the horror of that. There was so much grief and heartbreak. I couldn't believe my parents had done such heinous things to me. My family had been so proper and clean, they squeaked. Unknown to me, all my life I'd been living my family's lie.

Because of the way my inside kids got me through the abuse, each of them held a different piece of the memories. That's why the memories didn't make sense at first. It was less painful to think I was crazy. If I hadn't been around other survivors talking about their experiences, I wouldn't have had any idea this stuff even existed. People have said to me, "Oh, you just copied what you heard someone else say." But how do you copy the feelings? How do you explain the scars on my body? How do you explain the pain?

I've used my 12-step and 12-tradition program for healing. I taught my little inside kids the principles, at their age level, in language they could understand. I let them talk and tell, and I listen. I love and nurture my inside kids. They have a loving higher power. For me, that's Jesus.

I'LL DO THE FOOTWORK

When the memories first came through I looked for a 12-step and 12-tradition program specifically for incest. There was one for overeating, for alcohol. I knew there needed to be one for incest, but I didn't think I had what it took to start it. I kept waiting for someone else to do it, but finally I just threw in the towel and said, "All right. I'll do the footwork. This brilliant person is going to come along and take it over. But I'll get things started because I have to show some faith."

Little by little, by working closely with other survivors in Incest Survivors Anonymous, I got stronger. I learned I needed to deprogram all those triggers I'd been brainwashed with so many years ago. I learned the more I gave my strength away, the more I got back, one hundred fold.

Sometimes I stop and think, why didn't I die of shock, of grief, of heartbreak when I was a little girl? I used to beg God to let me stay in green pastures. I didn't want to come back. But I came back for a reason. I came back to tell and to speak for those who died. This isn't an isolated thing that only happened to me. I traced it back in my little town three generations. And it happens in other towns too. It's happening to kids today. I've had more than a hundred calls about ritual abuse. It's starting to break into the papers. And people are starting to believe it. That's the only way it's going to stop.

Sandi Gallant: Ritual-Abuse Investigator

Sandi Gallant is a policewoman and an investigator in the Intelligence Division of the San Francisco Police Department. She has been investigating cases involving ritualistic crime for the past eight years and has consulted with other investigators nationwide. She's also led extensive training groups with therapists, teachers, police officers, and parents.

The mere fact that you mention the words "satanic abuse" turns a lot of people right off. Society is in a state of denial about this, just as they have been about child sexual abuse. In law enforcement the term "ritual abuse" didn't even exist until a few years ago. It's going to take some time before law enforcement and the public at large accept that these things actually happen. My personal feeling is that it is not a widespread phenomenon. But it does happen. And it's very traumatic to the victim.

Ritual abuse is surfacing now because we've started to talk openly about the sexual abuse of children. More and more adults are remembering what happened to them when they were young.

The best description I've heard of ritual abuse is from Larry Pazder, the psychologist who wrote the book *Michelle Remembers*. He calls it "a systematic series of emotional, physical and/or sexual abuses." There's a se-

RESOURCES FOR RITUAL ABUSE SURVIVORS

There are currently very few resources for adult survivors of ritual abuse. It's important to see a therapist who knows, believes, and understands the issue. The organizations listed here can be contacted for referrals.

Believe the Children
P.O. Box 1358
Manhattan Beach, CA 90266
(213) 379-3514

The Cult Awareness Network
2421 West Pratt Blvd., Suite 1173
Chicago, IL 60645

The Cult Hotline
1651 Third Avenue
New York, NY 10028
(212) 860-8533

Incest Survivors Anonymous
P.O. Box 5613
Long Beach, CA 90805-0613
(send a self-addressed, stamped envelope)
(213) 428-5599

National Center for Missing and Exploited Children
1835 K Street NW, Suite 700
Washington, DC 20006
(800) 843-5678 or (202) 634-9836

VOICES in Action, Inc.
P.O. Box 148309
Chicago, IL 60614
(312) 327-1500
(calls will be returned collect)

ries of events taking place on a regular basis with multiple suspects and multiple victims.

When Satanism is involved, the child is used by the adults to align themselves more closely with their spiritual leader—in their eyes, Satan. Often these rituals are scheduled according to a set calendar, and are accompanied by the wearing of robes, chanting, mock marriage ceremonies, orgies, and the mutilation of animals. Frequently they take place in cemeteries or mortuaries and center around death themes. Trickery and illusion are often involved. It's all very secretive. A lot of threats are used to ensure the victims' cooperation and silence.

Many adult survivors believe they're at risk talking about these things. In some cases this may be true, but in many cases I think they're feeding off the threats and intimidation they experienced as children. I've never been threatened, and I've been the most outspoken person in law enforcement in the country on this issue.

The reason so few of these cases are successfully prosecuted is that the information is so unpleasant that no one wants to believe it. The investigators hear these stories and they say to themselves, "No, this can't be true," and so they don't write it down, they don't document it. There's often a lack of physical evidence. The prosecutors don't want to hurt their careers by taking cases they're unlikely to prove in court. So these cases are frequently dropped rather than dealt with.

The most unfortunate thing is that the victims are so often accused of making all this up. The victims end up being the suspects, and the suspects end up being the victims. That's a real travesty. People say children invent these stories after watching TV, but before there was any media coverage of these cases, the allegations these kids made were extremely consistent with the allegations other kids were making in other parts of the country. These kids weren't networking with each other. Nobody was talking about it. Children don't make up stories like these.

Society has got to stop denying. Technologically we've advanced to a great degree and people think that means the human animal has advanced to that same degree. But that isn't true. We're the same basic animal we've always been. If people can imagine these things going on four and five hundred years ago, then they have to start believing that they are happening today. It's time for people to get out of the denial stage so we can stop it.

DIANE HUGS

Diane Hugs is a thirty-two-year-old writer who has been struggling with memories of her childhood abuse for the last ten years.* She's had multiple sclerosis for the last twelve. MS is a degenerative condition of the central nervous system, with symptoms that vary greatly from person to person. In Diane's case, she has been paraplegic for six years and legally blind for the past year. Diane connects her disease with the severe abuse she experienced, starting in infancy.

In the past two and a half years, Diane has become aware that she has multiple personalities—more than thirty of them, ranging in age from three to thirty. As she eloquently expresses, women with multiple personalities can heal.

---

* Diane Hugs is using her own name.

From the time I was a very young child, I had experiences which were so traumatic they split my personality wide open. There was no way for my young mind to cope with the brutality and random acts of sadism that I experienced. Instead, I completely forgot the incidents and created a totally new personality. Within two years, I went in and out of three such changes: from being an introverted, shy pacifist, to being the leader of a girls' gang that went after known rapists and child molesters, to becoming an academic scholar. Each of these personalities began without the old scars, without the old terror, without the anger. Each had her own coping mechanisms, approaching the world in a completely different way. I, as the core personality, was totally unaware of their existence. Every time I wiped the slate clean, a new and different personality would come out to take over so that I might survive. There were many times as a child when I questioned whether I would survive. The ultimate threat was always "I will kill you if you tell, if you . . . if you . . ."

It wasn't until I was much older that I realized I had multiple personalities—more than thirty of them. I also realized that I had blocks of time which I did not remember. I had always accepted that as being normal. I thought everyone occasionally spaced out and found themselves in another city or in the midst of a conversation with no idea what was being talked about.

Accepting each of these parts of myself and then integrating them into my personality is a long process. And it's often very painful, as each of these splits, each of these personalities, has memories and feelings separate from my own experience. So to integrate means to accept those feelings and to accept those memories which I have successfully blocked since I was a child. Sometimes, accepting how I coped in order to survive is extremely painful. Imagine integrating an eighteen-year-old part who is a prostitute when you've been a lesbian for over ten years.

Usually, when one of these personalities takes control, so to speak, I lose time. It seems to me as if seconds have gone by, when in reality minutes, hours, or a day has gone by with this other personality functioning in my place. As I begin to accept the feelings and the parts of me that have split off, instead of losing time with that particular personality, I hear a voice in my head which is that other personality talking. Sometimes it's totally against what I'm thinking or feeling, so I have a lot of inner arguments as part of the process of integration.

After the arguments comes a blending where I not only accept those parts of me, but am strengthened by the knowledge, the courage, whatever it is that each part holds. It's as if each personality holds a special part of my life, not only a painful part of my life. And each time I integrate one, I'm integrating another part of myself that adds to my understanding.

One of the major aspects of healing from childhood abuse is to begin to love yourself. With multiple personalities, this task is much more difficult, because I have to love parts of myself that have been so walled off, so blocked from the conscious personality, that I don't even know them. Over and over, I have to figure out ways to get through those walls so I can know other parts of me. Before I can love myself, I have to know myself.

MULTIPLE PERSONALITIES

This information is taken from an excellent group of articles, "Multiple Personality—Mirrors of a New Model of Mind?" by Brendan O'Regan and Thomas J. Hurley III, published by Investigations *of the Institute of Noetic Sciences.**

People with multiple-personality disorder (often called "multiples") have two or more distinct and complex personalities.

---

* This special double issue (Volume 1:3/4) presents a comprehensive analysis of multiple personalities and offers recommendations for treatment. To order, write to: The Institute of Noetic Sciences, 475 Gate Five Road, Suite 300, Sausalito, CA 94965.

These personalities, who may or may not be aware of each other, alternately control the physical body. When personalities switch, other features may switch also. Voice, posture, gestures and expressions, handedness, brain-wave patterns, allergic reactions, physical abilities, and the ability to speak different languages all may change.

Virtually everyone who is diagnosed as being multiple has been severely abused—sexually, physically, or psychologically—as a young child. To cope with this trauma, the child blocks the feelings and memories from consciousness and another self, the "alter" personality, takes over and functions. If there is no chance for nurturing, healing experiences, the child continues to split as a way to deal with stress and pain. Over time, the alternate personalities assume an independent existence.

Most multiples have personalities who are children and personalities of the opposite sex. Personalities with conflicting values or differing lifestyles are also common. Frequently different personalities perform distinct functions and express distinct emotional states.

Multiples frequently experience amnesia and thus become confused and disoriented, often having to lie about lost time. They can also suffer from severe headaches, periods of fear and panic, internal conflict, and self-destructive behavior. But multiple-personality disorder is not always incapacitating. In fact, some multiples have extraordinary capacities—the ability to withstand pain, to heal rapidly, or to function at an unusual level of productivity.

The initial split into an alter personality usually occurs before the age of five, but most multiples are not diagnosed until adulthood, and the vast majority have been misdiagnosed at least once. In recent years there has been a surge of interest in multiple personality (along with an increased interest in child sexual abuse), and therapists who work with multiples have learned more about approaches that are helpful to healing.

KRISHNABAI

The first twenty-five years of my life were an experience of despair. They were just incredibly painful. There's something devastating about a child who does not feel loved. And I've really turned that around in my life. I have experienced healing and I just feel incredibly blessed.

Krishnabai is thirty-five years old.* She lives in the Boston area, does workshops for survivors, and works as a consultant.

Krishnabai grew up in a rural area of New

Jersey. "I had no feeling of being part of a family. It was like being a member of a boarding house. Although I was close to my father, I had no relationship whatsoever with my mother."

When she was nine years old, Krishnabai was sexually abused one time by her great-uncle. As is true for many women, Krishnabai's sexual abuse was just one of the factors that shaped her early development. Her story clearly demonstrates the way sexual abuse can exacerbate already existing problems.

Krishnabai says she was psychotically de-

---

* Krishnabai is using her own name. She received the name "Krishnabai" while living in the ashram of Baba Muktananda. She changed her name legally and says, "It was a real release of the past. That name I had, which I don't even say anymore, is gone. It marks the end of an era. Using 'Krishnabai' makes me vulnerable, but it also gives me strength."

pressed for most of the first twenty-five years of her life. In the ten years since then, she has healed herself through a combination of therapy, reparenting, and spirituality.

I was molested once by my mother's uncle during the summer between fifth and sixth grades. I was already a very isolated, withdrawn child. My uncle got drunk one night and pounced on me, and started kissing me and feeling me up. I was unable to get away. He was in the process of getting undressed when my aunt walked in. She sent me to my room, yelled at him, and then came upstairs and said to me, "It's really obvious that no one loves you and you're just a sad little kid. I'm really sorry this happened, but you must never, ever tell anyone." And I didn't tell anyone for years.

I already had a very shaky foundation, and this just destroyed me. My mother had been unable to make any kind of emotional connection with me. She once said to me, "I should never have been a mother." She didn't know how to nurture, how to open up, how to express love. And so I already felt unlovable.

After the sexual abuse, my behavior took a radical turn toward the bizarre. I thought if people touched me it would kill me. I thought there were people in the trees. I thought there were cameras in the house, staring at me. I was getting messages from the universe. I had to plug my teddy bears into invisible oxygen tubes at night before I went to sleep, so they wouldn't suffocate. I had an incredible amount of ritualistic behavior going on, trying to control my environment. I started wearing black shroudy clothes. Weight, which was always an issue, became much worse. I was throwing up every morning.

I was very isolated. I went into therapy in ninth grade. I was given Librium. I continued having visions and hearing voices but I knew not to tell anyone about them.

I was bright and I excelled at school. I went to Europe between my junior and senior year of high school to study at the University of London. It was 1968. I got immersed in the hippie scene. I came back and I got into drugs and acting out sexually. I got into freedom. Everything just blew wide open, and it was supported by the times.

I went to college for a year, and then quit and moved to Boston. I got a job as a cashier. I lived in this hippie crash pad. You never knew who was going to be there. I have no idea how many people I fucked. It was just this continuous "Whatever you want is fine with me 'cause I don't know who 'me' is." I was totally bland, because I had killed my feelings. I got into drugs because they made me feel real. So I took a lot of them, including LSD.

I JUST CRUMBLED

When I was twenty my dad died, and I just crumbled. My dad had been my one link to the world. He had been a gentle and beautiful man, so when he died I just fell apart. I went into intensive therapy. They loaded me up on psychotropic drugs. They considered hospitalizing me.

I couldn't work. I was totally fogged out. I was put into a program through Massachusetts Rehabilitation. They put me in cooking school, figuring maybe I could function on that level if they trained me to be a cook. I ended up working as a cook in a snack bar at a mental hospital. There I was flipping hamburgers in this snack bar, and the patients started talking to me. They had decreased my drugs at that point, and my intellect got aroused. The clinical staff started to notice that these patients could talk to me, that there was a real relationship going on. And so I got invited onto the clinical staff.

I only worked the night shift, which was perfect, because no psychiatrist ever saw me. I dealt with people in their most difficult moments, which I could totally understand. It helped me so much to help them.

Right about that time, I got into a car accident. A drunken driver plowed into me. I went into the hospital and the doctor said, "Well, I think you're okay. But I don't want you to be alone for the night. Do you have a roommate?"

I said, "No."

And he said, "Do you have a friend you can call?"

I said "No."

He said, "Do you have any family you can call?"

I said, "No."

And he looked at me with this incredible compassion and said, "Is there anyone there for you in your life?"

And I thought about it, and I said, "No."

He ended up having me call a co-worker to tell her what had happened. I went home and was terribly depressed. I decided to kill myself that night by hanging myself with the telephone cord, and just then, the woman I had called phoned to check in with me. She talked to me for two hours on the phone, and then came and got me. I started to tell her how I really felt. And she said, "I think you need to see somebody."

I went to this psychiatrist at the hospital where I worked, and I said, "Look, I need help, and I don't know how to get it." And so she agreed to take me on. And then in the process of unfolding me, she kind of went, "Oh, my God! We've got this person on our staff!"

She listened to me for maybe five sessions and she said, "Something is really wrong here. You've never experienced connection. You've never experienced happiness in your life. I think there's something going on with you biologically and I want to try some drugs on you." Well, I had nothing to lose.

She put me on Tofranil, which was a brand-new drug at that time. One day a few weeks later, I woke up and I felt really weird. It was about four in the afternoon. I'd worked the night before. I called her up and I said, "I don't know what's going on, but I feel really weird." And I kept talking, and she got really excited. And she said, "You've got to come right over here."

So I went over and she said to me, "You're starting to have feelings! I can't believe it! It's working! These are emotions you're feeling! This is what everybody has. Your TV is going from black-and-white to color and you don't understand because you've never seen color before."

We spent the next six months in therapy with her saying, "This is sadness. This is happiness." She described different feelings to me and helped put them in a framework that I could understand. I was like a baby looking out at the world and beginning to understand things for the first time. And my life really started to change.

When I got access to my feelings, the psychotic episodes dropped down a whole lot. Some kind of pressure was released. I started to have more energy. I was so hungry to explore the world. I decided to go back to school and I did.

"GO TO THIS WORKSHOP"

I was working full time at night and going to school during the day. I was living in this alienating group house. There'd been a woman who lived there once who got all kinds of neat junk mail. And she got a circular saying, "Our friends Robbie and Judith Gass are going to be offering a brand-new workshop called *Opening the Heart,* and we want to invite all of you to come."

That was when I heard my clear inner voice for the very first time. It said, "Go to this workshop." All I'd had up until then was real traditional psychotherapy. I was still on the medication. I was so-called stabilized. So I wrote them a letter, asking all kinds of questions about the schedule and what they'd be doing. And Robbie wrote back a letter that said, "Don't worry. Just come. Love, Robbie."

And I said to myself, "Oh my God! I can't do this." But I sent my money in and I got back this list: Bring a baby picture, a picture of your parents, a blindfold! I'm like really flipping out, but this little part of me pushed me to go. And so I did.

I was terrified. I was the first one to show up. I was totally going on faith and I didn't know what faith was. The whole weekend was the most incredible experience. There was singing, there was bioenergetic work, there was meditation. We did yoga, visualization, and a lot of work in pairs. It was an experience of people letting go of the gates in their heart, releasing the blocks that have kept them from feeling love.

We did this exercise where we were supposed to lie on the floor, reach up our arms, and call for our mothers. I couldn't do it. I was terrified. Judith sat down next to me and said, "Let me hold you. Let me put you on my lap." And she pulled me onto her lap, put her arms around me. I had never experienced such tenderness.

Here was this beautiful woman holding me like that. I cracked right open. I bawled my eyes out. And she rocked me and she held me for so long. Robbie came over and joined us. The two of them saw some potential in me that I was not able to see. And they made this commitment that weekend to hold on to me and help me with my healing.

AT SPRING HILL

About two months later, I went to visit them at Spring Hill.* Judith put her arms around me and said, "I want you to come live with us. I think it would be really good for you." And so I moved in in the spring of 1977. I was twenty-six years old. I lived in their house, in the room right beneath them.

Judith was like this barnacle. She just hung on through all my acting out, all my fear, all my resistance. First I thought I was crazy. Then I thought they were crazy. My fears and doubts just got flushed right out of me.

Although I had made some progress before I came to Spring Hill, I was still a totally isolated person when I got there. I was functional in a work sense, but not in a people sense. I was terrified of people. I had no ability to have loving relationships. I was like

---

* Spring Hill is a community and conference center in Central Massachusetts that Robert and Judith Gass started. It's where the Opening the Heart workshops originated.

this little bubble floating in the universe with no connection.

I was split, like pieces in a basket, and Robbie and Judith picked up the basket, took it to Spring Hill, dumped the pieces out on the floor, and started putting them together, like a puzzle. And then when there was enough that they could recognize the picture, they made contact with me and said, "Well, is this the kind of picture you want to be?"

I couldn't cooperate for a long time because I didn't understand what they were trying to do. There was no sense of "me" in there. They could see the "me," but I couldn't. I couldn't do it. I was like a baby.

Judith just kept hanging in there with me. She'd say, "You're going to get through this. You are this incredible being. You just need a little bit of love. You just didn't get enough love, and I'm going to help you with that." And I bonded with her, and with Robbie, and they became my parents.

They did things like come to my college graduation. They gave me big birthday parties. Judith helped me with my appearance. She got me to start bathing. They encouraged me to have fun and to develop a sense of humor. They kept telling me it was okay to be me, and that I was lovable. They reparented me, and they loved me into life. For that I feel they really gave me life. They really birthed me.

I lived with them twenty-four hours a day, and on top of that, Judith was my therapist. Life was going off and having therapy, and then coming back and watching them practice what she had just told me about. I finally saw that there were two people on the earth who were trustworthy and consistent. And I had never known that before.

I got off my medication. That was terrifying for me. I had to take the gamble that if I lost it and had a psychotic break, Judith would be there for me. And that I could survive without those drugs. Because they had become like a lifeline for me. So what I did was transfer that lifeline over to Judith. And it worked. They literally saved my life.

"I'M NOT CRAZY ANYMORE"

One day, about six months after I came to Spring Hill, Judith and I had this amazing therapy session. She was trying to get me to talk about something that was real hard for me. I was shaking, and I felt myself losing grip with reality, and I kind of started to melt away. And she looked at me and she said, "Don't you understand? Your mother tried to kill your spirit. You did what you needed to do to survive. You did the right thing! You survived and now you can live."

This revelation swept through me. Instead of seeing myself as unworthy, I realized that I had done the right thing. I burst into tears, and I hung onto her, and I started weeping, and I said, "I'm not crazy anymore."

I realized at that moment how far I had come. I felt the integration happening right then. And Judith burst into tears, and she rocked me. And at that point, for the first time, I knew that I had a future. That I had hope, that I could change my life, and that my destiny was not to be psychotic, alienated, and a complete wreck for the rest of my life. It was in my control to heal myself. The past was over, and this was the beginning of the future.

I TOO HAVE WALKED IN THE LAND OF DREAMS

I believe we come into the world to learn certain lessons. The universe is like a central data bank, and each of us is like a terminal. I think we get what we need. I feel very provided for. I feel a lot of gratitude. And it's a natural spillover to want to help other people.

I'll tell you of a healing experience I had in that regard. I was at Ellen's workshop. I wasn't really sure why I was going. I felt like the sexual abuse stuff had been pretty much laid to rest, yet I had this intuition to go. So I went. There was a woman there who was so badly abused that she was also psychotic. And during the first day of the workshop, she went into that psychotic place and was speaking out from there. I was watching her, and I knew where she was. Ellen was working with her, and then there was a cooling-off period.

What was true was this woman was in pieces, and she wasn't able to pull herself back together again. She was kind of like this mess all over the floor. I looked at her and I knew I could say something to her that would have a very healing effect. But it meant exposing my history to a group of women that I didn't know.

Finally I asked myself, "What's more important—your safety or helping her?" And I knew it was to help her. I took a deep breath, and I looked over at her, and I said, "I too have walked in the land of dreams, and I have become real. And I know that you too can become real."

Well, it just broke us both up. I spent the next three and a half days with her in my lap almost all the time. It was an incredible connection. It showed her that it was possible for her to heal. It created the first tangible sign of hope that she had ever had. And what it did for me, on a very concrete level, was show me that I was completely on the other side of the river, and that I could now turn around and offer my hand to someone else. It was the last piece of really knowing that I was whole.

And consequently, the bond that happened between us was so potent that it's very alive for both of us. I feel like she's my kid, and I would do anything for her, because I know, the way Judith knew for me, that there's a way out. And I have dedicated myself to being a guidepost for her. I think helping other people heal is very important in our own healing, keeping it all a circle.

MICHELLE AND ARTEMIS

Because we're sisters, I think we blared through everything at an incredibly high intensity and speed. Having each other to bounce off of has really catalyzed things. As each one of us broke a barrier for ourselves, we broke a barrier for the other person.

Michelle Thomas is thirty-one years old.* She is a counselor and lives with her husband of four years, David, in Boulder, Colorado. Her sister Artemis is thirty-seven. She is a nurse and was recently divorced after a twelve-year marriage.

Michelle and Artemis grew up in Denver. They lived with their mother, their stepfather, and their younger sister, who is now twenty-five. Their stepfather worked for the military and earned a

good income, but they lived in poverty because he gambled. Frequently there was no food in the house.

Both parents were violent alcoholics, and both sexually abused the girls. Their mother abused them mostly in the context of "preparing" them for Ben, their stepfather. She was totally unpredictable—kind one minute and sadistic the next. He was particularly brutal in his abuse, often torturing the girls.

---

* Michelle Thomas and Artemis wanted to use their own names, but couldn't for legal reasons.

MICHELLE: When we were children we never talked about the abuse. It was almost as if we couldn't stand to look at each other—

you know, the victim hating the other victim syndrome.

ARTEMIS: You never knew what you were going to get from who, when. There was never a feeling of safety. When I was eleven, I had an abortion with my stepfather's child and almost died. Michelle was five years old and she was told to take care of me.

At the point of the abortion, I went amnesiac. I clinked out. I was standing at the living room window. It was raining and I just let go of any hold on reality and slipped into a gray fog. I just disappeared and nobody knew it. And I remember the intense feeling of isolation and hopelessness. That's when the splitting began.

There was a daytime Artemis and a nighttime Artemis. They did not know each other existed. The daytime Artemis was very sweet and accommodating. She was the Barbie Doll, whatever anybody needed or wanted me to be. And the other one, the nighttime Artemis, was just a dead person, like a beaten-up pulp of death. I remember I used to act out this thing with our cat. I would dress up in our mother's clothes and I would torture the shit out of this cat. And then I would throw it in the bathroom and lock the door. And then I would take my mother's clothes off and I'd be me, and I'd go take the cat out and really love it. I acted out the split continually. It was a ritual for me. I used to black out and not know how I'd gotten into certain places. Then suddenly I'd wake up and I'd be the daytime person. I only remember coming out of my fog once.

MICHELLE: That was the time we tried to kill our stepfather. I was seven and Artemis was thirteen. I basically talked her into it. I knew I was too small to do the job alone.

ARTEMIS: We made a pact, Michelle and I. Nighttime Artemis stuck a knife in his back when he was sleeping. We punctured his lung, but my mother's a nurse and he never went to the hospital. You know, live with a nurse and you can handle the abuse at home.

My sense of failure at that point was really amazing. I had come out of my fog to kill him for all of us, and I failed.

I remember the daytime Artemis asked my mother sometime in my teens, "I feel like I've tried to kill someone." And she said, "Artemis, you have such a wild imagination." And since the daytime Artemis really didn't remember what happened to the nighttime Artemis, the daytime bought it.

MICHELLE: My stepfather had my mom committed to a number of mental facilities. The message was, if you said anything or you crossed him in any way, it would be very easy for him to institutionalize any of us. And so it was progressively impressed upon us to not go to the outside.

ARTEMIS: And even when we did tell, no one believed us. Michelle told the principal in fifth grade. And I used to draw pictures of what was happening to me and leave them places. I got in a lot of trouble for drawing dirty pictures. I told people I baby-sat for. They'd just go on with their conversation as if I'd never said anything. I remember my exact thought: "I must be telling a lie. Why am I telling a lie?"

MICHELLE: I was just on a straight survival mode. I never did anything that would be your normal teenage routine. Life was very serious. I put myself through school. I worked, I crammed my life as full as I possibly could with outside stimulus. I was a zombie, just going through the motions of being alive.

And then there was my tough guy. We grew up in a tough neighborhood. I always used that as a cover: "I was just a hard kid because of where I grew up." Yet I never got into dope. I needed control much too much to allow myself to get stoned or drunk.

I was very withdrawn. I made sure that nobody knew me. And at the same time, I bounced around in a lot of relationships. There was a revolving door on my bedroom. That lasted until I met David.

I never split like Artemis did. I just stayed there and kicked ass as hard as I could. I made sure that the house ran at least on some existence level. As early as nine I did most of the shopping. I would always come in after the fact and clean up the mess, clean the blood off the kitchen floor, make sure my mom was going to survive, whatever.

ARTEMIS: My coping was very different. I learned the tremendous capabilities of the mind. I could keep myself from feeling pain. I took a lot of drugs. Nothing that addicted me—just so I stayed in the ozone. I screwed around. I hated men. I hated myself.

As an adult, I was either docile and helpless or I would fly into violent rages and get ugly as hell. I'd fix the house up very nice, and I'd try so hard to do things beautiful for myself and for my husband. But I couldn't handle it for long. He'd come home and the house would be in shambles. I would have demolished it.

And my husband would say, "Why did you do it?" And I'd say, "I don't know why."

Things would trigger me off and I'd run down the street just screaming. Or I'd be in a car and kick the windshield in or try to jump out. At this point I hadn't remembered anything about the abuse.

Once I took a knife to my husband. I realized later I was acting out the whole stabbing incident with my stepfather. And then I would turn around and be very nice. That's how split I was. Looking back, I have no idea how I was able to function as a nurse for all those years.

DON'T YOU KNOW I'M POISON?

MICHELLE: In sex I was always the controller and there was always a very fine knife edge between pain and pleasure. I would say where it was going to go, and when it was going to go, and how far.

I had an almost sadistic desire to watch the other person come to a point of pain. I knew how to string it out to a fine degree where they weren't sure if they were in pain or whether it was just slightly pleasurable. I would toy with other people to the point of being cruel. I had been extremely well trained. I was very adept at it.

I had lots of denial about being vulnerable and feminine. It wasn't until I came into a soft relationship with a strong woman that I learned not to be in that dominant role in sex. From her I learned to touch and to feel because it was safe.

ARTEMIS: I was never cruel or sadistic sexually. I was always just the victim. I would seduce a lot of people into bed, and then I'd disappear and not feel anything. I also had a big appetite for sex, a lot of actual physical desire, which confused me, and I hated it. It was the most disgusting, degrading thing to actually want sex.

With my husband, who was a very gentle man, I got more destructive. It was like "Don't love me. Don't you know I'm poison?" I would often get hysterical and start beating at him, screaming "I'm a whore. I'm a whore. Can't you see how ugly I am?"

And then he'd say, "Artemis, no." Because he loved me, he sincerely loved me. He'd say that and I'd go into absolute hysteria. I'd go about definitely proving to him how evil I was. I'd start smashing everything in the room or myself with a knife or everything in the room with a knife. It would then be a matter of him trying to save us both.

He'd say, "Artemis, don't close off to me. I'll stay right here till you're ready, but don't close off." And then he'd say, "Okay, can I reach out to you?" And he'd gradually reach out to me, and then slowly I'd be able to climb out of this hole I was in and reach out to him.

MICHELLE: When I first remembered the abuse, I went through long periods of "Don't touch me." Then when I started feeling sexual again, I tried to go back and do the same kind of sexual controlling I had always done with David, and it didn't work. I'd crack up laughing in the middle of it.

My domination and cruelty had been connected to my fear of feeling. People set up scenarios to keep from feeling particular things. If you're going to go to that elaborate way of making sure that you don't feel something soft, something's going on.

I didn't make serious changes in my sexuality until I was willing to make a commitment to my partner around monogamy. I mean monogamy was the equivalent of being imprisoned. It had the potential of a man being in control of me again. But it wasn't until I made that commitment that I was able to explore my own feelings of sexuality and sensuality.

ARTEMIS: And I remember coming to a place where I let myself admit that I loved my husband. That was a big taboo. I mean, you can let a man beat you, you can let him rape you, you can hate him, but you can't love a man. Sincerely care for a man? That was against all the rules of the universe and God was going to strike me down for sure. It's almost like that was more humiliating than being raped and being beaten and tortured. That fresh, wonderful feeling of just loving him. And I did love him.

IF I HAD BEEN ALONE, I WOULD NEVER HAVE BELIEVED IT

ARTEMIS: Before I even began remembering the abuse, I had a dream in which a friend stood at my bedroom window with a long scroll and said, "You have to remember, Artemis. You have to remember." And I had no idea what I was supposed to remember.

MICHELLE: I always remembered the alcohol and the neglect. But I didn't remember anything about the sexual abuse until I was in a very safe relationship. David and I were driving from Boulder to Denver. All of a sudden I saw my stepfather's face and knew what had happened. His face just kind of hung outside the window, and when I turned to look at David, he was Ben. I remember going very white and afraid, and throughout the rest of that night, I progressively became more conscious of what that fear and those feelings were. I knew why I hated him so much.

After I started remembering, I lost a couple of jobs because I couldn't handle being in the outside world. I virtually did not leave my house for three months. I thought I was insane. I would find myself sitting in a room and hearing my stepfather and my mother, or hearing scenes before I saw pictures. And I thought, "This is it. You're crazy, kid. You're hearing voices so you are possessed."

ARTEMIS: That thing of being possessed and being of the devil was something we were always told: "Devil's daughter. Devil's child. You're evil, and someday everybody's going to find out how evil you are."

MICHELLE: For the first couple of years, I didn't have any pictures. I knew that I had been sexually abused by my stepfather. I didn't know to what degree. I just started becoming aware that my actions toward other people, the way I would respond to things, everything I did from breathing onward, seemed related to what had happened as a child. There wasn't a part of me I liked.

ARTEMIS: I was the opposite of Michelle. I didn't start remembering until everything that was secure around me left. My husband and I separated.

Our youngest sister got married. Michelle and I were driving home from the wedding. I don't remember what led up to it, but Michelle looked at me and said, "Did anything happen to you?"

And I said, "No, nothing ever happened to me. But I always had these dreams." And so I told her the dreams and she looked me straight in the face and said, "Those were not dreams, Artemis." And it just cracked. It was like a lightning bolt hit me and my head opened up. And I knew. My God, they were not dreams.

That night I did not sleep. I kept the light on all night, and just remembered. I had no control over the memories. But I had done a lot of meditation, so I knew there was some part of my brain where I could sit in a calm and neutral place. In the midst of experiencing it very intensely, I climbed into that one little corner of myself that could view it neutrally.

MICHELLE: You get to the point where you realize that the memory is only a memory. You already lived through it the first time, and it can't hurt you anymore. And if you can just take the observer role and watch it, then the fear of going crazy goes away. But that fear was there for the longest time.

I remember coming up against a picture and fighting it for days: "No, I'm not going to see this. Because if I see this, I'll go crazy. If I see this, I'll disappear." And finally I came to a place where I knew I needed to see the pictures, and I would actually chase after them.

I believed the memories right away, but believing another human being could do those things to a child was where the doubt came in.

ARTEMIS: I never would have believed the memories if I hadn't been able to call Michelle and tell her, "This is what happened." And she'd say, "Yes, it did happen. And here's the other part of it." Between the two of us we were able to put the puzzle pieces together.

MICHELLE: For a long time, I didn't realize how bad these things were. It had been such a way of life that I just accepted it. It wasn't until I could bounce it off somebody else and see their reaction that it sank in.

ARTEMIS: There were times I felt I was going to go under with the memories. The agony was so awful, and the aloneness. The feeling was, nobody loves someone who needs. Everyone is afraid of the rawness of pure human need, so don't let anybody see.

But finally I said, "Fuck it! I'm going to look myself and I'm not going to be afraid to let anyone else see." Because everybody's human. So I just dove into that aloneness completely, and dove all the way through it until I was no longer afraid of the intensity of my need as a human being.

FACING THE SHAME

ARTEMIS: I've done everything in the damn book that's wrong, or had it done to me. And I realize the integrity of who I am in the face of all that. I'd worn that cloak of shame and it branded itself into my skin. But I found out that I could take it off, even if it meant taking my skin off along with it. I could grow back new skin that was healthy and good.

What helped me do that was allowing myself to be deeply loved. I allowed myself to be loved in the places where I felt the ugliest and most ashamed of myself. And I don't mean physical places.

MICHELLE: I'm in a marriage where there's total, unconditional love—to do the most horrible rotten things you can do to a person and to have them be accepting of you, and love that ugliness in you, until you yourself can love that ugliness. And that ugliness and that shame turns into something very soft and very warm and very beautiful inside of yourself.

The particular incident I'm thinking of is the time I was staying at Artemis's house. I remember reading, for the third time, *If I Die Before I Wake*. I was by myself. And I was in a total state of agony and numbness at the same time, if you can do that. The world could have disappeared and I wouldn't have known it. I was feeling the shame and the ugliness that had surrounded my life so intensely, and feeling horribly alone, like I had no right to be alive because I was the carrier of all this horrendous atrocity. And that day, I dove into that self-destructiveness because I knew I had to or I would never get to the other side.

There were knives in the house, which were my favorite tool as a child. As a kid I would sit and carve and just watch the blood to know I was alive. There are scars on my body and I have no idea where they came from. I couldn't tell you which ones I inflicted and which ones were inflicted upon me. When I was twelve, I realized I could kill myself, so I quit. This was the first time since then that I'd had that feeling again. And so I got myself out of the house.

I walked to the top of a steep cliff, watching the ocean and thinking about different ways that I could kill myself. I thought about jumping off the cliff. I thought of this whole series of things, one, to intensify the pain, and two, to get away from it. And I looked down and I happened to be sitting right in the middle of poison oak.

I remember very vividly thinking about my mother, thinking that staying alive didn't matter because she never loved me. She never cared. I finally faced that I'd never had a mother, and I never would.

And so, sobbing, I just picked up handfuls of poison oak and rubbed it into my skin from head to toe. After doing that I felt better. There was always a release with the carving—and this time with the poison oak—because somebody on the outside could see the pain that was a constant on the inside.

And then I went and sat on the steps outside Artemis's house and waited until somebody came home. And I told both David and Artemis what I had done.

ARTEMIS: You risked being vulnerable and we both were there for you. I think that was the day you lost your hard guy.

MICHELLE: Yeah. I did. You just loved me. Even with what I had done. So to heal shame, you just dive right into that shame and you risk letting somebody love you inside of that.

WE LITERALLY RERAISED OURSELVES

ARTEMIS: Bringing my two selves together was a long, slow process. There was a time when I had to go back to being a young child. I had to learn to feel and reach out and touch the world. For a while I went around and touched everything. It was so magical just to feel things that were soft. It was magical that I could feel my feet in shoes, my legs in my pants, how the cloth felt on my body. And be able to say, "It's safe to feel." Just the thing of feeling a pencil on paper. I was ecstatic.

MICHELLE: That's the intense integration process that happens. You raise that two-year-old to a five-year-old and then you bring the five-year-old up. You have to function in the outside world as an adult, but part of you inside is growing up. Remember the little notes we'd write and leave around the house?

ARTEMIS: Oh, yeah: "It's okay to feel safe in my room. It's okay to feel safe in my house." All these little reminders. I also remember when I became aware that I took up space. I had volume. I was not just a thought. I was not just flat; there was a behind to me, a side to me. And other people took up space too, and there was space between us through which we could reach. At first that was extremely threatening because that also meant there was a space between us that they could hurt me in.

NO LONGER WOULD ABUSE BE THE CAUSE AND MY LIFE THE EFFECT

MICHELLE: I had always considered myself a chalkboard that somebody erased really fast. And there was a little scratch of a piece of chalk here, and here. If you've ever had a sloppy teacher, you know what that looks like. And I was angry about that. I wanted to know where I'd been in this life. Yet there was a fear. What if it's just too horrible? And it *was* horrible. It was pretty damn close.

And then you get to the point of "Well, I lived through it once and it didn't kill me. Somehow I managed to survive it that time and I had a hell of a lot less resources than I do now. It's time to face it."

So you face, and you face, and you face, and you continue to face each aspect of yourself. You have to remember and claim each individual experience. Acknowledge that it happened. Acknowledge that you lived through it.

I realized why I would always position my bed in a particular part of the room. I realized there wasn't an aspect of my life that wasn't somehow a response to the abuse. The way I walked. The way I breathed. There was nothing about me, at some point during this healing process, that I haven't confronted and changed. I have totally metamorphosed.

And then I had to face that person who was my mother. And there was a period of "I hate you because you did that." And "Why did you do that?" You ask, "Was there some way as a child I unknowingly invited all of that?" And you come up with the answer, "No, there's no way."

And then I blamed my mother for being in her own agony so much that she wasn't willing to challenge herself, if for no other reason than to save her kids.

And you hate. And you hurt. And you hate yourself. And you hate the mess that you're in. And you'd love to run away. And I think as the stages progress, there are parts of the cycle that recur. Each time it *looks* like you're going

through the same thing, but it's elevated just a little bit. And you have to come to a position of trust that "Okay, I'm facing this thing again. There's a reason I need to face it from this particular position. There's something I didn't learn before."

Then I stepped out of my own life to see where my stepfather was coming from. He had also been sexually and physically abused by his parents. My mother told me that. And I know that she had been abused. I slowly started to see the other people's positions in the whole play. And once I did that, I was able to make that quantum leap of no longer identifying with my past.

ARTEMIS: For me the decision not to identify with the past was a decision, not just a change I went through in the healing process. I had to make a quantum leap that I was no longer going to have the abuse be the cause and my life be the effect. And to say "I am me, whole and complete." I'm able to do that because now I do have an identity, a whole person that I have given birth to, that the people who love me have given birth to.

MICHELLE: The identification as an abused person can be a prison in itself. I had to say, "I'm just going to risk who I am here and now, without that identity." It's almost a rebirthing. You change your birthright.

ARTEMIS: It's like "Where are you *now? Right now* you have to choose what standpoint you are going to live life from." And it's a constant choice. Every time I'm in a situation where I start acting in those same patterns and my mind says, "I need this security, I need these ways of manipulation, and it's because of what happened to me," I have to say, "No! *No!*" Sometimes I'll be in a state of terrible limbo because I'm not sure what to do instead.

It's still a constant decision for me. I've been alive for thirty-seven years and the groove on that record is pretty deep, but I pick up that needle and move it over.

For me the hardest part was letting go of the right to hate. It was letting go of the right to be confused and messed up because of what had happened to me. Because I did have a right to those things. And they were treasures, but if I wanted to heal all the way, I had to give them up.

I mean I grew up waking up in the morning in a pool of my own vomit and my own blood. And I grew up having to wake myself up in the morning, having to clean myself up and get ready for school alone. I lived it. I grew up being raped at knifepoint by somebody I was supposed to be able to trust. I had a right to hate. I had a right to get even. And I did!

Until finally I realized, "I'm destroying myself because of this. As long as I hold on to my right to hate, I am limiting myself. I'm the only one who's putting the prison walls around me now. Because there's no one raping me anymore. There's nobody torturing me anymore. I am surrounded now by nothing but loving people." I realized I loved myself too much to keep myself in that prison, and so I let go of my hate for *me*. It was a real inside job.

I experienced some damn heavy things and I've come through it. I've come through with an intense love for myself and an intense amount of love even for that man who was called my stepfather. I have struggled intensely, and I have come into a state of real forgiveness, to the point where I feel love for him. I have never seen him again, but I don't feel fear anymore. It goes all the way straight through me, clean.

MICHELLE: But you can't fake it. There's a fine line between denial and moving on. You can't forgive someone until you're ready. I went through a phase of trying to be magnanimous and forgive before I was ready, and I got smacked right in the face with it. It was like a boomerang.

There is no way to move on without total acceptance of each place where you are. You have to accept yourself as the awakener, as the victim, as not wanting to be the victim, and then as the survivor. And you have to go through all the pain and agony and pride of being that survivor before you can move beyond that to warrior status.

Each step becomes a sweater that you wear and it keeps you warm and it keeps you safe until you grow out of it. Then the sweater gets tight and starts pinching you. You say, "I'm never going to let go of this sweater." And it's not until that sweater becomes so outrageously uncomfortable that you just *have* to take it off that you take a chance that maybe you'll find something else to take its place. You have to be willing to accept the next void, at any given point in time, in order to be able to fill it.

ARTEMIS: I had a sense, even when I was in the deepest hell, of something that said "I'll get you out of this. Don't worry. Trust me." I don't know what to call it. I don't know if that's called spiritual awakening. But I trusted it. And that for me is where the healing really happened. When I felt connected to that part of myself, it healed the rest of me.

MICHELLE: I didn't go to much therapy. I wasn't inclined that way, to be honest, because I haven't found anybody who could stay ahead of me. "How am I going to give my trust over to somebody to guide me when I don't feel they're any more capable than I am?" Mostly I've utilized my own resources. I can process and analyze things up one side and down the other. And my stubbornness really helped.

ARTEMIS: I didn't go to therapy either. Because as a teenager it meant someone trying to throw me in the hospital and put me on drugs. And when I did try counseling they identified me so much as a victim that I could hardly get past their image of me.

But even though I didn't go to therapy, I did not do it alone. I had people around me who had deep insights into me as a person, who knew the reality of my intrinsic self, who were able to hold it for me even when I couldn't hold it for myself. Their belief in me was like a magnet which pulled me through.

I realized I didn't want to be loved *because* I had survived these things. I want to be loved and cared for for who I am. And it's a fine line. I'm not ashamed of what happened to me. But I don't want that to be an excuse through which some-

one loves me. Or the only reason I can say, "I need."

When I need, I immediately lapse into that person who was desperately needy and could not have any of those needs filled. I want to be able to say "I need" because I'm a woman alive *today*, without having to throw myself back into being the victim. I want to risk coming as a person needing *now*, because I'm a human being, not because of what happened to me.

COMING OVER THE RISE

MICHELLE: I think when I learned that I could have a sense of humor, that it was okay to laugh at things, that it was okay to be joyful in the world, was when I started having hope.

Now there's amusement in my life. I realized there were things in life that were actually designed to be enjoyable, that I didn't always have to struggle at being alive. It's like coming over a rise and all of a sudden you see in the horizon a world that you've never experienced before. You have no idea what's going to happen to you. It's all brand-new. The world starts opening up. You slow down enough to feel the trees. To notice light and shade and shadow. To notice sounds. And to start expanding your life in other ways. And that's an even bigger challenge than the one you just came from.

MARY McGRATH

Incest is not a taboo. Talking about it is a taboo.

Mary McGrath is forty-eight years old.* She grew up in Nevada. She is Scottish and French. Raised as a fundamentalist, she went to Lutheran churches throughout her teen years and early adulthood. At age twenty she married an alcoholic, and she stayed in that marriage for almost twenty years. She has five grown children. After leaving her husband, Mary came out as a lesbian. She now lives with her lover of two years and earns her living as a massage therapist.

Mary has one sister. They were both molested by their stepfather. The incest started when Mary was seven and continued through her teen years.

* Mary McGrath chose to use a pseudonym.

The two girls shared a room, and they would talk about what was going on: "Because we could give each other support, we were clear from the beginning that he was the bad guy, so we never had the confusion many victims have."

Three years after our stepfather started molesting us, we told our mother. Mother had a classic reaction: "You never liked him. He's so good to you. You're just making this up." Years later, when I was in my thirties, she told us she had believed us and had in fact told him to stop.

Sometime in high school the molestation stopped, but he still used to stand in the doorway and watch us dress, or leave us weird notes. His intrusive behavior continues even to this day if we're not really strong about setting limits and boundaries. Mother stayed married to him until she died last year. So we had to keep dealing with him.

I never had a warm relationship with my mother. It was mostly "Don't rock the boat." "Present this facade to the world and Mother will be happy." I never forgot the incest, but I did minimize it to please my mother for many years.

LIFE WAS DOING

I developed a victim stance in life. I married an alcoholic. Like a martyr I said, "You put up with. You hang in there." There was a whole lot of "I'll wait and see if this helps." I'd say, "It must be me. It must be how I keep house. It must be how I take care of the kids." I just kept waiting, and blaming myself. I was a co-alcoholic. I thought I could fix it: "I'll love him and he'll be fine."

My greatest denial of the incest had been presenting myself as this happy, bubbly kid. I did the same thing with my own family when I grew up. I presented myself to the world as a self-assured, fun, together person. "It doesn't matter what's really going on. Keep up appearances."

I did the same thing with the alcoholism that I did with the incest: Be active in church, be friendly with the neighbors. People were dumbfounded when they found out we had a problem.

I kept everything totally superficial. Life was doing. You got up and did what you had to around the house. You figured out bills and shopping and getting through the day. There were brief moments of intimacy, but intimacy wasn't something I thought of, or understood, or realized I needed.

The main exception was my sister. Because of our common experience, I could be more real with her. And then there were my kids. I got a lot of my needs for closeness met with my kids. I still do, but that's shifted. I know now I can't own my kids.

MY BODY IS AS MUCH A PART OF ME AS MY HEAD AND HEART

I didn't feel associated with my body for many years. I was really all mental until my mid-thirties. I've brought my center down out of my head after ten years of body work. Now I know my body is as much a part of me as my head or my heart. And as I've gotten in touch with my body, I've gotten in touch with my feelings and vice versa.

I had been totally alienated from my feelings. That's how I protected myself all those years. It took me forever to feel a feeling, much less express it. People would say to me, "How do you feel?" and I'd say, "Well, I think . . ." It was like learning a totally different language. It was a process of getting things intellectually, then at a feeling level, and finally being able to act from that position.

I did not view myself as a sexual person. I was a virgin when I married. My sexual relationship in my marriage was good compared to other marriages I knew. I was orgasmic. My sex life seemed satisfactory to me. But I was shut down in terms of being able to *be* a sexual person. Sex was something you *did* and once in a while you enjoyed it. The message was "Don't be a sexual person," or "Be one, but only in a compartmentalized way." I mean, obviously, if I was going to get married, I was going to have sex.

There were prescribed things that were okay, but I wasn't willing to explore. My husband wasn't complaining. He was happy with the number of times we had sex. So there was nothing pushing me to move those boundaries. And that's how it was throughout an eighteen-year marriage.

COMING OUT

As my marriage ended, I fell in love with a woman, and that was like the change between night and day. There's change that comes slow and you work on it, and then there's change that's like a complete reversal. The very first time I was with this woman, I had no inhibitions, no guardedness.

I guess I thought, "If I can do this (be with a woman at all), then I can let this side of me down." I didn't have any problem feeling it was sick or immoral. I knew there would be problems as far as how the world perceived me, but I didn't have any other issues with lesbianism, even though I'd been a churchgoer all that time. It was like being let out of a cage, and suddenly I was in touch with a part of me that I didn't even know was there.

Now I enjoy my sexuality tremendously. If I feel it, I express it. Even if it's a hug or a kiss on the ear. I won't ever shut it down again. It's not that my lover always has to respond. It's just that I won't ever say, "I can't show this part of myself. She's had a hard day at the office." Life is so much more of a turn-on being in touch with that. I don't mean wanting sex ten times a day. I mean

responding to things, visually and tactilely. It's put me in touch with my senses.

I WAS IN AND OUT OF THERAPY MOST OF THE TIME

Phase one of my healing was sharing it with my sister, never letting the memory get too far away from us. Phase two started when I was thirty-seven years old, and it's involved a good ten years of healing. During that time, if I felt like I needed to do body work, I'd work with a body work therapist. If I felt like I needed something else, I'd find the right person for that.

My first therapy experience was very cerebral, very verbal. We worked on feelings, but it was elementary. It probably was all I could handle. My therapist was a warm, nurturing, supportive person, and that's really what I needed at the time.

The second time, I was in couples therapy with my woman lover. That was a problem-solving kind of therapy.

At one point I did some body therapy work. I don't know if I would have made that leap if I hadn't been training to be a body worker myself. I knew those therapies existed, and I was willing to try it. But it was real scary.

I did work on a mat, trying to get in touch with the feelings in my body when my stepfather was about to molest me. I did lots of screaming and kicking. I remember at the time thinking, "This is dumb." But it helped me feel different *in* my body. I had real severe muscle spasms in my back on and off for years. They were crippling. They're almost totally gone now.

I did some rage work with Elisabeth

Kübler-Ross. I used to think, "You've been through this and you can't even feel rage? You have no rage? I find that hard to believe!" But I was just terrified—knowing I couldn't feel it, but that it was there.

Elisabeth Kübler-Ross tends to attract people who have had trauma in their lives. There were people who had been battered as children, people who had lost children through murder and accidents, all kinds of things.

She has people work in a large group with telephone books and rubber hoses. Her basic theory is that if feelings aren't expressed, they're internalized, and that's what contributes to us being physically sick and having pain. And as we release our feelings, we begin to heal.

Doing the actual rage work wasn't scary. In fact, it was very exciting. It's such a safe environment with so much love, you have the feeling you can do or say anything. It's okay if you bash in your stepfather's face with a rubber hose. I remember thinking, "This isn't so bad. This isn't going to kill anybody." Every once in a while I'd stop, look around the room, and think, "No way, that didn't come from me!" I had totally shredded a Denver phone book, just obliterated it, and still more to come. I'd have to catch my breath or blow my nose, and I remember looking at the devastation and thinking, "My God! That was all inside!" I was flabbergasted at how much rage there was.

After all that release, I started having powerful dreams. In one, I was lying in bed as a teenager. I felt my stepdad was in the room. I'd always thought if I could only scream, I could stop it. And in the dream, I did. I literally did. I let out a piercing, bloodcurdling scream. I was able to scream and stop it.

I HAVE TAKEN CONTROL

There were times when I thought I was through the whole healing process. About fifteen of those times! I'd say to myself, "Now I've done incest. Now I'm through." I understand, finally, that you never really get to the end. Not until you die.

For instance, my mother's death brought up the whole new thing: What do I do with my stepfather now that she's dead? Do I take responsibility for his connection with the children? What limits do I set, and what do I do if he doesn't honor those limits?

I don't want a warm, friendly relationship with him. I don't. Even if he hadn't been my incest offender, I still wouldn't want it. What I'd like to have—the ideal—would be no funny energy with him, where I could see him, say hello and talk on a surface level, and not feel I have to watch where I stand. I still feel real vulnerable. I have to be constantly on guard: "Is he going to try to corner me and talk about something that will make me feel weird?"

He doesn't ever quit. I would tell him not to hug me, and so he would sit *way* down on the other end of the couch and pout. In front of a roomful of my children he would say, "I *hope* this is acceptable."

When my mother died, my stepfather starting sending me and my sister incest articles. I thought, "This might be his convoluted way of saying 'I'm sorry,' " but my feeling was, "This is more incest offense. If he has something to say, he needs to learn to say it. And if he's working through something, then the victim is not who he works it through with. He goes to the shrink and he pays good money. I'm not going to be his therapist."

I sent the article back and I said, "I have never been real clear with you about what the boundaries were. Now I'm going to spell them out. The boundaries are no hugging, no touching except for a handshake. No discussion or information about sex, sexual preference, incest, sexual assault of any kind. What is acceptable is, 'How is your job going? How are the kids? What's the weather?' It has to be within these boundaries; watch my lips. And if you cannot honor this, then I am ready to discontinue communication with you." I also told him, "I am not willing to work this through with you. If indeed you are trying to say 'I'm sorry,' then you need to get a therapist to do that with you." I put all that in a letter. My sister did the same thing, and we mailed them to him.

I got no reply, except my usual little Christmas check. That's been all.

I think the most important thing for incest families is to have no more secrets and no more "We're not going to talk about this." To keep silent is to continue to protect the offender. Part of the result of his abusive behavior is that he has to deal with the consequences within his own family. Not only for the sake of that family, but for the sake of ending incest in America, we need to quit having any secrets about it at all.

We need to quit taking care of anybody. If Mother can't handle it that's her problem. If the incest offender can't handle it, that's his problem. We as survivors have to do what we have to do.

HEALING IS SOMETHING I'VE INTEGRATED INTO MY LIFE

A big part of healing for me has been learning that I have power and options. I decided I didn't like not being responsible for my own life: "If he would just stop drinking. If she would only get her shit together." That was nice in one way—there was always someone else to blame. But it kept me stuck. Finally I got tired of blaming. I decided I wasn't going to be a victim anymore. And instead of saying "I want to survive this," I started to say "I want my life to be different." I wanted more than just to be able to go back to my hometown without throwing up. I wanted to make real changes.

I take a lot of responsibility for my own healing. It's been pretty continuous, not like a roller coaster, more like a steady level with a couple of high peaks. One thing that's been helpful to me lately is not to try so hard. What I say to myself is "I don't have to *do* anything, but I have to *be* open to my feelings and not shut down." *Trying* shut me down. It kept me feeling bad about myself: "I'm not doing enough. I'm not doing it right." I don't feel I have to push through things anymore. I just have to be open. Healing isn't separate anymore. It's just a regular part of life.

GIZELLE

Though I still become caught in fear and anger, each day I become more aware of the power I possess to choose love. The most powerful words given me during this painful process of healing came from Martin Luther King, Sr.: "No matter what you do to me, I will not give you the power to make me hate."

Gizelle is forty-two years old and lives in Santa Cruz, California.* She was born in Newton, Massachusetts, the second of four girls in an Ital-ian Catholic family. Her father was a surgeon at a prominent New England hospital. Gizelle was dressed in Saks Fifth Avenue clothes, had ballet and piano lessons, and was sent to private schools and expensive colleges.

Gizelle has been married and divorced twice, and has a sixteen-year-old daughter, Adrienne. Gizelle has suffered much of her life with disabling illness. Just three and a half months before this interview took place, she remembered the violent rape she experienced at age three. She now under-

---

* Gizelle wanted to use her own name, but couldn't for legal reasons. Of her pseudonym Gizelle says, "The name I have chosen belongs to a Canadian friend, a woman who is making her own healing journey from sexual abuse. Her story and mine are not the same; however, I have chosen her name (with her permission) so that I can honor yet another brave and beautiful woman. This lessens the pain of having my own name deleted."

stands that this caused the emotional and physical problems she has had all her life.*

I WAS SOUND ASLEEP IN MY ROOM

It was soon after I was born that my father went away to Burma and spent two years in a MASH unit in the jungle, putting together blown-up bodies. When he came back, he was unable to work. He was in a lot of emotional difficulty. One of his best friends had committed suicide right after the war.

I really don't think my mother and he could relate when he came home. They hadn't seen each other in almost three years. She was expecting her husband to come home, and that's not really what came back.

And I was very small. All I had in my mind were pictures of Daddy. I was very open and very loving. And so, as I gather from my mother, he spent a great deal of time taking care of me. I was his human link to affection and comfort.

The rape happened the month of my third birthday, right after he returned. I was sound asleep in my bedroom. I woke up with my father's penis in my mouth. The impact of it thrust my head back and literally cut off my wind and I thought I was dying. I didn't know what was in my mouth. I didn't know what a penis was. I just woke up with this whatever-it-was shoved down my throat, suffocating, gagging.

And then he took his penis out of my mouth and began raping me vaginally. As soon as his penis left my mouth, I threw up. I didn't make a sound. I remember him banging, trying to get into me, and then he ripped me open and actually entered me and I let out a terrified scream. Within seconds he was gone, and I was alone and the room was empty.

And then within seconds after that, my mother came into the room and put on the light. She found me lying in bed covered with blood and vomit all over the sheets. And she went into immediate hysteric denial. She wouldn't compute. She refused to compute. So what she computed, in her craziness, was that I had done this to me. That I had somehow done this to myself.

She started screaming at me, "Bad, evil, wicked child." Even at that point, I still had my knowledge that I hadn't done this. I knew my father had been the one who had done it by his smell and the whole feel of him, even though it was dark.

And so I screamed back to my mother, "Mommy I didn't do it. I didn't do it. It was Daddy." Then my mother was hitting me, over and over again. "Don't you ever say that again. You lying, evil, dirty, filthy child." She just kept hitting me and hitting me.

She cleaned up the sheets, put me back in bed. She was still screaming, she was still hysterical. Through a lot of the beating I maintained, "I didn't do it, Mommy. I didn't do it." It's amazing that at age three, in the face of being raped and beaten, I was able to say that I was innocent.

Then my mother left the room. She was still screaming at my father. He hit her across the face, said for her to go to her room. "I'll take care of it." And then the next memory I have is my father, whose of-

---

* Since this interview, Gizelle has remembered other incidents of molestation that continued throughout her childhood.

fice was downstairs in our house, sewing my vagina back up, without any anesthetic. I was never taken to the hospital.

He put me back into bed. Then he left the room and I was alone. And I remember feeling my bed was all sticky and wet. That must have been the blood. I was a little girl, and I was thinking, "I'm a bad girl. I got my bed all sticky and wet." So by then I was beginning to buy the other reality.

Suddenly, as I was lying there, my grandmother, who was living with us, came quietly creeping down the hall and into my room. She put her hand on my head. My feeling as I reexperienced it was that if my grandmother had not come in and put her hand on my head, I was going into this no-man's-land where I might never come back. But when she put her hand on my head, it brought me back. I kept saying "Nanny, I'm a bad girl." She didn't say a word. She just kept stroking my head.

The next morning my mother and father went away on a vacation. I was left with my grandmother. I remember going to get out of bed. I wanted to play. But I couldn't move and I couldn't get out of bed. I said to my grandmother, "What happened? I can't get out of bed. I hurt." And her message to me was "Don't talk about it. Pretend it didn't happen. I'll take care of you. It'll go away." So I forgot it.

IT ALL FITS NOW

The effects of the abuse manifested through my body. I sleepwalked. I had high fevers that were life-threatening. And they could never find a cause. I had nightmares. I had severe asthma. I would just stop breathing. I was at the doctor's all the time. I was in the bed, always sick. My legs were turned out so badly that I could not walk without tripping over my own feet. I had to wear corrective shoes. It all fits now.

I had a great deal of compulsive behavior as a child. I structured my world so incredibly. I had to open and close doors twice and I'd have to hear them click. I had to do everything in pairs. I made everybody repeat things twice and I repeated everything twice. I developed a compulsive head spasm. The feeling was always that something was out of place and that if I could just shake my head, everything would click back into focus. It was always a feeling that something was just out of whack. So I developed all of these things to give some shape to my reality, to create some boundaries and some safety.

I split my father into two different people, because there was no other way to sit across the breakfast table from him. The man who came down and sat at the kitchen table was my father. The man who came in the middle of the night and molested me was a shadow. I made him into someone else.

And as I split him into two, I split myself into two. There was the little girl whose father taught her to ride a bike, who got A's and became a perfectionist. And then there was the little girl who played in the attic, felt that she was dying, wanted to commit suicide, had nightmares. But I never could speak of her. Her voice had been taken away.

I felt caught, trapped in my body. That's continued into adulthood. I never heard any messages from my body. I would be really sick and I'd stagger around and go to work. I made a lifetime dedication of not listening to my body, because if I had, I would have had to hear that I was raped, and I couldn't do that and survive.

I developed an eating disorder when I was eighteen, which they now call anorexia nervosa. I was at college. I felt obese if I weighed over ninety-five pounds. When I ate, I would eat alone. I would never let anyone see me eat. I'd starve myself. I'd have a hard-boiled egg and half a piece of toast and that would be my quota for the day. And I would do that for three or four days. Then I would go to the store for a quart of ice cream and eat it all in one sitting.

I understand now it was a terror of becoming a woman. That was just the age when I was beginning to integrate my sexuality. As I started to go out with men, the terror was there. There was no way to deal with it but to somehow stop myself from being a woman. If you stop eating, you don't have hips, you don't have breasts, your periods stop. You are not a woman; therefore you can't have sex, you can't be raped.

It wasn't until I was twenty-three and I got pregnant with my daughter that I began to eat like a normal human being. Having a healthy child became the most important thing to me, and so I taught myself to eat right.

I OWE MY DAUGHTER MY LIFE

From the moment my daughter was born, my instincts kicked in, and I was able to nurture her and be intimate with her. Somehow my love and my desire that this child would not be hurt were strong enough to overcome the obstacles that stopped me in other areas of my life. And I don't know how. I literally can say I owe my daughter my life because she awakened that ability to mother. Time and again, when for myself I would have died, I chose to live for her. I knew that somehow this had to stop with me and that I would not pass it on to my daughter. And I didn't even know what the "it" was.

I remember very distinctly that when my daughter was the age I had been when I was raped, I began to distance myself from her. She came to me in tears and said, "Mommy, you don't like me anymore." I put my arms around her and I said, "Adrienne, you've got to understand. Something happened to Mommy when she was very little. And you remind me of what happened. It's not you. You're fine. I love you. It's me. There's something in Mommy. I was hurt very badly when I was young, and that's why I'm not holding you." That's all I could tell her. I didn't even remember the rape at the time.

I COULDN'T GO ON

When Adrienne was five, I developed chronic back and hip problems. I became crippled by the pain. It got worse and worse. I was in and out of the hospital for back surgery. I lost the feeling in my left leg. I was in traction. And I was a single mother when this was happening.

I knew it was all connected to what was happening emotionally, so I went for counseling. But whatever I did, I was besieged with terror associated with severe nerve pain in my pelvis. I had anxiety attacks so bad I couldn't move. I was in severe depression. I cried all the time. I couldn't even read a book. I couldn't sleep. I couldn't eat.

One morning, when I was thirty-eight and my daughter was almost twelve, I took a lot of pills. I never said anything to anybody.

I just knew I couldn't go on in the kind of pain I was in, that I had tried everything I could think of. As I said, it was not just the physical pain, but the terror that hooked into the physical pain. The two completely overwhelmed me.

That suicide attempt didn't work, and I went into counseling again. The pain got worse and worse. I started receiving epidural blocks, which alleviated some of the pain. And they gave me antidepressants.

All through this, I was working with my dreams. I went to an American Indian power circle and something happened, like a dam breaking, and I started crying. There was an older Mexican-Indian woman there who worked with me. I did Lomi body work —a combination of breath and deep tissue massage. And I started moving through some of the pain.

And then everything froze and I began to get severe nerve pain in my neck, and a terror that was as bad as the terror around the pain in my pelvis. It totally immobilized me again. I couldn't even mother during that time. My daughter was mothering me. I felt like I was destroying my daughter's life. I felt guilty for being alive. I made the decision once again to kill myself. That led to suicide attempt number four.

This time all I can say is that my survival was a miracle. I took enough pills and alcohol to kill me twice over. I said a prayer just before I took the drugs. It was "I no longer can live and believe in a God of suffering." One of my last acts was to tear that God down, and I said, "If there is another reason for me being alive besides extended suffering, then I surrender into your hands."

I was not found for twenty-four hours. That was how I planned it. I was in a motel and the maid found me. I was in a coma. And they rushed me to the hospital. They said I wasn't going to live, and that if I did live, I wouldn't have a brain.

The doctors did a last-ditch measure where they took all the blood out of my body and recirculated it through a charcoal screen, and then put it back in my body. It worked, and I started to stabilize. The third day of the coma they said I would live, but that I might be a basket case. And then on the seventh day, I came out of the coma.

I had a vision as I was coming out of the coma which has stayed with me through my entire healing process. I had a vision of a tree which was in blossom. All over the tree were the most incredibly beautiful flowers I had ever seen in my life. And the tree was growing out of the desert.

I came out of the coma and I did have a brain.

Unbeknownst to me, my daughter had sat by my bed for seven days and seven nights. She was driving herself to the hospital. She was fourteen years old at the time. It was her life force that connected with mine and brought me back. I felt it the minute I came to. That was a year and a half ago.

WE BOTH NEEDED HELP

The psychiatrist gave me a list of counselors I could see and sent me home. I looked at Adrienne and I saw that she had no energy left whatsoever, that she had used every ounce she had to bring me back. So I took her by the hand and got in the car and drove down to the Parents Center and walked in the door and said, "We both need counseling. We both need help." I hooked my daughter up immediately. She had a lot of anger about the situation and we had to work that out.

Then I looked at the list the psychiatrist had given to me and I called a therapist and got started. I hooked up with Frank Lanou, who has been my counselor and guide through this whole thing.*

It was his belief in my strength that kept me moving forward. He'd say, "Look at what you've done. You're an incredibly strong woman." Time and time again when I lost belief in my healing, Frank would say: "Trust your process, *allow* it to lead you. *Trust* yourself, listen to yourself." The greatest gift Frank gave me was his unwavering faith in the wisdom and power of my own healing spirit. He listened so carefully to my feelings that I began to trust them, which led me to my discovery.

By spring I knew I was getting very close. The anxiety attacks were overwhelming again. A psychiatrist friend suggested I go back on antidepressants and I said, "No, I'm not going to put this to sleep again. If I do, it's going to kill me."

I asked Adrienne's stepfather if she could move in with him for a while. I said, "Look, I've *got* to do this. And it's too hard on Adrienne." The three of us talked about it, and she went to live with him.

OH MY GOD, IT'S MY FATHER

It was during that same month that I started to have the flashbacks. I was in the hospital getting my last siege of tests. I had needles stuck in my back. They had me on a drug and I started freaking out. I started

calling everybody motherfuckers, trying to pull the needles out, screaming, "Stop it now. Get out of my body. Take the needles out! I don't want to do it anymore." They had to hold me down to finish the test.

When I got back to my room, I somehow had the presence of mind to know that I was having flashbacks. I called Frank and he came to the hospital. I was extremely suicidal. All I could say was, "Frank, it's connected with the drug. I'm having flashbacks and I don't know what's happening." So I told the doctor to discontinue the drug, and I checked myself out of the hospital.

Within a week, Frank and I did a five-hour session and it all came up. We used a drug called MDMA as a therapeutic tool.†
I had been reading about this drug, and how it specifically worked in cases of severe repression by lowering the level of fear. And I said, "Frank, I want to use this, because whatever this is, I can't get close enough. The terror is too great." And Frank, who had never used drugs in his therapy, said, "I'll be with you."

The night before I planned to take the drug, I gave him a tape to listen to. I make a tape of all my dreams as soon as I wake up. And I just pulled one tape out, and I didn't even know what was on it, and I said, "Frank, my gut says for you to listen to this tape because the key is in it."

On the tape was a dream where I had been raped and I was a little girl. This little

---

* Frank Lanou is using his own name.

---

† When Gizelle used MDMA it was legal and she had the support of a skilled therapist. Other women have had negative reactions resulting in severe emotional stress. MDMA can be extremely dangerous and we do not recommend it.

girl who was autistic keeps saying, "I love you, Daddy. I love you, Daddy." And everybody thinks she's crazy or retarded. And I tell the people who come to take her away: "There's nothing wrong with her mind. She's been severely traumatized. If you take her and put her in a mental hospital, she'll never recover. She's got to stay with me because I have the key to her healing." And at the very end of the dream, I say, "I feel like I've been raped." They're the last words on the tape.

So Frank comes to the session with this tape. I took the MDMA and within twenty minutes, it all started coming up. First I said, "I feel numb." Then I said, "I feel trapped." Then I said, "I see this little girl, but she's on the other side of a screen and I can't get to her." We worked out how to get to the little girl. And as soon as I got to her, I said, "Frank, this sounds crazy, but I feel like I'm being raped. That's the feeling in my body." And then I said, "Who would do this to me?" And then the next moment, I said, "Oh my God, it's my father." And every part of my body just knew it.

But even then, the denial was so strong. Frank said to me, "What's happening?" And I said, "I don't know!" And then I'd go into hysteria where I couldn't breathe. And then I'd start choking. And then I would go numb and I wouldn't feel anything. We went around like that for three hours. I said to Frank, "You know what I'm feeling? I feel like I'm lying."

The next day, I called my father and said, "Dad, something happened between you and me. I was three years old and I was really hurt. Tell me! Tell me what it was." And he immediately said, "Nothing," but his voice started getting really shaky and weird. So then I said to him, "I know something happened. It was after you came back from the war, Dad. I know something happened."

So he rattled off all these things: "Well, there was one time I gave you a shot. And I started coming near you and you started screaming so bad I couldn't give it to you." And I said, "Nope, Dad. That wasn't it." And he said, "Well, there was a time you had a really bad asthma attack and we had to take you to the hospital and put you in an oxygen tent." And I said, "Nope." And he said, "I have all these things it could be, and you're not listening to me." And I said, "I'm listening, but they aren't what happened." It ended by him saying he would think about it. He said, "I'll talk with your mother and we'll see if we can come up with what it could have been."

Then I started feeling crazy. I felt that way on and off until the second MDMA session, when I had total recall. Within five hours the whole thing just came back, three-dimensional and solid. I remembered it all—not only the rape, but what my mother said, my grandmother, the doors opening and closing, who did what, when, how, where, exact words. It's all on tape. I'm talking like a three-year-old. And then I'm my mother, using my mother's voice, her exact tone of voice, the words she was using. It's like it's all recorded in your skin, in your body. We have in our bodies exact 100 percent recall of what's happened to us. All we have to do is connect with it.

This time I believed it right away. I knew it wasn't the drug. It was the kind of feeling that can't be denied. Every time I'd take a breath it went right to my core. I knew this was what I'd been looking for. It was instant click. This is it!! I got it!

"DAD, YOU MOLESTED ME"

After I discovered the details of the rape, I called up my father again and said, "Dad, I know what happened. You molested me." I nearly vomited getting the words out. And he said I was wrong. And I said to him, "Dad, I want you to know that I understand the context in which it happened. I understand you'd just come back from the war. My heart is breaking because I know the torment you were in at the time, and I know that you loved me. But I need to heal this."

Then he reversed everything he had said to me about the war, and he said, "There was nothing wrong with my mind when I came back from the war. I was perfectly fine. There has never been anything wrong with my mind. You're crazy."

Then my mother got on the phone and she was hysterical: "How can you say this about your father? How can you possibly say this?" And I said, "Mother, those are the exact words you screamed at me forty years ago. And they didn't make it go away then. And they can't make it go away now. This is what happened, Mom. I was molested. And your denial and my denial is not going to change it." She screamed that I was crazy and I needed to be institutionalized. And then she hung up the phone.

Then my father sent me a photograph. It was of me, before the molestation happened. I'm sitting on my mother's lap on a swing in the backyard. It was yellowed. He must have carried it in his wallet all those years. And he enclosed a postcard I had written as a teenager when he had sent me to Europe, saying I was having a wonderful time. And he enclosed a picture of the church. All in one letter! And he said, "See this little girl. See how happy she was. Does this look like a girl who was molested? And does this postcard sound like it comes from someone who's miserable? You were a very happy child growing up. An evil psychiatrist has implanted a hypnotic suggestion into your mind. As your father, and as a professional, I *demand* that you get a new psychiatrist, an *M.D.* And I want a letter from him stating that you are in his care. If you do not do this immediately, I will sever all further relationship with you. Love, Dad."

I wrote back and said, "First of all, it was not hypnotic implantation. I remember being molested. It's that simple. I remember how and when and where it happened. It's instant recall, Dad. Secondly, I'm not going to change counselors." I told my father that I was going to heal this wound, and that I'd do it with him or without him.

I'm glad I confronted him when I did. The initial step of picking up that phone and saying "I know" was empowering to me. It's moved me very quickly. I got on with my own healing, without wasting a lot of time fantasizing that my father would help me.

I NEEDED SOMEONE TO LISTEN

The immediate thing when I first realized I was molested was a feeling "I've got to talk." My mouth went twenty-four hours a day. I felt if I couldn't talk about it, I'd go crazy. When you have been sexually abused and your voice has been taken away, the child in you needs to speak. My child had been silenced for forty years. I began to hear her crying out in me: "Someone has to listen to me. No one's ever listened to me. No one's ever believed me." And that was her first need—to be listened to—if she was going to heal.

By that time, I had made a few good friends who stood by me. I started with a very sparse network of support, which has since spiraled, one person at a time. I felt so blessed with the support I had. I went home and made a list of all my dearest friends, female and male, and I said, "This is what I'm discovering. And I need someone to listen. I'm calling all my friends. I'm going to structure seven days, and I want you to tell me what day you can come, and if you can give me a commitment to come every Monday between two and four, it'd be great." And people came through. I talked and I talked. About my feelings. About the molestation. About my health. About my suicides. About my father. Giving it form. Giving it shape. Naming it. Feeling it. I just needed to have someone listen to me.

HEALING WITH MEN

If you can't be with men when you're healing, it's fine. You may need to get your power back with women. But there's a real treasure in doing some healing with men. It allows you to directly and dynamically work out your feelings toward your abuser. If you're able to speak your truths with a male friend, and hold your own, and ask for comfort, there's a real empowerment there, because you're doing it with the gender that has taken your power.

And for the man, it makes him aware of this whole issue and how it's affected women. It encourages him to look at himself and to start his own healing if he's out of balance.

Anybody that sits with you during your healing is going to start healing themselves.

It just works that way. It will be a healing for him, and hopefully he'll take it to another man. And that's how it will spread.

It has to. Because now it's "We rape your children in war. You rape our children in war. We throw a bomb at you. You throw a bomb at us." And if we as women stop at the stage where we're out just to cut off the nuts of all our persecutors, we're stopping short of our goal to heal ourselves, the earth, our children, and our world.

Men are out of synch and they need to be healed. We can't keep them out. We have to heal ourselves, but we need to bring them into the circle to be healed. If the men don't get healed, rape is going to continue. And they can't be healed through hatred. It's a vision I have.

I JUST KEEP BREATHING

I've gone through periods in the healing process where the terror is so great that I avoid breathing. I breathe very shallowly to avoid breathing into the pain. But then I have to lie down and breathe into it. When I breathe into it, I feel like I want to throw up.

What I've learned is to use my hands to massage any place that's tight or blocked. I breathe from my diaphragm and I use my hands to release the energy. If I feel a block in my throat, I put one hand there and another hand on my solar plexus. And I try to feel the channel between those two points. Then I'll put my hand over my heart, or on top of my head. It's pure instinct when I do it.

And as I breathe, I give my breath a sound. I just let out whatever sound comes out of my mouth. I don't plan it. I let my body speak. I give my child a voice. Because I was orally molested, my throat will often close up when I do this. It's like the penis is in my mouth again, and I'll gag or choke. Then I put my hand on my throat and keep my throat as open as I can, as I make the sound. Sometimes it comes out like the child is crying or like a lullaby, like the mother in me responding to my child's cry.

Music is another thing that's helped. I got a Walkman and I change the music on it all the time. Whatever sounds my child needs to hear—sometimes it's Bach's Mass in B Minor, all the angels in heaven singing through my ears, other times it may be gentle music, or sound of the ocean, or wolves howling. I've extended that into the use of my own voice. I don't know what to call it—it's not really singing, it's not really choking, it's just letting the sound out—but I do it now almost everyday. I do it with drums, or I do it with rattles. Music is very powerful—the ability to move it out through sound. There's a lot of power there to heal.

MY OUTRAGE COMES FROM LOVE

I had to learn to honor all my feelings, especially the anger and the outrage. I was outraged not only against my father, but against all of the men who are doing this.

This friend of mine said, "You know that you created this because you are the creator of your universe and your soul set this energy in motion. So take responsibility for it and stop mewling and whining and bellyaching about it. Just forgive and go on."

And I got *so* pissed! I was just choked with anger. When you're feeling anger, you need to honor that. If you try to get to the forgiveness before you deal with the anger, you're going to fuck the whole thing up. You have to work from where you are in your belly, not from where you think you should be in your head.

I go through real revenge periods. I imagine walking into my parents' house with a shotgun aimed right at my father's balls. "Okay, Dad. Don't move an inch. Not one step, you sucker. I'm gonna take 'em off one at a time. And I'm gonna take my sweet time about it, too!"

But at the same time, I believe that the only way to stop abuse is to come from a consciousness of love and forgiveness. Hate cannot be stopped with hate. Abuse cannot be stopped with abuse. That does not mean you don't stop the people who are doing this, or that you stop prosecuting them. But you do it from a place of love. If I didn't feel love for the child in me who had been raped, I would not have this outrage.

Sometimes I sit here and feel such compassion for my father, I weep. Other times I see myself taking a gun and shooting his balls off. I am letting it all come right on through. And the more I allow all of it to come up, the more I find myself moving toward love. The more I block the rage, the more I stay stuck. And so for me they're both right there. I reconcile it by saying I trust the process. I trust the validity of my outrage. The outrage is because I honor and value and love life.

SHE ALMOST LOST HER MOTHER

The incest affected every aspect of my relationship with Adrienne. We both went through a lot of sadness, a lot of aching. She almost lost her mother to madness and to suicide.

Everything would have been better if I'd known this twenty years ago. The one thing I couldn't give my daughter was my happiness, my love of myself. I was able to give her a love for herself, a feeling for her strength, but there was a lot of joy we were never able to share. I weep for that. However, it's coming. It's down the road.

And you know, I see all I couldn't give her and she sees all I gave her. That's a blessing. My daughter is a very strong, creative, emotionally healthy human being. I feel proud to watch her becoming a strong woman who refuses to be compromised or silenced.

My first feeling was not to tell Adrienne about the rape, to protect my father, who is her grandfather. And then I thought, "No, that's where this is passed on. This is the denial that allows this to happen. My daughter has a right to know the truth of what's going on."

So I sat down with her and told her, and she wept with me. We both sat there and cried. One of her first responses was, "How were you able to survive that and not become evil yourself?" And I didn't have an answer.

The rifts in our relationship are already mending. I do my work. She does her work. When we get together, each time it's shifting and moving, and there's a mutual healing and a mutual honoring that's starting to happen. She's doing a lot of writing about my attempted suicide, about my surgeries, about her love for me, about her anger, the whole nine yards. We share our writings. We talk. If I can mend me, we can mend the relationship. All I have to do is heal myself. In the process of healing myself, the relationship can heal.

EVERYTHING IN ME HAS CHANGED

Since it's come out, it's been the difference of night and day, of living in hell and living on the earth. Everything in me has changed—my perceptions of myself, of others, of the earth, of my power, of my strength, of my abilities, of my sanity—everything. It's been so fast, I can't believe it. In just three and a half months, there's incredible healing.

For so much of my life, I have fought death wishes. Now I feel grounded, very connected to the earth, very determined to stay. The purpose of my living is to help other men and women heal this, to give it a voice. Nothing is going to take me off of this one. Before, the thing that kept me here, despite all the pain and agony, was my daughter, and then even that wasn't enough.

My strength and energy to deal with my life is returning. My neck has begun to unlock. I've begun to feel a looseness in my hips that I never felt before. I feel life moving through my body. I walk around and say, "God, this is what life is about!" I am just deluged with feelings in my body—of warmth, of movement, of connectedness. I've never had them before. There is nothing that can't be healed in the spirit of life.

I really can't tell you how far my body can heal. I know I'll be able to free up my neck and the strength in my arms. As far as my back goes, there's been a lot of cutting down there, so I'm not sure. But I do know that I will heal physically enough to be able to lead a productive, full, and happy life, even if I have residual pain.

THERE'S A GREAT DEAL OF MAGIC IN THIS HEALING PROCESS

When I get into a crisis now, instead of saying, "Oh my God, I'm never going to heal," I see that it's like layers, and the more I work with it, the more they keep coming around. And even though it's like "But I was feeling good two days ago and now I'm shaking and crying and I can't sleep," I'm beginning to see that I'm not coming back to the same place, I'm coming back at a different level. It's a circling, an up and down, and I have to be with it, and ride it, and trust it. When I reach the next level where the tears are, where the fear is, where the tiredness is, I have to trust in my life energy —that where I am is where I need to be. And by being there as fully as I possibly can, I move to the next step.

I feel there's a great deal of magic involved in this healing process. And what I mean by magic is that the old ways of healing, that have been lost, are waking up. I'm awakening in my cells a lot of that old knowledge. It comes from the earth, from the spirit of the earth. It's the knowledge of women who have healed through the centuries. It's very mysterious and it's very in our gut. It doesn't come from books. It doesn't come from medicine. It doesn't channel through churches, or through yoga teachers, or through anything like that. It's ancient traditions that were passed down from mother to daughter until they were lost through witch hunts and the systematic elimination of women healers.

This knowledge connects with the capacity to heal the rift that has the world in crisis, that has us in danger of extinction. It's the healing power of mother earth. It's been taken away and lost. And She's coming back through us now.

Sometimes when I think that one man can molest thirty children, I feel hopeless. When I get in that space, I have to get in contact with the power of the Mother. She could line up a hundred bleeding women and Her power could touch each of those women and they could heal. Only She is more powerful than the forces of destruction and death.

To me She is the sweetest force, the most gentle healing force there is. She's so sweet it's almost too much to take, it's almost unbearable. And She's very powerful. This is the kind of healing force that heals so gently. It's like a feather. And I feel very strongly that She is what's needed to heal me and to heal all the destruction upon this earth.

HEALING RESOURCES

One counselor said to me, "You're at the center of your own healing process. I'm just one of your tools." I really liked that. That's the way healing should be.

—Saphyre

There is a wide variety of resources that can be of value in the healing process. In this chapter, we discuss individual counseling, support groups, self-help programs, and national organizations. In the following chapter, the Bibliography, you'll find suggested reading in a range of topics.

INDIVIDUAL COUNSELING

If you're considering therapy, there are many types of counselors to choose from, including religious counselors, lay counselors, peer counselors, psychiatrists, marriage, family, and child counselors, social workers, and psychologists.

There are also many types of therapeutic schools. There's talk therapy, where you sit in a room with your counselor and talk about your experiences and express your feelings. There are counselors who take this basic talk approach and incorporate massage, breath work, body work, movement, or role-playing. Some counselors use art, writing, or theater. Others use hypnosis to recover occluded memories.*

If you start working with someone and the counseling doesn't meet your needs, change to a new therapist. You may want to work with one person for part of the process and then switch later on. It's common for your needs to shift as you heal.

FINDING A COUNSELOR

Seeing someone who is already an expert on child sexual abuse has obvious advantages, but it isn't essential. The important thing is that your counselor is a skilled practitioner with whom you can build trust.

Be willing to do a fair amount of work to find a counselor. You don't have to go to the first person you see. Even if you are in crisis and feel you will die within the week if you don't get help, hold off on committing yourself to a long-term therapy relationship until you've looked around thoroughly.

Ask for recommendations from friends, other survivors, or family members. If your immediate circle of acquaintances doesn't offer any leads, check in the county listings in your phone book for the equivalent of Child Protective Services. Although these agencies work with current cases of child abuse, they may be able to refer you to counselors or groups who work with adult survivors. Battered women's shelters, rape crisis centers, parents' centers, and other women's programs are also likely places to get referrals.

You can save money and time by doing some preliminary screening on the phone. Counselors will have different policies about this. Many will talk to you for ten or fifteen minutes on the phone for free. Compare the counselors' orientations, how you feel when you talk to them, and cost.

Once you've narrowed down your choices over the telephone, talk to the two or three you liked most. One woman went to six counselors, a different one each week, until she found the person she wanted to work with. Go to the appointment with a prepared list of questions:

- Have you ever worked with survivors? What kind of training do you have in this work?
- How do you work with survivors? What are the techniques you use?
- If you haven't worked with survivors before, how would you educate yourself on the subject?
- Would you support my participation in a survivors group?
- Do you think sex with adults is always damaging to children?
- Do you think children ever willingly participate in sex with adults?
- Do you think women ever fantasize or exaggerate abuse?

---

* Hypnosis is often effective in recovering memories, but generally your protective defenses will allow you to remember only what you're ready to deal with.

If you're considering hypnosis, look for a hypnotist who's also a counselor. Or have your own therapist present for support. Be sure to choose a responsible practitioner.

- Do you see family reconciliation as a goal? Why (or why not)?
- What role do you think forgiveness plays in the healing process?
- What do you think about touching clients?
- (For lesbian clients.) Have you worked with many lesbians? Do you see lesbianism as an issue in therapy? Do you think sexual preference has anything to do with a history of sexual abuse?
- Do you think it's okay for therapists and clients to socialize or become friends during therapy or after it is over? Are there any circumstances where sex is appropriate?
- How much do you charge? (If the fee isn't within your means, ask if there's a sliding scale or the possibility of barter.)
- Can I call you at home? Schedule emergency sessions?

Ask the questions that are most important to you. Add others to determine whether your prospective counselor is sensitive to particular issues that matter to you. You may want someone familiar with alcoholism or eating disorders, for instance.

Many survivors prefer working with a woman because they feel safer, because they were molested by a man, or because they are more comfortable discussing intimate feelings with a woman. Other women have gained benefits from working with a man because they learned to trust and relate to a man in healthy ways. Choose whichever gender you want to work with. You may also prefer to choose a counselor of your race, economic background, sexual preference, or religion.

As a nun I felt more comfortable going to a nun because we could talk about spiritual things. If you get the wrong counselor, they say, "Spiritual, smiritual. There is no God." My counselor was a nun herself. So I was able to join a group for incest and rape survivors that was made up of just nuns. That way we didn't have to talk about our marriage partners or our sexual partners. We all had the issue of being "good," and we had a lot of the same guilts. I would have been very nervous as a religious to talk about sexual things in a secular group. I would have been very conscious of the fact that I was a nun, and that that was fascinating to people. This group was safe. We could focus on what was important.

Your needs may not be this specialized, and your options will vary depending on where you live. But it's worth trying to find the best person for you.

Once you've done your interviews, compare the way you felt when you were talking with each counselor. Whom did you feel the strongest connection with? Where were you most at ease? Think about the way each person answered your questions.

If this idea of shopping around is foreign to you, remember that the counselor is providing you with a service. You're paying for it. And you're going to have to live with it. You have a right to make a choice.

WHAT DOES EFFECTIVE COUNSELING FEEL LIKE?

When you work with a good counselor, you should feel understood and supported. You should feel warmth between you and your counselor. And that should happen early in the therapy process.

However, you can't judge whether it's good therapy by the way you feel in the moment. Some women experience counseling as a haven they can't wait to get to. Others dread every session and have to force themselves to go. One woman said, "There were times I was absolutely terrified of going to therapy. I don't know how I drove there, how I got out of my car, how I got through the door."

Counseling is not always comfortable, but you know you're with a good counselor when you develop more and more skills to heal yourself as time goes on. You become able to recognize your own patterns and to feel and interpret your own emotions. Even if there's an initial period of strong dependency, you should eventually become more independent. Frank Lanou was able to do this for Gizelle: *

I really owe a lot to my counselor. When I was struggling time and again and would say, "Where do I go from here? What should I do?" he would say, "Trust your process. Trust yourself. *You* know." The greatest gift he's given me is belief in myself. He constantly reflected to me my own knowing and my own power, my own ability to heal. He never gave me the answers. *He* never did the healing. It's very important to work with people who help you get back your power, who help you get back your trust in your body, in your instincts, in your gut, in your voice, in *you*.

---

* For more of Gizelle's story, see page 446.

IF YOU FEEL THERE'S A PROBLEM

If you don't feel respected, valued, or understood, or if your experience is being minimized or distorted, that's a sign that you're in bad therapy, or at least that there's a bad fit between you and the counselor. If you feel there is something wrong in the therapy relationship, or if you get upset or angry with your counselor, talk about it in your session. Afterward, you should feel you've been heard and understood. However, if your counselor discounts your feelings or responds defensively, then you're not getting the respect you need. Look elsewhere.

If a counselor ever wants to have a sexual relationship with you, get out right away. Report the therapist to the appropriate licensing board. If you have had a bad or abusive experience with a counselor, you have a right to be angry. And if you decide to try counseling again, carefully read the guidelines for picking a counselor to protect yourself in the future.

IF YOU'VE BEEN AVOIDING COUNSELING

Although it's right to choose carefully, don't be so cautious that no one can meet your qualifications.

I kept picking counselors that I could easily get rid of. I went to see seven different counselors for either one or two sessions. I would go to great lengths to find people who worked far away from where I lived, so I could say, "Oh well, this is too far to drive."

I would pick nontraditional therapies because I didn't want to work on things. One time I picked a past-life counselor, and you know that wasn't what I needed to work on!

I'd make the initial appointment because I felt desperate. Within one or two visits, I wouldn't be that desperate, and so I'd quit.

Soledad only wanted to see a lesbian Chicana counselor who had worked with sexual abuse.* Since there was no one who met these specifications in her area, she could have talked herself out of going to therapy. But she decided getting help was more important. She compromised and found a skilled woman who has effectively facilitated her healing.

PAYING FOR COUNSELING

Therapy can be very expensive, but there is often low-cost counseling available if you're willing to look for it. Clinics, women's health centers, and state counseling agencies frequently have sliding fee scales, so you are charged according to your income. Some counselors do trades, where you work off the cost by doing something for them in exchange: painting their house, or doing some carpentry, or giving a computer lesson. Other counselors will let you pay over time. One woman paid her counselor a flat rate every month no matter how many sessions she had. And medical insurance may pick up part of the fee. But remember, even if you're getting free or low-cost therapy, you still have the right to see a qualified, skilled counselor. Inexpensive help that isn't good is no bargain.

Some women have gone to court to get their abuser to pay for their therapy bills.† Every state also has a Victim's Compensation Fund, which gives money to victims of violent crime to cover the cost of injuries, lost income, rehabilitation training, and medical bills. The exact name of the program will vary from state to state, but your local district attorney's office will either run the program or know who does. Although some of these programs require that you must apply within one year of the date of the crime, there are adult survivors in California who have applied for compensation from childhood abuse and have received large settlements.

SUPPORT GROUPS

Being with other survivors is a critical part of the healing process, and joining a group is an ideal way to work with other women who've been abused. Group work is particularly useful for dealing with shame, isolation, and secrecy. If you're still fuzzy about what happened to you, hearing other women's stories can stimulate your memories. Their words can loosen buried feelings. Talking with other survivors is useful for problem solving, also. There's likely to be at least one other woman in the room who has suggestions for dealing with whatever issue you're facing.

In groups, survivors get together at a regularly scheduled time specifically to support each other in their healing. Groups can be organized for a set number of weeks or they can be ongoing. They can focus on a

---

* For more of Soledad's story, see page 373.

† For information on how this process works, see "Mary Williams: Attorney for Adult Survivors," page 307.

particular topic—like anger or sexuality—or they can be more general. In leaderless groups (these are usually free), all members share responsibility for running the group. Groups led by a trained facilitator or counselor usually have a weekly or monthly fee.

Being in a Group: Jennierose Lavender

When I joined a group with other survivors, it was the first time I ever felt connected with anybody. All my life I had felt alone. I had never trusted anyone. I had always isolated myself. All those years in therapy, I had just played psychiatrist with them. I told them the kinds of things I knew they wanted to hear. I never could talk about my fears or what was really bothering me.

But now I wasn't alone anymore. There were other people who had the same kind of symptoms I did, for the same kind of reasons. I started to reach out and make friends. It was an incredible relief.

Working in a group is the only helpful therapy I've gotten in my whole life, and I've been in therapy since I was six years old. That's forty-one years. Being in a group is better than being with a therapist because other survivors really understand—they weren't *taught* to understand. And hearing other people's stories has sparked things in my memory. I can see myself coming in and out of groups for years, maybe for my whole life. Group support is fantastic.

STARTING A GROUP

If there are no groups in your area, consider starting one. Tell people you know and ask them to spread the word. Try running a classified ad in the newspaper, put notices on bulletin boards, let the same agencies you called for referrals know that you are starting a group. Contact the groups mentioned in "Self-Help Programs," below, and let them know you want to reach other survivors.

For guidance in starting and running a self-help group, we recommend three books: *Solving Women's Problems, Talking It Out: A Guide to Groups for Abused Women,* and *In Our Own Hands: A Woman's Book of Self-Help Therapy.* All three are listed in the "Sexual Abuse" section of the Bibliography.

SELF-HELP PROGRAMS AND NATIONAL ORGANIZATIONS

Many successful self-help programs have been modeled on the 12-step program of Alcoholics Anonymous (AA). One of the newest is Incest Survivors Anonymous.

Incest Survivors Anonymous (I.S.A.) is a self-help peer program for incest survivors: "We meet to share our experience, strength and hope, so that we may recover from our incest experiences and no longer allow ourselves to be revictimized by our past. As survivors, we strive to recognize the negative behavior patterns developed as children and break free to a new understanding and a new peace of mind. Living and working the twelve steps and twelve traditions of I.S.A., we find a healing solution to our root causes."

There are I.S.A. groups nationwide.

Alcoholics Anonymous and **Narcotics Anonymous** are available for survivors recovering from alcoholism or drug addiction. If you come from an alcoholic family, there's

Al-Anon and, more recently, groups for Adult Children of Alcoholics. For survivors who have difficulties with intimate relationships and sexuality, many cities have branches of Sex and Love Addicts Anonymous. Larger cities may also have meetings that address your particular needs—gay and lesbian groups, women's groups, teen groups.

VOICES (Victims of Incest Can Emerge Survivors) in Action is a national network of incest survivors and pro-survivors (supporters of survivors) that was founded in 1980. They offer a free referral service, listing therapists, agencies, and self-help groups that have been recommended by other survivors. For an annual membership fee, you receive a survival packet of excellent resource material and a subscription to the organization's newsletter, *The Newsy Letter*. You can also attend the VOICES annual conference, take part in group leader training, and participate in special-interest support groups.

Through the special-interest groups, survivors who experienced certain types of abuse can contact each other. There are more than a hundred of these groups dealing abuse, multiple personalities, abuse by priests, and abuse by sadistic perpetrators. These support groups correspond in a systematic way and operate under strict confidentiality. They are the real foundation of the VOICES program.

VOICES in Action, Inc.
P.O. Box 148309
Chicago, IL 60614
(312) 327-1500 (phone calls will be returned collect)

Incest Resources provides multidimensional treatment for women survivors, "including cognitive, physical, educational, behavioral, and spiritual components." Among their services, Incest Resources offers individual and group therapy, drop-in discussion groups, a therapeutic aerobics program, a free referral service for individual and group therapy (for survivors, offenders, and family members), educational literature and national networking information, public speaking, legislative advocacy, and consultation and training. Write to:

Incest Resources
Women's Center
46 Pleasant Street
Cambridge, MA 02139
(617) 492-1818

Looking Up, incorporated in 1984, is a national organization formed to serve the needs of incest victims and survivors of all ages. (Victims are children still in the abusive situation; survivors are those for whom the abuse has stopped.) Based on a model of empowerment, Looking Up offers movement workshops, sponsors art exhibits and wilderness trips, and publishes a newsletter, *The Looking Up Times*.

Of special interest is Climb High, a week-long backpacking trip for survivors. This "challenge week" is designed to promote independence, build trust, and help survivors "reclaim their bodies' energies and strengths."

Looking Up also does public education, legislative lobbying, professional training, and consultation to support groups. Contact:

Looking Up
P.O. Box K
Augusta, ME 04330
(207) 626-3402

Parents United, which is based on the work of Henry and Anna Giarretto, has nationwide chapters that support families who have been through the trauma of incest. Parents United offers groups for offenders, child victims, and nonoffending parents, counseling for families, and Adults Molested As Children, or AMACs.

Parents United chapters vary greatly. Some are run by professionals; some use a self-help model. There are also nonaffiliated groups that use some Parents United principles.

Women have had both positive and negative experiences with Parents United. Some survivors have benefited greatly from the opportunity to directly confront and work with perpetrators. On the other hand, many Parents United chapters stress forgiveness and family reconciliation as goals, are not sufficiently supportive of women's anger, and do not adequately confront perpetrators. There is sometimes insufficient training for group leaders, lack of appropriate boundaries between counselors and clients, and homophobia. Investigate your individual chapter carefully. For information on Adults Molested as Children United, contact:

AMACU Coordinator
c/o Parents United
P.O. Box 952
San Jose, CA 95108
(408) 280-5055

SARAH, Inc. (Sexual Assault Recovery through Awareness and Hope) was founded by survivors of incest to serve the needs of sexual and physical abuse victims and survivors. Based on a model of peer support, women, men, and teenagers come together to share their experiences and struggle together to solve their problems. All newcomers are welcome and invited to "Keep coming back. We believe you." For more information, contact:

SARAH, Inc.
P.O. Box 20353
Bradenton, FL 34203
(813) 746-9114

SCAP (Survivors of Child Abuse Program) provides networking, training, consultation, advocacy, resources, and public education on abuse-related issues. For referrals and information, write or call their National Abuse Hotline:

SCAP
1345 El Centro Avenue
P.O. Box 630
Hollywood, CA 90028
(800) 422-4453

Survivors of Incest Anonymous is a 12-step recovery program for survivors of child sexual abuse. "We are learning that we are not alone and not to blame. Recovery is painful but at least now, we are no longer alone." They are glad to mail you their extensive literature (free of charge if you can't afford it). Write or call:

Survivors of Incest Anonymous
P.O. Box 21817
Baltimore, MD 21222
(301) 282-3400

BIBLIOGRAPHY

Most of the books included here are low-cost paperbacks. Some will be available at your local public library, but many are published by small presses that do not have widespread distribution. If there is a book on this list that is not available at your library, ask if they'll order it or locate it through an interlibrary loan system.

If your local bookstore does not have a certain title in stock, ask them to order it. Most bookstores will place a special order, even if it's not a title or a publisher they normally carry. You can also place orders by writing or calling the publisher directly.

SEXUAL ABUSE

ABOUT SEXUAL ABUSE

Butler, Sandra. *Conspiracy of Silence: The Trauma of Incest.* San Francisco: Volcano Press (330 Ellis St., San Francisco, CA 94102), 1985 (updated).
A classic. Feminist analysis of child sexual abuse.

Finkelhor, David. *Sexually Victimized Children.* New York: The Free Press, 1979.
Results of a landmark study on sex between adults and children. Combines survivors' accounts with data in a readable style. The follow-up, *Child Sexual Abuse: New Theory and Research*, cites the latest research on child sexual abuse.

Fortune, Marie M. *Sexual Violence: The Unmentionable Sin: An Ethical and Pastoral*

Perspective. New York: The Pilgrim Press (132 W. 31 St., New York, NY 10001), 1983.
Written from a Christian and feminist point of view, this groundbreaking book looks at the reasons why the church has ignored sexual abuse and rape, and explains why and how the church must deal with it now. A bridge-building book.

Herman, Judith. *Father-Daughter Incest.* Cambridge: Harvard University Press, 1981.
A well-researched book that combines a clinical approach with a feminist analysis. Herman does a good job of debunking long-standing myths.

Masson, Jeffrey Moussaieff. *The Assault on Truth: Freud's Suppression of the Seduction Theory.* New York: Farrar, Straus, & Giroux, 1984.
This book challenges Freud's seduction theory and has sent shock waves through the psychoanalytic community.

Miller, Alice. *Thou Shalt Not Be Aware: Society's Betrayal of the Child.* New York: New American Library, 1986.
Miller brilliantly rips apart the Oedipal theory and shows that sexual abuse is real. Required reading for every therapist. Miller has written two other excellent books: *The Drama of the Gifted Child: The Search for the True Self* and *For Your Own Good: Hidden Cruelty in Child-rearing and the Roots of Violence.*

Rush, Florence. *The Best Kept Secret: Sexual Abuse of Children.* Englewood Cliffs, NJ: Prentice-Hall, 1980.
A lucid feminist analysis of child sexual abuse from biblical times to the present.

Rush was the first to expose the Freudian cover-up.

Russell, Diana. *The Secret Trauma: Incest in the Lives of Girls and Women.* New York: Basic Books, 1986.
The result of eight years of comprehensive incest research. Full of statistical validation: Incest happens. It's damaging. Written in an academic style.

Terry, Morey. *The Ultimate Evil.* New York: Dolphin, 1987. A disturbing, frightening, suspenseful account of the trial of David Berkowitz, the "Son of Sam." Written by an investigative reporter, this book includes comprehensive information about satanic cults and ritual abuse.

SURVIVORS SPEAK OUT

Bass, Ellen, and Louise Thornton, eds. *I Never Told Anyone: Writings by Women Survivors of Child Sexual Abuse.* New York: Harper & Row, 1983.
These personal accounts of childhood abuse will let you know you're not alone.

Bates, Caroline, and Annette Brodsky. *Sex in the Therapy Hour: A Case of Professional Incest.* Guilford Publications, Inc. (Dept. EI, 72 Spring St., New York, NY 10012), 1989.
A woman writes about her damaging sexual relationship with her therapist and the frustrating process of suing for malpractice. At last, the silence is broken.

Brady, Katherine. *Father's Days: A True Story of Incest.* New York: Dell, 1979.
An honest first-person account of father-daughter incest.

Danica, Elly. *Don't: A Woman's Word. A Personal Chronicle of Childhood Incest and Adult Recovery.* San Francisco: Cleis Press, 1988.
A horrifying, vivid, and poetic chronicle of one woman's experience of incest, child pornography, and prostitution at the hands of her father. You'll need support to read the graphic description of abuse and pain. A hard read.

Donaforte, Laura. *I Remembered Myself: The Journal of a Survivor of Childhood Sexual Abuse.* Self-published, 1982. (Send $7.00 to P.O. Box 914, Ukiah, CA 95482.)
Tells the day-to-day struggles, pain, and triumphs of healing, in a very personal way. This window into Laura's life offers recognition, a survivor's sense of humor, and hope.

Evert, Kathy, and Inie Bijkerk. *When You're Ready: A Woman's Healing from Childhood Physical and Sexual Abuse by Her Mother.* Walnut Creek, CA: Launch Press, 1988.
A powerful resource for women molested by their mothers.

Gallagher, Sister Vera. *Speaking Out, Fighting Back: Women Who Have Survived Child Sexual Abuse in the Home.* Seattle: Madrona Publishers (P.O. Box 22667, Seattle, WA 98122), 1985.
First-person accounts of abuse and survival woven together with the voice of a member of the Good Shepherd Sisters who has done community-service work with troubled girls and women for fifty years. Warm and encouraging, with occasional bits of misinformation.

McNaron, Toni, and Yarrow Morgan, eds. *Voices in the Night: Women Speaking About Incest.* Minneapolis: Cleis Press (P.O. Box 8281, Minneapolis, MN 55408), 1982.
Women talk about their childhood experiences. Many lesbian stories.

Morris, Michelle. *If I Should Die Before I Wake.* New York: Dell, 1982.
A harrowing fictional account of one child's experience of incest. Guaranteed to evoke feelings and memories of your own. But please, have someone nearby you can talk to when you're through.

Randall, Margaret. *This Is About Incest.* Ithaca: Firebrand Books (141 The Commons, Ithaca, NY 14850), 1987.
Well known as a witness to Latin American progressive movements, Margaret Randall now writes about incest. Using words and photography, she documents her own healing from her grandfather's incestuous assault.

Sisk, Sheila, and Charlotte Foster Hoffman. *Inside Scars: Incest Recovery As Told by a Survivor and Her Therapist.* Gainesville, Florida: Pandora Press (P.O. Box 5723, Gainesville, FL 32602), 1987.
A brave, honest and valuable resource for both survivors and therapists. Affirms again that healing is possible.

Smith, Michelle, and Laurence Tazder. *Michelle Remembers.* New York: Pocket Books, 1980.
A ritual abuse survivor writes with her therapist about healing. Some survivors have objected to her spiritual interpretation of her experiences.

White, Louise. *The Obsidian Mirror: An Adult Healing From Incest.* Seattle: Seal Press

(3131 Western Ave., #410, Seattle, WA 98121-1028), 1988.

A first-person account by a counselor describing her own years-long, successful healing process through therapy, family confrontation, and powerful visualization techniques.

Periodicals and Newsletters

For Crying Out Loud, c/o Women's Center, 46 Pleasant St., Cambridge, MA 02139.
This fine quarterly newsletter is by and for women with a sexual abuse history. A one-year subscription costs $5.00.

The Freedom Voice, published by PACA (People Allied for Child Advocacy), P.O. Box 17005, Durham, NC 27705, (919) 493-3333.
A quarterly newsletter published by this child rights organization directed by victims and survivors of abuse. Champions the rights of children and supports the recovery of survivors. "PACA is proud to join the struggle of all people for equality, respect, and dignity." $6 per year.

Healing Journeys, P.O. Box 734, Centuck Station, NY 10710.
Healing Journeys is about healing together and sharing our strength and experience to create a network of support, caring, and hope. Members receive a newsletter, referrals, and other services. Membership fee is $35.00. Quarterly newsletter is only $9.95.

Incest Survivor Information Exchange, P.O. Box 3399, New Haven, CT 06515.
"Our purpose is to provide a forum for female and male survivors of incest to publish their thoughts, writings and art work, and to exchange information."
I.S.I.E. is financed primarily by donations, but the newsletter will be sent to anyone who needs it at no charge. Subscriptions are: $5.00 bulk mail, $7.00 first class. Sample issue: $1.00.

The "Looking Up" Times, RFD #1, Box 2620, Mt. Vernon, ME 04352, (207) 293-2750.
Looking Up not only produces this fine publication but also has excellent resources for Maine survivors of incest— therapy referrals, wilderness trips, art exhibits, training for therapists, legislative advocacy (see page 464). Their mailing list is confidential.

The Newsy Letter, published by VOICES in Action, Inc., P.O. Box 148309, Chicago, IL 60614, (312) 327-1500.
Available only as part of yearly membership in VOICES (see page 464).

The Survivor Newsletter, published by P.L.E.A., P.O. Box 22, West Zia Road, Santa Fe, NM 87505.
An excellent newsletter for male survivors. $20.00 for four issues. "We provide a communication network, share expertise, experience, and knowledge, and provide a mutual strength and support to adult male survivors."

ON HEALING

Bear, Evan, with Peter T. Dimock. *Adults Molested as Children: A Survivor's Manual for Women & Men.* Orwell, VT: The Safer Society Press (RR1, Box 24-B, Orwell, VT 05760-9756), 1988.
Written by survivors for survivors, this

manual is for adults who are beginning to explore the experience of abuse and the process of coming to terms with that experience in everyday life.

Courtois, Christine. *Healing the Incest Wound: Adult Survivors in Therapy*. New York: W. W. Norton, 1988.
A feminist psychologist writes a useful guidebook for therapists on healing.

Gil, Eliana. *Outgrowing the Pain: A Book for and about Adults Abused as Children*. San Francisco: Launch Press (P.O. Box 40174, San Francisco, CA 94140), 1983.
A good overview of the healing process for all kinds of abuse. Cartoon illustrations and simple, clear text. A helpful place to begin for women becoming aware of the role abuse has played in their lives. Her second book, *Treatment of Adult Survivors of Sexual Abuse*, is a practical guide for mental health professionals.

Ledray, Linda. *Recovering from Rape*. New York: Henry Holt, 1986.
An excellent guide for survivors of sexual assault, their partners, and families. Chapters on dealing with doctors, police, the legal system, emotional recovery, and preventing rape. Although the book focuses on the immediate aftermath of rape, it deals with long-term consequences and includes a chapter for survivors of childhood abuse.

Maltz, Wendy, and Beverly Holman. *Incest and Sexuality: A Guide to Understanding and Healing*. Lexington, MA: Lexington Books, 1987.
Written for adult survivors, intimate partners, and therapists, this book is the first publication to address the sexual effects of incest. Lots of practical guidelines and information. Includes a section about partners and how to work together as a couple. Has an appendix devoted to male incest survivors.

Poston, Carol, and Karen Lison. *Reclaiming Our Lives: Hope for Adult Survivors of Incest*. Boston: Little Brown, 1989.
Down-to-earth help for women survivors. Outlines a process for healing that explores issues of trust, power, control, sexuality, and intimacy.

RESOURCES FOR MALE SURVIVORS

Lew, Mike. *Victims No Longer: Men Recovering from Incest and Other Child Sexual Abuse*. New York: Harper & Row, 1990.
A book for men recovering from childhood sexual abuse. Written in basic English. A resource for healing and recovery.

For information and referrals, you can contact:

Mike Lew
The Next Step Counseling
10 Langley Road, Suite 200
Newton Centre, MA 02159

P.L.E.A. (Prevention, Leadership, Education and Assistance) is a non-profit organization of concerned professionals and non-professionals united to combat the widespread problem of male sexual, physical, and emotional abuse and neglect. P.L.E.A. exclusively serves non-offending male survivors. For information, contact:

P.L.E.A.
Hank Estrada, Founder and Director
Box 22, West Zia Road
Santa Fe, NM 87505
(505) 982-9184

Porter, Eugene. *Treating the Young Male Victim of Sexual Assault: Issues & Intervention Strategies.* Orwell, VT: The Safer Society Press (RR 1, Box 24-B, Orwell, VT 05760-9756), 1986.
Provides an understanding of the context in which male sexual victimization occurs, the ways in which boys are likely to respond, and clinical approaches to treatment.

COUNSELING AND SUPPORT GROUPS

Ernst, Sheila, and Lucy Goodwin. *In Our Own Hands: A Woman's Book of Self-Help Therapy.* Los Angeles: J. P. Tarcher, 1981.
Guidelines for starting a self-help group. Explores the politics of therapy and gives clear guidelines for picking a therapist. Feminist analysis of encounter groups, body work, massage, dance, psychodrama, gestalt, regression, and dream work. Practical exercises for each.

Gangi, Barbara, Fredda Bruckner-Gordon, and Gerry Wallman. *Making Therapy Work.* New York: Harper & Row, 1987.
A guide to "choosing, using, and ending therapy," it will help you evaluate and get the most out of therapy.

Hall, Marny. *The Lavender Couch: A Consumer's Guide to Psychotherapy for Lesbians and Gay Men.* Boston: Alyson Publications (P.O. Box 247, Boston, MA 02208), 1985.
Clear and simple.

NiCarthy, Ginny, Karen Merriam, and Sandra Coffman. *Talking It Out: A Guide to Groups for Abused Women.* Seattle: Seal Press (3131 Western Ave., Suite 410, Seattle, WA 98121-1028), 1984.
Although this book was written with battered women in mind, it offers a lot of sound advice about starting a group.

Wyckoff, Hogie. *Solving Women's Problems Through Awareness, Action and Contact.* New York: Grove Press, 1980.
From one of the founders of the Radical Psychiatry movement. If you can make your way around the somewhat dated language, you'll find an excellent critique of traditional psychiatry and clear guidelines for running a women's problem-solving group.

FOR SUPPORTERS OF SURVIVORS
(See also under "About Sexual Abuse")

Beneke, Timothy. *Men On Rape: What They Have to Say About Sexual Violence.* New York: St. Martin's Press, 1982.
If you think sexual violence toward women is someone else's problem, think again. All men should read this book, and do something about it. Pay special attention to Chapter 8, "An Advocate for Rape Victims Responds."

Maltz, Wendy, and Beverly Holman. *Incest and Sexuality: A Guide to Understanding and Healing.* Lexington, MA: Lexington Books, 1987.
Helpful for partners too.

McEnvoy, Alan, and Jeff Brookings. *If She Is Raped: A Book for Husbands, Fathers, and Male Friends.* Holmes Beach: Learning Publications (P.O. Box 1326, Holmes Beach, FL 33509), 1984.
Although some of the specifics apply only to rape, many of their guidelines can be helpful for supporters of survivors.

Sonkin, Daniel Jay, and Michael Durphy. *Learning to Live Without Violence: A Handbook for Men.* San Francisco: Volcano Press (330 Ellis St., Dept. B, San Francisco, CA 94102), 1985.
An excellent step-by-step workbook for the man who wants to stop being violent.

SAFE, STRONG, AND FREE
For Parents and Other Helpers of Children

Adams, Caren, and Jennifer Fay. *No More Secrets: Protecting Your Child from Sexual Assault.* San Luis Obispo: Impact Publishers (P.O. Box 1094, San Luis Obispo, CA 43406), 1981.
A fine practical guide.

Byerly, Carolyn. *The Mother's Book: How to Survive the Incest of Your Child.* Dubuque, Iowa: Kendall/Hunt Publishing, 1985.
This will be universally helpful to women whose children have been molested, with the exception of the chapter on religion, which is written solely from a mainstream Christian perspective. (To order, send $5.80 to Washington Coalition of Sexual Assault Programs, 1063 S. Capitol Way, Olympia, WA 98501. Price includes postage and handling.)

Child Assault Prevention Project. *Strategies for Free Children: A Leader's Guide to Child Assault Prevention.* Columbus: Child Assault Prevention Project (P.O. Box 02005, Columbus, OH 43202), 1985.
Guidelines for running CAP programs. Excellent how-to manual for anyone doing child abuse prevention.

Colao, Flora, and Tamar Hosansky. *Your Children Should Know.* New York: Harper & Row, 1987.
A top resource book for parents. Why, how, and when to talk to your children. What to do if assault occurs. Teaching children to be powerful.

Fay, Jennifer, et al. *"He Told Me Not to Tell."* Renton: King County Rape Relief (305 So. 43rd, Renton, WA 98055), 1979.
A parents' guide for talking to children about sexual assault. This clear, direct booklet is also available in Spanish.

Kraizer, Cheryll Kerns. *The Safe Child Book.* P.O. Box GG, Palisades, NY 10964.
This is a clear, practical guide for teaching children skills to protect themselves. Reassuring, direct language.

Nelson, Mary, and Kay Clark. *The Educator's Guide to Preventing Child Sexual Abuse.* Santa Cruz: Network Publications of ETR Associates (1700 Mission St., Suite 203, P.O. Box 1830, Santa Cruz, CA 95061-1830), 1987.
A valuable analysis of issues and guidelines for child assault prevention by the leaders in the field. Includes a comprehensive listing of national programs, audiovisual materials, books, and teaching

aids. Network Publications also publishes an excellent newsletter *Preventing Sexual Abuse* (subscriptions are $25.00 per year) and a large variety of educational books and pamphlets. Write for their free catalogue.

Sanford, Linda. *The Silent Children: A Parent's Guide to the Prevention of Child Sexual Abuse.* New York: McGraw-Hill, 1980. Detailed and practical. Resources for single parents, parents of children with disabilities, parents who are Asian, Native American, black, and Hispanic.

For Children

Bass, Ellen. *I Like You to Make Jokes with Me, But I Don't Want You to Touch Me.* Chapel Hill: Lollipop Power, 1981. (Available from Carolina Wren Press, 300 Barclay Rd., Chapel Hill, NC 27514).
A gentle picture book. Sara is a little girl who learns to tell a man that, though she wants to be his friend, she doesn't want him to touch her.

Blank, Joani. *The Playbook for Kids About Sex.* Burlingame: Down There Press (P.O. Box 2086, Burlingame, CA 94010), 1980.
A nonbiased, body-loving sex education workbook for children "whose bodies have not started to change into grownups' bodies." Every child should have a copy.

Gardner-Loulan, JoAnn, Bonnie Lopez, and Marcia Quackenbush. *Period.* San Francisco: Volcano Press (330 Ellis Street, #518, San Francisco, CA 94102), 1981.
Clear, well-illustrated sexual information for girls. A book that will give girls a strong, self-confident feeling about menstruation and their bodies. (Also available in a Spanish-language edition from same address.)

Freeman, Lory. *It's MY Body.* Seattle: Parenting Press (Suite 600, 7750 31st Ave. N.E., Seattle, WA 98115), 1986.
A picture book for preschoolers, this book has an accompanying parents' discussion guide titled *Protect Your Child from Sexual Abuse.* Also available in Spanish.

Johnson, Karen. *The Trouble with Secrets.* Seattle: Parenting Press, 1986.
A picture book that clearly explains what kinds of secrets should be kept and what kind should be broken.

Polese, Carolyn. *Promise Not to Tell.* New York: Human Sciences Press, 1985.
A book for eight- to twelve-year-olds. This moving, beautifully illustrated story encourages children to tell if they are being abused.

For Parents and Other Helpers of Teens

Adams, Caren, Jennifer Fay, and Jan Loreen-Martin. *NO Is Not Enough: Helping Teenagers Avoid Sexual Assault.* San Luis Obispo, CA: Impact Publishers, 1984.
How to talk to your teenager about sexual assault, acquaintance rape, and exploitation.

Bateman Py, and Gayle Stringer. *Where Do I Start? A Parents' Guide for Talking to Teens*

About Acquaintance Rape. Dubuque, Iowa: Kendall/Hunt Publishing, 1984.
Teaching children about personal safety shouldn't stop at adolescence. Strong sections on teens abused as children, and for parents who were victimized themselves.

Davidson, Sue. *The Second Mile: Contemporary Approaches in Counseling Young Women*. Tucson: New Directions for Young Women (738 N. 5th Ave., Tucson, AZ 85705), 1983.
An anthology of articles on the needs of young women, including those who've been abused.

Fortune, Marie M. *Sexual Abuse Prevention: A Study for Teenagers*. New York: United Church Press (132 W. 31 St., New York, NY 10001), 1984.
This excellent training guide outlines a five-session course of study for teenagers on sexual abuse. A must for anyone working with adolescents.

For Teenagers

Bateman, Py. *Acquaintance Rape: Awareness and Prevention for Teenagers*. Seattle: Alternatives to Fear (101 Nickerson, Suite 150, Seattle, WA 98109)
A useful booklet for teenage girls on how to stop unwanted touching and defend themselves from acquaintance rape. Bateman's *Macho? What Do Girls Really Want?* is a guide for boys to learn to date without being aggressive.

Bell, Ruth. *Changing Bodies, Changing Lives: A Book for Teens About Sex and Relationships*. New York: Random House, 1980.
A nonsexist, no-nonsense guide for teens. Clear definitions of sexual violence. An all-around reference book that every teen should have access to.

King County Rape Relief. *Top Secret: Sexual Assault Information for Teenagers Only*. (305 So. 43rd, Renton, WA 98055), 1982.
A well-designed, informative booklet, written directly for teens. Great for classroom use. Bulk discounts and a discussion guide for teachers also available.

NiCarthy, Ginny. *Assertion Skills for Young Women: A Manual*. Tucson: The National Female Advocacy Project (376 South Stone Ave., Tucson, AZ 85701).
A book that counters the normal cultural training for young women.

Reese, Lyn, Jean Wilkinson, and Phyllis Sheon Koppelman, eds. *I'm On My Way Running: Women Speak On Coming of Age*. New York: Avon Books, 1983.
Anthology of personal accounts from fiction, nonfiction, and poetry. Wonderful writing.

Terkel, Susan, and Janice Rench. *Feeling Safe, Feeling Strong: How to Avoid Sexual Abuse and What to Do if It Happens to You*. Minneapolis: Lerner Publications, 1984. (Distributed by ETR, 1700 Mission St., Suite 203, P.O. Box 1830, Santa Cruz, CA 95061-1830.)
Six fictionalized first-person stories about young people who dealt successfully with a variety of potentially dangerous situations.

ALCOHOLISM AND DRUG ABUSE

Black, Claudia. *It Will Never Happen to Me: Children of Alcoholics*. Denver: MAC Pub-

lishing (1850 High Street, Denver, CO 80218), 1981.
A groundbreaker. Still the best. Black has also published a workbook for adults, *Repeat After Me,* and one for children, *"My Dad Loves Me. My Dad Has a Disease."*

Sandmaier, Marian. *The Invisible Alcoholics: Women and Alcohol Abuse in America.* New York: McGraw-Hill, 1980.
Sandmaier outlines the reasons women's drinking has been hidden, discusses the hazards of traditional treatment, and provides a guide for getting real help. Full of profiles and first-person accounts.

Swallow, Jean, ed. *Out From Under: Sober Dykes and Our Friends.* San Francisco: Spinsters/Aunt Lute (P.O. Box 410687, San Francisco, CA 94141), 1983.
An inspiring book about lesbians recovering from alcohol and drug addiction.

V., Rachel, ed. *A Woman Like You: Life Stories of Women Recovering from Alcoholism and Addiction.* New York: Harper & Row, 1985.
Nineteen women of diverse backgrounds tell firsthand stories of addiction and recovery.

CO-DEPENDENCY

Norwood, Robin. *Women Who Love Too Much: When You Keep Wishing and Hoping He'll Change.* New York: Jeremy Tarcher, 1985.
Norwood explains the way women from dysfunctional families repeatedly choose inappropriate partners. She outlines the causes and the progression of "loving too much," and explains what's needed for recovery. Written with a complete assumption of heterosexual relationships.

Peele, Stanton. *Love and Addiction.* New York: New American Library, 1975.
Solid. Written before there was a co-dependency movement.

Schaef, Anne Wilson. *Co-Dependence: Misunderstood—Mistreated.* San Francisco: Harper & Row, 1986.
Traces the development of the concept of co-dependency and expands our understanding to include troubled and unhealthy relationships in general.

Wegscheider-Cruse, Sharon. *Choice-Making: For Co-Dependents, Adult Children, and Spirituality Seekers.* Pompano Beach: Health Communications (1721 Blount Road, Suite 1, Pompano Beach, FL 33069), 1985.
A recovery guide for anyone experiencing co-dependency: adult children of alcoholics, dependent partners, professional helpers. Helpful guidance on developing a spiritual practice.

Woititz, Janet Geringer. *Struggle for Intimacy.* Pompano Beach: Health Communications (1721 Blount Road, Suite 1, Pompano Beach, FL 33069), 1985.
Written with adult children of alcoholics in mind. A valuable resource for anyone who wants to achieve greater intimacy in her life.

BATTERING

Lobel, Kerry, ed. *Naming the Violence: Speaking Out About Lesbian Battering.* Seattle:

Seal Press (3131 Western Ave., Suite 410, Seattle, WA 98121-1028), 1986.
Another silence broken; it includes personal stories, a look at the homophobia that has kept lesbians from seeking help, and suggestions for services.

Martin, Del. *Battered Wives*. Revised Edition. San Francisco: Volcano Press (330 Ellis St., #518, Dept. B, San Francisco, CA 94102), 1981.
The pioneering book that framed the problem of wife-beating. Still the best overview available.

NiCarthy, Ginny. *Getting Free: A Handbook for Women in Abusive Relationships*. Revised Edition. Seattle: Seal Press (3131 Western Ave., Suite 410, Seattle, WA 98121-1028), 1986.
A must for any woman wanting to leave an abusive partner. Valuable information on both practical and emotional issues. Expanded edition has sections on lesbian abuse, teen abuse, and emotional abuse.

Pagelow, Mildred Daley. *Family Violence*. New York: Prager Publishers, 1984.
Comprehensive and readable. Includes chapters on sexual abuse.

Walker, Lenore. *The Battered Woman*. New York: Harper & Row, 1979.
Describes and documents the battering syndrome and provides practical recommendations for "the way out." A major contribution.

White, Evelyn C. *Chain Chain Change: For Black Women Dealing with Physical and Emotional Abuse*. Seattle: Seal Press (3131 Western Ave., Suite 410, 98121-1028), 1985.
Direct. Clearly written.

Zambrano, Myrna M. *Mejor Sola Que Mal Acompañada: Para la Mujer Golpeada/For the Latina in an Abusive Relationship*. Seattle: Seal Press (3131 Western Ave., Suite 410, Seattle, WA 98121-1028), 1985.
Bilingual. Excellent sections on institutionalized racism and barriers Latinas face in getting help.

VIOLENCE AGAINST WOMEN

Aegis: The Magazine on Ending Violence Against Women. Published quarterly by the National Communications Network, the Feminist Alliance Against Sexual Coercion, P.O. Box 21033, Washington, D.C. 20009.

Brownmiller, Susan. *Against Our Will: Men, Women and Rape*. New York: Bantam, 1975.
A comprehensive history and analysis of rape. A classic.

Griffin, Susan. *Pornography and Silence: Culture's Revenge Against Nature*. New York: Harper & Row, 1981.
Griffin looks at the ways pornography is woven through the texture of our society, and explores the role it plays in undermining our basic humanity and values. Griffin's *Women and Nature*, a beautifully written classic, parallels the violation of women with the continuing violation of the earth. *Rape: The Power of*

Consciousness is a series of powerful essays.

Lederer, Laura, ed. *Take Back the Night: Women on Pornography.* New York: William Morrow, 1980.
An anthology of the best feminist thinking on pornography.

McAllister, Pam, ed. *Reweaving the Web of Life: Feminism and Nonviolence.* Philadelphia: New Society Publishers, 1982.
The first substantial collection of writings by feminists on nonviolence. "By combining our rage with compassion, we live the revolution every day."

Russell, Diana E. H. *The Politics of Rape: The Victim's Perspective.* New York: Stein & Day, 1975.
Ninety women were interviewed for this incisive look at rape from the victim's point of view.

Russell, Diana E. H. and Nicole Van de Ven. *Crimes Against Women: Proceedings of the International Tribunal.* East Palo Alto: Frog in the Well Press (430 Oakdale Rd., East Palo Alto, CA 94303), 1984.
Women from around the world testify about the violence against women in their countries.

W.H.I.S.P.E.R. (Women Hurt in Systems of Prostitution Engaged in Revolt) is a newsletter "written by and for women engaged in systems of prostitution or who have escaped." *WHISPER* is based on the belief that prostitution exploits women, and is committed to "end the sexual enslavement of women." For a one-year subscription, send $15.00 to: *WHISPER,* P.O. Box 5514, Rockefeller Center Station, New York, NY 10185. Free distribution to women in need.

SELF-DEFENSE

Bart, Pauline, and Patricia O'Brien. *Stopping Rape: Successful Survival Strategies.* Elmsford: Pergamon Press (Maxwell House, Fairview Park, Elmsford, NY 10523), 1985.
A look at the strategies women have used to prevent rape, with an analysis of the factors in women's backgrounds that contribute to their capacity to defend themselves. Recommendations for society as a whole.

Caignon, Denise, and Gail Groves, eds. *Her Wits About Her: Self-Defense Success Stories by Women.* New York: Harper & Row, 1987.
These stories are inspiring; they'll help you sleep better night.

Sexual Coercion and Assault: Issues and Perspectives. Py Bateman edits this fine bimonthly journal on self-defense. For subscriptions, write to P.O. Box 2831, Bellingham, WA 98227.

FEELINGS AND SELF-ESTEEM

Adair, Margo. *Working Inside Out: Tools for Change.* Berkeley: Wingbow Press, (Bookpeople, 2929 Fifth St., Berkeley, CA 94710), 1984.
Adair's meditations for intuitive prob-

lem solving are gentle yet penetrating healing tools. They're also available on cassette.

Colgrove, Melba, Harold Bloomfield, and Peter McWilliams. *How to Survive the Loss of a Love.* New York: Bantam, 1976.
A classic. Dealing with grief and losses of all kinds. The subtitle: "58 Things to Do When There's Nothing to Be Done." A day at a time, this simple little book helps.

Inglehart, Hallie Austen. *Woman Spirit: A Guide to Women's Wisdom.* San Francisco: Harper & Row, 1983.
A guide to women healers, meditation, and dreams. Includes tools for creating personal mythology and rituals.

Lerner, Harriet. *The Dance of Anger: A Woman's Guide to Changing the Patterns of Intimate Relationships.* New York: Harper & Row, 1986.
Practical suggestions on handling anger and making meaningful changes in relationships.

Phelps, Stanlee, and Nancy Austin. *The Assertive Woman.* San Luis Obispo: Impact Publishers (P.O. Box 1094, San Luis Obispo, CA 43406), 1979.
An enjoyable book that teaches you step-by-step to become an assertive woman.
Watch the all-out slurs on aggressiveness. Sometimes it's needed.

Sanford, Linda Tschirhart, and Mary Ellen Donovan. *Women & Self-Esteem: Understanding and Improving the Way We Think and Feel About Ourselves.* New York: Penguin Books, 1986.

Brilliant analysis of why we think poorly of ourselves. Full of anecdotes and personal examples. "Blueprints for change" at the end of each chapter offer useful exercises for improving self-esteem.

Sonkin, Daniel Jay, and Michael Durphy. *Learning to Live Without Violence: A Handbook for Men.* San Francisco: Volcano Press (330 Ellis St., Dept. B, San Francisco, CA 94102), 1985.
Although designed for men who batter, this is a helpful guide for everyone who wants to learn to recognize and deal with their anger effectively.

YOUR BODY

The Boston Women's Health Book Collective. *The New Our Bodies, Ourselves.* New York: Simon & Schuster, 1984.
New and expanded. The complete, readable sourcebook on women's health-care issues from birthing to aging, from violence against women to occupational health hazards. (For the Spanish language edition, write to: *Nuestros Cuerpos, Nuestras Vidas,* Boston Women's Health Book Collective, 465 Mt. Auburn St., Watertown, MA 02172.)

Chernin, Kim. *The Obsession: Reflections on the Tyranny of Slenderness.* New York: Harper & Row, 1981.
An incisive, well-researched analysis of women's obsession with weight and body size.

Davis, Martha, Matthew McKay, and Elizabeth Tobbins Eshelman. *The Relaxation and Stress Reduction Workbook.* Oakland:

New Harbinger Publications (2200 Adeline, Suite 305, Oakland, CA 94607), 1982.
Practical step-by-step guidebook includes relaxation, self-hypnosis, meditation, imagination, nutrition, coping skills, assertiveness training, biofeedback, breathing, time management, exercise, thought stopping, and more.

Hendricks, Gay, and Russel Wills. *The Centering Book: Awareness Activities for Children, Parents, and Teachers.* New York: Prentice-Hall, 1975.
Designed for use with children, this simple volume is an easy-to-understand introduction to the world of dreams, meditation, centering, body awareness, yoga, and guided imagery.

Hutchinson, Marcia Germaine. *Transforming Body Image.* New York: Crossing Press (Box 640, Trumansburg, NY 14886), 1985.
Every woman should read this book. Step-by-step exercises to help you integrate your body, mind, and self-image, and to begin to love and accept yourself just the way you are.

Lidell, Lucinda. *The Book of Massage: The Complete Step-By-Step Guide to Eastern and Western Techniques.* New York: Simon & Schuster, 1984.
A beautifully illustrated guide that teaches the basics.

Roth, Geneen. *Feeding the Hungry Heart: The Experience of Compulsive Eating.* New York: Bobbs-Merrill, 1982.
Looks at bingeing, hunger, body image, and nourishment as issues far deeper than food. Her second book, *Breaking Free from Compulsive Eating,* is a practical how-to follow up.

Schoenfielder, Lisa, and Barb Wieser, eds. *Shadows on a Tightrope: Writings by Women on Fat Oppression.* San Francisco: Spinsters/Aunt Lute (P.O. Box 410687, San Francisco, CA 94141), 1983.
A powerful anthology of stories, articles, and poems from the fat liberation movement.

SEXUALITY

Barbach, Lonnie. *For Yourself: The Fulfillment of Female Sexuality.* Garden City: Anchor Press, 1975.
An enlightening guide for women wanting to develop their capacity for sexual pleasure. The sections on fantasy and pornography as aids to sexual arousal are *not* recommended and can be further damaging to survivors. Written mainly for a heterosexual audience, but helpful to any woman.

Blank, Joani. *Good Vibrations: The Complete Guide to Vibrators.* Burlingame: Down There Press (P.O. Box 2086, Burlingame, CA 94010), 1982.
It's all right here in black and white. There's nothing better than a vibrator for exploring your budding sexuality. Beg, borrow, or steal one, and read this book. Also fun is *The Playbook for Women About Sex.* A nonthreatening place to start a loving relationship with yourself.

Dodson, Betty. *Selflove & Orgasm.*
A sex-positive guide to masturbation. For a copy, send $5.00 to Betty Dodson, P.O. Box 1933, Murray Hill Station, New York, NY 10156.

Loulan, JoAnn. *Lesbian Sex.* San Francisco: Spinsters/Aunt Lute (P.O. Box 410687, San Francisco, CA 94141), 1984.
A good read about sexuality, sexual problems, and healing for *all* women, not just lesbians. Sections on sex and disability, sobriety, sexual abuse, motherhood, aging, and youth. The sequel, *Lesbian Passion: Loving Ourselves and Each Other,* includes chapters for incest survivors and their partners, for women in recovery from substance abuse, and for women who are celibate, single and dating, or in long-term relationships.

Maltz, Wendy. *Partners in Healing.* Independent Video Services (401 E. 10th Ave., Suite 160, Eugene, OR 97401), (503) 345-3455.
Groundbreaking video designed to help heterosexual couples identify sexual problems caused by childhood incest and begin working together toward sexual healing and emotional intimacy. Three incest survivors and their spouses discuss their experiences.

Mail-Order Stores for Vibrators and Other Sex Toys

Eve's Garden, Suite 1406, 119 West 57th St., New York, NY 10019. Readers get a free mail-order catalogue by mentioning this book.

Good Vibrations, 3416 22nd St., San Francisco, CA 94110. For a mail-order catalogue, send $1.00.

PARENTING

(See also under "Safe, Strong, and Free.")

Arcana, Judith. *Our Mother's Daughters.* Berkeley: Shameless Hussy Press (Box 3092, Berkeley, CA 94703), 1979.
Illuminates the mother-daughter relationship. Also valuable is *Every Mother's Son: The Role of Mothers in the Making of Men,* which explores the question, "Is it possible for us to bring up boys in a non-sexist way?" (Available from Seal Press, 3131 Western Ave., Suite 410, Seattle, WA 98121-1028.)

Boston Women's Health Collective. *Ourselves and Our Children.* New York: Random House, 1978.
A great all-around resource.

Chesler, Phyllis. *Mothers on Trial: The Battle for Children and Custody.* Seattle: Seal Press (3131 Western Ave., #410, Seattle, WA 98121-1028), 1986.
A landmark book exploring how "good enough" mothers are separated from their children in custody battles. A passionate indictment of a discriminatory system and a celebration of maternal love and heroism under siege. Also important is Chesler's *Women and Madness,* an impassioned indictment against a century of psychiatric theory and practice.

Dinnerstein, Dorothy. *The Mermaid and the Minotaur: Sexual Arrangements and Human Malaise.* New York: Harper & Row, 1977.
An extraordinary analysis of the ways in which traditional male and female roles in child-raising have operated as a destructive force thoughout history.

Duncan, Barbara. *The Single Mother's Survival Manual.* Saratoga: R&E Publishers (P.O. Box 2008, Saratoga, CA 95070), 1984.
Just what it says it is. The basics: practical, simple, and homophobic.

Gilbert, Lucy, and Paula Webster. *Bound by Love: The Sweet Trap of Daughterhood.* Boston: Beacon Press, 1982.
A lucid analysis of the "good girl" psychology that sets women up to be victims of physical and emotional violence.

Gordon, Dr. Thomas. *P.E.T. Parent Effectiveness Training.* New York: Peter Wyden Inc., 1970.
A resource that's helped millions of parents.

Planned Parenthood. *How to Talk with Your Child about Sexuality: A Parent's Guide.* New York: Doubleday, 1986.
Clear, direct, and helpful. Includes a chapter on protecting your child from abuse.

Pogrebin, Letty Cottin. *Growing Up Free: Raising Your Child in the 80s.* New York: McGraw-Hill, 1980.
A feminist guide to raising children.

Porterfield, Kay Marie. *Keeping Promises: The Challenge of a Sober Parent.* San Francisco: Harper & Row, 1984.
This book provides insight into how your children have coped in a chemically dependent family, but can offer valuable guidance helpful for any family whose members are beginning to change and heal.

Rich, Adrienne. *Of Woman Born: Motherhood as Experience and Institution.* New York: Bantam, 1977.
A feminist classic. If you've ever been a mother or a daughter, read this book.

Schulenberg, Joy. *Gay Parenting: A Complete Guide for Gay Men and Lesbians with Children.* Garden City: Anchor Press, 1985.
Practical and thorough. Readable. Includes a thorough resource section and bibliography.

WORK AND CREATIVITY

Bolles, Richard N. *A Practical Manual for Job-Hunters & Career-Changers: The 1986 What Color Is Your Parachute?* Berkeley: Ten Speed Press, 1986.
It's not only fun to read, it's the best, most helpful guide to dealing with today's work world. Cheaper and more friendly than many career counselors. His second book, *The Three Boxes of Life And How to Get Out of Them* deals with the way education, work, and leisure fit into your life.

Edwards, Betty. *Drawing on the Right Side of the Brain.* Los Angeles: J. P. Tarcher, 1979.

A classic on developing your creativity. A friendly, readable companion. The sequel, *Drawing on the Artist Within: A Guide to Innovation, Imagination, and Creativity,* is equally worthwhile.

Olsen, Tillie. *Silences.* New York: Delacorte Press, 1978.
An eloquent writer confronts the relationship between circumstances (class, race, sex, the times and climate into which one is born) and creativity.

Rico, Gabrielle. *Writing the Natural Way.* Los Angeles: J. P. Tarcher, 1986.
An innovative approach to writing (and fun ways to sneak past your censors).

Ruddick, Sara, and Pamela Daniels, eds. *Working It Out: 23 Women Writers, Artists, Scientists and Scholars Talk About Their Lives and Work.* New York: Pantheon Books, 1977.
If you've always longed for a mentor, here are twenty-three.

Sher, Barbara, with Annie Gottlieb. *Wishcraft.* New York: Ballantine, 1979.
As one of the blurbs says, this book "makes hope practical." A guide for getting what you want in life, this book presents a realistic blend of "you-control-your-own-reality" new-age consciousness with realistic goal setting and planning for change.

Winter, Nina. *Interview with the Muse: Remarkable Women Speak on Creativity and Power.* Berkeley: Moon Books (P.O. Box 9233, Berkeley, CA 94709), 1978.
Inspiring.

AGING

Adelman, Marcy, ed. *Long Time Passing: Lives of Older Lesbians.* Boston: Alyson Publications (40 Plympton St., Boston, MA 02118), 1986.
A truly invisible minority comes out. Inspiring stories of aging for all women.

Calyx Editorial Collective. *Women and Aging: An Anthology by Women.* Corvallis: Calyx Books (P.O. Box B, Corvallis, OR 97339), 1986.
Photography, essays, fiction, journal writing, profiles, art, poetry, and reviews. Compelling. Beautiful to look at.

Greenwood, Sadja. *Menopause Naturally: Preparing for the Second Half of Life.* San Francisco: Volcano Press (330 Ellis St., San Francisco, CA 94102), 1985.
Clear, instructive, and positive.

Painter, Charlotte, with photos by Pamela Valios. *Gifts of Age.* San Francisco: Chronicle Books (One Hallidie Plaza, San Francisco, CA 94102), 1985.
Portraits and essays about the lives of thirty-two extraordinary older women. A beautiful, thought-provoking book that shows old age as a time of creativity, change, and inspiration.

DISABLED WOMEN

Browne, Susan, Debra Conners, and Nanci Stern, eds. *With the Power of Each Breath:*

A Disabled Women's Anthology. San Francisco: Cleis Press (P.O. Box 14684, San Francisco, CA 94114), 1985.
Another silence broken. Educational.

Miller, Vassar, ed. *Despite This Flesh: The Disabled in Stories and Poems.* Austin: The University of Texas Press (Box 7819, Austin, TX 78713), 1985.
Forty-five physically disabled men and women contributed to this fine literary anthology.

Saxton, Marsha, and Florence Howe, eds. *With Wings: An Anthology of Literature by and about Women with Disabilities.* New York: The Feminist Press, 1987.
Dispelling stereotypes, this collection captures the striving for dignity, self-expression, love, and independence in the day-to-day reality of disabled women's lives.

Seattle Rape Relief. *Choices: Sexual Assault Prevention for Persons with Disabilities.* Seattle: Seattle Rape Relief (1825 South Jackson, Seattle, WA 98144), 1985.
Three self-help workbooks for people with physical disabilities and hearing and visual impairments. Available in braille and large print.

Weiner, Florence. *No Apologies: A Guide to Living with a Disability.* New York: St. Martin's Press, 1986.
Practical support and assistance around issues of work, education, sexuality, recreation, access, medical help, and independent living. Full of personal stories, essays, and extensive resource listings.

WOMEN OF COLOR

Brant, Beth, ed. *A Gathering of Spirit: Writing and Art by North American Indian Women.* Rockland: Sinister Wisdom Books (P.O. Box 1308, Montpelier, VT 05602), 1984.
A wonderfully woven tapestry, full of powerful images.

Calyx Editorial Collective. *Asian-American Women's Anthology.* Corvallis: Calyx (P.O. Box B, Corvallis, OR 97339), 1987.
Explores the concerns of Asian American women in poetry, fiction, essays, reviews, and art. Includes a bibliography.

Cochran, Jo, et al., eds. *Bearing Witness Sobreviviendo: An Anthology of Native American/Chicana/Latina Art and Literature.* Corvallis: Calyx (P.O. Box B, Corvallis, OR 97339), 1987.
"Crossing the borders of language and culture, the ancient spirits come to life."

Gomez, Alma, Cherríe Moraga, and Mariana Romo-Carmona, eds. *Cuentos: Stories by Latinas.* New York: Kitchen Table: Women of Color Press (P.O. Box 592, Van Brunt Station, Brooklyn, NY 11215), 1983.
The first of its kind. Stories in both Spanish and English.

Hull, Gloria T., Patricia Bell Scott, and Barbara Smith, eds. *All the Women Are White, All the Blacks Are Men, But Some of Us Are Brave.* New York: The Feminist Press, 1982.
A ground-breaking collection on the subject of black women, including politi-

cal theory, literary essays, guidelines for consciousness-raising about racism, and many other issues of concern to all women. Excellent annotated bibliographies.

Moraga, Cherrie, and Gloria Anzaldua, eds. *This Bridge Called My Back: Writings By Radical Women of Color*. New York: Kitchen Table: Women of Color Press (P.O. Box 592, Van Brunt Station, Brooklyn, NY 11215), 1981.
Prose, poetry, narrative, and analysis by Afro-American, Asian American, Latina, and Native American women. Compelling.

Morales, Aurora Levins, and Rosario Morales. *Getting Home Alive*. Ithaca, NY: Firebrand Books (141 The Commons, Ithaca, NY 14850), 1986.
Written by a Puerto Rican mother and her Puerto Rican/Jewish daughter, this well-crafted volume inspires and informs.

Smith, Barbara, ed. *Home Girls: A Black Feminist Anthology*. New York: Kitchen Table: Women of Color Press (P.O. Box 2753, Rockefeller Center Station, New York, NY 10185).
Excellent. Kitchen Table Press publishes wonderful books. Write for their listing of current titles.

LESBIANS

Clark, Don. *Loving Someone Gay*. New York: Signet, 1977.
If you think you might be gay or if you care about someone who is, this book challenges common stereotypes and gives basic facts.

Cruikshank, Margaret. *New Lesbian Writing*. San Francisco: Grey Fox Press (Subterranean Company, P.O. Box 10233, Eugene, OR 97440), 1984.
Beautiful poetry and prose from many cultures. Includes a thorough literature review.

Martin, Del, and Phyllis Lyon. *Lesbian Woman*. New York: Bantam, 1983.
A pioneering book that first told the truth about the lesbian experience.

Vida, Ginny, ed. *Our Right to Love: A Lesbian Resource Book*. Englewood Cliffs: Prentice-Hall, 1978.
Exactly what it says—a diversified resource book. Don't let the bright orange cover stop you.

PERIODICALS

Hot Wire, 1417 W. Thome, Chicago, IL 60660. (312) 274-8298.
An upbeat positive look at lesbian culture. Each issue includes interviews, articles on music and the arts, resources, upcoming events, and even a record. Available three times a year, the subscription price is $14.00.

Sinister Wisdom, P.O. Box 3252, Berkeley, CA 94703.

A beautifully written, inspiring quarterly journal of lesbian fiction, poetry, essays, and reviews. Subscriptions: $15.00 Hardship rate: $6.00.

FOR INSPIRATION

Allen, Paula Gunn. *The Woman Who Owned the Shadows.* San Francisco: Spinsters/ Aunt Lute (P.O. Box 410687, San Francisco, CA 94141), 1983.
The absorbing story of a Native American woman's journey back into her own culture.

Angelou, Maya. *I Know Why the Caged Bird Sings.* New York: Bantam, 1980.
A moving portrayal of incest and its effects in a wonderful novel that celebrates life.

Barnes, Liz. *hand me downs.* San Francisco: Spinsters/Aunt Lute (P.O. Box 410687, San Francisco, CA 94141), 1985.
A delightful autobiographical novel written from the point of view of a spunky five-year-old who is abused by her brother.

Bryant, Dorothy. *The Kin of Ata Are Waiting for You.* New York: Random House, 1971.
A visit to a world where people live in harmony with their dreams.

Davidson, Robyn. *Tracks.* New York: Pantheon Books, 1980.
Great adventure story of one woman's trek across the desert on a camel. All about women and courage.

Dickson, Margaret. *Maddy's Song.* Boston: Houghton Mifflin, 1985.
A beautifully written novel about a young girl's struggle to break free from a physically abusive father. Horrible, inspiring, and incredibly suspenseful, it's a tough book to put down.

Gearhart, Sally Miller. *The Wanderground: Stories of the Hill Women.* Boston: Alyson Publications (P.O. Box 247, Boston, MA 02208), 1984.
A novel about a society where women's psychic abilities have come to full fruition.

LeGuin, Ursula. *A Wizard of Earthsea.* New York: Bantam, 1975.
Compelling fantasy story about a young man's quest to seek out and conquer the dark shadows that chase him. Survivors of sexual abuse will have no trouble identifying with his denial, his search, and his recovery.

Marshall, Paule. *Praisesong for the Widow.* New York: E. P. Dutton, 1983.
A wonderful novel about a middle-class black woman's spiritual awakening and journey home.

Morrison, Toni. *The Bluest Eye.* New York: Pocket Books, 1970.
A beautiful novel about a young survivor.

Randall, Margaret. *Women Brave in the Face of Danger: Photographs and Writings by Latin and North American Women.* New York:

Crossing Press (Box 640, Trumansburg, NY 14886), 1985.
An extraordinary book about the courage, diversity, and strength of women. The photos and the poetry cannot help but move you.

Sarton, May. *A Reckoning*. New York: W. W. Norton, 1978.
A dying woman looks back at her life. Makes you appreciate the essentials of life.

Swallow, Jean. *Leave a Light On for Me*. San Francisco: Spinsters/Aunt Lute (P.O. Box 410687, San Francisco, CA 94141), 1986.
An insipiring novel about a lesbian relationship between an incest survivor and a recovering alcoholic, which actually works out in the end. Wonderful wisdom on friendship and being there for someone.

The Troops for Truddi Chase. *When Rabbit Howls*. New York: E. P. Dutton, 1987.
Truddie Chase has multiple personalities that began when, at the age of two, she was raped by her stepfather. Written by her numerous selves during therapy, this book shows intimately and vividly how the mind must work to cope with the horror of sexual abuse.

Walker, Alice. *The Color Purple*. New York: Pocket Books, 1982.
A young woman's letters to God. A passionate human story of triumph through adversity. Exquisitely written.

Wassmo, Herbjorg. *The House with the Blind Glass Windows*. Translated by Roseann Lloyd and Allen Simpson. Seattle: Seal Press (3131 Western Ave., Suite 410, Seattle, WA 98121-1028), 1987.
Set against the backdrop of a rural community in which hardship and isolation are a way of life, this sensitive Norwegian novel shows both the vulnerability and the resilience of a young girl who is sexually abused by her stepfather.

Zahava, Irene, ed. *Hear the Silence: Stories of Myth, Magic and Renewal*. New York: Crossing Press (P.O. Box 640, Main Street, Trumansburg, NY 14886), 1986.
Diverse cross-cultural stories of women and spirituality. A gorgeous anthology. Pace yourself to make them last longer. The first story is a knockout about sexual abuse and retribution.

INDEX

Abuser(s). *See also specific topics*
  advice for interacting with
    survivors for, 298–99
  current relationship with, 296,
    444
  sympathizing with, 123
Addiction(s), 217–18, 464
  as coping behavior, 49
  to relationship, 236
  remembering and, 78
  to sex, 259–60, 464
Adult Children of Alcoholics, 464
Adults Molested as Children United
    (AMACU), 465
Affirmations, 184–85, 208
  partners of survivors and, 343–44
  self-abuse and, 220
Agoraphobia, 383–84
Al-Anon, 155, 326*n*, 464
Alcoholics Anonymous (AA), 155,
    463, 464
Alcoholism, 38, 49, 216, 389–90,
    408, 409, 442
  violence and, 199
Alicia, 134, 140–41

Anger, 59, 122–32, 371, 379, 455
  abusive, 200–1
  action and, 131–32
  behavioral signs of, 199
  denying, 123
  directing, 124
  emotional release exercises for,
    200, 443
  fear of, 127
  feeling vs. expressing, 127
  getting in touch with, 124, 126–
    27
  as healthy response, 123
  intimacy and, 232
  lashing out, 123–24
  love and, 127–28
  at mother, 125
  of partners of survivors, 327–28,
    339
  as part of everyday life, 131
  physical signs of, 198–99
  positive expressions of, 129
  power of, 129–30
  revenge and, 128–29
  role-playing and, 126

Anger (*cont.*)
  self-abuse and, 220
  suicidal feelings and, 203
  supportive, 130
  verbal abuse as expression of, 124
  violence and, 123–24, 127, 128,
    198–201
Annette (pseud.), 417–21
Anorexia, 50, 218–19
Anxiety. *See* Panic
Artemis (pseud.), 209, 431–40
Asherah, Karen, xx
Assault, 220–21
*Assault on Truth: Freud's Suppression
    of the Seduction Theory* (Masson),
    347
Autobiography in Five Short Chapters
    (Nelson), 183

Barclay, Esther, 129–30
Bass, Ellen, 177
Bat Or, Rachel, 63–64, 188–90, 207
Battering, 220–21
Belief that it happened, 58, 86–91
  counselor's, 345–47

Belief that it happened (cont.)
  as gradual awakening, 91
  healing process and, 88, 90
Belly breathing, 214
Best Kept Secret, The (Rush), 347
Bioenergetics, 198
Blaming your mother, 125
Blaming yourself, 58, 104–10
  counseling and, 347–48
  need for affection and, 105–6
  sexual response to abuse and, 106, 361, 390
Body (body image), 207–22, 442. See also specific topics
  affirmation and, 208
  drawing yourself and, 209
  eating difficulties and, 50, 217–19, 361
  effects of sexual child abuse on, 36
  emotional release work and, 198, 200
  exercise and, 212
  feelings and, 192–95
  ignoring, 211–12
  insomnia and, 213
  learning to love, 208
  leaving, 43
  listening to, 211–12
  looking in the mirror and, 209
  massage and, 211
  one-inch exercise and, 208
  physical illness and, 213, 216, 422
  self-defense and, 220–22
  self-mutilation and, 219–20
  splitting and, 208–10
Body memories, 74–75
Body therapy, 442, 443
Boundaries, 34, 182–84, 444–45. See also Setting limits
  with children, 276
  intimate relationships and, 231–32
Breaking silence. See Disclosing and confronting; Telling
Breakthroughs, 157
Breathing, 454–55
  belly, 214
  numbness and, 210

Breathing (cont.)
  panic and, 201–3
  splitting and, 210
Brister, Jude, 98
"Bubba Esther" (Whitman), 108
Bulimia, 50, 218–19
Busyness, as coping behavior, 47
Butler, Sandra, 148, 208

Calming down, 201–3
C.A.P. (Child Assault Prevention Project), 281n
Carey, 93
Catherine, 66–68, 95, 144–45, 252
Celia, 134–35
"Change" (Bass), 177
Change, process of, 173–77
  acknowledging accomplishments, 176–77
  basic steps in, 174
  coping behaviors and, 54
  fear of, 175
  intimate relationships and, 225–26, 236
  obstacles to, 174–75
  patience and, 176
  patterns and, 175–76
  writing exercise for, 177
Chaos, coping and, 45
Child assault prevention programs, 107, 117
Child Assault Prevention Project (C.A.P.), 281n
Children
  abused by others, 282–85
  abused by yourself, 285–87
  adults' responsibility for, 107
  communication with, 274
  deciding whether or not to have, 217, 415–16
  family of origin and, 281–82
  feelings about, 38
  observing, 109–10
  partners of survivors and, 330–31
  protecting, 134, 140–41, 279–85, 444–45
  safe touch and, 277–79
  setting boundaries with, 276–79
  talking about your abuse with, 275–76, 369–70, 456

Children (cont.)
  as teachers, 271–72
  teaching them to protect themselves, 281–83
  telling by, 281, 282
Child within, 58, 111–15, 348
  anger at, 123
  coming to terms with, 112–13
  getting to know, 114–15
  making contact with, 113
  reassuring, 164
  writing exercise and, 115
Child witnesses, 93n
Choice-Making (Wegscheider-Cruse), 236
Climb High, 465
Co-dependency, 236, 236n, 326
Colao, Flora, 283
Commitment
  to healing, 58, 60–64
  of partners of survivors, 340–342
Communication
  partners of survivors and, 328–39
  sex and, 246–48, 337–38
  with your children, 274
Compassion. See Forgiving
Compulsive eating, 50, 217–18, 361
Conflict, intimacy and, 232
Confronting abuser. See Disclosing and confronting
Conspiracy of Silence (Butler), 148
Control
  coping and, 43–46
  partners of survivors and, 331
  sense of, 34
  sex and, 257–58, 364, 378, 392–93
Conversations with My Lover's Father (Dwight), 335
Coping (coping behaviors), 40–54, 443. See also specific topics
  addiction, 49
  avoiding intimacy, 52
  busyness, 47
  change and, 54
  chaos, 45
  control, 43–46
  denying, 42
  eating difficulties, 50, 361

Coping (coping behaviors) (*cont.*)
escape, 47
forgetting, 42–43
gambling, 51
humor and, 46–47
hyper-awareness, 46
isolation, 49
lack of integration, 43
leaving your body, 43
lying, 50
mental illness, 48
minimizing, 41
rationalizing, 41–42
religion and, 52
security and, 51–53
self-mutilation, 48
sexuality and, 53–54
spacing out, 45–46
splitting, 42–43
stealing, 50–51
suicide attempts, 48
workaholism, 51
writing exercise and, 54
Counseling (counselors), 345–53,
439–40
abuser and, 348
addictions of survivors and, 348
anger and, 349
attitude toward sexual abuse and,
346
avoiding, 461–62
believing the survivor, 345–47
choosing, 377, 459–60
confidence in healing process
and, 345
coping behaviors and, 349
drug therapy, 450–51
dynamic of counseling
relationship, 346
effective, 460–61
empathy of, 346
forgiveness and, 348
gender of, 346
hypnosis and, 459, 459n
individual, 458–62
needs of survivors and, 346–47
nurturing by, 352
pain of survivors and, 345, 352–
53
paying for, 462

Counseling (counselors) (*cont.*)
placing blame and, 347–48
problems with, 461
safe touch and, 351
sexual preference and, 349
sexual relationship with, 351, 461
shame and, 348
speaking out by survivors and,
349
support systems for survivors
and, 349
telling, 99
uncovering of abuse by, 349–51
C.O.Y.O.T.E. (Call Off Your Old
Tired Ethics), 261n
Creativity
getting in touch with your
feelings and, 194
sex and, 249–50

Daddy Kanagy (Asherah), xx
Dana, 78, 285, 293–94
Davis, Laura, 76–77
Death of abuser, 78–79, 143
Deciding to heal, 58, 60–64
Denial, 86–91
of anger, 123
coping and, 42
Dependency, 230–31
co-dependency, 236, 236n, 326
of partners of survivors, 326–27
Depression, 185
Disclosing and confronting, 59,
133–48, 364–65, 379, 401–4,
409, 453
choosing not to, 142–43
danger and, 140
dead or gone abuser, 143
deciding to, 134
fear of, 134–35, 139–40
initial confrontation, 139
motives for, 133–34
outside the family, 136
by partners of survivors, 334–36
preparing to, 137–39
protecting other children and,
134, 140–41, 284–85
reactions to, 135–36, 140–42
staying centered and, 138–39
symbolic, 143–44

Disclosing and confronting (*cont.*)
ways to, 139
writing exercise for, 148
Distancing, 229
Drawing
your feelings, 194
yourself, 209
Drug therapy, 450–51
Drug abuse, 216, 375
Narcotics Anonymous and, 464
violence and, 199
Durphy, Michael, 198
Dwight, Carol Anne, 335

Eating disorders, 50, 217–19, 361,
376
Eileen, 230
Ella, 74, 98, 271–72
Emergency stage of healing process,
58, 65–69, 411–12
partners of survivors and, 330–
31
Emily, 90
Emotional abuse, in adulthood,
235
Emotional release work, 198,
200
anger and, 198, 200, 443–44
self-abuse and, 220
Enemas, 262
Escape
coping and, 47
spirituality and, 159
Estrangement, from family of
origin, 292–93
ETR Associates (Education,
Training, Research), 281n
Eva, 185
Exercise(s), 212. *See also* Writing
exercises
breathing, 214
for connecting with your body,
214–15
emotional release, 198, 200, 442,
443
grounding, 214–15
relaxation, 214
self-abuse and, 220

Faith, healing and, 156–57. *See also*
Religion; Spirituality

Families of origin, 289–311
  assessing relationship with, 290–91
  effects of sexual child abuse on, 38–39
  estrangement from, 293
  holidays and, 297, 300
  hope for change in, 302–5
  love of, 300–1
  partners of survivors and, 333–34
  reaction of, 301–2
  reconstructing history of, 154
  separating from, 303–6
  setting limits with, 291–94, 296
  substitutes for, 306
  suing abuser and, 307–10
  as supporters, 318–20
  visiting, 297
  writing exercise and, 306
  your children and, 281–82
Fear
  of change, 175
  of confrontation, 134–35, 139–40
  of feelings, 205–6
  of happiness, 205–6
  of love, 230
Featherdancing, Kyos, 261, 394–99
Feelings, 191–206. *See also specific feelings*
  anger, 198–201, 203
  drawing, 194
  effects of sexual child abuse on, 35–36
  emotional release work and, 198, 200
  expressing, 197
  fear of, 205–76
  getting in touch with, 192–95
  grief, 200
  identifying, 194–95
  numbness and, 191–92, 208, 210–11
  as package deal, 192
  panic, 201–5
  physical sensations and, 192–93, 198–99
  positive, 205–6
  remembering and, 78–79
  splitting and, 210
  suicidal, 202–3

Feelings (*cont.*)
  support for, 196–97
  suppression of, 191–92
  tension, 199, 200
  thinking vs., 195
"First Light" (Morales), 89
Flashbacks
  while masturbating, 243
  during sex with a partner, 249, 253
Forgetting, coping and, 42–43
Forgiving (forgiveness), 59, 149–54, 365–66, 398
  definition of, 150
  paying attention to, 193–94
  pressure to, 150–51
  sense of freedom and, 152–53
  writing exercise for, 154
  your mother, 151–52
  yourself, 149, 151, 154
"For Neil, Because You Asked" (Krishnabai), 316
Fortune, Marie, 151*n*, 348*n*
Freud, Sigmund, 347
Freud and the Sexual Abuse of Children (Rush), 347*n*
Friendships
  intimacy and, 224
  reaching out and, 204, 210
Frustration, of partners of survivors, 337–39
Fuller, Elly, 60, 223
Fun, importance of, 237–38

Gallant, Sandi, 419–21
Gambling, as coping behavior, 51
Gass, Robert and Judith, 428*n*, 428–29
Gender-based conditioning, abusers and, 96–97*n*
Getting Free (NiCarthy), 234–35, 260
Gibbs, Experience, xix
Gift of Water, The (Vaughn), 265
Giving and receiving, intimacy and, 233–34
Gizelle (pseud.), 115, 256, 446–57, 461
Gold, Judy (pseud.), 359–66

Grieving and mourning, 59
  emotional release exercises for, 200
  rituals and, 120
  as transformative, 120
  writing exercise and, 121
Grounding exercises, 214–15
Groups for survivors. *See* Support groups

Habe, Jayne, 211–12, 352
Hamilton, Barbara, 64, 129, 282, 284
Happiness, fear of, 205–6
Healing crises, 65–69
  intimate relationships and, 233–34
  letting go of, 165–66
Healing process, 57–169. *See also* Anger; Belief that it happened; Blaming yourself; Child within; Disclosing and confronting; Forgiveness; Grieving and mourning; Remembering Resolution and moving on; Spirituality; Telling; *and specific topics*
  broader commitments and, 168–69
  commitment to, 58, 60–64
  crisis periods, 65–69
  denial and, 88, 90
  difficulty of, 62–63
  emergency stage, 58, 65–69, 411–12
  hardest and scariest parts of, 146–47
  as lifelong, 166–67
  safety and support and, 120
  self-esteem and, 178–79
  sexual healing, 266–67
  stages of, 58–59
  taking breaks and, 186
  trusting yourself, 59, 116–117
Healing resources, 458–65. *See also specific topics*
  counseling, 458–62
  support groups, 462–65
"Hearsay law" (proposed), child witnesses and, 93*n*

Holidays with family of origin, 297, 300
Hope, sources of, 69
Horning, Edith, vii, 130, 294–95
Hosansky, Tamar, 283
Hoyal, Maggie, xiii*n*, xix
Hugs, Diane (pseud.), 422–24
Humor, coping and, 46–47
Hurley, Thomas J., III, 423
Husbands. *See* Partners of survivors
Hutchinson, Marcia Germaine, 208*n*
Hyper-awareness, coping and, 46
Hypnosis, 459, 459*n*

Identity, as survivor of sexual abuse, 163–64
"I Gave Thanks for the Sky" (Strong), 84–85
Incest Survivors Anonymous (I.S.A.), 417, 419, 463–65
I Never Told Anyone: Writings by Women Survivors of Child Sexual Abuse, xiii–xiv, 130
I Never Told Anyone workshops, xiv, xxvii
Inner voice, 117
Insomnia, 213
Institute of Noetic Sciences, 423, 423*n*
Integration, 164–65
coping and, 43
Internalized messages, 179–82
Intimacy (intimate relationships), 223–38, 324, 370–71, 392–93. *See also* Partners of survivors; Sex
abusive, 234–35, 368
addiction and, 236
anger and, 232
avoiding, 52
bad, 234–36
calculated risks and, 226
change and, 232
conflict and, 232
coping and, 52
dependency and, 230–31
distancing and, 229
effects of sexual child abuse on, 36–37
friendships as, 224

Intimacy (intimate relationships) (*cont.*)
giving and receiving and, 233–34
healing crises and, 233–34
merging and, 231
non-sexual, 338–39
past and present, 228–29
patterns in, 234–37
quality of, 224–25
reaching out and, 204, 210
separating from, 236
setting limits and, 231–32
trust and, 223, 226–28
working on, 237–38
with your children, 276
Isolation, coping and, 49

Jesse, 338

Kaplan, Helen Singer, 254
Kathe Kollwitz (Rukeyser), 92
King, Martin Luther, 446
King, Susan, 164–65
Kingsolver, Barbara, 158
Klepfisz, Irena, 154
Krishnabai, 316, 425–30
Kübler-Ross, Elisabeth, 443–44

Lanou Frank, 451, 452, 461
Lashing out, 123–24
Laux, Dorianne, vii, 41, 44, 99
Lavender, Jennierose, 33, 75–77, 109, 287–88, 463
Lawyers, 311
Learning to Live Without Violence (Sonkin and Durphy), 198–99
Leaving your body, 43. *See also* Splitting
Legal issues
child witnesses and, 93*n*
lawyers handling cases for adult survivors, 311
revenge and, 128
suing your abuser, 307–10, 462
Lesbianism (lesbian relationships), 268–69, 349, 397
abuse in, 333
choosing, 268
coming out, 443
where both are survivors, 322–23

Levy, Emily, 101–3
Lieberman, Meryl, 344*n*
Littleford, Barbara, 128
Louise, 137–38
Loulan, JoAnn, 244*n*, 253–55
Love. *See also* Intimacy
anger and, 127–28
fear of, 230
spirituality and, 159
Lovers. *See* Lesbianism; Partners of survivors; Sex
Low, Denise, 278
Lying, as coping behavior, 50

McGrath, Mary, 441–45
McNaron, Toni, 106*n*
Malcolm, Evie (pseud.), 164, 381–86
Male genitals, fear of, 256
Male survivors, xxvi
Marilyn, 52–53, 114–15
Mary, 107, 157
Masson, Jeffrey, 347, 347*n*
Masters and Johnson, 254
Masturbation, 241–44
flashbacks during, 243
orgasm and, 243–44
MDMA, 451, 451*n*, 452
Media coverage of sexual abuse, 75
Memories. *See* Remembering
Men. *See also* Intimacy; Love; Partners of survivors; Sex
fear of genitals of, 256
healing with, 454
as survivors of child sexual abuse, xxvi
Mendoza, Alicia, 410–16
Mental illness. *See also* Multiple personalities; *and other specific topics*
coping and, 48
Merging, 231. *See also* Boundaries; Setting limits
Michelle Remembers (Pazder), 419
Mines, Julie, 113
Minimizing, as coping behavior, 41
Mirror, looking in, 209
Model Mugging, 221–22
Monetary compensation, 309–10, 462
Moonwater, Rose Z., 353

Morales, Aurora Levins, 89
Morgan, Yarrow, 106*n*
Mother
  blaming, 125
  forgiving, 151–52
Mother-daughter incest, 96–97, 387–93
Motherhood. *See* Parenthood
Multiple personalities, 43, 417, 423–24, 432–33, 435
"Multiple Personality-Mirrors of a New Model of Mind?" (O'Regan and Hurley), 423–24
Multiple sclerosis (MS), 422, 422*n*
Munyon, Jerilyn, 45, 227

"Name of My Own, A" (Bat Or), 188–90
Narcotics Anonymous, 464
Nelson, Patricia, 183
Newsy Letter, The, 464
NiCarthy, Ginny, 234, 260
1952, and Other Years (Gibbs), xix
No, saying, 34, 182–84, 406–7. *See also* Setting limits
  to sex, 241
Nonsexual needs, sex and, 259–60
Norwood, Robin, 236
"November" (Williams), 402–4
Numbness, 191–92, 208, 210–11, 371
  breathing and, 210
  compulsive eating and, 217
Nurturing parent exercise, 188
Nurturing yourself, 187
  body image and, 209
  compulsive eating and, 217

Obsessing, 65–68, 156–57
Oedipal theory, 347
"One Hundred and Fifty-Seven Ways to Tell My Incest Story" (Levy), 101–3
Opening the Heart workshop, 428
O'Regan, Brendan, 423
Orgasm, masturbation and, 243–44
Overeating, 50, 376
Overprotection of children, 280–81
"Own Your Own Pain" (Schwartz), 121

Panic (panic attacks), 201–5, 383, 408, 409
  breathing and, 201–3
  calming down, 201–3
  determining causes of, 204–5
  physical sensations and, 204
  reaching out and, 204
  safe spot and, 203–4
  self-abuse and, 220
  what to avoid during, 204–5
Parent effectiveness training (P.E.T.), 273, 273*n*
Parenting (parenthood), 270–88, 361, 449, 455–56
  abusing your children, 285–87
  choosing, 271
  communicating with your children, 274
  effects of sexual child abuse on, 38
  learning, 272–73
  "parent," use of word, 270
  protecting your children, 279–85
  remembering and, 78
  setting boundaries and, 276–79
  strengths and weaknesses and, 273–74
  support and, 318–19
  telling children about your own abuse, 275–76
Parents United, 465
Partners of survivors, 321–44, 323. *See also* Intimacy; Sex
  abuse by, 333
  abuser and, 333–36
  affirmations and, 343–44
  as allies, 327–28
  anger and, 123–24, 327–28, 339
  benefits of healing process for, 323–24, 339–40, 343, 413
  children and, 330–31
  as co-dependents, 326
  commitment and, 340–42
  communication and, 328–29
  confrontation by, 334–36
  control and, 331
  crisis periods and, 233–34, 330–31
  dependency of, 326–27
  doubts of, 341–42

Partners of survivors (*cont.*)
  family of origin and, 333–34
  frustration of, 337–39
  identified with abuser, 332–33
  intimacy and, 324
  needs of, 328–29, 337–39
  pain of survivor and, 330
  separating and, 342
  setting of limits by, 329
  sex and, 252, 258–59, 336–40
  shame of, 324–25
  suicide and, 331
  as supports, 334–36
  support for, 325–26
  taking a break from healing process, 343
  telling, 99, 363–64
  trust and, 332
Patience, change process and, 176
Patricia, 131
Pavat, Patricia, 345
Pazder, Larry, 419
Phil, 336
Phobias, 383–86
Phobic therapy, 384–85
Physical abuse, in adulthood, 234–35
Physical illness, 213, 216
  multiple sclerosis, 422, 422*n*
Physical sensations, 191–93, 198–99. *See also specific topics*
  anger and, 198–99
  numbness, 191–92, 208, 210–11
  panic and, 204
Pillow talk, 247–48
Pine, Amy, 194, 198*n*, 200, 214*n*
"Poem for My Mother's Birthday" (Stevens), 391
Positive feelings, fear of, 205
"Pray for the People" (Low), 278
Primal therapy, 198
Prostitution, 261
Pseudonyms, using, 357–58
Psychodrama, 198. *See also* Role playing
Psychological issues. *See* Counseling; Eating disorders; Mental illness; Multiple personalities; Phobias; *and specific topics*

Quitting smoking, 216–7

Rape, self-defense against, 220–21
Rationalizing, as coping behavior, 41–42
Reaching out
panic attacks and, 204
splitting and, 210
Rebirthing, 198
"Reconciliation" (Wade), 165
Relaxation exercises, 214
Religion, coping and, 52. *See also* Faith; Spirituality
Remembering (memories), 58, 70–85, 411, 434–35
addictions and, 78
believing, 86–91
body memories, 74–75
control of, 79–81
death and, 78–79
feelings and, 78–79
flashbacks, 73
lack of, 81–83
motherhood and, 78
regression and, 73–74
sense memories, 74–75
over time, 80–81
process of, 71, 75–78
types of, 72–75
writing exercise and, 83–84
"Remember the Moon Survives" (Kingsolver), 158
Resolution and moving on, 59, 438–39
the child within and, 164
integeration and, 164–65
letting go of the crisis, 165–66
letting go of the damage, 163–64
life in the present and, 166–67
limbo and, 166
relationships with abusers and family and, 162–63
stabilizing and, 162
Responsibility for children, 107
Revenge, 128–29, 455
Rich, Adrienne, 123
Ritual abuse, 417–21
Rituals, 188–90
anger and, 129
grief and mourning, 120

Rituals (*cont.*)
separating from family of origin and, 306
Roger, 328
Rogers, Carl, xiii
Role-playing. *See also* Psychodrama
anger and, 126
confrontations and, 138
setting limits and, 183
Rukeyser, Muriel, 92
Rush, Florence, 347, 347*n*

Sado-masochisim (SM), 262–64
Safe spot, creating, 203–4
Safe touch, 211
with children, 277–79
by therapist, 351
Safety
compulsive eating and, 217
coping and, 51–63
safe spot, 203–4
Saphyre, 106, 161, 173, 223–24, 263, 264, 458
Satanism, 417–21
Saying no, 34, 182–84, 406–7. *See also* Setting limits
to sex, 241
Schwartz, Patricia Roth, 121
Schweig, Lisa, 88
Seal Press, 236*n*
Security
coping and, 51–53
safe spot and, 203–4
Seifert, Jaroslav, 44
Self-absorption, 233
Self-defense, 220–22
Self-destructiveness, 179, 375, 408
Self-esteem, 178–90, 375
activities and, 184, 185
affirmations and visualizations and, 184–85
effects of sexual child abuse on, 34–35
internalized messages and, 179–82
living for yourself and, 184
nurturing yourself and, 187
in relationships, 186, 188

Self-esteem (*cont.*)
setting limits, 182–84
taking breaks and, 186
Self-hatred, 179, 185
Self-image, 184–85. *See also* Body
Self-massage, 211
Self-mutilation, 48, 219–20
Sense memory, 74–75
Separation (separating), 236
from family of origin, 303
from partners, 342
Setting limits, 182–84
with children, 276–79
with families of origin, 291–94, 296
in intimate relationships, 231–32
by partners of survivors, 329
Sex (sexuality), 239–69, 360–61, 414–15, 433, 442–43. *See also* Intimacy; Lesbianism; Love; Partners of survivors
abusive, 260–63
addiction to, 259–60
celibacy and, 241
choosing, 263–64
communication and, 246–48, 337–38
control and, 257–58, 364, 378, 392–93
coping and, 53–54
with counselors, 351
creativity and, 249–50
definition of, 245
desire and, 252–55
effects of sexual child abuse on, 37–38
fantasies and, 262–65
fear of, 255–56
flashbacks during, 249, 253
going slow, 246
intimacy and, 257, 338–39
new relationships and, 245–47
nonsexual needs and, 259–60
partners feelings and, 252, 258–59
pillow talk and, 247–48
reasons to work on, 244–45
re-awakening, 251
sado-masochistic, 262–64
saying no to, 241

Sex (cont.)
  setting boundaries with your
    children and, 277
  sexual healing, 266–67
  sexual response to abuse, 106,
    240–41, 254–55, 351, 390
  spacing out or splitting during,
    249
  taking a break from, 241, 253
  violence and, 261–63
  willingness and, 254–55
Sex and Love Addicts Anonymous,
  260n, 464
Sexual abuse. See also specific topics
  in adulthood, 234–35
  defining, xxi
Sexual Abuse Anonymous, 389n
Sexual Violence: The Unmentionable
  Sin (Fortune), 151n, 348n
Shama, 122
Shame, 104–6, 436–37
  counseling and, 348
  overcoming, 108–10
  of partners of survivors, 324–25
Shuster, Becky, 349
Siblings, 319–20. See also Families of
  origin
Simone, Nina, 69, 242
"Sisters of Rachel, The" (Bat Or),
  189–90
Sladek v. Moore, 307n
Smith, Eva (pseud.), 126–27, 367–
  72
Smoking, quitting, 216–17
Smolover, Miriam, 344n
Soledad (pseud.), vii, 128, 462, 373–
  80
Solving Women's Problems (Wyckoff),
  188
Sonkin, Daniel Jay, 198
Spacing out, 229
  as coping behavior, 45–46
  during sex, 249
Speaking publicly, 109
Spirituality, 59, 155–60. See also
  Faith; Religion
  defining, 156
  escape and, 159
  faith and, 156–57
  gaining perspectives and, 156

Spirituality (cont.)
  getting in touch with, 157, 159
  love and, 159
  as personal, 159–60
Splitting, 208–10, 448–49
  breathing and, 210
  as coping behavior, 42–43
  exercises for, 215
  feelings and, 210
  during love making, 249
  paying attention to, 210
  reaching out and, 210
Spring Hill, 428–29
Stealing, as coping behavior, 50–51
Stevens, Anna (pseud.), 78, 387–93
Strippers, 261
Strong, Teresa, 84–85
Suicidal feelings, 202–3
Suicide, 202–3, 436, 449–50
  coping and, 48
  partners of survivors and, 331
Suing your abuser, 307–10, 462
Sunny, 49–50
Supporters of survivors, 453–54
  advice for, 315–17
  parents as, 318–19
  partners as, 334–36
  siblings as, 319–20
Support groups, 316–17, 346–47,
  462–65
  overcoming shame and, 108–9
  telling and, 99
Supportive anger, 130

Taylor, Randi (pseud.), 201, 405–10
Telling, 58, 92–103. See also
    Disclosing and confronting
  by children, 92–94, 281, 282
  context for, 99–100
  how to, 100
  levels of, 98
  partner, 363–64
  response to, 92–94
  as transformative, 94–95, 98
  weeding and, 100–1
  whom to tell, 99
Temples, Phil, 321
Tension, emotional release exercises
  for, 200
Testing, 228

Therapists. See Counseling
Therapy. See also Counseling
  body, 442, 443
  phobic, 384–85
  working vs. talking, 372
"There Are Things" (Schweig), 88
"These Are the Things I
    Remember" (Hoyal), xiiin, xix
Thinking, feeling vs., 195
Thomas, Matt, 221
Thomas, Michelle (pseud.), 431–40
Time-outs, violence and, 199
"To My Dad" (Featherdancing),
  398–99
Topless dancers, 261
Toribio, Julio, 132
Touch, safe, 211, 277–79, 351
Transforming Body Image
    (Hutchinson), 208n
Trust, 223, 226–28
  partners of survivors and, 332
  reaching out and, 204, 210
  testing and, 228
Trusting yourself, 59, 116–17, 226–
  27
Twelve-Step programs, 155
"Two Pictures of My Sister" (Laux), 44

Validation, 86–91, 377
  counselors and, 345–47
Vaughn, Jeanne Marie, 265
Verbal abuse, 124
Vibrators, 243
Vicki, 90–91, 136
Victim's Compensation funds, 462
Violence
  alcohol and, 199
  anger and, 123–24, 127, 128,
    198–201
  drugs and, 199
  learning to live without, 198–99
  sex and, 261–63
  time-outs and, 199
Visiting your family, 297
Visualizations, 184–85
VOICES (Victims of Incest Can
    Emerge Survivors) in Action,
  464
Voices in the Night (McNaron and
    Morgan), 106

W.H.I.S.P.E.R. (Women Hurt In Systems of Prostitution Engaged in Revolt), 261n
Wade, Cheryl Marie, 165
Walking, 214–15
Wean, meaning of word, 292
Weeding, telling and, 100–1
Wegscheider-Cruse, Sharon, 236
"What My Father Told Me" (Laux), 41
"While Making Love" (Davis), 76–77
Whitman, Ruth, 108
Wicked Stance, 237n
Williams, Jean, 161

Williams, Lorraine (pseud.), 400–404
Williams, Mary R., 307–11
Willingness to have sex, 254
Women. *See also specific topics*
  abuse by, 96–97, 286
  anger and, 122
Women Against Rape, 139
Women Who Love Too Much (Norwood), 236
Workaholism, as coping behavior, 51
Work On It, 237
Writing as Healing Workshops, 148, 208

Writing exercises, xxvii–xix
  change process and, 177
  child within and, 115
  coping behaviors and, 54
  disclosing and confronting and, 148
  effects of abuse and, 39
  family of origin and, 306
  forgiveness and, 154
  grieving and mourning and, 121
  remembering and, 83–84
Wyckoff, Hogie, 188

Your Children Should Know (Colao and Hosansky), 283